Steps to Writing Well

with Additional Readings

Jean Wyrick

D1318617

CENGAGE
Learning·

Australia • Brazil • Japan • Korea • Mexico • Singapore • Spain • United Kingdom • United States

CENGAGE Learning

Steps to Writing Well: with Additional Readings

Steps to Writing Well with Additional Readings, 9th Edition
Jean Wyrick

© 2014 Cengage Learning. All rights reserved.

Senior Project Development Manager:
 Linda deStefano

Market Development Manager:
 Heather Kramer

Senior Production/
Manufacturing Manager:
 Donna M. Brown

Production Editorial Manager:
 Kim Fry

Sr. Rights Acquisition Account Manager:
 Todd Osborne

For product information and technology assistance, contact us at
Cengage Learning Customer & Sales Support, 1-800-354-9706

For permission to use material from this text or product,
submit all requests online at **cengage.com/permissions**
Further permissions questions can be emailed to
permissionrequest@cengage.com

This book contains select works from existing Cengage Learning resources and was produced by Cengage Learning Custom Solutions for collegiate use. As such, those adopting and/or contributing to this work are responsible for editorial content accuracy, continuity and completeness.

Compilation © 2013 Cengage Learning

ISBN-13: 978-1-285-91258-5

ISBN-10: 1-285-91258-6

Cengage Learning
5191 Natorp Boulevard
Mason, Ohio 45040
USA

Cengage Learning is a leading provider of customized learning solutions with office locations around the globe, including Singapore, the United Kingdom, Australia, Mexico, Brazil, and Japan. Locate your local office at:
international.cengage.com/region.
Cengage Learning products are represented in Canada by Nelson Education, Ltd.
For your lifelong learning solutions, visit **www.cengage.com /custom.**
Visit our corporate website at **www.cengage.com.**

Printed in the United States of America

Brief Contents

Part 1

The Basics
of the Short Essay

The first section of this text is designed to move you through the writing process as you compose a short essay, the kind you are most likely to encounter in composition class and in other college courses. Chapters 1 and 2, on prewriting and the thesis statement, will help you find a topic, purpose, and focus for your essay. Chapter 3, on paragraphs, will show you how to plan, organize, and develop your ideas; Chapter 4 illustrates ways you might begin, end, and title your essay. Chapter 5 offers suggestions for revising your writing, for sharpening your critical thinking skills, and for participating effectively in collaborative classroom activities and peer-revision workshops; this chapter also addresses the problems of procrastination and Writer's Block. Chapters 6 and 7 present additional advice on composing your sentences and selecting the best words. Chapter 8 explains the important reading-writing connection and shows how learning to read analytically can improve your writing skills.

Chapter 1

Prewriting

· ·

Getting Started (or Soup-Can Labels Can Be Fascinating)

For many writers, getting started is the hardest part. You may have noticed that when it is time to begin a writing assignment, you suddenly develop an enormous desire to straighten your books, water your plants, or clean out your closet. If this situation sounds familiar, you may find it reassuring to know that many professionals undergo these same strange compulsions before they begin writing. Jean Kerr, author of *Please Don't Eat the Daisies,* admitted that she often found herself in the kitchen

reading soup-can labels—or anything—to prolong the moments before taking pen in hand. John C. Calhoun, vice president under Andrew Jackson, insisted he had to plow his fields before he could write, and Joseph Conrad, author of *Lord Jim* and other novels, is said to have cried on occasion from the sheer dread of sitting down to compose his stories. Writer Ernest Hemingway once confessed that the most frightening thing he ever confronted in his life of adventures was "a blank sheet of paper," and contemporary horror-writer Stephen King agrees that the "scariest moment" of all occurs just before one starts writing.

To spare you as much hand-wringing as possible, this chapter presents some practical suggestions on how to begin writing your short essay. Although all writers must find the methods that work best for them, you may find some of the following ideas helpful.

But no matter how you actually begin putting words on paper, it is absolutely essential to maintain two basic ideas concerning your writing task. Before you write a single sentence, you should always remind yourself that

1. You have some valuable ideas to tell your reader, and
2. More than anything, you want to communicate those ideas to your reader.

These reminders may seem obvious to you, but without a solid commitment to your own opinions as well as to your reader, your prose will be lifeless and boring. If *you* don't care about your subject, you can't very well expect anyone else to. Have confidence that your ideas are worthwhile and that your reader genuinely wants, or needs, to know what you think.

Equally important, you must also have a strong desire to tell others what you are thinking. One of the most common mistakes inexperienced writers make is failing to move past early stages in the writing process in which they are writing for—or writing to—themselves only. In the first stages of composing an essay, writers frequently "talk" on paper to themselves, exploring thoughts, discovering new insights, making connections, selecting examples, and so on. The ultimate goal of a finished essay, however, is to communicate your opinions to *others* clearly and persuasively. Whether you wish to inform your readers, change their minds, or stir them to action, you cannot accomplish your purpose by writing so that only you understand what you mean. The burden of communicating your thoughts falls on *you,* not the reader, who is under no obligation to struggle through unclear prose, paragraphs that begin and end for no apparent reason, or sentences that come one after another with no more logic than lemmings following one another to the sea.

Therefore, as you move through the drafting and revising stages of your writing process, commit yourself to becoming increasingly aware of your reader's reactions to your prose. Ask yourself as you revise your drafts, "Am I moving beyond writing just to myself? Am I making myself clear to others who might not know what I mean?" Much of your success as a writer depends on an unflagging determination to communicate clearly with your readers.

Selecting a Subject

Once you have decided that communicating clearly with others is your ultimate goal, you are ready to select the subject of your essay. Here are some suggestions on how to begin:

Start early. Writing teachers since the earth's crust cooled have been pushing this advice—and for good reason. It's not because teachers are egoists competing for the dubious honor of having the most time-consuming course; it is because few writers, even experienced ones, can do a good job when rushed. You need time to mull over ideas, organize your thoughts, revise and polish your prose. Rule of thumb: Always give yourself twice as much time as you think you'll need to avoid the 2:00-A.M.-why-did-I-come to-college panic. (◆ For help overcoming procrastination, see pages 98–100.)

Find your best space. Develop some successful writing habits by thinking about your very own writing process. When and where do you usually do your best composing? Some people write best early in the morning; others think better later in the day. What time of day seems to produce your best efforts? Where are you working? At a desk? In your room or in a library? Do you start drafting ideas on a computer, or do you begin with paper or a yellow pad? With a certain pen or sharpened pencil? Most writers avoid noise and interruptions (the lure of social media sites, phone calls or texts, TV, friends, etc.), although some swear by playing music in the background. If you can identify a previously successful writing experience, try duplicating its location, time, and tools to help you calmly address your new writing task. Or consider trying new combinations of time and place if your previous choices weren't as productive as you would have liked. Recognition and repeated use of your most comfortable writing "spot" may shorten your hesitation to begin composing; your subconscious may recognize the pattern ("Hey, it's time to write!") and help you start in a positive frame of mind. (Remember that it's not just writers who repeat such rituals—think of the athletes you've heard about who won't begin a game without wearing their lucky socks. If it works for them, it can work for you.)

Select something in which you currently have a strong interest. If the essay subject is left to you, think of something fun, fascinating, or frightening you've done or seen lately, perhaps something you've already told a friend about. The subject might be the pleasure of a new hobby, the challenge of a recent book or movie, or even the harassment of registration—anything in which you are personally involved. If you aren't enthusiastic enough about your subject to want to spread the word, pick something else. Bored writers write boring essays.

Don't feel you have nothing from which to choose your subject. Your days are full of activities, people, joys, and irritations. Essays do not have to be written on lofty intellectual or poetic subjects—in fact, some of the world's best essays have been written on such subjects as china teacups, roast pig, and chimney sweeps. Think: what have you been talking or thinking about lately? What have you been doing that you're excited about? Or what about your past? Reflect a few moments on some of your most vivid memories; special people, vacations, holidays, childhood hideaways, your first job or first date—all are possibilities.

Still searching? Make a list of all the subjects on which you are an expert. None, you say? Think again. Most of us have an array of talents we hardly acknowledge. Perhaps you play the guitar or make a mean pot of chili or know how to repair a sports car. You've trained a dog or become a first-class house sitter or gardener. You know more about computers or old baseball cards than any of your friends. You play soccer or volleyball or Ping-Pong. In other words, take a fresh, close look at your life. You know things that others don't . . . now is your chance to enlighten them!

If a search of your immediate or past personal experience doesn't turn up anything inspiring, try looking in your local or campus newspaper for stories that arouse your strong feelings; don't skip the editorials or "Letters to the Editor" column. What are the current topics of controversy on your campus? How do you feel about a particular graduation requirement? Speakers or special-interest groups on campus? Financial aid applications? Registration procedures? Parking restrictions? Consider the material you are studying in your other classes: reading *The Jungle* in a literature class might spark an investigative essay on the hot dog industry today, or studying previous immigration laws in your history class might lead you to an argument for or against current immigration practices. Current news magazines or Internet news blogs might suggest timely essay topics on national or international affairs that affect your life. In addition, there are, according to the search engine Technorati, over 200 million individual English-language blogs (and perhaps a billion worldwide). Personal web logs today may offer information and opinions (often controversial) on almost any subject one can name, with topics including politics, cultural trends, business, travel, education, entertainment, and health issues, to name only a few examples. Some blogs are directed to specific groups with shared interests or professional objectives, while others may have more in common with personal diaries or daily logs. Although all readers should always carefully evaluate any information provided online, a professional or personal blog might present an idea or argument that invites your thoughtful investigation and response.

In other words, when you're stuck for an essay topic, take a closer look at your environment: your own life—past, present, and future; your hometown; your campus and college town; your state; your country; and your world. You'll probably discover more than enough subjects to satisfy the assignments in your writing class.

Narrow a large subject. Once you've selected a general subject to write on, you may find that it is too broad for effective treatment in a short essay; therefore, you may need to narrow it somewhat. Suppose, for instance, you like to work with plants and have decided to make them the subject of your essay. The subject of "plants," however, is far too large and unwieldy for a short essay, perhaps even for a short book. Consequently, you must make your subject less general. "Houseplants" is more specific, but, again, there's too much to say. "Minimum-care houseplants" is better, but you still need to pare this large, complex subject further so that you can treat it in depth in your short essay. After all, there are many houseplants that require little attention. After several more tries, you might arrive at more specific, manageable topics, such as "houseplants that thrive in dark areas" or "the easy-care Devil's Ivy."

Then again, let's assume you are interested in sports. A 500-to-800-word essay on "sports" would obviously be superficial because the subject covers so much ground. Instead, you might divide the subject into categories such as "sports heroes," "my years on the high school tennis team," "women in gymnastics," "my love of running," and so forth. Perhaps several of your categories would make good short essays, but after looking at your list, you might decide that your real interest at this time is running and that it will be the topic of your essay.

Finding Your Essay's Purpose and Focus

Even after you've narrowed your large subject to a more manageable topic, you still must find a specific *purpose* for your essay. Why are you writing about this topic? Do your readers need to be informed, persuaded, entertained? What do you want your writing to accomplish?

In addition to knowing your purpose, you must also find a clear *focus* or direction for your essay. You cannot, for example, inform your readers about every aspect of running. Instead, you must decide on a particular part of the sport and then determine the main point you want to make. If it helps, think of a camera: you see a sweeping landscape you'd like to photograph, but you know you can't get it all into one picture, so you pick out a particularly interesting part of the scene. Focus in an essay works in the same way; you zoom in, so to speak, on a particular part of your topic and make that the focus of your paper.

Sometimes part of your problem may be solved by your assignment; your teacher may choose the focus of your essay for you by asking for certain specific information or by prescribing the method of development you should use (compare running to aerobics, explain the process of running properly, analyze the effects of daily running, and so forth). But if the purpose and focus of your essay are decisions you must make, you should always allow your interest and knowledge to guide you. Often a direction or focus for your essay will surface as you narrow your subject, but don't become frustrated if you have to discard several ideas before you hit the one that's right. For instance, you might first consider writing on how to select running shoes and then realize that you know too little about the shoe market, or you might find that there's just too little of importance to say about running paths to make an interesting 500-word essay.

Let's suppose for a moment that you have thought of a subject that interests you—but now you're stuck. Deciding on something to write about this subject suddenly looks as easy as nailing Jell-O to your kitchen wall. What should you say? What would be the purpose of your essay? What would be interesting for you to write about and for readers to hear about?

At this point, you may profit from trying more than one prewriting exercise, designed to help you generate some ideas about your topic. The exercises described next are, in a sense, "pump primers" that will get your creative juices flowing again. Because all writers compose differently, not all of these exercises will work for you—in fact, some of them may lead you nowhere. Nevertheless, try all of them at least once or twice; you may be surprised to discover that some pump-primer techniques work better with some subjects than with others.

Pump-Primer Techniques
1. Listing

Try jotting down all the ideas that pop into your head about your topic. Free-associate; don't hold back anything. Try to brainstorm for at least ten minutes.

A quick list on running might look like this:

fun	training for races
healthy	both sexes
relieves tension	any age group
no expensive equipment	running with friend or spouse
shoes	too much competition
poor shoes won't last	great expectations
shin splints	good for lungs
fresh air	improves circulation
good for heart	firming
jogging paths vs. streets	no weight loss
hard surfaces	warm-ups before run
muscle cramps	cool-downs after run
going too far	getting discouraged
going too fast	hitting the wall
sense of accomplishment	marathons

As you read over the list, look for connections between ideas or one large idea that encompasses several small ones. In this list, you might first notice that many of the ideas focus on improving health (heart, lungs, circulation), but you discard that subject because a "running improves health" essay is too obvious; it's a topic that's been done too many times to say anything new. A closer look at your list, however, turns up a number of ideas that concern how *not* to run or reasons why someone might become discouraged and quit a running program. You begin to think of friends who might have stuck with running as you have if only they'd warmed up properly beforehand, chosen the right places to run, paced themselves more realistically, and so on. You decide, therefore, to write an essay telling first-time runners how to start a successful program, how to avoid a number of problems—from shoes to track surfaces—that might otherwise defeat their efforts before they've given the sport a chance.

2. Freewriting

Some people simply need to start writing to find a focus. Facing a blank page, give yourself at least ten to fifteen minutes, and begin writing whatever comes to mind on your subject. Don't worry about spelling, punctuation, or even complete sentences. Don't change, correct, or delete anything. If you run out of things to say, write "I can't think of anything to say" until you can find a new thought. At the end of the time period you may discover that by continuously writing you will have written yourself into an interesting topic.

Here are examples of freewriting from students who were given ten minutes to write on the general topic of "nature."

Student 1:

I'm really not the outdoorsy type. I'd rather be inside somewhere than out in Nature tromping through the bushes. I don't like bugs and snakes and stuff like that. Lots of my friends like to go hiking around or camping but I don't. Secretly, I think maybe one of the big reasons I really don't like being out in Nature is because I'm deathly afraid of bees. When I was a kid I was out in the woods and ran into a swarm of bees and got stung about a million times, well, it felt like a million times. I had to go to the hospital for a few days. Now every time I'm outside somewhere and something, anything, flies by me I'm terrified. Totally paranoid. Everyone kids me because I immediately cover my head. I keep hearing about killer bees heading this way, my worst nightmare come true.

Student 2:

We're not going to have any Nature left if people don't do something about the environment. Despite all the media attention to recycling, we're still trashing the planet left and right. People talk big about "saving the environment" but then do such stupid things all the time. Like smokers who flip their cigarette butts out their car windows. Do they think those filters are just going to disappear overnight? The parking lot by this building is full of butts this morning where someone dumped their car ashtray. This campus is full of pop cans, I can see at least three empties under desks in this classroom right now.

These two students reacted quite differently to the same general subject. The first student responded personally, thinking about her own relationship to "nature" (defined as being out in the woods), whereas the second student obviously associated nature with environmental concerns. More freewriting might lead student 1 to a humorous essay on her bee phobia or even to an inquiry about those dreaded killer bees; student 2 might write an interesting paper suggesting ways college students could clean up their campus or easily recycle their aluminum cans.

Often freewriting will not be as coherent as these two samples; sometimes freewriting goes nowhere or in circles. But it's a technique worth trying. By allowing our minds to roam freely over a subject, without worrying about "correctness" or organization, we may remember or discover topics we want to write about or investigate, topics we feel strongly about and wish to introduce to others.

3. Looping*

Looping is a variation on freewriting that works amazingly well for many people, including those who are frustrated rather than helped by freewriting.

Let's assume you've been assigned that old standby, "My Summer Vacation." Obviously, you must find a focus, something specific and important to say. Again, face a blank page and begin to freewrite, as described previously. Write for at least ten minutes. At the end of this period, read over what you've written and try to identify a central idea that has emerged. This idea might be an important thought that occurred to you in the middle or at the end of your writing, or perhaps it was the idea you liked best for

---

* This technique is suggested by Peter Elbow in *Writing Without Teachers* (New York: Oxford University Press, 1975).

whatever reason. It might be the idea that was pulling you onward when time ran out. In other words, look for the thought that stands out, that seems to indicate the direction of your thinking. Put this thought or idea into one sentence called the "center-of-gravity sentence." You have now completed loop 1.

To begin loop 2, use your center-of-gravity sentence as a jumping-off point for another ten minutes of freewriting. Stop, read what you've written, and complete loop 2 by composing another center-of-gravity sentence. Use this second sentence to start loop 3. You should write at least three loops and three center-of-gravity sentences. At the end of three loops, you may find that you have focused on a specific topic that might lead to a good essay. If you're not satisfied with your topic at this point, by all means try two or three more loops until your subject is sufficiently narrowed and focused.

Here's an example of one student's looping exercise:

Summer Vacation

Loop 1

I think summer vacations are very important aspects of living. They symbolize getting away from daily routines, discovering places and people that are different. When I think of vacations I think mostly of traveling somewhere too far to go, say, for a weekend. It is a chance to get away and relax and not think about most responsibilities. Just have a good time and enjoy yourself. Vacations can also be a time of gathering with family and friends.

Center-of-gravity sentence

Vacations are meant to be used for traveling.

Loop 2

Vacations are meant for traveling. Last summer my family and I drove to Yellowstone National Park. I didn't want to go at first. I thought looking at geysers would be dumb and boring. I was really obnoxious all the way up there and made lots of smart remarks about getting eaten by bears. Luckily, my parents ignored me and I'm glad they did, because Yellowstone turned out to be wonderful. It's not just Old Faithful—there's lots more to see and learn about, like these colorful boiling pools and boiling patches of mud. I got interested in the thermodynamics of the pools and how new ones are surfacing all the time, and how algae make the pools different colors.

Center-of-gravity sentence

Once I got interested in Yellowstone's amazing pools, my vacation turned out great.

Loop 3

Once I got interested in the pools, I had a good time, mainly because I felt I was seeing something really unusual. I knew I'd never see anything like this again unless I went to Iceland or New Zealand (highly unlikely!). I felt like I was learning a lot, too. I liked the idea of learning a lot about the inside of the earth without having to go to class and study books. I really hated to leave—Mom and Dad kidded me on the way back about how much I'd griped about going on the trip in the first place. I felt pretty dumb. But I was really glad I'd given the Park a closer look instead of holding on to my view of it as a boring bunch of water fountains. I would have had a terrible time, but now I hope to go back someday. I think the experience made me more open-minded about trying new places.

Center-of-gravity sentence

My vacation this summer was special because I was willing to put aside my expectations of boredom and learn some new ideas about the strange environment at Yellowstone.

At the end of three loops, this student has moved from the general subject of "summer vacation" to the more focused idea that her willingness to learn about a new place played an important part in the enjoyment of her vacation. Although her last center-of-gravity sentence still contains some vague words ("special," "new ideas," "strange environment"), the thought stated here may eventually lead to an essay that not only will say something about this student's vacation but may also persuade readers to reconsider their attitude toward taking trips to new places.

4. The Boomerang

Still another variation on freewriting is the technique called the "boomerang," named appropriately because, like the Australian stick, it invites your mind to travel over a subject from opposite directions to produce new ideas.

Suppose, for example, members of your class have been asked to write about their major field of study, which in your case is Liberal Arts. Begin by writing a statement that comes into your mind about majoring in the Liberal Arts, and then freewrite on that statement for five minutes. Then write a second statement that approaches the subject from an opposing point of view, and freewrite again for five minutes. Continue this pattern several times. Boomeranging, like looping, can help writers see their subject in a new way and consequently help them find an idea to write about.

Here's an abbreviated sample of boomeranging:

1. Majoring in the Liberal Arts is impractical in today's world.
   [Freewrite for five minutes.]

2. Majoring in the Liberal Arts is practical in today's world.
   [Freewrite for five minutes.]

3. Liberal Arts is a particularly enjoyable major for me.
   [Freewrite for five minutes.]

4. Liberal Arts is not always an enjoyable major for me.
   [Freewrite for five minutes.]

And so on.

By continuing to "throw the boomerang" across your subject, you may not only find your focus but also gain insight into other people's views of your topic, which can be especially valuable if your paper will address a controversial issue or one that you feel is often misunderstood.

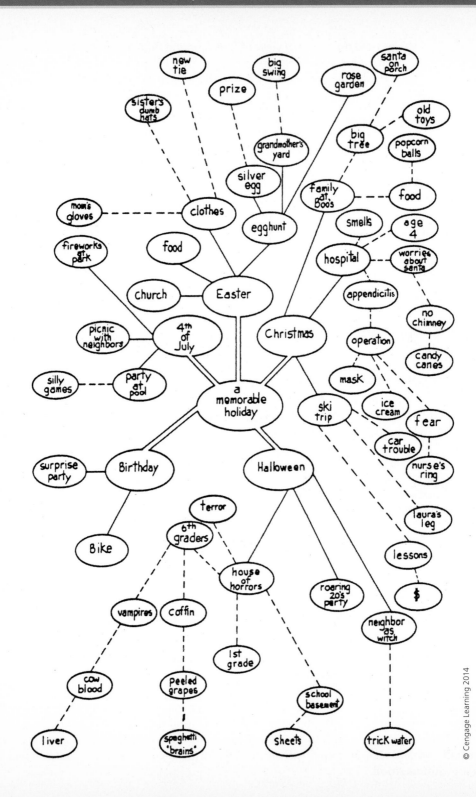

5. Clustering

Another excellent technique is clustering (sometimes called "mapping"). Place your general subject in a circle in the middle of a blank sheet of paper and begin to draw other lines and circles that radiate from the original subject. Cluster those ideas that seem to fall together. At the end of ten minutes, see if a topic emerges from any of your groups of ideas.

Ten minutes of clustering on the subject of "A Memorable Holiday" might look like the drawing on page 12.

This student may wish to brainstorm further on the Christmas he spent in the hospital with a case of appendicitis or perhaps on the Halloween he first experienced a house of horrors. By using clustering, he has recollected some important details about a number of holidays that may help him focus on an occasion he wants to describe in his paper.

6. Cubing

Still another way to generate ideas is cubing. Imagine a six-sided cube that looks something like the figure below.

Mentally, roll your subject around the cube and freewrite the answers to the questions that follow. Write whatever comes to mind for ten or fifteen minutes; don't concern yourself with the "correctness" of what you write.

a. **Describe it:** What does your subject look like? What size, colors, textures does it have? Does it have any special features worth noting?

b. **Compare or contrast it:** What is your subject similar to? What is your subject different from? In what ways?

c. **Free-associate it:** What does this subject remind you of? What does it call to mind? What memories does it conjure up?

d. **Analyze it:** How does it work? How are the parts connected? What is its significance?

e. **Argue for or against it:** What arguments can you make for or against your subject? What advantages or disadvantages does it have? What changes or improvements should be made?

f. **Apply it:** What are the uses of your subject? What can you do with it?

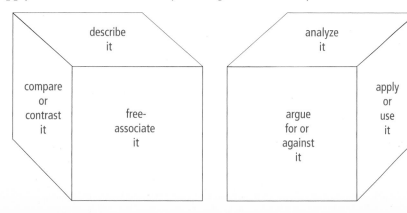

© Cengage Learning 2014

A student who had recently volunteered at a homeless shelter wrote the following responses about her experience:

a. **Describe it:** I and five other members of my campus organization volunteered three Saturdays to work at the shelter here in town. We mainly helped in the kitchen, preparing, serving, and cleaning up after meals. At the dinners we served about forty homeless people, mostly men but also some families with small children and babies.

b. **Compare or contrast it:** I had never done anything like this before so it's hard to compare or contrast it to anything. It was different though from what I expected. I hadn't really thought much about the people who would be there—or to be honest I think I thought they would be pretty weird or sad and I was kind of dreading going there after I volunteered. But the people were just regular normal people. And they were very, very polite to us.

c. **Free-associate it:** Some of the people there reminded me of some of my relatives! John, the kitchen manager, said most of the people were just temporarily "down on their luck" and that reminded me of my aunt and uncle who came to stay with us for a while when I was in high school after my uncle lost his job.

d. **Analyze it:** I feel like I got a lot out of my experience. I think I had some wrong ideas about "the homeless" and working there made me think more about them as real people, not just a faceless group.

e. **Argue for or against it:** I would encourage others to volunteer there. The work isn't hard and it isn't scary. It makes you appreciate what you've got and also makes you think about what you or your family might do if things went wrong for a while. It also makes you feel good to do something for people you don't even know.

f. **Apply it:** I feel like I am more knowledgeable when I hear people talk about the poor or the homeless in this town, especially those people who criticize those who use the shelter.

After you've written your responses, see if any one or more of them give you an idea for a paper. The student who wrote the preceding responses decided she wanted to write an article for her campus newspaper encouraging people to volunteer at the shelter not only to provide much-needed help, but also to challenge their own preconceived notions about the homeless in her college town. Cubing helped her realize she had something valuable to say about her experience and gave her a purpose for writing.

7. Interviewing

Another way to find a direction for your paper is through interviewing. Ask a classmate or friend to discuss your subject with you. Let your thoughts range over your subject as your friend asks you questions that arise naturally in the conversation. Or your friend might try asking what are called "reporter's questions" as she or he "interviews" you on your subject:

Who?   When?
What?   Why?
Where?   How?

Listen to what you have to say about your subject. What were you most interested in talking about? What did your friend want to know? Why? By talking about your subject, you may find that you have talked your way into an interesting focus for your paper. If, after the interview, you are still stumped, question your friend: if he or she had to publish an essay based on the information from your interview, what would that essay focus on? Why?

8. The Cross-Examination

If a classmate isn't available for an interview, try interviewing, or cross-examining, yourself. Ask yourself questions about your general subject, just as a lawyer might if you were on the witness stand. Consider using the five categories described below and on the next page, which are adapted from those suggested by Aristotle centuries ago to the orators of his day. Ask yourself as many questions in each category as you can think of, and then go on to the next category. Jot down brief notes to yourself as you answer.

Here are the five categories, plus six sample questions for each to illustrate the possibilities:

1. Definition
    a. How does the dictionary or encyclopedia define or explain this subject?
    b. How do most people define or explain it?
    c. How do I define or explain it?
    d. What do its parts look like?
    e. What is its history or origin?
    f. What are some examples of it?
2. Comparison and Contrast
    a. What is it similar to?
    b. What does it differ from?
    c. What does it parallel?
    d. What is its opposite?
    e. What is it better than?
    f. What is it worse than?
3. Relationship
    a. What causes it?
    b. What are the effects of it?
    c. What larger group or category is it a part of?
    d. What larger group or category is it in opposition to?
    e. What are its values or goals?
    f. What contradictions does it contain?
4. Circumstance
    a. Is it possible?
    b. Is it impossible?

     c. When has it happened before?

     d. What might prevent it from happening?

     e. Why might it happen again?

     f. Who has been or might be associated with it?

5. Testimony

     a. What do people say about it?

     b. What has been written about it?

     c. What authorities exist on the subject?

     d. Are there any relevant statistics?

     e. What research has been done?

     f. Have I had any direct experience with it?

Some of the questions suggested here, or ones you think of, may not be relevant to or useful for your subject. But some may lead you to ideas you wish to explore in more depth, either in a discovery draft or by using another prewriting technique described in this chapter, such as looping or clustering.

9. Sketching

Sometimes when you have found or been assigned a general subject, the words to explain or describe it just won't come. Although listing or freewriting or one of the other methods suggested here works well for some people, other writers find these techniques intimidating or unproductive. Some of these writers are visual learners—that is, they respond better to pictorial representations of material than they do to written descriptions or explanations. If, on occasion, you are stuck for words, try drawing or sketching or even cartooning the pictures in your mind.

    You may be surprised at the details that you remember once you start sketching. For example, you might have been asked to write about a favorite place or a special person in your life or to compare or contrast two places you have lived in or visited. See how many details you can conjure up by drawing the scenes or the people; then look at your details to see if some dominant impression or common theme has emerged. Your Aunt Sophie's insistence on wearing two pounds of costume jewelry might become the focus of a paragraph on her sparkling personality, or the many details you recalled about your grandfather's barn might lead you to a paper on the hardships of farm life. For some writers, a picture can be worth a thousand words—especially if that picture helps them begin putting those words on paper.

10. Dramatizing the Subject

Some writers find it helpful to visualize their subject as if it were a drama or play unfolding in their minds. Kenneth Burke, a thoughtful writer himself, suggests that writers might think about human action in dramatists' terms and then see what sorts of new insights arise as the "drama" unfolds. Burke's dramatists' terms might be adapted for our use and pictured this way:

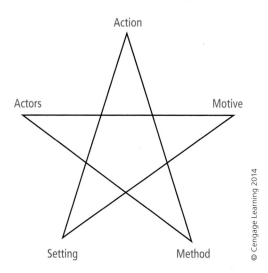

© Cengage Learning 2014

Just as you did in the cubing exercise, try mentally rolling your subject around the star and explore the possibilities that emerge. For example, suppose you want to write about your recent decision to return to college after a long period of working, but you don't know what you want to say about your decision. Start thinking about this decision as a drama and jot down brief answers to such questions as these:

Action: What happened?
          What were the results?
          What is going to happen?

Actors: Who was involved in the action?
          Who was affected by the action?
          Who caused the action?
          Who was for it and who was opposed?

Motive: What were the reasons behind the action?
          What forces motivated the actors to perform as they did?

Method: How did the action occur?
          By what means did the actors accomplish the action?

Setting: What were the time and place of the action?
          What did the place look like?
          What positive or negative feelings are associated with this time or place?

These are only a few of the dozens of questions you might ask yourself about your "drama." (If it helps, think of your "drama" as a murder mystery and answer the questions the police detective might ask: what happened here? to whom? who did it? why? with what? when? where? and so on.)

You may find that you have a great deal to write about the combination of actor and motive but very little to say in response to the questions on setting or method. That's fine—simply use the "dramatists' approach" to help you find a specific topic or idea you want to write about.

REMEMBER: If at any point in this stage of the writing process you are experiencing Writer's Block, you might turn to the suggestions for overcoming this common affliction that appear on pages 121–123 in Chapter 5. You might also find it helpful to read the section *Keeping a Journal,* pages 26–29, because writing in a relaxed mood on a regular basis may be the best long-term cure for your writing anxiety.

After You've Found Your Focus

Once you think you've found the focus of your essay, you may be ready to compose a *working thesis statement,* an important part of your essay discussed in great detail in the next chapter. If you've used one of the prewriting exercises outlined in this chapter, by all means hang on to it. The details and observations you generated as you focused your topic may be useful as you begin to organize and develop your body paragraphs.

Practicing What You've Learned

© Canstock Images, Inc./
Index Stock Imagery

A. Some of the subjects listed below are too broad for a 500-to-800-word essay. Identify those topics that might be treated in short papers and those that still need to be narrowed.

1. The role of the modern university

2. My first (and last) experience with skateboarding

3. The characters of William Shakespeare

4. Solar energy

5. Collecting baseball cards

6. Gun-control laws

7. Down with throwaway bottles

8. Computers

9. The best teacher I've ever had

10. Selecting the right bicycle

B. Select two of the large subjects that follow and, through looping or listing details or another prewriting technique, find focused topics that would be appropriate for essays of three to five pages.

1. Music

2. Cars

continued on next page

3. Education

4. Jobs

5. Television commercials

6. Politics

7. Animals

8. Childhood

9. Cell phones

10. Athletics

Discovering Your Audience

Once you have a focused topic and perhaps some ideas about developing your essay, you need to pause a moment to consider your *audience*. Before you can decide what information needs to go into your essay and what should be omitted, you must know who will be reading your paper and why. Knowing your audience will also help you determine what *voice* you should use to achieve the proper tone in your essay.

Suppose, for example, you are attending a college organized on the quarter system, and you decide to write an essay arguing for a switch to the semester system. If your audience is composed of classmates, your essay will probably focus on the advantages to the student body, such as better opportunities for in-depth study in one's major, the ease of making better grades, and the benefits of longer midwinter and summer vacations. However, if you are addressing the Board of Regents, you might emphasize the power of the semester system to attract more students, cut registration costs, and use professors more efficiently. If your audience is composed of townspeople who know little about either system, you will have to devote more time to explaining the logistics of each one and then discuss the semester plan's advantages to the local merchants, real estate agents, restaurateurs, and so on. *In other words, such factors as the age, education, profession, and interests of your audience can make a difference in determining which points of your argument to stress or omit, which ideas need additional explanation, and what kind of language to adopt.*

How to Identify Your Readers

To help you analyze your audience before you begin writing your working thesis statement and rough drafts, here are some steps you may wish to follow:

1. First, see if your writing assignment specifies a particular audience (editors of a journal in your field or the Better Business Bureau of your town, for example) or a general audience of your peers (your classmates or readers of the local newspaper, for instance). Even if your assignment does not mention an intended

audience, try to imagine one anyway. Imagining specific readers will help you stick to your goal of communicating clearly, in engaging detail.

2. If a specific audience is designated, ask yourself some questions about their motivation or *reasons for reading* your essay.

- What do these readers want to learn?
- What do they hope to gain?
- Do they need your information to make a decision? Formulate a new plan? Design a new project?
- What action do you want them to take?

The answers to such questions will help you find both your essay's purpose and its content. If, for example, you're trying to persuade an employer to hire you for a particular job, you certainly would write your application in a way that stresses the skills and training the company is searching for. You may have a fine hobby or a wonderful family, but if your prospective employer-reader doesn't need to hear about that particular part of your life, toss it out of this piece of writing.

3. Next, try to discover what *knowledge* your audience has of your subject.

- What, if anything, can you assume that your readers already know about your topic?
- What background information might they need to know to understand a current situation clearly?
- What facts, explanations, or examples will best present your ideas? How detailed should you be?
- What terms need to be defined? Equipment explained?

Questions like these should guide you as you collect and discard information for your paper. An essay written to your colleagues in electrical engineering, for instance, need not explain commonly used technical instruments; to do so might even insult your readers. But the same report read by your composition classmates would probably need more detailed explanation for you to make yourself understood. Always put yourself in your readers' place and then ask: what else do they need to know to understand this point completely?

4. Once you have decided what information is necessary for your audience, dig a little deeper into your readers' identities. Pose some questions about their *attitudes* and emotional states.

- Are your readers already biased for or against your ideas in some way?
- Do they have positive or negative associations with your subject?
- Are they fearful or anxious, reluctant or bored?
- Do they have radically different expectations or interests?

It helps enormously to know the emotional attitudes of your readers toward your subject. Let's suppose you are arguing for the admission of a young child with AIDS into a local school system, and your audience is the parent-teacher organization. Some of your readers might be frightened or even hostile; knowing this, you would wisely begin your argument with a disarming array of information showing that no cases of AIDS have developed from the casual contact of schoolchildren. In other words, the more you know about your audience's attitudes before you begin writing, the more convincing your prose, because you will make the best choices about both content and organization.

5. Last, think of any *special qualities* that might set your audience apart from any other.

- Are they older or younger than your peers?
- Do they share similar educational experiences or training?
- Are they from a particular part of the world or country that might affect their perspective? Urban or rural?
- Are they in positions of authority?

Knowing special facts about your audience makes a difference, often in your choice of words and tone. You wouldn't, after all, use the same level of vocabulary addressing a group of fifth-graders as you would writing to the children's teacher or principal. Similarly, your tone and word choice probably wouldn't be as formal in an e-mail to a friend as in a letter to a credit card company protesting your most recent bill.

Without question, analyzing your specific audience is an important step to take before you begin to shape your rough drafts. And before you move on to writing a working thesis, here are a few tips to keep in mind about *all* audiences, no matter who your readers are or what their reasons for reading your writing.

1. **Readers don't like to be bored.** Grab your readers' attention and fight to keep it. Remember the last dull movie you squirmed—or slept—through? How much you resented wasting not only your money but your valuable time as well? How you turned it off mentally and drifted away to someplace more exciting? As you write and revise your drafts, keep imagining readers who are as intelligent—and busy— as you are. Put yourself in their place: would you find this piece of writing stimulating enough to keep reading?

2. **Readers hate confusion and disorder.** Can you recall a time when you tried to find your way to a party, only to discover that a friend's directions were so muddled you wound up hours later, out of gas, cursing in a cornfield? Or the afternoon you spent trying to follow a friend's notes for setting up a chemistry experiment, with explanations that twisted and turned as often as a wandering stray cat? Try to relive such moments of intense frustration as you struggle to make *your* writing clear and direct.

3. **Readers want to think and learn (whether they realize it or not).** Every time you write, you strike a bargain of sorts with your readers: in return for their time and attention, you promise to inform and interest them, to tell them something new or show them something familiar in a different light. You may enlighten them or amuse them or even try to frighten them—but they must feel, in the end, that they've gotten a fair trade. As you plan, write, and revise, ask yourself, "What are my readers learning?" If the honest answer is "nothing important," you may be writing only for yourself. (If you yourself are bored rereading your drafts, you're probably not writing for anybody at all.)

4. **Readers want to see what you see, feel what you feel.** Writing that is vague keeps your readers from fully sharing the information or experience you are trying to communicate. Clear, precise language—full of concrete details and specific examples—lets your readers know that you understand your subject and that you want them to understand it, too. Even a potentially dull topic such as tuning up a car can become engaging to a reader if the right details are provided in the right places: your terror as blue sparks leap under your nose when the wrong wire is touched, the depressing sight of the screwdriver squirming from your greasy fingers and disappearing into the oil pan, the sudden shooting pain when the wrench slips and turns your knuckles to raw hamburger. Get your readers involved and interested—and they'll listen to what you have to say. (Details also persuade your reader that you're an authority on your subject; after all, no reader likes to waste time listening to someone whose tentative, vague prose style announces, "I only sort of know what I'm talking about here.")

5. **Readers are turned off by writers with pretentious, phony voices.** Too often, inexperienced writers feel they must sound especially scholarly, scientific, or sophisticated for their essays to be convincing. In fact, the contrary is true. When you assume a voice that is not yours, when you pretend to be someone you're not, you don't sound believable at all—you sound phony. Your readers want to hear what *you* have to say, and the best way to communicate with them is in a natural voice. You may also believe that to write a good essay it is necessary to use a host of unfamiliar, unpronounceable, polysyllabic words gleaned from the pages of your thesaurus. Again, the opposite is true. Our best writers agree with Mark Twain, who once said, "Never use a twenty-five-cent word when a ten-cent word will do." In other words, avoid pretension in your writing just as you do in everyday conversation. Select simple, direct words you know and use frequently; keep your voice natural, sincere, and reasonable. (◆ For additional help choosing the appropriate words and the level of your diction, see Chapter 7.)

Don't Ever Forget Your Readers!

Thinking about them as you write will help you choose your ideas, organize your information effectively, and select the best words.

Practicing What You've Learned

A. Practice identifying intended audiences by analyzing, first, the Geico insurance advertisement that appears on the next page and then at least two additional advertisements reprinted in other pages of this text, such as "Gas Heat Makes Me Nervous" (page 314) or "PETA Anti-Fur" (page 320). (A list of the ads in this text follows the Table of Contents.)

continued on next page

In each case, first determine the purpose of the ad and then describe the ad's target audience, explaining your reasons for your response. You may find it helpful to consider some of the following questions:

1. What age group does the ad target? Does it appeal primarily to males, females, or both? Is the intended audience of a particular social or economic class?

2. What concerns or strong interests might this audience have?

3. What kinds of arguments are used in the ad to persuade its intended audience?

4. What specific words or phrases are chosen to appeal to this particular audience?

Courtesy of Geico, Inc.

B. Select an essay or feature story from a magazine or journal of your choosing and identify the intended audience. Explain how you arrived at this conclusion by showing ways the writer effectively addresses his or her audience.

C. Find two advertisements for the same kind of common product (car, cell phone service, shoes, cosmetics, etc.) but with different brands (e.g., Ford and Toyota, AT&T and Verizon). Do the ads you have selected have different or similar target audiences? How do you know? Does one ad more effectively address its audience than the other, and if so, why?

Assignment

A. The article that follows appeared in newspapers across the country some time ago. Read about the diet called "Breatharianism" and then write one or more of the assignments that follow the article.

© CORBIS

continued on next page

The Ultimate in Diet Cults: Don't Eat Anything at All*

1   CORTE MADERA, CALIF.—Among those seeking enlightenment through diet cults, Wiley Brooks seemed to have the ultimate answer—not eating at all. He called himself a "Breatharian" and claimed to live on air, supplemented only by occasional fluids taken to counteract the toxins of urban environments.

2   "Food is more addictive than heroin," the tall, gaunt man told hundreds of people who paid $500 each to attend five-day "intensives," at which he would stand before them in a camel velour sweatsuit and talk for hours without moving, his fingers meditatively touching at their tips.

3   Brooks, 46, became a celebrity on the New Age touring circuit. ABC-TV featured him in October, 1980, as a weight lifter; he allegedly hoisted 1,100 pounds, about 10 times his own weight. He has also been interviewed on radio and in newspapers.

4   Those who went to his sessions during the past six months on the West Coast and in Hawaii were not just food faddists, but also physicians and other professionals who—though not necessarily ready to believe—thought this man could be onto something important. Some were convinced enough by what they saw to begin limiting their own diets, taking the first steps toward Breatharianism.

5   In his intensives, Brooks did not recommend that people stop eating altogether. Rather, he suggested they "clean their blood" by starting with the "yellow diet"— 24 food items including grapefruit, papaya, corn products, eggs, chicken, fish, goat's milk, millet, salsa piquante (Mexican hot sauce) and certain flavors of the Häagen Dazs brand ice cream, including "rum raisin." These foods, he said, have a less toxic effect because, among other things, "their vibrational quality is yellow."

6   Last week, however, aspirants toward Breatharianism were shocked by reports that Brooks had been eating—and what's more, eating things that to health food purists are the worst kind of junk.

7   Word spread that during an intensive in Vancouver, Brooks was seen emerging from a 7-Eleven store with a bag of groceries. The next morning there were allegedly room service trays outside his hotel room, while inside, the trash basket held empty containers of chicken pot pie, chili and biscuits.

8   Kendra Wagner, regional Breatharian coordinator, said she herself had seen Brooks drinking a Coke. "When I asked him about it he said, 'That's how dirty the air is here,'" she explained. "We (the coordinators) sat down with Wiley after the training and said, 'We want you to tell us the truth.' He denied everything. We felt tricked and deceived."

9   As the rumors grew, some Breatharians confronted their leader at a lecture in San Francisco. Brooks denied the story and said that the true message of Breatharianism did not depend on whether he ate or not, anyway.

10   The message in his promotional material reads that "modern man is the degenerate descendant of the Breatharian," and that "living on air alone leads to perfect health and perfect happiness." Though followers had the impression Brooks has not eaten for 18 years, his leaflets merely declare that "he does not eat, and seldom drinks any fluid. He sleeps less than seven hours a week and is healthier, more energetic and happier than he ever dreamed possible."

---

* "The Ultimate in Diet Cults: Don't Eat Anything at All" from the Bay Area Institute. Reprinted with permission.

11   In a telephone interview, Brooks acknowledged that this assertion is not quite correct. "I'm sure I've taken some fruit, like an apple or an orange, but it's better in public to keep it simple." He again staunchly denied the 7-Eleven story.

12   Among those who have been on the yellow diet for months is Jime Collison, 24, who earlier tried "fruitarianism," fasting and other special regimens, and moved from Texas to the San Francisco Bay area just to be around the Breatharian movement. "Now I'm a basket case," he said. "My world revolved around Wiley's philosophy." He had thought Wiley "made the jump to where all of us health food fanatics were going," Collison said.

13   Other Brooks disciples, though disappointed, feel they nevertheless benefited from their experience. Said a physician who has been on the yellow diet for four months: "I feel very good. I still don't know what the truth is, but I do know that Wiley is a good salesman. So I'll be patient, keep an open mind and continue to observe."

14   "Breatharianism is the understanding of what the body really needs, not whether Wiley eats or doesn't," said James Wahler, 35, who teaches a self-development technique called "rebirthing," in Marin County. "I'm realizing that the less I eat the better I feel." He also suggested that Brooks may have lied for people's own good, to get them to listen.

15   "Everyone has benefited from what I'm saying," Brooks said. "There will be a food shortage and a lot of unhappy people when they realize that I was trying to save their lives."

The assignments that follow are directed to different audiences, each unfamiliar with Breatharianism. What information does each audience need to know? What kinds of details will be the most persuasive? What sort of organization will work best for each purpose and audience?

1.   Write a single-page flyer advertising the five-day intensives. What appeals might persuade people to pay $500 each to attend a seminar to learn to eat air?

2.   Assume you are a regional Breatharian coordinator. Write a letter to your city council petitioning for a parade permit that will allow members of your organization to parade down your main street in support of this diet and its lifestyle. What do council members need to know before they vote on such a permit?

3.   You are a former Breatharian who is now unhappy with the diet and its unfulfilled promises. Write a report for the vice squad calling for an investigation into the organization. Convince the investigators that the organization is defrauding local citizens and should be stopped.

B. *Collaborative Activity:* In a small group of three or four classmates, exchange the assignments you have written. Which flyer, petition, and report does the group find most persuasive for its intended audience, and why? Present your group's analysis to the class.

Keeping a Journal (Talking to Yourself Does Help)

Many professional writers carry small notebooks with them so they can jot down ideas and impressions for future use. Still others write blogs, web logs intended for public reading and commentary.

In your composition class, you may find it useful to keep a private journal to help you with your writing process, or you may be assigned a journal or blog whose entries will be shared with your teacher or classmates. Whatever the exact medium, you might use a journal to explore your thoughts, experiment with prewriting techniques, save important ideas, respond to classroom readings or discussions, comment on other students' writing, remember important course material, or reflect on your own work, to name only a few possibilities. Devoting time to a journal can help you become a more confident, practiced writer.

Often, the journal is kept in a notebook you can carry with you (spiral is fine, although a prong or ring notebook allows you to add or remove pages when you wish); some writers prefer to collect their thoughts in designated computer files or web logs. Even if a journal is not assigned in your composition class, it is still a useful tool.

Writers who have found journal writing effective advise trying to write a minimum of three entries a week, with each entry at least a half page. To keep a carry-around notebook organized, start each entry on a new page and date each entry you write. You might also leave the backs of your notebook pages blank so that you can return and respond to an entry at a later date if you wish.

Uses of the Journal

Here are some suggested uses for your journal as you move through the writing process. You may want to experiment with a number of these suggestions to see which are the most productive for you.

1. **Use the journal, especially in the first weeks of class, to confront your fears of writing, to conquer the blank page.** Write anything you want to—thoughts, observations, notes to yourself, letters home, anything at all. Best your enemy by writing down that witty retort you thought of later and wished you had said. Write about your ideal job, vacation, car, or home. Write a self-portrait or make a list of all the subjects on which you are (or would like to become) an "authority." The more you write, the easier writing becomes—or at least, the easier it is to begin writing because, like a sword swallower, you know you have accomplished the act before and lived to tell about it.

2. **Improve your powers of observation.** Record interesting snippets of conversations you overhear or catalog noises you hear in a ten-minute period in a crowded place, such as your student center, a bookstore, or a mall. Eat something with multiple layers (a piece of fruit such as an orange) and list all the tastes, textures, and smells you discover. Look around your room and write down a list of everything that is yellow. By becoming sensitive to the sights, sounds, smells, and textures around you, you may find that your powers of description and explanation

will expand, enabling you to help your reader "see" what you're talking about in your next essay.

3. **Save your own brilliant ideas.** Jot down those bright ideas that might turn into great essays. Or save those thoughts you have now for the essay you know is coming later in the semester so you won't forget them. Expand or elaborate on any ideas you have; you might be able to convert your early thoughts into a paragraph when it's time to start drafting.

4. **Save other people's brilliant ideas.** Record interesting quotations, facts, and figures from other writers and thinkers. You may find some of this information useful in one of your later essays. It's also helpful to look at the ways other writers make their words emphatic, moving, and arresting so you can try some of their techniques in your own prose. (Important: Don't forget to note the source of any material you record, so if you do quote any of it in a paper later, you will be able to document it properly.)

5. **Be creative.** Write a poem or song or story or joke. Parody the style of someone you've heard or read. Become an inanimate object and complain to the humans around you (for example, what would a soft-drink machine like to say to those folks constantly beating on its stomach?). Become a little green creature from Mars and convince a human to accompany you back to your planet as a specimen of Earthlings (or be the invited guest and explain to the creature why you are definitely not the person to go). The possibilities are endless, so go wild.

6. **Keep pre- and post-reading notes.** As a composition student, you may be asked to read and analyze selections by professional writers, and your journal is a fine place to record your responses. In addition, many of the professional essays in this text have pre-reading/thinking questions designed to encourage your preliminary consideration of the writer's topic or point of view; you might reply to those questions in a journal entry or perhaps freewrite on a subject they suggest.

   After you've read your assignment, try a split-page entry. Draw a line down the middle of a page in your journal, and on the left side of the page write a summary of what you've read or perhaps list the main points. Then on the right side of the same page, write your responses to the material. Your responses might be your personal reaction to the content (what struck you hardest? why?) or your agreement or disagreement with a particular point or two. Or the material might call up some long-forgotten idea or memory. By thinking about your class material both analytically and personally, you almost certainly will remember it for class discussion. You might also find that a good idea for an essay will arise as you think about the reading assignments in different ways.

7. **Record responses to class discussions.** A journal is a good place to note your reactions to what your teacher and your peers are saying in class. You can ask yourself questions ("What did Megan mean when she said . . .") or note any confusion ("I got mixed up when . . .") or record your own reactions ("I disagreed

with Jamal when he argued that . . .”). Again, some of your reactions might become the basis of a good essay.

8. **Focus on a problem.** You can restate the problem or explore the problem or solve the problem. Writing about a problem often encourages the mind to flow over the information in ways that allow discoveries to happen. Sometimes, too, we don't know exactly what the problem is or how we feel about it until we write about it. Remember the encouraging words of the philosopher Voltaire: “No problem can withstand the assault of thinking.” Writing *is* thinking.

9. **Practice audience awareness.** Write letters to different companies, praising or panning their product; then write advertising copy for each product. Become the third critic on a popular movie-review program and show the other two commentators why your review of your favorite movie is superior to theirs. Thinking about a specific audience when you write will help you plan the content, organization, and tone of each writing assignment.

10. **Describe your own writing process.** It's helpful sometimes to record how you go about writing your essays. How do you get started? How much time do you spend getting started? Do you write an “idea” draft or work from an outline? How do you revise? Do you write multiple drafts? These and many other questions may give you a clue to any problems you might have as you write your next essay. If, for example, you see that you're having trouble again and again with conclusions, you can turn to Chapter 4 for some extra help. Sometimes it's hard to see that there's a pattern in our writing process until we've described it several times.

11. **Write a progress report.** List all the skills you've mastered as the course progresses. You'll be surprised at how much you have learned. Read the list over if you're ever feeling frustrated or discouraged, and take pride in your growth.

12. **Become sensitive to language.** Keep a record of jokes and puns that play on words. Record people's weird-but-funny uses of language (overheard at the dorm cafeteria: “She was so skinny she was emancipated” and “I'm tired of being the escape goat”). Rewrite some of today's bureaucratic jargon or retread a cliché. Come up with new images of your own. Playing with language in fun or even silly ways can make writing tasks seem less threatening. (A newspaper recently came up with this language game: change, add, or subtract one letter in a word and provide a new definition. Examples: intoxication/intaxication—the giddy feeling of getting a tax refund; graffiti/giraffiti—spray paint that appears on tall buildings; sarcasm/sarchasm—the gulf between the witty speaker and the listener who doesn't get it.)

13. **Write your own textbook.** Take notes on material that is important for you to remember. For instance, make your own grammar or punctuation handbook with only those rules you find yourself referring to often. Or keep a list of spelling rules that govern the words you misspell frequently. Writing out the rules

in your own words and having a convenient place to refer to them may help you teach yourself quicker than studying any textbook (including this one).

These suggestions are some of the many uses you may find for your journal once you start writing in one on a regular basis. Obviously, not all the suggestions here will be appropriate for you, but some might be. If it's helpful, consider using multiple files or, in a notebook, a set of divider tabs to separate the different functions of your journal (one section or file for class responses, one section for your own thoughts, one for your own handbook, and so on).

You may find, as some students have, that the journal is especially useful during the first weeks of your writing course, when putting words on a page is often hardest. Many students, however, continue to use the journal throughout the entire course, and others adapt their journals to record their responses to their other college classes and experiences. Whether you continue using a journal beyond this course is up to you, but consider trying the journal for at least six weeks. You may find that it will improve your writing skills more than anything else you have tried before.

Chapter 1 Summary

Here is a brief summary of what you should know about the prewriting stage of your writing process:

1. Before you begin writing anything, remember that you have valuable ideas to tell your readers.

2. It's not enough that these valuable ideas are clear to you, the writer. Your single most important goal is to communicate those ideas clearly to your readers, who cannot know what's in your mind until you tell them.

3. Whenever possible, select a subject to write on that is of great interest to you, and always give yourself more time than you think you'll need to work on your essay.

4. Try a variety of prewriting techniques to help you find your essay's purpose and a narrowed, specific focus.

5. Review your audience's knowledge of and attitudes toward your topic before you begin your first draft; ask yourself questions such as "Who needs to know about this topic, and why?"

6. Consider keeping a journal to help you explore good ideas and possible topics for writing assignments in your composition class.

Chapter 2

The Thesis Statement

The famous American author Thomas Wolfe had a simple formula for beginning his writing: "Just put a sheet of paper in the typewriter and start bleeding." For some writers, the "bleeding" method works well. You may find that, indeed, you are one of those writers who must begin by freewriting or by writing an entire "discovery draft" to find your purpose and focus—you must write yourself into your topic, so to speak.* Other writers are more structured; they may prefer prewriting in lists, outlines, or cubes. Sometimes writers begin certain projects by composing one way, whereas other kinds of writing tasks profit from another method. There is no right or wrong way to find a topic or to begin writing; simply try to find the methods that work best for you.

Let's assume at this point that you have identified a topic you wish to write about—perhaps you found it by working through one of the prewriting activities mentioned in Chapter 1 or by writing in your journal. Perhaps you had an important idea you had been wanting to write about for some time, or perhaps the assignment in your class suggested the topic to you. Suppose that through one of these avenues you had focused on a topic and you have given some thought to a possible audience for your paper. You may now find it helpful to formulate a *working thesis*.

What Is a Thesis? What Does a "Working Thesis" Do?

The thesis statement declares the main point or controlling idea of your entire essay. Frequently located near the beginning of a short essay, the thesis answers these questions: "What is the subject of this essay?" "What is the writer's opinion on this subject?" "What is the writer's purpose in this essay?" (to explain something? to argue a position? to move people to action? to entertain?).

---

*◆ If you do begin with a discovery draft, you may wish to turn at this point to the manuscript suggestions on pages 94–95 in Chapter 5.

Consider a "working thesis" a statement of your main point in its trial or rough-draft form. Allow it to "work" for you as you move from prewriting through drafts and revision. Your working thesis may begin as a very simple sentence. For example, one of the freewriting exercises on nature in Chapter 1 (pages 8–9) might lead to a working thesis such as "Our college needs an on-campus recycling center." Such a working thesis states an opinion about the subject (the need for a center) and suggests what the essay will do (give arguments for building such a center). Similarly, the prewriting list on running (page 8) might lead to a working thesis such as "Before beginning a successful program, novice runners must learn a series of warm-up and cool-down exercises." This statement not only tells the writer's opinion and purpose (the value of the exercises) but also indicates an audience (novice runners).

A working thesis statement can be your most valuable organizational tool. Once you have thought about your essay's main point and purpose, you can begin to draft your paper to accomplish your goals. *Everything in your essay should support your thesis.* Consequently, if you write your working thesis statement at the top of your first draft and refer to it often, your chances of drifting away from your purpose should be reduced.

Can a "Working Thesis" Change?

It's important for you to know at this point that there may be a difference between the working thesis that appears in your rough drafts and your final thesis. As you begin drafting, you may have one main idea in mind that surfaced from your prewriting activities. But as you write, you may discover that what you really want to write about is different. Perhaps you discover that one particular part of your essay is really what you want to concentrate on (instead of covering three or four problems you have with your current job, for instance, you decide you want to explore in depth only the difficulties with your boss), or perhaps in the course of writing you find another approach to your subject more satisfying or persuasive (explaining how employees may avoid problems with a particular kind of difficult boss instead of describing various kinds of difficult bosses in your field).

Changing directions is not uncommon: *writing is an act of discovery.* Frequently, we don't know exactly what we think or what we want to say until we write it. A working thesis appears in your early drafts to help you focus and organize your essay; don't feel it's carved in stone.

A warning comes with this advice, however. If you do write yourself into another essay—that is, if you discover as you write that you are finding a better topic or main point to make—consider this piece of writing a "discovery draft," extended prewriting that has helped you find your real focus. Occasionally, your direction changes so slightly that you can rework or expand your thesis to accommodate your new ideas. But more frequently you may find that it's necessary to begin another draft with your newly discovered working thesis as the controlling idea. When this is the case, don't be discouraged—this kind of "reseeing" or revision of your topic is a common practice among experienced writers. (◆ For more advice on revising as rethinking, see Chapter 5.) Don't be tempted at this point to leave your original thesis in an essay that has clearly changed its point, purpose, or approach—in other words, don't try to pass off an old head on the body of a new statue! Remember that ultimately you want your thesis to guide your readers rather than confuse them by promising an essay they can't find as they read on.

Guidelines for Writing a Good Thesis

To help you draft your thesis statement, here is some advice:

A good thesis states the writer's clearly defined opinion on some subject. You must tell your reader what you think. Don't dodge the issue; present your opinion specifically and precisely. For example, if you were asked to write a thesis statement expressing your position on the national law that designates twenty-one as the legal minimum age to purchase or consume alcohol, the first three theses listed here would be confusing:

Poor	Many people have different opinions on whether people under twenty-one should be permitted to drink alcohol, and I agree with some of them. [The writer's opinion on the issue is not clear to the reader.]
Poor	The question of whether we need a national law governing the minimum age to drink alcohol is a controversial issue in many states. [This statement might introduce the thesis, but the writer has still avoided stating a clear opinion on the issue.]
Poor	I want to give my opinion on the national law that sets twenty-one as the legal age to drink alcohol and the reasons I feel this way. [What is the writer's opinion? The reader still doesn't know.]
Better	To reduce the number of highway fatalities, our country needs to enforce the national law that designates twenty-one as the legal minimum age to purchase and consume alcohol. [The writer clearly states an opinion that will be supported in the essay.]
Better	The legal minimum age for purchasing alcohol should be eighteen rather than twenty-one. [Again, the writer has asserted a clear position on the issue that will be argued in the essay.]

If you want to write about a personal experience but are finding it difficult to clearly define your thesis idea, try asking yourself questions about the topic's significance or value. (Examples: Why is this topic important to me? What was so valuable about my year on the newspaper staff? What was the most significant lesson I learned? What was an unexpected result of this experience?) Often the answer to one of your questions will show you the way to a working thesis. (Example: Writing for the school newspaper teaches time-management skills that are valuable both in and out of class.)

A good thesis asserts one main idea. Many essays drift into confusion because the writer is trying to explain or argue two different, large issues in one essay. You can't effectively ride two horses at once; pick one main idea and explain or argue it in convincing detail.

Poor	The proposed no-smoking ordinance in our town will violate a number of our citizens' civil rights, and no one has proved that secondhand smoke is danger-ous anyway. [This thesis contains two main assertions—the ordinance's violation of rights and secondhand smoke's lack of danger—that require two different kinds of supporting evidence.]
Better	The proposed no-smoking ordinance in our town will violate our civil rights. [This essay will show the various ways the ordinance will infringe on personal liberties.]
Better	The most recent U.S. Health Department studies claiming that secondhand smoke is dangerous to nonsmokers are based on faulty research. [This essay will also focus on one issue: the validity of the studies on secondhand smoke danger.]
Poor	High school athletes shouldn't have to maintain a "B" or better grade-point average in all subjects to participate in school sports, and the value of sports for some students is often overlooked. [Again, this thesis moves in two different directions.]
Better	High school athletes shouldn't have to maintain a "B" or better grade-point average in all subjects to participate in school sports. [This essay will focus on one issue: reasons why a particular average shouldn't be required.]
Better	For some students, participation in sports may be more valuable than achiev-ing a "B" grade-point average in all subjects. [This essay will argue that the benefits of sports sometimes outweigh those of elective classes.]

Incidentally, at this point you may recall from your high school days a rule about always expressing your thesis in one sentence. Writing teachers often insist on this rule to help you avoid the double-assertion problem just illustrated. Although not all essays have one-sentence theses, many do, and it's a good habit to strive for in this early stage of your writing.

A good thesis has something worthwhile to say. Although it's true that almost any subject can be made interesting with the right treatment, some subjects are more predictable and therefore more boring than others. Before you write your thesis, think hard about your subject: does your position lend itself to stale or overly obvious ideas? For example, most readers would find the following theses tiresome unless the writers had some original method of developing their essays:

Poor	Dogs have always been man's best friends. [This essay might be full of ho-hum clichés about dogs' faithfulness to their owners.]
Poor	Friendship is a wonderful thing. [Again, watch out for tired truisms that restate the obvious.]
Poor	The food in my dorm is horrible. [Although this essay might be enlivened by some vividly repulsive imagery, the subject itself is ancient.]

Frequently in composition classes you will be asked to write about yourself; after all, you are the world's authority on that subject, and you have many significant interests to talk about whose subject matter will naturally intrigue your readers. However, some topics you might consider writing about may not necessarily appeal to other readers because the material is simply too personal or restricted to be of general interest. In these cases, it often helps to *universalize* the essay's thesis so your readers can also identify with or learn something about the general subject, while learning something about you at the same time:

Poor	The four children in my family have completely different personalities. [This statement may be true, but would anyone other than the children's parents really be fascinated by this topic?]
Better	Birth order can influence children's personalities in startling ways. [The writer is wiser to offer this controversial statement, which is of more interest to readers than the preceding one because many readers have brothers and sisters of their own. The writer can then illustrate her claims with examples from her own family, and from other families, if she wishes.]
Poor	I don't like to take courses that are held in big lecture classes at this school. [Why should your reader care one way or another about your class preference?]
Better	Large lecture classes provide a poor environment for the student who learns best through interaction with both teachers and peers. [This thesis will allow the writer to present personal examples that the reader may identify with or challenge, without writing an essay that is exclusively personal.]

In other words, try to select a subject that will interest, amuse, challenge, persuade, or enlighten your readers. If your subject itself is commonplace, find a unique approach or an unusual, perhaps even controversial, point of view. If your subject is personal, ask yourself if the topic alone will be sufficiently interesting to readers; if not, think about universalizing the thesis to include your audience. Remember that a good thesis should encourage readers to read on with enthusiasm rather than invite groans of "Not this again" or shrugs of "So what?"

A good thesis is limited to fit the assignment. Your thesis should show that you've narrowed your subject matter to an appropriate size for your essay. Don't allow your thesis to promise more of a discussion than you can adequately deliver in a short essay. You want an in-depth treatment of your subject, not a superficial one. Certainly you may take on important issues in your essays; don't feel you must limit your topics to local or personal subjects. But one simply cannot refight the Vietnam War or effectively defend U.S. foreign policy in Central America in five to eight paragraphs. Focus your essay on an important part of a broader subject that interests you. (◆ For a review of ways to narrow and focus your subject, see pages 7–18.)

Poor	Nuclear power should be banned as an energy source in this country. [Can the writer give the broad subject of nuclear power a fair treatment in three to five pages?]
Better	Because of its poor safety record during the past two years, the Collin County nuclear power plant should be closed. [This writer could probably argue this focused thesis in a short essay.]

Poor   The parking permit system at this college should be completely revised. [An essay calling for the revision of the parking permit system would involve discussion of permits for various kinds of students, faculty, administrators, staff, visitors, delivery personnel, and so forth. Therefore, the thesis is probably too broad for a short essay.]

Better   Because of the complicated application process, the parking permit system at this college penalizes students with disabilities. [This thesis is focused on a particular problem and could be argued in a short paper.]

Poor   African-American artists have always contributed a lot to many kinds of American culture. ["African-American artists," "many kinds," "a lot," and "culture" cover more ground than can be dealt with in one short essay.]

Better   Scott Joplin was a major influence in the development of the uniquely American music called ragtime. [This thesis is more specifically defined.]

A good thesis is clearly stated in specific terms. More than anything, a vague thesis reflects lack of clarity in the writer's mind and almost inevitably leads to an essay that talks around the subject but never makes a coherent point. Try to avoid words whose meanings are imprecise and those that depend largely on personal interpretation, such as "interesting," "good," and "bad."

Poor   The women's movement is good for our country. [What group does the writer refer to? How is it good? For whom?]

Better   The Colorado Women's Party is working to ensure the benefits of equal pay for equal work for both males and females in our state. [This tells who will benefit and how—clearly defining the thesis.]

Poor   Registration is a big hassle. [No clear idea is communicated here. How much trouble is a "hassle"?]

Better   Registration's alphabetical fee-paying system is inefficient. [The issue is specified.]

Poor   Living in an apartment for the first time can teach you many things about taking care of yourself. ["Things" and "taking care of yourself" are both too vague. What specific ideas does the writer want to discuss? And who is the "you" the writer has in mind?]

Better   By living in an apartment, a first-year student can learn valuable lessons in financial planning and time management. [The thesis is now clearly defined and directed.]

A good thesis is easily recognized as the main idea and is often located in the first or second paragraph. Many students are hesitant to spell out a thesis at the beginning of an essay. To quote one student, "I feel as if I'm giving everything away." Although you may feel uncomfortable "giving away" the main point so soon, the alternative of waiting until the last page to present your thesis can seriously weaken your essay.

Without an assertion of what you are trying to prove, your reader does not know how to assess the supporting details your essay presents. For example, if your roommate comes home one afternoon and points out that the roof on your apartment leaks, the rent is too high, and the closet space is too small, you may agree but you may also be confused. Does your roommate want you to call the owner or is this merely a gripe session?

The Great Wave at Kanagawa, 1831, by Katsushika Hokusai

To avoid feeling swamped as you gather your prewriting thoughts, craft a working thesis to help steer you through your first draft.

How should you respond? On the other hand, if your roommate first announces that he wants the two of you to look for a new place, you can put the discussion of the roof, rent, and closets into its proper context and react accordingly. Similarly, you write an essay to have a specific effect on your readers. You will have a better chance of producing this effect if readers easily and quickly understand what you are trying to do.

Granted, some essays whose position is unmistakably obvious from the outset can get by with a strongly *implied thesis,* and it's true that some essays, often those written by professional writers, are organized to build dramatically to a climax. But if you are an inexperienced writer, the best choice at this point still may be a direct statement of your main idea. It is, after all, your responsibility to make your purpose clear, with as little expense of time and energy on the readers' part as possible. Readers should not be forced to puzzle out your essay's main point—it's your job to tell them.

Remember: An essay is not a detective story, so don't keep your readers in suspense until the last minute. Until you feel comfortable with more sophisticated patterns of organization, plan to put your clearly worded thesis statement near the beginning of your essay.

Avoiding Common Errors in Thesis Statements

Here are five mistakes to avoid when forming your thesis statements:

1. Don't make your thesis merely an announcement of your subject matter or a description of your intentions. State an attitude toward the subject.

Poor	The subject of this essay is my experience with a pet boa constrictor. [This is an announcement of the subject, not a thesis.]
Poor	I'm going to discuss boa constrictors as pets. [This represents a statement of intention but not a thesis.]
Better	Boa constrictors do not make healthy indoor pets. [The writer states an opinion that will be explained and defended in the essay.]
Better	My pet boa constrictor, Sir Pent, was a much better bodyguard than my dog, Fang. [The writer states an opinion that will be explained and illustrated in the essay.]

2. Don't clutter your thesis with such expressions as "in my opinion," "I believe," and "in this essay I'll argue that. . . ." These unnecessary phrases weaken your thesis statement because they often make you sound timid or uncertain. This is your essay; therefore, the opinions expressed are obviously yours. Be forceful: speak directly, with conviction.

Poor	My opinion is that the federal government should devote more money to solar energy research.
Poor	My thesis states that the federal government should devote more money to solar energy research.
Better	The federal government should devote more money to solar energy research.
Poor	In this essay I will present lots of reasons why horse racing should be abolished in Texas.
Better	Horse racing should be abolished in Texas.

3. Don't be unreasonable. Making irrational or oversimplified claims will not persuade your reader that you have a thorough understanding of the issue. Don't insult any reader; avoid irresponsible charges, name-calling, and profanity.

Poor	Radical religious fanatics across the nation are trying to impose their right-wing views by censoring high school library books. [Words such as "radical," "fanatics," "right-wing," and "censoring" will antagonize many readers immediately.]
Better	Only local school board members—not religious leaders or parents—should decide which books high school libraries should order.
Poor	Too many corrupt books in our high school libraries selected by liberal, atheistic educators are undermining the morals of our youth. [Again, some readers will be offended.]
Better	To ensure that high school libraries contain books that reflect community standards, parents should have a voice in selecting new titles.

4. Don't merely state a fact. A thesis is an assertion of opinion that leads to discussion. Don't select an idea that is self-evident or dead-ended.

Poor	Child abuse is a terrible problem. [Yes, of course, who wouldn't agree that child abuse is terrible?]
Better	Child-abuse laws in this state are too lenient for repeat offenders. [This thesis will lead to a discussion in which supporting arguments and evidence will be presented.]
Poor	Advertisers often use attractive models in their ads to sell products. [True, but rather obvious. How could this essay be turned into something more than a list describing one ad after another?]
Better	A number of liquor advertisers, well known for using pictures of attractive models to sell their products, are now using special graphics to send subliminal messages to their readers. [This claim is controversial and will require persuasive supporting evidence.]

Better   Although long criticized for its negative portrayal of women in television commercials, the auto industry is just as often guilty of stereotyping men as brainless idiots unable to make a decision. [This thesis makes a point that may lead to an interesting discussion.]

5. Don't express your thesis in the form of a question unless the answer is already obvious to the reader.

Poor   Why should every college student be required to take two years of foreign language?

Better   Chemistry majors should be exempt from the foreign-language requirement.

REMEMBER: Many times writers "discover" a better thesis near the end of their first draft. That's fine—consider that draft a prewriting or focusing exercise and begin another draft, using the newly discovered thesis as a starting point.

Practicing What You've Learned

© Canstock Images, Inc./
Index Stock Imagery

A. Identify each of the following thesis statements as adequate or inadequate. If the thesis is weak or insufficient in some way, explain the problem.

1. I think *Schindler's List* is a really interesting movie that everyone should see.

2. Which cars are designed better, Japanese imports or those made in the United States?

3. Some people think that the state lottery is a bad way to raise money for parks.

4. My essay will tell you how to apply for a college loan with the least amount of trouble.

5. During the fall term, final examinations should be given before Winter Break, not after the holidays as they are now.

6. Raising the cost of tuition will be a terrible burden on the students and won't do anything to improve the quality of education at this school.

7. I can't stand to even look at people who are into body piercing, especially in their face.

8. The passage of the newly proposed health-care bill for the elderly will lead to socialized medicine in this country.

9. People over seventy-five should be required to renew their driver's licenses every year.

continued on next page

   10. Having a close friend you can talk to is very important.

B. Rewrite the following sentences so that each one is a clear thesis statement. Be prepared to explain why you changed the sentences as you did.

   1. Applying for a job can be a negative experience.

   2. There are many advantages and disadvantages to the county's new voting machines.

   3. Buying baseball tickets online is one big headache.

   4. In this paper I will debate the pros and cons of the controversial motorcycle helmet law.

   5. We need to do something about the billboard clutter on the main highway into town.

   6. The insurance laws in this country need to be rewritten.

   7. Bicycle riding is my favorite exercise because it's so good for me.

   8. In my opinion, Santa Barbara is a fantastic place.

   9. The Civil Rights Movement of the 1960s had a tremendous effect on this country.

   10. All my friends like the band Thriving Ivory, and it's too bad they don't play more venues around here.

Assignment

© CORBIS

Narrow the subject and write one good thesis sentence for five of the following topics:

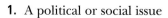

   1. A political or social issue

   2. College or high school

   3. Family

   4. A hobby or pastime

   5. A recent book or movie

   6. Vacations

   7. An environmental issue

   8. A current fad or fashion

   9. A job or profession

   10. A rule, law, or regulation

Using the Essay Map*

Many thesis sentences will benefit from the addition of an *essay map,* a brief statement in the introductory paragraph introducing the major points to be discussed in the essay. Consider the analogy of beginning a trip by checking your map to see where you are headed. Similarly, an essay map allows the readers to know in advance where you, the writer, will be taking them in the essay.

Let's suppose you have been assigned the task of praising or criticizing some aspect of your campus. You decide that your thesis will be "The Study Skills Center is an excellent place for first-year students to receive help with basic courses." Although your thesis does take a stand ("excellent place"), your reader will not know why the Center is helpful or what points you will cover in your argument. With an essay map added, the reader will have a brief but specific idea where the essay is going and how it will be developed:

Thesis

Essay map (underlined)

The Study Skills Center is an excellent place for first-year students to receive help with basic courses. <u>The Center's numerous free services, well-trained tutors, and variety of supplementary learning materials can often mean the difference between academic success and failure for many students.</u>

Thanks to the essay map, the reader knows that the essay will discuss the Center's free services, tutors, and learning materials.

Here's another example—this time let's assume you have been frustrated trying to read books your teacher has placed "on reserve" in your campus library, so you have decided to criticize your library's reserve facility:

Thesis

Essay map (underlined)

The library's reserve facility is badly managed. <u>Its unpredictable hours, poor staffing, and inadequate space discourage even the most dedicated students.</u>

After reading the introductory paragraph, the reader knows the essay will discuss the reserve facility's problematic hours, staff, and space. In other words, the thesis statement defines the main purpose of your essay, and the essay map indicates the route you will take to accomplish that purpose.

The essay map often follows the thesis, but it can also appear before it. It is, in fact, frequently part of the thesis statement itself, as illustrated in the following examples:

Thesis with underlined essay map

<u>Because of its free services, well-trained tutors, and useful learning aids,</u> the Study Skills Center is an excellent place for students seeking academic help.

Thesis with underlined essay map

For those students who need extra help with their basic courses, the Study Skills Center is one of the best resources <u>because of its numerous free services, well-trained tutors, and variety of useful learning aids.</u>

---

*I am indebted to Susan Wittig Albert for this useful concept, introduced in *Steps to Structure: An Introduction to Composition and Rhetoric* (Cambridge, MA: Winthrop Publishers, 1975).

Thesis with
underlined essay
map

<u>Unreasonable hours, poor staffing, and inadequate space</u> make the library's reserve facility difficult to use.

In addition to suggesting the main points of the essay, the map provides two other benefits. It will provide a set of guidelines for organizing your essay, and it will help keep you from wandering off into areas only vaguely related to your thesis. A clearly written thesis statement and essay map provide a skeletal outline for the sequence of paragraphs in your essay, frequently with one body paragraph devoted to each main point mentioned in your map. (Chapter 3, on paragraphs, will explain in more detail the relationships among the thesis, the map, and the body of your essay.) Note that the number of points in the essay map may vary, although three or four may be the number found most often in 500-to-800-word essays. (◆ More than four main points in a short essay might result in underdeveloped paragraphs; see pages 58–61 for additional information.)

Some important advice: although essay maps can be helpful to both writers and readers, they can also sound too mechanical, repetitive, or obvious. If you choose to use a map, always strive to blend it with your thesis as smoothly as possible.

Poor   The Study Skills Center is a helpful place for three reasons. The reasons are its free services, good tutors, and lots of learning materials.

Better   Numerous free services, well-trained tutors, and a variety of useful learning aids make the Study Skills Center a valuable campus resource.

If you feel your essay map is too obvious or mechanical, try using it only in your rough drafts to help you organize your essay. Once you're sure it isn't necessary to clarify your thesis or to guide your reader, consider dropping it from your final draft.

Practicing What You've Learned

© Canstock Images, Inc./
Index Stock Imagery

A. Identify the thesis and the essay map in the following sentences by underlining the map.

1. *Citizen Kane* deserves to appear on a list of "Top Movies of All Time" because of its excellent ensemble acting, its fast-paced script, and its innovative editing.

2. Our state should double the existing fines for first-offense drunk drivers. Such a move would lower the number of accidents, cut the costs of insurance, and increase the state revenues for highway maintenance.

3. To guarantee sound construction, lower costs, and personalized design, more people should consider building their own log cabin home.

4. Apartment living is preferable to dorm living because it's cheaper, quieter, and more luxurious.

5. Not everyone can become an astronaut. To qualify, a person must have intelligence, determination, and training.

continued on next page

6. Through unscrupulous uses of propaganda and secret assassination squads, Hitler was able to take control of an economically depressed Germany.

7. Because it builds muscles, increases circulation, and burns harmful fatty tissue, weightlifting is a sport that benefits the entire body.

8. The new tax bill will not radically reform the loophole-riddled revenue system: deductions on secondary residences will remain, real estate tax shelters will be untouched, and nonprofit health organizations will be taxed.

9. Avocados make excellent plants for children. They're inexpensive to buy, easy to root, quick to sprout, and fun to grow.

10. His spirit of protest and clever phrasing blended into unusual musical arrangements have made Bob Dylan a recording giant for more than fifty years.

B. Review the thesis statements you wrote for the Assignment on page 39. Write an essay map for each thesis statement. You may place the map before or after the thesis, or you may make it part of the thesis itself. Identify which part is the thesis and which is the essay map by underlining the map.

C. *Collaborative Activity:* Write a thesis sentence with an essay map for an essay you might write for this or another class. Exchange your work with that of a classmate and, drawing on the advice of this chapter, reconfirm strengths or offer suggestions for revision.

Assignment

Use one of the following quotations to help you think of a subject for an essay of your own. Don't merely repeat the quotation itself as your thesis statement but, rather, allow the quotation to lead you to your subject and a main point of your own creation that is appropriately narrowed  and focused. Don't forget to designate an audience for your essay, a group of readers who need or want to hear what you have to say.

1. "Opportunity is missed by most people because it is often dressed in overalls and looks like work."—Thomas Edison, inventor

2. "The world is a book and those who don't travel read only a page." —St. Augustine, cleric

3. "It is never too late to be what one might have been."—George Eliot (Mary Ann Evans), writer

continued on next page

4. "Sports do not build character. They reveal it."—Heywood Hale Broun, sportscaster

5. "Noncooperation with evil is as much a moral obligation as is cooperation with good."—Martin Luther King, Jr., statesman and civil-rights activist

6. "When a thing is funny, search it carefully for a hidden truth."—George Bernard Shaw, writer

7. "I am a great believer in luck, and I find the harder I work the more I have of it."—Stephen Leacock, economist and humorist

Jackie Robinson, who with exemplary courage ended segregation of American pro-baseball, steals home plate during the 1955 World Series.

©Bettmann / Corbis

8. "It is never too late to give up your prejudices."—Henry Thoreau, writer and naturalist

9. "When an old person dies, a library burns to the ground."—African proverb

10. "No person is your friend who demands your silence or denies your right to grow" –Alice Walker, writer

11. "Education is the most powerful weapon. You can use it to change the world."—Nelson Mandela, anti-apartheid activist and former President of South Africa

12. "The journey is the reward."—Taoist proverb

13. "You can discover more about a person in an hour of play than in a year of conversation."—Plato, philosopher

14. "Nobody can make you feel inferior without your consent."—Eleanor Roosevelt, stateswoman

15. "Never doubt that a small group of thoughtful, committed people can change the world. Indeed, it is the only thing that ever has."—Margaret Mead, anthropologist

16. "If you are patient in one moment of anger, you will escape a hundred days of sorrow."—Chinese proverb

17. "Let your hook be always cast; in the pool where you least expect it, there will be a fish."—Ovid, Roman poet

continued on next page

18. "Even if you are on the right track, you will get run over if you just sit there."—Will Rogers, humorist and writer

19. "No matter what accomplishments you make, somebody helps you." —Althea Gibson, tennis champion

20. "Only when the well runs dry do we learn the wealth of water." —Benjamin Franklin, statesman

21. "Pearls lie not on the seashore. If thou desirest one, thou must dive for it."—Chinese proverb

22. "I took the [road] less traveled by, and that has made all the difference."—from "The Road Not Taken" by Robert Frost, poet (◆ For the complete poem, see page 480.)

Early Snow, ca. 1827, by Caspar David Friedrich

bpk, Berlin/Hamburger Kunsthalle/Art Resource, NY

Chapter 2 Summary

Here's a brief review of what you need to know about the thesis statement:

1. A thesis statement declares the main point of your essay; it tells the reader what clearly defined opinion you hold.
2. Everything in your essay should support your thesis statement.
3. A good thesis statement asserts one main idea, narrowed to fit the assignment, and is stated in clear, specific terms.
4. A good thesis statement makes a reasonable claim about a topic that is of interest to its readers as well as to its writer.
5. The thesis statement is often presented near the beginning of the essay, frequently in the first or second paragraph, or is so strongly implied that readers cannot miss the writer's main point.
6. A "working" or trial thesis is an excellent organizing tool to use as you begin drafting because it can help you decide which ideas to include.
7. Because writing is an act of discovery, you may write yourself into a better thesis statement by the end of your first draft. Don't hesitate to begin a new draft with the new thesis statement.
8. Some writers may profit from using an essay map, a brief statement accompanying the thesis that introduces the supporting points discussed in the body of the essay.

Chapter 3

The Body Paragraphs

•••

The middle—or *body*—of your essay is composed of paragraphs that support the thesis statement. By citing examples, explaining causes, offering reasons, or using other strategies in these paragraphs, you supply enough specific evidence to persuade your reader that the opinion expressed in your thesis is a sensible one. Each paragraph in the body usually presents and develops one main point in the discussion of your thesis. Generally, but not always, a new body paragraph signals another major point in the discussion.

Planning the Body of Your Essay

Many writers like to have a plan before they begin drafting the body of their essay. To help you create a plan, first look at your thesis. If you used an essay map, as suggested in Chapter 2, you may find that the points mentioned there will provide the basis for the body paragraphs of your essay. For example, recall from Chapter 2 a thesis and essay map praising the Study Skills Center: "Because of its free services, well-trained tutors, and useful learning aids, the Study Skills Center is an excellent place for students seeking academic help." Your plan for developing the body of your essay might look like this:

Body paragraph one: discussion of free services
Body paragraph two: discussion of tutors
Body paragraph three: discussion of learning aids

At this point in your writing process you may wish to sketch in some of the supporting evidence you will include in each paragraph. You might find it helpful to go back to your prewriting activities (listing, looping, freewriting, mapping, cubing, and so on) to see what ideas surfaced then. Adding some examples and supporting details might make an informal outline of the Study Skills paper appear like this:

I. Free services

    A. Minicourse on improving study skills

    B. Tutoring ⟨ composition / math

    C. Weekly seminars ⟨ stress management / test anxiety / building vocabulary

    D. Testing for learning disabilities

II. Tutors

    A. Top graduate students in their fields

    B. Experienced teachers

    C. Some bilingual

    D. Have taken training course at Center

III. Learning aids

    A. Supplementary texts

    B. Workbooks

    C. Audiovisual aids

Notice that this plan is an *informal* or *working outline* rather than a *formal outline*—that is, it doesn't have strictly parallel parts nor is it expressed in complete sentences. Unless your teacher requests a formal sentence or topic outline, don't feel you must make one at this early stage. Just consider using the informal outline to plot out a tentative plan that will help you start your first draft.

Here's an example of an informal outline at work: let's suppose you have been asked to write about your most prized possession, and you've chosen your 1966 Mustang, a car you have restored. You already have some ideas, but as yet they're scattered and too few to make an interesting, well-developed essay. You try an informal outline, jotting down your ideas thus far:

    I. Car is special because it was a gift from Dad

    II. Fun to drive

    III. Looks great—new paint job

    IV. Engine in top condition

    V. Custom features

    VI. Car shows—fun to be part of

©Bettmann / Corbis

After looking at your outline, you see that some of your categories overlap and could be part of the same discussion. For example, your thoughts about the engine are actually part of the discussion of "fun to drive," and "custom features" are what make the car look great. Moreover, the outline may help you discover new ideas. For example, custom features could be divided into those on the interior as well as those on the exterior of the car. The revised outline might look like this:

I.   Gift from Dad
II. Fun to drive
   A. Engine
   B. Steering
III. Looks great
   A. New paint job
   B. Custom features
      1. exterior
      2. interior
IV. Car shows

You could continue playing with this outline, even moving big chunks of it around; for example, you might decide that what really makes the car so special is that it was a graduation gift from your dad and that is the note you want to end on. So you move "I. Gift from Dad" down to the last position in your outline.

The important point to remember about an informal or working outline is that it is there to help you—not control you. The value of an outline is its ability to help you plan, to help you see logical connections between your ideas, and to help you see obvious places to add new ideas and details. (The informal outline is also handy to keep around in case you're interrupted for a long period while you're drafting; you can always check the outline to see where you were and where you were going when you stopped.) In other words, *don't be intimidated by the outline!*

Here's one more example of an informal outline, this time for the thesis and essay map on the library reserve facility, from Chapter 2:

Thesis–Essay Map: Unpredictable hours, poor staffing, and inadequate space make the library's reserve facility difficult for students to use.

I.   Unpredictable hours
   A. Hours of operation vary from week to week
   B. Unannounced closures
   C. Closed on some holidays, open on others
II. Poor staffing
   A. Uninformed personnel at reserve desk
   B. Too few on duty at peak times
III. Inadequate space
   A. Room too small for number of users
   B. Too few chairs, tables
   C. Weak lighting

You may have more than three points to make in your essay. And, on occasion, you may need more than one paragraph to discuss a single point. For instance, you might discover that you need two paragraphs to explain fully the many services at the Study Skills Center. (◆ For advice on splitting the discussion of a single point into two or more paragraphs, see page 61.) At this stage, you needn't bother trying to guess whether you'll need more than one paragraph per point; just use the outline to get going. Most writers don't know how much they have to say before they begin writing—and that's fine because *writing itself is an act of discovery and learning.*

When you are ready to begin drafting, read Chapter 5 for advice on composing and revising. ◆ Remember, too, that Chapter 5 contains suggestions for beating Writer's Block, should this condition arise while you are working on any part of your essay, as well as some specific hints on formatting your draft that may make revision easier.

Composing the Body Paragraphs

There are many ways to organize and develop body paragraphs. Paragraphs developed by common patterns, such as example, comparison, and definition, will be discussed in specific chapters in Part Two; at this point, however, here are some comments about the general nature of all good body paragraphs that should help as you draft your essay.

> REMEMBER: Most of the body paragraphs in your essay will profit from a focused *topic sentence.* In addition, body paragraphs should have adequate *development, unity,* and *coherence.*

The Topic Sentence

Most body paragraphs present one main point in your discussion, expressed in a *topic sentence.* The topic sentence of a body paragraph has three important functions:

1. It supports the thesis by clearly stating a main point in the discussion.
2. It announces what the paragraph will be about.
3. It controls the subject matter of the paragraph. The entire discussion—the examples, details, and explanations—in a particular paragraph must directly relate to and support the topic sentence.

Think of a body paragraph (or a single paragraph) as a kind of mini-essay in itself. The topic sentence is, in a sense, a smaller thesis. It too asserts one main idea on a limited subject that the writer can explain or argue in the rest of the paragraph. Like the thesis, the topic sentence should be stated in as specific language as possible.

To see how a topic sentence works in a body paragraph, study this sample:

Essay Thesis: The Study Skills Center is an excellent place for students who need academic help.

Topic Sentence
1. The topic sentence supports the thesis by stating a main point (one reason the Center provides excellent academic help).

The Center offers students a variety of free services designed to improve basic skills. Those who discover their study habits are poor, for instance, may enroll in a six-week minicourse in study skills that offers advice on such topics as how to read a text, take notes, and organize material for review. Students whose math or writing skills are below par can sign up for free tutoring sessions held five days a week throughout each semester. In addition, the Center presents weekly seminars on

2. The topic sentence announces the subject matter of the paragraph (a variety of free services that improve basic skills).

3. The topic sentence controls the subject matter (all the examples—the minicourse, the tutoring, the seminars, and the testing—support the claim of the topic sentence).

special topics such as stress management and overcoming test anxiety for those students who are finding college more of a nerve-wracking experience than they expected; other students can attend evening seminars in such worthwhile endeavors as vocabulary building or spelling tips. Finally, the Center offers a series of tests to identify the presence of any learning disabilities, such as dyslexia, that might prevent a student from succeeding academically. With such a variety of free services, the Center can help almost any student.

The Library, 1960, by Jacob Lawrence

Smithsonian American Art Museum, Washington, DC / Art Resource, NY. ©2012 The Jacob and Gwendolyn Lawrence Foundation, Seattle / Artists Rights Society (ARS), NY

Here's another example from the essay on the library reserve facility:

Essay Thesis: The library's reserve facility is difficult for students to use.

Topic Sentence

1. The topic sentence supports the thesis by stating a main point (one reason the facility is difficult to use).

2. The topic sentence announces the subject matter of the paragraph (the unpredictable hours).

The library reserve facility's unpredictable hours frustrate even the most dedicated students. Instructors who place articles or books on reserve usually ask students to read them by a certain date. Too often, however, students arrive at the reserve desk only to find it closed. The facility's open hours change from week to week: students who used the room last week on Tuesday morning may discover that this week on Tuesday the desk is closed, which means another trip. Perhaps even more frustrating are the facility's sudden, unannounced closures. Some of these closures allow staff members to have lunch or go on breaks, but, again, they occur without notice on no regular schedule. A student arrives, as I did two weeks ago, at the desk to find a "Be Back Soon"

3. The topic sentence controls the subject matter (all the examples— the changing hours, the sudden closures, the erratic holiday schedule— support the claim of the topic sentence).

sign. In my case, I waited for nearly an hour. Another headache is the holiday schedule, which is difficult to figure out. For example, this year the reserve room was closed without advance notice on Presidents' Day but open on Easter; open during Winter Break but closed some days during Spring Break, a time many students use to catch up on their reserve assignments. Overall, the reserve facility would be much easier for students to use if it adopted a set schedule of operating hours, announced these times each semester, and maintained them.

Always be sure your topic sentences actually support the particular thesis of your essay. For example, the second topic sentence presented here doesn't belong in the essay promised by the thesis:

Thesis: Elk hunting should be permitted because it financially aids people in our state.

Topic Sentences

1. Fees for hunting licenses help pay for certain free, state-supported social services.
2. Hunting helps keep the elk population under control.
3. Elk hunting offers a means of obtaining free food for people with low incomes.

Although topic sentence 2 is about elk and may be true, it doesn't support the thesis's emphasis on financial aid and therefore should be revised or tossed out of this essay.

Here's another example:

Thesis: During the past fifty years, movie stars have often tried to change the direction of America's politics.

Topic Sentences

1. During World War II, stars sold liberty bonds to support the country's war effort.
2. Many stars refused to cooperate with the blacklisting of their colleagues during the McCarthy Era in the 1950s.
3. Some stars were actively involved in protests against the Vietnam War.
4. More recently, stars have appeared in Congress criticizing the lack of legislative help for struggling farmers.

Topic sentences 2, 3, and 4 all show how stars have tried to effect a change. But topic sentence 1 says only that stars sold bonds to support, not *change,* the political direction of the nation. Although it does show stars involved in politics, it doesn't illustrate the claim of this particular thesis.

Sometimes a topic sentence needs only to be rewritten or slightly recast to fit:

Thesis: The recent tuition hike may discourage students from attending our college.

Topic Sentences

1. Students already pay more here than at other in-state schools.

2. Out-of-state students will have to pay an additional "penalty" to attend.

3. Tuition funds should be used for scholarships.

As written, topic sentence 3 doesn't show why students won't want to attend the school. However, a rewritten topic sentence does support the thesis:

3. Because the tuition money will not be used for scholarships, some students may not be able to afford this higher-priced school.

In other words, always check carefully to make sure that *all* your topic sentences clearly support your thesis's assertion.

Focusing Your Topic Sentence

A vague, fuzzy, or unfocused topic sentence most often leads to a paragraph that touches only on the surface of its subject or that wanders away from the writer's main idea. On the other hand, a topic sentence that is tightly focused and stated precisely will not only help the reader to understand the point of the paragraph but will also help you select, organize, and develop your supporting details.

Look, for example, at these unfocused topic sentences and their revisions:

Unfocused	Too many people treat animals badly in experiments. [What people? Badly how? What kinds of experiments?]
Focused	The cosmetic industry often harms animals in unnecessary experiments designed to test products.
Unfocused	Grades are an unfair pain in the neck. [Again, the focus is too broad. All grades? Unfair how?]
Focused	A course grade based on two multiple-choice exams doesn't accurately measure a student's knowledge of the subject.
Unfocused	Finding the right job is important and can lead to rewarding experiences. [Note both vague language and a double focus: "important" and "can lead to rewarding experiences."]
Focused	Finding the right job can lead to an improved sense of self-esteem.

◆ Before you practice writing focused topic sentences, you may wish to review pages 32–38, the advice on composing good thesis statements, as the same rules generally apply.

Placing Your Topic Sentence

Although the topic sentence most frequently occurs as the first sentence in the body paragraph, it also often appears as the second or last sentence. A topic sentence that directly follows the first sentence of a paragraph usually does so because the first sentence provides an introductory statement or some kind of "hook" to the preceding paragraph. A topic sentence frequently appears at the end of a paragraph that first presents particular details and then concludes with its central point. Here are two paragraphs in which the topic sentences do not appear first:

Introductory
sentence

Topic sentence

Millions of Americans have watched the elaborate Rose Bowl Parade televised nationally each January from Pasadena, California. *Less well known, but growing in popularity, is Pasadena's Doo Dah Parade, an annual parody of the Rose Bowl spectacle, which specializes in wild-and-crazy participants.* Take this year's Doo Dah Precision Drill Team, for instance. Instead of marching in unison, the members cavorted down the avenue displaying—what else—a variety of precision electric drills. In heated competition with this group was the Synchronized Briefcase Drill Team, whose members wore gray pinstripe suits and performed a series of tunes by tapping on their briefcases. Another crowd-pleasing entry was the Citizens for the Right to Bare Arms, whose members sang while carrying aloft unclothed mannequin arms. The zany procession, led this year as always by the All-Time Doo Dah Parade Band, attracted more than 150,000 fans and is already preparing for its next celebration.

In the preceding paragraph, the first sentence serves as an introduction leading directly to the topic sentence. In the following example, the writer places the topic sentence last to sum up the information in the paragraph:

Topic sentence

Rumors certainly fly around Washington's Capitol Building—but ghosts, too? According to legend, the building was cursed in 1808 by construction superintendent John Lenthall, who was crushed by a falling ceiling following a feud with his architect over the wisdom of ceiling braces. Some workers in the building swear they have heard both the ghostly footsteps of James Garfield, who was assassinated after only four months as president, and the spooky last murmurings of John Quincy Adams, who died mid-speech on the House floor. Others claim to have seen a demon cat, so large and terrifying that it caused a guard to suffer a fatal heart attack. Perhaps the most cheerful ghosts appear on the night of a new president's swearing-in ceremony when the statues in Statuary Hall are said to leave their pedestals and dance at their own Inaugural Ball. *Whether these stories are true or merely the products of rich imaginations, the U.S. Capitol Building boasts the reputation as one of the most haunted buildings in America.*

As you can see, the position of topic sentences largely depends on what you are trying to do in your paragraph. And it's true that the purposes of some paragraphs are so obvious that no topic sentences are needed. However, if you are a beginning writer, you may want to practice putting your topic sentences first for a while to help you organize and unify your paragraphs.

Some paragraphs with a topic sentence near the beginning also contain a concluding sentence that makes a final general comment based on the supporting details. The last sentence of the following paragraph, for example, reemphasizes the main point.

Topic sentence

Of all nature's catastrophes, tornadoes may cause the most bizarre destruction. Whirling out of the sky at speeds up to 300 miles per hour, tornadoes have been known to drive broom handles through brick walls and straws into tree trunks. In one extreme case, a Kansas farmer reported that his prize rooster had been sucked into a two-gallon distilled-water bottle. More commonly, tornadoes lift autos and deposit them in fields miles away or uproot trees and drop them on lawns in neighboring towns. One tornado knocked down every wall in a house but one—luckily, the very wall shielding the terrified family. *Whenever a tornado touches the earth, spectacular headlines are sure to follow.*

Concluding
sentence

Warning: Although topic sentences may appear in different places in a paragraph, there is one common error you should be careful to avoid. Do *not* put a topic sentence at the end of one body paragraph that belongs to the paragraph that follows it. For example, let's suppose you are writing an essay discussing a job you held recently, one that you enjoyed because of the responsibilities you were given, the training program you participated in, and the interaction you experienced with your coworkers. The body paragraph describing your responsibilities may end with its own topic sentence or with a concluding sentence about those responsibilities. However, that paragraph should not end with a sentence such as "Another excellent feature of this job was the training program for the next level of management." This "training program" sentence belongs in the *following* body paragraph as its topic sentence. Similarly, you would not end the paragraph on the training program with a topic sentence praising your experience with your coworkers.

If you feel that your paragraphs are ending too abruptly, consider using a concluding sentence, as described previously. Later in this chapter you will also learn some ways to smooth the flow from one paragraph to the next by using transitional devices and "idea hooks" (pages 76–77). For now, remember: Do *not* place a topic sentence that introduces and controls paragraph "B" at the end of paragraph "A." In other words, always place your topic sentence in the paragraph to which it belongs, to which it is topic-related, not at the end of the preceding paragraph.

Practicing What You've Learned

© Canstock Images, Inc./
Index Stock Imagery

A. Point out the topic sentences in the following paragraphs; identify those paragraphs that also contain concluding sentences. Cross out any stray topic sentences that belong elsewhere.

Denim is one of America's most widely used fabrics. It was first introduced during Columbus's voyage, when the sails of the *Santa Maria* were made of the strong cloth. During our pioneer days, denim was used for tents, covered wagons, and the now-famous blue jeans. Cowboys found denim an ideal fabric for protection against sagebrush, cactus, and saddle sores. World War II also gave denim a boost in popularity when sailors were issued jeans as part of their dress code. Today, denim continues to be in demand as more and more casual clothes are cut from the economical cloth. Because of its low cost and durability, manufacturers feel that denim will continue as one of America's most useful fabrics.

continued on next page

Adlai Stevenson, American statesman and twice an unsuccessful presidential candidate against Eisenhower, was well known for his intelligence and wit. Once on the campaign trail, after he had spoken eloquently and at length about several complex ideas, a woman in the audience was moved to stand and cheer, "That's great! Every thinking person in America will vote for you!" Stevenson immediately retorted, "That's not enough. I need a majority!" Frequently a reluctant candidate but never at a loss for words, Stevenson once defined a politician as a person who "approaches every question with an open mouth." Stevenson was also admired for his work as the Governor of Illinois and, later, as Ambassador to the United Nations.

Almost every wedding tradition has a symbolic meaning that originated centuries ago. For example, couples have been exchanging rings to symbolize unending love for over a thousand years. Most often, the rings are worn on the third finger of the left hand, which was thought to contain a vein that ran directly to the heart. The rings in ancient times were sometimes made of braided grass, rope, or leather, giving rise to the expression "tying the knot." Another tradition, the bridal veil, began when marriages were arranged by the families and the groom was not allowed to see his bride until the wedding. The tossing of rice at newlyweds has long signified fertility blessings, and the sweet smell of the bride's bouquet was intended to drive away evil spirits, who were also diverted by the surrounding bridal attendants. Weddings may vary enormously today, but many couples still include ancient traditions to signify their new life together.

You always think of the right answer five minutes after you hand in the test. You always hit the red light when you're already late for class. The one time you skip class is the day of the pop quiz. Back-to-back classes are always held in buildings at opposite ends of campus. The one course you need to graduate will not be offered your last semester. If any of these sound familiar, you've obviously been a victim of the "Murphy's Laws" that govern student life.

Want to win a sure bet? Then wager that your friends can't guess the most widely sold musical instrument in America today. Chances are they won't get the answer right—not even on the third try. In actuality, the most popular instrument in the country is neither the guitar nor the trumpet but the lowly kazoo. Last year alone, some three and one-half million kazoos were sold to music lovers of all ages. Part of the instrument's popularity arises from its availability, since kazoos are sold in variety stores and music centers nearly everywhere; another reason is its inexpensiveness—it ranges from the standard thirty-nine-cent model to the five-dollar gold-plated special. But perhaps the main reason for the kazoo's popularity is the ease with which it can be played by almost anyone—as can testify the members of the entire Swarthmore College marching band, who have now added a marching kazoo number to their repertoire. Louis Armstrong, move over!

It's a familiar scenario: Dad won't stop the car to ask directions, despite the fact that he's been hopelessly lost for over forty-five minutes. Mom keeps nagging Dad to slow down and finally blows up because your little sister suddenly

continued on next page

remembers she's left her favorite doll, the one she can't sleep without, at the rest stop you left over an hour ago. Your legs are sweat-glued to the vinyl seats, you need desperately to go to the bathroom, and your big brother has just kindly acknowledged that he will relieve you of your front teeth if you allow any part of your body to extend over the imaginary line he has drawn down the backseat. The wonderful tradition known as the "family vacation" has begun.

B. Rewrite these topic sentences so that they are clear and focused rather than fuzzy or too broad.

1. My personality has changed a lot in the last year.

2. His date turned out to be really great.

3. The movie's special effects were incredible.

4. The Memorial Day celebration was more fun than ever before.

5. The evening with her parents was an unforgettable experience.

C. Add topic sentences to the following paragraphs:

Famous inventor Thomas Edison, for instance, did so poorly in his first years of school that his teachers warned his parents that he'd never be a success at anything. Henry Ford, the father of the auto industry, also had trouble in school with both reading and writing. But perhaps the best example is Albert Einstein, whose parents and teachers suspected that he was mentally disabled because he responded to questions so slowly and in a stuttering voice. Einstein's high school record was poor in everything but math, and he failed his college entrance exams the first time. Even out of school the man had trouble holding a job—until he announced the theory of relativity.

A 1950s felt skirt with Elvis's picture on it, for example, now sells for $150, and Elvis scarves go for as much as $300. Elvis handkerchiefs, originally 50 cents or less, fetch $150 in today's market; 1956 wallets imprinted with the singer's face have sold for over $400 each. Original posters from the Rock King's movies can sell for $750, and cards from the chewing gum series can run $30 apiece. Perhaps one of the most expensive collectors' items is the Emenee Elvis toy guitar that can cost a fan up to $1,000, regardless of musical condition.

When successful playwright Jean Kerr once checked into a hospital, the receptionist asked her occupation and was told, "Writer." The receptionist said, "I'll just put down 'housewife.'" Similarly, when a British official asked W. H. Auden, the award-winning poet and essayist, what he did for a living, Auden replied, "I'm a writer." The official jotted down "no occupation."

Cumberland College, for example, set the record back in 1916 for the biggest loss in college ball, having allowed Georgia Tech to run up 63 points in the first quarter and ultimately succumbing to them with a final score of 222 to nothing. In pro ball, the Washington Redskins are the biggest losers, going down in

continued on next page

defeat 73 to 0 to the Chicago Bears in 1940. The award for the longest losing streak, however, goes to Northwestern University's team, who by 1981 had managed to lose 29 consecutive games. During that year, morale was so low that one disgruntled fan passing a local highway sign that read "Interstate 94" couldn't resist adding "Northwestern 0."

D. Write a focused topic sentence for five of the following subjects:

1. Job interviews
2. Friends
3. Food
4. Money
5. Selecting a major or occupation
6. Clothes
7. Music
8. Dreams
9. Housing
10. Childhood

Assignment

Review the thesis statements with essay maps you wrote for the Practice "B" exercise on page 42. Choose two, and from each thesis create at least three topic sentences for possible body paragraphs.

© CORBIS

Applying What You've Learned to *Your* Writing

© Keith Brofsky/
Photodisc/Getty Images

If you currently have a working thesis statement you have written in response to an assignment in your composition class, try sketching out an outline or a plan for the major ideas you wish to include. After you write a draft, underline the topic sentences in your body paragraphs. Do your topic sentences directly support your thesis? If you find that they do not clearly support your thesis, you must decide if you need to revise your draft's organization or whether you have, in fact, discovered a new, and possibly better, subject to write about. If the latter is true, you'll need to redraft your essay so that your readers will not be confused by a paper that announces one subject but discusses another. (◆ See Chapter 5 for more information on revising your drafts.)

Paragraph Development

Possibly the most serious—and most common—weakness of all essays by novice writers is the lack of effectively developed body paragraphs. The information in each paragraph must adequately explain, exemplify, define, or in some other way support your topic sentence. Therefore, you must include enough supporting information or evidence in each paragraph to make your readers understand your topic sentence. Moreover, you must make the information in the paragraph clear and specific enough for the readers to accept your ideas.

The next paragraph is *underdeveloped*. Although the topic sentence promises a discussion of Jesse James as a Robin Hood figure, the paragraph does not provide enough specific supporting evidence (in this case, examples) to explain this unusual view of the gunfighter.

> Although he was an outlaw, Jesse James was considered a Robin Hood figure in my hometown in Missouri. He used to be generous to the poor, and he did many good deeds, not just robberies. In my hometown people still talk about how lots of the things James did weren't all bad.

Rewritten, the paragraph might read as follows:

> Although he was an outlaw, Jesse James was considered a Robin Hood figure in my hometown in Missouri. Jesse and his gang chose my hometown as a hiding place, and they set out immediately to make friends with the local people. Every Christmas for four years, the legend goes, he dumped bags of toys on the doorsteps of poor children. The parents knew the toys had been bought with money stolen from richer people, but they were grateful anyway. On three occasions, Jesse gave groceries to the dozen neediest families—he seemed to know when times were toughest—and once he supposedly held up a stage to pay for an old man's operation. In my hometown, some people still sing the praises of Jesse James, the outlaw who wasn't all bad.

The topic sentence promises a discussion of James's generosity and delivers just that by citing specific examples of his gifts to children, the poor, and the sick. The paragraph is therefore better developed.

The following paragraph offers reasons but no specific examples or details to support its claims:

> Living with my ex-roommate was unbearable. First, she thought everything she owned was the best. Second, she possessed numerous filthy habits. Finally, she constantly exhibited immature behavior.

The writer might provide more evidence this way:

> Living with my ex-roommate was unbearable. First, she thought everything she owned, from clothes to cosmetics, was the best. If someone complimented my pants, she'd point out that her designer jeans looked better and would last longer because they were made of better material. If she borrowed my shampoo, she'd let me know that it didn't get her hair as clean and shiny as hers did. My hand cream wasn't as smooth; my suntan lotion wasn't as protective; not even my wire clothes hangers

were as good as her padded ones! But despite her pickiness about products, she had numerous filthy habits. Her dirty dishes remained in the sink for days before she felt the need to wash them. Piles of the "best" brand of tissues were regularly discarded from her upper bunk and strewn about the floor. Her desk and closets overflowed with heaps of dirty clothes, books, cosmetics, and whatever else she owned, and she rarely brushed her teeth (when she did brush, she left oozes of toothpaste in the sink). Finally, she constantly acted immaturely by throwing tantrums when things didn't go her way. A poor grade on an exam or paper, for example, meant books, shoes, or any other small object within her reach would hit the wall flying. Living with such a person taught me some valuable lessons about how not to win friends or keep roommates.

By adding more supporting evidence—specific examples and details—to this paragraph, the writer has a better chance of convincing the reader of the roommate's real character.

Where does evidence come from? Where do writers find their supporting information? Evidence comes from many sources. Personal experiences, memories, observations, hypothetical examples, reasoned arguments, facts, statistics, testimony from authorities, many kinds of studies and research—all these and more can help you make your points clear and persuasive. In the paragraph on Jesse James, for example, the writer relied on stories and memories from his hometown. The paragraph on the obnoxious roommate was supported by examples gained through the writer's personal observation. The kind of supporting evidence you choose for your paragraphs depends on your purpose and your audience; as the writer, you must decide what will work best to make your readers understand and accept each important point in your discussion. (◆ For advice on ways to think critically about evidence, see Chapter 5; for more information on incorporating research material into your essays, see Chapter 14.)

Having a well-developed paragraph is more than a matter of adding material or expanding length, however. The information in each paragraph must effectively explain or support your topic sentence. *Vague generalities or repetitious ideas are not convincing.* Look, for example, at the following paragraph, in which the writer offers only generalities:

We ought to ban the use of cell phones in moving vehicles. Some people who have them think that's a really good idea, but a lot of us don't agree. Using a phone while driving causes too many dangerous accidents to happen, and even if there's no terrible accident, people using them have been known to do some really stupid things in traffic. Drivers using phones are constantly causing problems for other drivers; pedestrians are in big trouble from these people too. I think this is getting to be a really dangerous situation, and we ought to do something about it soon.

This paragraph is weak because it is composed of repetitious general statements using vague, unclear language. None of its general statements is supported with specific evidence. Why is phone use when driving not a "good" idea? How can it cause accidents? What are the "problems" and "trouble" the writer refers to? What exactly does "do something about it" mean? The writer obviously had some ideas in mind, but these ideas are not clear to the reader because they are not adequately developed with specific evidence and language.

By adding supporting examples and details, the writer might revise the paragraph this way:

> Although cell phones are a time-saving convenience for busy people, they are too distracting for use by drivers of moving vehicles, whose lack of full attention poses a serious threat to other drivers and to pedestrians. The simple act of answering a phone, for example, may take a driver's eyes away from traffic signals or other cars. Moreover, involvement in a complex or emotional conversation could slow down a driver's response time just when fast action is needed to avoid an accident. Last week I drove behind a man using his phone. As he drove and talked, I could see him gesturing wildly, obviously agitated with the other caller. His speed repeatedly slowed and then picked up, slowed and increased, and his car drifted more than once, on a street frequently crossed by schoolchildren. Because the man was clearly not in full, conscious control of his driving, he was dangerous. My experience is not isolated; a recent study by the Foundation for Traffic Safety maintains that using a cell phone is more distracting to drivers than listening to the radio or talking to a rider. With additional studies in progress, voters in our state should soon demand legislation to restrict phone use to passengers or to drivers when the vehicles are not in motion.

The reader now has a better idea why the writer feels such cell phone use is distracting and, consequently, dangerous. By using two hypothetical examples (looking away, slowed response time), one personal experience (observing the agitated man), and one reference to research (the safety study), the writer offers the reader three kinds of supporting evidence for the paragraph's claim.

After examining the following two paragraphs, decide which explains its point more effectively.

1   Competing in an Ironman triathlon is one of the most demanding feats known to amateur athletes. First, they have to swim many miles, and that takes a lot of endurance. Then, they ride a bicycle a long way, which is also hard on their bodies. Last, they run a marathon, which can be difficult in itself but is especially hard after the first two events. Competing in the triathlon is really tough on the participants.

2   Competing in an Ironman triathlon is one of the most demanding feats known to amateur athletes. During the first stage of the triathlon, the competitors must swim 2.4 miles in the open ocean. They have to battle the constantly choppy ocean, the strong currents, and the frequent swells. The wind is often an adversary, and stinging jellyfish are a constant threat. Once they have completed the ocean swim, the triathletes must ride 112 miles on a bicycle. In addition to the strength needed to pedal that far, the bicyclists must use a variety of hand grips to ensure the continued circulation in their fingers and hands as well as to ease the strain on the neck and shoulder muscles. Moreover, the concentration necessary to steady the bicycle, as well as the attention to the inclines on the course and the consequent shifting of gears, causes mental fatigue for the athletes. After completing these two grueling segments, the triathletes must then run 26.2 miles, the length of a regular marathon. Dehydration is a constant concern, as is the prospect of cramping. Even the pain and swelling of a friction blister can be

enough to eliminate a contestant at this late stage of the event. Finally, disorientation and fatigue can set in and distort the athlete's judgment. Competing in an Ironman triathlon takes incredible physical and mental endurance.

The first paragraph contains, for the most part, repetitious generalities; it repeats the same idea (the triathlon is hard work) and gives few specific details to illustrate the point presented in the topic sentence. The second paragraph, however, does offer many specific examples and details—the exact mileage figures, the currents, jellyfish, inclines, grips, blisters, and so forth—that help the reader understand why the event is so demanding.

Joseph Conrad, the famous novelist, once remarked that a writer's purpose was to use "the power of the written word to make you hear, to make you feel . . . before all, to make you *see*. That—and no more, and it is everything." By using specific details instead of vague, general statements, you can write an interesting, convincing essay. Ask yourself as you revise your paragraphs, "Have I provided enough information, presented enough clear, precise details to make my readers see what I want them to?" In other words, a well-developed paragraph effectively makes its point with *an appropriate amount of specific supporting evidence*. (Remember that a paragraph in a handwritten rough draft will look much shorter when it is typed. Therefore, if you can't think of much to say about a particular idea, you should gather more information or consider dropping it as a major point in your essay.)

Paragraph Length

"How long is a good paragraph?" is a question novice writers often ask. Like a teacher's lecture or a preacher's sermon, paragraphs should be long enough to accomplish their purpose and short enough to be interesting. In truth, there is no set length, no prescribed number of lines or sentences, for any of your paragraphs. In a body paragraph, your topic sentence presents the main point, and the rest of the paragraph must give enough supporting evidence to convince the reader. Although unnecessary or repetitious detail is boring, too little discussion will leave the reader uninformed, unconvinced, or confused.

Although paragraph length varies, beginning writers should avoid the one- or two-sentence paragraphs frequently seen in newspapers or magazine articles. (Journalists have their own rules to follow; paragraphs are shorter in newspapers, for one reason, because large masses of print in narrow columns are difficult to read quickly.) Essay writers do occasionally use the one-sentence paragraph, most often to produce some special effect, when the statement is especially dramatic or significant and needs to call attention to itself or when an emphatic transition is needed. For now, however, you should concentrate on writing well-developed body paragraphs.

One more note on paragraph length: sometimes you may discover that a particular point in your essay is so complex that your paragraph is growing far too long—nearly a page, for instance. If this problem occurs, look for a logical place to divide your information and start a new paragraph. For example, you might see a convenient dividing point in a series of actions you're describing or a break in the chronology of a narrative or between explanations of arguments or examples. Just make sure you begin your next paragraph with some sort of transitional phrase or key words to let the reader know that you are still discussing the same point as before ("Still another problem caused by the computer's faulty memory circuit is . . .").

Practicing What You've Learned

A. Analyze the following paragraphs. Explain how you might improve the development of each one.

1. Professor Wilson is the best teacher I've ever had. His lectures are interesting, and he's very concerned about his students. He makes the class challenging but not too hard. On tests he doesn't expect more than one can give. I think he's a great teacher.

2. Newspaper advice columns are pretty silly. The problems are generally stupid or unrealistic, and the advice is out of touch with today's world. Too often the columnist just uses the letter to make a smart remark about some pet peeve. The columns could be put to some good uses, but no one tries very hard.

3. Driving tests do not adequately examine a person's driving ability. Usually the person being tested does not have to drive very far. The test does not require the skills that are used in everyday driving situations. Supervisors of driving tests tend to be very lenient.

4. Nursing homes are often sad places. They are frequently located in ugly old buildings unfit for anyone. The people there are lonely and bored. What's more, they're sometimes treated badly by the people who run the homes. It's a shame something better can't be done for the elderly.

5. There is a big difference between acquaintances and friends. Acquaintances are just people you know slightly, but friends give you some important qualities. For example, they can help you gain self-esteem and confidence just by being close to you. By sharing their friendship, they also help you feel happy about being alive.

B. Practice developing paragraphs by choosing two of the following three topics, fleshing out each paragraph with an example from your own experience or that of a close friend. Use vivid, specific details to make each paragraph clear and interesting. (If you cannot think of an appropriate example, you may rework the topic sentence; for instance, in the first paragraph, you might change the topic to a product or service that exceeded your expectations rather than one that disappointed you.)

1. Too many products today have expensive advertising campaigns but simply don't live up to their claims. For instance,

continued on next page

© Canstock Images, Inc./Index Stock Imagery

2. Sooner or later, almost everyone experiences that dreaded moment when he or she suddenly forgets something familiar. Someone forgets a friend's name in the middle of an introduction; someone else experiences memory loss standing in front of the ATM or just after volunteering to answer a question in class. I too have temporarily "gone blank," but eventually regained my composure. For example,

3. Unexpected help is a miracle that often comes just in time to prevent a disaster or foolish move. Such help can come from a variety of sources—from friends, family, or even strangers. For example,

Assignment

A. Find two well-developed paragraphs in an essay or book; explain why you think the paragraphs are successfully developed.

B. Select one of the paragraphs from Practicing What You've Learned exercise "A" (page 62) and rewrite it, adding enough specific details to make a well-developed paragraph.

C. *Collaborative Activity:* Exchange paragraphs with a classmate. Mark any weaknesses you see in the topic sentence or in the paragraph's development. Rewrite at least one problematic area so that the paragraph is stronger, with enough appropriate supporting detail. In a sentence or two, explain why you made the changes you did.

Applying What You've Learned to *Your* Writing

If you are currently drafting an essay, look closely at your body paragraphs. Find the topic sentence in each paragraph, and circle the key words that most clearly communicate the main idea of the paragraph. Then ask yourself whether the information in each paragraph effectively supports, explains, or illustrates the main idea of the paragraph's topic sentence. Is there enough information? If you're not sure, try numbering your supporting details. Are there too few to be persuasive? Does the paragraph present clear, specific supporting material, or does it contain too many vague generalities to be convincing? Where could you add more details to help the reader understand your ideas better and to make each paragraph more interesting? (◆ For more help revising your paragraphs, see Chapter 5.)

Paragraph Unity

Every sentence in a body paragraph should relate directly to the main idea presented by the topic sentence. A paragraph must stick to its announced subject; it must not drift away into another discussion. In other words, a good paragraph has *unity*.

Examine the following unified paragraph; note that the topic sentence clearly states the paragraph's main point and that each sentence thereafter supports the topic sentence.

(1)Frank Lloyd Wright, America's leading architect of the first half of the twentieth century, believed that his houses should blend naturally with their building sites. (2)Consequently, he designed several "prairie houses," whose long, low lines echoed the flat earth plane. (3)Built of brick, stone, and natural wood, the houses shared a similar texture with their backgrounds. (4)Large windows were often used to blend the interior and exterior of the houses. (5)Wright also punctuated the lines and spaces of the houses with greenery in planters to further make the buildings look like part of nature.

The first sentence states the main idea, that Wright thought houses should blend with their locations, and the other sentences support this assertion:

Topic Sentence: (1) Wright's houses blend with their natural locations

- **(2)** Long, low lines echo flat prairie
- **(3)** Brick, stone, wood provide same texture as location
- **(4)** Windows blend inside with outside
- **(5)** Greenery in planters imitates the natural surroundings

Now look at the next paragraph, in which the writer strays from his original purpose:

Frank Lloyd Wright's Fallingwater House in Bear Run, Pennsylvania

©Richard A. Cooke / Corbis

(1)Cigarette smoke is unhealthy even for people who don't have the nicotine habit themselves. (2)Secondhand smoke can cause asthmatics and sufferers of sinusitis serious problems. (3)Doctors regularly advise heart patients to avoid confined smoky areas because coronary attacks might be triggered by the lack of clean air. (4)Moreover, having the smell of smoke in one's hair and clothes is a real nuisance. (5)Even if a person is without any health problems, exhaled smoke doubles the amount of carbon monoxide in the air, a condition that may cause lung problems in the future.

Sentence 4 refers to smoke as a nuisance and therefore does not belong in a paragraph that discusses smoking as a health hazard to nonsmokers.

Sometimes a large portion of a paragraph will drift into another topic. In the following paragraph, did the writer wish to focus on her messiness or on the beneficial effects of her engagement?

I have always been a very messy person. As a child, I was a pack rat, saving every little piece of insignificant paper that I thought might be important when I grew up. As a teenager, I filled my pockets with remnants of basketball tickets, hall passes, gum wrappers, and other important articles from my high school education. As a college student, I became a boxer—not a fighter, but someone who cannot throw anything away and therefore it winds up in a box in my closet. But my engagement has changed everything. I'm really pleased with the new stage of my life, and I owe it all to my fiancé. My overall outlook on life has changed because of his influence on me. I'm neater, much more cheerful, and I'm even getting places on time like I never did before. It's truly amazing what love can do.

Note shift from the topic of messiness

This writer may wish to discuss the changes her fiancé has inspired and then use her former messiness, tardiness, and other bad habits as examples illustrating those changes; however, as presented here, the paragraph is not unified around a central idea. On the contrary, it first seems to promise a discussion of her messiness but then wanders into comments on "what love can do."

Also beware a tendency to end your paragraph with a new idea. A new point calls for an entirely new paragraph. For example, the following paragraph focuses on the *origins* of Muzak; the last sentence, on Muzak's *effects* on workers, should be omitted or moved to a paragraph on Muzak's uses in the workplace.

Muzak, the ever-present background music that pervades elevators, office buildings, and reception rooms, was created nearly eighty years ago by George Owen Squier, an army general. A graduate of West Point, Squier was also an inventor and scientist. During World War I he headed the Signal Corps, where he began experimenting with the notion of transmitting simultaneous messages over power lines. When he retired from the army in 1922, he founded Wired Radio, Inc., and later, in 1934, the first Muzak medley was heard in Cleveland, Ohio, for homeowners willing to pay the great sum of $1.50 a month. That year he struck upon the now-famous name, which combined the idea of music with the name of the country's then-most popular camera, Kodak. *Today, experiments show that workers get more done when they listen to Muzak.*

Breaks unity

In general, think of paragraph unity in terms of the following diagram:

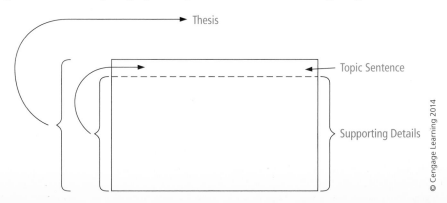

Thesis

Topic Sentence

Supporting Details

© Cengage Learning 2014

The sentences in the paragraph support the paragraph's topic sentence; the paragraph, in turn, supports the thesis statement.

Practicing What You've Learned

© Canstock Images, Inc./
Index Stock Imagery

In each of the following examples, delete or rewrite any information that interferes with the unity of the paragraph or begins to drift off topic:

In the Great Depression of the 1930s, American painters suffered severely because few people had the money to spend on the luxury of owning art. To keep our artists from starving, the government ultimately set up the Federal Art Project, which paid then little-known painters such as Jackson Pollock, Arshile Gorky, and Willem de Kooning to paint murals in post offices, train stations, schools, housing projects, and other public places. During this period, songwriters were also affected by the Depression, and they produced such memorable songs as "Brother, Can You Spare a Dime?" The government-sponsored murals, usually depicting familiar American scenes and historical events, gave our young artists an opportunity to develop their skills and new techniques; in return, our country obtained thousands of elaborate works of art in over one thousand American cities. Sadly, many of these artworks were destroyed in later years as public buildings were torn down or remodeled.

After complaining in vain about the quality of food in the campus restaurant, University of Colorado students are having their revenge after all. The student body voted to rename the grill after Alferd Packer, the only American ever convicted of cannibalism. Packer was a Utah prospector trapped with an expedition of explorers in the southwest Colorado mountains during the winter of 1874; the sole survivor of the trip, he was later tried by a jury and sentenced to hang for dining on at least five of his companions. Colorado students are now holding an annual "Alferd Packer Day" and have installed a mural relating the prospector's story on the main wall of the restaurant. Some local wits have also suggested slogans for the bar and grill, including "Have a friend for lunch!" and "Serving our fellow man since 1874." Another well-known incident of cannibalism in the West occurred in the winter of 1846, when the Donner party, a wagon train of eighty-seven California-bound immigrants, became trapped by ice and snow in the Sierra Nevada mountain range.

Inventors of food products often name their new creations after real people. In 1896 Leo Hirshfield hand-rolled a chewy candy and named it after his daughter Clara, nicknamed Tootsie. In 1920 Otto Schnering gave the world the Baby Ruth candy bar, named after the daughter of former President Grover Cleveland. To publicize his new product, Schnering once dropped the candy tied to tiny parachutes from an airplane flying over Pittsburgh. One of our most popular soft drinks was named by a young suitor who sought to please his sweetheart's physi-

continued on next page

cian father, none other than old Dr. Pepper. Despite the honor, the girl's father never approved of the match, and the young man, Wade Morrison, married someone else.

States out West have often led the way in recognizing women's roles in politics. Wyoming, for example, was the first state to give women the right to vote and hold office, back in 1869 while the state was still a territory. Colorado was the second state to grant women's suffrage; Idaho, the third. Wyoming was also the first state to elect a woman as governor, Nellie Tayloe Ross, in 1924. Montana elected Jeannette Rankin as the nation's first congresswoman in 1916. Former U.S. Representative from Colorado, Patricia Schroeder, claims to be the first person to take the congressional oath of office while clutching a handbag full of diapers. Ms. Schroeder later received the National Motherhood Award.

Living in a college dorm is a good way to meet people. There are activities every weekend, such as game night and parties where one can get acquainted with all kinds of students. Even just sitting by someone in the cafeteria during a meal can start a friendship. Making new friends from foreign countries can teach students more about international relations. A girl on my dorm floor, for example, is from Peru, and I've learned a lot about the customs and culture in her country. She's also helping me with my study of Spanish. I hope to visit her in Peru some day.

Applying What You've Learned to *Your* Writing

© Keith Brofsky/ Photodisc/Getty Images

If you have written a draft of an essay, underline the topic sentence in each body paragraph and circle the key words. For example, if in an essay on America's growing health consciousness, one of your topic sentences reads, "In an effort to improve their health, Americans have increased the number of vitamins they consume," you might circle "Americans," "increased," and "vitamins." Then look closely at your paragraph. All the information in that paragraph should support the idea expressed in your topic sentence; nothing should detract from the idea of showing that Americans have increased their vitamin consumption. Now study the paragraphs in your draft, one by one. Cross out any sentence or material that interferes with the ideas in your topic sentences. If one of your paragraphs begins to drift away from its topic-sentence idea, you will need to rethink the purpose of that paragraph and rewrite it so that the reader will understand what the paragraph is about. (◆ For additional help revising your drafts, turn to Chapter 5.)

Paragraph Coherence

In addition to unity, *coherence* is essential to a good paragraph. Coherence means that all the sentences and ideas in your paragraph flow together to make a clear, logical point about your topic. Your paragraph should not be a confusing collection of ideas set down in random order. The readers should be able to follow what you have written and see easily and quickly how each sentence grows out of, or is related to, the preceding sentence. To achieve coherence, you should have a smooth connection or transition between the sentences in your paragraphs.

There are five important means of achieving coherence in your paragraphs:

1. A natural or easily recognized order
2. Transitional words and phrases
3. Repetition of key words
4. Substitution of pronouns for key nouns
5. Parallelism

These transitional devices are similar to the couplings between railroad cars; they enable the controlling engine to pull the train of thought along as a unit.

A Recognizable Ordering of Information

Without consciously thinking about the process, you may often organize paragraphs in easily recognized patterns that give the reader a sense of logical movement and order. Four common patterns of ordering sentences in a paragraph are discussed here.

The Order of Time

Some paragraphs are composed of details arranged in chronological order. You might, for example, explain the process of changing an oil filter on your car by beginning with the first step, draining the old oil, and concluding with the last step, installing the new filter. Here is a paragraph on black holes in which the writer chronologically orders the details:

> A black hole in space, from all indications, is the result of the death of a star. Scientists speculate that stars were first formed from the gases floating in the universe at the beginning of time. In the first stage in the life of a star, the hot gas is drawn by the force of gravity into a burning sphere. In the middle stage—our own sun being a middle-aged star—the burning continues at a regular rate, giving off enormous amounts of heat and light. As it grows old, however, the star eventually explodes to become what is called a nova, a superstar. But gravity soon takes over again, and the exploded star falls back in on itself with such force that all the matter in the star is compacted into a mass no larger than a few miles in diameter. At this point, no heavenly body can be seen in that area of the sky, as the tremendous pull of gravity lets nothing escape, not even light. A black hole has thus been formed.

The Order of Space

When your subject is a physical object, you should select some orderly means of describing it: from left to right, top to bottom, inside to outside, and so forth. For example, you might describe a sculpture as you walk around it from front to back. In the following paragraph describing a cowboy, the writer has ordered the details of the description in a head-to-feet pattern:

> Big Dave was pure cowboy. He wore a black felt hat so big that it kept his face in perpetual shade. Around his neck was knotted a red bandana stained with sweat from long hot days in the saddle. An oversized blue denim shirt hung from his shoulders to give him plenty of arm freedom, and his faded jeans were held up by a broad leather belt with a huge silver buckle featuring a snorting bronc in full buck. His boots, old and dirt-colored, kicked up little dust storms as he sauntered across the corral.

Deductive Order

A paragraph ordered deductively moves from a generalization to particular details that explain or support the general statement. Perhaps the most common pattern of all paragraphs, the deductive paragraph begins with its topic sentence and proceeds to its supporting details, as illustrated in the following example:

> If a group of 111 ninth-graders is typical of today's teenagers, spelling and social science teachers may be in for trouble. In a recent experiment, not one of the students tested could write the Pledge of Allegiance correctly. In addition, the results showed that the students apparently had little understanding of the pledge's meaning. For example, several students described the United States as a "nation under guard" instead of "under God," and the phrase "to the Republic for which it stands" appeared in several responses as "of the richest stand" or "for Richard stand." Many students changed the word "indivisible" to the phrase "in the visible," and over nine percent of the students, all of whom are Americans from varying racial and ethnic backgrounds, misspelled the word "America."

Inductive Order

An inductive paragraph begins with an examination of particular details and then concludes with a larger point or generalization about those details. Such a paragraph often ends with its topic sentence, as does the following paragraph on Little League baseball:

> At too many Little League baseball games, one or another adult creates a minor scene by yelling rudely at an umpire or a coach. Similarly, it is not uncommon to hear adults whispering loudly with one another in the stands over which child should have caught a missed ball. Perhaps the most astounding spectacle of all, however, is an irate parent or coach yanking a child off the field after a bad play for a humiliating lecture in front of the whole team. Sadly, Little League baseball today often seems intended more for childish adults than for the children who actually play it.

Transitional Words and Phrases

Some paragraphs may need internal transitional words to help the reader move smoothly from one thought to the next so that the ideas do not appear disconnected or choppy.

Here is a list of common transitional words and phrases and their uses:

giving examples	for example, for instance, specifically, in particular, namely, another, other, in addition, to illustrate
comparison	similarly, not only . . . but also, in comparison
contrast	although, but, while, in contrast, however, though, on the other hand, nevertheless
sequence	first . . . second . . . third, finally, moreover, also, in addition, next, then, after, furthermore, and, previously
results	therefore, thus, consequently, as a result

Notice the difference the use of transitional words makes in the following paragraphs:

Working in the neighborhood grocery store as a checker was one of the worst jobs I've ever had. In the first place, I had to wear an ugly, scratchy uniform cut at least three inches too short. My schedule of working hours was another inconvenience; because my hours were changed each week, it was impossible to make plans in advance, and getting a day off was out of the question. In addition, the lack of working space bothered me. Except for a half-hour lunch break, I was restricted to three square feet of room behind the counter and consequently felt as if I were no more than a gerbil in a cage.

The same paragraph rewritten without transitional words sounds choppy and childish:

Working in the neighborhood grocery store as a checker was one of the worst jobs I've ever had. I had to wear an ugly, scratchy uniform. It was cut at least three inches too short. My schedule of working hours was inconvenient. My hours changed each week. It was impossible to make plans in advance. Getting a day off was out of the question. The lack of working space bothered me. Except for a half-hour break, I was restricted to three square feet of room behind the counter. I felt like a gerbil in a cage.

Although transitional words and phrases are useful in bridging the gaps between your ideas, don't overuse them. Not every sentence needs a transitional phrase, so use one only when the relationship between your thoughts needs clarification. It's also a mistake to place the transitional word in the same position in your sentence each time. Look at the paragraph that follows:

It's a shame that every high school student isn't required to take a course in first aid. *For example,* you might need to treat a friend or relative for drowning during a family picnic. Or, *for instance,* someone might break a bone or receive a snakebite on a camping trip. *Also,* you should always know what to do for a common cut or burn. *Moreover,* it's important to realize when someone is in shock. *However,* very few people take the time to learn the simple rules of first aid. *Thus,* many injured or sick people suffer more than they should. *Therefore,* everyone should take a first aid course in school or at the Red Cross center.

As you can see, a series of sentences each beginning with a transitional word quickly becomes repetitious and boring. To hold your reader's attention, use transitional words only when necessary to avoid choppiness, and vary their placement in your sentences.

Repetition of Key Words

Important words or phrases (and their synonyms) may be repeated throughout a paragraph to connect the thoughts into a coherent statement:

> One of the most common, yet most puzzling, phobias is the *fear* of *snakes*. It's only natural, of course, to be afraid of a poisonous *snake*, but many people are just as frightened of the harmless varieties. For such people, a tiny green grass *snake* is as terrifying as a cobra. Some researchers say this unreasonable *fear* of any and all *snakes* is a legacy left to us by our cave-dwelling ancestors, for whom these *reptiles* were a real and constant danger. Others maintain that the *fear* is a result of our associating the *snake* with the notion of evil, as in the Garden of Eden. Whatever the reason, the fact remains that for many otherwise normal people, the mere sight of a *snake* slithering through the countryside is enough to keep them city dwellers forever.

The repeated words "fear" and "snake" and the synonym "reptile" help tie one sentence to another so that the reader can follow the ideas easily.

Pronouns Substituted for Key Nouns

A pronoun is a word that stands for a noun. In your paragraph you might use a key noun in one sentence and then use a pronoun in its place in the following sentences. The pronoun "it" often replaces "shark" in the description that follows:

> (1)The great white shark is perhaps the best equipped of all the ocean's predators. (2)*It* can grow up to twenty-one feet and weigh three tons, with two-inch teeth that can replace themselves within twenty-four hours when damaged. (3)The shark's sense of smell is so acute that *it* can detect one ounce of fish blood in a million ounces of water. (4)In addition, *it* can sense vibrations from six hundred feet away.

Sentences 2, 3, and 4 are tied to the topic sentence by the use of the pronoun "it."

Parallelism

Parallelism in a paragraph means using the same grammatical structure in several sentences to establish coherence. The repeated use of similar phrasing helps tie the ideas and sentences together. Next, for example, is a paragraph predominantly unified by its use of grammatically parallel sentences:

> (1)The weather of Texas offers something for everyone. (2)If you are the kind who likes to see snow drifting onto mountain peaks, a visit to the Big Bend area may satisfy your eye. (3)If, on the other hand, you demand a bright sun to bake your skin a golden brown, stop in the southern part of the state. (4)And for hardier souls, who ask from nature a show of force, the skies of the Panhandle regularly release ferocious springtime tornadoes. (5)Finally, if you are the fickle type, by all means come to central Texas, where the sun at any time may shine unashamed throughout the most torrential rainstorm.

The parallel structures of sentences 2, 3, and 5 ("if you" + verb) keep the paragraph flowing smoothly from one idea to the next.

Using a Variety of Transitional Devices

Most writers use a combination of transitional devices in their paragraphs. In the following example, three kinds of transitional devices are circled: transitional words, repetition of pronouns, and repetition of key words. See whether you can identify each one.

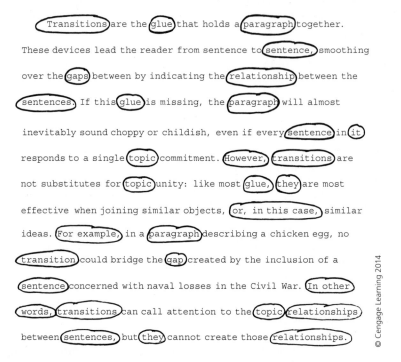

Transitions are the glue that holds a paragraph together. These devices lead the reader from sentence to sentence, smoothing over the gaps between by indicating the relationship between the sentences. If this glue is missing, the paragraph will almost inevitably sound choppy or childish, even if every sentence in it responds to a single topic commitment. However, transitions are not substitutes for topic unity: like most glue, they are most effective when joining similar objects, or, in this case, similar ideas. For example, in a paragraph describing a chicken egg, no transition could bridge the gap created by the inclusion of a sentence concerned with naval losses in the Civil War. In other words, transitions can call attention to the topic relationships between sentences, but they cannot create those relationships.

© Cengage Learning 2014

Avoiding Whiplash

The preceding example not only illustrates a variety of transitional devices, but also makes an important point about their use—and their limitations. Transitional devices show connections between sentences, but they alone cannot create a logical flow of ideas if none exists. For example, notice in the following sample the "disconnect" between the first three sentences and sentence 4:

> [1]Despite our growing dependency on computers, one of our most useful household tools is still the lowly pencil. [2]Cheap, efficient, and long-lasting, the pencil may be operated by children and adults alike, without the necessity of a user's manual or tech support. [3]According to the Incense Cedar Institute, today's pencil can draw a line 70 miles long, be sharpened 17 times, and write an average of 45,000 words. [4]Chinese factories don't have to follow as many environmental regulations, and their workers are paid less than their American counterparts. [5]Many pencils used in this country are still manufactured in China because of the cheaper cost.

Did you suffer "reader's whiplash" as your mind experienced the sudden jerk from the discussion of pencil use to "Chinese factories"? No addition of a simple transitional word will fix this problem; the writer needs to revise the paragraph's internal logic and flow or perhaps even consider a new paragraph on cost or production. In other words, don't rely on transitional devices when deep-structure revision for coherence is needed. Make your reader's trip through your prose an enjoyable one by avoiding sudden stops and starts in thought, and then smooth that ride with appropriate transitional devices when they are necessary.

Practicing What You've Learned

© Canstock Images, Inc./ Index Stock Imagery

A. Identify each of the following paragraphs as ordered by time, space, or parallelism:

My apartment is so small that it will no longer hold all my possessions. Every day when I come in the door, I am shocked by the clutter. The wall to my immediate left is completely obscured by art and movie posters that have become so numerous they often overlap, even hiding each other. Along the adjoining wall is my sound system: CDs are stacked several feet high on two long, low tables. The big couch that runs across the back of the room is always piled so high with schoolbooks and magazines that a guest usually ends up sitting on the floor. To my right is a large sliding glass door that opens onto a balcony—or at least it used to, before it was permanently blocked by my tennis gear, golf clubs, and bicycle. Even the tiny closet next to the front door is bursting with clothes, both clean and dirty. I think the time has come for me to move.

Once-common acts of greeting may be finding renewed popularity after three centuries. According to one historian, kissing was at the height of its popularity as a greeting in seventeenth-century England, when ladies and gentlemen of the court often saluted each other in this affectionate manner. Then the country was visited by a strange plague, whose cause was unknown. Because no one knew how the plague was spread, people tried to avoid physical contact with others as much as possible. Both kissing and the handshake went out of fashion and were replaced by the bow and curtsy, so people could greet others without having to touch them. The bow and curtsy remained in vogue for over a hundred years, until the handshake—for men only—returned to popularity in the nineteenth century. Today, both men and women may shake hands upon meeting others, and kissing as a greeting is making a comeback—especially among the jet-setters and Hollywood stars.

Students have diverse ways of preparing for final exams. Some stay up the night before, trying to cram into their brains what they avoided all term. Others pace themselves, spending a little time each night going over the notes they took in class that day. Still others just cross their fingers, assuming they absorbed enough along the way from lectures and readings. In the end, though, everyone hopes the tests are easy.

continued on next page

B. Circle and identify the transitional devices in the following paragraphs:

Each year I follow a system when preparing firewood to use in my stove. First, I hike about a mile from my house with my bow saw in hand. I then select three good-size oak trees and mark them with orange ties. Next, I saw through the base of each tree about two feet from the ground. After I fell the trees, not only do I trim away the branches, but I also sort the scrap from the usable limbs. I find cutting the trees into manageable-length logs is too much for one day; however, I roll them off the ground so they will not begin to rot. The next day I cut the trees into eight-foot lengths, which allows me to handle them more easily. Once they are cut, I roll them along the fire lane to the edge of the road, where I stack them neatly but not too high. The next day I borrow my uncle's van, drive to the pile of logs, and load as many logs as I can, thus reducing the number of trips. When I finally have all the logs in my backyard, I begin sawing them into eighteen-inch lengths. I create large piles that consequently have to be split and finally stacked. The logs will age and dry until winter, when I will make daily trips to the woodpile.

Fans of professional baseball and football argue continually over which is America's favorite spectator sport. Though the figures on attendance for each vary with every new season, certain arguments remain the same, spelling out both the enduring appeals of each game and something about the people who love to watch. Football, for instance, is a quicker, more physical sport, and football fans enjoy the emotional involvement they feel while watching. Baseball, on the other hand, seems more mental, like chess, and attracts those fans who prefer a quieter, more complicated game. In addition, professional football teams play sixteen games a season, usually providing fans with a week between games to work themselves up to a pitch of excitement and expectation. Baseball teams, however, play almost every day for six months, so that the typical baseball fan is not so crushed by missing a game, knowing there will be many other chances to attend. Finally, football fans seem to love the halftime pageantry, the cheerleaders, and the mascots, whereas baseball fans are often more content to concentrate on the game's finer details and spend the breaks between innings filling out their own private scorecards.

C. The following paragraph lacks common transitional devices. Fill in the blanks with appropriate transitional words or key words.

Scientists continue to debate the cause of the dinosaurs' disappearance. One group claims the _____ vanished after an asteroid smashed into the Earth; dust and smoke _____ blocked the sun for a long time. _____ of no direct sunlight, the Earth underwent a lengthy "winter," far too cold for the huge _____ to survive. A University of California paleontologist, _____, disputes this claim. He argues that _____ we generally think of _____ living in swampy land, fossils found in Alaska show that _____ could live in cold climates _____ warm ones. _____

continued on next page

group claims that the _____ became extinct following an intense period of global volcanic activity. _____ to killing the _____ themselves, these scientists _____ believe the volcanic activity killed much of the plant life that the _____ ate and, _____, many of the great _____ who survived the volcanic eruptions starved to death. Still _____ groups of _____ claim the _____ were destroyed by acid rain, by a passing "death star," _____ even by viruses from outer space.

D. The sentences below are out of order. By noting the various transitional devices, arrange the sentences into a coherent paragraph.

How to Purchase a New Car

a. If you're happy with the car's performance, find out about available financing arrangements.

b. Later, at home, study your notes carefully to help you decide which car fits your needs.

c. After you have discussed various loans and interest rates, you can negotiate the final price with the salesperson.

d. A visit to the showroom also allows you to test-drive the car.

e. Once you have agreed on the car's price, feel confident that you have made a well-chosen purchase.

f. Next, a visit to a nearby showroom should help you select the color, options, and style of the car of your choice.

g. First, take a trip to the library to read the current auto magazines and consumers' guides.

h. As you read, take notes on models and prices.

E. *Collaborative Activity:* Rearrange a paragraph you have written so that your sentences are listed out of order, in similar fashion to those in the preceding exercise. Exchange your sentences with those of a classmate. If the original paragraphs were written with logical unity and enough transitional devices for a smooth flow, it should be easy for both of you to reassemble the sentences into their proper cohesive order. If you cannot solve your classmate's paragraph puzzle or if you experience "reader's whiplash," explain the problem, offering suggestions for revision.

Paragraph Sequence

The order in which you present your paragraphs is another decision you must make. In some essays, the subject matter itself will suggest its own order.* For instance, in an essay designed to instruct a beginning runner, you might want to discuss the necessary

---

* ◆ For more information on easily recognized patterns of order, see pages 68–69.

equipment—good running shoes, loose-fitting clothing, and a sweatband—before moving to a discussion of where to run and how to run. Other essay topics, however, may not suggest a natural order, in which case you must decide which order will most effectively reach and hold the attention of your audience. Frequently, writers withhold their strongest point until last. (Lawyers often use this technique; they first present the jury with the weakest arguments, then pull out the most incriminating evidence—the "smoking gun." Thus, the jury members retire with the strongest argument freshest in their minds.) Sometimes, however, you'll find it necessary to present one particular point first so that the other points make good sense. Study your own major points, and decide which order will be the most logical, successful way of persuading your reader to accept your thesis.

Transitions between Paragraphs

As you already know, each paragraph usually signals a new major point in your discussion. These paragraphs should not appear as isolated blocks of thought but rather as parts of a unified, step-by-step progression. To avoid a choppy essay, link each paragraph to the one before it with *transitional devices.* Just as the sentences in your paragraphs are connected, so are the paragraphs themselves; ◆ therefore, you can use the same transitional devices suggested on pages 69–71.

The first sentence of most body paragraphs frequently contains the transitional device. To illustrate this point, here are some topic sentences lifted from the body paragraphs of a student essay criticizing a popular sports car, renamed the 'Gator to protect the guilty and to prevent lawsuits. The transitional devices are italicized.

> **Thesis:** The *'Gator* is one of the worst cars on the market.

- When you buy a *'Gator,* you buy physical inconvenience. [repetition of key word from thesis]
- *Another* reason the *'Gator* is a bad buy is the cost of insurance. [transitional word, key word]
- You might overlook the *inconvenient* size and exorbitant *insurance* rates if the *'Gator* were a strong, reliable car, *but* this automobile constantly needs repair. [key words from preceding paragraphs, transitional word]
- When you decide to sell this *car,* you face *still another* unpleasant surprise: the extremely low resale value. [key word, transitional phrase]
- The most serious drawback, *however,* is the *'Gator's* safety record. [transitional word, key word]

Sometimes, instead of using transitional words or repetition of key words or their synonyms, you can use an *idea hook.* The last idea of one paragraph can lead you smoothly into your next paragraph. Instead of repeating a key word from the previous discussion, find a phrase that refers to the entire idea just expressed. If, for example, the previous paragraph discussed the highly complimentary advertising campaign for the 'Gator, the next paragraph might begin, "This view of the 'Gator as an economy car is ridiculous to anyone who has pumped a week's salary into this gas guzzler." The phrase "this view" connects the idea of the first paragraph with the one that follows. Idea hooks also work well with transitional words: "This view, however, is ridiculous. . . ."

If you do use transitional words, don't allow them to make your essay sound mechanical. For example, a long series of paragraphs beginning "First . . . Second . . . Third . . ." quickly becomes boring. Vary the type and position of your transitional devices so that your essay has a subtle but logical movement from point to point.

Applying What You've Learned to *Your* Writing

© Keith Brofsky/
Photodisc/Getty Images

If you are currently working on a draft of an essay, check each body paragraph for coherence, the smooth connection of ideas and sentences in a logical, easy-to-follow order. You might try placing brackets around key words, pronouns, and transitional words that carry the reader's attention from thought to thought and from sentence to sentence. Decide whether you have enough ordering devices, placed in appropriate places, or whether you need to add (or delete) others. (◆ For additional help revising your drafts, turn to Chapter 5.)

Chapter 3 Summary

Here is a brief restatement of what you should know about the paragraphs in the body of your essay:

1. Each body paragraph usually contains one major point in the discussion promised by the thesis statement.

2. Each major point is presented in the topic sentence of a paragraph.

3. Each paragraph should be adequately developed with clear supporting detail.

4. Every sentence in the paragraph should support the topic sentence.

5. There should be an orderly, logical flow from sentence to sentence and from thought to thought.

6. The sequence of your essay's paragraphs should be logical and effective.

7. There should be a smooth flow from paragraph to paragraph.

8. The body paragraphs should successfully persuade your reader that the opinion expressed in your thesis is valid.

Chapter 4

Beginnings and Endings

· ·

As you work on your rough drafts, you might think of your essay as a coherent, unified whole composed of three main parts: the introduction (lead-in, thesis, and essay map), the body (paragraphs with supporting evidence), and the conclusion (final address to the reader). These three parts should flow smoothly into one another, presenting the reader with an organized, logical discussion. The following pages will suggest ways to begin, end, and also name your essay effectively.

How to Write a Good Lead-In

The first few sentences of your essay are particularly important; first impressions, as you know, are often lasting ones. The beginning of your essay, then, must catch the readers' attention and make them want to keep reading. Recall the way you read a magazine: if you are like most people, you probably skim the magazine, reading a paragraph or two of each article that looks promising. If the first few paragraphs hold your interest, you read on. When you write your own introductory paragraph, assume that you have only a few sentences to attract your reader. Consequently, you must pay particular attention to making those first lines especially interesting and well written.

In some essays, your thesis statement alone may be controversial or striking enough to capture the readers. At other times, however, you will want to use the introductory device called a *lead-in.** The lead-in (1) catches the readers' attention; (2) announces the subject matter and tone of your essay (humorous, satiric, serious, etc.); and (3) sets up, or leads into, the presentation of your thesis and essay map.

---

* Do note that for some writing assignments, such as certain kinds of technical reports, attention-grabbing lead-ins are not appropriate. Frequently, these reports are directed toward particular professional audiences and have their own designated format; they often begin, for example, with a statement of the problem under study or with a review of pertinent information or research.

Here are some suggestions for and examples of lead-ins:

1. A paradoxical or intriguing statement

    "Eat two chocolate bars and call me in the morning," says the psychiatrist to the patient. Such advice sounds like a sugar fanatic's dream, but recent studies have indeed confirmed that chocolate positively affects depression and anxiety.

2. An arresting statistic or shocking statement

    One of every eight women in the U.S. will develop invasive breast cancer over the course of a lifetime, according to a recent report prepared by the American Cancer Society.

3. A question

    What are more and more Americans doing these days to stay in touch with friends and family? Overwhelmingly, the answer is text messaging: a whopping 4.1 billion of them a day, according to CTIA, the International Association for the Wireless Telecommunications Industry. That's approximately fourteen texts a day for every man, woman, and child in this country.

4. A quotation from a recognized authority, historical figure, or literary source

    Confucius wisely noted that "our greatest glory is not in never falling, but in rising every time we fall." Despite a frustrating series of close losses, my soccer team faced every new game with optimism and determination. My teammates' never-give-up attitudes have shown me that the value of sport is not winning but learning how to face defeat and begin again.

Note too that sometimes writers may challenge the wisdom of authorities or use their words in humorous ways to introduce lighthearted essays:

    When Einstein wrote that the "most beautiful thing we can experience is the mysterious," I don't believe he was thinking about the mystery smell coming from our attic last summer.

5. A relevant story, joke, or anecdote

    Writer and witty critic Dorothy Parker was once assigned a remote, out-of-the-way office. According to the story, she became so lonely, so desperate for company, that she ultimately painted "Gentlemen" on the door. Although this university is large, no one on this campus needs to feel as isolated as Parker obviously did: our excellent Student Activity Office offers numerous clubs, programs, and volunteer groups to involve students of all interests.

6. A description, often used for emotional appeal

    With one eye blackened, one arm in a cast, and third-degree burns on both her legs, the pretty, blond two-year-old seeks corners of rooms, refuses to speak, and shakes violently at the sound of loud noises. Tammy is not the victim of a war or a natural disaster; rather, she is the helpless victim of her parents, one of the thousands of children who suffer daily from America's hidden crime, child abuse.

7. A factual statement or a summary who-what-where-when-why lead-in

Texas's first execution of a woman in twenty-three years occurred September 14, 2005, at the Huntsville Unit of the state's Department of Corrections, despite the protests of various human-rights groups around the country.

8. An analogy or comparison

The Romans kept geese on their Capitol Hill to cackle alarm in the event of attack by night. Modern Americans, despite their technology, have hardly improved on that old system of protection. According to the latest Safety Council report, almost any door with a standard lock can be opened easily with a common plastic credit card.

9. A contrast or a before-and-after scenario

I used to search for toast in the supermarket. I used to think "blackened"—as in blackened Cajun shrimp—referred to the way I cooked anything in a skillet. "Poached" could only have legal ramifications. But all that has changed! Attending a class in basic cooking this summer has transformed the way I purchase, prepare, and even talk about food.

10. A personal experience

I first realized times were changing for women when I overheard my six-year-old nephew speaking to my sister, a prominent New York lawyer. As we left her elaborate, luxurious office one evening, Tommy looked up at his mother and queried, "Mommy, can little boys grow up to be lawyers, too?"

11. A catalog of relevant examples or facts

A two-hundred-pound teenager quit school because no desk would hold her. A three-hundred-pound chef who could no longer stand on his feet was fired. A three-hundred-fifty-pound truck driver broke furniture in his friends' houses. All these people are now living healthier, happier, and thinner lives, thanks to the remarkable intestinal bypass surgery first developed in 1967.

12. Statement of a problem or a popular misconception

Some people believe that poetry is written only by aging beatniks or solemn, mournful men and women with suicidal tendencies. The Poetry in the Schools Program is working hard to correct that erroneous point of view.

13. Brief dialogue to introduce the topic

"Be bold! You can do it!" said my roommate again and again during the weeks before choir tryouts, despite my whimpering cries of "I can't, I can't." For a shy person like me, the thought of singing in a public audition was agony. But thanks to the ABC Relaxation Method suggested by the Counseling Center, I performed so well I was chosen for a solo. The ABC method, incorporating visualization and proper breathing techniques, is a helpful process every shy person should practice regularly.

14. A proverb, maxim, or motto

"One falsehood spoils a thousand truths," says the African proverb. Caught in the biggest lie of his political career, once-popular local mayor Paul TerGhist is learning the meaning of this old saying the hard way, as his former friends and supporters are now deserting him.

15. A recognition, revelation, or insight

> As someone who earned "A's" throughout my Spanish classes, I thought I had a good grasp of the language. However, immersion in the Tres Amigos Building Project in Monterrey, Mexico, over Spring Break this year showed me I had much to learn about conversational speech patterns.

16. An appeal to a common or imagined experience

> Come on, you know you've done it . . . in your bedroom, bathroom, car, wherever you've listened to hard rock music. You played your air guitar—and you're good, but maybe not great. If you keep practicing, though, you might be able to join the best air-shredders in the country as they compete annually in front of sold-out crowds at the national Air Guitar Championships.

Thinking of a good lead-in is often difficult when you sit down to begin your essay. Many writers, in fact, skip the lead-in until the first draft is written. They compose their working thesis first and then write the body of the essay, saving the lead-in and conclusion for last. As you write the middle of your essay, you may discover an especially interesting piece of information you might want to save to use as your lead-in.

Avoiding Errors in Lead-Ins

In addition to the previous suggestions, here is some advice to help you avoid common lead-in errors:

Make sure your lead-in introduces your thesis. A frequent weakness in introductory paragraphs is an interesting lead-in but no smooth or clear transition to the thesis statement. To avoid a gap or awkward jump in thought in your introductory paragraph, you may need to add a connecting sentence or phrase between your lead-in and thesis. Study the following paragraph, which uses a comparison as its lead-in. The italicized transitional sentence takes the reader from a general comment about Americans who use wheelchairs to information about those in Smallville, smoothly preparing the reader for the thesis that follows.

Lead-in   In the 1950s African-Americans demanded the right to sit anywhere they pleased on public buses. Today, Americans who use wheelchairs are fighting for the right to board those same buses. *Here in Smallville,*

Transitional
sentence

Thesis

the lack of proper boarding facilities often denies citizens with physical disabilities basic transportation to jobs, grocery stores, and medical centers. To give people using wheelchairs the same opportunities as other residents, the City Council should allocate the funds necessary to convert every bus in the public transportation system.

Keep your lead-in brief. Long lead-ins in short essays often give the appearance of a tail wagging the dog. Use a brief, attention-catching hook to set up your thesis; don't make your introduction the biggest part of your essay.

Don't begin with an apology or complaint. Such statements as "It's difficult to find much information on this topic . . ." and "This controversy is hard to understand, but . . ." do nothing to entice your reader.

Don't assume your audience already knows your subject matter. Identify the pertinent facts even though you know your readers know the assignment. ("The biggest problem with the new college requirement. . . ." What requirement?) If you are writing about a particular piece of literature or art, identify the title of the work and its author or artist, using the full name in the first reference.

Stay clear of overused lead-ins. If composition teachers had a nickel for every essay that began with a dry dictionary definition, they could all retire to Bermuda. Leave Webster's alone and find a livelier way to begin. Asking a question as your lead-in is becoming overworked, too, so use it only when it is obviously the best choice for your opener.

Practicing What You've Learned

© Canstock Images, Inc./
Index Stock Imagery

Describe the lead-ins in the following paragraphs. Did any of the writers blend more than one kind of lead-in?

1. In the sixth century, Lao-Tzu, the father of Taoism, described the "good traveler" as someone who has "no fixed plans and is not intent on arriving." If that ancient Chinese philosopher is correct, then my aimless but eventful wanderings across the South last fall qualify me as a World-Class Traveler.

2. Ever wonder if those long hours hitting the books are worth it? Do grades really matter to employers? According to a survey by the National Association of Colleges and Employers, the answer is . . . yes. Strong grades and a go-getter attitude are the keys to securing a good job after college.

3. An average can of soda may contain ten or more teaspoons of sugar. If you are one of the college students who drinks a can or two of pop

continued on next page

every day, you could be consuming as much as thirty-two pounds of sugar every year! Cutting back on soft drinks is an easy way people can achieve a healthier diet.

4. I used to think bees were my friends. They make the honey I like to eat, and they help pollinate the flowers I like to smell. But after being stung multiple times and spending three days in the hospital last summer, I have come to see the little creatures in a totally different light. For those of us who are allergic to their venom, bees are flying killers whose buzz sends us scurrying for cover.

5. On May 6, 1937, the *Hindenburg*, a luxurious German airship with cabins for fifty, exploded into flames as it tried to land in New Jersey, killing thirty-six people and ending zeppelin passenger service forever. Theories about the cause of this mysterious explosion include lightning and static electricity, but the most intriguing explanation involves sabotage and betrayal.

© Bettmann / Corbis

Assignment

© CORBIS

A. Find three good lead-ins from essays, magazine articles, or newspaper feature stories. Identify the kinds of lead-ins you found, and tell why you think each effectively catches the reader's attention and sets up the thesis.

B. *Collaborative Activity:* Select an example of a successful lead-in from an essay or article. Join a group of three classmates and share your choices. Of the four lead-ins, which is the most effective, and why? Report your decision to the class.

How to Write a Good Concluding Paragraph

Like a good story, a good essay should not stop in the middle. It should have a satisfying conclusion, one that gives the reader a sense of completion on the subject. Don't allow your essay to drop off or fade out at the end—instead, use the concluding paragraph to emphasize the validity and importance of your thinking. Remember that the concluding paragraph is your last chance to convince the reader. (As one cynical but realistic student pointed out, the conclusion may be the last part of your essay the teacher reads before putting a grade on your paper.) Therefore, make your conclusion count.

Some people feel that writing an essay shares a characteristic with a romantic fling—both activities are frequently easier to begin than they are to end. If you find, as many writers do, that you often struggle while searching for an exit with the proper emphasis and grace, here are some suggestions, by no means exhaustive, that might spark some good ideas for your conclusions:

1.   A summary of the thesis and the essay's major points (most useful in long essays)

> The destruction of the rain forests must be stopped. Although developers protest that they are bringing much-needed financial aid into these traditionally poverty-stricken areas, no amount of money can compensate for what is being lost. Without the rain forests, we are not only contributing to the global warming of the entire planet, we are losing indigenous trees and plants that might someday provide new medicines or vaccines for diseases. Moreover, the replacement of indigenous peoples with corporation-run ranches robs the world of cultural diversity. For the sake of the planet's well-being, Project Rainforest should be implemented.

2.   An evaluation of the importance of the essay's subject

> These amazing, controversial photographs of the comet will continue to be the subject of debate because, according to some scientists, they yield the most important clues yet revealed about the origins of our universe.

3.   A statement of the essay's broader implications

> Because these studies of feline leukemia may someday play a crucial role in the discovery of a cure for AIDS in human beings, the experiments, as expensive as they are, must continue.

4.   A recommendation or call to action

> The specific details surrounding the death of World War II hero Raoul Wallenberg are still unknown. Although Russia has recently admitted—after fifty years of denial—that Wallenberg was murdered by the KGB in 1947, such a confession is not enough. We must write our congressional representatives today urging their support for the new Swedish commission investigating the circumstances of his death. No hero deserves less.

5.   A warning based on the essay's thesis

> Understanding the politics that led to the destruction of Hiroshima is essential for all Americans—indeed, for all the world's peoples. Without such knowledge, the frightful possibility exists that somewhere, sometime, someone might drop the bomb again.

6.   A quotation from an authority or someone whose insight emphasizes the main point

> Even though I didn't win the fiction contest, I learned so much about my own powers of creativity. I'm proud that I pushed myself in new directions. I know now

I will always agree with Herman Melville, whose writing was unappreciated in his own time, that "it is better to struggle with originality than to succeed in imitation."

7. An anecdote or brief example that emphasizes or sums up the point of the essay

   Bette Davis's role on and off the screen as the catty, wisecracking woman of steel helped make her an enduring star. After all, no audience, past or present, could ever resist a dame who drags on a cigarette and then mutters about a passing starlet, "There goes a good time that was had by all."

8. An image or description that lends finality to the essay

   As the last of the Big Screen's giant ants are incinerated by the Army scientist, one can almost hear the movie audiences of the 1950s breathing a collective sigh of relief, secure in the knowledge that once again the threat of nuclear radiation had been vanquished by the efforts of the U.S. military.

   (◆ For another last image that captures the essence of an essay, see the "open house" scene that concludes "To Bid the World Farewell," page 220.)

9. A rhetorical question that makes the readers think about the essay's main point

   No one wants to see hostages put in danger. But what nation can afford to let terrorists know they can get away with blackmail?

10. A forecast based on the essay's thesis

    "Reality" TV shows that are competition-based (contestants singing, dancing, cooking, etc.) will continue to be popular not only because they invite viewers to imagine themselves as powerful judges but also because such shows are easier and cheaper for networks to produce than scripted dramas or comedies.

11. An ironic twist, witticism, pun, or playful use of words (often more appropriate in lighthearted essays)

    After analyzing and understanding the causes of my procrastination, I now feel better, more determined to change my behavior. In fact, I've decided that today is the day for decisive action! I will choose a major! Hmmmm . . . or maybe not. I need to think about it some more. I'll get back to you, okay? Tomorrow. Really.

12. Return to the technique used in your lead-in (answer a question you asked, circle back to a story, extend a quotation, etc.)

    So was Dorothy right in *The Wizard of Oz*? After the tough summer I spent on our ranch in Wyoming, mending barbed-wire fences and wrestling angry calves, I could think of nothing but Dorothy's words on the long bus ride back to school. As eager as I had been to leave, I couldn't wait to get back there. It wasn't Kansas, but Dorothy and I knew the truth: There's no place like home.

◆ **Hint:** After reading the preceding suggestions, if you are still struggling with your conclusion, turn back to the advice for writing lead-ins on pages 78–81. One of the suggestions there may trigger a useful idea for closing your essay. In fact, following a first draft, you may decide that the technique you chose to open your essay might be used more effectively to conclude it.

Avoiding Errors in Conclusions

Try to omit the following common errors in your concluding paragraphs:

Avoid a boring, mechanical ending. One of the most common weaknesses in student essays is a conclusion that merely restates the thesis, word for word. A brief essay of 500 to 750 words rarely requires a flat, point-by-point conclusion; in fact, such an ending often insults the readers' intelligence by implying that their attention spans are extremely short. Only after reading long essays do most readers need a precise recap of all the writer's main ideas. Instead of recopying your thesis and essay map, try finding an original, emphatic way to conclude your essay—or, as a well-known newspaper columnist described it, a good ending should snap with grace and authority, like the close of an expensive sports car door.

© Jack Hollingsworth / Corbis

Don't introduce new points or irrelevant material. Treat the major points of your essay in separate body paragraphs rather than in your exit. Stay focused on your essay's specific thesis and purpose; don't allow any unimportant or off-subject comments to drift into your concluding remarks.

Don't tack on a conclusion. There should be a smooth, logical flow of thought from your last body paragraph into your concluding statements.

Don't change your stance. Sometimes writers who have been critical of something throughout their essays will soften their stance or offer apologies in their last paragraph. For instance, someone complaining about the poor quality of a particular college course might abruptly conclude with statements that declare the class wasn't so bad after all, maybe she should have worked harder, or maybe she really did learn something after all. Such reneging may seem polite, but in actuality it undercuts the thesis and confuses the reader who has taken the writer's criticisms seriously. Instead of contradicting themselves, writers should stand their ground, forget about puffy clichés or "niceties," and find an emphatic way to conclude that is consistent with their thesis.

Avoid trite expressions. Don't begin your conclusion by declaring, "In conclusion," "In summary," or "As you can see, this essay proves my thesis that. . . ." End your essay so that the reader clearly senses completion; don't merely announce that you're finished.

Don't insult or anger your reader. No matter how right you feel you are, resist the temptation to set up an "either-or" conclusion in an argumentative essay: either you agree with me or you are an ignorant/wrong/selfish/immoral person. Don't exaggerate your claims or moralize excessively as you exit. Remember that your purpose is to inform and persuade your readers, not to annoy them to the point of rejecting your thesis out of sheer irritation. Conclude on a positive note, one that encourages readers to see matters your way.

Practicing What You've Learned

Identify the weaknesses you see in the following conclusions. How might these writers revise to create more satisfactory endings for their essays?

1. My thesis in this essay stated that I believe that having to change schools does not harm children for three reasons. Children at new schools learn how to make new friends. They learn how to get along with a variety of people. They also learn about different teaching styles. For these three reasons, I believe that having to change schools does not harm children.

2. "A journey of a thousand miles must begin with a single step" (Lao Tzu). As I discussed in this causal analysis essay, I would have never started painting again if I hadn't gone back to school. I'm the first to admit that it was a long, hard road to get my degree, and sometimes I really questioned the value of certain courses I had to take (like algebra, for example, which I think is a totally useless course for artists. The entire math requirement needs revision, in my opinion). But going back to school was the right choice for me and, who knows, maybe it would be for others.

3. In conclusion, as I have shown here, our country's forest conservation policies are just plain stupid. If you don't stand up and join the fight against them, I hope you will enjoy living in a tent because pretty soon there isn't going to be any lumber for houses left. After selling out to the tree-huggers, will you be able to look at yourself in the mirror?

Assignment

Find three good concluding paragraphs. Identify each kind of conclusion, and tell why you think it is an effective ending for the essay or article.

How to Write a Good Title

As in the case of lead-ins, your title may be written at any time, but many writers prefer to finish their essays before naming them. A good title is similar to a good newspaper headline in that it attracts the readers' interest and makes them want to investigate the essay. Like the lead-in, the title helps announce the tone of the essay. An informal or humorous essay, for instance, might have a catchy, funny title. Some titles show the writer's wit and love of wordplay; a survey of recent magazines revealed these titles: "Bittersweet News about Saccharin," "Coffee: New Grounds for Concern," and "The Scoop on the Best Ice Cream."

On the other hand, a serious, informative essay should have a more formal title that suggests its content as clearly and specifically as possible. Let's suppose, for example, that you are researching the meaning of color in dreams, and you see an article in a database list titled merely "Dreams." You don't know whether you should bother to read it. To avoid such confusion in your own essay and to encourage readers' interest, always use a specific title: "Interpreting Animal Imagery in Dreams," "Dream Research: An Aid to Diagnosing Depression," and so forth. Moreover, if your subject matter is controversial, let the reader know which side you're on (e.g., "The Advantages of Solar Power"). Never substitute a mere label, such as "Football Games" or "Euthanasia," for a meaningful title. And never, never label your essays "Theme One" or "Comparison and Contrast Essay." In all your writing, including the title, use your creativity to attract the readers' attention and to invite their interest in your ideas.

If you're unsure about how to present your title, here are three basic rules:

1. Your own title should not be underlined, italicized, or put in quotation marks. It should be written at the top of page one of your essay or on an appropriate title page with no special marks of punctuation.

2. Capitalize the first, last, and important words of your title. Generally, do not capitalize such words as "an," "and," "a," or "the," or prepositions, unless they appear as the first or last words of the title or follow a colon within the title.

3. Sometimes writers craft a title that presents a word or phrase followed by a colon introducing a definition, a revealing image, a question, or some other kind of explanatory material to interest the reader.

Examples	"Stephen Crane: Daredevil Reporter"
	"Memories Carved in Stone: Tennessee Pioneer Memorials"
	"Intervention in Iran: A Recipe for Disaster"
	"Yoga: Does Twisting Like a Pretzel Really Help?"

You may use such titles to clarify a work's scope or perhaps to set the appropriate tone for your reader, but be careful not to overuse this structure. (Note that the word after the colon is capitalized as if it were the first word of the title.)

Practicing What You've Learned

© Canstock Images, Inc./Index Stock Imagery

Describe any weaknesses you see in the following titles. How might each one be revised to clarify its essay's content and to attract more reader interest?

1. Advice for College Freshmen

2. Essay Assignment #3: "Review of a Favorite Movie"

3. Learning to Play Texas Hold'em

4. A Comparison of Two Heroes

continued on next page

5. The Problem of Abandoned Pets and Its Solution

6. Steroids and Athletes Today

7. The Effects of Three Popular Diets

8. The Best Laptop on the Market

9. An Explanation of the Human Genome Project

10. My Interpretation of Auden's "The Unknown Citizen"

Assignment

© CORBIS

A. Read one of the student or professional essays in this text and evaluate the title. Explain why you think the title is or is not effective. Or, if you prefer, write a new title for one of the essays in this book. Why is your choice as effective as (or even better than) that of the original writer?

B. *Collaborative Activity:* Bring to class three titles or headlines from print or online articles. In a small group of classmates, compare all the samples. Which ones would encourage members of the group to read on? Which one is the least interesting or helpful? (If time permits, select one effective title to read to the class as a whole.) How might your choices influence your crafting of a title for your next essay?

Applying What You've Learned to *Your* Writing

© Keith Brofsky/
Photodisc/Getty Images

Look at the draft of the essay you are currently working on, and ask yourself these questions:

- Does the opening of my essay make my reader want to continue reading? Does the lead-in smoothly set up my thesis, or do I need to add some sort of transition to help move the reader to my main idea? Is the lead-in appropriate in terms of the tone and length of my essay?
- Does the conclusion of my essay offer an emphatic ending, one that is consistent with my essay's purpose? Have I avoided a mechanical, trite, or tacked-on closing paragraph? Have I refrained from adding a new point in my conclusion that belongs in the body of my essay or in another essay?
- Does my title interest my reader? Are its content and tone appropriate for this particular essay?

If you have answered "no" to any of these questions, you should continue revising your essay. (◆ For more help revising your prose, turn to Chapter 5.)

Chapter 4 Summary

Here is a brief restatement of what you should remember about writing introductions, conclusions, and titles:

1. Many essays will profit from a lead-in, the first sentences of the introductory paragraph that attract the reader's attention and smoothly set up the thesis statement.

2. Essays should end convincingly, without being repetitious or trite, with thoughts that emphasize the writer's main purpose.

3. Titles should invite the reader's interest by indicating the general nature of the essay's content and its tone.

Chapter 5

Drafting and Revising: Creative Thinking, Critical Thinking

· ·

> " *There is no good writing, only rewriting.* "
>
> —James Thurber, author and humorist

> " *When I say writing, O, believe me, it is rewriting that I have chiefly in mind.* "
>
> —Robert Louis Stevenson, novelist and essayist

The absolute necessity of revision cannot be overemphasized. All good writers rethink, rearrange, and rewrite large portions of their prose. The French novelist Colette, for instance, wrote everything over and over. In fact, she often spent an entire morning working on a single page. Hemingway, to cite another example, rewrote the ending to *A Farewell to Arms* thirty-nine times "to get the words right." Although no one expects you to make thirty-nine drafts of each essay, the point is clear: writing well means revising. **All good writers revise their prose.**

What Is Revision?

Revision is a *thinking process* that occurs any time you are working on a writing project. It means looking at your writing with a "fresh eye"—that is, reseeing your writing in ways that will enable you to make more effective choices throughout your essay. Revision often entails rethinking what you have written and asking yourself questions about its effectiveness; it involves discovery as well as change. As you write, new ideas surface, prompting you to revise what you have planned or have just written. Or perhaps these new ideas will cause changes in earlier parts of your essay. In some cases, your new ideas will encourage you to begin an entirely new draft with a different focus or approach. Revision means making important decisions about the best ways to focus, organize, develop, clarify, and emphasize your ideas.

When Does Revision Occur?

Revision, as previously noted, occurs throughout your writing process. Early on, you are revising as you sort through ideas to write about, and you almost certainly revise as you define your purpose and audience and sharpen your thesis. Some revising may be done in your head, and some may be on paper or computer screen as you plan, sketch, or "discovery-write" your ideas. Later, during drafting, revision becomes more individualized and complex. Many writers find themselves sweeping back and forth over their papers, writing for a bit and then rereading what they wrote, making changes, and then moving ahead. Some writers like to revise "lumps," or pieces of writing, perhaps reviewing one major idea or paragraph at a time. Frequently, writers discover that a better idea is occurring almost at the very moment they are putting another thought on a page. And virtually all writers revise after "reseeing" a draft in its entirety.

   Revision, then, occurs before drafting, during drafting, between parts of drafts, and at the ends of drafts. You can revise a word, a sentence, a paragraph, or an entire essay. If you are like most writers, you sometimes revise almost automatically as you write (deleting one word or line and quickly replacing it with another as you move on, for example), and at other times you revise very deliberately (concentrating on a conclusion you know is weak, for example). Revision is "rethinking," and that activity can happen any time, in many ways, in any part of your writing.

Myths about Revision

If revision is rethinking, what is it not? Three misconceptions about revision are addressed here.

   1. **Revision is not autopsy.** Revision is not an isolated stage of writing that occurs *only* after your last draft is written or right before your paper is due. Revising is not merely a postmortem procedure, to be performed only after your creative juices have ceased to flow. Good writing, as the popular writer James Thurber noted, *is* revision, and revision occurs throughout the writing process.

2. **Revision is not limited to editing or proofreading.** Too many writers mistakenly equate revision with editing and proofreading. *Editing* means revising for "surface errors"—mistakes in spelling, grammar, punctuation, sentence sense, and word choice. Certainly, good writers comb their papers for such errors, and they edit their prose extensively for clarity, conciseness, and emphasis, too. *Proofreading* to search out and destroy errors and typos that distort meaning or distract the reader is also important. Without question, both editing and proofreading are essential to a polished paper. But revision is not *limited* to such activities. It includes them but also encompasses those larger, global changes writers may make in purpose, focus, organization, and development. Writers who revise effectively not only change words and catch mechanical errors but also typically add, delete, rearrange, and rewrite large chunks of prose. In other words, revision is not cosmetic surgery on a body that may need major resuscitation.

3. **Revision is not punishment or busywork.** At one time or another, most of us have found ourselves guilty of racing too quickly through a particular job and then moving on. And perhaps just as often we have found ourselves redoing such jobs because the results were so disappointing. Some people may regard revising in a similar light—as the repeat performance of a job done poorly the first time. But that attitude isn't productive. Revising isn't punishment for failing to produce a perfect first draft. Rarely, if ever, does anyone—even our most admired professional writers—produce the results he or she wants without revising.* Remember that revising is not a tacked-on stage, nor is it merely a quick touch-up; it's an integral part of the entire writing process itself. It's an ongoing opportunity to discover, remember, reshape, and refine your ideas.

If you've ever created something you now treasure—a piece of jewelry, furniture, painting, or music—recall the time you put into it. You probably thought about it from several angles, experimented with it, crafted it, worked it through expected and unexpected problems, and smoothed out its minor glitches, all to achieve the results you wanted. Similarly, with each revision you make, your paper becomes clearer, truer, more satisfying to you and to your readers. With practice, you will produce writing you are proud of—and you will discover that revising has become not only an essential but also a natural part of your writing process.

Can I Learn to Improve My Revision Skills?

Because revision is such a multifaceted and individual activity, no textbook can guide you through all the rethinking you may do as you move through each sentence of every writing project. But certainly you can learn to improve your ability to think both

---

*All of us have heard stories about famous essays or poems composed at one quick sitting. Bursts of creativity do happen. But it's also possible that authors of such pieces revise extensively in their heads before they write. They may rattle ideas around in their brains for such a prolonged period that the actual writing does in fact flow easily or may even seem "dictated" by an inner voice. This sort of lengthy internal "cooking" may work well at various times for you, too.

creatively and analytically about your prose. To sharpen your critical thinking and revision skills, this chapter will suggest a step-by-step method of self-questioning designed to help you achieve your writing goals.

Preparing to Draft: Some Time-Saving Hints

Before you begin drafting (either a "discovery" draft or a draft from your working thesis), remember this important piece of advice: no part of your draft is sacred or permanent. No matter what you write at this point, you can always change it. Drafting is discovering and recollecting as well as developing ideas from your earlier plans. Take the pressure off yourself: no one expects blue-ribbon prose in early drafts. (◆ If you can't seem to get going or if you do become stuck along the way, reread pages 98–100 and 121–123 of this chapter for help triumphing over your procrastination or case of Writer's Block.)

At this point, too, you might consider the actual format of your drafts. Because you will be making many changes in your writing, you may find revising less cumbersome and time-consuming if you prepare your manuscripts as described here.

1. If you are handwriting your first drafts, always write on one side of your paper only, in case you want to cut and tape together portions of drafts or you want to experiment with interchanging parts of a particular draft. (If you have written on both sides, you may have to copy the parts of your essay you want to save; your time is better spent creating and revising.)

2. Leave big margins on *both* sides of any handwritten pages so you can add information later or jot down new ideas as they occur. (Some writers also skip lines for this reason. If you choose to write on every other line, however, do remember that you may not be getting a true picture of your paragraph development or essay length. A handwritten double-spaced body paragraph, for example, may appear skimpy in your typed final copy.)

3. Devise a system of symbols (circles, stars, checks, asterisks, etc.) that will remind you of changes you want to make later. For example, if you're in hot pursuit of a great idea but can't think of the exact word you want, put down a word that's close, circle it (or type three XXXs by it), and go on so that your thinking is not derailed. Similarly, a check in the margin might mean "return to this tangled sentence." A question mark might mean a fuzzy idea, and a star, a great idea that needs expanding. A system of symbols can save you from agonizing over every inch of your essay while you are still trying to discover and clarify your ideas.

4. If your ideas are flowing well but you realize you need more supporting evidence for some of your points, consider leaving some blank spots to fill in later. For example, let's say you are writing about the effects of television commercials on our presidential elections; your ideas are good, but in a particular body paragraph you decide some statistics on commercial frequency would be most convincing. Or perhaps you need to cite an example of a particular kind of advertisement, but you just can't think of a good one at that moment. Leave a spot for the piece of evidence with a key word or two to remind you of what's needed, and keep

writing. Later, when you come back to that spot, you can add the appropriate support; if you can't find or think of the right supporting evidence to insert, you may decide to omit that point.

5. If you do decide to rewrite or omit something—a sentence or an entire passage—in a handwritten draft, mark a single "X" or line through it lightly. Don't scratch it out or destroy it completely; you may realize later that you want to reinsert the material there or move it to another, better place. If you are composing on a computer, italicize or put brackets around material you may want to use elsewhere. Or consider moving a larger chunk of prose to a "holding page" or to the end of the current draft so you can take another look at it later.

6. If you begin with a handwritten draft, do eventually work on a print copy. The more compact spacing of typed prose allows you to see more clearly the relationship of the parts in your essay, making it easier for you to organize and develop your ideas. It is also far more likely that you will catch spelling and other mechanical errors in a printed draft.

7. Always keep your notes, outlines, drafts, and an extra copy of your final paper. Never burn your bridges—or your manuscripts! Sometimes essays change directions, and writers find they can return to prewriting or earlier drafts to recover ideas, once rejected, that now work well. Drafts also may contain ideas that didn't work in one paper but look like great starts for another assignment. Tracking revisions from draft to draft can give writers a sense of accomplishment and insight into their composing processes. And drafts can be good insurance in case final copies of papers are lost or accidentally destroyed.

Writing with Computers

Most college students today are accustomed to using computers at school, home, or work, and feel quite comfortable drafting and revising at their keyboards. If this has been your experience, you probably already know how helpful computers can be in all stages of the writing process. You can, for example, compose and store your prewriting activities, journal entries, notes, or good ideas in various files until you need to recall certain information—and you can easily produce extra copies of your drafts or finished essays without having to search out a copy machine and correct change. Spell-checkers and dictionaries can help you correct many of your errors and typos.

But the most important use of the computer to a writer may be what it can do as you draft and revise your prose. A word-processing program enables you to add, delete, or change words easily; it allows you to move words, sentences, and even paragraphs or larger pieces

© Rick Gomez/Corbis

of your essay. On a computer, for example, you can play "what if" by dropping below what you have written and phrasing your idea in another way. With some programs, you can even compare drafts side by side or with special "windows" that help you see your choices more clearly; tracking tools allow a record of changes, additions, and deletions. In other words, computers can help us as writers do the kind of deep-structure revision necessary to produce our best, most effective prose—the kind of major changes that, in the past, we may have been hesitant to make because of the time involved in recopying or retyping major portions of our drafts.

Although computers have made composing and revising easier and more effective for many writers, such technology provides its own special temptations and potential problems. Here, in addition to the hints in the previous section, are a few more suggestions for drafting and revising your essay on a computer:

1. To avoid the "agony of delete," always save what you have composed every ten minutes or so, and consider printing out your work (or copying it to a portable storage device) after each drafting session in case your system crashes or gobbles your pages. Remember that all sorts of events, from electrical storms to carpet cleaning, have caused the tiny leprechauns in computers to behave badly; having copies of your notes and latest revisions will help you reconstruct your work should disaster strike. If you have drafts in multiple files, add the date to each file name (Rafting 4-10); for multiple versions on the same date, add a letter (Rafting 4-10a, Rafting 4-10b). (Also, if you are working on multiple writing tasks, as most students are, or if you are just the forgetful type, develop the habit of noting on each print copy the name you have given the file. Doing so may save you from a frustrating search through your list of existing documents, especially if several days have elapsed between drafts.)

2. Do learn to use the editing tools that your word-processing program offers. In addition to allowing you to make changes and move text, most programs offer a dictionary to help you check the proper spelling, meaning, and use of your words; a thesaurus can help you expand your vocabulary, avoid repetition of words, or find just the right word to express the shade of meaning you want. Even the "word count" command can help writers who want to trim the fat from their essays.

   One of the most prized tools the computer offers writers is the spell-checker. For poor spellers and bad typists, the invention of the spell-checker ranks right up there with penicillin as a boon to humankind. The spell-checker performs minor miracles as it asks writers to reconsider certain words as typed on the page. If you have one available, by all means run it! But be aware of its limitations: spell-checkers highlight only words whose order of assembled letters they do not recognize or whose capitalization they question. They do not recognize confused words (*its/it's, you're/your, their/there, to/too*), incorrect usage of words, or typos that are correctly spelled words. To underscore this point, here's a sample of writing that any spell-checker would happily pass over:

   > Eye have a knew spell checker
   > That tells me wrong from write;
   > It marks four me miss steaks
   > My ayes kin knot high light.

> I no its let her perfect,
> Sew why due I all ways get
> Re quests to proof reed bet her
> Win my checker says I'm set?

The message of this brilliantly crafted poem? Don't rely on your spell-checker to catch all the errors in your final draft! Learn to edit, question your word choice, and proofread carefully with your own eyes and brain. (The same advice holds true for grammar-check and "style" programs, too. Although such programs have improved over the past several years, they are still limited in their ability to catch errors and see distinctions among usage and punctuation choices. Such programs may help you take a second look at your grammar, punctuation, or word choice, but do not rely on *any* computer program to do your editing and proofreading work for you.)

3. Use the computer to help you double-check for your own common errors. By using the "search," "find," or similar command, writers can highlight words they know they frequently misuse. For example, on a final sweep of editing, you might take one last look at each highlighted "its" you wrote to determine whether the usage truly calls for the possessive pronoun "its" or rather should be the contraction for "it is" (it's). Or perhaps you have an ongoing struggle with the uses of "affect" and "effect" and know that you have used these words often in your essay. Reviewing your word-choice decisions in the proofreading stage could make an important difference to your readers, who wish to travel smoothly through the ideas in your essay without annoying errors flagging down their attention. Also consider searching for and replacing words that you know you overuse or those that are lazy or vague. For example, until you break yourself of the habit, highlight any use of the word "thing." In each case, are you really discussing an unknown quantity—or do you need to press yourself to find a more specific or vivid word to communicate what you mean?

4. Even if you are comfortable drafting on your computer, resist doing all your work there. It's a good idea from time to time to read your screen version in its printed form—the format your readers may see. Many effective writers move back and forth multiple times between the computer screen and printed copies of their drafts. Experiment to discover the best ways for you to revise. Remember that a neatly printed draft can look professional but may still need much rethinking, restructuring, and polishing!

Writing Centers, Computer Classrooms, and Electronic Networks

Today, many schools have professionally staffed writing centers and computer labs open to composition students. The writing center or laboratory computers may have a variety of software designed to help you brainstorm, focus your ideas, organize a working structure, compose your drafts, revise your essay, and proofread. These computers also can help you to research a topic by allowing you to check information available in your campus library as well as providing access to other libraries and sources on the Internet. Many writing centers have special tutors on hand to answer your questions about your drafts as well as to explain effective uses of the available computer programs. In addition, many schools now have labs and special classrooms in which the computers are part of a network, linked together so that a specific group of writers can communicate with each other and/or with their instructor. In such a lab or classroom, for example, students might read each other's drafts and make suggestions or post comments about a current reading assignment on an electronic bulletin board for their classmates to consider.

Whether the program you are using at home or at school is a series of simple commands or an elaborate instructional system, make a point of getting to know how to use the computer in the most effective ways. Study the advice that accompanies your word-processing program, and don't be afraid to ask your instructor or computer-lab tutor for assistance. The more you practice using your program to help you organize, develop, and revise your prose, the better your writing will be.

Procrastination: Enemy of Critical Thinking, Thief of Time

Now that you have a good understanding of the continual interplay between writing and revision and have your writing tools at hand, you are ready to get down to business, to begin that first draft. You're going to start this very afternoon. Or maybe early tomorrow morning would be better. Or in that free hour between classes on Tuesday. Or, let's see, over the weekend. Or . . .

Let's talk about *procrastination*. Yes, right now, not later.

Procrastination refers to the human practice of postponing action and/or thought. It's a common response; all of us at one time or another have put off activities—chores, jobs, confrontations, responsibilities—that we'd rather not do. So we stall, finding excuses, and often discover ourselves stressed out, doing poor last-minute work, sometimes taking longer to do the job than if we had just jumped in right away.

Although putting off an assignment may feel good temporarily, doing so may ultimately produce more time-wasting anxiety in the long run, as you guiltily fret and dodge each time thoughts of your project surface. As the famous psychologist William James once said, "Nothing is so fatiguing as the eternal hanging on of an uncompleted task."

But procrastination often produces a worse effect than creeping anxiety: it is likely to defeat your best chance of success. Waiting too long to begin means less time to think about what you are writing. Rather than thoroughly exploring your ideas and shaping them effectively for your purpose and audience, you may only skim your subject's surface or veer off course without time to revise. *Critical thinking*—the careful consideration of ideas, claims, and evidence—takes time, effort, and some objective distance, as will be discussed in more detail on pages 102–106. Even if your initial ideas are good ones, a last-minute draft may mean you have inadequate time for creating clear organization or careful editing of contorted sentences or distracting errors. Worst-case scenario: the pressure to produce prose at the eleventh hour is so great you develop paralyzing Writer's Block and can't finish your assignment at all.

So if you want to avoid self-sabotage, challenge yourself to overcome your procrastination. Avoid what we might call, using a football metaphor, the fourth down and long "desperation punt-draft." That is, don't get yourself into a crunch situation in which, facing the crashing onrush of a deadline, you sit at the computer, write whatever comes to mind, rip the draft from the printer, and turn in feeble drivel. Triumph unlikely.

Despite the lack of success it may bring, procrastination can be a hard habit to break. How can you change such a pattern? First, understand its causes. For many people, procrastination results from insecurity, the fear that we aren't up to the task at hand. The work is too hard; it won't be good enough. Arm yourself against these self-doubts by realizing that you do know how to begin a discovery draft (review earlier chapters in this book if necessary) and that you don't have to instantly produce perfect prose. Begin early and let it be a comfort that you have given yourself plenty of time to think, rethink, stop, start, and revise in stages (following the steps outlined in this chapter will help). If you are a habitual procrastinator in many areas of your life, focus on your larger, long-range goals rather than on short-term ease. Consider: If I want to be ultimately successful at "X," what choices today will best accomplish this? And remember, busy is not the same as productive.

Mental attitude is key, but here are some additional hints to help you conquer procrastination during your writing process:

1. As soon as you receive and understand your assignment, break your writing task into parts (working thesis, rough outline, first major point, etc.). Make a list of these parts and give yourself a specific deadline to accomplish each one ("Have draft of first body paragraph finished by Wednesday noon."). Be sure to set aside an extra day for time away from your last draft and enough time after that day to "resee" and polish your essay however necessary. Check and revise your list each day; try to stay up with or even ahead of your schedule. Yes, Life Happens, but if you have started early enough, you can miss a deadline and still be all right.

2. Promise yourself a "carrot" or reward after you successfully complete an item on your list, even if the gift to yourself is as small as a coffee break or a short walk outside.

3. Procrastinators are often easily distracted. Leave your friends; close the door. Turn off your phone and TV; do not allow yourself to check e-mail or your social media pages while you are working. If you can't resist the sound of temptation, use your technology's mute button. (Your brain has a mute button, too; use it to silence non-writing thoughts and stay on task.)

4. Find a suitable place to work, one that is comfortable but not too cozy or near distractions. Although it may be tempting to write as you flop on a couch or prop up in bed, the time-to-begin function in your brain will probably turn on quicker if you are sitting upright at a desk or table, squarely facing the task at hand. (Hint: Some writers have discovered that they perform better on in-class exams and essays if they prepare in an environment similar to the classroom or testing center, such as a library or study room.)

5. Remember that no first draft is perfect and that revision is recursive; it occurs throughout your writing process in both large and small ways. As you move toward completion of a rough draft, familiarize yourself with the suggested

six-stage revision procedure that follows this section, to ensure that you do not derail yourself by trying to revise every part of your essay at the same time.

Conquering your procrastination should help you produce successful results: a thoughtful, well-written essay. If at any time during your drafting you do become temporarily stuck, don't panic—after all, you've left yourself plenty of time, right? ◆ Turning to the suggestions for beating Writer's Block, at the end of this chapter, will help you start moving again.

A Revision Process for Your Drafts

Let's assume at this point that you have completed a draft, using the first four chapters of this book as a guide. You feel you've chosen an interesting topic and collected some good ideas. Perhaps the ideas came quickly or perhaps you had to coax them. However your thoughts came, they're now in print—you have a draft with meaning and a general order, although it's probably much rougher in some spots than in others. Now it's time to "resee" this draft in a comprehensive way.

But wait. If possible, put a night's sleep or at least a few hours between this draft and the advice that appears on the next few pages. All writers become tired when they work on any project for too long at one sitting, and then they lose a sense of perspective. When you've looked at a piece of prose again and again, you may begin to read what's written in your head instead of what's on the page—that is, you may begin to "fill in" for yourself, reading into your prose what you meant to say rather than what your reader will actually see. Always try to start your writing process early enough to give yourself a few breaks from the action. You'll find that you will be better able to evaluate the strengths and weaknesses of your prose when you are fresh.

When you do return to your draft, *don't try to look at all the parts of your paper, from ideas to organization to mechanics, at the same time.* Trying to resee everything at once is rarely possible and will only overload and frustrate you. It may cause you to overlook some important part of your paper that needs your full attention. Overload can also block your creative ideas. Therefore, instead of trying to revise an entire draft in one swoop, break your revising process into a series of smaller, more manageable steps. Here is a suggested process:

I.	rethink	purpose, thesis, and audience
II.	rethink	ideas and evidence
III.	rethink	organization
IV.	rethink	clarity and style
V.	edit	grammar, punctuation, and spelling
VI.	proofread	entire essay

IMPORTANT: Please note that these steps are not necessarily distinct, nor must you always follow this suggested order. You certainly might, for instance, add details to a paragraph when you decide to move or reorder it. Or you might replace a vague word with a specific one after thinking about your audience and their needs. After strengthening a particular point, you might decide to offer it last, and therefore you rearrange the order of your paragraphs. In other words, the steps offered here are not part of a forced march—they are here simply to remind you to rethink and improve any part of your essay that needs work.

Now let's look at each of the steps in the revision process suggested here in more detail.

I. Revising for Purpose, Thesis, and Audience

To be effective, writers need a clear sense of purpose and audience. Their essays must present (or clearly imply) a main idea or thesis designed to fulfill that purpose and to inform their audience. As you reread your draft, ask yourself the following questions:

- Have I fulfilled the objectives of my assignment? (For example, if you were asked to analyze the causes of a problem, did you merely describe or summarize it instead?)
- Did I follow directions carefully? (If you were given a three-part assignment, did you treat all parts as requested?)
- Do I understand the purpose of my essay? Am I trying to inform, persuade, or amuse my readers? Spur them to action? Convince them to change their minds? Give them a new idea? Am I myself clear about my exact intent—what I want to do or say—in this essay?
- Does my essay reflect my clearly understood purpose by offering an appropriately narrowed and focused thesis? (After reading through your essay once, could a reader easily state its purpose and main point?)
- Do I have a clear picture of my audience—their character, knowledge, and expectations?
- Have I addressed both my purpose and my readers' needs by selecting appropriate strategies of development for my essay? (For example, would it be better to write an essay primarily developed with examples illustrating the community's need for a new hospital, or should you present a more formal argument that also rebuffs objections to the project? Should you narrate the story of your accident or analyze its effects on your family?)

If you feel that your draft needs work in any of these areas, make changes. ◆ You might find it helpful to review Chapters 1 and 2 of this text to guide you as you revise.

II. Revising for Ideas and Evidence

If you're satisfied that your purpose and thesis are clear to your readers, begin to look closely at the development of your essay's ideas.

You want your readers to accept your thesis. To achieve this goal, you must offer body paragraphs whose major points clearly support that main idea. As you examine the body of your essay, you might ask yourself questions such as these:

- Is there a clear relationship between my thesis and each of the major points presented in the body of my essay? That is, does each major point in my essay further my readers' understanding, and thus their acceptance, of my thesis's general claim?

- Did I write myself into a new or slightly different position as I drafted my essay? If so, do I need to begin another draft with a new working thesis?

- Have I included all the major points necessary to the readers' understanding of my subject or have I omitted pertinent ones? (On the other hand, have I included major ideas that aren't relevant or that actually belong in a different essay?)

- Are my major points located and stated clearly in specific language so that readers can easily see what position I am taking in each part of my discussion?

If you are happy with your choice and presentation of the major ideas in the body of your essay, it's time to look closely at the evidence you are offering to support those ideas (which, in turn, support the claim of your thesis). To choose the best supporting evidence for their major points, effective writers use *critical thinking skills*.

What Is Critical Thinking?

Critical thinking refers to the ability to reflect upon and evaluate the merits of our own ideas and those of others as we decide what to believe, what to do, or how to act. To think "critically" about ideas doesn't mean being hostile or negative; it means undertaking a close, reasonable examination of opinions, logic, and evidence before we accept certain claims or pass them along to others.

Critical thinking, in your classes, professional work, or personal life, calls for questioning and evaluation. Is the idea or claim under consideration clear, fair, relevant? Is the supporting evidence accurate, logical, reasonable? Is its source reliable, current, balanced? Critical thinking employs these and other similar questions as we examine various kinds of assertions and beliefs.

Here's a common situation in which critical thinking comes into play: two of your friends are arguing over the use of animals in medical research. Each friend has many points to offer; each is presenting statistics, case studies, the words of experts, and hypothetical situations that might arise. Many of the statistics and experts on one side of the argument seem to contradict directly the figures and authorities on the other side. Which side do you take? Why? Are there other points of view to consider? How can you know what to think?

Every day we are faced with just such decisions. Practicing critical thinking skills in your composition course will help you learn to judge what you hear and read, ultimately strengthening your confidence in your choice of beliefs and actions.

Thinking Critically as a Writer

As a writer, you will be thinking critically in two important ways. First, you will need to think critically about any information you may be collecting to use as evidence in your essay. You will, for example, need to be a critical reader as you consider information from books, journals, or electronic sources. (◆ For specific advice to help you become an effective critical reader, see the steps outlined in Chapter 8. For more discussion on the evaluation and selection of reliable print and online sources, turn to pages 386–388 in Chapter 14.)

As you draft and revise your essay, you must become a critical thinker in a second way: you must become your own toughest reader-critic. To convince your readers that your essay has merit, you must stand back and assess objectively what you have written. Are your ideas clear not only to you but to your readers as well? Will readers find your opinions well developed, logical, and supported? In other words, to revise more effectively, try role-playing one of your own most thoughtful critical readers, someone who will be closely examining the ideas and evidence in your essay before agreeing with its position.

Here are six suggestions to help you think critically as you draft and revise:

1. **Learn to distinguish fact from opinion.** A *fact* is an accepted truth whose verification is not affected by its source. No matter who presents it, a fact remains true. We accept some statements as facts because we can test them personally (fire is hot) or because they have been verified frequently by others (penguins live in Antarctica). We accept as fact, for example, that Martin Luther King, Jr., was murdered on April 4, 1968, at the Lorraine Motel in Memphis, Tennessee. However, even though much investigation and debate have focused on the assassination, the question of who was responsible for the murder is, for many people, still a matter of *opinion*. Although some people think that James Earl Ray was the lone gunman, a number of others believe in other explanations, holding local racists, Memphis police, the FBI, or the Mafia responsible to varying degrees. Opinions are often based on one's awareness and interpretation of information and can often be influenced by personal feelings. Therefore, as you write, be careful that you don't present your personal opinions as facts accepted by everyone. Opinions are debatable, and therefore you must always support them before your readers will be convinced.

2. **Support your opinions with evidence.** To support your opinions, you must offer evidence of one or more kinds. You have a variety of options to choose from. You might support one idea by using personal experiences. Or you might describe the experiences of friends or family. In another place you might decide to offer detailed examples or to cite statistics or to quote an expert on your subject. You can also use hypothetical examples, researched material, vivid descriptions, reasoned arguments, revealing comparisons, case studies, or testimony of relevant participants, just to name a few other strategies. Consider your purpose and your audience, review the possibilities, and choose the most effective kind of support. The more convincing the support, the more likely your readers are to accept your opinions as true. (◆ If you need to review some sample paragraphs developed by various types of evidence, turn to pages 58–61 of Chapter 3.)

3. **Evaluate the strength and source of your evidence.** As you choose your evidence, you should consider its value for the particular point it will support. Use your critical thinking skills to scrutinize the nature and source of your evidence carefully. If you are using examples, do they clearly illustrate your claim? Does this example or a different one (or both?) provide the best illustration of your particular point? Is description alone enough support here? Are your statistics or researched material

from a reliable, current source? Was information from your research collected in a careful, professional way? Are your experts unbiased authorities in the field under discussion? Where did your experts obtain their information? (For example, are you claiming that a certain vitamin drink possesses healing powers because a TV celebrity said so and she sounded reasonable to you? Just how much do you know about the source of a particular Web site? Or the knowledge of a blogger?) Asking yourself the kinds of questions posed here will help you develop a critical eye for choosing the best evidence to support your opinions. (◆ For more discussion on choosing reliable sources, see pages 386–388.)

IMPORTANT REMINDER: If you decide to include the ideas, opinions, or research of others to support your ideas, you must not only use your critical thinking skills to evaluate the evidence, but you must also cite the sources of your borrowed material carefully. ◆ For information on selecting and accurately documenting research data, such as studies, statistics, or the testimony of authorities, see Chapter 14 on the writing of the research paper. Remember that if you include the specific ideas of others in your paper, you must give proper credit, even if you do not quote the material word for word. Learning to identify and document your sources correctly for your readers will strengthen your claims and also prevent any unintentional plagiarism.

4. **Use enough specific supporting evidence.** Readers need to see strong, relevant supporting evidence throughout your essay. You must be sure, therefore, that you have enough clearly stated evidence for each of your major points. If you present, for instance, too few examples or only a vague reference to an event that supports one of your ideas, a reader may remain unconvinced or may even be confused. As you revise, ask yourself questions such as these: "Do I need to provide additional information here?" "Do I need more details to clarify my supporting evidence?" "Is any of my evidence clouded by vague or fuzzy language?" If you feel additional supporting evidence or details are needed, take another look at any prewriting you did or use one of the "pump-primer" techniques described in Chapter 1 to discover some new creative thoughts. For some topics, you may need to do more research or interviewing to find the information you need. (Writers occasionally need to prune ideas too, especially if they're repetitious or off the topic. But, in general, most early drafts are thin or overly general and will profit from more, rather than less, specific supporting evidence.)

5. **Watch for biases and strong emotions that may undermine evidence.** As you think critically about evidence you are using, monitor any biases and emotional attitudes that may distort information you wish to incorporate into your essay. If you are using personal experiences, for example, have you calmed down enough from your anger over your landlord's actions to write about the clash in a rational, persuasive way? In an essay criticizing a particular product, are you so familiar with the frustrating item that you are making ambiguous claims? (If you write,

"The new instructions for assembly are more confusing than ever," have you shown that they were confusing in the first place? Or why they are more so now?) Be sensitive to any racial, ethnic, cultural, religious, or gender-based assumptions you or your sources may have. Opinions based on generalizations and stereotypes ("Japanese cars are good buys because Asians are more efficient workers than Americans"; "Women should stay home out of the workplace because they are better with children than men") are not convincing to thinking readers.

6. **Check your evidence for logical fallacies.** Thinking critically about your drafts should help you support your ideas with reasonable, logical explanations and arguments. Logical fallacies are common errors in reasoning that good writers try to avoid. ◆ Those fallacies found most often today are explained on pages 295–299 of this text; reviewing them will enable you to identify problems in logic that might appear in the writing of others or in your own drafts.

Critical thinking is not, of course, limited to the suggestions offered here. But by practicing this advice, you will begin to develop and sharpen analytical skills that should improve any writing project.

A Special Note: Critical Thinking and Visual Literacy

Using critical thinking to analyze and evaluate the written and spoken claims of others is an essential skill. In today's media-saturated world, however, you also need to sharpen your *visual literacy*—that is, your ability to "read" and assess the validity of messages presented through all kinds of images. In particular, photographs that may appear in newsprint, advertisements, Web pages, posters, and billboards (to list only a few sources) may be altered in ways to manipulate your response. Most of us know that the faces of models in cosmetic ads are frequently airbrushed to lure us to a particular product and that tabloids have been routinely guilty of staging attention-grabbing pictures (space invaders? Big Foot?) to sell their newspapers. Photoshopped pictures making the rounds on the Internet may be silly fun (deer heads on humans) or wry satire (the California university police officer casually pepper-spraying protestors transported into other settings, including famous art works such as the signing of the Constitution).

But on a much more serious note, be aware that photoshopped and other kinds of altered pictures have been used dishonestly as evidence for political and social claims in order to arouse fear, encourage prejudice, or substantiate false statements. For example, in recent years, a presidential candidate was "inserted" into a photo taken at a controversial rally he never attended, while, in another picture, a different candidate at a speaking event had soldiers magically cloned throughout the crowd in an attempt to exaggerate his support from military personnel. While some photos are just plain dishonest in their altered states, others lack validity because they are taken out of context or are not current.

Just as you would not accept all written or spoken communication as true or valid without thoughtful scrutiny, do not be taken in by visual images that also need your close, critical examination. Be especially careful with images circulated on the Internet, which, unlike many print sources, has no designated fact-checker or other methods of "quality control."

© Sepah News/Handout/Document Iran/Corbis

Don't believe everything you see! Iran's Revolutionary Guard distributed this altered picture (on left) in 2008 to exaggerate its missile strength; the photograph appeared on the front pages of widely distributed newspapers, including the *Los Angeles Times* and the *Chicago Tribune*, before being exposed as fake.

III. Revising for Organization

In reality, you have probably already made several changes in the order and organization of ideas in your draft. As noted before, it's likely that when you thought about your essay's meaning—its major points and their supporting evidence—you also thought about the arrangement of those ideas. As you take another look at your draft's organization, use these questions as a guide:

- Am I satisfied with the organizational strategy I selected for my purpose? (For example, would an essay developed primarily by comparison and contrast achieve your purpose better than a narrative approach?)
- Are my major points ordered in a logical, easy-to-follow pattern? Would readers understand my thinking better if certain paragraphs or major ideas were rearranged? Added? Divided? Omitted? Expanded?
- Are my major points presented in topic sentences that state each important idea clearly and specifically? (If any of your topic sentences are implied rather than stated, are you absolutely, 100 percent sure that your ideas cannot be overlooked or even slightly misunderstood by your readers?)
- Is there a smooth flow between my major ideas? Between paragraphs? Within paragraphs? Have I used enough transitional devices to guide the reader along?
- Are any parts of my essay out of proportion? Too long or too brief to do their job effectively?
- Do my title and lead-in draw readers into the essay and toward my thesis?
- Does my conclusion end my discussion thoughtfully? Emphatically or memorably?

Don't be afraid to restructure your drafts. Most good writers rearrange and recast large portions of their prose. Describing his writing process, the admired novelist Bernard Malamud once said, "First drafts are for learning what one's [writing] wants him to say. Revision works with that knowledge to enlarge and enhance an idea, to reform it." ◆ Reviewing Chapters 3 and 4 may help you address questions about organization, beginnings, or endings.

IV. Revising for Clarity and Style

As you've revised for purpose, ideas, and organization, you have also taken steps to clarify your prose. Making a special point now of focusing on sentences and word choice will help ensure your readers' complete understanding of your thinking. Read through your draft, asking these kinds of questions:

- Is each of my sentences as clear and precise as it could be for readers who do not know what I know? Are there sentences that contain misplaced words or convoluted phrases that might cause confusion?

- Are there any sentences that are unnecessarily wordy? Is there deadwood that could be eliminated? (Remember that concise prose is more effective than wordy, "fat" prose because readers can more easily find and follow key ideas and terms. Nearly every writer has a wordiness problem that chokes communication, so now is the season to prune.)

- Do any sentences run on for too long to be fully understood? Can any repetitive or choppy sentences be combined to achieve clarity and a pleasing variation of sentence style? (To help you decide whether you need to combine sentences, you might try this experiment. Select a body paragraph and count the number of words it contains. Then, count the number of sentences; divide the number of words by the number of sentences to discover the average number of words per sentence. If your score is less than 15–18, you might need to combine *some* sentences. Good prose offers a variety of sentence lengths and patterns.)

- Are all my words and their connotations accurate and appropriate?

- Can I clarify and energize my prose by adding "showing" details and by replacing bland, vague words with vivid, specific ones? By using active verbs rather than passive ones?

- Can I eliminate any pretentious or unnecessary jargon or language that's inappropriate for my audience? Replace clichés and trite expressions with fresh, original phrases?

- Is my voice authentic, or am I trying to sound like someone else? Is my tone reasonable, honest, and consistent?

◆ The issues raised by these questions—and many others—are discussed in detail in Chapters 6 and 7, on effective sentences and words, which offer more advice on clarifying language and improving style.

V. Editing for Errors

Writers who are proud of the choices they've made in content, organization, and style are, to use a baseball metaphor, rounding third base and heading for home. But there's more to be done. Shift from a baseball metaphor to car maintenance for a moment. All good essays are not only fine-tuned but also waxed and polished—they are edited and proofread repeatedly for errors until they shine. To help you polish your prose by correcting errors in punctuation, grammar, spelling, and diction, here are some hints for effective editing:

Read aloud. In addition to repeatedly reading your draft silently, reading your draft aloud is a good technique because it allows your ears to hear ungrammatical "clunks" or unintended gaps in sense or sound you may otherwise miss. (Reading aloud may also flag omitted words. If, for example, the mother had reread this note to her child's teacher, she might have noticed a missing word: "Please excuse Ian for being. It was his father's fault.")

Know your enemies. Learn to identify your particularly troublesome areas in punctuation and grammar, and then read through your draft for one of these problems at a time: once for fragments, once for comma splices, once for run-ons, and so on. (If you try to look for too many errors at each reading, you'll probably miss quite a few.)

Read backwards. Try reading your draft one sentence at a time starting at the *end* of your essay and working toward the beginning. Don't read each sentence word-for-word backwards—just read the essay one sentence at a time from back to front. When writers try to edit (or proofread) starting at the beginning of their essays, they tend to begin thinking about the ideas they're reading rather than concentrating on the task of editing for errors. By reading one sentence at a time from the back, you will find that the sentences will still make sense but that you are less likely to wander away from the job at hand.

Learn some tricks. There are special techniques for treating some punctuation and grammar problems. ◆ If you have trouble with comma splices, for example, turn to the FANBOYS hint on page 146. If fragments plague your writing, try the "It is true that" test explained on page 129. Consider designating a special part of your journal or class notebook to record in your own words these tricks and other useful pieces of advice so that you can refer to them easily and often.

Eliminate common irritants. Review your draft for those diction and mechanical errors many readers find especially annoying because they often reflect sheer carelessness. For example, look at these frequently confused words: *it's/its, your/you're, there/their/they're, who's/whose* (◆ other often-confused words are listed on page 155). Some readers are ready for a national march to protest the public's abandonment of the apostrophe, the Amelia Earhart of punctuation. (Apostrophes *can* change the meaning of sentences: "The teacher called the students names." Was the instructor being rude or just taking roll?) It's a grammatical jungle out there, so be sensitive to your weary readers.

Use your tools. Keep your dictionary handy to check the spelling, usage, and meanings of words in doubt. A thesaurus can also be useful if you can restrain any tendencies you might have for growing overly exotic prose. If you are using a computer spell-checker, by all means run it after your last revisions are completed. Do remember, as noted earlier in this chapter, that such programs only flag words whose spelling they don't recognize; they will not alert you to omitted or confused words (*affect/effect*), nor will they signal when you've typed in a wrong, but correctly spelled, word (*form* for *from*).

◆ Use Part Four of this text to help resolve any questions you may have about grammar, mechanics, and spelling. Advice on untangling sentences and clarifying word choice in Chapters 6 and 7 may be useful, too.

VI. Proofreading

Proofread your final draft several times, putting as much time between the last two readings as possible. Fresh eyes catch more typographical or careless errors. Remember that typing errors—even the simple transposing of letters—can change the meaning of an entire thought and occasionally bring unintended humor to your prose. (Imagine, for example, the surprise of restaurant owners whose new lease instructed them to "Please sing the terms of the agreement." Or consider the ramifications of the newspaper ad offering "Great dames for sale" or the 1716 Bible whose advice "sin no more" was misprinted as "sin on more.")

Make sure, too, that any hard-copy paper looks professional before you turn it in. You wouldn't, after all, expect to be taken seriously if you went to an executive job interview dressed in scruffy jeans. Turning in a paper with a coffee stain or ink smear on it has about the same effect as a blob of spinach in your teeth—it distracts folks from hearing what you have to say. If your final copy has typos or small blemishes, you may use correction tape or fluid to conceal them; but if you've patched so frequently that your paper resembles the medicine-dotted face of a kindergartner with chicken pox, reprint or photocopy your pages for a fresh look.

Check to be sure you've formatted your paper exactly as your assignment requested. Some instructors ask for a title page; others want folders containing all your drafts and prewriting. Most teachers requiring print copy want essays with pages that are numbered, ordered correctly, and paper-clipped or stapled, with clean edges (no sheets violently ripped from a spiral notebook still dribbling angry confetti down one side; no pages mutilated at the corners by the useless "tear-and-fold-tab" technique). Putting your name on each page will identify your work if papers from a particular class are accidentally mixed up.

> As it's often been said, essays are never really done—only due. Take a last reading using the checklist that follows, make some notes on your progress as a writer and thinker, and congratulate yourself on your fine efforts and accomplishment.

A Final Checklist for Your Essay

If you have written an effective essay, you should be able to answer "yes" to the following questions:

1. Do I feel I have something important to say to my reader?

2. Am I sincerely committed to communicating with my reader and not just with myself?

3. Have I considered my audience's needs? (See Chapter 1.)

4. Do my title and lead-in attract the reader's attention and help set up my thesis? (See Chapter 4.)

5. Does my thesis statement assert one main, clearly focused idea? (See Chapter 2.)

6. Does my thesis and/or essay map give the reader an indication of what points the essay will cover? (See Chapter 2.)

7. Do my body paragraphs contain the essential points in the essay's discussion, and are those points expressed in clearly stated or implied topic sentences? (See Chapter 3.)

8. Is each major point in my essay well developed with enough detailed supporting evidence? (See Chapter 3.)

9. Does each body paragraph have unity and coherence? (See Chapter 3.)

10. Are all the paragraphs in my essay smoothly linked in a logical order? (See Chapter 3.)

11. Does my concluding paragraph provide a suitable ending for the essay? (See Chapter 4.)

12. Are all my sentences clear, concise, and coherent? (See Chapter 6.)

13. Are my words accurate, necessary, and meaningful? (See Chapter 7.)

14. Have I edited and proofread for errors in grammar, punctuation, spelling, and typing? (See Part Four.)

And most important:

15. Has my essay been effectively revised so that I am proud of this piece of writing?

Practicing What You've Learned

© Canstock Images, Inc./ Index Stock Imagery

A. The draft of the following student essay has been annotated by its own writer according to some—*but not all*—of the questions presented in this chapter's discussion of revision. As you read the draft and the writer's marginal comments, think of specific suggestions you might offer to help this writer improve her essay. What changes, in addition to the ones mentioned here, would you encourage this writer to make? What strengths do you see in this draft?

continued on next page

Dorm Life

My title and lead-in are too bland to attract reader's attention.

Would my thesis be clearer if I said what I did find?

My supporting examples could use more "showing" details so the readers can really see the unfriendliness.

Contradicts my point

This paragraph has some specific details, but it rambles and repeats ideas. Needs tighter organization.

Contradicts my ¶'s point

Dorm life is not at all what I had expected it to be. I had anticipated meeting friendly people, quiet hours for studying, eating decent food, and having wild parties on weekends. My dreams, I soon found out, were simply illusions, erroneous perceptions of reality.

My roommate, Kathy, and I live in Holland Hall on the third floor. The people on our dorm floor are about as unfriendly as they can possibly be. I wonder whether or not they're just shy and afraid or if they are simply snobs. Some girls, for example, ignore my roommate and me when we say "hello." Occasionally, they stare straight ahead and act like we aren't even there. Other girls respond, but it's as if they do it out of a sense of duty rather than being just friendly. The guys seem nice, but some are just as afraid or snobby as the girls.

I remember signing up for "quiet hours" when I put in my application for a dorm room last December. Unfortunately, I was assigned to a floor that doesn't have any quiet hours at all. I am a person who requires peace and quiet when studying or reading. The girls in all the rooms around us love to stay up until early in the morning and yell and turn up their music full blast. They turn music on at about eight o'clock at night and turn it off early in the morning. There is always at least one girl who has music playing at maximum volume. Now, I am very appreciative of music, but listening to hard rock until three in the morning isn't really my idea of what fun is. The girls right across from us usually play soft rock or country artists, and I enjoy them. On the other hand, though, the girls on either side of our room love to listen to growling punk bands into the wee hours of the morning. It is these girls who run up and down the hall, yell at each other, laugh obnoxiously, and try to attract attention. All this continuous racket makes it nearly impossible to study, read, or get any sleep. Kathy and I usually end up going to the library or student cafeteria to study. As far as sleep goes, it doesn't matter what time we go to bed, but rather it depends on how noisy it is and how late the music is on. Sometimes the noise gets so loud and goes on for so long that even when it stops, my ears are ringing and my stomach keeps churning. It is on nights like this that I never go to sleep. I wish the people here were a little more considerate of the people around them.

continued on next page

This paragraph doesn't support my thesis claim—do I mean the dorm has no good parties or not enough parties? Rethink so my point is clear.

Parties, on weekends, are supposedly the most important part of dorm life. Parties provide the opportunity to meet others and have a good time. Holland Hall has had two parties that are even worth mentioning. One of them was a Fifties dance held in the courtyard approximately three weeks ago. Unfortunately, all the other dormitories, the fraternities, and the sororities heard about it, and by eight o'clock at night there were masses of people. It was so packed that it was hard to move around. The other party, much to my dismay, turned out to be a luau party. I do not really care for roast pig, and my stomach turned from the scent of it when I entered the room. Our floor never has parties. Everyone leaves their doors open, turns up the music, and yells back and forth. I suppose that there will be more floor parties once everyone becomes adjusted to this life and begins to socialize.

As stated, this topic sentence contradicts my thesis.
Some good examples—could I use even more descriptive language?
Unity?

Dorm food is what I anticipated it would be, terrible, and I was right, it is awful. Breakfast is probably the hardest meal to digest. The bacon and sausage are cold, slightly uncooked, and very greasy. Sometimes, it's as though I am eating pure grease. The eggs look and taste like nothing I ever had before. They look like plastic and they are never hot. I had eggs once, and I vowed I would never have another one as long as I lived in Holland Hall. The most enjoyable part of breakfast is the orange juice. It's always cold and it seems to be fresh. No one can say dorm food is totally boring because the cooks break up the monotony of the same food by serving "mystery meat" at least once every two weeks. This puts a little excitement in the student's day because everyone cracks jokes and wonders just what's in this "mystery meat." I think a lot of students are afraid to ask, fearful of the answer, and simply make snide remarks and shovel it in.

Can I conclude emphatically without switching positions?

All in all, I believe dorm life isn't too great, even though there are some good times. Even though I complain about dorm food, the people, the parties, and everything else, I am glad I am here. I am happy because I have learned a lot about other people, responsibilities, consideration, and I've even learned a lot about myself.

B. As you work on strengthening your own revision skills, you may find it easier in the beginning to practice on the writing of others. Assume the writer of the draft that follows is directing these comments to a group of high school students contemplating their college choices. By offering helpful marginal comments and questions, guide this writer to a revised draft with more effective arguments, organization, and clarity.

continued on next page

Maybe You Shouldn't Go Away to College

Going away to college is not for everyone. There are good reasons why a student might choose to live at home and attend a local school. Money, finding stability while changes are occurring, and accepting responsibility are three to consider.

Money is likely to be most important. Not only is tuition more expensive, but extra money is needed for room and board. Whether room and board is a dorm or an apartment, the expense is great.

Most students never stop to consider that the money that could be saved from room and board may be better spent in future years on graduate school, which is likely to be more important in their careers.

Going to school is a time of many changes anyway, without adding the pressure of a new city or even a new state. Finding stability will be hard enough, without going from home to a dorm. Starting college could be an emotional time for some, and the security of their home and family might make everything easier.

When students decide to go away to school, sometimes because their friends are going away, or maybe because the school is their parents' alma mater, something that all need to decide is whether or not they can accept the responsibility of a completely new way of life.

Everyone feels as if they are ready for total independence when they decide to go away to college, but is breaking away when they are just beginning to set their futures a good idea?

Going away to school may be the right road for some, but those who feel that they are not ready might start looking to a future that is just around the corner.

C. Practice your editing and proofreading skills by correcting all the errors you see in the paragraph that follows. Look carefully for problems in grammar, punctuation, spelling, word confusion, and sentence sense, as well as typos. Some proofreaders find it useful to place a blank piece of paper or index card under each line to help them focus as they read.

One fo the most interesting books I've read lately is Bold Spirit, by Linda Lawrence

Hunt. Its the true story of Hega Estby's 1896 walk across america, form Eastern

Washingto to New york City; in order to win a $10,000 prize to save the family farm.

Acompanied by her teen age daughter Clara the two sets out with only $5 dollars

continued on next page

each and walked 3500 miles on foot in Victorian clothes. Despite alot bad wheather

and dangerous encounter along the the way. Helga and her daughter did arrive safely,

but, unfortunately they weren't never able too collect there prize money. Worse then

that, tho, Helgas family afterwards r so embarrsssed about her walk thatthey burned

her diary, her notes & newspaper clippings, her story only came to light recently be

cause a daughter-inlaw had secretly saved and album of clippings from the fire

Assignment

© CORBIS

Select a body paragraph from "Dorm Life" (pages 111–112) or "Maybe You Shouldn't Go Away to College" (page 113) and revise it, making effective changes in focus, development, organization, sentence construction, and word choice. (Feel free to elaborate on or delete any supporting details to improve the paragraph's content.)

Applying What You've Learned To *Your* Writing

© Keith Brofsky/
Photodisc/Getty Images

If you have completed a draft of an essay, you have already revised many parts of it—changing ideas, sentences, and words as you wrote. Now begin to revise by moving through the stages outlined in this chapter. Remember, you cannot revise for everything at once, so this process calls for multiple readings—and rewriting. After another look at your work, are you satisfied that it accomplishes your purpose, that it addresses the needs of your specific audience? Using your best critical thinking skills, strengthen any weak development of your ideas; then tackle questions of order and coherence. You may find that you need another draft at this point to accommodate new material or deep-structure changes.

Once you are happy with your essay's larger issues of content and organization, work on clarity by polishing rough sentences and substituting better words. Proofread your draft for surface errors at least twice! Until a revision process becomes second nature to you, use the checklist on pages 109–110 as a guide.

Collaborative Activities: Group Work, Peer Revision Workshops, and Team Projects

Writers in both the business and academic worlds often consult their colleagues for advice; they might, for example, ask for help with a difficult explanation, a complex description, or a twisted sentence. Sometimes they may write together as part of a task force or committee. Similarly, you may find that working on composing and revising strategies with your colleagues—your classmates—can be enormously helpful.

You may have already noticed a practice exercise or assignment earlier in this text identified as a Collaborative Activity. "Collaborative" simply means working together, and these assignments are designed so you and your classmates can help each other improve particular writing skills. By offering reactions, suggestions, and questions (not to mention moral support), your classroom colleagues may become some of your best writing teachers.

Collaborative activities in composition courses take many forms and may occur in any stage of the writing process. Here are three of the most common types:

1. **Group Work:** Frequently in writing classes an instructor will ask three to five students to form a discussion or activity group. For example, students might be asked to evaluate a writing sample or to respond to an exercise or to ask for feedback on their own drafts. The possibilities are numerous, and small-group discussions can be especially useful early on as writers brainstorm on and focus their topics, as well as later in the writing process when they are striving for well-developed content and clear organization.

2. **Peer Revision Workshops:** On some days, instructors may ask students to respond to each other's drafts in writing. Sometimes teachers will give student-reviewers a list of tasks to perform ("Underline the thesis") or questions to answer ("How successful is the conclusion?"); at other times, the writers themselves will create the inquiries. Although many workshops are orga-  nized as one-on-one exchanges of papers in the classroom, an increasing number of schools today have the electronic means to post students' drafts on protected sites so that a variety of student-reviewers may comment on them both in and out of class. Structured in many effective ways, peer workshops allow writers to see their drafts from a reader's point of view.

   © C. Devan/Corbis

3. **Team Projects:** Sometimes students will be asked to work together to produce a single piece of writing. Because many organizations today require a set of members

or employees to prepare such projects as proposals, position papers, or grants, the practice of writing together as a committee or team can provide a valuable experience. A "blended" project might call for members of a team to write individually and then compare their efforts, selecting and revising the best ideas and prose as they craft the final piece together. A "composite" approach might ask students to assign each team member a different task (investigate a problem, research a study, conduct an interview, etc.) or a particular section to write, with the group responsible for smoothly meshing the parts into a whole.

◆ Panel discussions, debates, and other kinds of oral presentations are often important parts of team-project assignments. For advice on preparing and delivering your written work or research in the classroom, turn to pages 455–457 in Chapter 15.

There are, of course, numerous other ways instructors may create collaborative activities, depending upon the lesson, goals, and logistics. In one format or another, working collaboratively can frequently help writers consider alternative ways of thinking and that, in turn, may encourage clearer, more effective prose.

Benefiting from Collaborative Activities

Collaborative activities can be extremely useful, but working with other writers may also present challenges. To receive the most benefit from interaction with your classmates, you'll need to develop both a sense of cooperation and good communication skills. The following section offers suggestions for gaining the most value from one-on-one revision workshops as well as some advice for successful participation in small-group discussions.

Guidelines for Peer Revision Workshops

Students taking part in revision workshops for the first time often have questions about the reviewing process. Some student-reviewers may feel uneasy about their role, wondering, "What if I can't think of any suggestions for the writer? How can I tell someone that the essay is really terrible? What if I sense something's wrong but I'm not sure what it is—or how to fix it?" Writers, too, may feel apprehensive or even occasionally defensive about receiving criticism of their papers. Because these concerns are genuine and widespread, here is some advice for you in the roles of both writer and reviewer.

When you are the **writer:**

1. **Develop a constructive attitude.** Admittedly, receiving criticism—especially on a creation that has required hard work—can sometimes be difficult, particularly if your self-image has become mixed up with your drafts. Try to realize that your reviewer is not criticizing you personally but rather is trying to help you by offering fresh insights. All drafts can be improved, and no writer need feel embarrassed

about seeking or receiving advice. (Take comfort in the words of writer Somerset Maugham: "Only the mediocre person is always at his best.") See the workshop as a nonthreatening opportunity to reconsider your prose and improve your audience awareness.

2. **Come prepared.** If your workshop structure permits, tell your reviewer what sort of help you need at this point in your drafting or revising process. Ask for suggestions to fix a particularly troublesome area, or ask for feedback on a choice you've made but are feeling unsure of. Don't hesitate to ask your reviewer for assistance with any part of your essay.

3. **Evaluate suggestions carefully.** Writing isn't math; most of the time there are no absolutely right or wrong answers—just better or worse rhetorical choices. That is, there are many ways to communicate an idea to a set of readers. You, as the writer, must decide on an effective way, the way that best serves your purpose and your readers' needs. Sometimes your reviewer will suggest a change that is brilliant or one so obviously right you will wonder why in the world you didn't think of it yourself. At other times you may weigh your reviewer's suggestion and decide that your original choice is just as good or perhaps even better. Be open to suggestions, but learn to trust thyself as well.

4. **Find the good in bad advice.** Occasionally, you may have a reviewer who seems to miss a crucial point or misunderstands your purpose entirely, whose suggestions for revising your paper seem uniformly unproductive for one reason or another. You certainly shouldn't take bad advice—but do think about the issues it raises. Although it's helpful to receive a dynamite suggestion you can incorporate immediately, the real value of a revision workshop is its ability to encourage you to rethink your prose. Readers' responses (yes, even the bizarre ones) challenge writers to take still another look at their rhetorical choices and ask themselves, "Is this clear after all? Does this example really work here? Did something in my essay throw this reader off the track?" Revision workshops offer you benefits, even if you ultimately decide to reject many of your reviewer's suggestions.

When you are the **reviewer:**

1. **Develop a constructive attitude.** Sometimes it's hard to give honest criticism— most of us are uncomfortable when we think we might hurt someone's feelings— but remember that the writer has resolved to develop a professional attitude, too. The writer expects (and is sometimes desperately begging for) sincere feedback, so be honest as you offer your best advice.

2. **Be clear and specific.** Vague or flippant responses ("Confusing"; "Huh?") don't help writers know what or how to revise. Try putting some of your comments into this format: your response to X, the reason for your response, a request for change, and, if possible, a specific suggestion for the change. ("I'm confused when you say you enjoy some parts of breakfast because this seems to contradict your

thesis claim of 'wretched dorm food.' Would it be clearer to modify your thesis to exclude breakfast or to revise this paragraph to include only discussion of the rubbery eggs?")

3. **Address important issues.** Unless you have workshop directions that request certain tasks, read through the draft entirely at least once and then comment on the larger issues first. Writers want to know if they are achieving their overall purpose, if their thesis is clear and convincing, if their major points and evidence make sense, and if their paper seems logical and ordered. Editing tips are fine, too, but because workshops encourage authors to rewrite large portions of their prose, attention to minor details may be less valuable early on than feedback on ideas, organization, and development. (Of course, an editing workshop later in the revision process might be exclusively focused on sentence, word, and mechanical errors. Workshops may be designed to specifically address any set of problems that writers face.)

4. **Encourage the writer.** Writers with confidence write and revise better than insecure or angry writers. Praise honestly wherever you can, as specifically as you can. When weaknesses do appear, show the writer that you know she or he is capable of doing better work by linking the weakness to a strength elsewhere in the draft. ("Could you add more 'showing' details here so that your picture of the dentist is as vivid as your description of the drill?") Substitute specific responses and suggestions for one-word labels such as "awk" (awkward) or "unclear." Even positive labels don't always help writers repeat effective techniques. ("Good!" enthusiastically inscribed in the margin by a well-developed paragraph feels nice but might cause the writer to wonder, "'Good' what? Good point? Good supporting evidence? Good detail? How can I do 'good' again if I don't know exactly what it is?")

5. **Understand your role as critical reader.** Sometimes it's easy for a reviewer to take ownership of someone else's paper. Keep the writer's purpose in mind as you respond; don't insist on revisions that produce the essay that's in *your* head. Be sensitive to your own voice and language as a reviewer. Instead of making authoritative pronouncements that might offend, ask reader-based questions ("Will all your readers know the meaning of this technical term?" "Would some readers profit from a brief history of this controversy?"). If you're unsure about a possible error, request verification ("Could you recheck this quotation? Its wording here is confusing me because . . ."). Practice offering criticism in language that acknowledges the writer's hard work and accentuates the positive nature of revision ("Would citing last year's budget figures make your good argument against the fish market even stronger?").

Last, always look over your own draft in light of the insightful suggestions you are offering your classmates. You may feel at first that it is far simpler to analyze someone else's writing than your own. As you participate in revision workshops, however, you will find it increasingly easy to transfer those same critical reading skills to your own work. Becoming a good reader-reviewer for your composition colleagues can be an important part of your training as a first-rate writer.

Guidelines for Small-Group Work

Much of the previous advice for participation in peer workshops holds true for student involvement in many kinds of classroom group activities. In addition, consider these suggestions for participation in groups of three to five members:

1. **Start informed.** Quickly acknowledge everyone's first name, and be sure everyone has a copy of the assignment or other materials necessary to the task at hand.

2. **Know your purpose.** Make sure everyone in your group clearly understands the goal of the activity. Consult your teacher if there are any questions about the instructions or the expected results.

3. **Create a plan with a time schedule.** In discussion groups that ask participants to give opinions or offer help, estimate the time allowed so that each person has an equal opportunity to talk. If your assignment has multiple parts, figure out how much time should be devoted to each task. (Larger team projects may call for an action plan that stretches over a number of days, with appropriate deadlines for the various jobs.)

4. **Consider appointing roles.** In some groups it's helpful to have a moderator or facilitator to keep participants focused and on track; sometimes it's useful to have a recorder to take notes, a timekeeper to call out when discussions need to move on, or a friendly "devil's advocate" to offer counter opinions. Some groups may designate a reporter to present the results of the activity to the class as a whole. Assigning roles or specific responsibilities may encourage each participant to remain engaged in the group's work.

5. **Stay focused.** It's easy to drift off topic or bog down. Keep yourself and your class-mates on target; be polite but firm if one of your group begins to wander off task. At times it may be helpful to stop a discussion and summarize what has been done thus far and what has yet to be accomplished.

6. **Be a good listener as well as a good talker.** Be willing to entertain the opinions of others in your group; stay open to criticism, suggestions, and diverse approaches. If there are conflicting opinions in the group, note differences but avoid personal hostility or sarcastic remarks. Lively debates can be exhilarating, but heated arguments may become irrational and unproductive.

7. **Set a good example.** Model behavior that promotes the good of the group; always do your share of the work. Consider taking on a leadership role: encourage the quieter members of the group by asking questions to draw out more details. Be grateful for help you receive from your classmates, even if it only means taking a second hard look at your own opinions or prose choices.

Most importantly, after the activity is finished, think about what you have learned. Every group discussion or exercise is a lesson created to improve your thinking, writing, and reading skills. Ask yourself what ideas and strategies you can apply to your own writing to make it more effective—and then revise your work accordingly!

Practicing What You've Learned*

© Canstock Images, Inc./ Index Stock Imagery

Collaborative Activity: Working with two or three classmates, first designate a recorder to take notes on the discussion of the following letter (if your group is larger, consider appointing a facilitator and perhaps a time-keeper as well). Assist poor Bubba by compiling a list of five specific suggestions to help him revise this draft so that it better addresses his audience and accomplishes his purpose. Rank order your suggestions and be prepared to report them to the class as a whole.

Dear Mom and Dad,

This week at college has been very interesting.

My roommate is gone and so is my wallet and computer. I tried to tell the police that the stacks of phony $3 bills by his copier weren't mine but I don't know if they believed me.

And, hey, the car thing isn't my fault either. Despite the testimony of all those witnesses. Who knew the entire back end would crumple like that? The other guy's lawyer will be in touch.

Without any transportation, I don't know when I can come home. Maybe at Thanksgiving. The doctor says the rash shouldn't be contagious by then. The arm, after the fight at the party, is another matter altogether.

I have a new girlfriend! Bambi's real nice and the age difference between us is no big deal. I hope you like her, despite how you feel about tattoos. I have a funny story to tell you about how the stuff in her face set off the airport metal detector last weekend. I just wish her sick grandmother didn't need me to help out so much with her expensive operation. Bambi and her brother are pressuring me a lot.

As you can plainly see, I need more financial help! Please send money right away!

Your devoted son,
Bubba

---

*Special note: Many other peer-based exercises appear throughout this text. If you find working with classmates helpful, look in the index of this book under "collaborative activities" to discover more ideas for focusing and revising your prose.

© CORBIS

Assignment

Collaborative Activity: Ask a classmate to read a draft on which you are currently working. Include at the end of the draft three questions you have about rough patches in your work—areas, for instance, where you think your ideas are fuzzy or your organization is unclear or your prose has missed the mark. Ask your classmate to respond to your concerns as a reader-reviewer who can help you revise. Once you understand the suggestions for your paper, provide similar assistance to your classmate by changing roles. (If possible, in a later follow-up discussion, show each other the revised work, explaining what changes were incorporated and why.)

Some Last Advice: How to Play with Your Mental Blocks

Most writers, sooner or later, will suffer a form of Writer's Block, the inability to move forward in some stage of their drafting process. Writers may begin with creativity and enthusiasm, but then at some point become "stuck"; the necessary ideas or words to express them simply won't come no matter how hard they're called. Symptoms may include sweaty palms, pencil chewing, and a pronounced, sudden desire to organize a sock drawer or clean out a closet. Although not every "cure" works for everyone, here are a few suggestions to help minimize your misery:

Try to give yourself as much time as possible to write your essay. Don't try to write the entire paper in one sitting at the last minute. By doing so, you place yourself under too much pressure. Writer's Block often accompanies the "up against the wall" feeling that strikes at 2:00 A.M. the morning your essay is due at 9:00. Make a start on your assignment as soon as you can; prewriting, notes, and rough outlines are all good first steps. (*Special note:* ◆ If you are a habitual writing-procrastinator—that is, if you are the king or queen of delaying tactics and have trouble getting started at all—turn back now to pages 98–100 in this chapter for encouragement and advice.)

Because most of us have had more experience talking than writing, try verbalizing your ideas. Sometimes it's helpful to discuss your ideas with friends or classmates. Their questions and comments (not to mention their sympathy for your temporary block) will often trigger the thoughts you need to begin writing again. In some cases, especially if you're stuck while drafting an argument or persuasive paper, it's useful to ask someone to role-play your Cranky Opposition. Forcing yourself to answer his or her objections to your position might lead you out of your bog-down into new or stronger points to include in your draft.

When an irresistible force meets an immovable object, something's going to give. Conquer the task: break the paper into manageable bits. Instead of drooping with

Sometimes Writer's Block makes you want to . . .

Erich Lessing/Art Resource, NY. © 2012 The Munch Museum/The Munch-Ellingsen Group/Artists Rights Society (ARS), NY

The Scream, 1893, by Edvard Munch

despair over the thought of a ten-page research paper, think of it as a series of small parts (explanation of the problem, review of current research, possible solutions, etc.). Then tackle one part at a time, and reward yourself when that section is done.

Get the juices flowing and the pen (or keys) moving. Try writing the easiest or shortest part of your essay first. A feeling of accomplishment may give you the boost of confidence you need to undertake the other, more difficult sections. If no part looks easy or inviting, try more prewriting exercises, as described in Chapter 1, until you feel prepared to begin the essay itself.

Play "Let's Make a Deal" with yourself. Sometimes we just can't face the failure that we are predicting for ourselves. Strike a bargain with yourself: promise yourself that you are going to work on your paper for only twenty minutes—absolutely, positively only twenty minutes, not a second more, no sir, no way. If in twenty minutes, you're onto something good, ignore your promise to yourself and keep going. If you're not, then leave and come back for another twenty-minute session later (if you started early enough, you can do this without increasing your anxiety).

Give yourself permission to write garbage. Take the pressure off yourself by agreeing in advance to tear up the first page or two of whatever you write. You can always change your mind if the trash turns out to be treasure. If it isn't, so what? You said you were going to tear it up anyway.

Imagine that your brain is a water faucet. If you're like most people, you've probably lived in a house or apartment containing a faucet that needed to run for a few minutes before the hot water came out. Think of your brain in the same way, and do some other, easier writing task to warm up. Write a letter, send an e-mail, make a grocery list, copy notes, whatever, to get your brain running. When you turn to your essay, your ideas may be hotter than you thought.

Remove the threat by addressing a friendly face. Sometimes we can't write because we are too worried about what someone else will think about us, or maybe we can't write because we can't figure out who would want to read this stuff anyway. Instead of writing into a void or to an audience that seems threatening, try writing to a friend. Imagine what that friend's responses might be and try to elaborate or clarify wherever necessary. If it helps, write the first draft as a letter ("Dear Clyde, I want to tell you what happened to me last week."), and then redraft your ideas as an essay when you've found your purpose and focus, making whatever changes in tone or development are necessary to fit your real audience.

If Writer's Block does hit, remember that it is a temporary bog-down, not a permanent one. Other writers have had it—and survived to write again. Try leaving your draft and taking a walk outdoors or at least into another room. Think about your readers—what should they know or feel at this point in your essay? As you walk, try to complete this sentence: "What I am trying to say is. . . ." Keep repeating this phrase and your responses aloud until you find the answer you want.

Sometimes while you're blocked at one point, a bright idea for another part of your essay will pop into your head. If possible, skip the section that has you stuck, and start working on the new part. (At least jot down the new idea somewhere so it won't be lost when you need it later.)

"Feelings, woo-o-o, nothing more than feelings . . ." You've hit a wall: you now despise your essay topic; you can't face that draft one more time. Turn that fear and loathing into something more positive. Put the draft away. Go to a blank page or screen and pour out your feelings toward your essay's *subject.* Why did you care about this topic in the first place? What's meaningful about it? Why did you want others to think about it? Reconnecting with your subject matter, rather than arm wrestling the same draft again and again, may suggest a new start with a clearer purpose. (And if this suggestion doesn't work, you may have at least helped yourself to a good night's rest. According to studies by James Pennebaker, a University of Texas psychology professor, writing about your feelings "reduces stress and allows for better sleep." A good snooze may be just what you need to tackle your essay with renewed energy.)

Change partners and dance. If you're thoroughly overcome by the vast white wasteland on the desk (or screen) before you, get up and do something else for a while. Exercise, balance your checkbook, or put on music and dance. (Mystery writer Agatha Christie claimed she did her best planning while washing the dishes.) Give your mind a break and refresh your spirit. When you come back to the paper, you may be surprised to discover that your subconscious writer has been working while the rest of you played.

Here's the single most important piece of advice to remember: relax. No one—not even the very best professional writer—produces perfect prose every time pen hits paper. If you're blocked, you may be trying too hard; if your expectations of your first draft are too high, you may not be able to write at all for fear of failure. You just might be holding yourself back by being a perfectionist at this point. You can always revise and polish your prose in another draft—the first important step is jotting down your ideas. Remember that once the first word or phrase appears on your blank page or screen, a major battle has been won.

Chapter 5 Summary

Here is a brief summary of what you should remember about drafting and revising your writing:

1. Revision is an activity that occurs in all stages of the writing process.

2. All good writers revise and polish their prose.

3. Revision is not merely editing or last-minute proofreading; it involves important decisions about the essay's ideas, organization, and development.

4. To revise effectively, novice writers might review their drafts in stages to avoid the frustration that comes with trying to fix everything at once.

5. Critical thinking skills are vitally important to all good readers and writers.

6. Collaborative activities can help writers draft and revise in a number of useful ways.

7. Most writers experience Writer's Block at some time but live through it to write again.

Effective Sentences

··

An insurance agent was shocked to open his mail one morning and read the following note from one of his clients: "In accordance with your instructions, I have given birth to twins in the enclosed envelope." However, he may not have been more surprised than the congregation who read this announcement in their church bulletin: "There will be a discussion tomorrow on the problem of adultery in the minister's office." Or the patrons of a health club who learned that "guest passes will not be given to members until the manager has punched each of them first."

Certainly, there were no babies born in an envelope, nor was there adultery in the minister's office, and no one believes the club manager was planning to assault the membership. But the implications (and the unintended humor) are nevertheless present—solely because of the faulty ways in which the sentences were constructed.

To improve your own writing, you must express your thoughts in clear, coherent sentences that produce precisely the reader response you want. Effective sentences are similar to the threads in a piece of knitting or weaving: each thread helps form the larger design; if any one thread becomes tangled or lost, the pattern becomes muddled. In an essay, the same is true: if any sentence is fuzzy or obscure, the reader may lose the point of your discussion and, in some cases, never

Robert Brenner/PhotoEdit

bother to regain it. Therefore, to retain your reader, you must concentrate on writing informative, effective sentences that continuously clarify the purpose of your essay.

Many problems in sentence clarity involve errors in grammar, punctuation, word choice, and usage; the most common of these errors are discussed in Chapter 7, "Word Logic," and throughout Part Four, the handbook section of this text. In this chapter you'll find some general suggestions for writing clear, concise, engaging sentences. However, *don't try to apply all the rules to the first draft of your essay.* Revising sentences before your ideas are firmly in place may be a waste of effort if your essay's stance or structure changes. Concentrate your efforts in early drafts on your thesis, the development of your important supporting points, and the essay's general organization; then, in a later draft, rework your sentences so that each one is informative and clear. Your reader reads only the words on the page, not those in your mind—so it's up to you to make sure the sentences in your essay express the thoughts in your head as closely and vividly as possible.

> **REMEMBER:** All good writers revise and polish their sentences.

Developing a Clear Style

When you are ready to revise the sentences in your rough draft for clarity, consider the following six rules.

Give Your Sentences Content

Fuzzy sentences are often the result of fuzzy thinking. When you examine your sentences, ask yourself, "Do I know what I'm talking about here? Or are my sentences vague or confusing because I'm really not sure what my point is or where it's going?" Look at this list of content-poor sentences taken from student essays; how could you put more information into each one?

- If you were to observe a karate class, you would become familiar with all the aspects that make it up.
- The meaning of the poem isn't very clear the first time you read it, but after several readings, the poet's meaning comes through.
- One important factor that is the basis for determining a true friend is the ability that person has for being a real human being.
- Listening is important because we all need to be able to sit and hear all that is said to us.

Don't pad your paragraphs with sentences that run in circles, leading nowhere; rethink your ideas and revise your writing so that every sentence—like each brick in a wall—contributes to the construction of a solid discussion. In other words, commit yourself to a position and make each sentence contain information pertinent to your point; leave the job of padding to mattress manufacturers.

Sometimes, however, you may have a definite idea in mind but still continue to write "empty sentences"—statements that alone do not contain enough information to make a specific point in your discussion. Frequently, an empty sentence can be revised by combining it with the sentence that follows, as shown in the examples that follow. The empty, or overly general, sentences are underlined.

Poor   There are many kinds of beautiful tropical fish. The kind most popular with aquarium owners is the angelfish.

Better   Of the many kinds of beautiful tropical fish, the angelfish is the most popular with aquarium owners.

Poor   D. W. Griffith introduced many new cinematic techniques, Some of these techniques were contrast editing, close-ups, fade-outs, and freeze-frame shots.

Better   D. W. Griffith made movie history by introducing such new cinematic techniques as contrast editing, close-ups, fade-outs, and the freeze-frame shot.

Poor   There is a national organization called The Couch Potatoes, The group's 8,000 members are devoted television watchers.

Better   The Couch Potatoes is a national organization whose 8,000 members are devoted television watchers.

◆ For more help on combining sentences, see pages 146–149.

Make Your Sentences Specific

In addition to containing an informative, complete thought, each of your sentences should give readers enough clear details for them to "see" the picture you are creating. Sentences full of vague words produce blurry, boring prose and drowsy readers. Remember your reaction the last time you asked a friend about a recent vacation? If the only response you received was something like, "Oh, it was great—a lot of fun," you probably yawned and moved on to a new topic. But if your friend had begun an exciting account of a wilderness rafting trip, with detailed stories about narrow escapes from freezing white water, treacherous rocks, and uncharted whirlpools, you'd probably have stopped and listened. The same principle works in your writing—clear, specific details are the only sure way to attract and hold the reader's interest. Therefore, make each sentence contribute something new and interesting to the overall discussion.

The following examples first show sentences that are far too vague to sustain anyone's attention. Rewritten, these sentences contain specific details that add clarity and interest:

Vague   She went home in a bad mood. [What kind of a bad mood? How did she act or look?]

Specific She stomped home, hands jammed in her pockets, angrily kicking rocks, dogs, small children, and anything else that crossed her path.

Vague   His neighbor bought a really nice old desk. [Why nice? How old? What kind of desk?]

Specific His neighbor bought an oak roll-top desk made in 1885 that contains a secret drawer triggered by a hidden spring.

Vague   My roommate is truly horrible. ["Horrible" in what ways? To what extent? Do you "see" this person?]

Specific My thoughtless roommate leaves dirty dishes under the bed, sweaty clothes in the closet, and toenail clippings in the sink.

◆ For more help selecting specific "showing" words, see pages 141–142 in this chapter, pages 162–166 in Chapter 7, and pages 324–327 in Chapter 11.

Avoid Overpacking Your Sentences

Because our society is becoming increasingly specialized and highly technical, we tend to equate complexity with excellence and simplicity with simplemindedness. This assumption is unfortunate because it often leads to a preference for unnecessarily complicated and even contorted writing. In a recent survey, for example, a student chose a sample of bureaucratic hogwash over several well-written paragraphs, explaining his choice by saying that it must have been better because he didn't understand it.

Our best writers have always worked hard to present their ideas simply and specifically so that their readers could easily understand them. Mark Twain, for instance, once praised a young author this way: "I notice that you use plain simple language, short words, and brief sentences. This is the way to write English. It is the modern way and the best way. Stick to it." And when a critic asked Hemingway to define his theory of writing, he replied, "[I] put down what I see and what I feel in the best and simplest way I can tell it."

In your own writing, therefore, work for a simple, direct style. Avoid sentences that are overpacked (too many ideas or too much information at once) as in the following example on racquetball:

> John told Phil that to achieve more control over the ball, he should practice flicking or snapping his wrist, because this action is faster in the close shots and placing a shot requires only a slight change of the wrist's angle instead of an acute movement of the whole arm, which gives a player less reaction time.

To make the overpacked sentence easier to understand, try dividing the ideas into two or more sentences:

> John told Phil that to achieve more control over the ball, he should practice flicking or snapping his wrist, because this action is faster in the close shots. Placing a shot requires only a slight change of the wrist's angle instead of an acute movement of the whole arm, which gives a player less reaction time.

Don't ever run the risk of losing your reader in a sentence that says too much to comprehend in one bite. This confusing notice, for example, came from a well-known credit card company:

> The Minimum Payment Due each month shall be reduced by the amounts paid in excess of the Minimum Payment Due during the previous three months which have not already been so applied in determining the Minimum Payment Due in such earlier months, unless you have exceeded your line of credit or have paid the entire New Balance shown on your billing statement.

Or consider the confusion of soccer players whose coach warned them in this manner:

> It is also a dangerous feeling to consider that where we are in the league is of acceptable standard because standard is relevant to the standards we have set, which thereby may well indicate that we have not aspired to the standard which we set ourselves.

Try, too, for a straightforward construction. This sentence by Ronald Reagan early in his campaign for the presidency, for example, takes far too many twists and turns for anyone to follow it easily on the first reading:

My goal is an America where something or anything that is done to or for anyone is done neither because of nor in spite of any difference between them, racially, religiously, or ethnic-origin-wise.

◆ If any sentences in your rough draft are overpacked or contorted, try rephrasing your meaning in shorter sentences and then combining thoughts where most appropriate. (Help with sentence variety may be found on pages 146–149 of this chapter.)

Fix Major Sentence Errors

Rather than creating overpacked sentences, some writers have the opposite problem. They write *sentence fragments,* dropping thoughts here or there without forming them into complete, comprehensible grammatical units. Such fragments are confusing to readers, who must struggle to fill in the connecting link between the writer's ideas.

A complete sentence has both a subject (the thing that performs the action or maintains the state of being) and a predicate (the verb and any modifiers or complements). A sentence fragment is often missing its subject, as shown in the following example.

Fragment	David bought a gopher ranch. *Hoping to strike it rich.*
Correct	David bought a gopher ranch, hoping to strike it rich.
Correct	David bought a gopher ranch. He hoped to strike it rich.

Other fragments have the essential sentence components but are considered fragments because they begin with a subordinating conjunction (such as "although," "if," or "when") or a relative pronoun (such as "who," "which," "whose," or "that").

Fragment	David bought a gopher ranch. *Although he knew nothing about rodents.*
Correct	David bought a gopher ranch, although he knew nothing about rodents.
Fragment	David bought a gopher ranch. *Which was for sale at a low price.*
Correct	David bought a gopher ranch, which was for sale at a low price.

If you are having problems recognizing whether a group of words is a fragment or a complete sentence, try the "It is true that" test. When you suspect a fragment, say, "It is true that" in front of the words in question. In most cases, a complete sentence will still make sense, but a fragment will not.*

- It is true that . . . David bought a gopher ranch. [Makes sense: complete sentence]
- It is true that . . . hoping to strike it rich. [No sense: fragment]
- It is true that . . . which was for sale at a low price. [No sense: fragment]

Although they can appear anywhere, fragments most often "belong" to the thought in front of them. To make a fragment fully meaningful, consider connecting it to the preceding or following sentence, as appropriate, or simply rewrite it as a complete sentence (for examples, see the first two "Correct" sentences in this section).

---

*The "It is true that" test does not work on questions, elliptical responses or exclamations (such as "Hello," "Yes," "Help!"), or commands ("Go to your room right now").

In some cases a writer will intentionally use a fragment for a particular purpose, often for emphasis or to create a specific tone ("She felt rotten. Worse than rotten. Miserable-rotten."). But unless you clearly know how to use a fragment for effect and are certain that the tone it creates is appropriate for your essay and audience, stick to writing complete sentences.

◆ For more help with fragments, see pages 563–564 in the Handbook. See also pages 146–149 in this chapter, which will suggest ways to combine thoughts through coordination and subordination.

In addition to unintentional fragments, another construction that may confuse meaning for readers is called a *run-on* (or *fused*) sentence. Run-ons are most often two complete sentences joined together without any punctuation. Such sentences may be corrected by making separate sentences, by placing a semicolon between the complete thoughts, by using a comma plus a coordinating conjunction, or by subordinating one clause.

Run-on	Peter the Penguin was disappointed at the airport's security checkpoint he learned he was on the no-fly list.
Corrected with semicolon	Peter the Penguin was disappointed at the airport's security checkpoint; he learned he was on the no-fly list.
Corrected with subordination	Peter the Penguin was disappointed at the airport's security checkpoint when he learned he was on the no-fly list.

Don't, however, correct a run-on sentence by merely inserting a comma without a coordinating conjunction between the two sentences; doing so will likely result in another major sentence error called a *comma splice.*

Comma splice	My economics professor says success is a great teacher, my yoga teacher says adversity may be an even greater one.
Corrected with a comma and a coordinating conjunction	My economics professor says success is a great teacher, but my yoga teacher says adversity may be an even greater one.

The common coordinating conjunctions are "and," "or," "but," "for," "so," "nor," and "yet." ◆ For more information on coordination, turn to pages 146–147 in this chapter. (For more help correcting the run-on sentence and the comma splice, see pages 565–567 in the Handbook.)

Pay Attention to Word Order

The correct word order is crucial for clarity. Always place a modifier (a word or group of words that affects the meaning of another word) near the word it modifies. The position of a modifier can completely change the meaning of your sentence; for example, each sentence presented here offers a different idea because of the placement of the modifier "only."

1. Eliza said she loves only me.

   [Eliza loves me and no one else.]

2. Only Eliza said she loves me.

[No other person said she loves me.]

3. Eliza said only that she loves me.

[Eliza said she loves me, but said nothing other than that.]

4. Eliza said only she loves me.

[Eliza said no one else loves me.]

To avoid confusion, therefore, place your modifiers close to the words or phrases they describe.

A modifier that seems to modify the wrong part of a sentence is called "misplaced." Not only can misplaced modifiers change or distort the meaning of your sentence, they can also provide unintentional humor, as illustrated by the following excerpt from the 1929 Marx Brothers movie *The Cocoanuts:*

Woman: There's a man waiting outside to see you with a black mustache.
Groucho: Tell him I've already got one.

Of course, the woman didn't mean to imply that the man outside was waiting with (that is, accompanied by) a mustache; she meant to say, "There's a man with a black mustache waiting outside."

A poster advertising a lecture on campus provided this opportunity for humor: "Professor Elizabeth Sewell will discuss the latest appearance of Halley's Comet in room 104." Under the announcement a local wit had scribbled, "Shall we reserve room 105 for the tail?" Or take the case of this startling headline: "Calf Born to Rancher with Two Heads."

Here are some other examples of misplaced modifiers:

Misplaced   Dilapidated and almost an eyesore, Shirley bought the old house to restore it to its original beauty. [Did the writer mean that Shirley needed a beauty treatment?]
Revised   Shirley bought the old house, which was dilapidated and almost an eyesore, to restore it to its original beauty.
Misplaced   Because she is now thoroughly housebroken, Sarah can take the dog almost anywhere. [Did the writer mean that Sarah once had an embarrassing problem?]
Revised   Because the dog is now thoroughly housebroken, Sarah can take her almost anywhere.
Misplaced   Three family members were found bound and gagged by the grandmother. [Did the writer mean that the grandmother had taken up a life of crime?]
Revised   The grandmother found the three family members who had been bound and gagged.
Misplaced   The lost child was finally found wandering in a frozen farmer's field. [Did the writer mean to say that the farmer was that cold?]
Revised   The lost child was finally found wandering in a farmer's frozen field.

In each of the preceding examples, the writer forgot to place the modifying phrase so that it modifies the correct word. In most cases, a sentence with a misplaced modifier can be corrected easily by moving the word or phrase closer to the word that should be modified.

In some sentences, however, the word being modified is missing entirely. Such a phrase is called a "dangling modifier." Think of these phrases as poor orphans, waiting out in the cold, without a parent to accompany them. Most of these errors can be corrected by adding the missing "parent"—the word(s) described by the phrase. Here are some examples followed by their revisions:

Dangling	Waving farewell, the plane began to roll down the runway. [Did the writer mean the plane was waving farewell?]
Revised	Waving farewell, <u>we</u> watched as the plane began to roll down the runway.
Dangling	After spending hours planting dozens of strawberry plants, the gophers came back to the garden and ate every one of them. [Did the writer mean that the gophers had a good meal after putting in such hard work?]
Revised	After spending hours planting dozens of strawberry plants, <u>Ralph</u> realized that the gophers had come back to the garden and eaten every one of them.
Dangling	While telling a joke to my roommate, a cockroach walked across my soufflé. [Did the writer mean that the cockroach was a comedian?]
Revised	While telling a joke to my roommate, <u>I</u> noticed a cockroach walking across my soufflé.
Dangling	Having tucked the children into bed, the cat was put out for the night. [Did the writer mean that the family pet had taken up nanny duties?]
Revised	Having tucked the children into bed, <u>Mom and Dad</u> put the cat out for the night.

Misplaced and dangling modifiers (and many other kinds of sentence errors) often occur as you write your first "idea" drafts. Later, when you are satisfied with your content and organization, you can smooth out these confusing or unintentionally humorous constructions. At first you may agree with well-known essayist Annie Dillard, who notes that writing sometimes feels like alligator wrestling: "With your two bare hands, you hold and fight a sentence's head while its tail tries to knock you over." By practicing good revision skills, however, you soon should be able to wrestle your sentence problems to the ground. (◆ For additional examples of misplaced and dangling modifiers, see page 562 in the Handbook.)

Avoid Mixed Constructions and Faulty Predication

Sometimes you may begin with a sentence pattern in mind and then shift, midsentence, to another pattern—a change that often results in a generally confusing sentence. In many of these cases, you will find that the subject of your sentence simply doesn't fit with the rest of the sentence (the predicate). Look at the following examples and note their corrections:

Faulty	Financial aid is a growing problem for many college students. [Financial aid itself isn't a problem; rather, it's the lack of aid.]
Revised	College students are finding it harder to obtain financial aid.

Faulty	Pregnant cows are required to teach a portion of two courses in Animal Science, AS100 (Breeding of Livestock) and AS200 (Problems in Reproduction of Cattle). [Obviously, the cows will not be the instructors for the classes.]
Revised	The Animal Science Department needs to purchase pregnant cows for use in two courses, AS100 (Breeding of Livestock) and AS200 (Problems in Reproduction of Cattle).
Faulty	Love is when you start rehearsing dinner-date conversation before breakfast. [A thing is never a "when" or a "where"; rewrite all "is when" or "is where" constructions.]
Revised	You're in love if you start rehearsing dinner-date conversation before breakfast.
Faulty	My math grade is why I'm so depressed. [A grade is not a "why"; rewrite "is why" constructions.]
Revised	I'm so depressed because of my math grade.
Faulty	"Fans, don't fail to miss tomorrow's game." [A contorted line from Dizzy Dean, baseball star and sportscaster.]
Revised	"Fans, don't miss tomorrow's game."

Many mixed constructions occur when a writer is in a hurry; read your rough drafts carefully to see if you have sentences in which you started one pattern but switched to another. (◆ For more help on faulty predications and mixed constructions, see pages 570–571 in Part Four.)

Clear, straightforward sentences keep readers from feeling as though they are lost in an Escher maze. *Convex and Concave*, 1955, by M.C. Escher.

Practicing What You've Learned

A. In this exercise, you will find sentences that contain some of the problems discussed thus far in this chapter. Rewrite any sentences that you find vague, confusing, overly simplistic, or overpacked; correct any sentence fragments, run-ons, or comma splice errors. You may divide or combine sentences and replace vague words to improve clarity.

1. There's a new detective show on television. Starring Phil Noir. It is set in the 1940s. According to *TV Guide*.

2. Roger was an awesome guy he was really a big deal in his company.

3. I can't help but wonder whether or not he isn't unwelcome.

4. The book *Biofeedback: How to Stop It* is a good book because of all the good ideas the writer put into it.

5. His assistant stole the magician's bag of tricks. The magician became disillusioned.

6. Afraid poor repair service will ruin your next road trip? Come to the Fix-It Shop and be sure. If your car has a worn-out part, we'll replace it with one just like it.

7. I've signed up for a course at my local college, it is "Cultivating the Mold in Your Refrigerator for Fun and Profit."

8. I'm not sure but I think that Lois is the author of *The Underachiever's Guide to Very Small Business Opportunities* or is she the writer of *Whine Your Way to Success* because I know she's written several books since she's having an autograph party at the campus bookstore either this afternoon or tomorrow.

9. For some people, reading your horoscope is a fun way to learn stuff about your life. Although some people think it's too weird.

10. Upon being asked if she would like to live forever, one contestant in a Miss USA contest replied: "I would not live forever, because we should not live forever, because if we were supposed to live forever, then we would live forever, but we cannot live forever, which is why I would not live forever."

B. The following sentences contain misplaced words and phrases as well as other faulty constructions. Revise them so that each sentence is clear.

1. If you are accosted in the subway at night, you should learn to escape harm from the police.

continued on next page

2. The bride was escorted down the aisle by her stepfather wearing an antique family wedding gown.

3. Almost dead for five years now, I miss my dog so much.

4. For sale: unique gifts for that special, hard-to-find person in your life.

5. The reason why I finally got my leg operated on over Thanksgiving break is because it had been hanging over my head for years.

6. We need to hire two three-year-old teachers for preschool kids who don't smoke.

7. The story of Rip Van Winkle is one of the dangers endured by those who oversleep.

8. We gave our waterbed to friends we didn't want anymore.

9. People who are allergic to chocolate and children should not be given the new vaccine.

10. "I remember meeting a mother of a child who was abducted by the North Koreans right here in the Oval Office."—George W. Bush, 2008

Developing a Concise Style

Almost all writing suffers from wordiness—the tendency to use more words than necessary. When useless words weigh down your prose, the meaning is often lost, confused, or hidden. Flabby prose calls for a reducing plan: put those obese sentences on a diet by cutting out unnecessary words, just as you avoid eating too many fatty foods to keep yourself at a healthy weight. Mushy prose is ponderous and boring; crisp, to-the-point writing, on the other hand, is both accessible and pleasing. Beware, however, a temptation to overdiet—you don't want your prose to become so thin or brief that your meaning disappears completely. Therefore, cut out only the *unessential* words and phrases.

Wordy prose is frequently the result of using one or more of the following: (1) deadwood constructions, (2) redundancies, (3) passive constructions, and (4) pretentious diction.

Avoid Deadwood Constructions

Always try to cut empty "deadwood" from your sentences. Having a clear, concise style does not mean limiting your writing to choppy, childish Dick-and-Jane sentences; it only means that all unnecessary words, phrases, and clauses should be deleted. Here are some sentences containing common deadwood constructions and ways they may be pruned:

Poor   The *reason* the starving novelist drove fifty miles to a new restaurant was because it was serving his favorite chicken dish, Pullet Surprise. ["The reason . . . was because" is both wordy and ungrammatical. If you have a reason, you don't need a "reason because."]

Revised	The starving novelist drove fifty miles to a new restaurant because it was serving his favorite chicken dish, Pullet Surprise.
Poor	The land settlement *was an example where* my client, Ms. Patti O. Furniture, did not receive fair treatment.
Revised	The land settlement was unfair to my client, Ms. Patti O. Furniture.
Poor	Because *of the fact that* his surfboard business failed after only a month, my brother decided to leave Minnesota.
Revised	Because his surfboard business failed after only a month, my brother decided to leave Minnesota.

Other notorious deadwood constructions include the following:

regardless of the fact that	(use "although")
due to the fact that	(use "because")
the reason is that	(omit)
as to whether or not to	(omit "as to" and "or not")
at this point in time	(use "now" or "today")
it is believed that	(use a specific subject and "believes")
concerning the matter of	(use "about")
by means of	(use "by")
these are the kinds of . . . that	(use "these" plus a specific noun)
on account of	(use "because")

Watch a tendency to tack on empty "fillers" that stretch one word into a phrase:

Wordy	Each candidate will be evaluated *on an individual basis.*
Concise	Each candidate will be evaluated *individually.*
Wordy	Television does not portray violence in a *realistic fashion.*
Concise	Television does not portray violence *realistically.*
Wordy	The New York blackout produced a *crisis-type situation.*
Concise	The New York blackout produced a *crisis.*

To retain your reader's interest and improve the flow of your prose, trim all the fat from your sentences.

"There are," "It is." These introductory phrases are often space wasters. When possible, omit them or replace them with specific subjects, as shown in the following:

Wordy	*There are* ten dental students on Full-Bite Scholarships attending this university.
Revised	Ten dental students on Full-Bite Scholarships attend this university.
Wordy	*It is* true that the County Fair still offers many fun contests, including the ever-popular map fold-off.
Revised	The County Fair still offers many fun contests, including the ever-popular map fold-off.

"Who" and "which" clauses. Some "who" and "which" clauses are unnecessary and may be turned into modifiers placed before the noun:

Wordy	The getaway car, *which* was stolen, turned the corner.
Revised	The stolen getaway car turned the corner.

Wordy	The chef, *who* was depressed, ordered his noisy lobsters to simmer down.
Revised	The depressed chef ordered his noisy lobsters to simmer down.

When adjective clauses are necessary, the words "who" and "which" may sometimes be omitted:

Wordy	Sarah Bellam, *who* is a local English teacher, was delighted to hear that she had won the annual lottery, *which* is sponsored by the Shirley Jackson Foundation.
Revised	Sarah Bellam, a local English teacher, was delighted to hear that she had won the annual lottery, sponsored by the Shirley Jackson Foundation.

"To be." Most "to be" phrases are unnecessary and ought not to be. Delete them every time you can.

Wordy	She seems *to be* angry.
Revised	She seems angry.
Wordy	Herb's charisma-bypass operation proved *to be* successful.
Revised	Herb's charisma-bypass operation proved successful.
Wordy	The chef wanted his favorite horror movie, *The Texas Coldslaw Massacre*, *to be* awarded the film festival's top prize.
Revised	The chef wanted his favorite horror movie, *The Texas Coldslaw Massacre*, awarded the film festival's top prize.

"Of" and infinitive phrases. Many "of" and infinitive ("to" plus verb) phrases may be omitted or revised by using possessives, adjectives, and verbs, as shown here:

Wordy	At the time *of registration,* students are required *to make* payment *of their library fees.*
Revised	At registration students must pay their library fees.
Wordy	The producer fired the mother *of the director of the movie.*
Revised	The producer fired the movie director's mother.

Including deadwood phrases makes your prose puffy; streamline your sentences to present a simple, direct style.

Avoid Redundancy

Many flabby sentences contain *redundancies* (words that repeat the same idea or whose meanings overlap). Consider the following examples, currently popular in the Department of Redundancy Department:

- *In this day and age*, people expect to live at least seventy years. ["Day" and "age" present a similar idea. "Today" is less wordy.]
- He repeated the winning bingo number *over again.* ["Repeated" means "to say again," so there is no need for "over again."]

- The *group* consensus *of opinion* was that the pizza crust tasted like cardboard. ["Consensus" means "collective opinion," so it's unnecessary to add "group" or repeat "opinion."]
- She thought his hot-lava necklaces were *really very* unique. [Because "unique" means "being the only one of its kind," the quality described by "unique" cannot vary in degree. Avoid adding modifiers such as "very," "most," or "somewhat" to the word "unique."]

Some other common redundancies include the following:

reverted ~~back~~	~~new~~ innovation
reflected ~~back~~	red ~~in color~~
retreated ~~back~~	burned ~~down~~ /~~up~~
fell ~~down~~	~~pair of~~ twins/~~two~~ twins
climb ~~up~~	~~resulting~~ effect (or "result")
a ~~true~~ fact	~~final~~ outcome
large ~~in size~~	at this point ~~in time~~ (or "now")
joined ~~up~~	8 p.m. ~~at night~~

Carefully Consider Your Passive Verbs

When the subject of the sentence performs the action, the verb is *active;* when the subject of the sentence is acted on, the verb is *passive.* You can recognize some sentences with passive verbs because they often contain the word "by," telling who performed the action.

Passive	The wedding date *was announced* by the young couple.
Active	The young couple *announced* their wedding date.
Passive	His letter of resignation *was accepted* by the Board of Trustees.
Active	The Board of Trustees *accepted* his letter of resignation.
Passive	The trivia contest *was won* by the popular Boulder team, The Godzillas Must Be Crazy.
Active	The popular Boulder team, The Godzillas Must Be Crazy, *won* the trivia contest.

In addition to being wordy and weak, passive sentences often disguise the performer of the action in question. You might have heard a politician, for example, say something similar to this: "It was decided this year to give all the senators an increase in salary." The question of *who* decided to raise salaries remains foggy—perhaps purposefully so. In your own prose, however, you should strive for clarity and directness; therefore, use active verbs as often as you can except when you wish to stress the person or thing that receives the action, as shown in the following examples:

- Their first baby was delivered September 30, 1980, by a local midwife.
- The elderly man was struck by a drunk driver.

Special note: Authorities in some professional and technical fields prefer the passive construction because they wish to emphasize the experiment or process rather than the people performing the action. If the passive voice is preferred in your field, you should abide by that convention when you are writing reports or papers for your professional colleagues.

Avoid Pretentiousness

Another enemy of clear, concise prose is *pretentiousness*. Pompous, inflated language surrounds us, and because too many people think it sounds learned or official, we may be tempted to use it when we want to impress others with our writing. But as George Orwell, author of *1984,* noted, an inflated style is like "a cuttlefish squirting out ink." If you want your prose easily understood, write as clearly and plainly as possible.

To illustrate how confusing pretentious writing can be, here is a copy of a government memo announcing a blackout order, issued in 1942 during World War II:

> Such preparations shall be made as will completely obscure all Federal buildings and non-Federal buildings occupied by the Federal government during an air raid for any period of time from visibility by reason of internal or external illumination.

President Franklin Roosevelt intervened and rewrote the order in plain English, clarifying its message and reducing the number of words by half:

> Tell them that in buildings where they have to keep the work going to put something across the windows.

By translating the obscure original memo into easily understandable language, Roosevelt demonstrated that a natural prose style can communicate necessary information to readers more quickly and efficiently than bureaucratic jargon. (◆ For more advice on ridding your prose of jargon, see pages 166–168.)

REMEMBER: In other—shorter—words, to attract and hold your readers' attention and to communicate clearly and quickly, make your sentences as informative, straightforward, specific, and concise as possible.

Practicing What You've Learned

© Canstock Images, Inc./ Index Stock Imagery

The following sentences are filled with deadwood, redundancies, awkward phrases, and passive constructions. Rewrite each one so that it is concise and direct.

1. In point of fact, the main reason he lost the editing job was primarily because of his being too careless and sloppy in his proofreading work.

2. It was revealed to us by staff members today that there were many adults at the company picnic throwing their trash on the ground as well as their children.

continued on next page

3. My brother Austin, who happens to be older than me, can't drive to work this week due to the fact that he was in a wreck in his car at 2:00 A.M. early Saturday morning.

4. In this modern world of today, we often criticize or disapprove of advertising that is thought to be damaging to women by representing them in an unfair way.

5. When the prosecution tried to introduce the old antique gun, this was objected to by the attorney defending the two twin brothers.

6. It seems to me in my opinion that what the poet is trying to get across to the reader in the poem "Now Is the Winter of Our Discount Tent" is her feeling of disgust with camping.

7. We very often felt that although we expressed our deepest concerns and feelings to our boss, she often just sat there and gave us the real impression that she was taking what we said in a very serious manner although, in our opinion, she did not really and truly care about our concerns.

8. It is a true fact that certainly bears repeating over and over again that learning computer skills and word processing can help you perform in a more efficient way at work and school and also can save you lots of time in daily life too.

9. Personally, I believe that there are too many people who go to eat out in restaurants who always feel they must continually assert their superior natures by acting in a rude, nasty fashion to the people who are employed to wait on their tables.

10. In order to enhance my opportunities for advancement in the workplace at this point in time, I arrived at the decision to seek the hand of my employer's daughter in the state of matrimony.

Assignment

Collaborative Activity: Write a paragraph of at least five sentences as clearly and concisely as you can. Then rewrite this paragraph, filling it with as many vague words, redundancies, and deadwood constructions as possible. Exchange this rewritten paragraph for a similarly faulty one written by a classmate; give yourselves fifteen minutes to "translate" each other's sentences into effective prose. Compare the translations to the original paragraphs. Which version is clearer? Why?

© CORBIS

Developing an Engaging Style

Good writing demands clarity and conciseness—but that's not all. Good prose should also be appealing and interesting. Each line should encourage the reader to the next. Consider, for example, a dull article you've read recently. It may have been written clearly, but perhaps it failed to interest or inform because of its insufferably bland tone; by the time you finished a few pages, you had discovered a new cure for insomnia.

You can prevent your readers from succumbing to a similar case of the blahs by developing an inviting prose style that continually engages and pleases them. As one writer has pointed out, all subjects—with the possible exceptions of sex and money—are dull until somebody makes them interesting. As you revise your rough drafts, remember: bored readers are not born but made. As playwright Anton Chekov once said, "Don't tell me the moon is shining; show me the glint of light on broken glass."

To help you transform ho-hum prose into lively sentences and paragraphs, here are some practical suggestions:

Use specific, descriptive verbs. Avoid bland verbs that must be supplemented by modifiers.

Bland	His fist *broke* the window *into many little pieces*.
Better	His fist *shattered* the window.
Bland	Dr. Love *asked* his congregation about donating money to his "love mission" *over and over again*.
Better	Dr. Love *hounded* his congregation into donating money to his "love mission."
Bland	The exhausted runner *went* up the last hill *in an unsteady way*.
Better	The exhausted runner *staggered* up the last hill.

To cut wordiness that weighs down your prose, try to use an active verb instead of a noun plus a colorless verb such as "to be," "to have," "to get," "to do," and "to make." Avoid unnecessary uses of "got."

Wordy	At first the players and managers *had an argument* over the money, but finally they *came to an agreement that got* the contract dispute settled.
Better	At first the players and managers *argued* over the money, but finally they *settled* the contract dispute.
Wordy	The executives *made the decision* to *have another meeting* on Tuesday.
Better	The executives *decided* to *meet again* on Tuesday.
Wordy	The family *made many enjoyable trips* to Hawaii before their daughter *got married* there in 2009.
Better	The family *enjoyed* many trips to Hawaii before their daughter *married* there in 2009.

Use specific, precise modifiers that help the reader see, hear, or feel what you are describing. Adjectives such as "good," "bad," "many," "more," "great," "a lot," "important," and "interesting" are too vague to paint the reader a clear picture. Similarly, the adverbs "very," "really," "too," and "quite" are overused and add little to sentence clarity. The following are examples of weak sentences and their revisions:

Imprecise	The potion changed the scientist into a *really old* man.
Better	The potion changed the scientist into a *one-hundred-year-old* man.
Imprecise	Aricelli is a *very interesting* person.
Better	Aricelli is *witty, intelligent,* and *talented.*
Imprecise	The vegetables tasted *funny.*
Better	The vegetables tasted *like moss mixed with Krazy Glue.*

(◆ For more advice on using specific, colorful words, see pages 162–166 in Chapter 7 and pages 324–327 in Chapter 11.)

Emphasize people when possible. Try to focus on human beings rather than abstractions whenever you can. Next to our fascinating selves, we most enjoy hearing about other people. Although all the sentences in the first paragraph that follows are correct, the second one, revised by a class of composition students at Brown University, is clearer and more useful because the jargon has been eliminated and the focus changed from the tuition rules to the students.

Original	Tuition regulations currently in effect provide that payment of the annual tuition entitles an undergraduate-degree candidate to full-time enrollment, which is defined as registration for three, four, or five courses per semester. This means that at no time may an undergraduate student's official registration for courses drop below three without a dean's permission for part-time status and that at no time may the official course registration exceed five. (Brown University Course Announcement)
Revised	If students pay their tuition, they may enroll in three, four, or five courses per semester. Fewer than three or more than five can be taken only with a dean's permission.

Here's a similar example with a bureaucratic focus rather than a personal one:

Original	The salary deflations will most seriously impact the secondary educational profession.
Revised	High school teachers will suffer the biggest salary reductions.

Obviously, the revised sentence is the more easily understood of the two because the reader knows exactly who will be affected by the pay cuts. In your own prose, wherever appropriate, try to replace vague abstractions, such as "society," "culture," "administrative concerns," and "programmatic expectations," with the human beings you're thinking about. In other words, remember to talk *to* people *about* people.

Vary your sentence style. Don't force readers to wade through annoying paragraphs full of identically constructed sentences. To illustrate this point, the following are a few sentences composed in the all-too-common "subject + predicate" pattern:

Soccer is the most popular sport in the world. Soccer exists in almost every country. Soccer players are sometimes more famous than movie stars. Soccer teams compete every few years for the World Soccer Cup. Soccer fans often riot if their team loses. Soccer fans even commit suicide. Soccer is the only game in the world that makes people so crazy.

Excruciatingly painful, yes? Each of us tends to repeat a particular sentence pattern (though the choppy "subject + predicate" is by far the most popular); you can often detect your own by reading your prose aloud. To avoid overdosing your readers with the same pattern, vary the length, arrangement, and complexity of your sentences. Of course, this doesn't mean that you should contort your sentences merely for the sake of illustrating variety; just read your rough draft aloud, listening carefully to the rhythm of your prose so you can revise any monotonous passages or disharmonious sounds. (Try also to avoid the hiccup syndrome, in which you begin a sentence with the same word that ends the preceding sentence: "The first president to install a telephone on his desk was Herbert *Hoover*. *Hoover* refused to use the telephone booth outside his office.")

Avoid overuse of any one kind of construction in the same sentence. Don't, for example, pile up too many negatives, "who" or "which" clauses, and prepositional or infinitive phrases in one sentence.

- He *couldn't* tell whether she *didn't* want him to go or *not*.
- I gave the money to my brother, *who* returned it to the bank president, *who* said the decision to prosecute was up to the sheriff, *who* was out of town.
- I went to the florist *for* my roommate *for* a dozen roses *for* his date.

Try also to avoid stockpiling nouns, one on top of another, so that your sentences are difficult to read. Although some nouns may be used as adjectives to modify other nouns ("baseball bat," "gasoline pump," "food processor"), too many nouns grouped together sound awkward and confuse readers. If you have run too many nouns together, try using prepositional phrases ("an income tax bill discussion" becomes "discussion of an income tax bill") or changing the order or vocabulary of the sentence:

Confusing	The legislators are currently considering the *liability insurance multiple-choice premium proposal.*
Clearer	The legislators are currently considering the proposal that suggests *multiple-choice premiums* for *liability insurance.*
Confusing	We're concerned about the low *female labor force participation figures* in our department.
Clearer	We're concerned about the low *number of women working* in our department.

Don't change your point of view between or within sentences. If, for example, you begin your essay referring to students as "they," don't switch midway—or midsentence—to "we" or "you."

Inconsistent	Students pay tuition, which should entitle *them* to some voice in the university's administration. Therefore, *we* deserve one student on the Board of Regents.

Consistent	Students pay tuition, which should entitle *them* to some voice in the university's administration. Therefore, *they* deserve one student on the Board of Regents.
Inconsistent	*I* like my photography class because *we* learn how to restore *our* old photos and how to take better color portraits of *your* family.
Consistent	*I* like my photography class because *I'm* learning how to restore *my* old photos and how to take better color portraits of *my* family.

Perhaps this is a good place to dispel the myth that the pronoun "I" should never be used in an essay; on the contrary, many of our best essays have been written in the first person. Some of your former teachers may have discouraged the use of "I" for these two reasons: (1) personal opinion does not belong in the essay, and (2) writing in the first person often produces too many empty phrases, such as "I think that" and "I believe that." Nevertheless, if the personal point of view is appropriate in a particular assignment, you may use the first person in moderation, making sure that every other sentence doesn't begin with "I" plus a verb.

Practicing What You've Learned

© Canstock Images, Inc./ Index Stock Imagery

Replace the following underlined words so that the sentences are clear and vivid. In addition, rephrase any awkward constructions or unnecessarily abstract words you find.

1. Judging from the <u>crazy</u> sound of the reactor, it isn't obvious to me that nuclear power as we know it today isn't a technology with a less than wonderful future.

2. The City Council felt <u>bad</u> because the revised tourist development activities grant fund application form letters were mailed without stamps.

3. To watch Jim Bob eat pork chops was <u>most interesting</u>.

4. For sale: <u>very nice</u> antique bureau suitable for ladies or gentlemen with thick legs and extra-large side handles.

5. We <u>don't want anybody to not</u> have fun.

6. My roommate is <u>sort of different</u>, but he's a <u>good</u> guy at heart.

7. After reading the <u>great</u> new book, *The Looter's Guide to Riot-Prone Cities*, Eddie <u>asked to have</u> a transfer <u>really soon</u>.

8. The wild oats soup was <u>fantastic</u>, so we drank <u>a lot of it very fast</u>.

9. When his new cat Chairman Meow won the pet show, owner Warren Peace got <u>pretty excited</u>.

10. The new diet <u>made me feel awful</u>, and it <u>did many horrible things</u> to my body.

Assignment

A. Find a short piece of writing you think is too bland, boring, vague, or confusing. (Possible sources: your college catalog, a business contract, a form letter, or your student health insurance policy.) In a well-written paragraph of your own, identify the sample's major problems, and offer some specific suggestions for improving the writing.

B. *Collaborative Activity*: Following your work on Assignment "A," you might participate in this peer activity. After the class has separated into small sets of three or four students, listen as each person in your group reads aloud his or her original sample. What makes each one so bland, boring, or confusing? Together, select the worst offender to share with the class as a whole. When all the groups have reported, vote one the winner of the Most Lifeless Prose Award. Vow to avoid any such blandness and/or vagueness in your own writing!

C. Continue working on a clear, concise style by writing a public service announcement (PSA) as a caption for the following photo. Think of a charity, service organization, or social program and use your words plus the picture to promote one of their goals (consider, for example, advertising a fund-raising activity, an awareness event, or an open house). Or, if you prefer, announce a new campus regulation or remind readers of a current policy. Assume your text and the picture will appear in a local or campus newspaper, and because print space is expensive, you must accomplish your task in three or four highly effective sentences. Be ready to read your caption to your classmates.

Blend Images/SuperStock

Developing an Emphatic Style

Some words and phrases in your sentences are more important than others and therefore need more emphasis. Three ways to vary emphasis are by (1) word order, (2) coordination, and (3) subordination.

Word Order

The arrangement of words in a sentence can determine which ideas receive the most emphasis. To stress a word or phrase, place it at the end of the sentence or at the beginning of the sentence. Accordingly, a word or phrase receives least emphasis when buried in the middle of the sentence. Compare the following examples, in which the word "murder" receives varying degrees of emphasis:

Least emphatic	For Colonel Mustard *murder* was the only solution.
Emphatic	*Murder* was Colonel Mustard's only solution.
Most emphatic	Colonel Mustard knew only one solution: *murder.*

Another use of word order to vary emphasis is *inversion,* taking a word out of its natural or usual position in a sentence and relocating it in an unexpected place.

Usual order	Parents who give their children both roots and wings are *wise.*
Inverted order	*Wise* are the parents who give their children both roots and wings.

Not all your sentences will contain words that need special emphasis; good writing generally contains a mix of some sentences in natural order and others rearranged for special effects.

Coordination

When you want to stress two closely related ideas equally, coordinate them.* In coordination, you join two sentences with a coordinating conjunction. To remember the coordinating conjunctions ("for," "and," "nor," "but," "or," "yet," "so"), think of the acronym FANBOYS; then always join two sentences with a comma and one of the FANBOYS. Here are two samples:

Choppy	The most popular girl's name in the U.S. last year was Sophia. The most popular boy's name in the U.S. last year was Jacob.
Coordinated	The most popular girl's name in the U.S. last year was Sophia, *and* the most popular boy's name was Jacob.
Choppy	The patient requested a chocolate I.V. The nurse said no.
Coordinated	The patient requested a chocolate I.V., *but* the nurse said no.

---

*To remember that the term "coordination" refers to equally weighted ideas, think of other words with the prefix *co* such as "copilots," "co-authors," or "cooperation."

You can use coordination to show a relationship between ideas and to add variety to your sentence structures. Be careful, however, to select the right words while linking ideas, unlike the sentence that appeared in a church newsletter: "The ladies of the church have discarded clothing of all kinds, and they have been inspected by the minister." In other words, writers often need to slow down and make sure their thoughts are not joined in unclear or even unintentionally humorous ways: "For those of you who have children and don't know it, we have a nursery downstairs."

Sometimes when writers are in a hurry, they join ideas that are clearly related in their own minds but whose relationship is confusing to the reader:

Confusing	My laboratory report isn't finished, and today my sister is leaving for a visit home.
Clear	I'm still working on my laboratory report, so I won't be able to catch a ride home with my sister who's leaving today.

You should also avoid using coordinating conjunctions to string too many ideas together like linked sausages:

Poor	We went inside the famous cave and the guide turned off the lights and we saw the rocks that glowed.
Revised	After we went inside the famous cave, the guide turned off the lights so we could see the rocks that glowed.

Subordination

Some sentences contain one main statement and one or more less emphasized elements; the less important ideas are subordinate to, or are dependent on, the sentence's main idea.* Subordinating conjunctions introducing dependent clauses show a variety of relationships between the clauses and the main part of the sentence. Here are four examples of subordinating conjunctions and their uses:

1. To show time **without subordination**	Superman stopped changing his clothes. He realized the phone booth was made of glass.
with subordination	Superman stopped changing his clothes *when* he realized the phone booth was made of glass.
2. To show cause **without subordination**	The country-western singer failed to gain success in Nashville. She sadly returned to Snooker Hollow to work in the sequin mines.
with subordination	*Because* the country-western singer failed to gain success in Nashville, she sadly returned to Snooker Hollow to work in the sequin mines.

*To remember that the term "subordination" refers to sentences containing dependent elements, think of such words as "a subordinate" (someone who works for someone else) or a post office "substation" (a less important branch of the main post office).

3. To show condition **without subordination**	Susan ought to study the art of tattooing. She will work with colorful people.
with subordination	*If* Susan studies the art of tattooing, she will work with colorful people.
4. To show place **without subordination**	Bulldozers are smashing the old movie theater. That's the place I first saw Roy Rogers and Dale Evans ride into the sunset.
with subordination	Bulldozers are smashing the old movie theater *where* I first saw Roy Rogers and Dale Evans ride into the sunset.

Subordination is especially useful in ridding your prose of choppy Dick-and-Jane sentences and those "empty sentences" discussed on pages 126–127. Here are some examples of choppy, weak sentences and their revisions, which contain subordinate clauses:

Choppy	Lew makes bagels on Tuesday. Lines in front of his store are a block long.
Revised	When Lew makes bagels on Tuesday, lines in front of his store are a block long.
Choppy	I have fond memories of Zilker Park. My husband and I met there.
Revised	I have fond memories of Zilker Park because my husband and I met there.

Effective use of subordination is one of the marks of a sophisticated writer because it presents adequate information in one smooth flow instead of in monotonous drips. Subordination, like coordination, also adds variety to your sentence construction.

Generally, when you subordinate one idea, you emphasize another, so to avoid the tail-wagging-the-dog problem, put your important idea in the main clause. Also, don't let your most important idea become buried under an avalanche of subordinate clauses, as in the sentence that follows:

When he was told by his boss, *who* had always treated him fairly, *that* he was being fired from a job *that* he had held for twenty years at a factory *where* he enjoyed working *because* the pay was good, Henry felt angry and frustrated.

Practice blending choppy sentences by studying the following sentence-combining exercise. In this exercise, a description of a well-known movie has been chopped into simple sentences and then combined into one complex sentence.

1. *Psycho* (1960)
   Norman Bates manages a motel.
   It is remote.
   It is dangerous.
   Norman has a mother.
   She seems overly fond of knives.
   He tries to protect his mom.

In a remote—and dangerous—motel, manager Norman Bates tries to protect his mother, who seems overly fond of knives.

2. *King Kong* (1933)
   A showman goes to the jungle.
   He captures an ape.
   The ape is a giant.
   The ape is taken to New York City.
   He escapes.
   He dies fighting for a young woman.
   He loves her.
   She is beautiful.

A showman captures a giant ape in the jungle and takes him to New York City, where he escapes but dies fighting for the beautiful young woman he loves.

3. *Casablanca* (1942)
   Rick is an American.
   He is cynical.
   He owns a café.
   He lives in Casablanca.
   He meets his former love.
   She is married.
   Her husband is a French resistance fighter.
   Rick helps the couple.
   He regains self-respect.

When Rick, a cynical American café owner in Casablanca, helps his former love and her husband, a French resistance fighter, he regains his self-respect.

Please note that the sentences in these exercises may be combined effectively in a number of ways. For instance, the description of *King Kong* might be rewritten this way: "After a showman captures him in the jungle, a giant ape escapes in New York City but dies fighting for the love of a beautiful young woman." How might you rewrite the other two sample sentences?

Practicing What You've Learned

© Canstock Images, Inc./Index Stock Imagery

A. Revise the following sentences so that the underlined words receive more emphasis.

1. A remark attributed to the former heavyweight boxing champion <u>Joe Louis</u> is "I don't really like money, but it quiets my nerves."

2. According to recent polls, <u>television</u> is where most Americans get their news.

3. Of all the world's problems, it is <u>hunger</u> that is most urgent.

continued on next page

4. I enjoyed visiting many foreign countries last year, <u>Greece</u> being my favorite of all of them.

5. The annoying habit of <u>knuckle-cracking</u> is something I can't stand.

B. Combine the following sentences using coordination or subordination.

1. The guru rejected his dentist's offer of novocaine. He could transcend dental medication.

2. John failed his literature test. John incorrectly identified Harper Lee as the author of the south-of-the-border classic *Tequila Mockingbird*.

3. Peggy Sue's house burned. She tapped a "9." She couldn't find "11" on the phone keypad.

4. The police had only a few clues. They suspected Jean and David had strangled each other in a desperate struggle over control of the thermostat.

5. Bubba's favorite movie is *Sorority Babes in the Slimeball Bowl-O-Rama* (1988). A film critic called it "a pinhead chiller."

6. We're going to the new Psychoanalysis Restaurant. Their menu includes banana split personality, repressed duck, shrimp basket case, and self-expresso.

7. Kato lost the junior high spelling bee. He could not spell *DNA*.

8. Colorado hosts an annual BobFest to honor all people named Bob. Events include playing softbob, bobbing for apples, listening to bob-pipes, and eating bob-e-que.

9. The earthquake shook the city. Louise was practicing primal-scream therapy at the time.

10. In 1789 many Parisians bought a new perfume called "Guillotine." They wanted to be on the cutting edge of fashion.

C. Combine the following simple sentences into one complex sentence. See if you can guess the name of the book or movie described in the sentences. (Answers appear on page 153.)

1. A boy runs away from home.
His companion is a runaway slave.
He lives on a raft.
The raft is on the Mississippi River.
He has many adventures.
The boy learns many lessons.
Some lessons are about human kindness.
Some lessons are about friendship.

continued on next page

2. A young man returns from prison.
   He returns to his family.
   His family lives in the Dust Bowl.
   The family decides to move.
   The family expects to find jobs in California.
   The family finds intolerance.
   They also find dishonest employers.

3. A scientist is obsessed.
   He wants to re-create life.
   He creates a monster.
   The monster rebels against the scientist.
   The monster kills his creator.
   The villagers revolt.
   The villagers storm the castle.

Assignment

© CORBIS

A. *Collaborative Activity*: Make up your own sentence-combining exercise by finding or writing one-sentence descriptions of popular or recent movies, books, or television shows. Divide the complex sentences into simple sentences and exchange papers with a classmate. Give yourselves ten minutes to combine sentences and guess the titles.

B. The following two paragraphs are poorly written because of their choppy, wordy, and monotonous sentences. Rewrite each passage so that it is clear, lively, and emphatic.

1. There is a new invention on the market. It is called a "dieter's conscience." It is a small box to be installed in one's refrigerator. When the door of the refrigerator is opened by you, a tape recorder begins to start. A really loud voice yells, "You eating again? No wonder you're getting fat." Then the very loud voice says, "Close the door; it's getting warm." Then the voice laughs a lot in an insane and crazy fashion. The idea is one that is designed to mock people into a habit of stopping eating.

2. In this modern world of today, man has come up with another new invention. This invention is called the "Talking Tombstone." It is made by the Gone-But-Not-Forgotten Company, which is located in Burbank, California. This company makes a tombstone that has a device in it that

continued on next page

makes the tombstone appear to be talking aloud in a realistic fashion when people go close by it. The reason is that the device is really a recording machine that is turned on due to the simple fact of the heat of the bodies of the people who go by. The closer the people get, the louder the sound the tombstone makes. It is this device that individual persons who want to leave messages after death may utilize. A hypochondriac, to cite one example, might leave a recording of a message that says over and over again in a really loud voice, "See, I told you I was sick!" It may be assumed by one and all that this new invention will be a serious aspect of the whole death situation in the foreseeable future.

Applying What You've Learned to *Your* Writing

If you have drafted a piece of writing and are satisfied with your essay's ideas and organization, begin revising your sentences for clarity, conciseness, and emphasis. As you move through your draft, think about your readers. Ask yourself, "Are any of my sentences too vague, overpacked, or contorted for my readers to understand? Can I clarify any of my ideas by using more precise language or by revising confusing or fragmented sentence constructions?"

If you can't easily untangle a jumbled sentence, try following the sentence-combining exercise described on pages 150–151 of this chapter—but in reverse. Instead of combining ideas, break your thought into a series of simpler sentences. Think about what you want to say, and put the person or thing of most importance in the *subject* position at the beginning of the sentences. Then select a verb and a brief phrase to complete each of the sentences. You will most likely need several of these simpler constructions to communicate the complexity of your original thought. Once you have your thought broken into smaller, simpler units, carefully begin to combine some of them as you strive for clarity and sentence variety. (◆ If you are concerned about fragment sentences, use the "It is true that" test described on page 129.)

Remember that it's not enough for you, the writer, to understand what your sentences mean—your readers must be able to follow your ideas, too. When in doubt, always revise your writing so that it is clear, concise, and inviting. (◆ For more help, turn to Chapter 5, on revision.)

Chapter 6 Summary

Here is a brief summary of what you should remember about writing effective sentences:

1. All good writers revise and polish their sentences.

2. You can help clarify your ideas for your readers by writing sentences that are informative, straightforward, and precise.

3. You can communicate your ideas more easily to your readers if you cut out deadwood, redundancies, confusing passives, and pretentious language.

4. You can maintain your readers' interest in your ideas if you cultivate an engaging style offering a variety of pleasing sentence constructions.

Answers to sentence-combining exercise (pages 150–151):

1. *Huckleberry Finn*

2. *The Grapes of Wrath*

3. *Frankenstein*

Word Logic

•••

The English language contains nearly one million words—quite a selection for you as a writer to choose from. But such a wide choice can make you feel like a starving person confronting a six-page, fancy French menu. Which choice is best? How do I choose? Is the choice so important?

Word choice can make an enormous difference in the quality of your writing for at least one obvious reason: if you substitute an incorrect or vague word for the right one, you risk being misunderstood. Ages ago, Confucius noted the same point: "If language is incorrect, then what is said is not meant. If what is said is not meant, then what ought to be done remains undone." It isn't enough that you know what you mean; you must transfer your thoughts onto paper in the proper words so that others clearly understand your ideas.

To help you think critically about diction—that is, word choice—this chapter offers some practical suggestions for selecting words that are not only accurate and appropriate but also memorable and persuasive.

Selecting the Correct Words
Accuracy: Confused Words

- Unless I get a bank loan soon, I will be forced to lead an *immortal* life.
- Dobermans make good pets if you train them with enough *patients*.
- He dreamed of eating *desert* after *desert*.
- She had dieted for so long that she had become *emancipated*.
- The young man was completely in *ah* of the actress's beauty.
- Socrates died from an overdose of *wedlock*.

The preceding sentences share a common problem: each one contains an error in word choice. In each sentence, the italicized word is incorrect, causing the sentence to be nonsensical or silly. (Consider a sign recently posted in a local night spot: "No miners allowed." Did the owner think the lights on their hats would bother the other customers? Did the student with "duel majors" imagine that his two areas of study were squaring off with pistols at twenty paces?) To avoid such confusion in word choice, check your words for *accuracy*. Select words whose precise meaning, usage, and spelling you know; consult your dictionary for any words whose definitions (or spellings) are fuzzy to you. As Mark Twain noted, the difference between the right word and the wrong one is the difference between lightning and the lightning bug.

Here is a list of words that are often confused in writing. Use your dictionary to determine the meanings or usage of any word unfamiliar to you.

its/it's	lead/led	choose/chose
to/too/two	cite/sight/site	accept/except
there/their/they're	affect/effect	council/counsel
your/you're	good/well	reign/rein
complement/compliment	who's/whose	lose/loose
stationary/stationery	lay/lie	precede/proceed
capitol/capital	than/then	illusion/allusion
principal/principle	insure/ensure	farther/further

Special note: Some "confused" words don't even exist! Here are four commonly used non-existent words and their correct counterparts:

No Such Word or Spelling	Use Instead
irregardless	regardless
alright	all right
alot	a lot
its'	its or it's

Accuracy: Idiomatic Phrases

Occasionally, you may have an essay returned to you with words marked "awkward diction" or "idiom." In English, as in all languages, we have word groupings that seem governed by no particular logic except the ever-popular "that's-the-way-we-say-it" rule. Many of these idiomatic expressions involve prepositions that novice writers sometimes confuse or misuse. Some common idiomatic errors and their corrected forms are listed here.

regardless ~~to~~ of	different ~~than to~~ from	relate ~~with~~ to
insight ~~of~~ into	must ~~of~~ have known	capable ~~to~~ of
similar ~~with~~ to	superior ~~than~~ to	aptitude ~~toward~~ for
comply ~~to~~ with	~~to~~ in my opinion	prior ~~than~~ to
off ~~of~~	meet ~~to~~ her standards	should ~~of~~ have

To avoid idiomatic errors, consult your dictionary and read your essay aloud; often your ears will catch mistakes in usage that your eyes have overlooked.*

Levels of Language

In addition to choosing the correct word, you should select words whose status is suited to your purpose. For convenience here, language has been classified into three categories, or levels, of usage: (1) colloquial, (2) informal, and (3) formal.

Colloquial language is the kind of speech you use most often in conversation with your friends, classmates, and family. It may not always be grammatically correct ("it's me"); it may include fragments, contractions, some slang, words identified as nonstandard by the dictionary (such as "yuck" or "lousy"), and shortened or abbreviated words ("grad school," "LOL"). Colloquial speech is everyday language, and although you may use it in some informal writing (text messages, personal e-mail and letters, social media, and so forth), you should think carefully about using colloquial language in most college essays or in professional letters or reports because such a choice implies a casual relationship between writer and reader. (◆ For more discussion of appropriate audiences for texting and Internet language, see page 166.)

Informal language is called for in most college and professional assignments. The tone is more formal than in colloquial writing or speech, and no slang or nonstandard words are permissible. Informal writing consistently uses correct grammar; fragments are used for special effect or not at all. Authorities disagree on the use of contractions in informal writing: some say avoid them entirely; others say they're permissible; still others advocate using them only to avoid stilted phrases ("let's go," for example, is preferable to "let us go"). Most, if not all, of your essays in English classes will be written in informal language.

Formal language is found in important documents and in serious, often ceremonial, speeches. Characteristics include an elevated—but not pretentious—tone, no

---

*You may not immediately recognize what's wrong with words your teacher has labeled "diction" or "idiom." If you're uncertain about an error, ask your teacher for clarification; after all, if you don't know what's wrong with your prose, you can't avoid the mistake again. To illustrate this point, here's a true story: A bright young woman was having trouble with prepositional phrases in her essays and, although her professor repeatedly marked her incorrect expressions with the marginal note "idiom," she never improved. Finally, one day near the end of the term, she approached her teacher in tears and wailed, "Professor Jones, I know I'm not a very good writer, but must you write 'idiot,' 'idiot,' 'idiot' all over my papers?" The moral of this story is simple: it's easy to misunderstand a correction or misread your teacher's writing. Because you can't improve until you know what's wrong, always ask when you're in doubt.

contractions, and correct grammar. Formal writing often uses inverted word order and balanced sentence structure. John F. Kennedy's 1960 Inaugural Address, for example, was written in a formal style ("Ask not what your country can do for you; ask what you can do for your country"). Most people rarely, if ever, need to write formally; if you are called on to do so, however, be careful to avoid diction that sounds pretentious, pompous, or phony.

Tone

Tone is a general word that describes writers' attitudes toward their subject matter and audience. There are as many different kinds of tones as there are emotions. Depending on how the writer feels, an essay's "voice" may sound lighthearted, indignant, sarcastic, or solemn, to name but a few of the possible choices. In addition to presenting a specific attitude, a good writer gains credibility by maintaining a tone that is generally reasonable, sincere, and authentic.

Although it is impossible to analyze all the various kinds of tones one finds in essays, it is nevertheless beneficial to discuss some of those that repeatedly give writers trouble. Here are some tones that should be used carefully or avoided altogether:

Invective

Invective is unrestrained anger, usually expressed in the form of violent accusation or denunciation. Let's suppose, for example, you hear a friend argue, "Anyone who votes for Joe Smith is a Fascist pig." If you are considering voting for Smith, you are probably offended by your friend's abusive tone. Raging emotion, after all, does not sway the opinions of intelligent people; they need to hear the facts presented in a calm, clear discussion. Therefore, in your own writing, aim for a reasonable tone. You want your readers to think, "Now here is someone with a good understanding of the situation, who has evaluated it with an unbiased, analytical mind." Keeping a controlled tone doesn't mean you shouldn't feel strongly about your subject—on the contrary, you certainly should—but you should realize that a hysterical or outraged tone defeats your purpose by causing you to sound irrational and therefore untrustworthy. For this reason, you should avoid using profanity in your essays; the shock value of an obscenity is probably not worth what you might lose in credibility. The most effective way to make your point is by persuading, not offending, your reader.

Sarcasm

In most of your writing you'll discover that a little sarcasm—bitter, derisive remarks—goes a long way. As with invective, too much sarcasm can damage the reasonable tone your essay should present. Instead of saying, "The last time we had a judge like him, people were burned at the stake," give your readers some reasons why you believe the judge is a poor one. Sarcasm can be effective, but realize that it often backfires by causing the writer to sound like a childish name-caller rather than a judicious commentator.

Irony

Irony is a figure of speech whereby the writer or speaker says the opposite of what is meant; for the irony to be successful, however, the audience must understand the writer's true intent. For example, if you have slopped to school in a rainstorm and your drenched teacher enters the classroom saying, "Ah, nothing like this beautiful, sunny weather," you know that your teacher is being ironic. Perhaps one of the most famous cases of irony occurred in 1938, when Sigmund Freud, the famous Viennese psychiatrist, was arrested by the Nazis. After being harassed by the Gestapo, he was released on the condition that he sign a statement swearing he had been treated well by the secret police. Freud signed it, but, as the story goes, he added a few words after his signature: "I can heartily recommend the Gestapo to everyone." Looking back, we easily recognize Freud's jab at his captors; the Gestapo, however, apparently overlooked the irony and let him go.

Although irony is often an effective device, it can also cause great confusion, especially when it is written rather than spoken. Unless your readers thoroughly understand your position in the first place, they may become confused by what appears to be a sudden contradiction. Irony that is too subtle, too private, or simply out of context merely complicates the issue. Therefore, you must make certain that your reader has no trouble realizing when your tongue is firmly embedded in your cheek. And unless you are assigned to write an ironic essay (in the same vein, for instance, as Jonathan Swift's "A Modest Proposal"), don't overuse irony, whose effectiveness may be reduced with overkill.

Flippancy or Cuteness

If you sound too flip, hip, or bored in your essay ("People with IQs lower than their sunscreen number will object . . ."), your readers will not take you seriously and, consequently, will disregard whatever you have to say. Writers suffering from cuteness will also antagonize their readers. For example, let's assume you're assigned the topic "Which Person Did the Most to Arouse the Laboring Class in Twentieth-Century England?" and you begin your essay with a discussion of the man who invented the alarm clock. Although that joke might be funny in an appropriate situation, it's not likely to impress your reader, who's looking for serious commentary. How much cuteness is too much is often a matter of taste, but if you have any doubts about the quality of your humor, leave it out. Also, omit personal messages or comic asides to your reader (such as "Ha, ha, just kidding!" or "I knew you'd love this part"). Humor is often effective, but remember that the purpose of any essay is to persuade an audience to accept your thesis, not merely to entertain with freestanding jokes. In other words, if you use humor, make sure it is appropriate for your subject matter and that it works to help you make your point.

Sentimentality

Sentimentality is the excessive show of cheap emotions—"cheap" because they are not deeply felt but evoked by clichés and stock, tear-jerking situations. In the nineteenth century, for example, a typical melodrama played on the sentimentality of the audience by presenting a black-hatted, cold-hearted, mustache-twirling villain tying a golden-haired, pure-hearted "Little Nell" to the railroad tracks after driving her ancient, sickly mother out into a snowdrift. Today, politicians (among others) often appeal to our sentimentality by conjuring up images they feel will move us emotionally rather than rationally to take their side: "My friends," says Senator Stereotype, "this fine nation of ours was founded by men like myself, dedicated to the principles of family, flag, and freedom. Vote for me, and let's get back to those precious basics that make life in America so grand." Such gush is hardly convincing; good writers and speakers use evidence and logical reason to persuade their audience. In personal essays, guard against becoming too carried away by emotion, as did this student: "My dog, Cuddles, is the sweetest, cutest, most precious little puppy dog in the whole wide world, and she will always be my best friend." In addition to sending the reader into sugar shock, this description fails to present any specific reasons why anyone should appreciate Cuddles. In other words, be sincere in your writing, but don't lose so much control of your emotions that you become mushy or maudlin.

Preachiness

Even if you are so convinced of the rightness of your position that a burning bush couldn't change your mind, try not to sound smug about it. No one likes to be lectured by someone perched atop the mountain of morality. Instead of preaching, adopt a tone that says, "I believe my position is correct, and I am glad to have this opportunity to explain why." Then give your reasons and meet objections in a positive but not holier-than-thou manner.

Pomposity

The "voice" of your essay should sound as natural as possible; don't strain to sound scholarly, scientific, or sophisticated. If you write, "My summer sojourn through the Western states of this grand country was immensely pleasurable" instead of "My vacation last summer in the Rockies was fun," you sound merely phony, not dignified and learned. Select only words you know and can use easily. Never write anything you wouldn't say in an intelligent classroom conversation. (◆ For more information on correcting pretentious writing, see page 139 and pages 166–169.)

> To achieve the appropriate tone, be as sincere, forthright, and reasonable as you can. Let the tone of your essay establish a basis of mutual respect between you and your reader.

Denotation and Connotation

A word's *denotation* refers to its literal meaning, the meaning defined by the dictionary; a word's *connotation* refers to the emotional associations surrounding its meaning. For example, "home" and "residence" both may be defined as the place where one lives, but "home" carries connotations of warmth, security, and family that "residence" lacks. Similarly, "old" and "antique" have similar denotative meanings, but "antique" has the more positive connotation because it suggests something that also has value. Reporters and journalists do the same job, but the latter name somehow seems to indicate someone more sophisticated and professional. Because many words with similar denotative meanings do carry different connotations, good writers must be careful with their word choice. *Select only words whose connotations fit your purpose.* If, for example, you want to describe your grandmother in a positive way as someone who stands up for herself, you might refer to her as "assertive" or "feisty"; if you want to present her negatively, you might call her "aggressive" or "pushy."

In addition to selecting words with the appropriate connotations for your purpose, be careful to avoid offending your audience with particular connotations. For instance, if you were trying to persuade a group of politically conservative doctors to accept your stand on a national health-care program, you would not want to refer to your opposition as "right-wingers" or "reactionaries," extremist terms that have negative connotations. Remember, you want to inform and persuade your audience, not antagonize them.

You should also be alert to the use of words with emotionally charged connotations, especially in advertising and propaganda of various kinds. Car manufacturers, for example, have often used names of swift, bold, or graceful animals (Jaguar, Cougar, Impala) to sway prospective buyers; cosmetics manufacturers have taken advantage of the trend toward lighter makeup by associating such words as "nature," "natural," and "healthy glow" with their products. Consumers are now deluged with "light" beverages, "organic" food, and "green" household products, despite the vagueness of those labels. Politicians, too, are heavy users of connotation; they often drop in emotionally positive, but virtually meaningless, words and phrases such as "defender of the American Way," "friend of the common man," and "visionary" to describe themselves, while tagging their opponents with such negative, emotionally charged labels as "radical," "elitist," and "anti-family."

Intelligent readers, like intelligent voters and consumers, want more than emotion-laden words; they want facts and logical argument. Therefore, as a good writer, you should use connotation as only one of many persuasive devices to enhance your presentation of evidence; never depend solely on an emotional appeal to convince your audience that your position—or thesis—is correct.

Practicing What You've Learned

A. Some of the following underlined words are used incorrectly; some are correct. Substitute the accurate word wherever necessary.

© Canstock Images, Inc./ Index Stock Imagery

1. Vacations of <u>to</u> weeks with <u>to</u> friends are always <u>to</u> short, and although <u>you're</u> <u>to</u> tired <u>to</u> return <u>to</u> work, <u>your</u> <u>to</u> broke not <u>to.</u>

2. The professor, <u>whose</u> famous for his <u>photogenic</u> memory, graciously <u>excepted</u> a large <u>amount</u> of <u>complements.</u>

3. <u>Its</u> <u>to</u> bad you don't like <u>they're</u> brand of <u>genetic</u> paper towels since <u>their</u> giving six <u>roles</u> of it <u>to</u> you for <u>you're</u> camping trip.

4. The finances of the chicken ranch are in <u>fowl</u> shape because the hens <u>r</u> <u>lying</u> down on the job.

5. Sara June said she deserved an "A" in math, <u>irregardless</u> of her 59 average in the <u>coarse,</u> but her arguments were in <u>vein.</u>

6. Did <u>u</u> <u>chose</u> to put the pamphlet "Ridding Your Home of Pesky <u>Aunts</u>" in the domestic-relations area of the library?

continued on next page

7. Did the high school <u>principal</u> <u>loose</u> <u>you're</u> heavy <u>medal</u> CD and <u>it's</u> case <u>too</u>?

8. The new city <u>counsel</u> parade ordinance will <u>effect</u> everyone in the <u>capitol</u> city <u>except</u> members of the Lawn Chair Marching Band.

B. The following sentences contain words and phrases that interfere with the sincere, reasonable tone good writers try to create. Rewrite each sentence, replacing sentimentality, cuteness, and pretentiousness with more appropriate language.

1. The last dying rays of day were quickly ebbing in the West as if to signal the feline to begin its lonely vigil.

2. Because of seasonal unproductivity, it has been deemed an unfortunate fiscal necessity to terminate your valuable association with our store in order to meet our projected growth estimates.

3. I was desirous of acquiring knowledge about members of our lower income brackets.

4. If the bill to legalize medical marijuana is passed, we can safely assume that the whole county will soon be going to pot (heh, heh!).

5. I just love to look at those little critters with their itty-bitty mousey eyes.

C. In each of the following groups of words, identify the words with the most pleasing and the least positive (or even negative) connotations.

1. dull/drab/quiet/boring/colorless/serene

2. slender/slim/skinny/thin/slight/anorexic

3. famous/notorious/well known/infamous

4. wealthy/opulent/rich/affluent/privileged

5. teacher/instructor/educator/professor/lecturer

D. Replace the underlined words in the following sentences with words that arouse more positive feelings:

1. The <u>stench</u> from Jean's kitchen meant that dinner was ready and was about to be served.

2. My neighbor was a <u>fat spinster lady</u> known for finding <u>cheap deals</u> on the Internet.

3. The coach had <u>rigid</u> rules for all her players.

4. His <u>obsession</u> with his yard pleased the city's beautification committee.

5. The <u>slick</u> car salesman made a <u>pitch</u> to the <u>old geezer</u> who walked in the door.

continued on next page

6. Textbook writers admit to having a few <u>bizarre</u> habits.

7. Carol was a <u>mediocre</u> student.

8. His <u>odd</u> clothes made Mary think he was a <u>bum.</u>

9. The High Priest explained his tribe's <u>superstitions.</u>

10. Many of the board members were amazed to see how Algernon <u>dominated</u> the meeting.

Selecting the Best Words

In addition to selecting the correct word and appropriate tone, good writers choose words that firmly implant their ideas in the minds of their readers. The best prose not only makes cogent points but also states these points memorably. To help you select the best words to express your ideas, the following is a list of do's and don'ts covering the most common diction (word choice) problems in writing today.

Do make your words as precise as possible. Consider choosing active verbs, specific nouns, and engaging modifiers. "The big tree was hit by lightning," for example, is not as informative or interesting as "Lightning splintered the neighbors' thirty-foot oak." *Don't* use words whose meanings are unclear:

Vague Verbs

Unclear	She *got involved* in a lawsuit. [How?]
Clear	She is suing her dentist for filling the wrong tooth.
Unclear	Tom can *relate* to Jennifer. [What's the relationship?]
Clear	Tom understands Jennifer's financial problem.
Unclear	He won't *deal* with his ex-wife. [In what way?]
Clear	He refuses to speak to his ex-wife.
Unclear	Clyde *participated* in an off-Broadway play. [How?]
Clear	Clyde held the cue cards for the actors in an off-Broadway play.

Vague Nouns

Unclear	The burglar took several valuable *things* from our house.* [What items?]
Clear	The burglar took a *television*, a *cell phone*, and a *microwave oven* from our house.
Unclear	When I have my car serviced, there is always *trouble*. [What kind?]
Clear	When I have my car serviced, *the mechanics always find additional repairs and never have the car ready when it is promised.*

---

*Advice that bears repeating: banish the word "thing" from your writing. In nine out of ten cases it is a lazy substitute for some other word. Unless you mean a nameless inanimate object, replace "thing" with the specific word it represents.

Unclear	When I have *problems,* I always call my friends for advice. [What problems?]
Clear	*If my girlfriend breaks up with me, my roof needs repairing, or my dog needs surgery,* I always call my friends for advice.
Unclear	I like to have *fun* while I'm on vacation. [What sort of activities?]
Clear	I like to *eat in fancy restaurants, fly stunt kites,* and *walk along the beach* when I'm on vacation.

Vague Modifiers

Unclear	His *terrible* explanation left me *very* confused. [Why "terrible"? How confused?]
Clear	His *disorganized* explanation left me *too confused to begin the project.*
Unclear	The boxer hit the punching bag *really* hard. [How hard?]
Clear	The boxer hit the punching bag *so hard it split open.*
Unclear	*Casablanca* is a *good* movie *with something for everyone.* [Why "good" and for everyone?]
Clear	*Casablanca* is a *witty, sentimental* movie that *successfully combines an adventure story and a romance.*

To help you recognize the difference between general and specific language, consider the following series of words:

General → → → → → → → → → → → → → → → → → → → **Specific**
food→snack food→chips→potato chips→Red Hot Jalapeño Potato Chips
car→red car→red sports car→classic red Corvette→1966 red Corvette convertible
building→house→old house→big old fancy house→19th-century Victorian mansion

The preceding examples illustrate varying degrees of generality, with the words becoming more specific as they move to the right. Sometimes in your writing you will, of course, need to use general words to communicate your thought. However, most writers need practice finding specific language to substitute for bland, vague, or overly general diction that doesn't clearly present the precise picture the writer has in mind. For instance, look at the difference between these two sentences:

- My date arrived at the restaurant in an older car and then surprised us by ordering snack food.

- My date arrived at the restaurant in a rusted-out, bumperless '52 Cadillac DeVille and then surprised us by ordering a large, expensive bowl of imported cheese puffs.

Which description better conveys the start of an unusual evening? Which sentence would make you want to hear more?

Not all occasions call for specific details, to be sure. Don't add details that merely clutter if they aren't important to the idea or mood you are creating. If all your readers need to know is "I ate dinner alone and went to bed early," you don't need to write "Alone, I ate a dinner of lasagna, green salad, and ice cream before putting on my Gap cowgirl pajamas and going to sleep under my yellow comforter at nine o'clock."

Most of the time, however, writers can improve their drafts by giving their language a close look, considering places where a vigorous verb or a "showing" adjective or a specific noun might make an enormous difference to the reader. As you revise and polish your own essays, ask yourself if you can clarify and enliven your writing by replacing dull, lifeless words with engaging, vivid, specific ones. Challenge yourself to find the best words possible—it's a writing habit that produces effective, reader-pleasing results. (◆ For more help in converting vague sentences to clear, inviting prose, see page 127 in Chapter 6.)

Do make your word choices as fresh and original as possible. Instead of saying, "My hometown is very quiet," you might say, "My hometown's definition of an orgy is a light burning after midnight." In other words, if you can make your readers admire and remember your prose, you have a better chance of persuading them to accept your ideas.

Conversely, to avoid ho-hum prose, *don't* fill your sentences with clichés and platitudes—overworked phrases that cause your writing to sound lifeless and trite. Although we use clichés in everyday conversation, good writers avoid them in writing because (1) they are often vague or imprecise (just how pretty is "pretty as a picture"?) and (2) they are used so frequently that they rob your prose style of personality and uniqueness ("It was raining cats and dogs"—does that phrase help your reader "see" the particular rainstorm you're trying to describe?).

Novice writers often include trite expressions because they do not recognize them as clichés; therefore, here is a partial list (there are literally thousands more) of phrases to avoid. Instead of using a cliché, try substituting an original phrase to describe what you see or feel. Never try to disguise a cliché by putting it in quotation marks—a baboon in dark glasses and a wig is still a baboon.

crack of dawn	needle in a haystack	gentle as a lamb
a crying shame	bed of roses	blind as a bat
white as a sheet	cold as ice	strong as an ox
depths of despair	hard as nails	sober as a judge
dead of night	white as snow	didn't sleep a wink
shadow of a doubt	almighty dollar	face the music
hear a pin drop	busy as a bee	out like a light
blessed event	to make a long story short	the last straw
first and foremost	pale as a ghost	solid as a rock

It would be impossible, of course, to memorize all the clichés and trite expressions in our language, but do check your prose for recognizable, overworked phrases so that your words will not be predictable and, consequently, dull. If you aren't sure whether a phrase is a cliché, but you've heard it used frequently, your prose will probably be stronger if you substitute an original phrase for the suspected one.

Some overused words and phrases might better be called "Insta-Prose" rather than clichés. Similar to those instant "just add water and stir" food mixes on grocery shelves, Insta-Prose occurs when writers grab for the closest words within thought-reach rather than taking time to create an original phrase or image. It's easy, for example, to recognize such overused phrases as "last but not least," "easier said than done," and "when all was said and done." But Insta-Prose may pop up in essays almost without a writer's awareness. For instance, using your very first thoughts, fill in the blanks in the following sentence:

> After years of service, my old car finally _____, _____, and _____ by the side of the road.

If your immediate responses were the three words printed at the bottom of page 177, don't be surprised! Most people who have taken this simple test responded that way too, either entirely or in part. So what's the problem, you might ask. The writer describing the car wanted her readers to see *her* particular old car, not some bland image identically reproduced in her readers' minds. To show readers her car—as opposed to thousands of other old cars—she needs to substitute specific, "showing" language for the Insta-Prose.* (Retest yourself: what might she have said about this car that would allow you, the reader, to see what happened that day?)

As a writer, you also want your readers to "see" your specific idea and be engaged by your prose rather than skipping over canned-bland images. When you are drafting for ideas early in the writing process, Insta-Prose pours out—and that's to be expected because you are still discovering your thoughts. But, later, when you revise your drafts, be sensitive to predictable language in all its forms. Stamp out Insta-Prose! Cook up some fresh language to delight your reader.

Don't use trendy expressions or slang in your essays. Slang generally consists of commonly used words made up by special groups to communicate among themselves. Slang has many origins, from sports to space travel; for example, surfers gave us the expression "to wipe out" (to fail), soldiers lent "snafu" (from the first letters of "situation normal—all fouled up"), astronauts provided "A-OK" (all systems working), and boxing managers contributed "throw in the towel" (to quit).

Although slang often gives our speech color and vigor, it is unacceptable in most writing assignments for several reasons. First, slang often originates as part of a private language understood only by members of a particular professional, social, or age group. Second, slang often presents a vague picture or one that changes meanings from person to person or from context to context. Different people may hold unique definitions for a particular slang expression, and although these definitions may overlap, they may not be precisely the same. Consequently, your reader could interpret your words in one way although you intend them in another—a dilemma that might result in total miscommunication (imagine, for example, the reaction of your grandmother who hears you say, "That's sick!").

Too often, beginning writers rely on vague, popular phrases ("The party was way awesome") instead of thinking of specific words to explain specific ideas. Slang expressions frequently contain nontraditional grammar and diction that are inappropriate for college work. Moreover, slang becomes dated quickly, and almost nothing sounds as silly

---

*Some prose is so familiar that it is now a joke. The phrase "It was a dark and stormy night," the beginning of an 1830 novel by Edward George Bulwer-Lytton, has been frequently parodied (and plagiarized without shame by Snoopy in the *Peanuts* comic strip). It has also prompted a bad-writing contest sponsored since 1982 by the English Department at San José State University, in which entrants are challenged to "compose the opening sentence to the worst of all possible novels."

as yesterday's "in" expressions. (Can you seriously imagine addressing a friend as "Daddy-O" or joyfully proclaiming "twenty-three skidoo"?)

Try to write so that your prose will be as fresh and pleasing ten years from now as it is today. Don't allow slang to give your writing a tone that detracts from a serious discussion. Putting slang in quotation marks isn't the solution—omit the slang and use precise words instead.

Refrain from using texting language and Webspeak in your academic or professional writing. Millions of people worldwide are chatting daily online and through their cell phone screens, with the number of messages increasing with each technological advance. But the language often used there—with its shorthand spelling (GR8, C U 2morrow), abbreviations (BTW, IMO, IDK), pictograms (what's ^?, I <3 U), and incomplete or "imposter" words (txtspk, cuz)—is not appropriate for your college assignments or traditional business correspondence.

Texting lingo thrives because it is fast and easy to type on a palm-sized keypad and quickly reduces content in small-screen messages that may be confined to a limited number of characters (for example, Twitter's 140-character cap for "tweets"). Despite its frequent use in casual messaging, such language is too informal for many other writing situations and audiences. More importantly, some readers may not understand all the acronyms, and even commonly used abbreviations may be misinterpreted (Does LOL here mean "laughing out loud" or "lots of love"? Consider, too, that someone's failure to understand a message marked NSFW as "not suitable for work" might lead to a professional disaster.). In addition, some readers may see incomplete or misspelled words simply as errors or as indications of carelessness; other readers may wonder if a lack of proper capitalization or incorrect punctuation reveals ignorance rather than chat-style. Still others may regard such language as juvenile slang, since keyboard symbols and emoticons [:-)] are so frequently used by younger teens.

Good writers understand that standards and levels of English vary from situation to situation and that to be successful in their communications, all effective writers must both respect and respond to the needs of different kinds of readers. Keep your shorthand symbols in their appropriate informal places, not in your college and professional work. But anywhere, at any time, if there's a chance the meaning of your message might be lost, take the extra minute to write out those words!

Do select simple, direct words your readers can easily understand. Don't use pompous or pseudo-sophisticated language in place of plain speech. Wherever possible, avoid *jargon*—that is, words and phrases that are unnecessarily technical, pretentious, or abstract.

Technical jargon—terms specific to one area of study or specialization—should be omitted or clearly defined in essays directed to a general audience because such language is often inaccessible to anyone outside the writer's particular field. By now, most of us are familiar with bureaucratese, journalese, and psychobabble, in addition to gobbledygook from business, politics, advertising, and education. If, for example, you worry that "a self-actualized person such as yourself cannot transcend either your hostile environment or your passive-aggressive behavior to make a commitment to a viable lifestyle and meaningful interpersonal relationships," you are indulging in psychological or sociological jargon; if you "review existing mechanisms of consumer input, thruput, and output via the consumer communications channel module," you are speaking business jargon. Although most professions do have their own terms, you should limit your use of specialized language to writing aimed solely at your professional colleagues; always try to avoid technical jargon in prose directed at a general audience.

Today the term "jargon" also refers to prose containing an abundance of abstract, pretentious, multisyllabic words. The use of this kind of jargon often betrays a writer's attempt to sound sophisticated and intellectual; actually, it only confuses meaning and delays communication. Here, for instance, is a sample of incomprehensible jargon from a college president who obviously prefers twenty-five-cent words to simple, straightforward, nickel ones: "We will divert the force of this fiscal stress into leverage energy and pry important budgetary considerations and control out of our fiscal and administrative procedures." Or look at the thirty-eight-word definition of "exit" written by an Occupational Safety and Health Administration bureaucrat: "That portion of a means of egress which is separated from all spaces of the building or structure by construction or equipment as required in this subpart to provide a protected way of travel to the exit discharge." Such language is not only pretentious and confusing, but almost comic in its wordiness.

Legal jargon, complicating even the smallest transaction, has become so incomprehensible that some lawmakers and consumers have begun to fight back. Today in Texas, for example, any firm lending $500 or less must use a model plain-English contract or submit its contract for approval to the Office of Consumer Credit. The new, user-friendly contract replaces "Upon any such default, and at any time thereafter, Secured party may declare the entire balance of the indebtedness secured hereby, plus any other sums owed hereunder, immediately due and payable without demand or notice, less any refund due, and Secured Party shall have all the remedies of the Uniform Commercial Code" with a clear, easy-to-understand statement: "If I break any of my promises in this document, you can demand that I immediately pay all that I owe." Hooray for the gobbledygook squashers in the Lone Star State!

To avoid such verbal litter in your own writing, follow these rules:

1. Always select the plainest, most direct words you know.

   Jargon   The editor wanted to halt the proliferation of the product because she discovered an error on the page that terminates the volume.

   Revised   The editor wanted to stop publishing the book because she found an error on the last page.

2. Replace nominalizations (nouns that are made from verbs and adjectives, usually by adding endings such as *-tion, -ism, -ness,* or *-al*) with simpler verbs and nouns.

> **Jargon**   The departmental head has come to the recognition that the utilization of verbose verbalization renders informational content inaccessible.
>
> **Revised**   The head of the department recognizes that wordiness confuses meaning.

3. Avoid adding *-ize* or *-wise* to verbs and adverbs.

> **Jargon**   *Weatherwise,* it looked like a good day to *finalize* her report on wind tunnels.
>
> **Revised**   The day's clear weather would help her finish her report on wind tunnels.

4. Drop out meaningless tack-on words such as "factor," "aspect," and "situation."

> **Jargon**   The convenience *factor* of the neighborhood grocery store is one *aspect* of its success.
>
> **Revised**   The convenience of the neighborhood grocery store contributes to its success.

Remember that good writing is clear and direct, never wordy, cloudy, or ostentatious. (◆ For more hints on developing a clear style, see pages 126–133.)

Do call things by their proper names. Don't sugarcoat your terms by substituting *euphemisms*—words that sound nice or pretty applied to subjects some people find distasteful. For example, you've probably heard someone say, "she passed away" instead of "she died" or "he was under the influence of alcohol" instead of "he was drunk." Flight attendants refer to a "water landing" rather than an ocean crash. "Senior Citizens" (or, worse, the "chronologically advantaged") may receive special discounts. Often, euphemisms are used to soften names of jobs: "sanitary engineer" for garbage collector, "field representative" for salesperson, "information processor" for typist, "vehicle appearance specialist" for car washer, and so forth.

Some euphemisms are dated and now seem plain silly: in Victorian times, for example, the word "leg" was considered unmentionable in polite company, so people spoke of "piano limbs" and asked for the "first joint" of a chicken. The phrases "white meat" and "dark meat" were euphemisms some people used to avoid asking for a piece of chicken breast or thigh.

Today, euphemisms still abound. Though our generation is perhaps more direct about sex and death, many current euphemisms gloss over unpleasant or unpopular business, military, and political practices. Some stockbrokers, for example, once referred to an October market crash as "a fourth-quarter equity retreat," and General Motors didn't really shut down one of its plants—the closing was merely a "volume-related production schedule adjustment." Similarly, Chrysler didn't lay off workers; it simply "initiated a career alternative enhancement program." Nuclear power plants no longer have dumps; they have "containment facilities" with radiation "migration" rather than leaks and "inventory discrepancies" rather than thefts of plutonium. Simple products are now complex technology: clocks are "analog temporal displacement monitors," toothbrushes are "home plaque removal instruments," sinks are part of the "hygienic hand-washing media," and pencils are "portable handheld communications inscribers." Vinyl is now "vegetarian leather."

Euphemisms abound in governments and official agencies when those in charge try to hide or disguise the truth from the public. On the national level, a former budget director gave us "revenue enhancements" instead of new taxes, and a former Secretary of Health, Education, and Welfare once tried to camouflage cuts in social services by calling them "advance downward adjustments." Wiretaps once became "technical collection sources" used by "special investigators units" instead of burglars, and plain lying became on one important occasion merely "plausible deniability." Other lies or exaggerations have been "strategic misrepresentations" and convenient "reality augmentations." Interestingly enough, even Washington staff members in charge of prettying up the truth for the public have earned their own euphemistic title: "spin doctors."

In a large Southwestern city, people might have been surprised to learn that there were no potholes in the streets—only "pavement deficiencies." Garbage no longer stinks; instead, it "exceeds the odor threshold." In some jails, a difficult prisoner who once might have been sent to solitary confinement is now placed in the "meditation room" or the "adjustment center." In some hospitals, sick people do not die—they experience "negative patient care outcome"; if they died because of a doctor's mistake, they underwent a "diagnostic misadventure of a high magnitude." Incidentally, those patients who survive no longer receive greeting cards; instead, they open "social expression products." During their recovery, patients might watch the "choreographed reality" of TV wrestling, while their dogs enjoy "play activities" at a local "pet lodge."

Perhaps the military is the all-time winner of the "substitute-a-euphemism" contest. Over the years, the military has used a variety of words, such as "neutralization," "pacification," and "liberation," to mean the invasion and destruction of towns, countries, and governments. During the first Gulf War with Iraq, for example, bombs that fell on civilians were referred to as "incontinent ordnance," with the dead becoming "collateral damage." Earlier, to avoid publicizing a retreat, the military simply called for "backloading our augmentation personnel." On the less serious side, the Navy changes ocean waves into "climatic disturbances at the air-sea interface," and the Army, not to be outdone, transforms the lowly shovel into a "combat emplacement evacuator."*

Although many euphemisms seem funny and harmless, too many of them are not, because people—often those with power to shape public opinion—have intentionally designed them to obscure the reality of a particular situation or choice of action. Because euphemisms can be used unscrupulously to manipulate people, you should always avoid them in your own prose and be suspicious of them in the writing of others. As Aldous Huxley, author of *Brave New World,* noted, "An education for freedom is, among other things, an education in the proper uses of language."

In addition to weakening the credibility of one's ideas, euphemisms can make prose unnecessarily abstract, wordy, pretentious, or even silly. For a clear and natural prose style, use terms that are straightforward and simple. In other words, call a spade a spade, not "an implement for use in horticultural environments."

Avoid sexist language. Most people will agree that language helps shape thought. Consequently, writers should avoid using language that promotes any kind of exclusion or demeaning stereotypes. In particular, sexist language, by consistently identifying certain groups, jobs, or actions as male, subtly suggests that only men, rather than both

---

* ◆ For more examples of euphemisms and doublespeak, see the "To the Student" essay in the front of this text.

men and women, appear in those roles. To make your writing as inclusive and unbiased as possible, here are some simple suggestions for writing nonsexist prose:

1. Try using plural nouns to eliminate the need for the singular pronouns "he" and "she."

   Original Today's *doctor* knows *he* must carry extra malpractice insurance.
   Revision Today's *doctors* know *they* must carry extra malpractice insurance.

2. Try substituting gender-neutral occupational titles for those ending in "man" or "woman."

   Original The *fireman* and the *saleslady* watched the *policeman* arrest the former *chairman* of the Physics Department.
   Revision The *firefighter* and the *sales clerk* watched the *police officer* arrest the former *chair* of the Physics Department.

3. Don't contribute to stereotyping by assigning particular roles solely to men or women.

   Original *Mothers* concerned about the possibility of Reyes syndrome should avoid giving aspirin to their sick children.
   Revision *Parents* concerned about the possibility of Reyes syndrome should avoid giving aspirin to their sick children.

4. Try substituting such words as "people," "persons," "one," "voters," "workers," "students," and so on, for "man" or "woman."

   Original Any *man* who wants to become a corporation executive before thirty should buy this book.
   Revision *Anyone* who wants to become a corporation executive before thirty should buy this book.

5. Don't use inappropriate diminutives.

   Original In the annual office picture, the photographer asked the men to stand behind the *girls*.
   Revision In the annual office picture, the photographer asked the men to stand behind the *women*.

6. Consider avoiding words that use "man" to describe the characteristics of a group or that refer to people in general.

   Original Rebuilding the space shuttle will call for extra money and *manpower*, but such an endeavor will benefit *mankind* in the generations to come.
   Revision Rebuilding the space shuttle will call for extra money and *employees*, but such an endeavor will benefit future *generations*.

   Similarly, substitute more specific words for "man" used as a verb or as an adjective.

   Original We needed someone to *man* the booth at the fair where we were selling *man-made* opals.
   Revision We needed someone to *staff* the booth at the fair where we were selling *synthetic* opals.

7. Be consistent in your treatment of men's and women's names, marital status, professional titles, and physical appearances.

Original   Neither Herman Melville, the inspired novelist, nor *Miss* Emily Dickinson, the *spinster poetess* of Amherst, gained fame or fortune in their lifetimes.

Revision   Neither Herman Melville, the novelist, nor Emily Dickinson, the *poet,* gained fame or fortune in their lifetimes.

8. If a situation demands multiple hypothetical examples, consider including or alternating references to both genders, when appropriate.

Original   In a revision workshop, one writer may request help with *his* concluding paragraph. Another writer may want reaction to *his* essay's introduction.

Revision   In a revision workshop, one writer may request help with *his* concluding paragraph. Another writer may want reaction to *her* essay's introduction.

Revising your writing to eliminate certain kinds of gender-specific references does not mean turning clear phrases into awkward or confusing jumbles of "he/she told him/her that the car was his/hers." By following the previous suggestions, you should be able to make your prose both clear and inoffensive to all members of your audience.*

Do enliven your writing with figurative language, when appropriate. Figurative language produces pictures or images in a reader's mind, often by comparing something unfamiliar to something familiar. The two most common figurative devices are the simile and the metaphor. A *simile* is a comparison between two people, places, feelings, or things, using the word "like" or "as"; a more forceful comparison, omitting the word "like" or "as," is a *metaphor.* Here are two examples:

Simile   George eats his meals like a hog.
Metaphor   George is a hog at mealtime.

In both sentences, George, whose eating habits are unfamiliar to the reader, is likened to a hog, whose sloppy manners are generally well known. By comparing George to a hog, the writer gives the reader a clear picture of George at the table. Figurative language not only can help you present your ideas in clear, concrete, economical ways but also can make your prose more memorable—especially if the image or picture you present is a fresh, arresting one. Here are some examples of striking images designed to catch the reader's attention and to clarify the writer's point:

- An hour away from him felt like a month in the country.
- The atmosphere of the meeting room was as tense as a World Series game tied in the ninth inning.
- The woman's earrings were as big as butter plates.
- The angry accusation flew like a spear: once thrown, it could not be retrieved and it cut deeply.

---

*Some writers now use "s/he" to promote gender inclusivity in their informal prose. Be aware, however, that this usage is nontraditional and not accepted universally. Always check with your instructors, or the publication for which you are writing, for the appropriate and preferred style.

- Out of the night came the convoy of brown trucks, modern-day buffalo thundering single file across the prairie, eyes on fire.
- Behind her broad polished desk, Matilda was a queen bee with a swarm of office drones buzzing at her door.
- The factory squatted on the bank of the river like a huge black toad.

Sometimes, in appropriate writing situations, exaggerated similes and metaphors may be used humorously to underscore a particular point: "I felt so stupid that day. I'm sure my colleagues thought my brain was so small that if they placed it on the head of a pin, it would roll around like a marble on a six-lane highway."

Figurative language can spice up your prose, but like any spice, it can be misused, thus spoiling your soup. Therefore, don't overuse figurative language; not every point needs a metaphor or simile for clarity or emphasis. Too many images are confusing. Moreover, don't use stale images. (Clichés—discussed on pages 164–165—are often tired metaphors or similes: "snake in the grass," "hot as fire," "quiet as a mouse," etc.) If you can't catch your readers' attention with a fresh picture, don't bore them with a stale one.

Advertising often uses figurative language to sell products. What is the metaphor in this ad?

Business is a series of battles.
We make the chariots.

//UNITED

A STAR ALLIANCE MEMBER

It's time to fly.

Finally, don't mix images—this too often results in a confusing or unintentionally comic scene. For example, a former mayor of Denver once responded to a question about city fiscal requirements this way: "I think the proper approach is to go through this Garden of Gethsemane that we're in now, give birth to a budget that will come out of it, and then start putting our ducks in order with an appeal and the backup we would need to get something done at the state level." Or consider the defense attorney who didn't particularly like his client's plea-bargaining deal but nevertheless announced, "Given the attitude of the normal jury on this type of crime, I feel we would be paddling up a stream behind the eight ball." Perhaps a newspaper columnist wins the prize for confusion with this triple-decker: "The Assemblymen also were miffed at their Senate counterparts because they have refused to bite the bullet that now seems to have grown to the size of a millstone to the Assemblymen whose necks are on the line."

Think of figurative language as you might regard a fine cologne on the person sitting next to you in a crowded theater: just enough is engaging; too much is overpowering.

(◆ For more discussion of similes, metaphors, and other figurative language, see pages 326–327 in Chapter 11.)

Do vary your word choice so that your prose does not sound wordy, repetitious, or monotonous. Consider the following sentence:

> According to child psychologists, depriving a child of sensory stimulation in the earliest stages of childhood can cause the child brain damage.

Reworded, the following sentence eliminates the tiresome, unnecessary repetition of the word "child":

> According to child psychologists, depriving infants of sensory stimulation can cause brain damage.

By omitting or changing repeated words, you can add variety and crispness to your prose. Of course, don't ever change your words or sentence structure to achieve variety at the expense of clarity or precision; at all times, your goal is to make your prose clear to your readers.

Do remember that wordiness is a major problem for all writers, even the professionals. State your thoughts directly and specifically in as few words as necessary to communicate your meaning clearly. ◆ In addition to the advice given here on avoiding wordy or vague jargon, euphemisms, and clichés, you might also review the sections on simplicity and conciseness in Chapter 6.

THE MOST IMPORTANT KEY TO EFFECTIVE WORD CHOICE IS REVISION. As you write your first draft, don't fret about selecting the best words to communicate your ideas; in later drafts, one of your main tasks will be replacing the inaccurate or imprecise words with better ones. (Dorothy Parker, famous for her witty essays, once lamented, "I can't write five words but that I change seven.") All good writers rewrite, so revise your prose to make each word count.

© Canstock Images, Inc./
Index Stock Imagery

Practicing What You've Learned

A. Underline the vague nouns, verbs, and modifiers in the sentences that follow. Then rewrite each sentence so that it says something clear and specific.

   1. The experiment had very bad results.

   2. The speaker came up with some odd items.

   3. The house was big, old, and ugly.

   4. The man was a nice guy with a good personality.

   5. I felt that the whole ordeal was quite an experience.

   6. The machine we got was missing a few things.

   7. The woman was really something special.

   8. The classroom material wasn't interesting.

   9. The child made a lot of very loud noises.

   10. The cost of the unusual meal was amazing.

B. Rewrite the following sentences, eliminating all clichés, slang, mixed metaphors, and euphemisms; change any texting or sexist language you find.

   1. Anyone who wants to be elected the next congressman from our state must clearly recognize that our tourist industry is sitting on a launching pad, ready to flex its muscles and become a dynamo.

   2. BTW, I thought the whole deal was sweet, but then my sister got a special delivery from the duh truck and 4gt 2 pick me ^ . G2G, thx, Dude!

   3. After all is said and done, agricultural producers may be forced to relocate to urban environments, settling in substandard housing with other members of the disadvantaged class until the day they expire.

   4. Both Ron Howard and Shirley Temple were popular child actors; careerwise, Howard moved on to directing movies, but Shirley left show biz to serve Old Glory by becoming ambassadoress to Ghana and Czechoslovakia.

   5. Each commander realizes that he might one day be called upon to use the peacekeepers to depopulate an emerging nation in a lethal intervention.

   6. Although Jack once regarded her as sweet and innocent, he knew then and there that Jill was really a wolf in sheep's clothing with a heart of stone.

continued on next page

7. The city councilman was stewing in his juices when he learned that his goals-impaired son had been arrested for fooling around with the funds for the fiscal underachievers' home.

8. NVR rite lik ds n yr skool r prowork. Srsly. Tlk 2 u l8r.

9. The U.S. Embassy in Budapest once warned its employees: "It must be assumed that available casual indigenous female companions work for or cooperate with the Hungarian government security establishment."

10. At a press conference on the war in Iraq, former Defense Secretary Donald Rumsfeld announced the following: "Reports that say something hasn't happened are always interesting to me, because as we know, there are known knowns, there are things we know we know. We also know there are known unknowns; that is to say we know there are some things we do not know. But there are also unknown unknowns— the ones we don't know we don't know."*

Assignment

A. Sometimes something as simple as changing your bland verbs to action words can make an enormous difference in creating prose that is interesting, lively, and emphatic. Practice such revision by first finding a sports section of a newspaper and circling any verbs in the headlines that you think help readers "see" the events. (Do teams *trounce* their opponents? *Charge, sneak,* or *sail* to victory? Does a contender *crumble* or *smash* a record?) Next, look at a current draft you are polishing, and take a second look at any sentences that might profit from replacing a "blah" verb (like "got" or "make") with a stronger one.

B. *Collaborative Activity:* In a group with three classmates, fill in the blanks with colorful words. You may make the paragraph as exciting or humorous as you wish, but avoid clichés and Insta-Prose (those predictable phrases that first come to mind). Work together to make your responses as original and creative as possible. When your story is finished, select a member of the group to read your paragraph to the class as whole. After all the groups have read their versions of the story, which images or details remain the most memorable, and why?

continued on next page

---

*Incidentally, this comment won Rumsfeld the "Foot in Mouth" prize for the most confusing public statement of that year, awarded by Britain's Plain English Campaign, a group dedicated to ridding the language of jargon and legalese.

As midnight approached, Janet and Brad _____ toward
the _____ mansion to escape the _____
storm. Their _____ car had _____
on the road nearby. The night was _____, and Brad
_____ at the shadows with _____
and _____. As they _____ up the
_____ steps to the _____ door, the
_____ wind was filled with _____ and
_____ sounds. Janet _____ on the
door, and moments later, it opened to reveal the _____
scientist, with a face like a _____. Brad and Janet
_____ at each other and then _____
(complete this sentence and then end the paragraph and the story).

C. To continue practicing effective word choice, turn to one of the many paintings or photographs in this text. Write several sentences that vividly describe the image you see. For instance, how might you describe the scene in *The Subway* (page 252)? Or the woman's face in *Migrant Mother* (page 338)? What sensory details might be appropriate in a description of *Starry Night* (page 471)? (For a list of all artworks in this text, see the page following the Table of Contents.)

Applying What You've Learned to *Your* Writing

© Keith Brofsky/
Photodisc/Getty Images

If you have drafted a piece of writing and you are satisfied with the development and organization of your ideas, you may want to begin revising your word choice. First, read your draft for accuracy, looking up in your dictionary any words you suspect may have been used incorrectly. Then focus your attention on your draft's tone, on the "voice" your words are creating. Have you selected the right words for your purpose, subject, and audience?

If you need a word with a slightly different connotation, use your thesaurus to suggest choices (for example, is the person you're discussing best described as smart, intellectual, studious, or wise?). Next, go on a Bland Word Hunt. Try to replace colorless verbs (such as "are," "get," or "make") with active, vivid ones. Revise vague nouns ("thing") and dull adjectives ("very," "really"); if you're stuck, think of words with strong sensory appeal (sight, smell, taste, sound, touch) to enliven your prose. Last, mine-sweep for any clichés, slang, or jargon. Make each word count: each choice should clarify, not muddy, your meaning.

Chapter 7 Summary

Here is a brief restatement of what you should remember about word choice:

1. Consult a dictionary if you are in doubt about the meaning or usage of a particular word.

2. Choose words that are appropriate for your purpose and audience.

3. Choose words that are clear, specific, and fresh rather than vague, bland, or clichéd.

4. Avoid language that is sexist or trendy or that tries to disguise meaning with jargon or euphemisms.

5. Work for prose that is concise rather than wordy, precise rather than fuzzy.

Answer for page 165:

Most people respond with "coughed, sputtered, and died."

The Reading–Writing Connection

It's hardly surprising that good readers often become good writers themselves. Good readers note effectiveness in the writing of others and use these observations to help clarify their own ideas and rhetorical choices about organization, development, and style. Analogies abound in every skill: singers listen to vocalists they admire, tennis players watch championship matches, actors evaluate their colleagues' award-winning performances, medical students observe famous surgeons, all with an eye to improving their own craft. Therefore, to help you become a better writer, your instructor may ask you to study some of the professional essays included in other sections of this text. Learning to read these essays analytically will help when you face your own writing decisions. To sharpen your reading skills, follow the steps suggested in this chapter. After practicing these steps several times, you should discover that the process is becoming a natural part of your reading experience.

How Can Reading Well Help Me Become a Better Writer?

Close reading of the professional essays in this text should help you become a better writer in several ways. First, understanding the opinions expressed in these essays may spark interesting ideas for your own essays; second, discovering the various ways other writers have organized and explained their material should give you some new ideas about selecting your own strategies and supporting evidence. Familiarizing yourself with the effective stylistic devices and diction of other writers may also encourage you to use language in ways you've never tried before.

Perhaps most importantly, analyzing the prose of others should make you more aware of the writing process itself. Each writer represented in this text faced a series of decisions regarding choice of ideas, organization, development of details, and style, just as you do when you write. By asking questions (Why did the writer begin the essay this way? Why compare this event to that one? Why use a personal example in that paragraph?), you will begin to see how the writer put the essay together— and that knowledge will help you plan and shape your own essay. Looking carefully at the rhetorical choices of other writers should also help you revise your prose because it promotes the habit of asking yourself questions that con-

Michael Newman/PhotoEdit

sider the reader's point of view (Does the point in paragraph 3 need more evidence to convince my reader? Will the reader be confused if I don't add a smoother transition from paragraph 4 to 5? Does the conclusion fall flat?).

In other words, the skills you practice as an analytical reader are those you'll use as a good writer.

How Can I Become an Analytical Reader?

Becoming an analytical reader may, at first, demand more time—and involvement— than you have previously devoted to a reading assignment. Analytical reading requires more than allowing your eyes to pass over the words on the page; it's not like channel surfing through late-night TV shows, stopping here or there as interest strikes. Analytical reading asks you not only to apply your critical thinking skills to understanding the writer's ideas, but also to consider *how* those ideas were presented, *why* the writer presented them that way, and whether that presentation was *effective*. To gain the most benefits from the reading–writing connection, plan on two readings of any assigned essay, some note-taking, and some marking of the text (called *annotating*). This procedure may seem challenging at first, but the payback to you as both reader and writer will be well worth the extra minutes.

Steps to Reading Well

1. Before you begin the essay itself, note the *title* of the selection. Does it draw you into the essay? Does it suggest a particular tone or image?

2. Note any *publication information* and *biographical data* about the author of the selection you are about to read. In this textbook, such information may be found in a paragraph that precedes each professional essay. Consider: Does the author seem qualified to write about this subject? Where and when was the essay

originally published, and for what audience? Is the subject matter still timely, or is it now dated? Is there any other helpful introductory material? For example, many of the professional essays in Part Two of this book are accompanied by *pre-reading questions* designed to focus your connection to the essay's subject matter (and perhaps even suggest a topic for an essay of your own).

3. You're now ready to begin your first reading of the essay. Some readers like to read through the essay without stopping; others feel comfortable at this point underlining a few main ideas or making checks in the margins. You may also have to make a dictionary stop if words you don't know appear in key places in the essay. Many times you can figure out definitions from context—that is, from the words and ideas surrounding the unknown word—but don't miss the point of a major part of an essay because of failure to recognize an important word, especially if that word is repeated or emphasized in some way.

   When you finish this reading, write a sentence or two summarizing your general impression of the essay's content or ideas. Consider the author's *purpose:* what do you think the writer was trying to do? Overall, how well did he or she succeed? (A typical response might be "argued for tuition hike—unconvincing, boring—too many confusing statistics.")

   Now prepare to take another, closer look at the essay. Make some notes in the margins or in another convenient place as you respond to the following tasks and questions. Remember that analytical reading is not a horse race: there are no trophies for finishing quickly! Fight the bad habit of galloping at breakneck speed through an essay; slow down to admire the verbal roses the writer has tried to place in your path.

4. Look at the *title* (again) and at the essay's *introductory paragraph(s)*. Did they effectively set up your expectations? Introduce the essay's topic, main idea, tone? (Would some other title or introductory "hook" have worked better?)

5. Locate the writer's main point or *thesis;* this idea may be stated plainly or it may be clearly implied. If you didn't mark this idea on your first reading, do so now by placing a "T" in the margin so you can refer to the thesis easily. (If the thesis is implied, you may wish to mark places that you think most clearly indicate the writer's stance.)

6. As you reread the essay, look for important statements that support or illustrate the thesis. (As you know, these are often found as *topic sentences* occurring near the beginning or end of the body paragraphs.) Try numbering these supporting points or ideas and jotting a key word by each one in the margin.

7. After you identify each important supporting point, ask yourself how the writer develops, explains, or argues that idea. For example, does the writer clarify or support the point by providing examples, testimony, or statistics? By comparing or contrasting one idea to another? By showing a cause-effect relationship? Some other method? A combination of methods? A writer may use one or many methods of development, but each major point in an essay should be explained clearly and logically. Make brief marginal notes to indicate how well you think the writer has succeeded ("convincing example," "generalization

without support," "questionable authority cited," "good comparison," etc.). Practice using marginal symbols, such as stars (for especially effective statements, descriptions, arguments) or question marks (for passages you think are confusing, untrue, or exaggerated). Make up your own set of symbols to help yourself remember your evaluations of the writer's ideas and techniques.

8. Look back over the essay's general *organization*. Did the writer use one of the expository, descriptive, narrative, or argumentative strategies to structure the essay? Some combination of strategies? Was this choice effective? (Always consider alternative ways: would another choice have allowed the writer to make his or her main point more emphatically? Why or why not?)

9. Does the essay flow logically and coherently? If you are having trouble with *unity* or *coherence* in your own essays, look closely at the transitional devices used in a few paragraphs; bracketing transitional words or phrases you see might show you how the writer achieved a sense of unity and flow.

10. Consider the writer's *style* and the essay's *tone*. Does the writer use figurative language in an arresting way? Specialized diction for a particular purpose? Repetition of words or phrases? Any especially effective sentence patterns? Does the writer's tone of voice come through clearly? Is the essay serious, humorous, angry, consoling, happy, sad, sarcastic, or something else? Is the tone appropriate for the purpose and audience of this essay? Writers use a variety of stylistic devices to create prose that is vivid and memorable; you might mark new uses of language you would like to try in essays of your own.

Now is also the time to look up meanings of any words you felt you could skip during your first time through the essay, especially if you sense that these words are important to the writer's tone or use of imagery.

Once you have completed these steps and added any other comments that seem important to the analysis of the essay, review your notes. Is this an effective essay? Is the essay's thesis explained or supported adequately with enough logically developed points and evidence? Is the essay organized as effectively as it could have been? What strengths and weaknesses did you find after this analytical reading? Has your original evaluation of this essay changed in any way? If so, write a new assessment, adding any other notes you want to help you remember your evaluation of this essay.

Finally, after this close reading of the essay, did you discover any new ideas, strategies, or techniques you might incorporate into *your* current piece of writing?

Sample Annotated Essay

Here is a professional essay annotated according to the steps listed on the previous pages.

By closely reading and annotating the professional essays in this text, you can improve your own writing in numerous ways. Once you have practiced analyzing essays by other writers, you may discover that you can assess your own drafts' strengths and weaknesses with more confidence.

Our Youth Should Serve*

Steven Muller

— *title forecasts thesis*

Steven Muller is President Emeritus of The Johns Hopkins University, founded *educator*
in 1876 in Baltimore, Maryland. This essay first appeared in *Newsweek* in
1978, and its ideas have been debated often. Currently, Dr. Muller is a *general audience*
trustee of the German Marshall Fund of the United States and executive
committee member of the Atlantic Council of the United States, a public
policy think-tank.

1   Too many young men and women now leave school without a
well-developed sense of purpose. If they go right to work after high
school, many are not properly prepared for careers. But if they enter
college instead, many do not really know what to study or what to do
afterward. Our society does not seem to be doing much to encourage   *Introductory*
and use the best instincts and talents of our young.   *paragraphs*
2   On the other hand, I see the growing problems of each year's   *present the*
new generation of high-school graduates. After twelve years of school-   *problem*
ing—and television—many of them want to participate actively in
society; but they face either a job with a limited future or more years
in educational institutions. Many are wonderfully idealistic: they have
talent and energy to offer, and they seek the meaning in their lives
that comes from giving of oneself to the common good. But they feel
almost rejected by a society that has too few jobs to offer them and that *Problem for youth:*
asks nothing of them except to avoid trouble. They want to be part of a *idealism, talent, and*
new solution; instead society perceives them as a problem. They seek a *energy but too few*
cause; but their elders preach only self-advancement. They need expe- *jobs and too little*
rience on which to base choice; yet society seems to put a premium on *experience*
the earliest possible choice, based inescapably on the least experience. *Problem for society:*
3   On the other hand, I see an American society sadly in need of *social services are*
social services that we can afford less and less at prevailing costs of *needed but labor*
labor. Some tasks are necessary but constitute no career; they should *costs are high*
be carried out, but not as anyone's lifetime occupation. Our democracy
profoundly needs public spirit, but the economy of our labor system
primarily encourages self-interest. The Federal government spends   *✱ Thesis: Youth*
billions on opportunity grants for post-secondary education, but some   *should volunteer to*
of us wonder about money given on the basis only of need. We ask the   *serve America's pub-*
young to volunteer for national defense, but not for the improvement   *lic service needs*
of our society. As public spirit and public services decline, so does the
quality of life. So I ask myself why cannot we put it all together and ask   *¶ clarifies proposal*
our young people to volunteer in peacetime to serve America.   *by contrast :*
4   I recognize that at first mention, universal national youth service   *not like military,*
may sound too much like compulsory military service or the Hitler   *not political,*
Youth or the Komsomol. I do not believe it has to be like that at all. It   *not required*
need not require uniforms or camps, nor a vast new Federal bureau-   *(Komsomol: youth*
   section of the

* "Our Youth Should Serve" by Steven Muller as appeared in NEWSWEEK, July
10, 1978. Reprinted by permission of the author.

   Soviet Communist
   Party)

cracy, nor vast new public expenditures. And it should certainly <u>not</u> <u>be compulsory</u>.

5   A voluntary program of universal national youth service does of course require compelling <u>incentives</u>. Two could be provided. Guaranteed <u>job training</u> would be one. Substantial <u>Federal assistance</u> toward <u>post-secondary education</u> would be the other. This would mean that today's complex measures of Federal aid to students would be ended, and that there would also be no need for tuition tax credits for post-secondary education. Instead, prospective <u>students would</u> <u>*earn* their assistance</u> for post-secondary education by volunteering for national service, and only those who earned assistance would receive it. Present Federal expenditures for the assistance of students in post-secondary education would be converted into a <u>simple grant</u> <u>program</u>, modeled on the post–World War II GI Bill of Rights.

1. Incentives
—job training
—Federal money for
  college

Comparison: education
grants like those given to
returning WWII soldiers

6   But what, you say, would <u>huge numbers of high-school gradu-</u> <u>ates do as volunteers in national service?</u> They could be interns in public agencies, local, state, and national. They could staff day-care programs, neighborhood health centers, centers to counsel and work with children; help to maintain public facilities, including highways, railbeds, waterways and airports; engage in neighborhood-renewal projects, both physical and social. Some would elect military service, others the Peace Corps. Except for the latter two alternatives and others like them, they could <u>live anywhere</u> they pleased. They would not wear uniforms. They would be employed and supervised by people already employed locally in public-agency careers.

2. Kinds of jobs

examples

7   Volunteers would be <u>paid only a subsistence wage</u>, because they would receive the benefits of job training (not necessarily confined to one task) as well as assistance toward post-secondary education if they were so motivated and qualified. If cheap mass <u>housing</u> for some groups of volunteers were needed, supervised participants in the program could rebuild decayed dwellings in metropolitan areas. . . .

3. Support costs
—wages
—housing

problem?

8   The <u>direct benefits</u> of such a universal national-youth-service pro- gram would be significant. Every young man and woman would face a <u>meaningful role in society</u> after high school. Everyone would receive <u>job training</u>, and the right to <u>earn assistance</u> toward post-secondary education. Those going on to post-secondary education would have their education interrupted by a constructive <u>work experience.</u> There is <u>evidence</u> that they would thereby <u>become more highly motivated</u> and successful students, particularly if their work experience related closely to subsequent vocational interests. Many participants might locate careers by means of their national-service assignments.

4. Direct benefits for
youth:
—meaningful role in
society
—job training
—money for education
—work experience
—success in school
—career direction

such as?

9   No union jobs need be lost, because skilled workers would be needed to give job training. Many <u>public services would be per-</u> formed by cheap labor, but there would be no youth army. And the intangible indirect benefits would be the greatest of all. Young people could regard themselves as more <u>useful and needed</u>. They could

addresses possible
criticism

serve this country for a two-year period as volunteers, and earn job training and/or assistance toward post-secondary education. There is more self-esteem and motivation in earned than in unearned benefits. Universal national youth service may be no panacea. But in my opinion the idea merits serious and imaginative consideration.

First impression: Muller proposes a volunteer youth corps to provide some public services. Many benefits for both country and young people.

Notes: Muller uses comparisons, contrasts, and examples to explain the proposed youth corps, and he clearly shows the benefits (training, grants, self-esteem). His arguments might be even more effective if he had added some specific examples and testimony from participants in similar kinds of service programs, such as AmeriCorps?

Personal response: Although the low wages might be a problem for many people, I like this program. It might have helped me decide on a career path sooner and definitely would help with tuition now.

Conclusion summarizes advantages, emphasizes the benefit of earning self-esteem, and calls for consideration of this proposal

(panacea: cure for all ills)

Practicing What You've Learned

Select one of the professional essays reprinted in this text, and annotate it according to the steps described in this chapter. Note at least one strength in the essay that you would like to incorporate into your own writing.

Assignment

Select one of the professional essays in this text to read analytically and annotate. Then write a one-page explanation of the essay's major strengths (or weaknesses), showing how the writer's rhetorical choices affected you, the reader.

Writing a Summary

Frequently, writing teachers will ask students to read an essay and briefly summarize it. A *summary* is an objective, condensed version of a reading selection, containing the author's main ideas. Although summaries are always more concise than the original texts, the length of a particular summary often depends on the length and complexity of the original reading and the purpose of the summary.

Learning to summarize reading material is a valuable skill, useful in many classes and in professional work. In one of your college classes, for example, your instructor might ask you to summarize an article pertinent to an upcoming lecture or class discussion, thus ensuring that you have thoroughly understood the information; at other times, you may need to summarize material for your own research. On a job, you might want to share a summary of an important report with colleagues, or you might be asked to present a summary of project results to your boss.

Because summarizing is such a useful skill, here are a few guidelines:

1. Read the selection carefully, as many times as it takes for you to understand and identify the author's thesis and main ideas. You might underline or take notes on the key ideas as you read, using the suggestions in the previous pages of this chapter to help you.

2. When you begin to draft your summary, always include the author's name and the title of the original text in your first sentence. Many times it's important to include the source of the work and its publication date, too.

3. Using your own words, present the author's thesis and other main ideas in a few concise sentences. Do not merely copy sentences directly from the original text. Use your own words to convey the main ideas as clearly and concisely as possible.

4. Omit all references to the supporting examples and details in the selection, unless you have been instructed to include these.

5. If, for clarity or emphasis, you do need to include an exact word or phrase from the original text, be certain to enclose the words in quotation marks.

6. Do not give your own opinion or interpretation of the material you are summarizing. Your goal is an objective, accurate, condensed overview of the selection that does not reveal your attitude toward the ideas presented.

To illustrate the preceding guidelines, here is a brief summary of the essay that appears on pages 182–184 of this chapter.

> In the *Newsweek* essay "Our Youth Should Serve," Steven Muller proposes a voluntary youth corps that would address America's need for social services and benefit our nation's youth. Muller, a former university president, believes the talents of too many bright, idealistic, but inexperienced high school graduates are wasted because the students must choose too soon between a low-paying job or more education with an undefined goal. Muller argues that a voluntary, nonpartisan civilian youth corps would provide cheap labor for short-term public service projects while offering young people job training, work experience, assistance toward post-secondary education, and a sense of self-esteem.

Note that the writer of the summary did not offer her opinion of Muller's proposal, but, instead, objectively presented the essay's main ideas.

◆ For additional discussion clarifying the difference between *summary* and *paraphrase*, see page 390 in Chapter 14. ◆ For suggestions on writing the assignment known as the "summary-and-response essay," see pages 449–451 in Chapter 15; this section also contains a sample student paper written in response to Steven Muller's essay "Our Youth Should Serve."

Practicing What You've Learned

Read one of the professional essays in this textbook, and annotate it according to the steps outlined earlier in this chapter. After you are sure you clearly understand the author's thesis and main ideas, write a one-paragraph summary of the essay. Use your own words to convey the essay's main ideas, but remember to remain objective in your summary.

© Canstock Images, Inc./ Index Stock Imagery

Benefiting from Class Discussions

If you have been practicing the steps for close reading of essays, you are on your way to becoming a better writer. By analyzing the rhetorical choices of other writers, you are gathering new ideas and techniques as well as improving your ability to look thoughtfully at your own drafts. To continue this progress, your composition instructor may devote class time to discussing sample professional or student essays that appear in this text.

Active participation in these discussions will contribute to your growth as a writer as you share ideas about effective prose with your classmates. To benefit from such discussions, consider these suggestions for improving your classroom skills:

Try to arrive a few minutes before class begins so that you can look over the reading and your marginal notes (and any other homework assigned to accompany the essay, such as questions or a summary).* Remind yourself that it is time to become an "active listener," so if sitting by friends or near a window is a distraction, move to another seat. Sitting up front is encouraged not only because you can hear your instructor better, but also because he or she can see and hear you more clearly if you have questions. (Be sure you have turned off your cell phone, media player, or any other electronic device, and remember that gum popping, pencil tapping, pen clicking, and knuckle cracking may lead to bad-karma thoughts from nearby students who are also trying to listen without distraction.)

During the class period, your teacher may ask for responses to questions that follow selected essays in this text or he or she may pose new questions. If you've prepared by closely reading and annotating the assigned essay as outlined on pages 179–181, you should be able to join these discussions. Listen carefully to your classmates' opinions; offer your own insights and be willing to voice agreement or polite disagreement. If participating in class makes you nervous, prepare one or two comments out of class in such clear detail that speaking about them will be easier for you, and then volunteer when those topics arise in the discussion. Don't hesitate to ask questions or request additional explanations; remember that if you don't understand something, it's a good bet others in the class are puzzled too.

As discussion of a sample essay unfolds, practice thinking critically on two levels. First, think of the essay as a draft in which the writer made certain choices to communicate meaning, just as you do in your essays. Trading ideas with your classmates may help you

---

* ◆ If you're having a difficult time remembering details in the essays you've been assigned to read, try the split-page journal technique, described on page 27.

see why the writer chose as he or she did—and whether those decisions work effectively. As you gain a clear understanding of the strengths and weaknesses in the sample essay, move to the second level by considering the choices you are making in your own writing. For example, if you struggle with conclusions to your essays, listen attentively to the discussion of the writer's choice and then consider whether this kind of ending might work in your essay. If a writer has failed to provide enough examples or details to illustrate a particular point, think about a paragraph in your current rough draft. Do you now see a similar problem in need of revision? In other words, as you and your classmates analyze essays in class, *actively make the essential connection between the readings and your own work.*

To remember important points in any class discussion, sharpen your note-taking skills. If you use a paper notebook for this course, you may find it helpful to leave a wide margin on the left side of each page, giving yourself space to write key words, questions, or ideas for your own writing. Start each day's notes on a new page with the day's date to help you locate material later. Acquire the habit of stapling or taping handouts to blank

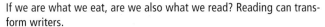

If we are what we eat, are we also what we read? Reading can transform writers.

Erich Lessing/Art Resource, NY

The Librarian, 1566, by Guiseppe Arcimboldo

pages that immediately follow notes from a particular class period (handouts stuck in your textbook or in your backpack are easily lost). As you take notes, pay special attention to any words your teacher considers significant enough to repeat in learning aids such as handouts, classroom or electronic boards, or slide presentations. Be sensitive to the verbal cues your instructor uses to emphasize essential material (words such as "key terms," "main reasons," and "central idea," as well as repetition or even a slightly louder tone of voice).

Because class discussion often moves quickly, you'll need to develop a shorthand method of note-taking. Some students write out an important term the first time (development) and then abbreviate it thereafter (dev). You can devise your own system of symbols, but included here are some abbreviations common to note-taking you may find handy. Most of these abbreviations are for notes only, although some (such as *e.g., i.e., cf.,* and *ca.*) may be used in college and professional writing; consult your instructor or the appropriate style manual if you are in doubt.

b/c = because	→ = causes, leads to, produces
b/4 = before	cf. = compare
w/ = with	↑ = increases, higher than
w/o = without	↓ = decreases, lower than
w/i = within	esp. = especially
e.g. = for example	re = regarding
i.e. = that is	ca. = approximately (use with dates or figures)
& = and	∴ = therefore
@ = at	≠ = not equal to, not the same, differs from
# = number	N.B. = "nota bene," Latin for "note well"

Later, after class, you may want to underline, star, or highlight important material. Fill in any gaps and rewrite any illegible words now before you forget what you meant. Make some notes about applying the ideas and techniques discussed in class to your own writing. Reread these notes before you begin drafting or revising your essay.

Here's the last, and possibly most important, piece of advice for every student of writing: *attend every class session!* There is a logical progression in all composition courses; each day's lesson reemphasizes and builds on the previous one. By conscientiously attending every class discussion and actively participating in your own learning process, you *will* improve your writing skills.

Practicing What You've Learned

© Canstock Images, Inc./ Index Stock Imagery

Collaborative Activity: Listen attentively and take notes on a classroom discussion of a sample essay or on another lesson your instructor has just presented. In a group of two or three classmates, compare your notes. As a group, describe the lesson's purpose and determine which points in the discussion were the most important, and why. In what ways will this class lesson help you improve your writing? What questions, if any, do you still have about this particular lesson?

Chapter 8 Summary

Here is a brief summary of what you should remember about the reading–writing connection.

1. Reading and analyzing essays can improve your writing skills.

2. Learning to recognize and evaluate the strategies and stylistic techniques of other writers will help you plan and shape your own essays.

3. Reading analytically takes time and practice but is well worth the extra effort.

4. Learning to summarize reading material accurately and objectively is an important skill, useful in school and at work.

5. Active participation in class discussions of sample essays can help you strengthen your own writing.

Part One Summary:

The Basics of the Short Essay

Here are ten suggestions to keep in mind while you are working on the rough drafts of your essay:

1. Be confident that you have something important and interesting to say.

2. Identify your particular audience and become determined to communicate effectively with them.

3. Use prewriting techniques to help you focus on one main idea that will become the thesis of your essay.

4. Organize your essay's points logically, in a persuasive and coherent order.

5. Develop each of your ideas with enough evidence and specific details.

6. Delete any irrelevant material that disrupts the smooth flow from idea to idea.

7. Compose sentences that are clear, concise, and informative; choose accurate, vivid words.

8. Improve your writing by learning to read analytically.

9. Revise your prose.

10. Revise your prose!

Part 2

Purposes, Modes, and Strategies

Communication may be divided into four types (or "modes" as they are often called): exposition, argumentation, description, and narration. Although each one will be explained in greater detail in this section of the text, the four modes may be defined briefly as follows:

Exposition

The writer intends to explain or inform.

Argumentation

The writer intends to convince or persuade.

Description

The writer intends to create in words a picture of a person, place, object, or feeling.

Narration

The writer intends to tell a story or recount an event.

Although we commonly refer to exposition, argumentation, description, and narration as the basic types of prose, in reality it is difficult to find any one mode in a pure form. In fact, almost all essays are combinations of two or more modes; it would be virtually impossible, for instance, to write a story—narration—without including description or to argue without also giving some information. Nevertheless, by determining a writer's main purpose, we can usually identify an essay or prose piece as primarily exposition, argumentation, description, or narration. In other words, an article may include a brief description of a new mousetrap, but if the writer's main intention is to explain how the trap works, then we may designate the essay as exposition. In most cases, the primary mode of any essay will be readily apparent to the reader.

In Part Two of this text, you will study each of the four modes in detail and learn some of the patterns of development, called *strategies*, that will enable you to write the kind of prose most frequently demanded in college and professional work. Mastering the most common prose patterns in their simplest forms now will help you successfully assess and organize any kind of complex writing assignment you may face in the future. Chapter 13 concludes this section by discussing the more complex essay, developed through use of multiple strategies.

Chapter 9

Exposition

· ·

Exposition refers to prose whose primary purpose is giving information. Some familiar examples of expository writing include encyclopedias, dictionaries, news magazines, and textbooks. In addition, much of your own college work may be classified as exposition: book reports, political analyses, laboratory and business reports, and most essay exams, to cite only a few of the possibilities.

Although expository writing does present information, a good expository essay is more than a collection of facts, figures, and details. First, each essay should contain a thesis statement clarifying the writer's purpose and position. Then the essay should be organized so that the body paragraphs explain and support that thesis. In an expository essay the writer says, in effect, here are the facts *as I see them*; therefore, the writer's main purpose is not only to inform readers but also to convince them that this essay explains the subject matter in the clearest, most logical way.

The Strategies of Exposition

There are a variety of ways to organize an expository essay, depending on your purpose. The most common strategies, or patterns, of organization include development by *example, process analysis, comparison and contrast, definition, classification,* and *causal analysis.* However, an essay is rarely developed completely by a single strategy (an essay developed by comparison and contrast, for instance, may also contain examples; a classification essay may contain definitions, and so forth); therefore, as in the case of the four modes, we identify the kind of expository essay by its *primary* strategy of development. To help you understand every expository strategy thoroughly before going on to the next, each is presented here separately. Each discussion section follows a similar pattern, which includes explanation of the strategy, advice on developing your essay, a list of essay topics, a topic proposal sheet, a revision checklist, sample essays (by students and by professional writers), and a progress report.

Strategy One: Development by Example

Perhaps you've heard a friend recently complain about a roommate. "Tina is an inconsiderate boor, impossible to live with," she cries. Your natural response might be to question your friend's rather broad accusation: "What makes her so terrible? What does she do that's so bad?" Your friend might then respond with specific examples of Tina's insensitivity: she never washes her dishes, she ties up the bathroom for hours, and she borrows clothes without asking. By citing several examples, your friend clarifies and supports her general criticism of Tina, thus enabling you to understand her point of view.

Examples in an essay work precisely the same way as in the preceding hypothetical story: they *support, clarify, interest,* and *persuade.*

In your writing assignments, you might want to assert that dorm food is cruel and inhuman punishment, that recycling is a profitable hobby, or that the cost of housing near campus is rising dramatically. But without some carefully chosen examples to show the truth of your statements, these remain unsupported generalities or mere opinions. Your task, then, is to provide enough specific examples to support your general statements, to make them both clear and convincing. Here is a statement offering the reader only hazy generalities:

> Our locally supported TV channel presents a variety of excellent educational shows. The shows are informative on lots of different subjects for both children and adults. The information they offer makes channel 19 well worth the public funds that support it.

Rewritten, the same paragraph explains its point clearly through the use of specific examples:

> Our locally supported TV channel presents a variety of excellent educational shows. For example, young children can learn their alphabet and numbers from *Sesame Street;* imaginative older children can be encouraged to create by watching *Kids' Writes,* a show on which four hosts read and act out stories written and sent in by youngsters from eight to fourteen. Adults may enjoy learning about antiques and collectibles from a program called *The Collector;* each week the show features an in-depth look at buying, selling, trading, and displaying collectible items, from Depression glass to teddy bears to Shaker furniture. Those folks wishing to become handy around the home can use information on repairs from plumbing to wiring on *This Old House,* while the nonmusical can learn the difference between scat singing and arias on such programs as *Jazz!* and *Opera Today.* Money-minded viewers may profit from interviews with financial leaders on *Nightly Business Report.* The information offered makes these and other educational shows on channel 19 well worth the public funds that support the station.

Although the preceding example is based on real shows, you may also use personal experiences, hypothetical situations, anecdotes, research material, facts, testimony, or any combination thereof, to explain, illustrate, or support the points in your essays.

In some cases you may find that a series of short examples fits your purpose, illustrating clearly the idea you are presenting to your reader:

In the earlier years of Hollywood, actors aspiring to become movie stars often adopted new names that they believed sounded more attractive to the public. Frances Ethel Gumm, for instance, decided to change her name to Judy Garland long before she flew over any rainbows, and Alexander Archibald Leach became Cary Grant on his way from England to America. Alexandra Cymboliak and Merle Johnson, Jr., might not have set teenage hearts throbbing in the early 1960s, but Sandra Dee and Troy Donahue certainly did. Although some names were changed to achieve a smoother flow (Frederic Austerlitz to Fred Astaire, for example), some may have also been changed to ensure a good fit on movie theater marquees as well as a place in their audience's memory: the teenage Turner girl, Julia Jean Mildred Frances, for instance, became just Lana.

Or you may decide that two or three examples explained in some detail provide the best support for your topic, rather than a series of short examples. In the paragraph that follows, the writer chose to develop two examples to illustrate her point about the unusual dog her family owned when she was a young girl in the late 1970s:

Our family dog Sparky always let us know when he wasn't getting enough attention. For instance, if he thought we were away from home too much, he'd perform his record trick. While we were out, Sparky would push an album out of the record rack and then tap the album cover in just such a way that the record would roll out. Then he would chomp the record! We'd return to find our favorite LP (somehow, always our current favorite) chewed into tiny bits of black vinyl scattered about the room. Another popular Sparky trick was the cat-sit. If the family was peacefully settled on the porch, not playing with him, Sparky would grab the family cat by the ear and drag her over to the steps, whereupon he would sit on top of her until someone paid attention to him. He never hurt the cat; he simply sat on her as one would sit on a fine cushion, with her head poking out under his tail, and a silly grin on his face that said, "See, if you'd play with me, I wouldn't get into such mischief."

You may also find that in some cases, one long, detailed example (called an *extended example*) is more useful than several shorter ones. If you were writing a paragraph urging the traffic department to install a stop sign at a particularly dangerous corner, you probably should cite numerous examples of accidents there. On the other hand, if you were praising a certain kind of local architecture, you might select one representative house and discuss it in detail. In the following paragraph, for instance, the writer might have supported his main point by citing a number of cases in which lives had been saved by seat belts; he chose instead to offer one detailed example, in the form of a personal experience:

Wearing seat belts can protect people from injury, even in serious accidents. I know because seat belts saved me and my dad two years ago when we were driving to see my grandparents who live in California. Because of the distance, we had to travel late on a rainy, foggy Saturday night. My dad was driving, but what he didn't know was that there was a car a short way behind us driven by a drunk who was following our car's taillights in order to keep himself on the road. About midnight, my dad decided to check the map to make sure we were headed in the right direction, so he signaled, pulled over to the shoulder, and began to stop. Unfortunately for us, the drunk didn't see the signal and moved his car over to the shoulder thinking that the main road must have curved slightly since our car had gone that way. As Dad slowed our car, the other car plowed into us at a speed estimated later by the police as over eighty miles an hour. The car hit us like Babe Ruth's bat hitting a slow pitch; the force of the speeding car slammed us hard into the dashboard but not through the windshield and out onto the rocky shoulder, because, lucky for us, we were wearing our seat belts. The highway patrol, who arrived quickly on the scene, testified later at the other driver's trial that without question my dad and I would have been seriously injured, if not killed, had it not been for our seat belts restraining us in the front seat.

The story of the accident illustrates the writer's claim that seat belts can save lives; without such an example, the writer's statement would be only an unsupported generalization.

In addition to making general statements specific and thus more convincing, good examples can explain and clarify unfamiliar, abstract, or difficult concepts for the reader. For instance, Newton's law of gravity might be more easily understood once it is explained through the simple, familiar example of an apple falling from a tree.

Moreover, clear examples can add vivid details to your prose that hold the reader's attention while you explain your points. A general statement decrying animal abuse, for instance, may be more effective accompanied by several examples detailing the brutal treatment of one particular laboratory's research animals.

The use of good examples is not, however, limited only to essays primarily developed by example. In reality, you will probably use examples in every essay you write. You couldn't, for instance, write an essay classifying kinds of popular teen movies without including examples to help identify your categories. Similarly, you couldn't write an essay defining the characteristics of a good teacher or comparing two schools without a generous use of specific illustration. Examples are essential in essays whose main purpose is evaluation—that is, essays that assert the advantages, benefits, or worth (or, conversely, the disadvantages or negative aspects) of a particular place, person, idea, or thing. An essay recommending your favorite restaurant, for instance, wouldn't be at all convincing without some examples of its delicious dishes.

To illustrate the importance of examples in all patterns of essay development, here are two excerpts from student essays reprinted in other parts of this textbook. The first excerpt comes from an essay classifying the Native American eras at Mesa Verde National Park (pages 264–266). In his discussion of a particular time period, the writer uses Balcony House pueblo as an example illustrating the Ancestral Puebloans' skills in building construction.

> The third period lasted until 1300 c.e. and saw the innovation of pueblos, or groups of dwellings, instead of single-family units. Nearly eight hundred dwellings show the large number of people who inhabited the complex, tunneled houses, shops, storage rooms, courtyards, and community centers whose masonry walls, often elaborately decorated, were three and four stories high. At the spacious Balcony House pueblo, for example, an adobe court lies beneath another vaulted roof; on three sides stand two-story houses with balconies that lead from one room to

the next. In back of the court is a spring, and along the front side is a low wall that kept the children from falling down the seven-hundred-foot cliff to the canyon floor below. Balcony House pueblo also contains two kivas, circular subterranean ceremonial chambers that show the importance of fellowship and religion to the people of this era.

Another student uses a personal example to help support a point in her essay that contrasts a local food co-op to a big chain grocery store (pages 232–235). By using her friend's experience as an example, the writer shows the reader how a co-op can assist local producers in the community:

> Direct selling offers two advantages for producers: they get a better price for their wares than by selling them through wholesalers, and at the same time they establish an independent reputation for their business, which can be immensely valuable to their success later on. In Fort Collins, for example, Luna tofu (bean curd) stands out as an excellent illustration of this kind of mutual support. Several years ago my friend Carol Jones began making tofu in small batches to sell to the co-op as a way to earn a part-time income as well as to contribute to the co-op. Her enterprise has now grown so well that last year her husband quit his job to go into business with her full time. She currently sells to distributors and independent stores from here to Denver; even Lane Grocer, which earlier would not consider selling her tofu even on a trial basis, is now thinking about changing its policy.

Learning to support, explain, or clarify your assertions by clear, thoughtful examples will help you develop virtually every piece of writing you are assigned, both in school and on the job. Development by example is the most widely used of all the expository strategies and by far the most important.

Developing Your Essay

An essay developed by example is one of the easiest to organize. In most cases, your first paragraph will present your thesis; each body paragraph will contain a topic sentence and as many effectively arranged examples as necessary to explain or support each major point; your last paragraph will conclude your essay in some appropriate way. Although the general organization is fairly simple, you should revise the examples in your rough draft by asking these questions:

Are all my examples relevant? Each specific example should support, clarify, or explain the general statement it illustrates; each example should provide readers with additional insight into the subject under discussion. Keep the purpose of your paragraphs in mind: don't wander off into an analysis of the causes of theft on your campus if you are only supposed to show various examples of it. Keep your audience in mind, too: which examples will provide the kinds of information that your particular readers need to understand your point?

Are my examples well chosen? To persuade your readers to accept your opinion, you should select those examples that are the strongest and most convincing. Let's say you were writing a research paper exposing a government agency's wastefulness. To illustrate your claim, you would select those cases that most obviously show gross or ridiculous expenditures rather than asking your readers to consider some unnecessary but minor expenses. And you would try to select cases that represent recent or current examples of wastefulness rather than discussing expenditures too dated to be persuasive. In other words, when you have a number of examples to choose from, evaluate them and then select the best ones to support your point.

Are there enough examples to make each point clear and persuasive? Put yourself in your reader's place: would you be convinced with three brief examples? Five? One extended example? Two? Use your own judgment, but be careful to support or explain your major points adequately. It's better to risk over-explaining than to leave your reader confused or unconvinced.

Problems to Avoid

By far, the most common weakness in essays developed by example is a lack of specific detail. Too often, novice writers present a sufficient number of relevant, well-chosen examples, but the illustrations themselves are too general, vague, or brief to be helpful. Examples should be clear, specific, and adequately detailed so that the reader receives the full persuasive impact of each one. For instance, in an essay claiming that junior high football has become too violent, don't merely say, "Too many players were hurt last year." Such a statement only hints; it lacks enough development to be fully effective. Go into more detail by giving actual examples of jammed fingers, wrenched backs, fractured legs, crushed kneecaps, and broken dreams. Present these examples in specific, vivid language; once your readers begin to "see" that field covered with blood and bruised bodies, you'll have less trouble convincing them that your point of view is accurate. (◆ For more help incorporating specific details into your paragraph development, review pages 58–62 in Chapter 3 and pages 162–165 in Chapter 7.)

The second biggest problem in example essays is the lack of coherence. The reader should never sense an interruption in the flow of thought from one example to the next in paragraphs containing multiple examples. Each body paragraph of this kind should be more than a topic sentence and a choppy list of examples. You should first arrange the examples in an order that best explains the major point presented by your topic sentence; then carefully check to make sure each example is smoothly connected in thought to the statements preceding and following it. You can avoid a listing effect by using transitional devices where necessary to ensure easy movement from example to example and from point to point. A few common transitional words often found in essays of example include "for instance," "for example," "to illustrate," "another," and "in addition." (◆ For a list of other transitional words and additional help on writing coherent paragraphs, review pages 68–73 and pages 76–77.)

Essay Topics

© Inspirestock/CORBIS

Consider one of the following eighteen general statements as a prompt to help you discover a focused essay topic of your own design, or choose one of the two more specific assignments, numbers 19 and 20. ◆ For additional ideas, turn to the "Suggestions for Writing" section following the professional essay (page 206); the quotations on pages 42–44 may also spark topics.

1. Failure is a better teacher than success.

2. First impressions are often the best/worst means of judging people.

3. Product X (e.g., cell phone, bicycle, e-reader, backpack) is the best choice in its field for college students.

4. Time spent on social networking sites interferes with/promotes good interpersonal skills.

5. The willingness to undertake adventure is a necessary part of a satisfying existence.

6. Everyone should see/flee this movie. (◆ See Chapter 17 for help with this topic.)

7. Complaining can produce unforeseen results.

8. Travel can be the best medicine.

9. Visits to the doctor/dentist can prove more traumatic than the illness.

10. Failure to keep my mouth shut (or some other bad habit) leads me into trouble.

11. Participation in (a sport, club, hobby, event) teaches valuable lessons.

12. Modern technology can produce more inconvenience than convenience.

13. A superstition or lucky charm has made me perform better in certain situations. (Or, conversely, my over-the-top fear of X [snakes, spiders, heights, flying, etc.] has affected my behavior in odd ways.)

14. Moving frequently has its advantages (or disadvantages).

15. Good deeds can backfire (or make a wonderful difference).

16. Many required courses are/are not relevant to a student's education.

17. My hometown has much/little to offer young people.

18. One important event can change the course of a life.

continued on next page

19. *Collaborative Activity:* With two classmates, brainstorm on the topic of time-management tips for college students. From your discussion, select one piece of good advice, and then choose at least two examples that most effectively show the benefit of your recommendation. Together, draft a one-page mini-essay presenting your suggestion to a group of incoming students.

20. To encourage people to use their products or services, companies often offer advertisements containing examples of satisfied customers or clients. Analyze the ad that follows plus one of your own choosing that is also developed by examples. As you look at each ad, consider: how and why are the examples used? Are the examples well chosen for the particular target audience? Are there too many or too few? Overall, what part does the use of example play in the success of the ad? (Hint: In your search for other ads using examples, you might turn to pages 310–320 in this text for some possible choices.)

JACQUELINE GOLSON,
CERVICAL CANCER

LUIS RIVERA,
BRAIN CANCER

PATTY HILL,
PANCREATIC CANCER

SANDY PIERCE,
MELANOMA

Cancer strikes indiscriminately. When it does, it's critical to choose the best team possible to help you in your battle. These people were once faced with just such decisions. They didn't ask for cancer. But they did ask lots of questions. And in doing so, they chose the nation's number-one rated cancer hospital as their ally. It's a decision they'll celebrate for the rest of their lives.

THE UNIVERSITY OF TEXAS
MD ANDERSON
CANCER CENTER
Making Cancer History®

WHEN YOU'RE READY TO FIGHT, CALL 1-800-392-1611 OR VISIT WWW.MDANDERSON.ORG.
RATED THE NUMBER-ONE CANCER HOSPITAL IN AMERICA BY *U.S.NEWS & WORLD REPORT*.

A Topic Proposal for Your Essay

Selecting the right subject matter is important to every writer. To help you clarify your ideas and strengthen your commitment to your topic, here is a proposal sheet that asks you to describe some of your preliminary ideas about your subject before you begin drafting. Although your ideas may change as you draft (they will almost certainly become more refined), thinking through your choice of topic now may help you avoid several false starts.

1. In a few words, identify the subject of your essay as you have narrowed and focused it for this assignment. Write a rough statement of your opinion or attitude toward this topic.

2. Why are you interested in this topic? Do you have a personal or professional connection to the subject? State at least one reason for your choice of topic.

3. Is this a significant topic of interest to others? Why? Who specifically might find it interesting, informative, or entertaining?

4. Describe in one or two sentences the primary effect you would like to have on your audience. After they read your essay, what do you want your audience to think, feel, or do? (In other words, what is your *purpose* in writing this essay?)

5. Writers use examples to explain and clarify their ideas. Briefly list two or three examples you might develop in your essay to support discussion of your chosen topic.

6. What difficulties, if any, might this topic present during your drafting? For example, do you know enough about this topic to illustrate it with specific rather than vague examples? Might the topic still be too broad or unfocused for this assignment? Revise your topic now or make notes for an appropriate plan of action to resolve any difficulties you foresee.

Sample Student Essay

Study the use of specific examples in the brief student essay that follows. If the writer were to revise this essay, where might he add more examples or details?

Paragraphs in the Sample Student Essays are numbered for ease of discussion; do not number your own paragraphs.

RIVER RAFTING TEACHES WORTHWHILE LESSONS

1   Sun-warmed water slaps you in the face, the blazing sun beats down on your shoulders, and canyon walls speed by as you race down rolling waves of water. No experience can equal that of river rafting. In addition to being fun and exciting, rafting has many educational advantages

Introduction: A description

Thesis

as well, especially for those involved in school-sponsored rafting trips. River trips teach students how to prevent some of the environmental destruction that concerns the park officials, and, in addition, river trips teach students to work together in a way few other experiences can.

2 The most important lesson a rafting trip teaches students is respect for the environment. When students are exposed to the outdoors, they can better learn to appreciate its beauty and feel the need to preserve it. For example, I went on a rafting trip three summers ago with the biology department at my high school. Our trip lasted seven days down the Green River through the isolated Desolation Canyon in Utah. After the first day of rafting, I found myself surrounded by steep canyon walls and saw virtually no evidence of human life. The starkly beautiful, unspoiled atmosphere soon became a major influence on us during the trip. By the second day I saw classmates, whom I had previously seen fill an entire room with candy wrappers and empty soda cans, voluntarily inspecting our campsite for trash. And when twenty-four high school students sacrifice washing their hair for the sake of a suds-less and thus healthier river, some new, better attitudes about the environment have definitely been established.

3 In addition to the respect for nature a rafting trip encourages, it also teaches the importance of group cooperation. Since school-associated trips put students in command of the raft, the students find that in order to stay in control, each member must be reliable, be able to do his or her own part, and be alert to the actions of others. These skills are quickly learned when students see the consequences of noncooperation. Usually this occurs the first day, when the left side of the raft paddles in one direction, and the right the other way, and half the crew ends up seasick from going in circles. An even better illustration is another experience I had on my river trip. Because an upcoming rapid was usually not too rough, our instructor said a few of us could jump out and swim

---

Margin annotations:

Essay map

Topic sentence one: Trip teaches respect for environment

Two brief examples illustrating respect:
1. Cleaning up trash
2. Foregoing suds in river

Topic sentence two: Trip teaches cooperation

Two examples of the need for cooperation:

1. Difficulties in paddling raft

in it. Instead of deciding as a group who should go, though, five eager swimmers bailed out. This left me, our angry instructor, and another student to steer the raft. As it turned out, the rapid was fairly rough, and we soon found ourselves heading straight for a huge hole (a hole is formed from swirling funnel-like currents and can pull a raft under). The combined effort of the three of us was not enough to get the raft completely clear of the hole, and the raft tipped up vertically on its side, spilling us into the river. Luckily, no one was hurt, and the raft did not topple over, but the near loss of our food rations for the next five days, not to mention the raft itself, was enough to make us all more willing to work as a group in the future.

2. A near accident

4　　Despite the obvious benefits rafting offers, the number of river permits issued to school groups continues to decline because of financial cutbacks. It is a shame that those in charge of these cutbacks do not realize that in addition to having fun and making discoveries about themselves, students are learning valuable lessons through rafting trips—lessons that may help preserve the rivers for future rafters.

Conclusion: Importance of lessons

Professional Essay*

So What's So Bad about Being So-So?**

Lisa Wilson Strick

Lisa Wilson Strick is a freelance writer who publishes in a variety of magazines, frequently on the subjects of family and education. She is co-author of *Learning Disabilities, A to Z: A Parent's Complete Guide to Learning Disabilities from Preschool to Adulthood* (1997). This essay first appeared in *Woman's Day* in 1984.

Pre-reading Thoughts: As a participant in your favorite sport, game, or other recreational activity, does strong competition make you a better or worse player? Why?

1　　The other afternoon I was playing the piano when my seven-year-old walked in. He stopped and listened awhile, then said: "Gee, Mom, you don't play that thing very well, do you?"

*◆ To help you read this essay analytically, review pages 179–181.
** "So What's So Bad About Being So-So?" by Lisa Wilson Strick. First appeared in WOMAN'S DAY Magazine, April 14, 1984. Copyright © 1984 by Lisa Wilson Strick. Reprinted by permission of the author.

2   No, I don't. I am a piano lesson dropout. The fine points of fingering totally escape me. I play everything at half-speed, with many errant notes. My performance would make any serious music student wince, but I don't care. I've enjoyed playing the piano badly for years.

3   I also enjoy singing badly and drawing badly. (I used to enjoy sewing badly, but I've been doing that so long that I finally got pretty good at it.) I'm not ashamed of my incompetence in these areas. I do one or two other things well and that should be enough for anybody. But it gets boring doing the same things over and over. Every now and then it's fun to try something new.

4   Unfortunately, doing things badly has gone out of style. It used to be a mark of class if a lady or a gentleman sang a little, painted a little, played the violin a little. You didn't have to be *good* at it; the point was to be fortunate enough to have the leisure time for such pursuits. But in today's competitive world we have to be "experts"—even in our hobbies. You can't tone up your body by pulling on your sneakers and slogging around the block a couple of times anymore. Why? Because you'll be laughed off the street by the "serious" runners—the ones who log twenty-plus miles a week in their headbands, sixty-dollar running suits and fancy shoes. The shoes are really a big deal. If you say you're thinking about taking up almost any sport, the first thing the aficionados will ask is what you plan to do about shoes. Leather or canvas? What type of soles? Which brand? This is not the time to mention that the gym shoes you wore in high school are still in pretty good shape. As far as sports enthusiasts are concerned, if you don't have the latest shoes you are hopelessly committed to mediocrity.

5   The runners aren't nearly so snobbish as the dance freaks, however. In case you didn't know, "going dancing" no longer means putting on a pretty dress and doing a few turns around the ballroom with your favorite man on Saturday night. "Dancing" means squeezing into tights and a leotard and leg warmers, then sweating through six hours of warm-ups and five hours of ballet and four hours of jazz classes. Every week. Never tell anyone that you "like to dance" unless this is the sort of activity you enjoy. (At least the costume isn't so costly, as dancers seem to be cultivating a riches-to-rags look lately.)

6   We used to do these things for fun or simply to relax. Now the competition you face in your hobbies is likely to be worse than anything you run into on the job. "Oh, you've taken up knitting," a friend recently said to me. "Let me show you the adorable cable-knit, popcorn-stitched cardigan with twelve tiny reindeer prancing across the yoke that I made for my daughter. I dyed the yarn myself." Now why did she have to go and do that? I was getting a kick out of watching my yellow stockinette muffler grow a couple of inches a week up till then. And all I wanted was something to keep my hands busy while I watched television anyway.

7   Have you noticed what this is doing to our children? "We don't want that dodo on our soccer team," I overheard a ten-year-old sneer the other day. "He doesn't know a goal kick from a head shot." As it happens, the boy was talking about my son, who did not—like some of his friends—start soccer instruction at age three (along with preschool diving, creative writing and Suzuki clarinet). I'm sorry, Son, I guess I blew it. In *my* day when we played softball on the corner lot, we expected to give a little instruction to the younger kids who didn't know how. It didn't

matter if they were terrible; we weren't out to slaughter the other team. Sometimes we didn't even keep score. To us, sports were just a way of having a *good time.* Of course we didn't have some of the nifty things kids have today—such as matching uniforms and professional coaches. All we had was a bunch of kids of various ages who enjoyed each other's company.

8   I don't think kids have as much fun as they used to. Competition keeps getting in the way. The daughter of a neighbor is a nervous wreck worrying about getting into the *best* gymnastics school. "I was a late starter," she told me, "and I only get to practice five or six hours a week, so my technique may not be up to their standards." The child is nine. She doesn't want to *be* a gymnast when she grows up; she wants to be a nurse. I asked what she likes to do for fun in her free time. She seemed to think it was an odd question. "Well, I don't actually *have* a lot of free time," she said. "I mean homework and gymnastics and flute lessons kind of eat it all up. I have flute lessons three times a week now, so I have a good shot at getting into the all-state orchestra."

9   Ambition, drive and the desire to excel are all admirable within limits, but I don't know where the limits are anymore. I know a woman who has always wanted to learn a foreign language. For years she has complained that she hasn't the time to study one. I've pointed out that an evening course in French or Italian would take only a couple of hours a week, but she keeps putting it off. I suspect that what she hasn't got the time for is to become completely fluent within the year—and that any lesser level of accomplishment would embarrass her. Instead she spends her evenings watching reruns on television and tidying up her closets—occupations at which no particular expertise is expected.

10   I know others who are avoiding activities they might enjoy because they lack the time or the energy to tackle them "seriously." It strikes me as so silly. We are talking about *recreation.* I have nothing against self-improvement. But when I hear a teenager muttering "practice makes perfect" as he grimly makes his four-hundred-and-twenty-seventh try at hooking the basketball into the net left-handed, I wonder if some of us aren't improving ourselves right into the loony bin.

11   I think it's time we put a stop to all this. For sanity's sake, each of us should vow to take up something new this week—and to make sure we never master it completely. Sing along with grand opera. Make peculiar-looking objects out of clay. I can tell you from experience that fallen soufflés still taste pretty good. The point is to enjoy being a beginner again; to rediscover the joy of creative fooling around. If you find it difficult, ask any two-year-old to teach you. Two-year-olds have a gift for tackling the impossible with zest; repeated failure hardly discourages them at all.

12   As for me, I'm getting a little out of shape so I'm looking into tennis. A lot of people I know enjoy it, and it doesn't look too hard. Given a couple of lessons I should be stumbling gracelessly around the court and playing badly in no time at all.

Questions on Content, Structure, and Style

1. Why does Strick begin her essay with the comment from her son and the list of activities she does badly?

2. What is Strick's thesis? Is it specifically stated or clearly implied?

3. What examples does Strick offer to illustrate her belief that we no longer take up hobbies for fun? Are there enough well-chosen examples to make her position clear?

4. What is the effect, according to Strick, of too much competition on kids? In what ways does she show this effect?

5. Does Strick use enough details in her examples to make them clear, vivid, and persuasive? Point out some of her details to support your answer.

6. What does Strick gain by using dialogue in some of her examples?

7. What solution to the problem does Strick offer? How does she clarify her suggestion?

8. Characterize the tone of Strick's essay. Is it appropriate for her purpose and for her intended audience? Why, or why not?

9. Evaluate Strick's conclusion. Does it effectively wrap up the essay?

10. Do you agree or disagree with Strick? What examples could you offer to support your position?

Vocabulary*

errant (2)   aficionados (4)   fluent (9)
incompetence (3)   mediocrity (4)   zest (11)

Suggestions for Writing

Try using Lisa Strick's essay "So What's So Bad about Being So-So?" as a stepping-stone, moving from one or more of her ideas to a subject for your own essay. For instance, you might write an essay based on your personal experience that illustrates or challenges Strick's view that competition is taking all the fun out of recreation. Or perhaps Strick's advice urging her readers to undertake new activities might lead you to an essay about your best or worst "beginner" experience. Look through Strick's essay once more to find other springboard ideas for *your* writing.

A Revision Worksheet

© Ryan McVay/
Photodisc/Getty Images

As you write your rough drafts, consult Chapter 5 for guidance through the revision process. In addition, here are a few questions to ask yourself as you revise your example essay:

1. Is the essay's thesis clear to the reader?

2. Do the topic sentences support the thesis?

3. Does each body paragraph contain examples that effectively illustrate the claim of the topic sentence rather than offering mere generalities?

*Numbers in parentheses following vocabulary words refer to paragraphs in the essay.

4. Are there enough well-chosen examples to make each point clear and convincing?

5. Is each example developed in enough specific detail? Where could more details be added? More precise language?

6. If a paragraph contains multiple examples, are they arranged in the most effective order, with a smooth transition from one to another?

7. If a paragraph contains an extended example, does the discussion flow logically and with coherence?

Collaborative Activity: After you've revised your essay extensively, exchange rough drafts with a classmate and answer these questions for each other, making specific suggestions for improvement wherever appropriate. (◆ For advice on productive participation in classroom workshops, see pages 116–120.)

Reviewing Your Progress

After you have completed your essay developed by examples, take a moment to measure your progress as a writer by responding to the following questions. Such analysis will help you to recognize growth in your writing skills and may enable you to identify areas that are still problematic.

1. What is the best feature of your essay? Why?

2. After considering your essay's supporting examples, which one do you think most effectively explains or illustrates your ideas? Why?

3. What part of your essay gave you the most trouble? How did you overcome the problem?

4. If you had more time to work on this essay, what would receive additional attention? Why?

5. What did you learn about your topic from writing this essay? About yourself as a writer?

Strategy Two: Development by Process Analysis

Process analysis identifies and explains what steps must be taken to complete an operation or procedure. There are two kinds of process analysis essays: directional and informative.

A *directional process* tells the reader how to do or make something. In simple words, it gives directions. You are more familiar with directional process than you might think. For example, when you tell friends how to find your house, you're asking them to follow a directional process. When you use a computer, you can learn how to transfer files or download attachments or any one of hundreds of other options by following step-by-step directions often found in a "Help" menu. The most widely read books in American libraries fall into the how-to-do-it (or how-to-fix-it) category: how to wire a house, how to repair a car, how to play winning poker, how to save more money, and so forth. And almost every home contains at least one cookbook full of recipes providing directions for preparing various dishes. (Even Part One of this text is, in detailed fashion, a directional process telling how to write a short essay, beginning with the selection of a topic and concluding with advice on revision.)

An *informative process* tells the reader how something is or was made or done or how something works. Informative process differs from directional process in that it is not designed primarily to tell people how to do it; instead, it describes the steps by which someone other than the reader does or makes something (or how something was made or done in the past). For example, an informative process essay might describe how scientists discovered polio vaccine, how a bill passes through Congress, how chewing gum is made, how contact lenses were invented, or how an engine propels a jet. In other words, this type of essay gives information on processes that are not intended to be—or cannot be—duplicated by the individual reader.

Developing Your Essay

Of all the expository essays, students usually agree that the process paper is the easiest to organize, mainly because its material is most often presented in a logical, chronological (time-ordered) sequence. To prepare a well-written process essay, you should remember the following advice:

Select an appropriate subject. First, make sure you know your subject thoroughly; one fuzzy step could wreck your entire process. Second, choose a process that is simple and short enough to describe in detail. In a 500-to-800-word essay, for instance, it's better to describe how to build a ship in a bottle than how to construct a life-size replica of Noah's Ark. On the other hand, don't choose a process so simpleminded, mundane, or mechanical that it insults your readers' intelligence or bores them silly ("How to Boil Water"). Be sensitive to the needs, experience, and knowledge of the audience you wish to address; an essay offering advice for purchasing a bicycle to parents buying a first bike for a child would differ in significant ways from an essay directed at a skilled adult rider.

Describe any necessary equipment and define special terms. In some process essays, you will need to indicate what equipment, ingredients, or tools are required. Such information is often provided in a paragraph following the thesis, before the process itself is described; in other cases the explanation of proper equipment is presented as the need arises in each step of the process. As the writer, you must decide which method is best for your subject. The same is true for any terms that need defining. Don't lose your reader by using terms only you, the specialist, can comprehend. Always remember that you're trying to tell people about a process they don't know or understand.

Include all the necessary steps in a logical order. Obviously, if someone wanted to know how to bake bread, you wouldn't begin with "Put the prepared dough in the oven." Start at the beginning and carefully follow through, step by step, until the process is completed. In many "how to do or make" essays the subject matter will necessitate a strict adherence to a chronological order to ensure that the proper result is achieved; think, for example, of a magic trick whose progress must be carried out precisely from A to B to C. In other essays, you may have to choose the most effective order of the information you present. In an essay offering college students a plan for creating a better diet, some of the steps might be accomplished at the same time or in a slightly different order without sabotaging the process, so you must select the best organization. What is important, in any kind of process essay, is that your readers see a logical progression of thought, not just pieces of information in a random or confusing order.

Don't omit any necessary steps or directions, no matter how insignificant or obvious they might seem to you, the expert. Without complete instructions, for example, the baker mentioned previously might end up with a gob of sticky dough rather than a crusty loaf of bread—simply because the directions didn't say to pre-heat the oven to a certain temperature.

Explain each step clearly, sufficiently, and accurately. If you've ever tried to assemble a child's toy or a piece of furniture, you probably already know how frustrating—and infuriating—it is to work from vague, inadequate directions. Save your readers from tears and tantrums by describing each step in your process as clearly as possible. Use enough specific details to distinguish one step from another. As the readers finish each step, they should know how the subject matter is supposed to look, feel, smell, taste, or sound—whatever is appropriate—at that stage of the process. You might also explain why a particular step is necessary ("Cutting back the young avocado stem is necessary to prevent a spindly plant"; "Senator Snort then had to win over the chair of the Arms Committee to be sure his bill would go to the Senate floor for a vote"). In some cases, especially in directional processes, it's helpful to give warnings ("When you begin tightrope walking, the condition of your shoes is critical; make sure the soles are not uneven or slick") or descriptions of errors and how to rectify them ("If you pass a white church, you've gone a block too far, so turn right at the church and circle back on Candle Lane"; "If the sauce appears thin, add one teaspoon more of cornstarch to thicken the gravy").

Organize your steps effectively. If you have a few big steps in your process, you might devote a paragraph to each one. On the other hand, if you have many small steps, you might organize them into several manageable units. For example, in the essay "How to Prepare Fresh Fish," the list of small steps on the left has been grouped into three larger units, each of which becomes a body paragraph:

1. scaling	I. Cleaning
2. beheading	A. scaling
3. gutting	B. beheading
4. washing	C. gutting
5. seasoning	II. Cooking
6. breading	A. washing
7. frying	B. seasoning
8. draining	C. breading
9. portioning	D. frying
10. garnishing	III. Serving
	A. draining
	B. portioning
	C. garnishing

In addition, don't forget to use enough transitional devices between steps to avoid the effect of a mechanical list. Some frequently used linking words in process essays include the following:

next	first, second, third, etc.
then	at this point
now	following
to begin	when
finally	at last
before	afterward

Vary your transitional words sufficiently so that your steps are not linked by a monotonous repetition of "and then" or "next."

Problems to Avoid

Don't forget to include a thesis. You already know, of course, that every essay needs a thesis, but the advice bears repeating here because for some reason some writers often omit the statement in their process essays. Your thesis might be (1) your reason for presenting this process—why you feel it's important or necessary for the readers to know it ("Because rescue squads often arrive too late, every adult should know how to administer CPR to accident victims") or (2) an assertion about the nature of the process itself ("Needlepoint is a simple, restful, fun hobby for both men and women"). Here are some other subjects and sample theses:

- Donating blood is not the painful process one might suspect.
- The raid on Pearl Harbor wasn't altogether unexpected.
- Returning to school as an older-than-average student isn't as difficult as it may look.
- Sponsoring a five-mile run can be a fun way for your club or student organization to raise money for local charities.
- Challenging an undeserved speeding ticket can be a time-consuming, energy-draining, but financially rewarding endeavor.
- The series of escalating demonstrations outside the White House influenced the 1920 passage of the Nineteenth Amendment, giving American women the right to vote.

Presenting a thesis and referring to it appropriately gives your essay unity and coherence, as well as ensuring against a monotonous list of steps.

Pay special attention to your conclusion. Don't allow your essay to grind to an abrupt halt after the final step. You might conclude the essay by telling the significance of the completed process or by explaining other uses it may have. Or, if it is appropriate, finish your essay with an amusing story or emphatic comment. However you conclude, leave the reader with a feeling of satisfaction, with a sense of having completed an interesting procedure. (◆ For more information on writing good conclusions, see pages 83–87.)

Essay Topics

Here are suggested topics for both directional and informative process essays. Some of the topics may be used in humorous essays, such as "How to Flunk a Test," "How to Remain a Bench Warmer," or "How to Say Nothing in Eight Hundred Words." ◆ For additional ideas, turn to the "Suggestions for Writing" sections following the professional essays (page 221 and page 224).

1. How you arrived at a major decision or solved an important problem
2. How to survive the first week of college
3. How to begin a collection or hobby or acquire a skill
4. How to buy a computer, cell phone, media player, camera, or other product
5. How a popular product or fad originated or grew
6. How to manage stress, stage fright, homesickness, or an irrational fear
7. How something in nature works or was formed
8. How you learned to drive (or mastered some other complex activity)
9. How a piece of equipment, a machine, or a product works
10. How to cure a cold, the hiccups, insomnia, or some other common ailment
11. How to improve physical fitness or a mental activity (e.g., study habits; ways to remember all those passwords)
12. How to stop smoking (or break some other bad habit)
13. How to select a car (new or used), house, apartment, roommate
14. How to earn money quickly or easily (and legally)
15. How a famous invention or discovery occurred
16. How to lodge a complaint and win
17. How to succeed or fail in a job or class (or in some other important endeavor)
18. How to build or repair a household item or create something online (e.g., blog, Web site, social network page)
19. How to plan the perfect party, holiday, birthday, or road trip
20. How a historical event occurred or an important law was passed (e.g., Rosa Parks's arrest; the 1773 Boston Tea Party; the passage of Title IX, ensuring equal athletic opportunities for female students)

Rosa Parks, whose refusal to give up her bus seat in Montgomery, Alabama, in 1955 helped to ignite the Civil Rights Movement.

A Topic Proposal for Your Essay

Selecting the right subject matter is important to every writer. To help you clarify your ideas and strengthen your commitment to your topic, here is a proposal sheet that asks you to describe some of your preliminary ideas about your subject before you begin drafting. Although your ideas may change as you write (they will almost certainly become more refined), thinking through your choice of topic now may help you avoid several false starts.

1. What process will you explain in your essay? Is it a directional or an informative process? Can you address the complexity of this process in a short essay?

2. Why did you select this topic? Are you personally or professionally interested in this process? Cite at least one reason for your choice.

3. Why do you think this topic would be of interest to others? Who might find it especially informative or enjoyable?

4. Describe in one or two sentences the ideal response from your readers. What would you like them to do or know after reading about your topic?

5. List at least three of the larger steps or stages in the process.

6. What difficulties might this topic present during your drafting? Will this topic require any additional research on your part?

Sample Student Essay

The following essay is a directional process telling readers how to run a successful garage sale. To make the instructions clear and enjoyable, the writer described seven steps and offered many specific examples, details, and warnings.

CATCHING GARAGE SALE FEVER

Introduction:
A series of
questions to
hook the reader

1   Ever need some easy money fast? To repay those incredible overdue library fines you ran up writing your last research paper? Or to raise money for that much-needed vacation to Florida you put on credit cards last Spring Break? Or maybe you feel you simply have to clear out some junk before the piles block the remaining sunlight from your windows? Whether the problem is cash flow or trash flow, you can solve it easily by holding what is fast becoming an all-American sport: the weekend garage sale. As a veteran of some half-dozen successful ventures, I can testify that garage sales are the easiest way to make quick money, with a

Thesis   minimum of physical labor and the maximum of fun.

2   Most garage sale "experts" start getting ready at least two weeks before the sale by taking inventory. Look through your closets and junk drawers to see if you actually have enough items to make a sale worthwhile. If all you have is a mass of miscellaneous small items, think about waiting or joining a friend's sale, because you do need at least a couple of larger items (furniture is always a big seller) to draw customers initially. Also, consider whether the season is appropriate for your items: sun dresses and shorts, for example, sell better in the spring and summer; coats and boots in the fall. As you collect your items, don't underestimate the "saleability" of some of your junk—the hideous purple china bulldog Aunt Clara gave you for Christmas five years ago may be perfect for someone's Ugly Mutt Collection.

Step one: Taking inventory

3   As you sort through your closets, begin thinking about the time and place of your sale. First, decide if you want a one- or two-day sale. If you opt for only one day, Saturdays are generally best because most people are free that day. Plan to start early—by 8 A.M. if possible—because the experienced buyers get up and get going so they can hit more sales that way. Unless you have nothing else to do that day, plan to end your sale by mid-afternoon; most people have run out of buying energy (or money) by 3 P.M. Deciding on the location of your sale depends, of course, on your housing situation, but you still might need to make some choices. For instance, do you want to put your items out in a driveway, a front yard, or actually in the garage (weather might affect this decision)? Or perhaps a side yard gets more passers-by? Wherever you decide, be sure that there are plenty of places for customers to park close by without blocking your neighbors' driveways.

Step two: Deciding when and where

4   Unless you live in a very small town or on a very busy street, you'll probably want to place an ad in your local newspaper or online classified service, scheduled to run a day or two before, and the day of, your sale. Your ad should tell the times and place of the sale (give brief directions

Step three: Advertising the sale

or mention landmarks if the location is hard to find) as well as a short list of some of your items. Few people will turn out for "household goods" alone; some popular items include bookcases, antiques, books, fans, jewelry, toys, baby equipment, and name-brand clothes. One other piece of advice about the ad copy: it should include the phrase "no early sales" unless you want to be awakened at 6:30 A.M., as I was one Saturday, by a bunch of semipro garage sale buyers milling restlessly around in your yard, looking like zombies out of a George Romero horror movie. In addition to your other ads, you may also wish to put up posters in places frequented by lots of people; laundromats and grocery stores often have bulletin boards for such announcements. You can also put up signs on nearby well-traveled streets, but one warning: in some towns it's illegal to post anything on utility poles or traffic signs, so be sure to check your local ordinances first.

A warning

Another warning

Step four: Pricing the merchandise

5   Tagging your items with their prices is the least fun, and it can take a day or a week depending on how many items you have and how much time each day you can devote to the project. You can buy sheets of little white stickers or use pieces of masking tape to stick on the prices, but if you want to save time, consider grouping some items and selling them all for the same price—all shirts, for example, are 50¢. Be realistic about your prices; the handcrafted rug from Greece may have been expensive and important to you, but to others, it's a worn doormat. Some experts suggest pricing your articles at about one-fourth their original value, unless you have special reasons not to (an antique or a popular collectors' item, for instance, may be more valuable now than when you bought it). Remember that you can always come down on your prices if someone is interested in a particular item.

Step five: Setting up your sale

A note on equipment

6   By the day before your sale you should have all your items clean and tagged. One of the beauties of a garage sale is that there's very little equipment to collect. You'll need tables, benches, or boards supported by

bricks to display your goods; a rope tied from side to side of your garage can double as a clothes rack. Try to spread out your merchandise rather than dumping articles in deep boxes; customers don't want to feel like they're rummaging through a trash barrel. Most important, you'll need a chair and a table to hold some sort of money box, preferably one with a lock. The afternoon before the sale, take a trip to the bank if you need to, to make sure you have enough one-dollar bills and coins to make plenty of change. The evening before the sale, set up your items on your display benches in the garage or indoors near the site of your sale so that you can quickly set things out in the morning. Get a good night's sleep so you can get up to open on time: the early bird does get the sales in this business.

7   The sale itself is, of course, the real fun. Half the enjoyment is haggling with the customers, so be prepared to joke and visit with the shoppers. Watching the different kinds of people who show up is also a kick—you can get a cross section from college students on a tight budget to harried mothers toting four kids to real eccentrics in fancy cars who will argue about the price of a 75¢ item (if you're a creative writer, don't forget to take notes for your next novel). If the action slows in the afternoon, you can resort to a half-price or two-for-one sale by posting a large sign to that effect; many shoppers can't resist a sale at a sale!

Step six: Running the sale

8   By late afternoon you should be richer and junk-free, at least to some extent. If you do have items left after the half-price sale, decide whether you want to box them up for the next sale or drop them by a charitable organization such as Goodwill (some organizations will even pick up your donations; others have convenient drop boxes). After you've taken your articles inside, don't forget to take down any signs you've posted in the neighborhood; old, withered garage sale signs fluttering in the breeze are an eyesore. Last, sit down and count your profits, so you can go out in the evening to celebrate a successful business venture.

Step seven: Closing up

Conclusion: A summary of the benefits and a humorous warning

9   The money you make is, of course, the biggest incentive for having one or two sales a year. But the combination of money, clean closets, and memories of the characters you met can be irresistible. Garage sales can rapidly get in your blood; once you hold a successful one, you're tempted to have another as soon as the junk starts to mount up. And having sales somehow leads to attending them too, as it becomes fun to see what other folks are selling at bargain prices. So be forewarned: you too can be transformed into a garage sale junkie, traveling with a now-popular car bumper sticker that proudly proclaims to the world: "Caution! I brake for garage sales"!

Professional Essays*

Because there are two kinds of process essays, informative and directional, this section presents two professional essays so that each type is illustrated.

I. The Informative Process Essay

To Bid the World Farewell**

Jessica Mitford

As an investigative reporter, Jessica Mitford wrote many articles and books, including *Kind and Unusual Punishment: The Prison Business* (1973), *A Fine Old Conflict* (1977), *Poison Penmanship* (1979), and *The American Way of Birth* (1992). This essay is from her best-selling book *The American Way of Death* (1963), which Mitford began revising before she died in 1996. *The American Way of Death Revisited* was completed by her husband Robert Trehaft and published in 1998.

Pre-reading Thoughts: Investigative reporting can reveal disturbing details. Have you ever read a journalistic investigation, or perhaps watched a documentary, that changed your mind about a product, activity, or person?

1   Embalming is indeed a most extraordinary procedure, and one must wonder at the docility of Americans who each year pay hundreds of millions of dollars for its perpetuation, blissfully ignorant of what it is all about, what is done, how it is done.

---

* ◆ To help you read this essay analytically, review pages 179–181.
** "To Bid the World Farewell" from THE AMERICAN WAY OF DEATH by Jessica Mitford. Reprinted by permission of The Estate of Jessica Mitford. Copyright © 1963, 1978 by Jessica Mitford, all rights reserved.

Not one in ten thousand has any idea of what actually takes place. Books on the subject are extremely hard to come by. They are not to be found in most libraries or bookshops.

2   In an era when huge television audiences watch surgical operations in the comfort of their living rooms, when, thanks to the animated cartoon, the geography of the digestive system has become familiar territory even to the nursery school set, and in a land where the satisfaction of curiosity about almost all matters is a national pastime, the secrecy surrounding embalming can, surely, hardly be attributed to the inherent gruesomeness of the subject. Custom in this regard has within this century suffered a complete reversal. In the early days of American embalming, when it was performed in the home of the deceased, it was almost mandatory for some relative to stay by the embalmer's side and witness the procedure. Today, family members who might wish to be in attendance would certainly be dissuaded by the funeral director. All others, except apprentices, are excluded by law from the preparation room.

3   A close look at what does actually take place may explain in large measure the undertaker's intractable reticence concerning a procedure that has become his major *raison d'être*. Is it possible he fears that public information about embalming might lead patrons to wonder if they really want this service? If the funeral men are loath to discuss the subject outside the trade, the reader may, understandably, be equally loath to go on reading at this point. For those who have the stomach for it, let us part the formaldehyde curtain. . . .

4   The body is first laid out in the undertaker's morgue—or rather, Mr. Jones is reposing in the preparation room—to be readied to bid the world farewell.

5   The preparation room in any of the better funeral establishments has the tiled and sterile look of a surgery, and indeed the embalmer-restorative artist who does his chores there is beginning to adopt the term "dermasurgeon" (appropriately corrupted by some mortician-writers as "demisurgeon") to describe his calling. His equipment, consisting of scalpels, scissors, augers, forceps, clamps, needles, pumps, tubes, bowls and basins, is crudely imitative of the surgeon's as is his technique, acquired in a nine- or twelve-month post-high-school course in an embalming school. He is supplied by an advanced chemical industry with a bewildering array of fluids, sprays, pastes, oils, powders, creams, to fix or soften tissue, shrink or distend it as needed, dry it here, restore the moisture there. There are cosmetics, waxes and paints to fill and cover features, even plaster of Paris to replace entire limbs. There are ingenious aids to prop and stabilize the cadaver: a Vari-Pose Head Rest, the Edwards Arm and Hand Positioner, the Repose Block (to support the shoulders during the embalming), and the Throop Foot Positioner, which resembles an old-fashioned stocks.

6   Mr. John H. Eckels, president of the Eckels College of Mortuary Science, thus describes the first part of the embalming procedure: "In the hands of a skilled practitioner, this work may be done in a comparatively short time and without mutilating the body other than by slight incision—so slight that it scarcely would cause serious inconvenience if made upon a living person. It is necessary to remove the blood, and doing this not only helps in the disinfecting, but removes the principal cause of disfigurement due to discoloration."

7   Another textbook discusses the all-important time element: "The earlier this is done, the better, for every hour that elapses between death and embalming will add to the problems and complications encountered. . . ." Just how soon should one get going on the embalming? The author tells us, "On the basis of such scanty information made available to this profession through its rudimentary and haphazard system of technical research, we must conclude that the best results are to be obtained if the subject is embalmed before life is completely extinct—that is, before cellular death has occurred. In the average case, this would mean within an hour after somatic death." For those who feel that there is something a little rudimentary, not to say haphazard, about this advice, a comforting thought is offered by another writer. Speaking of fears entertained in early days of premature burial, he points out, "One of the effects of embalming by chemical injection, however, has been to dispel fears of live burial." How true; once the blood is removed, chances of live burial are indeed remote.

8   To return to Mr. Jones, the blood is drained out through the veins and replaced by embalming fluid pumped in through the arteries. As noted in *The Principles and Practices of Embalming*, "every operator has a favorite injection and drainage point—a fact which becomes a handicap only if he fails or refuses to forsake his favorites when conditions demand it." Typical favorites are the carotid artery, femoral artery, jugular vein, subclavian vein. There are various choices of embalming fluid. If Flextone is used, it will produce a "mild flexible rigidity. The skin retains a velvety softness, the tissues are rubbery and pliable. Ideal for women and children." It may be blended with B. and G. Products Company's Lyf-Lyk tint, which is guaranteed to reproduce "nature's own skin texture . . . the velvety appearance of living tissue." Suntone comes in three separate tints: Suntan; Special Cosmetic Tint, a pink shade "especially indicated for young female subjects"; and Regular Cosmetic Tint, moderately pink.

9   About three to six gallons of a dyed and perfumed solution of formaldehyde, glycerin, borax, phenol, alcohol and water is soon circulating through Mr. Jones, whose mouth has been sewn together with a "needle directed upward between the upper lip and gum and brought out through the left nostril," with the corners raised slightly "for a more pleasant expression." If he should be bucktoothed, his teeth are cleaned with Bon Ami and coated with colorless nail polish. His eyes, meanwhile, are closed with flesh-tinted eye caps and eye cement.

10   The next step is to have at Mr. Jones with a thing called a trocar. This is a long, hollow needle attached to a tube. It is jabbed into the abdomen, poked around the entrails and chest cavity, the contents of which are pumped out and replaced with "cavity fluid." This done, and the hole in the abdomen sewn up, Mr. Jones' face is heavily creamed (to protect the skin from burns which may be caused by leakage of the chemicals), and he is covered with a sheet and left unmolested for a while. But not for long—there is more, much more, in store for him. He has been embalmed, but not yet restored, and the best time to start the restorative work is eight to ten hours after embalming, when the tissues have become firm and dry.

11   The object of all this attention to the corpse, it must be remembered, is to make it presentable for viewing in an attitude of healthy repose. "Our customs require the presentation of our dead in the semblance of normality . . . unmarred by the

ravages of illness, disease or mutilation," says Mr. J. Sheridan Mayer in his *Restorative Art*. This is rather a large order since few people die in the full bloom of health, unravaged by illness and unmarked by some disfigurement. The funeral industry is equal to the challenge: "In some cases the gruesome appearance of a mutilated or disease-ridden subject may be quite discouraging. The task of restoration may seem impossible and shake the confidence of the embalmer. This is the time for intestinal fortitude and determination. Once the formative work is begun and affected tissues are cleaned or removed, all doubts of success vanish. It is surprising and gratifying to discover the results which may be obtained."

12   The embalmer, having allowed an appropriate interval to elapse, returns to the attack, but now he brings into play the skill and equipment of sculptor and cosmetician. Is a hand missing? Casting one in plaster of Paris is a simple matter. "For replacement purposes, only a cast of the back of the hand is necessary; this is within the ability of the average operator and is quite adequate." If a lip or two, a nose or an ear should be missing, the embalmer has at hand a variety of restorative waxes with which to model replacements. Pores and skin texture are simulated by stippling with a little brush, and over this cosmetics are laid on. Head off? Decapitation cases are rather routinely handled. Ragged edges are trimmed, and head joined to torso with a series of splints, wires and sutures. It is a good idea to have a little something at the neck—a scarf or high collar—when time for viewing comes. Swollen mouth? Cut out tissue as needed from inside the lips. If too much is removed, the surface contour can easily be restored by padding with cotton. Swollen necks and cheeks are reduced by removing tissue through vertical incisions made down each side of the neck. "When the deceased is casketed, the pillow will hide the suture incisions . . . as an extra precaution against leakage, the suture may be painted with liquid sealer."

13   The opposite condition is more likely to present itself—that of emaciation. His hypodermic syringe now loaded with massage cream, the embalmer seeks out and fills the hollowed and sunken areas by injection. In this procedure the backs of the hands and fingers and the under-chin area should not be neglected.

14   Positioning the lips is a problem that recurrently challenges the ingenuity of the embalmer. Closed too tightly, they tend to give a stern, even disapproving expression. Ideally, embalmers feel, the lips should give the impression of being ever so slightly parted, the upper lip protruding slightly for a more youthful appearance. This takes some engineering, however, as the lips tend to drift apart. Lip drift can sometimes be remedied by pushing one or two straight pins through the inner margin of the lower lip and then inserting them between the two front teeth. If Mr. Jones happens to have no teeth, the pins can just as easily be anchored in his Armstrong Face Former and Denture Replacer. Another method to maintain lip closure is to dislocate the lower jaw, which is then held in its new position by a wire run through holes which have been drilled through the upper and lower jaws at the midline. As the French are fond of saying, *il faut souffrir pour être belle.**

15   If Mr. Jones has died of jaundice, the embalming fluid will very likely turn him green. Does this deter the embalmer? Not if he has intestinal fortitude. Masking

---

* "One must suffer to be beautiful."

pastes and cosmetics are heavily laid on, burial garments and casket interiors are color-correlated with particular care, and Jones is displayed beneath rose-colored lights. Friends will say, "How *well* he looks." Death by carbon monoxide, on the other hand, can be rather a good thing from the embalmer's viewpoint: "One advantage is the fact that this type of discoloration is an exaggerated form of a natural pink coloration." This is nice because the healthy glow is already present and needs but little attention.

16   The patching and filling completed, Mr. Jones is now shaved, washed and dressed. Cream-based cosmetic, available in pink, flesh, suntan, brunette and blond, is applied to his hands and face, his hair is shampooed and combed (and, in the case of Mrs. Jones, set), his hands manicured. For the horny-handed son of toil special care must be taken; cream should be applied to remove ingrained grime, and the nails cleaned. "If he were not in the habit of having them manicured in life, trimming and shaping is advised for better appearance—never questioned by kin."

17   Jones is now ready for casketing (this is the present participle of the verb "to casket"). In this operation his right shoulder should be depressed slightly "to turn the body a bit to the right and soften the appearance of lying flat on the back." Positioning the hands is a matter of importance, and special rubber positioning blocks may be used. The hands should be cupped slightly for a more lifelike, relaxed appearance. Proper placement of the body requires a delicate sense of balance. It should lie as high as possible in the casket, yet not so high that the lid, when lowered, will hit the nose. On the other hand, we are cautioned, placing the body too low "creates the impression that the body is in a box."

18   Jones is next wheeled into the appointed slumber room where a few last touches may be added—his favorite pipe placed in his hand or, if he was a great reader, a book propped into position. (In the case of little Master Jones a Teddy bear may be clutched.) Here he will hold open house for a few days, visiting hours 10 A.M. to 9 P.M.

Questions on Content, Structure, and Style

1. By studying the first three paragraphs, summarize both Mitford's reason for explaining the embalming process and her attitude toward undertakers who wish to keep their patrons uninformed about this procedure.

2. Does Mitford use enough specific details to help you visualize each step as it occurs? Point out examples of details that create vivid descriptions by appealing to your sense of sight, smell, or touch.

3. How does the technique of using the hypothetical "Mr. Jones" make the explanation of the process more effective? Why didn't Mitford simply refer to "the corpse" or "a body" throughout her essay?

4. What is Mitford's general attitude toward this procedure? The overall tone of the essay? Study Mitford's choice of words and then identify the tone in each of the following passages:

   • "The next step is to have at Mr. Jones with a thing called a trocar." (10)*

---

*Numbers in parentheses following quoted material and vocabulary words refer to paragraphs in the essay.

- "The embalmer, having allowed an appropriate interval to elapse, returns to the attack. . . ." (12)
- "Friends will say, 'How *well* he looks.'" (15)
- "On the other hand, we are cautioned, placing the body too low 'creates the impression that the body is in a box.'" (17)
- "Here he will hold open house for a few days, visiting hours 10 A.M. to 9 P.M." (18)

What other words and passages reveal Mitford's attitude and tone?

5. Why does Mitford repeatedly quote various undertakers and textbooks on the embalming and restorative process ("'needle directed upward between the upper lip and gum and brought out through the left nostril'")? Why is the quotation in paragraph 7 that begins "'On the basis of such scanty information made available to this profession through its rudimentary and haphazard system of technical research'" particularly effective in emphasizing Mitford's attitude toward the funeral industry?

6. What does Mitford gain by quoting euphemisms used by the funeral business, such as "dermasurgeon," "Repose Block," and "slumber room"?

7. What are the connotations of the words "poked," "jabbed," and "left unmolested" in paragraph 10? What effect is Mitford trying to produce with the series of questions (such as "Head off?") in paragraph 12?

8. Does this process flow smoothly from step to step? Identify several transitional devices connecting the paragraphs.

9. Evaluate Mitford's last sentence. Does it successfully sum up the author's attitude and conclude the essay?

10. By supplying information about the embalming process, did Mitford change your attitude toward this procedure or toward the funeral industry? Are there advantages Mitford fails to mention?

Vocabulary

docility (1)
perpetuation (1)
inherent (2)
mandatory (2)
intractable (3)
reticence (3)

raison d'être (3)
ingenious (5)
cadaver (5)
somatic (7)
rudimentary (7)
dispel (7)

pliable (8)
semblance (11)
ravages (11)
stippling (12)
emaciation (13)

Suggestions for Writing

Try using Jessica Mitford's "To Bid the World Farewell" as a stepping-stone to your own writing. Mitford's graphic details and disparaging tone upset some readers who feel funerals are important for the living. If you agree, consider writing an essay that challenges Mitford's position. Or adopt Mitford's role as an investigative reporter exposing a controversial process. For example, how is toxic waste disposed of at the student health center? Dangerous chemicals from science labs? What happens to unclaimed animals at your local shelter? Or try a more lighthearted investigation: just how do they obtain that mystery meat served in the student center cafeteria? Use Mitford's vivid essay as a guide as you present your discoveries.

II. The Directional Process Essay

Preparing for the Job Interview: Know Thyself*

Katy Piotrowski

Katy Piotrowski, M.Ed., is the owner of Career Solutions Group, through which she provides career and job-search support, and the author of five books in the *Career Cowards Guide* series. Her essay, which originally appeared in 2005 in her "On the Job" column for the Fort Collins, Colorado, *Coloradoan* newspaper, has been slightly revised for this text.

Pre-reading Thoughts: Have you ever successfully interviewed for a job or for a position in a school or community organization? What factors contributed to your effective interview?

1   "I have a job interview this afternoon!" Shawn told me. "Are you ready for it?" I asked. "I'm not sure," she confessed. So, drawing on my work as a career-search consultant, I helped her through an interview-readiness procedure, a quick, six-step process that can successfully prepare almost anyone for a job interview.

2   First, I asked, can you identify the top two or three responsibilities of the job? Shawn hesitated, so I asked her to reread the position description and tell me which parts or key words stood out most. "Evaluating the effectiveness of health-care programs" and "coordinating information exchange in the hospital," she determined. With the key responsibilities in mind, we were ready for the next step. For each of the primary responsibilities, can you describe at least three examples from your past that demonstrate your expertise in those areas? Shawn had one example ready to share, but she needed more. "Tell me about a time when you evaluated the effectiveness of health-care or coordinated information among people or agencies," I prompted her. Within minutes, she'd created a longer list of examples.

3   Moving on, I asked Shawn to think of other experiences in her professional background that would show her as an attractive candidate for this job. Shawn's responses were unfocused, so I taught her a simple three-step STAR process for answering a number of interview questions: 1) describe the **s**ituation or **t**asks, 2) talk about the **a**ctions you took, 3) finish with the **r**esults of your efforts. Try to frame your answers concisely but in a compelling way, using action verbs that show leadership, such as "designed," "coordinated," "implemented," "created," and "managed," when such words are appropriate. Shawn practiced the process, and soon her answers were much more effective.

4   In addition to questions about specific qualifications, interviewers often ask general questions designed to reveal a candidate's "fit" as an employee in their

---

business. "Tell me a little about yourself" is a common request; it may even come at the beginning of an interview when you are the most nervous, so it helps to have some prepared (though not stiffly memorized) thoughts. Shawn's response included highlights of her work history, information about her education, and a statement about why she was excited about the job opening. Variations on this line of questioning might include "As a worker in this field, what is your greatest strength? Biggest weakness?" or "How have you handled a difficult situation?" Shawn had impressive responses to these kinds of questions; she just needed to practice them several more times.

5   As well as presenting themselves to companies, interviewees also need to know something about the companies to which they are applying. Whether you are asked directly or not, it's important to be acquainted with the goals, products, and services of your prospective employer. A quick online search may lead you to a company Web page and any recent publicity. Knowing current information about your prospective employer may better help you respond to questions such as "What knowledge or skills can you bring to our company?" with specific answers that happily fit their needs.

6   Often interviewers' final question may be "Do you have any questions for us?" so the last step in your preparation process calls for thinking of at least one good response. You might ask about the ways this position fits into the larger organization or the company's future plans or ask for more details about the advertised position. You might ask them to describe the most successful employees they've ever hired for this job. (At this time, you probably do not want to negotiate salary, especially if you are an entry-level applicant.) If it seems appropriate, you may also ask how you should proceed: would they prefer for you to contact them or to wait for their response? Is there any other information you can provide that would be helpful in furthering your application for this job? (Don't forget, I reminded Shawn, at the close of your meeting, to thank the interviewers for their time.)

7   Within an hour, following these few steps, Shawn was much more prepared for her interview. Though few people can be totally relaxed during an interview, she was calmed with the knowledge that she was ready to effectively give meaningful responses to a variety of questions. And, yes, she *did* get the job.

Questions on Content, Structure, and Style

1. What process is explained in this essay? What is Piotrowski's main purpose?

2. Although Piotrowski describes her conversation with Shawn, why may this article be considered a directional process essay for its readers?

3. What are the primary steps in this process?

4. Piotrowski uses an actual job applicant, Shawn, to show how the interview-preparation process works. What benefits for the reader does this choice of organization present?

5. Consider ways in which Piotrowski explains each step of the process. How does she clarify her advice by using examples?

6. Cite some ways Piotrowski moves her reader from one step in the preparation process to the next. What transitional words or phrases help guide the reader through the steps?

7. Effective writers of process essays often offer warnings or point out what not to do. Where does Piotrowski use this technique?

8. In paragraph 3, how does Piotrowski use an *acronym* (a word formed from the first letters or parts of other words) to explain her advice?

9. Describe Piotrowski's tone or "voice" in this essay. Is it appropriate and effective? Cite some examples of her language to support your answer.

10. Evaluate Piotrowski's conclusion. How does it wrap up the essay? In particular, what is the effect of the last sentence?

Vocabulary

expertise (2)
implemented (3)
prospective (5)

Suggestions for Writing

Try using Piotrowski's essay as a stepping-stone to your own writing. Think of a job that you would like to have soon, perhaps this summer or after you finish your education. Following Piotrowski's procedure for interview preparation, write an essay showing why you are the best candidate for the position. Keep this essay for later use when you face a real interview or for help designing a résumé. (Or, if you prefer, try writing a light-hearted, tongue-in-cheek process essay that makes a serious point by humorously advising readers what *not* to do in the workplace: how not to impress your boss, how not to cooperate with your co-workers, how not to get a raise, and so on.)

A Revision Worksheet

As you write your rough drafts, consult Chapter 5 for guidance through the revision process. In addition, here are a few questions to ask yourself as you revise your process essay:

© Ryan McVay/
Photodisc/Getty Images

1. Is the essay's purpose clear to the reader?

2. Has the need for any special equipment been noted and explained adequately? Are all terms unfamiliar to the reader defined clearly?

3. Does the essay include all the steps (and warnings, if appropriate) necessary to understanding the process?

continued on next page

4. Is each step described in enough detail to make it understandable to all readers? Where could more detail be effectively added?

5. Are all the steps in the process presented in an easy-to-follow, logical order, with smooth transitions between steps or stages?

6. Are there any steps that might be combined in a paragraph describing a stage in the process?

7. Does the essay have a pleasing conclusion?

Collaborative Activity: After you've revised your essay extensively, exchange rough drafts with a classmate and answer the preceding questions for each other, making specific suggestions for improvement wherever appropriate. (◆ For advice on productive participation in classroom workshops, see pages 116–120.)

Reviewing Your Progress

After you have completed your process essay, take a moment to measure your progress as a writer by responding to the following questions. Such analysis will help you to recognize growth in your writing skills and may enable you to identify areas that are still problematic.

1. Which part of your essay is most successful? Why?

2. Select two details that contribute significantly to the clarity of your explanation. Why are these details effective?

3. What part of your essay gave you the most trouble? How did you overcome the problem?

4. If you had more time to work on this essay, what would receive additional attention? Why?

5. What did you learn about your topic from writing this essay? About yourself as a writer?

Strategy Three: Development by Comparison and Contrast

Every day you exercise the mental process of comparison and contrast. When you get up in the morning, for instance, you may contrast two choices of clothing—a short-sleeved shirt versus a long-sleeved one—and then make your decision after hearing the weather forecast. Or you may contrast and choose between Sugar-Coated Plastic Pops and Organic Millet Kernels for breakfast, between the health advantages of walking to campus and the speed afforded by your car or bicycle. Once on campus, preparing to register, you may first compare both professors and courses; similarly, you probably compared the school you attend now to others before you made your choice. In short, you frequently use the process of comparison and contrast to come to a decision or make a judgment about two or more objects, persons, ideas, or feelings.

When you write a comparison or contrast essay, your opinion about the two elements* in question becomes your thesis statement; the body of the paper then shows why you arrived at that opinion. For example, if your thesis states that Mom's Kum-On-Back Hamburger Haven is preferable to McPhony's Mystery Burger Stand, your body paragraphs might contrast the two restaurants in terms of food, service, and atmosphere, revealing the superiority of Mom's on all three counts.

Developing Your Essay

There are two principal patterns of organization for comparison or contrast essays. For most short papers you should choose one of the patterns and stick with it throughout the essay. Later, if you are assigned a longer essay, you may want to mix the patterns for variety as some professional writers do, but do so only if you can maintain clarity and logical organization.

Pattern One: Point by Point

This method of organization calls for body paragraphs that compare or contrast the two subjects first on point one, then on point two, then point three, and so on. Study the following example:

Thesis: Mom's Hamburger Haven is a better family restaurant than McPhony's because of its superior food, service, and atmosphere.

Point 1:   Food
        A. Mom's
        B. McPhony's
Point 2:   Service
        A. Mom's
        B. McPhony's
Point 3:   Atmosphere
        A. Mom's
        B. McPhony's
Conclusion

If you select this pattern of organization, you must make a smooth transition from subject "A" to subject "B" in each discussion to avoid a choppy seesaw effect. Be consistent: present the same subject first in each discussion of a major point. In the essay just outlined, for instance, Mom's is always introduced before McPhony's.

Pattern Two: The Block

This method of organization presents body paragraphs in which the writer first discusses subject "A" on points one, two, three, and so on, and then discusses subject "B" on the same points. The following model illustrates this Block Pattern:

---

*It is possible to compare or contrast more than two elements. But until you feel confident about the organizational patterns for this kind of essay, you should probably stay with the simpler format.

Thesis: Mom's Hamburger Haven is a better family restaurant than McPhony's because of its superior food, service, and atmosphere.

    A. Mom's
        1. Food
        2. Service
        3. Atmosphere

    B. McPhony's
        1. Food
        2. Service
        3. Atmosphere

Conclusion

If you use the Block Pattern, you should discuss the three points—food, service, atmosphere—in the same order for each subject. In addition, you must include in your discussion of subject "B" specific references to the points you made earlier about subject "A" (see outline). In other words, because your statements about Mom's superior food may be several pages away by the time your comments on McPhony's food appear, the readers may not remember precisely what you said. Gently, unobtrusively, remind them with a specific reference to the earlier discussion. For instance, you might begin your paragraph on McPhony's service like this: "Unlike the friendly, attentive help at Mom's, service at McPhony's features grouchy employees who wait on you as if they consider your presence an intrusion on their privacy." The discussion of atmosphere might begin, "McPhony's atmosphere is as cold, sterile, and plastic as its decor, in contrast to the warm, homey feeling that pervades Mom's." Without such connecting phrases, what should be one unified essay will look more like two distinct mini-essays, forcing readers to do your job of comparing or contrasting for themselves.

Which Pattern Should You Use?

As you prepare to compose your first draft, you might ask yourself, "Which pattern of organization should I choose—Point by Point or Block?" Indeed, this is not your simple "paper or plastic" supermarket choice. It's an important question—to which there is no single, easy answer.

For most writers, choosing the appropriate pattern of organization involves thinking time in the prewriting stage, before beginning a draft. Many times, your essay's subject matter itself will suggest the most effective method of development. The Block Pattern might be the better choice when a complete, overall picture of each subject is desirable. For example, you might decide that your "then-and-now" essay (your disastrous first day at a new job contrasted with your success at that job today) would be easier for your readers to understand if your description of "then" (your first day) was presented in its entirety, followed by the contrasting discussion of "now" (current success). Later in this section, you will see that Mark Twain chose this method in his essay "Two Ways of Viewing the River" to contrast his early and later impressions of the Mississippi.

On the other hand, your essay topic might best be discussed by presenting a number of distinct points for the reader to consider one by one. Essays that evaluate, that argue the superiority or advantage of one thing over another ("A cat is a better pet for students than a dog because . . ."), often lend themselves to the Point-by-Point Pattern because each of the writer's claims may be clearly supported by the side-by-side details. "Bringing Back the Joy of Market Day," a student essay in this section, employs this method to emphasize three ways in which a small food cooperative is preferable to a chain grocery store.

However, none of the preceding advice always holds true. There are no hard-and-fast rules governing this rhetorical choice. Each writer must decide which method of organization works best in any particular comparison/contrast essay. Before drafting begins, therefore, writers are wise to sketch out an informal outline or rough plan using one method and then the other to see which is more effective for their topic, their purpose, and their audience. By spending time in the prewriting stage "auditioning" each method of development, you may spare yourself the frustration of writing an entire draft whose organization doesn't work well for your topic.

Problems to Avoid

The single most serious error is the "so-what" thesis. Writers of comparison and contrast essays often wish to convince their readers that something—a restaurant, a movie, a product—is better (or worse) than something else: "Mom's Haven is a better place to eat than McPhony's." But not all comparison or contrast essays assert the absolute superiority or inferiority of their subjects. Sometimes writers simply want to point out the similarities or differences in two or more people, places, or objects, and that's fine, too—*as long as the writer avoids the "so-what" thesis problem.*

Too often, novice writers will present thesis statements such as "My sister and I are very different" or "Having a blended family with two stepbrothers and a stepsister has advantages and disadvantages for me." To such theses, readers can only respond, "So what? Who cares?" There are many similarities and differences (or advantages and disadvantages) between countless numbers of things—but why should your readers care about those described in your essay? Comparing or contrasting for no apparent reason is a waste of the readers' valuable time; instead, find a purpose that will draw in your audience. You may indeed wish to write an essay contrasting the pros and cons of your blended family, but do it in a way that has a universal appeal or application. For instance, you might revise your thesis to say something like "Although a blended family often does experience petty jealousies and juvenile bickering, the benefits of having stepsiblings as live-in friends far outweigh the problems," and then use your family to show the advantages and disadvantages. In this way, your readers realize they will learn something about the blended family, a common phenomenon today, as well as learning some information about you and your particular family.

Another way to avoid the "so-what" problem is to direct your thesis to a particular audience. For instance, you might say that "Although Stella's Sweatateria and the Fitness Fanatics Gym are similar in their low student-membership prices and excellent instructors, Stella's is the place to go for those seeking a variety of exercise classes rather than hard-core bodybuilding machines." Or your thesis may wish to show a particular relationship between two subjects. Instead of writing "There are many similarities between the movie *Riot of the Killer Snails* and Mary Sheeley's novel *Salt on the Sidewalk*," write "The many similarities in character and plot (the monster, the scientist, and vegetable garden scene) clearly suggest that the movie director was greatly influenced by—if not actually guilty of stealing—parts of Mary Sheeley's novel."

In other words, tell your readers your point and then use comparison or contrast to support that idea; don't just compare or contrast items in a vacuum. Ask yourself, "What is the significant point I want my readers to learn or understand from reading this comparison/contrast essay? Why do they need to know this?"

Describe your subjects clearly and distinctly. To comprehend a difference or a similarity between two things, the reader must first be able to "see" them as you do. Consequently, you should use as many vivid examples and details as possible to describe both your subjects. Beware a tendency to over elaborate on one subject and then grossly skimp on the other, an especially easy trap to fall into in an essay that asserts "X" is preferable to "Y." By giving each side a reasonable treatment, you will do a better job of convincing your reader that you know both sides and have made a valid judgment.

Avoid a choppy essay. Whether you organize your essay by the Point-by-Point Pattern or the Block Pattern, you need to use enough transitional devices to ensure a smooth flow from one subject to another and from one point to the next. Without transitions, your essay may assume the distracting movement of a Ping-Pong game, as you switch back and forth between discussions of your two subjects. Listed here are some appropriate words to link your points:

Comparison	Contrast
also	however
similarly	on the contrary
too	on the other hand
both	in contrast
like	although
not only . . . but also	unlike
have in common	though
share the same	instead of
in the same manner	but

(◆ For a review of other transitional devices, see pages 69–72.)

Essay Topics

© Inspirestock/CORBIS

Here are some topics that may be compared or contrasted. Remember to narrow your subject, formulate a thesis that presents a clear point, and follow one of the two organizational patterns discussed on pages 226–228.

◆ For additional ideas, turn to the "Suggestions for Writing" sections following the professional essays (page 241 and page 243).

1. An expectation and its reality

continued on next page

2. A memory of a person or place and a more recent encounter (or a first impression and a later point of view)

3. Two views of a current controversial issue (campus, local, national)

4. Two conflicting theories you are studying in another college course

5. Coverage of the same story by two newspapers or magazines (the *National Enquirer* and the *Dallas Morning News,* for example, or *Time* and *Newsweek*)

6. A hero today and yesterday

7. Two essays or pieces of literature with similar themes but different styles

8. Two kinds of classes (online and on campus; lecture and lab; high school and college, etc.)

9. Two pieces of technology or two pieces of sports equipment (or an older and newer version of a product)

10. Two paintings/photographs/posters (You might select any of the many images in this text; a list of the artworks follows the Table of Contents. You could choose two portraits or a portrait and a self-portrait [for example, *Migrant Mother, Repose,* or *The Two Fridas*]; two landscapes [*Early Snow, Starry Night,* or *Moonrise, Hernandez, New Mexico*]; two scenes of action [*The Third of May, Tornado over Kansas*]; or two pictures with contrasting themes, styles, or media or two that share certain themes or techniques [the surrealism of *The Persistence of Memory, Birthday,* or *The Scream,* for example]. (◆ For help writing about artworks, see Chapter 17.)

11. One of today's popular entertainments, games, or magazines and one from an earlier era

12. Two places you've lived or visited or two schools you've attended

13. Two instructors or coaches whose teaching styles are effective but different

14. Two movies; a book and its movie; a movie and its sequel; an older movie and its remake (◆ For help writing about film, see Chapter 18.)

15. Two jobs, bosses, or employers (or your current job and your dream job)

16. Two people, places, or pets that are special for you in different ways

17. An opinion you held before coming to college that has changed

18. Your attitude toward a social custom or political belief and your parents' (or grandparents') attitude toward that belief or custom

continued on next page

19. *Collaborative Activity*: Interview a classmate who grew up in a different town, state, or country. In comparison to your own experience, what are some important similarities or differences? Advantages/disadvantages? Given a choice between the two places, in which area would you relocate today, and why?

20. Compare or contrast two advertisements that are themselves developed by comparison/contrast or analogy. (Consider, for example, the ad shown here. What is its purpose and who is its target audience? How does the ad incorporate the strategy of contrast to sell its product? What other appeals are used? Is this ad effective? Why, or why not? For another ad developed by contrast, see page 312.)

YOUR LEFT HAND LIVES FOR LOVE. YOUR RIGHT HAND LIVES FOR THE MOMENT. YOUR LEFT HAND WANTS TO BE HELD. YOUR RIGHT HAND WANTS TO BE HELD HIGH. **WOMEN OF THE WORLD, RAISE YOUR RIGHT HAND.** A DIAMOND IS FOREVER

THE NEW DIAMOND RIGHT HAND RING. MODERN VINTAGE, FLORAL, ROMANTIC AND CONTEMPORARY STYLES AT ADIAMONDISFOREVER.COM

A Topic Proposal for Your Essay

Selecting the right subject matter is important to every writer. To help you clarify your ideas and strengthen your commitment to your topic, here is a proposal sheet that asks you to describe some of your preliminary ideas about your subject before you begin drafting. Although your ideas may change as you write (they will almost certainly become more refined), thinking through your choice of topic now may help you avoid several false starts.

1. What two subjects will your essay discuss? In what ways are these subjects similar? Different?

2. Do you plan to compare or contrast your two subjects?

3. Write one or two sentences describing your attitude toward these two subjects. Are you stating a preference for one or are you making some other significant point? In other words, what is the purpose of this essay?

4. Why would other people find this topic interesting and important? Would a particular group of people be more affected by your topic than others? Are you avoiding the "so-what" thesis problem?

5. List three or four points of comparison or contrast that you might include in this essay.

6. What difficulties might this topic present during your drafting? For example, would your topic be best explained using the Block or Point-by-Point Pattern?

Sample Student Essay

Because there are two popular ways to develop comparison/contrast essays, this section offers two student essays so that each pattern is illustrated.

I. The Point-by-Point Pattern

Note that this writer takes a definite stand—that local food co-ops are superior to chain grocery stores—and then contrasts two local stores, Lane Grocer and the Fort Collins, Colorado, Co-op, to prove her thesis. She selected the Point-by-Point Pattern to organize her essay, contrasting prices, atmosphere, and benefits to local producers. See if you can identify her transitional devices as well as some of her uses of detail that make the essay more interesting and convincing.

BRINGING BACK THE JOY OF MARKET DAY

1   Now that the old family-run corner grocery is almost extinct, many people are banding together to form their own neighborhood stores as food cooperatives. Locally owned by their members, food co-ops such as the one here in Fort Collins are welcome alternatives to the impersonal chain-store markets such as Lane Grocer. In exchange for volunteering a few hours each month, co-op members share savings and a friendly experience while they shop; local producers gain loyal, local support from the members as well as better prices for their goods in return for providing the freshest, purest food possible.

2   Perhaps the most crucial distinction between the two kinds of stores is that while supermarkets are set up to generate profit for their corporations, co-ops are nonprofit groups whose main purpose is to provide their members and the community with good, inexpensive food and basic household needs. At first glance, supermarkets such as Lane

Thesis

Essay map

Point one: Prices

Grocer may appear to be cheaper because they offer so many specials, which they emphasize heavily through ads and in-store promotions. These special deals, known as "loss-leaders" in the retail industry, are more than compensated by the extremely high markups on other products. For example, around Thanksgiving Lane Grocer might have a sale on flour and shortening and then set up the displays with utmost care so that as customers reach for the flour they will be drawn to colorful bottles of pie spices, fancy jars of mincemeat, or maybe an inviting bin of fresh-roasted holiday nuts, all of which may be marked up 100% or more—way above what is being lost on the flour and shortening.

3   The Fort Collins Co-op rarely bothers with such pricing gimmicks; instead, it tries to have a consistent markup—just enough to meet overhead expenses. The flour at the co-op may cost an extra few cents, but that same fancy spice bottle that costs over $2.00 from the supermarket display can be refilled at the co-op for less than 50¢. The nuts, considered by regular groceries as a seasonal "gourmet" item, are sold at the co-op for about two-thirds the price. Great savings like these are achieved by buying in bulk and having customers bag their own groceries. Recycled containers are used as much as possible, cutting down substantially on overhead. Buying in bulk may seem awkward at first, but the extra time spent bagging and weighing their own food results in welcome savings for co-op members.

Examples of Lane Grocer's prices contrasted to examples of co-op prices

4   Once people have become accustomed to bringing their own containers and taking part in the work at the co-ops, they often find that it's actually more fun to shop in the friendly, relaxed atmosphere of the co-ops. At Lane Grocer, for example, I often find shopping a battle of tangled metal carts wielded by bored customers who are frequently trying to manage one or more cranky children. The long aisles harshly lit by rows of cold fluorescent lights and the bland commercial music don't make the chore of shopping any easier either. On the other hand, the

Point two: Atmosphere

Description of Lane Grocer's atmosphere contrasted to description of the co-op's atmosphere

Fort Collins Co-op may not be as expertly planned, but at least the chaos is carried on in a friendly way. Parents especially appreciate that they can safely let their children loose while they shop because in the small, open-spaced co-op even toddlers don't become lost as they do in the aisles of towering supermarket shelves. Moreover, most members are willing to look after the children of other members if necessary. And while they shop, members can choose to listen to the FM radio or simply to enjoy each other's company in relative quiet.

Point three: Benefits to local producers

5   As well as benefiting member consumers, co-ops also help small local producers by providing a direct market for their goods. Large chain stores may require minimum wholesale quantities far beyond the capacity of an individual producer, and mass markets like Lane Grocer often feel they are "too big" to negotiate with small local producers. But because of their small, independent nature, co-ops welcome the chance to buy direct from the grower or producer. Direct selling offers two advantages for producers: they get a better price for their wares than by selling them through wholesalers, and at the same time they establish an independent reputation for their business, which can be immensely valuable to their success later on. In Fort Collins, for example, Luna tofu (bean curd) stands out as an excellent illustration of this kind of mutual support. Several years ago my friend Carol Jones began making tofu in small batches to sell to the co-op as a way to earn a part-time income as well as to contribute to the co-op. Her enterprise has now grown so well that last year her husband quit his job to go into business with her full time. She currently sells to distributors and independent stores from here to Denver; even Lane Grocer, which earlier would not consider selling her tofu even on a trial basis, is now thinking about changing its policy.

No benefits at Lane Grocer contrasted to two benefits at the co-op

Conclusion: Summarizing the advantages of co-ops over chain stores

6   Of course, not all co-ops are like the one here in Fort Collins, but that is one of their best features. Each one reflects the personalities of its members, unlike the supermarket chain stores that vary only slightly.

> Most important, though, while each has a distinctive character, co-ops share common goals of providing members with high-quality, low-cost food in a friendly, cooperative spirit.

II. The Block Pattern

After thinking through both methods of development, a second student writer chose the Block Pattern to contrast two kinds of backyards. He felt it was more effective to give his readers a complete sense of his first backyard, with its spirit of wildness, instead of addressing each point of the contrast separately, as did the first student writer in this section. Do you agree with his choice? Why or why not? Note, too, the ways in which this writer tries to avoid the "split essay" problem by making clear connections between the new yard and the older one.

BACKYARDS: OLD AND NEW

1   Most of the time I like getting something new—new clothes, new CDs, new video games. I look forward to making new friends and visiting new places. But sometimes new isn't better than old. Five years ago, when my family moved to a house in a new area, I learned that a new, neat backyard can never be as wonderful as a rambling, untamed yard of an older house.

Thesis

2   My first yard, behind our older house, was huge, the size of three normal backyards, but completely irregular in shape. Our property line zagged in and out around old, tall trees in a lot shaped like a large pie piece from which some giant had taken random bites. The left side was taken up by a lopsided garden that sometimes grew tomatoes but mainly wild raspberries, an odd assortment of overgrown bushes, and wildflowers of mismatched shapes and sizes. The middle part had grass and scattered shade trees, some that were good for climbing. The grassy part drifted off into an area with large old evergreen trees surrounded

Block A: The older, "untamed" backyard

(Landscape variety: Irregular lot size and shape; trees, rambling mix of bushes, flowers, berries, and vines)

by a tall tangle of vines and bushes that my parents called "the Wild Spot," which they had carefully ignored for years. The whole yard sloped downhill, which with the irregular shape and the trees, made my job of mowing the grass a creative challenge.

3   Despite the mowing problem, there was something magical about that untamed yard. We kids made a path through the Wild Spot and had a secret hideout in the brush. Hidden from adult eyes, my friends and I sat around a pretend fire ring, made up adventures (lost in the jungle!), asked each other Important Questions (better to be a rock star or a baseball player?), and shared our secret fears (being asked to dance). The yard's grassy section was big enough for throwing a football with my brother (the here-and-there trees made catching long passes even more spectacular), and my twin sisters invented gymnastic routines that rolled them downhill. Mom picked vegetables and flowers when she felt like it. It seemed like someone, family or friend, was always in our yard doing something fun.

(Many activities)

4   When all the kids were teenagers, my parents finally decided we needed more space, so we moved into a house in a new development. Although the house itself was better (more bathrooms), the new backyard, in comparison to our older one, was a total disappointment. New Backyard was neat, tidy, tiny, flat, square, and completely fenced. There were not only no big old trees for shade or for climbing—there were no trees at all. My parents had to plant a few, which looked like big twigs stuck in the ground. No untamed tangles of bushes and flowers there—only identical fire hydrant–sized shrubs planted evenly every few feet in narrow, even beds along the fence. The rest of this totally flat yard was grass, easy to mow in mere minutes, but no challenge either. No wild berry bushes or rambling vegetable gardens were allowed in the new development. No wild anything at all, to be exact.

Transition to Block B: The new backyard (contrasting bland landscape)

5   Nothing wild and no variety: that was the problem. To put it bluntly, the yard was neat but boring. Every inch of it was open to inspection; it held no secret spaces for the imagination to fill. There was no privacy either as our yard looked directly into the almost duplicate bland yards of the neighbors on all sides. The yard was too small to do any real physical activity in it; going out for a long pass would mean automatic collision with the chain link fence in any direction. My sisters' dance routines soon dissolved under our neighbors' eyes, and our tomatoes came from the grocery store. With no hidden nooks, no interesting landscape, and no tumbling space, our family just didn't go into the backyard very often. Unlike the older, overgrown backyard that was always inviting someone to play, the new backyard wasn't fun for anyone.

(Few activities)

6   Over the last five years, the trees have grown and the yard looks better, not so sterile and empty. I guess all new yards are on their way to becoming old yards eventually. But it takes decades and that is too slow for me. New houses have lots of modern conveniences, but I hope if I am lucky enough to own my own place someday, I will remember that when it comes to backyards, old is always better than new.

Conclusion: A future preference based on essay's thesis

Professional Essays*

Because there are two common ways to develop comparison/contrast essays, this section offers two professional essays so that each pattern is illustrated.

I. The Point-by-Point Pattern

Grant and Lee: A Study in Contrasts**

Bruce Catton

Bruce Catton, an authority on the Civil War, won both the Pulitzer Prize for historical work and the National Book Award in 1954. He wrote numerous books, including *Mr. Lincoln's Army* (1951), *A Stillness at Appomattox* (1953), *Never Call Retreat* (1966), and

---

* ◆ To help you read these essays analytically, review pages 179–181.
** "Grant and Lee: A Study in Contrasts" by Bruce Catton. Copyright © U.S. Capitol Historical Society, all rights reserved. Reprinted with permission.

Gettysburg: The Final Fury (1974). This classic essay is from *The American Story* (1956), a collection of essays by noted historians. In 1977, the year before he died, Catton was awarded the Presidential Medal of Freedom, the nation's highest civil honor.

Pre-reading Thoughts: Consider the most important character traits of two people you admire. Do these two people have similar backgrounds, strengths, or goals? Do they share common values or virtues?

1   When Ulysses S. Grant and Robert E. Lee met in the parlor of a modest house at Appomattox Court House, Virginia, on April 9, 1865, to work out the terms for the surrender of Lee's Army of Northern Virginia, a great chapter in American life came to a close, and a great new chapter began.

2   These men were bringing the Civil War to its virtual finish. To be sure, other armies had yet to surrender, and for a few days the fugitive Confederate government would struggle desperately and vainly, trying to find some way to go on living now that its chief support was gone. But in effect it was all over when Grant and Lee signed the papers. And the little room where they wrote out the terms was the scene of one of the poignant, dramatic contrasts in American history.

3   They were two strong men, these oddly different generals, and they represented the strengths of two conflicting currents that, through them, had come into final collision.

4   Back of Robert E. Lee was the notion that the old aristocratic concept might somehow survive and be dominant in American life.

5   Lee was tidewater Virginia, and in his background were family, culture, and tradition . . . the age of chivalry transplanted to a New World which was making its own legends and its own myths. He embodied a way of life that had come down through the age of knighthood and the English country squire. America was a land that was beginning all over again, dedicated to nothing much more complicated than the rather hazy belief that all men had equal rights, and should have an equal chance in the world. In such a land Lee stood for the feeling that it was somehow of advantage to human society to have a pronounced inequality in the social structure. There should be a leisure class, backed by ownership of land; in turn, society itself should be keyed to the land as the chief source of wealth and influence. It would bring forth (according to this ideal) a class of men with a strong sense of obligation to the community; men who lived not to gain advantage for themselves, but to meet the solemn obligations which had been laid on them by the very fact that they were privileged. From them the country would get its leadership; to them it could look for the higher values—of thought, of conduct, of personal deportment—to give it strength and virtue.

6   Lee embodied the noblest elements of this aristocratic ideal. Through him, the landed nobility justified itself. For four years, the Southern states had fought a desperate war to uphold the ideals for which Lee stood. In the end, it almost seemed as if the Confederacy fought for Lee; as if he himself was the Confederacy . . . the best thing that the way of life for which the Confederacy stood could ever have to offer. He had passed into legend before Appomattox. Thousands of tired,

underfed, poorly clothed Confederate soldiers, long-since past the simple enthusiasm of the early days of the struggle, somehow considered Lee the symbol of everything for which they had been willing to die. But they could not quite put this feeling into words. If the Lost Cause, sanctified by so much heroism and so many deaths, had a living justification, its justification was General Lee.

7   Grant, the son of a tanner on the Western frontier, was everything Lee was not. He had come up the hard way, and embodied nothing in particular except the eternal toughness and sinewy fiber of the men who grew up beyond the mountains. He was one of a body of men who owed reverence and obeisance to no one, who were self-reliant to a fault, who cared hardly anything for the past but who had a sharp eye for the future.

8   These frontier men were the precise opposites of the tidewater aristocrats. Back of them, in the great surge that had taken people over the Alleghenies and into the opening Western country, there was a deep, implicit dissatisfaction with a past that had settled into grooves. They stood for democracy, not from any reasoned conclusion about the proper ordering of human society, but simply because they had grown up in the middle of democracy and knew how it worked. Their society might have privileges, but they would be privileges each man had won for himself. Forms and patterns meant nothing. No man was born to anything, except perhaps to a chance to show how far he could rise. Life was competition.

9   Yet along with this feeling had come a deep sense of belonging to a national community. The Westerner who developed a farm, opened a shop, or set up in business as a trader could hope to prosper only as his own community prospered— and his community ran from the Atlantic to the Pacific and from Canada down to Mexico. If the land was settled, with towns and highways and accessible markets, he could better himself. He saw his fate in terms of the nation's own destiny. As its horizons expanded, so did his. He had, in other words, an acute dollars-and-cents stake in the continued growth and development of his country.

10   And that, perhaps, is where the contrast between Grant and Lee becomes most striking. The Virginia aristocrat, inevitably, saw himself in relation to his own region. He lived in a static society which could endure almost anything except change. Instinctively, his first loyalty would go to the locality in which that society existed. He would fight to the limit of endurance to defend it, because in defending it he was defending everything that gave his own life its deepest meaning.

11   The Westerner, on the other hand, would fight with an equal tenacity for the broader concept of society. He fought so because everything he lived by was tied to growth, expansion, and a constantly widening horizon. What he lived by would survive or fall with the nation itself. He could not possibly stand by unmoved in the face of an attempt to destroy the Union. He would combat it with everything he had, because he could only see it as an effort to cut the ground out from under his feet.

12   So Grant and Lee were in complete contrast, representing two diametrically opposed elements in American life. Grant was the modern man emerging; beyond him, ready to come on the stage, was the great age of steel and machinery, of crowded cities and a restless, burgeoning vitality. Lee might have ridden down from the old age of chivalry, lance in hand, silken banner fluttering over his head. Each man was the perfect champion of his cause, drawing both his strengths and his weaknesses from the people he led.

13   Yet it was not all contrast, after all. Different as they were—in background, in personality, in underlying aspiration—these two great soldiers had much in common. Under everything else, they were marvelous fighters. Furthermore, their fighting qualities were really very much alike.

14   Each man had, to begin with, the great virtue of utter tenacity and fidelity. Grant fought his way down the Mississippi Valley in spite of acute personal discouragement and profound military handicaps. Lee hung on in the trenches at Petersburg after hope itself had died. In each man there was an indomitable quality . . . the born fighter's refusal to give up as long as he can still remain on his feet and lift his two fists.

15   Daring and resourcefulness they had, too; the ability to think faster and move faster than the enemy. These were the qualities which gave Lee the dazzling campaigns of Second Manassas and Chancellorsville and won Vicksburg for Grant.

16   Lastly, and perhaps greatest of all, there was the ability, at the end, to turn quickly from war to peace once the fighting was over. Out of the way these two men behaved at Appomattox came the possibility of a peace of reconciliation. It was a possibility not wholly realized, in the years to come, but which did, in the end, help the two sections to become one nation again . . . after a war whose bitterness might have seemed to make such a reunion wholly impossible. No part of either man's life became him more than the part he played in their brief meeting in the McLean house at Appomattox. Their behavior there put all succeeding generations of Americans in their debt. Two great Americans, Grant and Lee—very different, yet under everything very much alike. Their encounter at Appomattox was one of the great moments of American history.

Questions on Content, Style, and Structure

1. What is Catton's thesis?

2. According to Catton, how did Lee view society? What "ideal" did he embody? Why do you think Catton avoided mentioning slavery in this description?

3. Who did Grant represent? How did they view the country's social structure?

4. After carefully studying paragraphs 4 through 16, describe the pattern of organization Catton uses to present his discussion.

5. What new means of development begins in paragraph 13?

6. How does Catton avoid the choppy seesaw effect as he compares and contrasts his subjects? Point out ways in which Catton makes a smooth transition from point to point.

7. Evaluate Catton's ability to write unified, coherent paragraphs with clearly stated topic sentences. Are his paragraphs adequately developed with enough specific detail? Cite evidence to support your answer.

8. What is the advantage or disadvantage of having only one sentence in paragraph 3? In paragraph 4?

9. What is Catton's opinion of these men? Select words and passages to support your answer. How does Catton's attitude affect the tone of this essay? Is his tone appropriate? Why, or why not?

10. Instead of including a separate paragraph, Catton presents his concluding remarks in paragraph 16, in which he discusses his last major point about Grant and Lee. Many essays lacking concluding paragraphs end too abruptly or merely trail off; how does Catton avoid these weaknesses?

Vocabulary

chivalry (5)   tenacity (11)   indomitable (14)
deportment (5)   diametrically (12)   reconciliation (16)
embodied (6)   burgeoning (12)

Suggestions for Writing

Try using Bruce Catton's "Grant and Lee: A Study in Contrasts" as a stepping-stone to your writing. Comparing public figures is a familiar activity. People often discuss the styles and merits of various politicians, writers, business leaders, humanitarians, sports celebrities, and media stars. Write your own essay about two public figures who interest you. Similar or different, these people may have lived in the same times (Winston Churchill and Franklin D. Roosevelt, Ernest Hemingway and F. Scott Fitzgerald, Babe Didrikson Zaharias and Babe Ruth), or you might choose two people from different eras (Clara Barton and Mother Teresa, Mozart and Madonna, Susan B. Anthony and Cesar Chavez, Harriet Tubman and Martin Luther King, Jr.). The possibilities are endless and thought-provoking; use your essay to make an interesting specific point about the fascinating (and perhaps heretofore unrecognized) differences/similarities between the people you choose.

II. The Block Pattern

Two Ways of Viewing the River*

Samuel Clemens

Samuel Clemens, whose pen name was Mark Twain, is regarded as one of America's most outstanding writers. Well known for his humorous stories and books, Twain was also a pioneer of fictional realism and local color. His most famous novel, *Adventures of Huckleberry Finn* (1884), is often hailed as a masterpiece. This selection is from the autobiographical book *Life on the Mississippi* (1883), which recounts Clemens' job as a riverboat pilot.

> **Pre-reading Thoughts:** Have you ever revisited a place and discovered that your perception of it had greatly changed over time? What might have caused this change? Did the place itself change—or did you?

1   Now when I had mastered the language of this water and had come to know every trifling feature that bordered the great river as familiarly as I knew the letters of the alphabet, I had made a valuable acquisition. But I had lost something, too. I had lost something which could never be restored to me while I lived. All the grace, the beauty, the poetry, had gone out of the majestic river! I still kept in

---

* Mark Twain, "Two Ways of Viewing the River"

mind a certain wonderful sunset which I witnessed when steamboating was new to me. A broad expanse of the river was turned to blood; in the middle distance the red hue brightened into gold, through which a solitary log came floating, black and conspicuous; in one place a long, slanting mark lay sparkling upon the water; in another the surface was broken by boiling, tumbling rings, that were as many-tinted as an opal; where the ruddy flush was faintest, was a smooth spot that was covered with graceful circles and radiating lines, ever so delicately traced; the shore on our left was densely wooded and the somber shadow that fell from this forest was broken in one place by a long, ruffled trail that shone like silver; and high above the forest wall a clean-stemmed dead tree waved a single leafy bough that glowed like a flame in the unobstructed splendor that was flowing from the sun. There were graceful curves, reflected images, woody heights, soft distances, and over the whole scene, far and near, the dissolving lights drifted steadily, enriching it every passing moment with new marvels of coloring.

2   I stood like one bewitched. I drank it in, in a speechless rapture. The world was new to me and I had never seen anything like this at home. But as I have said, a day came when I began to cease from noting the glories and the charms which the moon and the sun and the twilight wrought upon the river's face; another day came when I ceased altogether to note them. Then, if that sunset scene had been repeated, I should have looked upon it without rapture, and should have commented upon it inwardly after this fashion: "This sun means that we are going to have wind tomorrow; that floating log means that the river is rising, small thanks to it; that slanting mark on the water refers to a bluff reef which is going to kill somebody's steamboat one of these nights, if it keeps on stretching out like that; those tumbling 'boils' show a dissolving bar and a changing channel there; the lines and circles in the slick water over yonder are a warning that that troublesome place is shoaling up dangerously; that silver streak in the shadow of the forest is the 'break' from a new snag and he has located himself in the very best place he could have found to fish for steamboats; that tall dead tree, with a single living branch, is not going to last long, and then how is a body ever going to get through this blind place at night without the friendly old landmark?"

3   No, the romance and beauty were all gone from the river. All the value any feature of it had for me now was the amount of usefulness it could furnish toward compassing the safe piloting of a steamboat. Since those days, I have pitied doctors from my heart. What does the lovely flush in a beauty's cheek mean to a doctor but a "break" that ripples above some deadly disease? Are not all her visible charms sown thick with what are to him the signs and symbols of hidden decay? Does he ever see her beauty at all, or doesn't he simply view her professionally and comment upon her unwholesome condition all to himself? And doesn't he sometimes wonder whether he has gained most or lost most by learning his trade?

Questions on Content, Structure, and Style

1. What is Clemens contrasting in this essay? Identify his thesis.
2. What organizational pattern does he choose? Why is this an appropriate choice for his purpose?

3. How does Clemens make a smooth transition to his later view of the river?

4. Why does Clemens refer to doctors in paragraph 3?

5. What is the purpose of the questions in paragraph 3? Why is the last question especially important?

6. Characterize the language Clemens uses in his description in paragraph 1. Is his diction appropriate?

7. Point out several examples of similes in paragraph 1. What do they add to the description of the sunset?

8. How does the language in the description in paragraph 2 differ from the diction in paragraph 1? What view of the river is emphasized there?

9. Identify an example of personification in paragraph 2. Why did Clemens add it to his description?

10. Describe the tone of this essay. Does it ever shift?

Vocabulary

trifling (1)   ruddy (1)
acquisition (1)   wrought (2)
conspicuous (1)   compassing (3)

Suggestions for Writing

Try using Samuel Clemens' "Two Ways of Viewing the River" as a stepping-stone to your own writing. Consider, as Clemens did, writing about a subject before and after you experienced it from a more technically informed point of view. Did your appreciation of your grandmother's quilt increase after you realized how much skill went into making it? Did a starry night have a different appeal after your astronomy course? Did your admiration of a story or poem diminish or increase after you studied its craft? Clemens felt that a certain loss came with his expertise, but was this the case in your experience?

A Revision Worksheet

As you write your rough drafts, consult Chapter 5 for guidance through the revision process. In addition, here are a few questions to ask yourself as you revise your comparison/contrast essay:

© Ryan McVay/
Photodisc/Getty Images

1. Does the essay contain a thesis that makes a significant point instead of a "so-what" thesis?

2. Is the material organized into the best pattern for the subject matter?

3. If the essay is developed by the Point-by-Point Pattern, are there enough transitional words used to avoid the seesaw effect?

continued on next page

4. If the essay is developed by the Block Pattern, are there enough transitional devices and references connecting the two subjects to avoid the split-essay problem?

5. Are the points of comparison/contrast presented in a logical, consistent order that the reader can follow easily?

6. Are both subjects given a reasonably balanced treatment?

7. Are both subjects developed in enough specific detail so that the reader clearly understands the comparison or contrast? Where might more detail be added?

Collaborative Activity: After you've revised your essay extensively, exchange rough drafts with a classmate and answer these questions for each other, making specific suggestions for improvement wherever appropriate. (◆ For advice on productive participation in classroom workshops, see pages 116–120.)

A Special Kind of Comparison: The Analogy

In the past few pages of this text, you've learned about essays developed by comparison/contrast, which generally point out similarities and differences between two things with enough common ground to merit meaningful discussion (two apartments, two computers, a book and its movie, etc.). In comparison/contrast essays, two subjects ("X" and "Y") are explained to make a point. An *analogy* is slightly different: it is a comparison that uses one thing ("X") only to clarify or argue a second thing ("Y"). In an analogy, one element is the main focus of attention.

You've probably heard several colorful analogies this week. Perhaps a friend who holds a hectic, dead-end job has tried to explain life at that moment by comparing herself to a crazed gerbil on a cage treadmill—always running, getting nowhere, feeling trapped in a never-changing environment. Or perhaps your science teacher explained the behavior of cancer cells by comparing them in several ways to an invading army on a destructive mission. If you read the Preface to this text, you were asked to see your writing instructor as a coach who helps you practice your skills, gives constructive criticism, and encourages your successes. Analogies are plentiful in our conversations and in both our reading and writing.

Writers often find analogies useful in three ways:

1. **To clarify and explain:** Most often writers use analogies to clarify an abstract, unfamiliar, or complex element by comparing it to something that is familiar to the reader, often something that is more concrete or easier to understand. For example, raising children has often been compared to nourishing baby birds, with parents feeding and nurturing but ultimately nudging offspring out of the nest. A relationship might be explained as having grown from a seed that eventually blossomed into a flower (or a weed!). Popular novelist Stephen King has used a roller coaster analogy to explain some people's enjoyment of horror movies.

    Frequently, scientific and medical topics profit from analogies that a general audience of readers can more readily understand. A technical discussion of the human eye, for instance, might be explained using the analogy of a camera lens; photosynthesis might be compared to the process of baking bread. One biology teacher explains the semipermeability of a cell membrane with a football analogy: the offensive line wants to let out the running back with the ball but keep the defensive line in. In short, analogies can make new or difficult material easier to grasp.

2. **To argue and persuade:** Writers often use analogies to try to convince their audience that what is true about "X" would also be true about "Y" because the two elements have so many important similarities. For example, someone against new anti-drug laws might argue that they are similar to those passed under Prohibition, the banning of alcohol in the 1930s, and thus the drug laws are doomed to failure. Or perhaps a NASA official might argue for more money for space exploration by comparing trips into outer space with those expeditions to the New World by explorers such as Columbus. How convincing an analogy is depends to a large extent on how similar the two elements appear to be. Remember, however, that analogies by themselves cannot *prove* anything; they can merely suggest similarities between two cases or things.

3. **To dramatize or capture an image:** Writers (and speakers) often use analogies because they wish their audience to remember a particular point or to see something in a new way. Using a vivid analogy—sometimes referred to as an extended metaphor or simile—can effectively impress an image upon the reader's or listener's mind ("Using crack is like burning down your own house. And the insurance policy ran out a long time ago . . ."). Analogies can be enjoyable too for their sheer inventiveness and their colorful language. Perhaps one of the most well-known analogies in American literature is Thoreau's description, in *Walden*, of a battle between two ant colonies, with the tiny creatures drawn as rival warriors fighting to the death in classical epic style. Analogies may even be used for comic effect in appropriate situations (moving into your basement apartment in sweltering August heat as analogous to a trip to the Underworld, for instance). Fresh, creative analogies can delight your readers and hold their attention.

Although analogies can be helpful and memorable, they can also present problems if they are trite, unclear, or illogical. Analogies can be especially harmful to a writer's credibility in an argument if readers don't see enough logical similarities to make the comparison convincing. Some faulty analogies may seem acceptable on first glance but fall apart when the details of the comparison are considered closely. For example, perhaps you have seen a bumper sticker that reads "Giving money and power to the government is like giving whisky and car keys to teenage boys." Are the two situations really alike? Do government agencies/officials and adolescents share many similarities in maturity, experience, and goals? Does financial support have the same effect as alcohol? If too many points of comparison are weak, readers will not find the analogy persuasive. Or perhaps you have read that "America is like a lifeboat already full of people; letting in more immigrants will cause the boat to sink." If readers do not accept the major premise—that America, a country with many renewable resources, closely resembles a lifeboat, a confined space with unchanging dimensions—they are likely to reject the argument.

Also be wary of those writers who try to substitute an analogy in place of any other kind of evidence to support their points in an argument, and be especially suspicious of those using analogies as "scare tactics" ("This proposed legislation is just like laws passed in Nazi Germany"). As a writer, use only those analogies that will help your reader understand, remember, or accept your ideas; as a reader, always protect yourself by questioning the validity of the analogy offered to you. (◆ For more on *faulty analogy* as a logical fallacy, see page 298.)

To illustrate use of analogy, here are three examples from professional writers. In each case, what was the writer's purpose? How is "X" used to clarify or argue for "Y"? Which of these analogies do you find the most effective, and why?

> A good lab course is an exercise in *doing* science. As such it differs totally in mission from a good lecture course where the object is learning *about* science. In the same way that one can gain vastly greater insight into music by learning to play an instrument, one can experience the doing of science only by going into the lab and trying one's hand at measurement.
>
> —*Miles Pickering, "Are Lab Courses a Waste of Time?"*

> For a long time now, since the beginning, in fact, men and women have been sparring and dancing around with each other, each pair trying to get it together and boogie to the tune called Life. For some people, it was always a glide, filled with grace and ease. For most of us, it is a stumble and a struggle, always trying to figure out the next step, until we find a partner whose inconsistencies seem to fit with ours, and the two of us fit into some kind of rhythm. Some couples wind up struggling and pulling at cross purposes; and of course, some people never get out on the floor, just stand alone in the corners, looking hard at the dancers.
>
> —*Jay Molishever, "Changing Expectations of Marriage"*

> One afternoon while we were there at that lake a thunderstorm came up. It was like the revival of an old melodrama that I had seen long ago with childish awe. The second-act climax of the drama of the electrical disturbance over a lake in America had not changed in any important respect. This was the big scene, still the big scene. The whole thing was so familiar, the first feeling of oppression and heat and a general air around camp of not wanting to go very far away. In midafternoon (it was all the same) a curious darkening of the sky, and a lull in everything that had made life tick; and then the way the boats suddenly swung the other way at their moorings with the coming of a breeze out of the new quarter, and the premonitory rumble. Then the kettle drum, then the snare, then the bass drum and cymbals, then crackling light against the dark. . . . Afterward the calm, the rain steadily rustling in the calm lake, the return of light and hope and spirits, and the campers running out in joy.
>
> —*E. B. White, "Once More to the Lake"*

Analogies come in a variety of lengths, from several sentences to an entire essay, depending upon the writer's purpose. As you practice your writing in this composition class, you may find that incorporating an analogy into one of your essays is an effective way to explain, emphasize, or help support an idea.

Reviewing Your Progress

After you have completed your essay developed by comparison/contrast, take a moment to measure your progress as a writer by responding to the following questions. Such analysis will help you to recognize growth in your writing skills and may enable you to identify areas that are still problematic.

1. Which part of your essay do you like the best? Why?

2. Which point of comparison or contrast do you think is the most successful? Why is it effective?

3. What part of your essay gave you the most trouble? How did you overcome the problem?

4. If you had more time to work on this essay, what would receive additional attention? Why?

5. What did you learn about your topic from writing this essay? About yourself as a writer?

Strategy Four: Development by Definition

Frequently in conversation we must stop to ask, "What do you mean by that?" because in some cases our failure to comprehend just one particular term may lead to total misunderstanding. Suppose, for example, in a discussion with a friend, you refer to a new law as a piece of "liberal legislation"; if you and your friend do not share the same definition of "liberal," your remark may be completely misinterpreted. Here's another example: if you tell your grandparents that you are "headed for the man-cave for some plasma and tweets," will they think you are going for a blood transfusion and bird watching in a natural area or that you are headed to the basement rec room for TV and text messaging? In other words, a clear understanding of terms or ideas is often essential to meaningful communication.

Sometimes a dictionary definition or a one- or two-sentence explanation is all a term needs (Hemingway, for example, once defined courage as "grace under pressure"). And sometimes a brief, humorous definition can cut right to the heart of the matter (e.g., Destinesia: wandering into a room and forgetting what you came for).*

Frequently, however, you will find it necessary to provide an *extended definition*—that is, a longer, more detailed explanation that thoroughly defines the subject. Essays of extended definitions are quite common; think, for instance, of the articles you've seen on "mercy killing," "assisted suicide," or abortion that define "life" in a variety of ways. Other recent essays have grappled with defining such complex concepts as free speech, animal rights, pornography, affirmative action, and gun control.

Discussions of many nationwide issues often contain confusing or controversial terms. Hearing about the state of American finances, you might wish for a clearer understanding of words such as "recession," "bailout," or "toxic assets." Ecological proposals often

---

*Even graffiti employ definition. One bathroom wall favorite: "Death is Nature's way of telling you to slow down." Another, obviously written by an English major: "A double negative is a no-no."

talk about "sustainability" and "green" choices. Following the events of September 11, 2001, the definitions of many divisive words continue to be debated nationally. Who is a "terrorist"? Are procedures such as waterboarding "enhanced interrogation techniques" or "torture"? What is the difference between an "enemy combatant," a "detainee," and a "political prisoner"? Is it "patriotic" to oppose military actions of one's country? Today we need to clearly understand specific meanings of language before we can make intelligent decisions or take appropriate actions.

Why Do We Define?

Essays of extended definition are usually written for one or more of the following reasons:

1. To clarify an abstract term or concept ("hero," "success," "friendship," "loyalty")

2. To provide a personal interpretation of a term that the writer feels is vague, controversial, misused, or misunderstood ("feminist," " meme," "eco-terrorist," "multiculturalism")

3. To explain a new or unusual term or phrase found in popular culture, slang, or dialect, or within a particular geographic area, age set, or cultural group ("hip-hop," "Twittersphere," "flashmob," "helicopter parent," "boomerang kids," "lagniappe")

4. To make understandable the language or technical terms of a particular field of study, a profession, or an industry ("deconstruction," "identity spoofing," "retinitis pigmentosa," "subprime mortgage")

5. To offer information about a term or an idea to a particular interested audience (antique collectors learning about "Depression glass," movie buffs understanding "film noir," home decorators exploring "Feng Shui")

6. To inform and entertain by presenting the colorful history, uses, effects, or examples of a word, expression, concept, group, or group activity ("comfort food," "Zydeco music," "urban legends," "Kwanzaa," "power yoga")

Developing Your Essay

Here are four suggestions to help you prepare your essay of extended definition:

Know your purpose. Sometimes we need to define a term as clearly and objectively as possible. As a laboratory assistant, for instance, you might need to explain a technical measuring instrument to a group of new students. At other times, however, we may wish to persuade as well as inform our readers. People's interpretations of words, especially abstract or controversial terms, can, and often do, differ greatly depending on their point of view. After all, one person's protest march can be another person's street riot. Consequently, before you begin writing, decide on your purpose. If your readers need objective information only, make your definition as unbiased as you can; if your goal is to convince them that your point of view is the right or best one, you may adopt a variety of persuasive techniques as well as subjective (or even humorous) language.

For example, readers of a paper entitled "The Joys of Catching Bronco-mania" should quickly realize they are not getting an objective medical analysis of Colorado football fever.

Give your readers a reason to read. One way to introduce your subject is to explain the previous use, misuse, or misunderstanding of the term; then present your new or better interpretation of the term or concept. An introduction and thesis defining a new word in popular usage might state, "Although people who suffer from weak immune systems might suddenly fear breathing the same air as someone suffering from affluenza, they needn't worry. 'Affluenza' isn't germ-laden; it's simply a colorful term describing the out-of-control consumerism spreading like an epidemic through America today." Or consider this introduction and thesis aimed at a word the writer feels is unclear to many readers: "When the credits roll at the end of a movie, much of the audience may be perplexed to see the job of 'best boy' listed. No, the 'best boy' isn't the nicest kid on the set—he (or she) is, in fact, the key electrician's first assistant, who helps arrange the lights for the movie's director of photography."

Keep your audience in mind to anticipate and avoid problems of clarity. Because you are trying to present a new or improved definition, you must strive above all for clarity. Ask yourself, "Who is my intended audience? What terms or parts of my definition are strange to them?" You don't help your audience, for example, by defining one campus slang expression in terms of other bits of unfamiliar slang. If, in other words, you discuss "mouse potatoes" as "Google bombers," you may be confusing some readers more than you are informing them. If your assignment doesn't specify a particular audience, you may find it useful to imagine one. You might pretend, for instance, that you're defining current campus slang for your parents, clarifying a local expression for a foreign visitor, or explaining a computer innovation to a technophobic friend. Remember that your definition is effective only if your explanation is clear, not just to you but to those unfamiliar with or confused about the term or concept under discussion.

Use as many strategies as necessary to clarify your definition. Depending on your subject, you may use any number of the following methods in your essay to define your term:

1. Describe the parts or distinguishing characteristics.*
2. Offer some examples.
3. Compare to or contrast with similar terms.
4. Explain an operation or a process.
5. State some familiar synonyms.
6. Define by negation (that is, tell what the term doesn't mean).
7. Present the history or trace its development or changes from the original linguistical meaning.

---

*With some topics, it may also be useful to describe the genus, class, or species to which the subject belongs.

8. Discuss causes or effects.

9. Identify times/places of use or appearance.

10. Associate it with recognizable people, places, or ideas.

To illustrate some of the methods suggested here, let's suppose you want to write an extended definition of "crossover" country music. You might choose several of these methods:

- Describe the parts: lyrics, musical sound, instruments, typical subject matter.
- Compare to or contrast with other kinds of music, such as traditional country music, "pop," and Rockabilly.
- Give some examples of famous "crossover" country songs and artists.
- Trace its historical development from traditional country music to its present state.

In the paper on "crossover" country music or in any definition essay, you should, of course, use only those methods that will best define your term. Never include methods purely for the sake of exhibiting a variety of techniques. You, the writer, must decide which method or methods work best, which should receive the most emphasis, and in which order the chosen methods of definition should appear.

Problems to Avoid

Here is a list of "don'ts" for the writer of extended-definition essays:

Don't present an incomplete definition. An inadequate definition is often the result of choosing a subject too broad or complex for your essay. You probably can't, for instance, do a good job of defining "twentieth-century modern art" in all its varieties in a short essay; you might, however, introduce your reader to some specific school of modern art, such as Cubism or Surrealism. Always narrow your subject to a manageable size and then define it as thoroughly as possible.

Don't begin every definition essay by quoting Webster. If you must include a standard definition of your term, try to find a unique way of blending it into your discussion, perhaps as a point of contrast to your explanation of a word's new or expanded meaning. Dictionary definitions are generally so overused as opening sentences that they can drive composition teachers to seek more interesting jobs, such as measuring spaghetti in a pasta factory. Don't bore your audience to death; it's a terrible way to go.

Don't define vaguely or by using generalities. As always, use specific, vivid details to explain your subject. If, for example, you define a shamrock as "a green plant with three leaves," you have also described hundreds of other plants, including poison ivy. Consequently, you must select details that will make your subject distinct from any other. Including concrete examples is frequently useful in any essay but especially so when you are defining an abstract term, such as "pride," "patriotism," or "prejudice." To make your definition both interesting and clear, always add as many precise details as possible. (◆ For a review of using specific, colorful language, see pages 127, 141–142, and 162–166.)

Don't offer circular definitions. To define a poet as "one who writes poetry" or the American Dream as "the dream most Americans hold dear" is about as helpful as a doctor telling a patient, "Your illness is primarily a lack of good health." Explain your subject; don't just rename it.

Essay Topics

© Inspirestock/CORBIS

Here are several suggestions for terms or concepts whose meanings might be unclear to a particular audience. Narrow any topic that seems too broad for your assignment, and decide before writing whether your definition will be objective or subjective, as appropriate for your purpose and readers. (Student writers, by the way, often note that abstract concepts are harder to define than the more concrete subjects, so proceed at your own risk, and remember to use plenty of specific detail in your essay.) ◆ For additional ideas, turn to the "Suggestions for Writing" section following the professional essay (page 258).

1. A current slang, campus, local, or popular culture expression

2. A term from your field of study

3. A slob (or some other annoying kind of roommate, friend, relative, or coworker)

4. Student success or failure

5. A good/bad teacher, clerk, coach, friend, parent, date, or spouse

6. Heroism or cowardice

7. A term from science or technology

8. A kind of music, painting, architecture, or dance

9. Cyberbullying (or some other form of social harassment)

10. A current fad or style or one from the past

11. A rebel or conformist

12. A family or hometown expression

13. A good/bad restaurant, store, movie theater, nightspot, class

14. Self-respect

15. Prejudice or discrimination

16. An important historical movement or group

continued on next page

17. A controversial political idea or term

18. A term from a hobby or sport

19. A medical term or condition

20. Select a painting or photograph in which you think the artist offers a visual definition of the subject matter (e.g., heroism, sorrow, mortality, prosperity). Explain this definition by examining the artist's choice and arrangement of details in the picture. For example, study George Tooker's painting *The Subway*. What aspect of urban life is represented here? What parts of the picture illustrate and clarify this point of view? Or consider another picture in this text, such as *The Scream* (page 122). (A list of artworks follows the Table of Contents.)

The Subway, 1950, by George Tooker

George Tooker, 1920-2011, *The Subway*, 1950. Egg tempera on composition board: 18 1/8 x 36 1/8 in. (46.04 x 91.76 cm). Whitney Museum of American Art, New York; Purchase, with funds from the Juliana Force Purchase Award 50.23.

A Topic Proposal for Your Essay

Selecting the right subject matter is important to every writer. To help you clarify your ideas and strengthen your commitment to your topic, here is a proposal sheet that asks you to describe some of your ideas about your subject before you begin drafting. Although your ideas may change as you write (they will almost certainly become more refined), thinking through your topic now may help you avoid several false starts.

1. What subject will your essay define? Will you define this subject objectively or subjectively? Why?

2. Why are you interested in this topic? Do you have a personal or professional connection to the subject? State at least one reason for your choice of topic.

3. Is this a significant topic of interest to others? Why? Who specifically might find it interesting, informative, or entertaining?

4. Is your subject a controversial, ambiguous, or new term? What will readers gain by understanding this term as defined from your point of view?

5. Writers use a variety of techniques to define terms. At this point, list at least two techniques you think you might use to help readers understand your topic.

6. What difficulties, if any, can you foresee during the drafting of this essay? For example, do you need to do any additional reading or interviewing to collect information for your definition?

Sample Student Essay

A student with an interest in running wrote the following essay defining "runner's high." Note that he uses several methods to define his subject, one that is difficult to explain to those who have not experienced it firsthand.

BLIND PACES

1   After running the Mile-Hi ten-kilometer race in my hometown, I spoke with several of the leading runners about their experiences in the race. While most of them agreed that the course, which passed through a beautifully wooded yet overly hilly country area, was difficult, they also agreed that it was one of the best races of their running careers. They could not, however, explain why it was such a wonderful race but could rather only mumble something about the tall trees, cool air, and sandy path. When pressed, most of them didn't even remember specific details about the course, except the start and finish, and ended their descriptions with a blank—but contented—stare. This self-satisfied, yet almost indescribable, feeling is often the result of an experienced runner running, a feeling often called, because of its similarities to other euphoric experiences, "runner's high."

Introduction: An example and a general definition of the term

2   Because this experience is seemingly impossible to define, perhaps a description of what runner's high is not might, by contrast, lead to

---

a better understanding of what it is. I clearly remember—about five

Definition
by negation,
contrast

years ago—when I first took up running. My first day, I donned my tennis shorts, ragged T-shirt, and white discount-store tennis shoes somewhat ashamedly, knowing that they were symbolic of my novice status. I plodded around my block—just over a half mile—in a little more than four minutes, feeling and regretting every painful step. My shins and thighs revolted at every jarring move, and my lungs wheezed uncontrollably, gasping for air, yet denied that basic necessity. Worst of all, I was conscious of every aspect of my existence—from the swinging of my arms to the slap of my feet on the road, and from the sweat dripping into my eyes and ears and mouth, to the frantic inhaling and exhaling of my lungs. I kept my eyes carefully peeled on the horizon or the next turn in the road, judging how far away it was, how long it would take me to get there, and how much torture was left before I reached home. These first few runs were, of course, the worst—as far from any euphoria or "high" as possible. They did, however, slowly become easier as my body became accustomed to running.

3   After a few months, in fact, I felt serious enough about this new pursuit to invest in a pair of real running shoes and shorts. Admittedly, these changes added to the comfort of my endeavor, but it wasn't until two full years later that the biggest change occurred—and I experienced my first real "high." It was a fall day. The air was a cool sixty-five degrees, the sun was shining intently, the sky was a clear, crisp blue, and a few dead leaves were scattered across the browning lawn. I stepped out onto the road and headed north towards a nearby park for my routine jog.

Personal
example

The next thing I remember, however, was not my run through the park, but rather my return, some forty-two minutes and six miles later, to my house. I woke, as if out of a dream, just as I slowed to a walk, cooling

Effects of the
"high"

down from my run. The only memory I had of my run was a feeling of floating on air—as if my real self were somewhere above and detached from my body, looking down on my physical self as it went through its blind paces. At first, I felt scared—what if I had run out in front of a car? Would I have even known it? I felt as if I had been asleep or out of control, that my brain had, in some real sense, been turned off.

4   Now, after five years of running and hundreds of such mystical experiences, I realize that I had never lost control while in this euphoric state—and that my brain hadn't been turned off, or, at least, not completely. But what does happen is hard to prove. George Sheehan, in a column for *Runner's World*, suggests that "altered states," such as runner's high, result from the loss of conscious control, from the temporary cessation of left-brain messages and the dominance of right-brain activity (the left hemisphere being the seat of reason and rationality; the right, of emotions and inherited archetypal feelings) (14). Another explanation comes from Dr. Jerry Lynch, who argues, in his book *The Total Runner*, that the "high" results from the secretion of natural opiates, called beta endorphins, in the brain (213). My own explanation draws on both these medical explanations and is perhaps slightly more mystical. It's just possible that indeed natural opiates do go to work and consequently our brains lose track of the ins and outs of everyday activities—of jobs and classes and responsibilities. And because of this relaxed, drugged state, we are able to reach down into something more fundamental, something that ties us not only to each other but to all creation, here and gone. We rejoin nature, rediscovering the thread that links us to the universe.

Possible causes of the feeling: Two authorities

The writer's explanation

5   My explanation is, of course, unscientific and therefore suspect. But I found myself, that day of the Mile-Hi Ten K run, eagerly trying to discuss my experience with the other runners: I wanted desperately to discover where I had been and what I had been doing during the race for which I received my first trophy. I didn't discover the answer from my fellow runners that day, but it didn't matter. I'm still running and still feeling the glow—whatever it is.

Conclusion: An incomplete understanding doesn't hamper enjoyment

WORKS CITED*

Lynch, Jerry. *The Total Runner: A Complete Mind-Body Guide to Optimal Performance*. Englewood Cliffs: Prentice, 1987. Print.

Sheehan, George. "Altered States." *Runner's* World Aug. 1988: 14. Print.

Professional Essay**

THE MUNCHAUSEN MYSTERY†

Don R. Lipsitt

As a clinical professor of psychiatry at Harvard Medical School, Don R. Lipsitt has written over one hundred articles on mental health and coedited five books, including *Hypochondriasis: Modern Perspectives on an Ancient Malady* (2001) and the *Handbook of Studies on General Hospital Psychiatry* (1991). In 2001 he was awarded a Lifetime Achievement Award from the Association of Academic Psychiatry. He published this article in *Psychology Today* in 1983.

Pre-reading Thoughts: Recall the last time someone clearly explained a new concept to you, perhaps in a class, at work, or during recreation. By what means was this subject defined and clarified for you—examples, description, comparisons, analysis of parts, or other techniques?

1   In Thomas Mann's *Confessions of Felix Krull, Confidence Man*, young Felix fabricates an illness and convinces both his mother and the family doctor that he is sick. Felix describes the intense pleasure that his performance brings him. "I was delirious with the alternate tension and relaxation necessary to give reality, in my own eyes and others, to a condition that did not exist."

2   I estimate that in any given year in the United States, every general hospital with 100 or more beds admits an average of two patients who deliberately mimic symptoms of disease so convincingly that they deceive reasonably competent physicians. The patients' ages range from 11 to 60, but most are men in their 20s and 30s. Often these strange imposters wander from hospital to hospital, but even if we count only one patient per hospital, we are left with the staggering figure of approximately 4,000 people each year who devote their energies to fooling medical practitioners. If each incurs a cost of $1,000 to $10,000—bills that are not unusual, and that are rarely paid—the annual drain on health services alone is between $4 million and $40 million.

---

*Editor's note: In a formal research paper, the "Works Cited" list appears on a separate page.

** ◆ To help you read this essay analytically, review pages 179–181.

† "The Munchausen Mystery" by Don R. Lipsitt from PSYCHOLOGY TODAY, February 1983.

3   What do these people hope to gain? Nothing more, experience and research suggest, than the opportunity to assume the role of patient—in some cases, all the way to the operating table.

4   Unlike hypochondriacs, who really believe that they are ill, these people intentionally use varied and often sophisticated deceptions to duplicate medical problems. These deceptions include: blood "spit up" from a rubber pouch concealed in the mouth; genital bleeding deliberately caused by sharp objects; hypoglycemia (low blood sugar) induced by insulin injections; and skin infections or abscesses caused by injecting oneself with feces, sputum, or laboratory cultures of bacteria. A patient who called himself "the Duncan Hines of American hospitals" logged about 400 admissions in 25 years. Another patient, dubbed the "Indiana cyclone," was hospitalized in at least 12 states and two countries. The dramatic fabrication and extensive wandering often observed in such individuals prompted the late British physician Richard Asher in 1951 to label their "condition" the Munchausen Syndrome, after a flamboyant 18th-century teller of tall tales fictionalized in *The Adventures of Baron von Munchausen,* by Rudolph Erich Raspe. But as Asher himself came to realize, the name is somewhat misleading. While stories of the Baron's escapades are always palpably absurd, the accounts of patients whose condition bears his name are generally quite feasible. "Indeed," says Asher, "it is the credibility of their stories that makes these patients such a perpetual and tedious problem."

5   For obvious reasons, Munchausen patients have been difficult to study—they usually flee once their fictions are exposed. But research to this point provides a minimal portrait. In addition to being primarily men in their 20s and 30s, most have high IQs (as their imaginative inventions indicate), often abuse but are not necessarily addicted to drugs, come from a background in which a doctor was an important figure, are employed in health care, and are productive citizens between episodes.

6   What produces their medical madness? There are three main explanations:

7   The psychoanalytic interpretation draws attention to the unconscious. The Munchausen patient, by feigning illness, presents himself simultaneously as victim and victimizer, and compulsively re-enacts unresolved conflicts: The weak child/patient is challenging and even defying the strong father/surgeon. Paradoxically, the weak patient controls the surgeon/parent—and risks death!—by "making" the doctor perform needless surgery. The psychoanalytic view also sees in the syndrome an attempt to continue into adulthood the game of "doctor," which characterizes a phase of childhood development.

8   A second explanation locates the source of Munchausen behavior in a personality trait known as borderline character disorder. According to Otto Kernberg, a psychoanalyst at Cornell who has most fully researched this trait, the core problems are untamed (often unconscious) rage and chronic feelings of boredom, two emotions that work against each other. The Munchausen character, for example, presents himself as a "sick" patient, a condition that should appeal to a dedicated physician—yet no accepting relationship can grow between a deceptive patient and a suspecting physician who is alternately idealized and despised.

9   The third explanation looks to excessive stress as the trigger that starts Munchausen patients on their medical odyssey. Many of them began their "wandering" and symptom mimicry in response to cumulative major disappointments,

losses, or damage to self-image. One patient first sought surgery for questionable persistent stomach pains after being jilted by a medical-student lover, beginning a long string of lies and hospitalizations.

10   We are beginning to identify the reasons for the behavior of Munchausen patients, but we are still far from knowing how to free them of their remarkably creative compulsion for self-destructive behavior.

Questions on Content, Structure, and Style

1. Why does Lipsitt begin his essay with reference to Thomas Mann's character in *Confessions of Felix Krull, Confidence Man*?

2. What effect does the essay's title have on readers? Why didn't Lipsitt simply call this essay "Munchausen Syndrome"?

3. Why does Lipsitt feel this syndrome is important to understand? How does this problem affect the health-care system?

4. Why explain the origin of the syndrome's name?

5. Why does Lipsitt use specific examples of "deceptions" to develop his extended definition?

6. Similarly, why does Lipsitt offer examples of actual patients? Would additional examples be helpful?

7. How does Lipsitt use contrast as a technique of definition in paragraph 4?

8. What other strategy of definition does Lipsitt employ in paragraphs 6–9? Why might readers interested in understanding this syndrome want such discussion?

9. Evaluate the essay's conclusion. Is it an effective choice for this essay?

10. After reading Lipsitt's descriptive details, examples, and analysis, do you feel you now have a general understanding of a new term? If the writer were to expand his definition, what might he add to make your understanding even more complete? More statistics? Case studies? Testimony from doctors or patients themselves?

Vocabulary

fabricates (1)	sputum (4)	psychoanalytic (7)
mimic (2)	palpably (4)	paradoxically (7)
incurs (2)	feasible (4)	odyssey (9)
hypochondriacs (4)		

Suggestions for Writing

Try using Don Lipsitt's "The Munchausen Mystery" as a stepping-stone to your essay. Select a puzzling or "mysterious" subject from a field of study (e.g., black holes in space) or from an interest you have explored (or would like to explore). Write an extended definition, as Lipsitt did, that explains this mystery for your readers. As appropriate, include information about its characteristics, parts, history, possible causes, effects, solutions, benefits, or dangers. Or investigate a well-known mystery, such as Stonehenge, the Bermuda Triangle, the Nazca path drawings, the Marfa lights, King Tut's "curse," Bigfoot, the Easter Island statues, or perhaps even a famous local ghost. Remember that your essay should offer in-depth explanation, not just general description.

A Revision Worksheet

© Ryan McVay/
Photodisc/Getty Images

As you write your rough drafts, consult Chapter 5 for guidance through the revision process. In addition, here are a few questions to ask yourself as you revise your extended-definition essay:

1. Is the subject narrowed to manageable size, and is the purpose of the definition clear to the readers?

2. If the definition is objective, is the language as neutral as possible?

3. If the definition is subjective, is the point of view obvious to the readers?

4. Are all the words and parts of the definition itself clear to the essay's particular audience?

5. Are there enough explanatory methods (examples, descriptions, history, causes, effects, etc.) used to make the definition clear and informative?

6. Have the various methods been organized and ordered in an effective way?

7. Does the essay contain enough specific details to make the definition clear and distinct rather than vague or circular? Where could additional details be added?

Collaborative Activity: After you've revised your essay extensively, exchange rough drafts with a classmate and answer these questions for each other, making specific suggestions for improvement wherever appropriate. (◆ For advice on productive participation in classroom workshops, see pages 116–120.)

Reviewing Your Progress

After you have completed your essay developed by definition, take a moment to measure your progress as a writer by responding to the following questions. Such analysis will help you to recognize growth in your writing skills and may enable you to identify areas that are still problematic.

1. What do you like best about your essay? Why?

2. After considering the various methods of definition you used in your essay, which one do you think offered the clearest or most persuasive explanation of your topic? Why was that particular technique effective in this essay?

3. What part of your essay gave you the most trouble? How did you overcome the problem?

4. If you had more time to work on this essay, what would receive additional attention? Why?

5. What did you learn about your topic from writing this essay? About yourself as a writer?

Strategy Five: Development by Division and Classification

To make large or complex subjects easier to comprehend, we frequently apply the principles of *division* or *classification*.

Division

Division is the act of separating something into its component parts so that it may be better understood or used by the reader. For example, consider a complex subject such as the national budget. Perhaps you have seen a picture on television or in the newspaper of the budget represented by a circle or a pie that has been divided into parts and labeled: a certain percentage or "slice" of the budget designated for military spending, another slice for social services, another for education, and so on. By studying the budget after it has been divided into its parts, taxpayers may have a better sense of how their money is being spent.

As a student, you see division in action in many of your college courses. A literature teacher, for instance, might approach a particular drama by dividing its plot into stages such as exposition, rising action, climax, falling action, and dénouement. Or your chemistry lab instructor may ask you to break down a substance into its components to learn how the parts interact to form the chemical compound. Even this textbook is divided into chapters to make it easier for you to use. When you think of *division*, then, think of dividing, separating, or breaking down one subject (often a large or complex or unfamiliar one) into its parts to help people understand it more easily.

Classification

While the principle of division calls for separating one thing into its parts, *classification* systematically groups a number of things into categories to make the information easier to grasp. Without some sort of imposed system of order, a body of information can be a jumble of facts and figures. For example, at some point you may have turned to the classified ads in a print newspaper or to an online site such as Craigslist. If the ads were not classified into categories such as "houses to rent," "cars for sale," and "jobs," you would have to search through numerous ads to find the service, opportunity, or item you needed.

Classification occurs everywhere around you. As a student, you may be classified as a freshman, sophomore, junior, or senior; you may also be classified by your major. If you vote, you may be categorized as a Democrat, Republican, Independent, Socialist, or something else; if you attend religious services, you may be classified as Baptist, Methodist, Catholic, Jewish, and so on. The books you buy may be grouped and shelved by the bookstore into "mysteries," "Westerns," "biographies," "science fiction," and other categories; the movies you see have already been typed as "G," "PG," "PG-13," "R," or "NC-17." Professionals classify almost every kind of knowledge: ornithologists classify birds; etymologists classify words by origins; botanists classify plants; zoologists classify animals.

Remember that *classification* differs from division in that it sorts and organizes *many* things into appropriate groups, types, kinds, or categories. *Division* begins with *one* thing and separates it into its parts.

Developing Your Essay

A classification or division paper is generally easy to develop. Each part or category is identified and described in a major part of the body of the essay. Frequently, one body paragraph will be devoted to each category. Here are three additional hints for writing your essay:

Select one principle of classification or division and stick to it. If you are classifying students by major, for instance, don't suddenly switch to classification by college: French, economics, psychology, *arts and sciences*, math, and chemistry. A similar error occurs in this classification of dogs by breeds because it includes a physical characteristic: spaniels, terriers, *long-haired*, hounds, and retrievers. Decide on what basis of division you will classify or divide your subject and then be consistent throughout your essay.

Make the purpose of your division or classification clear to your audience. Don't just announce that "There are four kinds of 'X'" or that "'Z' has three important parts." Why does your particular audience need this information? Consider these sample thesis statements:

- By recognizing the three kinds of poisonous snakes in this area, campers and backpackers may be able to take the proper medical steps if they are bitten.
- Knowing the four types of spinning reels will help those new to mullet fishing purchase the equipment best suited to their needs.
- Although karate has become a popular form of exercise as well as of self-defense, few people know what the ascending levels of achievement—or "belts" as they are called—actually stand for.

Organize your material for a particular purpose and then explain to your readers what that purpose is.

Account for all the parts in your division or classification. Don't, for instance, claim to classify all the evergreen trees native to your hometown and then leave out one or more species. For a short essay, narrow your ruling principle rather than omit categories. You couldn't, for instance, classify all the architectural styles in the United States in a short paper, but you might discuss the major styles on your campus. In the same manner, the enormous task of classifying all types of mental illness might be narrowed to the most common forms of childhood schizophrenia. However you narrow your topic, remember that in a formal classification, all the parts must be accounted for.

Like most rules, the preceding one has an exception. If your instructor permits, you can also write a satirical or humorous classification. In this sort of essay, you make up your own categories as well as your thesis. One writer, for example, recently wrote about the kinds of moviegoers who spoil the show for everyone else, such as "the babbling idiot," "the texting screen-flasher," and "the wandering dawdler." Another female student described blind dates to avoid, including "Mr. Neanderthal," "Timothy Timid," "Red, the Raging Rebel," and "Frat-Rat Freddie," among others. Still another student classified the various kinds of people who frequent the school library at 2 A.M. In this kind of informal essay, in which you're making a humorous or satirical point about your subject, your classification should be more than random silliness. Effective humor should ultimately make good sense, not nonsense.

Problems to Avoid

Avoid underdeveloped categories. A classification or division essay is not a mechanical list; each category should contain enough specific details to make it clearly recognizable and interesting. To present each category or part, you may draw on the methods of development you already know, such as example, comparison and contrast, and definition. Try to use the same techniques in each category so that no one category or part of your essay seems underdeveloped or unclear.

Avoid indistinct categories. Each category should be a separate unit; there should be no overlap among categories. For example, in a classification of shirts by fabric, the inclusion of flannel with silk, nylon, and cotton is an overlap because flannel is a kind of cotton. Similarly, in a classification of soft drinks by flavor, to include sugar-free with cola, root beer, orange, grape, and so on, is misleading because sugar-free drinks come in many different flavors. In other words, make each category unique.

Avoid too few or too many categories. A classification essay should have at least three categories, avoiding the either-or dichotomy. On the other hand, too many categories give a short essay the appearance of a list rather than a discussion. Whatever the number, don't forget to use transitional devices for easy movement from category to category.

Essay Topics

© Inspirestock/CORBIS

Narrow and focus your subject by selecting an appropriate principle of division or classification. Some of the following suggestions may be appropriate for humorous essays ("The Three Best Breeds of Cats for Antisocial People").

◆ For additional ideas, see the "Suggestions for Writing" section following the professional essays (pages 269 and 272).

continued on next page

1. Attitudes towards a current controversy

2. Theories explaining "X" (e.g., disappearance of dinosaurs, climate change in Antarctica)

3. Chronic moochers, dangerous drivers, annoying cell phone users, or some other irritating group

4. Heroes in a particular field

5. Reasons people participate in some activity (or excuses for not participating)

6. Summer or part-time jobs on campus

7. Customers at your work or at a business you frequent

8. Kinds of people gathered in a particular locale: in a waiting room, standing in a grocery store line, attending a particular concert or campus event, etc.

9. Specializations in your field of study

10. Approaches to studying a subject

11. Myths or common misperceptions about a person, place, or thing

12. Dogs, cats, birds, or other pets

13. Popular kinds of movies, music, or video games (or types within a larger category: kinds of teen vampire-movies or varieties of heavy-metal music)

14. Vacations or Spring Break trips

15. Most common distractions interfering with composition students' vows to revise their essays one more time

16. Methods of accomplishing a task (e.g., ways to conduct an experiment, ways to introduce a bill into Congress)

17. Bosses or co-workers to avoid or cultivate

18. Kinds of tools or equipment for a particular task in your field of study

19. Diets, exercise, or stress-reduction programs (or their participants)

20. Amateur athletes, coaches, or sports fans (including those you hope aren't sitting next to you at an athletic event)

Wisconsin Cheeseheads cheer on the Green Bay Packers.

Mark Richards/PhotoEdit

A Topic Proposal for Your Essay

Selecting the right subject matter is important to every writer. To help you clarify your ideas and strengthen your commitment to your topic, here is a proposal sheet that asks you to describe some of your preliminary ideas about your subject before you begin drafting. Although your ideas may change as you write (they will almost certainly become more refined), thinking through your choice of topic now may help you avoid several false starts.

1. What is the subject of your essay? Will you write an essay of classification or division?
2. What principle of classification or division will you use? Why is this a useful or informative principle for your particular topic and readers?
3. Why are you interested in this topic? Do you have a personal or professional connection to the subject? State at least one reason for your choice of topic.
4. Is this a significant topic of interest to others? Why? Who specifically might find it interesting, informative, or entertaining?
5. List at least three categories you are considering for development in your essay.
6. What difficulties, if any, might arise from this topic during the drafting of your essay? For example, do you know enough about your topic to offer details that will make each of your categories clear and distinct to your readers?

Sample Student Essay

In the following essay, the student writer divided the Mesa Verde Native American Era into three time periods that correspond to changes in the people's domestic skills, crafts, and housing. Note the writer's use of description and examples to help the reader distinguish one time period from another.

THE NATIVE AMERICAN ERA AT MESA VERDE

1   Visiting Mesa Verde National Park is a trip back in time to two and a half centuries before Columbus. The park, located in southwestern Colorado, is the setting of a silent stone city, ten ruins built into protective seven-hundred-foot cliffs that housed hundreds of people from the pre-Columbian era to the end of the thirteenth century. Visitors to the park often enjoy its architecture and history more if they know a little about the various people who lived there. The Native American Era may be

Introduction: Establishing a reason for knowing the classification

divided into three time periods that show growing sophistication in such activities as crafts, hunting, trade, and housing: Basket Maker (1–450 C.E.), Modified Basket Maker (450–750 C.E.), and Pueblo (750–1300 C.E.).*

Principle of division of the Native American Era

2   The earliest Mesa Verdeans, the Basket Makers, whose ancestors had been nomads, sought shelter from the dry plains in the cliff caves and became farmers. During growing seasons they climbed up toeholds cut in the cliffs and grew beans and squash on the green mesa above. Settling down also meant more time for crafts. They didn't make pottery yet but instead wove intricate baskets that held water. Instead of depending on raw meats and vegetables, they could now cook food in these baskets by dropping heated rocks into the water. Because the Basket Makers hadn't discovered the bow and arrow yet, they had to rely on the inaccurate spear, which meant little fresh meat and few animal skins. Consequently, they wore little clothing but liked bone, seed, and stone ornaments.

Time period one: Early cliff life

3   The second period, 450–750 C.E., saw the invention of pottery, the bow and arrow, and houses. Pottery was apparently learned from other tribes. From crude clay baked in the sun, the Mesa Verdeans advanced to clay mixed with straw and sand and baked in kilns. Paints were concocted from plants and minerals, and the tribe produced a variety of beautifully decorated mugs, bowls, jars, pitchers, and canteens. Such pots meant that water could be stored for longer periods, and perhaps a water supply encouraged more trade with neighboring tribes. These Mesa Verdeans also acquired the bow and arrow, a weapon that improved their hunting skills, and enlarged their wardrobes to include animal skins and feather blankets. Their individual living quarters, called pithouses, consisted of twenty-foot-wide holes in the ground with log, grasses, and earthen framework over them.

Time period two: New crafts, trade, and housing

---

* Last summer I worked at Mesa Verde as a student-guide for the Parks Service; the information in this paper is based on the tour I gave three times a week to hundreds of visitors to the park.

Time period
three: Expanded
community
living and trade

4   The third period lasted until 1300 C.E. and saw the innovation of
pueblos, or groups of dwellings, instead of single-family units. Nearly
eight hundred dwellings show the large number of people who inhabited
the complex tunneled houses, shops, storage rooms, courtyards, and
community centers whose masonry walls, often elaborately decorated,
were three and four stories high. At the spacious Balcony House pueblo,
for example, an adobe court lies beneath another vaulted roof; on three
sides stand two-story houses with balconies that lead from one room to
the next. In back of the court is a spring, and along the front side is a
low wall that kept the children from falling down the seven-hundred-
foot cliff to the canyon floor below. Balcony House pueblo also contains
two kivas, circular subterranean ceremonial chambers that show the
importance of fellowship and religion to the people of this era. During
this period the Mesa Verdeans were still farmers and potters, but cotton
cloth and other nonnative products found at the ruins suggest a healthy
trade with the south. But despite the trade goods, sophisticated pottery,
and such innovations in clothing as the "disposable" juniper-bark diapers
of babies, life was still simple; the Mesa Verdeans had no system of
writing, no wheel, and no metal.

5   Near the end of the thirteenth century, the cliff dwellings became
ghost towns. Archaeologists don't know for certain why the Mesa
Verdeans left their elaborate homes, but they speculate that a drought
that lasted some twenty years may have driven them south into New
Mexico and Arizona, where strikingly similar crafts and tools have been
found. Regardless of their reason for leaving, they left an amazing
architectural and cultural legacy. Learning about the people who lived in
Mesa Verde centuries ago provides an even deeper appreciation of the
cliff palaces that awe thousands of national park visitors every year.

Conclusion: The
importance of
understanding
Mesa Verde's
people

Professional Essay: Classification*

The Plot Against People**

Russell Baker

Russell Baker was a journalist and social commentator for over forty years before his retirement in 2004. His "Observer" columns, written for the *New York Times* and syndicated throughout the country, won him both the George Polk Award for Distinguished Commentary and a Pulitzer Prize for journalism. He has published numerous books, including *Growing Up* (1982), an autobiography that won him a second Pulitzer Prize; *The Good Times* (1989); and *Looking Back* (2002). This often-reprinted essay originally appeared in the *New York Times* in 1968.

Pre-reading Thoughts: What one possession or piece of technology in your life causes the most frustration for you? How do you successfully triumph over this misery?

1   Inanimate objects are classified into three major categories—those that don't work, those that break down and those that get lost.

2   The goal of all inanimate objects is to resist man and ultimately to defeat him, and the three major classifications are based on the method each object uses to achieve its purpose. As a general rule, any object capable of breaking down at the moment when it is most needed will do so. The automobile is typical of the category.

3   With the cunning typical of its breed, the automobile never breaks down while entering a filling station with a large staff of idle mechanics. It waits until it reaches a downtown intersection in the middle of the rush hour, or until it is fully loaded with family and luggage on the Ohio Turnpike.

4   Thus it creates maximum misery, inconvenience, frustration and irritability among its human cargo, thereby reducing its owner's life span.

5   Washing machines, garbage disposals, lawn mowers, light bulbs, automatic laundry dryers, water pipes, furnaces, electrical fuses, television tubes, hose nozzles, tape recorders, slide projectors—all are in league with the automobile to take their turn at breaking down whenever life threatens to flow smoothly for their human enemies.

6   Many inanimate objects, of course, find it extremely difficult to break down. Pliers, for example, and gloves and keys are almost totally incapable of breaking down. Therefore, they have had to evolve a different technique for resisting man.

7   They get lost. Science has still not solved the mystery of how they do it, and no man has ever caught one of them in the act of getting lost. The most plausible theory is that they have developed a secret method of locomotion which they are able to conceal the instant a human eye falls upon them.

8   It is not uncommon for a pair of pliers to climb all the way from the cellar to the attic in its single-minded determination to raise its owner's blood pressure. Keys have been known to burrow three feet under mattresses. Women's purses, despite their great weight, frequently travel through six or seven rooms to find hiding space under a couch.

---

* ◆ To help you read this essay analytically, review pages 179–181.
** "The Plot Against People" by Russell Baker from THE NEW YORK TIMES, June 18, 1968. Copyright © 1968 The New York Times Co. Reprinted by permission.

9   Scientists have been struck by the fact that things that break down virtually never get lost, while things that get lost hardly ever break down.

10   A furnace, for example, will invariably break down at the depth of the first winter cold wave, but it will never get lost. A woman's purse, which after all does have some inherent capacity for breaking down, hardly ever does; it almost invariably chooses to get lost.

11   Some persons believe this constitutes evidence that inanimate objects are not entirely hostile to man, and that a negotiated peace is possible. After all, they point out, a furnace could infuriate a man even more thoroughly by getting lost than by breaking down, just as a glove could upset him far more by breaking down than by getting lost.

12   Not everyone agrees, however, that this indicates a conciliatory attitude among inanimate objects. Many say it merely proves that furnaces, gloves and pliers are incredibly stupid.

13   The third class of objects—those that don't work—is the most curious of all. These include such objects as barometers, car clocks, cigarette lighters, flashlights and toy-train locomotives. It is inaccurate, of course, to say that they never work. They work once, usually for the first few hours after being brought home, and then quit. Thereafter, they never work again.

14   In fact, it is widely assumed that they are built for the purpose of not working. Some people have reached advanced ages without ever seeing some of these objects—barometers, for example—in working order.

15   Science is utterly baffled by the entire category. There are many theories about it. The most interesting holds that the things that don't work have attained the highest state possible for an inanimate object, the state to which things that break down and things that get lost can still only aspire.

16   They have truly defeated man by conditioning him never to expect anything of them, and in return they have given man the only peace he receives from inanimate society. He does not expect his barometer to work, his electric locomotive to run, his cigarette lighter to light or his flashlight to illuminate, and when they don't, it does not raise his blood pressure.

17   He cannot attain that peace with furnaces and keys and cars and women's purses as long as he demands that they work for their keep.

Questions on Content, Structure, and Style

1. What is Baker's purpose in writing this classification? What reaction do you think Baker wants to evoke from his newspaper audience?

2. Where is Baker's thesis statement? Would his essay be more effective if his thesis were preceded by a fully developed lead-in? Why, or why not?

3. Identify Baker's categories and principle of classification. What do these categories have in common?

4. Why does Baker give examples of items that belong to each category? Does this strengthen his essay? Why or why not?

5. Of the categories of inanimate objects discussed in the essay, which one is most effectively developed? List some examples of details.

6. Consider Baker's use of personification as he talks about inanimate objects. Give some examples of descriptions that give human qualities to these items. What effect does this have on tone and style?

7. How does Baker's word choice affect his tone? What does Baker's title contribute to his tone?

8. How does publication in a newspaper affect Baker's paragraphing style? How might paragraphs 7 and 8, for example, appear in essay format?

9. If Baker were to revise his article today, how might he change his word choice in paragraphs 2, 7, 11, 16, and 17 to make his language more gender inclusive?

10. Evaluate Baker's conclusion. Is it effective or too abrupt?

Vocabulary

inanimate (1)

cunning (3)

evolve (6)

locomotion (7)

virtually (9)

inherent (10)

constitutes (11)

conciliatory (12)

barometer (13)

Suggestions for Writing

Try using Russell Baker's "The Plot against People" as a stepping-stone to your writing. To parallel Baker's criticisms of objects that inflict misery, think about kinds of people or forces that you feel are secretly conspiring to destroy your peace of mind. Consider, for example, kinds of crazed drivers who are contributing to road rage today. Annoying telephone solicitors? Obnoxious wait-staffers or clerks? Grocery shoppers in the checkout line in front of you? Or consider the kinds of rules that govern your life. Inane parking regulations that ensure you will never find a space anywhere near campus? Financial-aid red tape only an accounting genius could cut through? Your essay might be humorous, like Baker's, or quite serious, as you expose still another "plot" against humankind.

Professional Essay: Division*

What Is REALLY in a Hot Dog?**

This 2008 article was written by the staff of SixWise, a Web site focused on family, career, and home safety advice. The mission of SixWise.com, and its newsletter, is to help its readers "be safe, live longer, and prosper."

Pre-reading Thoughts: Have you ever looked closely at the ingredients or the nutritional facts listed on a food or personal-use item and consequently rejected that product? In general, how important are healthful ingredients in your choice of favorite foods?

---

* To help you read this essay analytically, review pages 179–181.

** What Is Really in a Hot Dog? from www.sixwise.com.

1   Now that baseball season is wrapping up, and you've likely eaten your share of ballpark dogs (9 percent of all hot dogs purchased are bought at baseball stadiums, after all), it's the perfect time to delve into what's really in one of America's favorite foods: the hot dog. It's the subject of many urban legends, the object of many grade-schoolers' double dares: do hot dogs contain pig snouts and chicken feathers, or are they really made from high-quality meat?

2   The debate certainly hasn't put a damper on Americans' enthusiasm for the food. The U.S. population consumes about 20 billion hot dogs a year, according to the National Hot Dog and Sausage Council. That works out to about 70 hot dogs per person, per year. And, an estimated 95 percent of U.S. homes serve hot dogs at one meal or another. Wondering how many hot dogs are sold each year? In 2005, retail stores sold 764 million packages of hot dogs (not including Wal-Mart), which adds up to more than $1.5 billion in retail sales.

What's in a Hot Dog?

3   On to the million-dollar question: what are hot dogs made of? According to the National Hot Dog and Sausage Council:

> All hot dogs are cured and cooked sausages that consist of mainly pork, beef, chicken and turkey or a combination of meat and poultry. Meats used in hot dogs come from the muscle of the animal and looks much like what you buy in the grocer's case. Other ingredients include water, curing agents and spices, such as garlic, salt, sugar, ground mustard, nutmeg, coriander and white pepper.

However, there are a couple of caveats. "Variety meats," which include things like liver, kidneys and hearts, may be used in processed meats like hot dogs, but the U.S. Department of Agriculture requires that they be disclosed in the ingredient label as "with variety meats" or "with meat by-products." Further, watch out for statements like "made with mechanically separated meats (MSM)." Mechanically separated meat is "a paste-like and batter-like meat product produced by forcing bones, with attached edible meat, under high pressure through a sieve or similar device to separate the bone from the edible meat tissue," according to the U.S. Food Safety and Inspection Service (FSIS).

4   Although the FSIS maintains that MSM are safe to eat, mechanically separated beef is no longer allowed in hot dogs or other processed meats (as of 2004) because of fears of mad cow disease. Hot dogs can contain no more than 20 percent mechanically separated pork, and any amount of mechanically separated chicken or turkey. So if you're looking for the purest franks, pick those that are labeled "all beef," "all pork," or "all chicken, turkey, etc." Franks labeled in this way must be made with meat from a single species and do not include by-products. (But check the label anyway, just to be sure. Turkey and chicken franks, for instance, can include turkey or chicken meat and turkey or chicken skin and fat in proportion to a turkey or chicken carcass.)

Are Hot Dogs Unhealthy?

5   Eating lots of processed meats like hot dogs has been linked to an increased risk of cancer. Part of that risk is probably due to the additives used in the meats, namely sodium nitrite and MSG. Sodium nitrite (or sodium nitrate) is used as a preservative, coloring and flavoring in hot dogs (and other processed meats), and studies have found it can lead to the formation of cancer-causing chemicals called nitrosamines. MSG, a flavor enhancer used in hot dogs and many other processed foods, has been labeled as an "excitotoxin," which, according to Dr. Russell Blaylock, an author and neurosurgeon, are "a group of excitatory amino acids that can cause sensitive neurons to die."

6   If you love hot dogs and are looking for a healthier alternative, opt for nitrate-free, organic varieties (available in health food stores and increasingly in regular supermarkets) that contain all meat, no byproducts and no artificial flavors, colors or preservatives.

Questions on Content, Structure, and Style

1. How does this article illustrate division rather than classification?

2. What is the main purpose of this article? What kinds of readers might be especially interested in this topic?

3. Why include the figures on hot dog consumption and sales?

4. In terms of organization, why did the staff writers begin with a statement from the National Hot Dog and Sausage Council?

5. What is gained by quoting directly from such organizations as the U.S. Department of Agriculture and the U.S. Food Safety and Inspection Service?

6. What warnings about hot dog variety are presented through use of description, definition, and examples? Were any of the details surprising to you?

7. Paragraph 5 offers several claims about the links of hot dogs to cancer. How might these claims be better supported?

8. Why is Dr. Blaylock's testimony included in the paragraph?

9. Would you consider this article an objective or subjective treatment of its subject? What choices are the writers advocating?

10. Did this article successfully persuade you to follow the advice given in its conclusion? Why or why not?

Vocabulary

delve (1)   caveats (3)
snouts (1)   sieve (3)
damper (2)   carcass (4)

Suggestions for Writing

Use the article "What Is REALLY in a Hot Dog?" as a stepping-stone to your own essay. As a consumer, what other products would you like to know more about? What ingredients, for example, go into your favorite snack food? Soft drink? Energy bar? Chewing gum? Or nutritionally analyze a popular fast-food dinner: how healthful is a Happy Meal? What is the meat-filler "pink slime"? Or consider a household product. What's really in our deodorants, cosmetics, hair products, or mouthwash? Are your choices of detergents or other cleaners more toxic than "green"? Write an essay that not only gives information but also influences your readers to buy or reject the product. (◆ Consult Chapter 14 if you need help researching your topic.)

A Revision Worksheet

© Ryan McVay/
Photodisc/Getty Images

As you write your rough drafts, consult Chapter 5 for guidance through the revision process. In addition, here are a few questions to ask yourself as you revise your classification essay:

1. Is the purpose of the essay clear to the reader?

2. Is the principle of classification or division maintained consistently throughout the essay?

3. If the essay presents a formal division or classification, has the subject been narrowed so that all the parts are accounted for?

4. If the essay presents an informal or humorous division or classification, does the paper nevertheless make a significant or entertaining point?

5. Is each category developed with enough specific detail? Where might more details be effectively added?

6. Is each class distinct, with no overlap among categories?

7. Is the essay organized logically and coherently with smooth transitions between the discussions of the categories?

Collaborative Activity: After you've revised your essay extensively, you might exchange rough drafts with a classmate and answer these questions for each other, making specific suggestions for improvement wherever appropriate. (◆ For advice on productive participation in classroom workshops, see pages 116–120.)

Reviewing Your Progress

After you have completed your essay developed by classification or division, take a moment to measure your progress as a writer by responding to the following questions. Such analysis will help you to recognize growth in your writing skills and may enable you to identify areas that are still problematic.

1. What is the best feature of your essay? Why?

2. Which category do you think is the clearest or most persuasive in your essay? Why does that one stand above the others?

3. What part of your essay gave you the most trouble? How did you overcome the problem?

4. If you had more time to work on this essay, what would receive additional attention? Why?

5. What did you learn about your topic from writing this essay? About yourself as a writer?

Strategy Six: Development by Causal Analysis

Causal analysis explains the cause-and-effect relationship between two (or more) elements. When you discuss the condition producing something, you are analyzing *cause*; when you discuss the result produced by something, you are analyzing *effect*. To find examples of causal analysis, you need only look around you. If your car stops running on the way to class, for example, you may discover that the cause was an empty gas tank. On campus, in your history class, you may study the causes of the Civil War; in your economics class, the effects of teenage spending on the cosmetics market; and in your biology class, both the causes and effects of heart disease. Over dinner, you may discuss the effects of some crisis in the Middle East on American foreign policy, and as you drift to sleep, you may ponder the effects of your studying—or *not* studying—for your math test tomorrow.

To express it most simply, *cause* asks:

why did "X" happen?
or why does "X" happen?
or why will "X" happen?

Effect, on the other hand, asks:

what did "Y" produce?
or what does "Y" produce?
or what will "Y" produce?

Some essays of causal analysis focus primarily on the cause(s) of something; others mainly analyze the effect(s); still others discuss both causes and effects. If, for example, you wanted to concentrate on the major causes of the Wall Street crash of 1929, you might begin by briefly describing the effects of the crash on the economy, then devote your thesis and the rest of your essay to analyzing the major causes, perhaps allotting one major section (or one paragraph, depending on the complexity of the reasons) to each cause. Conversely, an effect paper might briefly note the causes of the crash and then detail the most important effects. An essay covering both the causes and effects of something often demands a longer paper so that each part will be clear. (Your assignment will frequently indicate which kind of causal analysis to write. However, if the choice is yours, let your interest in the subject be your guide.)

Developing Your Essay

Whether you are writing an essay that primarily discusses either causes or effects, or one that focuses on both, you should follow these rules:

Present a reasonable thesis statement. If your thesis makes dogmatic, unsupportable claims ("This national health care plan will lead to a complete collapse of quality medical treatment") or overly broad assertions ("Peer pressure causes alcoholism among students"), you won't convince your reader. Limit or qualify your thesis whenever necessary by using such phrases as "may be," "a contributing factor," "one of the main reasons," "two important factors," and so on ("Peer pressure is *one of the major causes* of alcoholism among students").

Limit your essay to a discussion of recent, major causes or effects. In a short paper you generally don't have space to discuss minor or remote causes or effects. If, for example, you analyzed your car wreck, you might decide that the three major causes were defective brakes, a hidden yield sign, and bad weather. A minor, or remote, cause might include being slightly tired because of less-than-usual sleep, less sleep because of staying out late the night before, staying out late because of an out-of-town visitor, and so on— back to the womb. In some cases you may want to mention a few of the indirect causes or effects, but do be reasonable. Concentrate on the most immediate, most important factors. Often, a writer of a 500-to-800-word essay will discuss no more than two, three, or four major causes or effects of something; trying to cover more of either frequently results in an underdeveloped essay that is not convincing.

Organize your essay clearly. Organization of your causal analysis essay will vary, of course, depending on whether you are focusing on the causes of something or the effects, or both. To avoid becoming tangled in causes and effects, you might try sketching out a drawing of your thesis and essay map before you begin your first draft. Here, for instance, are a couple of sketches for essays you might write on your recent traffic accident:

Thesis Emphasizing the Causes:

Cause (defective brakes)
Cause (hidden yield sign)　　　produced　　　＞ Effect (my car wreck)
Cause (bad weather)

Thesis Emphasizing the Effects:

　　　　　　　　　　　　　　　　　　　　　Effect (doctor bills)
Cause (my car wreck)　　　produced　　＞ Effect (loss of car)
　　　　　　　　　　　　　　　　　　　　　Effect (higher insurance rates)

Sometimes you may discover that you can't isolate "the three main causes/effects of 'X'"; some essays do in fact demand a narrative explaining a chain reaction of causes and effects. For example, a paper on the rebellion of the American colonies might show how one unjust British law or restriction after another led to the war for independence. In this kind of causal analysis essay, be careful to limit your subject so that you'll have the space necessary to show your readers how each step in the chain led to the next. Here's a sketch of a slightly different car-wreck paper presented in a narrative or chain-reaction format:

$$\text{Cause} \longrightarrow \underset{\text{(wet brakes)}}{\text{1st Effect}} \xrightarrow{\text{causes}} \underset{\text{(car wreck)}}{\text{2nd Effect}} \xrightarrow{\text{causes}} \underset{\text{(doctor bills)}}{\text{3rd Effect}}$$

Cause (bad weather) → 1st Effect (wet brakes) — causes → 2nd Effect (car wreck) — causes → 3rd Effect (doctor bills)

Sometimes your subject matter will suggest the plan for organizing your causal analysis paper; often, however, you'll have to devote some of your prewriting time to deciding, first, whether you want to emphasize causes or effects and, then, in what arrangement you will present your analysis.

Convince your reader that a causal relationship exists by showing how the relationship works. Let's suppose you are writing an essay in which you want to discuss the three major changes you've undergone since coming to college. Don't just state the changes and describe them; your job is to show the reader how college has *brought about* these changes. If, for instance, your study habits have improved, you must show

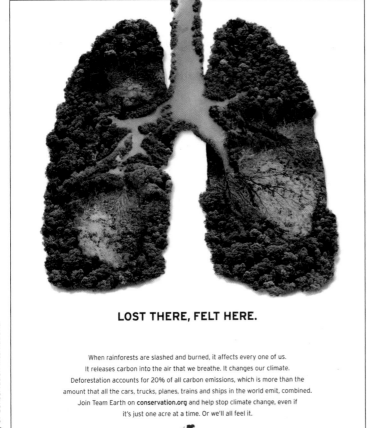

LOST THERE, FELT HERE.

When rainforests are slashed and burned, it affects every one of us.
It releases carbon into the air that we breathe. It changes our climate.
Deforestation accounts for 20% of all carbon emissions, which is more than the
amount that all the cars, trucks, planes, trains and ships in the world emit, combined.
Join Team Earth on **conservation.org** and help stop climate change, even if
it's just one acre at a time. Or we'll all feel it.

CONSERVATION
INTERNATIONAL

Courtesy of Conservation International

Advertisements often use short bursts of causal analysis to persuade their viewers to take action. What is the cause-effect relationship presented here, and do you find it effective?

the reader how the academic demands of your college courses caused you to change your habits; a simple description of your new study techniques is not enough. Remember that a causal analysis essay should stress *how* (and often *why*) "X" caused "Y," rather than merely describing "Y" as it now exists.

Problems to Avoid

Don't oversimplify by assigning one all-encompassing cause to some effect. Most complex subjects have more than one cause (or effect), so make your analysis as complete and objective as you can, especially when dealing with your own problems or beliefs. For example, was that car wreck really caused only by the bad weather—or also because of your carelessness? Did your friend do poorly in astronomy class only because the instructor didn't like her? Before judging a situation too quickly, investigate your own biases. Then provide a thoughtful, thorough analysis, effectively organized to convince your readers of the validity of your viewpoint.

Avoid the *post hoc* fallacy. This error in logic (from the Latin phrase *post hoc, ergo propter hoc*, meaning "after this, therefore because of this") results when we mistake a temporal connection for a causal relationship—or in other words, when we assume that because one event follows another in time, the first event caused the second. Most of our superstitions are *post hoc* fallacies; we now realize that bad luck after walking under a ladder is a matter of coincidence, not cause and effect. The *post hoc* fallacy provided the basis for a rather popular joke in the early debates over decriminalizing marijuana. Those against argued that marijuana led to heroin because most users of the hard drug had first smoked the weed. The proponents retorted that milk, then, was the real culprit, because both marijuana and heroin users had drunk milk as babies. The point is this: in any causal analysis, you must be able to offer proof or reasoned logic to show that one event *caused* another, not just that it preceded it in time.

Avoid circular logic. Often causal essays seem to chase their own tails when they include such circular statements as "There aren't enough parking spaces for students on campus because there are too many cars." Such a statement merely presents a second half that restates what is already implied in the first half. A revision might say, "There aren't enough parking spaces for students on campus because the parking permits are not distributed fairly." This kind of assertion can be argued specifically and effectively; the other is a dead end.

Important reminder: Many essays developed by causal analysis draw on personal experience; others, however, need research material to provide explanation, evidence, or background. For example, an essay analyzing the effects of an historical event (e.g., Lincoln's assassination) would need to provide readers with some facts about the event itself. Remember that any borrowed information (quoted directly or paraphrased) appearing in your essay—including ideas, statistics, or quotations—must be properly attributed to its source. ◆ To understand how to thoughtfully choose, incorporate, and document research material in your essay, consult Chapter 14 in this text.

Essay Topics

The following subjects may be developed into essays emphasizing cause or effect, or both. ◆ For additional ideas, turn to the "Suggestions for Writing" section following the professional essay (page 284).

1. A pet peeve or bad habit

2. A change of mind about some important issue or belief

3. An accident, a misadventure, a lucky break, or an unexpected turn of good fortune

4. A family story/tradition or an influential book

5. A move, a trip, or an experience in a different country or culture

6. The best gift you ever received or ownership of a particular possession

7. A radical change in your behavior or appearance

8. A hobby, sport, or class

9. The best (or worst) advice you ever gave, followed, or rejected

10. An important decision or choice

11. An act of heroism or sacrifice (your own or someone else's)

12. An important idea, event, or discovery in your field of study

13. A superstition or irrational fear

14. A currently popular kind of entertainment (e.g., social media sites, TV reality shows, superhero movies, vampire stories, graphic novels)

15. A disappointment or a success

16. Bullying, racism, sexism, or some other kind of discrimination or prejudice

17. An influential person (teacher, coach, friend, etc.)

18. A political action (campus, local, state, national), historical event, or social movement

19. A popular cultural trend (tattooing, piercing, clothing or hair styles, etc.)

20. A piece of visual art promoting a particular cause or point of view (Consider, for example, the famous image of Rosie the Riveter, who first appeared on a poster sponsored by the War Production Committee during World War II [see next page]. Considering the gender roles of

continued on next page

the time, why was such a poster needed? What effects was this image designed to have on both its male and female viewers? What specific elements in this picture produce these effects? What effect does this image have on viewers today? If you prefer, select another visual image reproduced in this text for analysis of its effects on the viewer, a famous photograph such as *Migrant Mother* [page 338] or perhaps one of the advertisements in Chapter 10 or in other chapters in this book. A list of all the artworks and ads in this text follows the Table of Contents. ◆ For help writing about art, see Chapter 17.)

The poster *Rosie the Riveter*, by graphic artist J. Howard Miller, was created in 1943 as part of a government campaign to encourage women to enter the factory workforce during World War II.

A Topic Proposal for Your Essay

Selecting the right subject matter is important to every writer. To help you clarify your ideas and strengthen your commitment to your topic, here is a proposal sheet that asks you to describe some of your preliminary ideas about your subject before you begin drafting. Although your ideas may change as you write (they will almost certainly become more refined), thinking through your choice of topic now may help you avoid several false starts.

1. What is the subject and purpose of your causal analysis essay? Is this subject appropriately narrowed and focused for a discussion of major causes or effects?

2. Will you develop your essay to emphasize primarily the effects or the causes of your topic? Or is a causal chain the most appropriate method of development?

3. Why are you interested in this topic? Do you have a personal or professional connection to the subject? State at least one reason for your choice of topic.

4. Is this a significant topic of interest to others? Why? Who specifically might find it interesting, informative, or entertaining?

5. List at least two major causes or effects that you might develop in the discussion of your topic.

6. What difficulties, if any, might arise during your drafting on this topic? For example, how might you convince a skeptical reader that your causal relationship is not merely a temporal one?

Sample Student Essay

In the following essay, a student explains why working in a local motel damaged her self-esteem, despite her attempts to do a good job. Note that the writer uses many vivid examples and specific details to show the reader how she was treated and, consequently, how such treatment made her feel.

IT'S SIMPLY NOT WORTH IT

1   It's hard to find a job these days, and with our county's unemployment rate reaching as high as seven percent, most people feel obligated to "take what they can get." But after working as a maid at a local motel for almost a year and a half, I decided no job is worth keeping if it causes a person to doubt his or her worth. My hard work rarely received recognition or appreciation, I was underpaid, and I was required to perform some of the most disgusting cleaning tasks imaginable. These factors caused me to devalue myself as a person and ultimately motivated me to return to school in hope of regaining my self-respect.

Introduction: Her job as a motel maid

Thesis: No appreciation, low pay, disgusting tasks (causes) produce damaged self-esteem and action (effects)

Cause one: Lack of appreciation

2   It may be obvious to say, but I believe that when a maid's hours of meticulous cleaning are met only with harsh words and complaints, she begins to lose her sense of self-esteem. I recall the care I took in making the motel's beds, imagining them as globs of clay and molding them into impeccable pieces of art. I would teeter from one side of a bed to the other, over and over again, until I smoothed out every intruding wrinkle or tuck. And the mirrors—I would vigorously massage the glass, erasing any toothpaste splotches or oil smudges that might draw my customer's disapproval. I would scrutinize the mirror first from the left side, then I'd move to the right side, once more to the left until every possible angle ensured an unclouded reflection. And so my efforts went, room after room. But, without fail, each day more than one customer would approach me, not with praise for my tidy beds or spotless mirrors, but with nitpicking complaints that undermined my efforts: "Young lady, I just checked into room 143 and it only has one ashtray. Surely for $69.95 a night you people can afford more ashtrays in the rooms."

3   If it wasn't a guest complaining about ashtrays, it was an impatient customer demanding extra towels or a fussy stay-over insisting his room be cleaned by the time he returned from breakfast at 8:00 A.M. "Can't you come to work early to do it?" he would urge thoughtlessly. Day after day, my spotless rooms went unnoticed, with no spoken rewards for my efforts from either guests or management. Eventually, the ruthless complaints and thankless work began wearing me down. In my mind, I became a servant undeserving of gratitude.

Cause two: Low pay

4   The lack of spoken rewards was compounded by the lack of financial rewards. The $7.30/hour appraisal of my worth was simply not enough to support my financial needs or my self-esteem. The measly $3.65 I earned for cleaning one room took a lot of rooms to add up, and by the end of the month I was barely able to pay my bills and buy some food. (My mainstay became ninety-two cent, generic macaroni and cheese dinners.)

Because the flow of travelers kept the motel full for only a few months of the year, during some weeks I could only work half time, making a mere $584.00 a month. As a result, one month I was forced to request an extension on my rent payment. Unsympathetically, my landlord threatened to evict me if I didn't pay. Embarrassed, yet desperate, I went to a friend and borrowed money. I felt uneasy and awkward and regretted having to beg a friend for money. I felt like a mooch and a bum; I felt degraded. And the constant reminder from management that there were hundreds of people standing in unemployment lines who would be more than willing to work for minimum wage only aided in demeaning me further.

5   In addition to the thankless work and the inadequate salary, I was required to clean some of the most sickening messes. Frequently, conventions for high school clubs booked the motel. Once I opened the door of a conventioneer's room one morning and almost gagged at the odor. I immediately beheld a trail of vomit that began at the bedside and ended just short of the bathroom door. At that moment I cursed the inventor of shag carpet, for I knew it would take hours to comb this mess out of the fibers. On another day I spent thirty minutes dislodging the bed linen from the toilet where it had been stuffed. And I spent what seemed like hours removing from one of my spotless mirrors the lipstick-drawn message that read, "Yorktown Tigers are number one." But these inconsiderate acts were relaying another message, a message I took personally: "Lady, you're not worth the consideration—you're a maid and you're not worth respecting."

Cause three: Repulsive duties

6   I've never been afraid to work hard or do jobs that weren't particularly "fun." But the line must be drawn when a person's view of herself becomes clouded with feelings of worthlessness. The thankless efforts, the inadequate wage, and the disgusting work were just parts of a total message that degraded my character and caused me to question my worth. Therefore, I felt compelled to leave this demeaning job in

Conclusion: Review of the problem and a brief explanation of the solution she chose

search of a way to rebuild my self-confidence. Returning to school has done just that for me. As my teachers and fellow students take time to listen to my ideas and compliment my responses, I feel once again like a vital, valued, and worthwhile person. I feel human once more.

Professional Essay*

Some Lessons from the Assembly Line**

Andrew Braaksma

Andrew Braaksma, from Portage, Michigan, was a junior at the University of Michigan studying history and French in the College of Literature, Science, and Arts when he won first place in a "Back to School" essay contest sponsored by *Newsweek* magazine. The award-winning essay was then published in *Newsweek's* "My Turn" column on September 12, 2005.

Pre-reading Thoughts: Consider one of the most challenging jobs or tasks outside your academic life you successfully accomplished sometime during the past several years. What was the most important lesson you learned about yourself from this experience?

1   Last June, as I stood behind the bright orange guard door of the machine, listening to the crackling hiss of the automatic welders, I thought about how different my life had been just a few weeks earlier. Then, I was writing an essay about French literature to complete my last exam of the spring semester at college. Now I stood in an automotive plant in southwest Michigan, making subassemblies for a car manufacturer.

Cultura Limited/SuperStock

2   I have worked as a temp in the factories surrounding my hometown every summer since I graduated from high school, but making the transition between school and full-time blue-collar work during the break never gets any easier. For a student like me who considers any class before noon to be uncivilized, getting to a factory by 6 o'clock each morning, where rows of hulking, spark-showering machines have replaced the lush campus and cavernous lecture halls of college life, is torture. There my time is spent

---

* ◆ To help you read this essay analytically, review pages 179–181.
** "Some Lessons from the Assembly Line" by Andrew Braaksma from NEWSWEEK, My Turn, September 12, 2005, p. 17. All rights reserved. Reprinted by permission.

stamping, cutting, welding, moving or assembling parts, the rigid work schedules and quotas of the plant making days spent studying and watching "SportsCenter" seem like a million years ago.

3   I chose to do this work, rather than bus tables or fold sweatshirts at the Gap, for the overtime pay and because living at home is infinitely cheaper than living on campus for the summer. My friends who take easier, part-time jobs never seem to understand why I'm so relieved to be back at school in the fall or that my summer vacation has been anything but a vacation.

4   There are few things as cocksure as a college student who has never been out in the real world, and people my age always seem to overestimate the value of their time and knowledge. After a particularly exhausting string of 12-hour days at a plastics factory, I remember being shocked at how small my check seemed. I couldn't believe how little I was taking home after all the hours I spent on the sweltering production floor. And all the classes in the world could not have prepared me for my battles with the machine I ran in the plant, which would jam whenever I absent-mindedly put in a part backward or upside down. As frustrating as the work can be, the most stressful thing about blue-collar life is knowing your job could disappear overnight. Issues like downsizing and overseas relocation had always seemed distant to me until my co-workers at one factory told me that the unit I was working in would be shut down within six months and moved to Mexico, where people would work for 60 cents an hour.

5   Factory life has shown me what my future might have been like had I never gone to college in the first place. For me, and probably many of my fellow students, higher education always seemed like a foregone conclusion: I never questioned if I was going to college, just where. No other options ever occurred to me. After working 12-hour shifts in a factory, the other options have become brutally clear. When I'm back at the university, skipping classes and turning in lazy rewrites seems like a cop-out after seeing what I would be doing without school. All the advice and public-service announcements about the value of an education that used to sound trite now ring true.

6   These lessons I am learning, however valuable, are always tinged with a sense of guilt. Many people pass their lives in the places I briefly work, spending 30 years where I spend only two months at a time. When fall comes around, I get to go back to a sunny and beautiful campus, while work in the factories continues. At times I feel almost voyeuristic, like a tourist dropping in where other people make their livelihoods. My lessons about education are learned at the expense of those who weren't fortunate enough to receive one. "This job pays well, but it's hell on the body," said one co-worker. "Study hard and keep reading," she added, nodding at the copy of Jack Kerouac's *On the Road** I had wedged into the space next to my machine so I could read discreetly when the line went down.

7   My experience will stay with me long after I head back to school and spend my wages on books and beer. The things that factory work has taught me—how lucky I am to get an education, how to work hard, how easy it is to lose that work once you have it—are by no means earth-shattering. Everyone has to come to grips with

*American novelist and poet Jack Kerouac was one of the 1950s "Beat Generation" writers.

them at some point. How and when I learned these lessons, however, has inspired me to make the most of my college years before I enter the real world for good. Until then, the summer months I spend in the factories will be long, tiring and every bit as educational as a French-lit class.

Questions on Content, Structure, and Style

1. What cause-effect relationship is presented in this essay? Does this essay focus primarily on causes or effects?
2. What are some of the important lessons Braaksma has learned? Learning these lessons at this point in his life inspired Braaksma in what new way?
3. What strategy does Braaksma use to begin his essay, and why? How is this strategy continued throughout the essay?
4. In paragraph 2, what descriptive details and verbs are particularly effective in characterizing the work that Braaksma did at the factories?
5. What specific examples does Braaksma include to help the reader understand his experiences and reactions?
6. Why does Braaksma often characterize himself and other college students in less than positive ways? Is such a characterization likely to appeal to or offend his readers?
7. Why does Braaksma mention that his lessons are "tinged with a sense of guilt"?
8. What does the use of dialogue in paragraph 6 add to this essay?
9. Evaluate Braaksma's conclusion. Why does he refer to his French-lit class?
10. Overall, how effective is Braaksma's essay? How would you compare this essay's effectiveness to that of the student essay on pages 279–282? Did either causal analysis essay change or reconfirm any of your beliefs about work or school?

Vocabulary

blue-collar (2)   cocksure (4)   voyeuristic (6)
lush (2)   downsizing (4)   discreetly (6)
cavernous (2)   tinged (6)

Suggestions for Writing

Use Andrew Braaksma's essay "Some Lessons from the Assembly Line" as a stepping-stone to your essay. If you have held full- or part-time jobs, think of how one affected you in specific ways that led to new insight or encouraged you to take new action. Perhaps your work changed your mind about your major or future profession, or perhaps your job helped you decide to begin or return to school. Or, if you prefer, consider any volunteer work you've done that made a difference in your life or in the lives of others. To help your readers understand the cause-effect relationship you're presenting, be sure to include enough logical explanation and vivid details to show clearly how "X" caused "Y."

A Revision Worksheet

As you write your rough drafts, consult Chapter 5 for guidance through the revision process. In addition, here are a few questions to ask yourself as you revise your causal analysis essay:

1. Is the thesis limited to a reasonable claim that can be supported in the essay?

2. Is the organization clear and consistent so that the reader can understand the purpose of the analysis?

3. Does the essay focus on the most important causes or effects, or both?

4. If the essay has a narrative form, is each step in the chain reaction clearly connected to the next?

5. Does the essay convincingly show the reader *how* or *why* relationships between the causes and effects exist, instead of merely naming and describing them?

6. Does the essay provide enough evidence to show the connections between causes and effects? Where could additional details be added to make the relationships clearer?

7. Has the essay avoided the problems of oversimplification, circular logic, and the *post hoc* fallacy?

Collaborative Activity: After you've revised your essay extensively, exchange rough drafts with a classmate and answer these questions for each other, making specific suggestions for improvement wherever appropriate. (◆ For advice on productive participation in classroom workshops, see pages 116–120.)

Reviewing Your Progress

After you have completed your essay developed by causal analysis, take a moment to measure your progress as a writer by responding to the following questions. Such analysis will help you to recognize growth in your writing skills and may enable you to identify areas that are still problematic.

1. What do you like best about your essay? Why?

2. After considering your essay's presentation of the major causes or effects, which part of your analysis do you think readers will find the most convincing? Why?

3. What part of your essay gave you the most trouble? How did you overcome the problem?

4. If you had more time to work on this essay, what would receive additional attention? Why?

5. What did you learn about your topic from writing this essay? About yourself as a writer?

Chapter 10

Argumentation

· ·

Almost without exception, each of us, every day, argues for or against something with somebody. The discussions may be short and friendly ("Let's go to this restaurant rather than that one") or long and complex ("Mandatory motorcycle helmets are an intrusion on civil rights"). Because we do argue our viewpoints so often, most of us realized long ago that shifting into high whine did not always get us what we wanted. On the contrary, we've learned that we usually have a much better chance at winning a dispute or having our plan adopted or changing someone's mind if we present our side of an issue in a calm, logical fashion, giving sound reasons for our position. This approach is just what a good argumentative essay does: it presents logical reasoning and solid evidence that will persuade your readers to accept your point of view.

Some argumentative essays declare the best solution to a problem ("Raising the drinking age will decrease traffic accidents"); others argue a certain way of looking at an issue ("Beauty pageants degrade women"); still others may urge adoption of a specific proposal or plan of action ("Voters should pass ordinance 10 to fund the new ice rink"). Whatever your exact purpose, your argumentative essay should be composed of a clear thesis and body paragraphs that offer enough sensible reasons and persuasive evidence to convince your readers to agree with you.

Developing Your Essay

Here are some suggestions for developing and organizing an effective argumentative essay:

Choose an appropriate topic. Selecting a good topic for any essay is important. Choosing a focused, appropriate topic for your argument essay will save you enormous time and energy even before you begin prewriting. Some subjects are simply too large and complex to be adequately treated in a three-to-five-page argumentative essay; selecting such a subject might produce a rough draft of generalities that will not be persuasive. If you have an interest in a subject that is too general or complex for the length of your assignment, try to find a more focused, specific issue within it to argue. For example, the large, controversial (and rather overdone) subject "capital punishment" might be narrowed and focused to a paper advocating time limits for the death-row appeal process or required use of DNA testing. A general opinion on "unfair college grading" might become a more interesting persuasive essay in which the writer takes a stand on the use of pluses and minuses (A–, B+, B–, etc.) on transcript grades. Your general annoyance with smokers might move from "All smoking should be outlawed forever" to an essay focused on the controversial smoking bans in open-air sports stadiums. The complex subject of gun control might be narrowed into an essay arguing support for or against new laws regarding concealed weapons on campuses or in national parks. In other words, while we certainly do debate large issues in our lives, in a short piece of writing it may be more effective, and often more interesting, to choose a focused topic that will allow for more depth in the arguments. You must ultimately decide whether your choice of subject is appropriate for your assignment, but taking a close, second look at your choice now may save you frustration later.

Explore the possibilities . . . and your opinions. Perhaps you have an interesting subject in mind for your argumentative essay, but you don't yet have a definite opinion on the controversy. Use this opportunity to explore the subject! Do some research; talk to appropriate people; investigate the issues. By discovering your own position, you can address others who may be similarly uncertain about the subject.

Many times, however, you may want to argue for a belief or position you already hold. But before you proceed, take some time to consider the basis of your strong feelings. Not surprisingly, we humans have been known, on various occasions, to spout opinions we can't always effectively support when challenged to do so. Sometimes we hold an opinion simply because on the surface it seems to make good sense to us or because it fits comfortably with our other social, ethical, or political beliefs. Or we may have inherited some of our beliefs from our families or friends, or perhaps we borrowed ideas from well-known people we admire. In some cases, we may have held an opinion for so long that we can't remember why we adopted it in the first place. We may also have a purely sentimental or emotional attachment to some idea or position. Whatever the origins of our beliefs, we need to examine the real reasons for thinking what we do before we can effectively convince others.

If you have a strong opinion you want to write about, try jotting down a list of the reasons or points that support your position. Then study the list—are your points logical and persuasive? Which aren't, and why not? After this bit of prewriting, you may discover that although you believe something strongly, you really don't have the kinds of factual evidence or reasoned arguments you need to support your opinion. In some cases, depending on your topic, you may wish to talk to others who share your position or you may decide to research your subject (◆ for help with research or interviewing, see Chapter 14); in other cases, you may just need to think longer and harder about your topic and your reasons for maintaining your attitude toward it. Keep an open mind; your exploration may lead you to a surprising new position. (Remember the words of humorist F. G. Burgess: "If in the last few years you haven't discarded a major opinion or acquired a new one, check your pulse. You may be dead.") But with or without formal research, the better you know your subject, the more confident you will be about writing your argumentative essay.

Anticipate opposing views. An argument assumes that there is more than one side to an issue. To be convincing, you must be aware of your opposition's views on the subject and then organize your essay to answer or counter those views. If you don't have a good sense of the opposition's arguments, you can't effectively persuade your readers to dismiss their objections and see matters your way. Therefore, before you begin your first rough draft, write down all the opposing views you can think of and an answer to each of them so that you will know your subject thoroughly. If you are unfamiliar with the major objections to your position, now is the time to investigate your subject further. (For the sake of clarity throughout this chapter, your act of responding to those arguments against your position will be called *refuting the opposition*; "to refute" means "to prove false or wrong," and that's what you will try to do to some of the arguments of those who disagree with you.)

Know and remember your audience. Although it's important to think about your readers' needs and expectations whenever you write, it is essential to consider carefully the audience of your argumentative essay both before and as you write your rough drafts. Because you are trying to persuade people to adopt some new point of view or perhaps to take some action, you need to decide what kinds of supporting evidence will be most convincing to your particular readers. Try to analyze your audience by asking yourself a series of questions. What do they already know about your topic? What information or terms do they need to know to understand your point of view? What biases might they already have for or against your position? What special concerns might your readers have that influence their receptiveness? ◆ To be convincing, you should consider these questions and others by carefully reviewing the discussion of audience on pages 19–22 *before* you begin your drafts.

Decide which points of argument to include. Once you have a good sense of your audience, your own position, and your opposition's strongest arguments, try making a Pro-and-Con Sheet to help you sort out which points you will discuss in your essay.

Let's suppose you want to write an editorial on the sale-of-class-notes controversy at your school. Should professional note-takers be allowed to sit in on a course and then sell their notes to class members? After reviewing the evidence on both sides, you have decided to argue that your school should prohibit professional note-taking services from attending large lecture classes and selling notes. To begin planning your essay, you list all the pro-and-con arguments you can think of concerning the controversy:

My Side: Against the Sale of Class Notes

1. Unfair advantage for some students in some classes

2. Note-taking is a skill students need to develop

3. Rich students can afford and poor can't

4. Prevents students from learning to organize for themselves

5. Encourages class cutting

6. Missing class means no chance to ask questions, participate in discussions

7. Notes taken by others are often inaccurate

8. Some professors don't like strangers in classroom

9. Students need to think for themselves

My Opposition's Side: For the Sale of Class Notes

1. Helps students to get better test, course grades

2. Helps students to learn, organize material

3. Helps if you're sick and can't attend class

4. Shows students good models for taking notes and outlining them

5. Other study guides are on the market, so why not these?

6. Gives starving graduate students jobs

7. No laws against sale of notes, free country

After making your Pro-and-Con Sheet, look over the list and decide which of your strongest points you want to argue in your paper and also which of your opposition's claims you want to refute. At this point you may also see some arguments on your list that might be combined and some that might be deleted because they're irrelevant or unconvincing. (Be careful not to select more arguments or counter-arguments to discuss than the length of your writing assignment will allow. It's far better to present a persuasive analysis of a few points than it is to give an underdeveloped, shallow treatment of a host of reasons.)

Let's say you want to cover the following points in your essay:

- Professional note-taking services keep students from developing their own thinking and organizational skills (combination of 4 and 9)

- Professional note-taking services discourage class attendance and participation (5 and 6)

- Unfair advantages to some students (1 and 3)

Your assignment calls for an essay of 750 to 1,000 words, so you figure you'll only have space to refute your opposition's strongest claim. You decide to refute this claim:

- Helps students to learn and organize material (2)

The next step is to formulate a working thesis. At this stage, you may find it helpful to put your working thesis in an "although-because" statement so you can clearly see both your opposition's arguments and your own. An "although-because" thesis for the note-taking essay might look something like this:

> *Although* some students maintain that using professional note-taking services helps them learn more, such services should be banned from our campus *because* they prevent students from developing their own thinking and organizational skills, they discourage class attendance, and they give unfair advantages to some students.

Frequently, your "although-because" statement will be too long and awkward to use in the later drafts of your essay. But for now, it can serve as a guide, allowing you to see your overall position before the writing of the first draft begins. (◆ To practice compiling a Pro-Con Sheet and writing an "although-because" working thesis, turn to the exercise on pages 299–300.)

Organize your essay clearly. Although there is no set model of organization for argumentative essays, here are some common patterns that you might use or that you might combine in some effective way.

Important note: For the sake of simplicity, the first two outlines present two of the writer's points and two opposing ideas. Naturally, your essay may contain any number of points and refuted points, depending on the complexity of your subject and the assigned length of your essay.

In Pattern A, you devote the first few body paragraphs to arguing points on your side and then turn to refuting or answering the opposition's claims.

> **Pattern A:** Thesis
> Body paragraph 1: you present your first point and its supporting evidence
> Body paragraph 2: you present your second point and its supporting evidence
> Body paragraph 3: you refute your opposition's first point
> Body paragraph 4: you refute your opposition's second point
> Conclusion

Sometimes you may wish to clear away the opposition's claims before you present the arguments for your side. To do so, you might select Pattern B:

> **Pattern B:** Thesis
> Body paragraph 1: you refute your opposition's first point
> Body paragraph 2: you refute your opposition's second point
> Body paragraph 3: you present your first point and its supporting evidence
> Body paragraph 4: you present your second point and its supporting evidence
> Conclusion

In some cases, you may find that the main arguments you want to present are the very same ones that will refute or answer your opposition's primary claims. If so, try Pattern

C, which allows each of your argumentative points to refute one of your opposition's claims in the same paragraph:

Pattern C: Thesis
Body paragraph 1: you present your first point and its supporting evidence, which also refutes one of your opposition's claims
Body paragraph 2: you present a second point and its supporting evidence, which also refutes a second opposition claim
Body paragraph 3: you present a third point and its supporting evidence, which also refutes a third opposition claim
Conclusion

Now you might be thinking, "What if my position on a topic as yet has no opposition?" Remember that almost all issues have more than one side, so try to anticipate objections and then answer them. For example, you might first present a thesis that calls for a new traffic signal at a dangerous intersection in your town and then address hypothetical counter-arguments, such as "The City Council may say that a stoplight at Lemay and Columbia will cost too much, but the cost in lives will be much greater" or "Commuters may complain that a traffic light there will slow the continuous flow of north-south traffic, but it is precisely the uninterrupted nature of this road that encourages motorists to speed." By answering hypothetical objections, you impress your readers by showing them you've thought through your position thoroughly before you asked them to consider your point of view.

You might also be thinking, "What if my opposition actually has a valid objection, a legitimate point of criticism? Should I ignore it?" Hoping that an obviously strong opposing point will just go away is like hoping the IRS will cancel income taxes this year—a nice thought but hardly likely. Don't ignore your opposition's good point; instead, acknowledge it, but then go on quickly to show your readers why that reason, though valid, isn't compelling enough by itself to motivate people to adopt your opposition's entire position. Or you might concede that one point while simultaneously showing why your position isn't really in conflict with that criticism, but rather with other, more important, parts of your opponent's viewpoint. By admitting that you see some validity in your opposition's argument, you can again show your readers that you are both fair-minded and informed about all aspects of the controversy.

If you are feeling confident about your ability to organize an argumentative essay, you might try some combination of patterns, if your material allows such a treatment. For example, you might have a strong point to argue, another point that simultaneously answers one of your opposition's strongest claims, and another opposition point you want to refute. Your essay organization might look like this:

Combination: Thesis
Body paragraph 1: a point for your side
Body paragraph 2: one of your points, which also refutes an opposition claim
Body paragraph 3: your refutation of another opposition claim
Conclusion

In other words, you can organize your essay in a variety of ways as long as your paper is logical and clear. Study your Pro-and-Con Sheet and then decide which organization best presents the arguments and counter-arguments you want to include. Try sketching out your essay following each of the patterns; look carefully to see which pattern (or variation of one of the patterns) seems to put forward your particular material most persuasively, with the least repetition or confusion. Sometimes your essay's material will clearly fall into a particular pattern of organization, so your choice will be easy. More often, however, you will have to arrange and rearrange your ideas and counter-arguments until you see the best approach. Don't be discouraged if you decide to change patterns after you've begun a rough draft; what matters is finding the most effective way to persuade the reader to your side.

If no organizational pattern seems to fit at first, ask yourself which of your points or counter-arguments is the strongest or most important. Try putting that point in one of the two most emphatic places: either first or last. Sometimes your most important discussion will lead the way to your other points and, consequently, should be introduced first; perhaps more often, effective writers and speakers build up to their strongest point, presenting it last as the climax of their argument. Again, the choice depends on your material itself, though it's rare that you would want to bury your strongest point in the middle of your essay.

Now let's return to the essay on note-taking first discussed on page 288. After selecting the most important arguments and counter-arguments (page 289), let's say that you decide that your main point concerns the development of students' learning skills. Since your opposition claims the contrary, that their service does promote learning, you see that you can make your main point as you refute theirs. But you also wish to include a couple of other points for your side. After trying several patterns, you decide to put the "thinking skills" rebuttal last for emphasis and present your other points first. Consequently, Pattern A best fits your plan. A sketchy outline might look like this:

- **Revised working thesis and essay map:** Professional note-taking services should be banned from our campus. Not only do they give some students unfair advantages and discourage class attendance, they prevent students from developing and practicing good learning skills.

- **Body paragraph 1 (a first point for the writer's side):** Services penalize some students—those who haven't enough money or take other sections or enroll in classes without lectures.

- **Body paragraph 2 (another point for the writer's side):** Services encourage cutting class so students miss opportunities to ask questions, participate in discussion, talk to instructor, see visual aids, etc.

- **Body paragraph 3 (rebuttal of the opposition's strongest claim):** Services claim they help students learn more, but they don't because they're doing the work students ought to be doing themselves. Students must learn to think and organize for themselves.

Once you have a general notion of where your essay is going, plan to spend some more time thinking about ways to make each of your points clear, logical, and persuasive to your particular audience. (◆ If you wish to see how one student actually developed an essay based on the preceding outline, turn to the sample student paper on pages 303–305.)

Argue your ideas logically. To convince your readers, you must provide sufficient reasons for your position. You must give more than mere opinion—you must offer logical arguments to back up your assertions. Some of the possible ways of supporting your ideas should already be familiar to you from writing expository essays; listed here are several methods and illustrations:

1. **Give examples (real or hypothetical):** "Cutting class because you have access to professional notes can be harmful; for instance, you might miss seeing some slides or graphics essential to your understanding of the lecture."

2. **Present a comparison or contrast:** "In contrast to reading 'canned' notes, outlining your own notes helps you remember the material."

3. **Show a cause-and-effect relationship:** "Dependence on professional notes may mean that some students will never learn to organize their own responses to classroom discussions."

4. **Argue by definition:** "Passively reading through professional notes isn't a learning experience in which one's mind is engaged."

The well-thought-out arguments you choose to support your case may be called *logical appeals* because they appeal to, and depend on, your readers' ability to reason and to recognize good sense when they see it. But there is another kind of appeal often used today: the *emotional appeal.*

Emotional appeals are designed to persuade people by playing on their feelings rather than appealing to their intellect. Rather than using thoughtful, logical reasoning to support their claims, writers and speakers using *only* emotional appeals often try to accomplish their goals by distracting or misleading their audiences. Frequently, emotional appeals are characterized by language that plays on people's fears, material desires, prejudices, or sympathies; such language often triggers highly favorable or unfavorable responses to a subject. For instance, emotional appeals are used constantly in advertising, where feel-good images, music, and slogans ("Come to Marlboro Country"; "The Heartbeat of America Is Today's Chevy Truck") are designed to sway potential customers to a product without their thinking about it too much. Some politicians also rely heavily on emotional appeals, often using scare tactics to disguise a situation or to lead people away from questioning the logic of a particular issue.

But in some cases, emotional appeals can be used for legitimate purposes. Good writers should always be aware of their audience's needs, values, and states of mind, and they may be more persuasive on occasion if they can frame their arguments in ways that appeal to both their readers' logic and their emotions. For example, when Martin Luther King, Jr., delivered his famous "I Have a Dream" speech to the crowds gathered in Washington, D.C., in 1963 and described his vision of little children of different races walking hand in hand, being judged not "by the color of their skin but by the content of their character," he certainly spoke with passion that was aimed at the hearts of his listeners. But King was not using an emotional appeal to keep his audience from thinking about his message; on the contrary, he presented powerful emotional images that he hoped would inspire people to act on what they already thought and felt, their deepest convictions about equality and justice.

Appeals to emotions are tricky: you can use them effectively in conjunction with appeals to logic and with solid evidence, but only if you use them ethically. Too many appeals to the emotions are also overwhelming; readers tire quickly from excessive tugs on the heartstrings. To prevent your readers from suspecting deception or feeling manipulated, support your assertions with as many logical arguments as you can muster, and use emotional appeals only when they legitimately advance your cause.

Offer evidence that effectively supports your claims. In addition to presenting thoughtful, logical reasoning, you may wish to incorporate a variety of convincing evidence to persuade your readers to your side. Your essay might profit from including, where appropriate, some of the following kinds of supporting evidence:

- Personal experiences
- The experiences or testimony of others whose opinions are pertinent to the topic
- Factual information you've gathered from research
- Statistics from current, reliable sources
- Hypothetical examples
- Testimony from authorities and experts
- Charts, graphs, or diagrams

You'll need to spend quite a bit of your prewriting time thinking about the best kinds of evidence to support your case. Remember that not all personal experiences or research materials are persuasive. For instance, the experiences we've had (or that our friends have had) may not be representative of a universal experience and consequently may lead to unconvincing generalizations. Even testimony from an authority may not be convincing if the person is not speaking on a topic from his or her field of expertise; famous football players, for instance, don't necessarily know any more about underwear or soft drinks than anyone else. Always put yourself in the skeptical reader's place and ask, "Does this point convince me? If not, why not?" (◆ For more information on incorporating research material into your essays, see Chapter 14. For more advice on the selection of evidence, see the section on critical thinking in Chapter 5.)

Find the appropriate tone. Sometimes when we argue, it's easy to get carried away. Remember that your goal is to persuade and perhaps change your readers, not alienate them. Instead of laying on insults or sarcasm, present your ideas in a moderate let-us-reason-together spirit. Such a tone will persuade your readers that you are sincere in your attempts to argue as truthfully and fairly as possible. If your readers do not respect you as a reasonable person, they certainly won't be swayed to your side of an issue. Don't preach or pontificate either; no one likes—or respects—a writer with a superior attitude. Write in your natural "voice"; don't adopt a pseudo-intellectual tone. In short, to argue effectively you should sound logical, sincere, and informed. (◆ For additional comments on tone, review pages 157–159.)

Consider using Rogerian techniques, if they are appropriate. In some cases, especially those involving tense situations or highly sensitive issues, you may wish to incorporate some techniques of the noted psychologist Carl Rogers, who developed a procedure for presenting what he called the nonthreatening argument. Rogers believed that people involved in a debate should strive for clear, honest communication so that the problem under discussion could be resolved. Instead of going on the defensive and trying to "win" the argument, each side should try to recognize common ground and then develop a solution that will address the needs of both parties.

A Rogerian argument uses these techniques:

1. A clear, objective statement of the problem or issue

2. A clear, objective summary of the opposition's position that shows you understand its point of view and goals

3. A clear, objective summary of your point of view, stated in nonthreatening language

4. A discussion that emphasizes the beliefs, values, and goals that you and your opposition have in common

5. A description of any of your points that you are willing to concede or compromise

6. An explanation of a plan or proposed solution that meets the needs of both sides

By showing your opposition that you thoroughly understand its position and that you are sincerely trying to effect a solution that is in everyone's—not just your—best interests, you may succeed in some situations that might otherwise be hopeless because of their highly emotional nature. Remember, too, that you can use some of these Rogerian techniques in any kind of argument paper you are writing, if you think they would be effective.

Problems to Avoid

Writers of argumentative essays must appear logical or their readers will reject their point of view. Here is a short list of some of the most common *logical fallacies*—that is, errors in reasoning. Check your rough drafts carefully to avoid these problems.

Students sometimes ask, "If a logical fallacy works, why not use it? Isn't all fair in love, war, and argumentative essays?" The honest answer is maybe. It's quite true that speakers and writers do use faulty logic and irrational emotional appeals to persuade people every day (one needs only to look at television or a newspaper to see example after example). But the cost of the risk is high: if you do try to slide one by your readers and they see through your trick, you will lose your credibility instantly. On the whole, it's far more effective to use logical reasoning and strong evidence to convince your readers to accept your point of view.

Common Logical Fallacies

Hasty generalization: The writer bases the argument on insufficient or unrepresentative evidence. Suppose, for example, you have owned two poodles and they have both bitten you. If you declare that all poodles are vicious dogs, you are making a hasty generalization. There are, of course, thousands of poodles who have not attacked any-one. Similarly, you're in error if you interview only campus athletes and then declare, "University students favor a new stadium." What about the opinions of the students who aren't athletes? In other words, when the generalization is drawn from a sample that is too small or select, your conclusion isn't valid.

***Non sequitur* ("it doesn't follow"): The writer's conclusion is not necessarily a logi-cal result of the facts.** An example of a *non sequitur* occurs when you conclude, "Profes-sor Smith is a famous chemist, so he will be a brilliant chemistry teacher." As you may have realized by now, the fact that someone knows a subject well does not automatically mean that he or she can communicate the information clearly in a classroom; hence, the conclusion is not necessarily valid.

Begging the question: The writer presents as truth what is not yet proven by the argument. For example, in the statement "All useless laws such as Reform Bill 13 should be repealed," the writer has already pronounced the bill useless without assuming responsibility for proving that accusation. Similarly, the statement "Professor Austin, one of the many instructors on our campus using their classrooms solely for preaching their political ideas, should be fired" begs the question (that is, tries like a beggar to get something for nothing from the reader) because the writer gives no evidence for what must first be argued, not merely asserted—that there are in fact professors on that par-ticular campus using class time solely for spreading their political beliefs.

Red herring: The writer introduces an irrelevant point to divert the readers' atten-tion from the main issue. This term originates from the old tactic used by escaped pris-oners of dragging a smoked herring, a strong-smelling fish, across their trail to confuse tracking dogs by making them follow the wrong scent. For example, roommate A might be criticizing roommate B for his repeated failure to do the dishes when it was his turn. To escape facing the charges, roommate B brings up times in the past when the other roommate failed to repay some money he borrowed. Although roommate A may indeed have a problem with remembering his debts, that discussion isn't relevant to the original argument about sharing the responsibility for the dishes. (By the way, you might have run across a well-known newspaper photograph of a California environmentalist group demonstrating for more protection of dolphins, whales, and other marine life; look closely to see, over in the left corner, almost hidden by the host of placards and banners, a fellow slyly holding up a sign that reads "Save the Red Herring!" Now, who says rhetori-cians don't have a good sense of humor?)

Post hoc, ergo propter hoc. See page 276.

Argument *ad hominem* ("to the man"): The writer attacks the opponent's character rather than the opponent's argument. The statement "Dr. Bloom can't be a competent marriage counselor because she's been divorced" may not be valid. Bloom's advice to her clients may be excellent regardless of her own marital status.

Faulty use of authority: The writer relies on "authorities" who are not convincing sources. Although someone may be well known in a particular field, he or she may not be qualified to testify in a different area. A baseball player in an ad for laser surgery may stress his need for correct vision, but he may be no more knowledgeable about eye care than anyone else on the street. In other words, name recognition is not enough. For their testimony to count with readers, authorities must have expertise, credentials, or relevant experience in the area under discussion. (◆ See also pages 294, 386–388, and "transfer of virtue" in the discussion of "bandwagon appeal" below.)

Argument *ad populum* ("to the people"): The writer evades the issues by appealing to readers' emotional reactions to certain subjects. For example, instead of arguing the facts of an issue, a writer might play on the readers' negative response to such words as "socialism," "terrorist," or "radical," and their positive response to words like "God," "country," "liberty," or "patriotic." In the statement "If you are a true American, you will vote against the referendum on flag burning," the writer avoids any discussion of the merits or weaknesses of the bill and merely substitutes an emotional appeal. Other popular "virtue words" include "duty," "common sense," "courage," and "healthy." (Advertisers, of course, also play on consumers' emotions by filling their ads with pictures of babies, animals, status objects, and sexually attractive men and women.)

Circular thinking. See page 276.

Either/Or: The writer tries to convince readers that there are only two sides to an issue—one right, one wrong. The statement "If you don't go to war against Iceland, you don't love your country" is irrational because it doesn't consider the other possibilities, such as patriotic people's right to oppose war as an expression of love for their country. A classic example of this sort of oversimplification was illustrated in the 1960s bumper sticker that was popular during the debate over the Vietnam War: "America: Love It or Leave It." Obviously, there are other choices ("Change It or Lose It," for instance, to quote another either/or bumper sticker of that era).

Hypostatization: The writer uses an abstract concept as if it were a concrete reality. Always be suspicious of a writer who frequently relies on statements beginning "History has always taught us . . ." or "Science has proven . . ." or "Research shows. . . ." The implication in each case is that history or science (or any other discipline) has only one voice, one opinion. On the contrary, "history" is written by a multitude of historians who hold a variety of opinions; doctors and scientists also frequently disagree. Instead of generalizing about a particular field, quote a respected authority or simply qualify your statement by referring to "many" or "some" scientists, historians, or other professionals.

Bandwagon appeal: The writer tries to validate a point by intimating that "everyone else believes in this." Such a tactic evades discussion of the issue itself. Advertising often uses this technique: "Everyone who demands real taste smokes Phooey cigarettes"; "Discriminating women use Smacky-Mouth lipstick." (The ultimate in "bandwagon" humor may have appeared on a recent Colorado bumper sticker: "Eat lamb—could 1000s of coyotes be wrong?") A variation of the "bandwagon" fallacy is sometimes referred to as "transfer of virtue," the sharing of light from someone else's sparkle. Advertisers often use this technique by paying attractive models or media stars to endorse their product. The underlying premise is this:

Popular/beautiful/"cool"/rich people use/buy/wear "X"; if you use "X," you too will be popular/beautiful/etc.

Intelligent readers and consumers know, of course, to suspect such doubtful causal relationships.

Straw man: The writer selects the opposition's weakest or most insignificant point to argue against, to divert the readers' attention from the real issues. Instead of addressing the opposition's best arguments and defeating them, the writer "sets up a straw man"—that is, the writer picks out a trivial (or irrelevant) argument against his or her own position and easily knocks it down, just as one might easily push over a figure made of straw. Perhaps the most famous example of the "straw man" occurred in 1952 when, during his vice-presidential campaign, Richard Nixon was accused of misappropriating campaign funds for his personal use. Addressing the nation on television, Nixon described how his six-year-old daughter, Tricia, had received a little cocker spaniel named Checkers from a Texas supporter. Nixon went on about how much his children loved the dog and how, regardless of what anyone thought, by gosh, he was going to keep that cute dog for little Tricia. Of course, no one was asking Nixon to return the dog; they were asking about the $18,000 in missing campaign funds. But Nixon's canine gift was much easier for him to defend, and the "Checkers" speech is now famous as one of the most notorious "straw man" diversions.

Faulty analogy: The writer uses an extended comparison as proof of a point. Look closely at all extended comparisons and metaphors to see if the two things being compared are really similar. For example, in a recent editorial a woman protested new laws requiring parents to use car seats for small children, arguing that if the state could require the seats, they could just as easily require mothers to breast-feed instead of using formula. Are the two situations alike? Car accidents are the leading cause of death of children under four; is formula deadly? Or perhaps you've read that putting teenagers in sex education classes is like taking an alcoholic to a bar. Is it? Is stem cell research the same as Nazi medical experiments on prisoners, as the leader of a family-outreach group has claimed? If readers don't see a close similarity, the analogy may not be persuasive. Moreover, remember that even though a compelling analogy may suggest similarities, it alone cannot *prove* anything. (◆ For more discussion of analogy, see pages 244–246.)

Quick fix: The writer leans too heavily on catchy phrases or empty slogans. A clever turn of phrase may grab one's attention, but it may lose its persuasiveness when scrutinized closely. For instance, a banner at a recent rally to protest a piece of anti-gun legislation read, "When guns are outlawed, only outlaws will have guns." Although the sentence had nice balance, it oversimplified the issue. The legislation in question was not trying to outlaw all guns, just the sale of the infamous Saturday Night Specials, most often used in crimes and domestic violence; the sale of guns for sport, such as hunting rifles, would remain legal. Other slogans sound good but are simply irrelevant: a particular soft drink, for example, may be "the real thing," but what drink isn't? The advertising slogan "The XYZ truck runs deep" means what, exactly? Look closely at clever lines substituted for reasoned argument; always demand clear terms and logical explanations.*

© Canstock Images, Inc./ Index Stock Imagery

Practicing What You've Learned

A. Imagine that you are writing an argumentative essay addressing the controversial question "Should home-schooled students be allowed to play on public school athletic teams?" You have investigated the topic and have noted the variety of opinions listed here. Arrange the statements into two lists: a "Pro" list (those statements that argue for allowing home schoolers to play) and a "Con" list (those statements that are against allowing home schoolers to play). Cross off any inappropriate or illogical statements you find; combine any opinions that overlap.

1. Parents of home schoolers pay the same taxes as public school parents.

2. Public school kids must meet grade requirements to be eligible.

3. School rules prohibit nonenrolled youth on campus.

4. Home schoolers shouldn't get the benefits of a school they've rejected.

5. Public school kids are bad influences on home schoolers.

6. Home schoolers need the social interaction.

7. Public school teams can always use more good athletes.

8. More students will overburden athletic facilities.

9. Home schoolers miss their public school friends, and vice versa.

10. Ten states allow home schoolers to play on teams.

11. Home schoolers will displace public school students on teams.

12. Public school students have to meet attendance rules to be eligible.

13. Athletic competition is good for everybody.

14. Home schoolers often have controversial political beliefs that will cause fights.

15. Team members need to share the same community on a daily basis.

16. Home schoolers aren't as invested in school pride.

continued on next page

*Sometimes advertisers get more for their slogans than they bargained for. According to one news source, a popular soft-drink company had to spend millions to revise its slogan after introducing its product into parts of China. Apparently the slogan "Come alive! Join the Blah-Blah-Cola Generation!" translated into some dialects as "Blah-Blah Cola Brings Your Ancestors Back from the Dead!"

Once you have your two lists, decide your own position on this topic. Then select two points you might use to argue your position and one opposing criticism you might refute. Put your working thesis into an "although-because" format, as explained on page 290. Compare your choices to those of your classmates.

B. Errors in reasoning can cause your reader to doubt your credibility. In the following mock essay, for example, the writer includes a variety of fallacies that undermine his argument; see if you can identify all his errors.

Ban Those Books!

1   A serious problem faces America today, a problem of such grave importance that our very existence as a nation is threatened. We must either cleanse our schools of evil-minded books, or we must reconcile ourselves to seeing our children become welfare moochers and homeless bums.

2   History has shown time and time again that placement of immoral books in our schools is part of an insidious plot designed to weaken the moral fiber of our youth from coast to coast. In Wettuckett, Ohio, for example, the year after books by Mark Twain, such as *Tom Sawyer* and *Huckleberry Finn*, were introduced into the school library by liberal free-thinkers and radicals, the number of students cutting classes rose by six percent. And in that same year, the number of high school seniors going on to college dropped from thirty to twenty-two.

3   The reason for this could be either a natural decline in intelligence and morals or the influence of those dirty books that teach our beloved children disrespect and irresponsibility. Since there is no evidence to suggest a natural decline, the conclusion is inescapable: once our children read about Twain's characters skipping school and running away from home, they had to do likewise. If they hadn't read about such undesirable characters as Huckleberry Finn, our innocent children would never have behaved in those ways.

4   Now, I am a simple man, a plain old farm boy—the pseudo-intellectuals call me redneck just like they call you folks. But I can assure you that, redneck or not, I've got the guts to fight moral decay everywhere I find it, and I urge you to do the same. For this reason I want all you good folks to come to the ban-the-books rally this Friday so we can talk it over. I promise you all your right-thinking neighbors will be there.

Assignment

Collaborative Activity: Out of class, search for one of the following:

© CORBIS

1.   An example of an advertisement that illustrates one or more of the fallacies or appeals discussed on pages 295–298;

continued on next page

2. An example of illogical or fallacious reasoning in a piece of writing (you might try looking at the editorial page or "Letters to the Editor" section of your local or campus newspaper);

3. An example of a logical, persuasive point in a piece of writing.

Be prepared to explain your analysis of your sample, but do not write any sort of identifying label or evaluation on the sample itself. Bring your ad or piece of writing to class and exchange it with that of a classmate. After ten minutes, compare notes. Do you and your classmate agree on the evaluation of each sample? Why, or why not?

Essay Topics

© Inspirestock/CORBIS

Write a convincing argument attacking or defending one of the following statements, or use them to help you think of your own topic. Remember to narrow and focus the topic as necessary. (◆ Note that essays on some of the topics presented here might profit from research material; see Chapter 14 for help.) For additional ideas, see the "Suggestions for Writing" section following the professional essays (page 309).

1. Students should/should not work throughout high school.

2. Drivers' use of cell phones while vehicles are in motion should/should not be prohibited.

3. Sixteen-year-olds should/should not be issued limited-privilege or "graduated" driver's licenses.

4. Academically qualified children of undocumented immigrants should/should not be allowed to apply for in-state tuition at public universities.

5. Violent video games should/should not be available for purchase by anyone under age eighteen.

6. Universities should/should not allow students to carry concealed handguns on campus.

7. A school voucher system should/should not be used in this state.

8. Students who do poorly in their academic courses should/should not be allowed to participate in athletic programs.

9. All schools should/should not adopt a "repeat/delete" policy, allowing students to retake a course and substitute a higher grade on their record.

continued on next page

10. Televised instant replays should/should not be used to determine controversial plays in major league baseball and other sports, just as they are in football.

11. Plastic shopping sacks should/should not be legally banned from grocery and other retail stores.

12. Sodas and high-sugar foods should/should not be sold in public school vending machines.

13. Public school districts should/should not be allowed to sell advertising inside or outside of school buses.

14. Americans should/should not be required to perform a year of public service after high school graduation.

15. Public school students should/should not be required to wear uniforms.

16. Employers should/should not be allowed to require social media passwords from job applicants.

17. Controversial names or symbols of athletic teams ("Redskins," the Confederate flag, the tomahawk chop) should/should not be changed.

18. A law prohibiting demonstrations close to military or other funerals (or some other controversial law, bill, or policy) should/should not be passed.

19. Individuals under age fourteen charged with felonies should/should not be tried as adults.

20. Advertising for "Product X" rarely/often relies on use of emotional appeals and faulty logic. (Focus on one kind of product—cars, cosmetics, computers, soft drinks, cell phones, etc.—or on one especially popular brand, and collect a number of its ads to analyze. What does your analysis reveal about the major ways the product is advertised to its target audience? Do the ads appeal to consumers' reason or do they employ logical fallacies? Some combination? Which ads are more effective, and why? If it's helpful, consider the appeals of ads reprinted in this text. A list of the ads follows the Table of Contents.)

A Topic Proposal for Your Essay

Selecting the right subject matter is important to every writer. To help you clarify your ideas and strengthen your commitment to your topic, here is a proposal sheet that asks you to describe some of your preliminary ideas about your subject before you begin drafting. Although your ideas may change as you write (they will almost certainly become more refined), thinking through your choice of topic now may help you avoid several false starts.

1. What is the subject of your argumentative essay? Write a rough statement of your opinion on this subject.

2. Why are you interested in this topic? Is it important to your personal, civic, or professional life? State at least one reason for your choice of topic.

3. Is this a significant topic of interest to others? Why? Is there a particular audience you would like to address?

4. At this point, can you list at least two reasons that support your opinion of your topic?

5. Who opposes your opinion? Can you state clearly at least one of your opposition's major criticisms of your position?

6. What difficulties, if any, might arise during drafting? For example, might you need to collect any additional evidence through reading, research, or interviewing to support your points or to refute your opposition?

Sample Student Essay

The student who wrote this essay followed the steps for writing an argumentative paper discussed in this chapter. His intended audience was the readers of his school newspaper, primarily students but instructors as well. To argue his case, he chose Pattern A, presenting two of his own points and then concluding with a rebuttal of an important opposing view. Notice that this writer uses a variety of methods to convince his readers, including hypothetical examples, causal analysis, analogy, and testimony. Does the writer persuade you to his point of view? Which are his strongest and weakest arguments? What might you change to make his essay even more persuasive?

STUDENTS, TAKE NOTE!

1   A walk across campus this week will reveal students, professors, and administrators arguing about class notes like never before. But they're not engaged in intellectual debates over chemical formulas or literary images. They're fighting over the taking of the notes themselves, as professional note-taking services in town are applying for permission to sit in on large lecture courses and then sell their notes to the students in those classes. Although the prospect of having "canned" notes looks inviting to many students, our administration should nevertheless ban these services from campus. Not only do such businesses give certain students unfair advantages and discourage class attendance, but they also

Introduction: Presenting the controversy

Thesis

Essay map

prohibit the development of students' important learning skills, despite the services' claims to the contrary.

A point for the writer's position: Note-taking services are unfair to some students

2   What is troubled for many of us about the professional-notes option is our sense of fair play. Let's face it: like it or not, school is, among other things, a place of competition, as students vie for the best academic records to send to prospective employers, graduate and professional schools, and in some cases, paying parents. In today's classes, all students have an equal opportunity to come to class, take notes, study, and pass or fail on their own merits. But the expensive professional notes, already organized and outlined, may give those with plenty of money some advantages that poorer students—those on scholarships or with families, for example—just can't afford. In addition, the notes may be available only to those students who take certain sections of a course and not others, thus giving some students an extra advantage. The same is true for students who satisfy a requirement by taking one course that has notes available rather than another that has not. Knowing that you're doing your own work may make you feel morally superior to a classmate who isn't, but frankly, on some other level, it just plain feels irritating and unfair, sort of like watching your roommate getting away with plagiarizing his paper for a class after you spent weeks researching yours.

Another point for the writer's position: Professional notes discourage students from attending and participating in class

3   In addition to being a potential source of conflict among students, the professional-note services aren't winning many friends among the faculty, either. Several instructors have complained that the availability of notes will encourage many students, especially the weaker ones, to cut classes, assuming that they have all the material necessary for understanding the lecture, discussion, or lab. But anyone who has ever had to use borrowed notes knows something vital is not there. Someone else's interpretation of the information is often hard or impossible to follow, especially if you must understand complex relationships and problems. Moreover, skipping class may mean missed opportunities for students to ask questions or to participate in experiments or in group discussions, all of which often

help clarify concepts under study. Not seeing visual aids or diagrams in person can also result in problems understanding the material. And, last, missing class can mean failure to become comfortably acquainted with the teacher, which, in turn, may discourage a student from asking for individual help when it's needed. All these possibilities are real; even Jeff Allridge, owner of the Quotable Notes service, has admitted to a campus reporter, "There *is* an incentive to skip class."

4   Despite the admission that professional note-taking encourages class-cutting, the services still promote themselves by claiming that students using their notes learn more. They support this claim by arguing that their notes offer students clearly organized information and, according to one advertising brochure, "good models" for students to follow in other classes. But such arguments miss the larger point: students should be learning how to develop their own note-taking, organizing, and thinking skills rather than swallowing the material whole as neatly packaged and delivered. Memorizing class material as outlined can be important, but it's not really as valuable in the long run as learning how to think about the material and use it to solve problems or come up with new ideas later. Taking your own notes teaches you how to listen and how to spot the important concepts; organizing your own notes teaches you how to pull ideas together in a logical way, all skills students will need in other classes, on jobs, and in life in general. Having memorized the outlines but not really mastered the thinking skills won't help the medical student whose patient's symptoms vary from the textbook description or the engineer whose airplane wings suddenly fail the stress test for no apparent reason.

Presentation and rebuttal of the opposition's claim that students learn more using professional notes

5   By appealing to students who believe professional notes will help them accomplish their educational goals easier and quicker, a variety of note-taking services now have franchises across the country. But our campus shouldn't allow them to move in. Students need to recognize that the difference between the services' definition of "learning" and the real learning experiences college can provide is of notable importance.

Conclusion: Restatement of thesis, ending on pun to emphasize the main idea

Professional Essays*

The following essays on the keeping of exotic and wild animals as pets were first published in *USA Today* in a "Today's Debate" column (2011). The first essay represents the view of the newspaper's editorial board; the second essay was written by Zuzana Kukol, president and co-founder of Responsible Exotic Animal Ownership (REXANO), who keeps a pet lion and tigers at her Nevada home. Although you may already hold an opinion on this controversial issue, try to objectively analyze the strengths and weaknesses of each essay. Which points are the most and least persuasive, and why?

> *Editor's note:* This debate was inspired by an Ohio event mentioned in both essays. When owner Terry Thompson released his collection of 56 animals into a populated area, local law officers, untrained in tranquilizer dart use, were forced to kill 49 of them, including lions, bears, wolves, and 18 rare Bengal tigers, of which only 1400 still exist in the wild.

Pre-reading Thoughts: Have you ever owned an unusual pet? Would you feel comfortable living near someone who kept an exotic or wild animal as a pet?

USA Today: Wild Animals Aren't Pets**

1   In many states, anyone with a few hundred dollars and a yen for the unusual can own a python, a black bear or a big cat as a "pet." For $8,000 a baby white tiger can be yours. Sometimes, wild animals are even offered free: "Siberian tigers looking for a good home," read an ad in the *Animal Finder's Guide.*

2   Until this week, though, few people knew how easy it is to own a wild animal as a pet. Or how potentially tragic.

3   But just as a 2007 raid on property owned by football star Michael Vick laid bare the little known and cruel world of dogfighting, a story that unfolded in a small Ohio city this week opened the public's eyes to the little known, distressing world of "exotic" pets. We're not suggesting that people who own these animals are cruel. Many surely love them. But public safety, common sense and compassion for animals all dictate the same conclusion: Wild animals are not pets.

4   If that weren't already obvious, it became more so on Tuesday, when collector Terry Thompson opened the cages on his Zanesville farm, springing dozens of lions, tigers, bears and other wild creatures before killing himself. With animals running loose and darkness closing in, authorities arrived with no good choices to protect the public. They shot all but a handful of the animals as the nation watched, transfixed and horrified.

5   Owners of "exotic" animals claim they rarely maim or kill. But is the death rate really the point?

6   In 2009, a 2-year-old Florida girl was strangled by a 12-foot-long Burmese python, a family pet that had gotten out of its aquarium. That same year, a Connecticut woman was mauled and disfigured by a neighbor's pet chimp. Last year, a caretaker was mauled to death by a bear owned by a Cleveland collector. This week

* ◆ For help reading these essays analytically, review pages 179–181.
** "Wild Animals Aren't Pets" AND "Let People Own Exotic Animals" from USA TODAY, September 15, 2011. Copyright © 2011. Used by permission.

in Zanesville, it was the animals themselves, including 18 rare Bengal tigers, who became innocent victims.

7   Trade in these beautiful creatures thrives in the USA, where thousands are bred and sold through classified ads or at auctions centered in Indiana, Missouri and Tennessee. There's too little to stop it.

8   A 2003 federal law, which forbids the interstate transport of certain big cats, has stopped much of the trade on the Internet, according to the Humane Society of the U.S. But monkeys, baboons and other primates were left out, and measures to plug that hole have twice stalled in Congress.

9   Only collectors who exhibit animals need a federal license. Those, such as Thompson, who keep the animals as "pets" are left alone, unless states intervene. And many do not. Eight—Alabama, Idaho, Ohio, Nevada, North Carolina, South Carolina, West Virginia and Wisconsin—have no rules, and in 13 others the laws are lax, according to Born Free USA, which has lobbied for years for stronger laws.

10   After the Cleveland bear-mauling, then-Ohio Gov. Ted Strickland issued an emergency order to ban possession of wild animals. While it exempted current owners, Thompson might have been forced to give up his menagerie because he had been cited for animal cruelty. We'll never know. Strickland's successor, John Kasich, let the order expire.

According to the National Parks Service, nearly two thousand Burmese pythons, some weighing almost 150 pounds, have been caught in the Florida Everglades. Some scientists estimate the python's population in the tens of thousands and believe that the original fast-breeding snakes were released by private owners or escaped from pet shops.

Zuana Kukol's Opposing View: Let People Own Exotic Animals

1   This week's tragedy in Zanesville, Ohio, brought back the question of whether private ownership of wild and exotic animals should be legal.

2   The simple answer is yes. Responsible private ownership of exotic animals should be legal if animal welfare is taken care of. Terry Thompson didn't represent the typical responsible owner. He had a criminal record and animal abuse charges. What Thompson did was selfish and insane; we cannot regulate insanity.

3   People keep exotic animals for commercial reasons and as pets. Most exotic animals—such as big cats, bears or apes—are in commercial, federally inspected facilities. These animals are born in captivity, and not "stolen" from the wild. Captive breeding eliminates the pressure on wild populations, and also serves as a backup in case the animals go extinct.

4   Dangers from exotic animals are low. On average in the United States, only 3.25 people per year are killed by captive big cats, snakes, elephants and bears. Most of these fatalities are owners, family members, friends and trainers voluntarily on the

property where the animals were kept. Meanwhile, traffic accidents kill about 125 people per day.

5   If we have the freedom to choose what car to buy, where to live, or what domestic animal to have, why shouldn't we have the same freedom to choose what species of wild or exotic animal to own and to love?

6   Would the Ohio situation be any different if the animals were owned by a government and their caretaker released them? Is this really about private ownership, or is it about certain people's personal issues with exotics in captivity?

7   If society overreacts and bans exotics because of actions of a few deranged individuals, then we need to ban kids, as that is the only way to totally stop child abuse, and we need to ban humans, because that is the only way to stop murder. Silly, isn't it?

Questions on Content, Structure, and Style

1. Evaluate the introduction in the *USA Today*'s essay. Does it effectively draw the reader into the essay's subject?

2. What is the opinion of the *USA Today* editorial board regarding private ownership of wild animals? What are the board's main reasons for this stance?

3. Why does the editorial board describe the event in Zanesville, Ohio, in some detail?

4. What is the purpose of the allusion to football quarterback Michael Vick in paragraph 3? Is this allusion successful? Why or why not?

5. How does the board address an opposing point? What role do examples play in this argument?

6. What action does the editorial board demand? Is this call for action a successful conclusion to the essay?

7. What is Kukol's view of private ownership of wild and exotic animals?

8. What are Kukol's main points in support of her view? How does she respond to the editorial board's claims?

9. Evaluate the analogies in Kukol's paragraphs 5 and 7. Do you find them persuasive? Why or why not?

10. What strengthens and weaknesses do you see in these two essays? Which essay is more persuasive, and why?

Vocabulary

USA Today's essay:	Kukol's essay:
yen (1)	extinct (3)
exotic (3)	fatalities (4)
mauled (6)	deranged (7)
intervene (9)	
lobbied (9)	
menagerie (10)	

Suggestions for Writing

Use the essays by the *USA Today*'s editorial board and Zuzana Kukol as a stepping stone to your essay. Perhaps drawing on your answers to the Questions following the essays, as well as any personal experience with the subject, write an editorial for your school or local newspaper arguing your position on wild animals as pets. You may wish to research the subject further, checking the laws governing ownership of pets in your area. Or perhaps you might explore another animal-related subject or controversy: medical experiments or product-testing on animals, no-kill shelters, service or therapy dogs, the wearing of fur, the maintenance of zoos, the licensing of commercial puppy mills, etc. (◆ If you wish to incorporate research material into your essay, see Chapter 14 for help.)

Analyzing Advertisements

Because they are designed to be persuasive, advertisements use a variety of logical and emotional appeals. Ads might be considered arguments in brief form, as they frequently try to convince the public to buy a product, take an action, vote for or against something, join a group, or change an attitude or a behavior. By analyzing the ads that follow, you can practice identifying a variety of persuasive appeals and evaluating their effectiveness. After discussing these ads, apply what you've learned about logical appeals, target audiences, and choice of language to your argumentative essay.*

Conflicting Positions: Gun Control

The three advertisements that follow address the controversial subject of gun control. The first ad is one of a series published by the National Rifle Association (NRA) to tell the public about its organization and its interpretation of the Second Amendment; other ads in this series have featured author Tom Clancy and basketball star Karl Malone. The second ad ("Well-Regulated Militia") counters the NRA position. This ad features Sarah Brady, who, following the shooting of her husband, White House Press Secretary James Brady, during an assassination attempt on President Ronald Reagan, became chair of the Center to Prevent Handgun Violence. The third ad uses an expository strategy and statistics to make its point about handgun regulation in America. Analyze the appeals used in each advertisement. Which methods of persuasion do you think are the most effective, and why? Do you find any of the logical fallacies previously described in this chapter?

---

* ◆ For additional practice analyzing the arguments and appeals of other advertisements that appear in this text, see the list that follows the Table of Contents.

REP. ALBERTO GUTMAN: Florida Legislator, Businessman, Husband, Member of the National Rifle Association.

"Being from a country that was once a democracy and turned communist, I really feel I know what the right to bear arms is all about. In Cuba, where I was born, the first thing the communist government did was take away everybody's firearms, leaving them defenseless and intimidated with fear. That's why our constitutional right to bear arms is so important to our country's survival.

"As a legislator I have to deal with reality. And the reality is that gun control does not work. It actually eliminates the rights of the law-abiding citizen, not the criminal. Criminals will always have guns, and they won't follow gun control laws anyway. I would like to see tougher laws on criminals as opposed to tougher laws on legitimate gun owners. We need to attack the problem of crime at its roots, instead of blaming crime on gun ownership and citizens who use them lawfully.

"It's a big responsibility that we face retaining the right to bear arms. That's why I joined the NRA. The NRA is instrumental in protecting these freedoms. It helps train and educate people, supporting legislation that benefits not only those who bear arms but all citizens of the United States. The NRA helps keep America free." **I'm the NRA.**

The NRA's lobbying organization, the Institute for Legislative Action, is the nation's largest and most influential protector of the constitutional right to keep and bear arms. At every level of government and through local grassroots efforts, the Institute guards against infringement upon the freedoms of law-abiding gun owners. If you would like to join the NRA or want more information about our programs and benefits, write J. Warren Cassidy, Executive Vice President, P.O. Box 37484, Dept. AG-15, Washington, D.C. 20013.

Paid for by the members of the National Rifle Association of America. Copyright 1986.

IS THIS THE "WELL REGULATED MILITIA" PROTECTED BY THE SECOND AMENDMENT?

"A well regulated Militia, being necessary to the security of a free State, the right of the people to keep and bear Arms, shall not be infringed."

—*Second Amendment to the U.S. Constitution*

For years, the National Rifle Association has spread the myth that gun control laws violate the Second Amendment. Now self-styled "citizen militias" invoke the Second Amendment as they stockpile weapons and train for warfare against what they perceive as a "tyrannical" federal government. The NRA declares that the paramilitary activity of these groups is an exercise of their "right to keep and bear arms." Echoing the extremist rhetoric of the "militias," an NRA official has called the Second Amendment "a loaded gun...held to the head of government." This is a perversion of our Constitution.

When our Founding Fathers wrote the Second Amendment more than 200 years ago, the "well regulated militia" was not a privately organized army formed to resist the government of the United States. It was the military arm of state government, formed to maintain public order.

The Supreme Court has ruled that the "obvious purpose" of the Second Amendment was to protect the "militia which the States were expected to maintain and train," and that "the National Guard is the modern militia."

Because laws regulating firearms do not interfere with the modern militia, no gun control law has ever been overturned by the federal courts on Second Amendment grounds. That's why former Supreme Court Chief Justice Warren Burger has called the NRA's Second Amendment propaganda a "fraud on the American public."

The Second Amendment is not a barrier to reasonable gun control laws. Nor is it a license for those who disagree with government policies to resist them by force of arms. It's time for the NRA to stop its Second Amendment fraud.

The Second Amendment protects the National Guard, not private armies preparing to take the law into their own hands.

Sarah Brady, Chair of the Center to Prevent Handgun Violence

☐ **Dear Sarah, I want to support your national education campaign to fight the NRA's Second Amendment fraud. Enclosed is my contribution for:**

☐ $15   ☐ $25   ☐ $50   ☐ Other _____

NAME _____

ADDRESS _____

CITY, STATE, ZIP _____

E-MAIL _____

Return to: Center to Prevent Handgun Violence, 1225 Eye Street, NW, Room 1100, Washington, DC 20005

Contributions to the Center to Prevent Handgun Violence are tax-deductible.

☐ **I'd like more Information on the Second Amendment and the Center to Prevent Handgun Violence.**

NAME _____

ADDRESS _____

CITY, STATE, ZIP _____

Return to: Center to Prevent Handgun Violence
1225 Eye Street, NW, Room 1100
Washington, DC 20005

Brought to you by the Center to Prevent Handgun Violence. Sarah Brady, Chair

TEDDY BEARS
HAVE TO MEET CONSUMER HEALTH & SAFETY STANDARDS

1 At least four types of federal safety standards cover teddy bears: sharp edges and points, small parts, hazardous materials, and flammability.

2 From 1994 to 1997, eight models of teddy bears were recalled by the United States Consumer Product Safety Commission due to possible choking hazards. The total number of teddy bears manufactured during this period was more than 750,000.

3 Teddy bears killed no one in the United States in 1997. From 1994 to 1997 there were 71 toy-related deaths in the United States.

BUT GUNS DON'T!

1 There are no federal safety standards for the domestic manufacture of firearms.

2 No federal health and safety agency has the authority to recall defective firearms or force changes in design.

3 Guns killed 32,436 people in the United States in 1997. From 1994 to 1997 there were 140,938 gun-related deaths in the United States. In 1997, for every time a firearm was used by a civilian to kill in self-defense, there were 4 unintentional deaths, 43 criminal homicides, and 75 suicides involving firearms.

THE SOLUTION

The Firearms Safety and Consumer Protection Act would end the gun industry's deadly exemption from health and safety regulation. Only then will America experience a meaningful reduction in firearms violence.

981 unintentional
367 undetermined
13,522 homicides
17,566 suicides

Violence Policy Center • 1140 19th Street • NW • Suite 600 • Washington • DC • 20036 • www.vpc.org

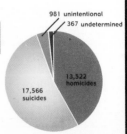

Competing Products: Sources of Energy

The advertisement by the Metropolitan Energy Council that follows argues for the use of oil to provide heating. What arguments are offered? What emotional appeals does this ad incorporate? To whom are these appeals directed? How does the next ad for Xcel Energy, a large Midwestern and Western natural gas utility company, try to respond to some of the first ad's arguments against using gas heat? Why might Xcel run a newspaper advertisement that appears to be primarily a public safety announcement?

The third advertisement (page 316) is part of a series sponsored by the U.S. Council for Energy Awareness to promote the building of more nuclear energy plants. How does it argue against both oil and gas? What emotional appeals do you see in this ad?

Considering both the language and the visual appeals of all three advertisements, which ad do you find the most persuasive, and why?

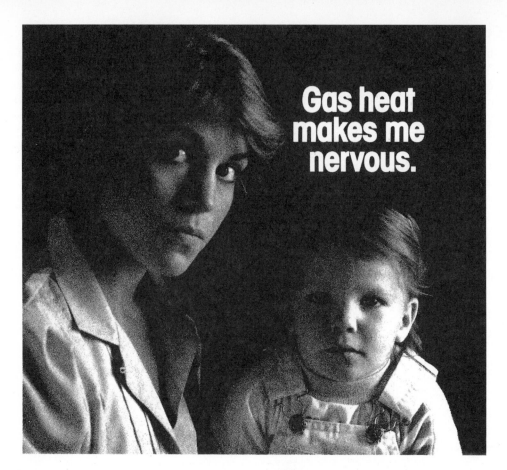

Gas comes from the big utility.
They don't know my name.
They don't know my family.

If you need prompt service from them,
you have to say, "I smell gas."

That's what scares me most. I think gas heat
is dangerous . . . too dangerous
for my home, my kids.

I heat with oil.

Oil heat...The Intelligent Choice
Metropolitan Energy Council, Inc.

66 Morris Ave., P.O. Box 359, Springfield, NJ 07081 • (201) 379-1100

www.xcelenergy.com   ©2005 Xcel Energy Inc.

"WE COULD MAKE NATURAL GAS SMELL LIKE LILACS OR BACON COOKING IN THE MORNING. BUT THAT WOULDN'T GET YOU OUT OF THE HOUSE."

"Natural gas is naturally odorless. So we mix a harmless chemical in with it that smells like sulfur or rotten eggs. If you ever smell that in your house, you could well have a dangerous gas leak. That's when you have to get everyone out of the house immediately, get to a neighbor's house, and call 1-800-895-2999 to get one of our inspectors over. In an emergency, call 911 first. Most people don't know this either, but if you suspect you have a leak, you should NEVER turn lights or appliances on or off. And NEVER use your phone or cell phone in a house that may be filling with gas. The spark from a switch or phone could cause an explosion. By the same token, don't be lighting a match or opening windows. Just get out of there. Then make that call for help. Remember: Stay away. Stay alive."

Timio, Lead Welder

For more safety tips, visit our website at www.xcelenergy.com.

Xcel Energy

Every time you flip a switch or turn a dial, you tap into the energy of over 12,000 people working to make your life better. Xcel Energy. You get all of our energy.

Courtesy of Xcel Energy

SOME ARGUMENTS FOR NUCLEAR ENERGY ARE SMALLER THAN OTHERS.

Around the nuclear electric plant on Florida's Hutchinson Island, endangered wildlife have a safe haven. The baby sea turtles hatching on nearby beaches are more evidence of the truth about nuclear energy: it peacefully coexists with the environment.

America's 110 operating nuclear plants don't pollute the air, because they don't burn anything to generate electricity. Nor do they eat up valuable natural resources such as oil and natural gas.

Still, more plants are needed—to help satisfy the nation's growing need for electricity without sacrificing the quality of our environment. For a free booklet on nuclear energy, write to the U.S. Council for Energy Awareness, P.O. Box 66080, Dept. TR01, Washington, D.C. 20035.

NUCLEAR ENERGY MEANS CLEANER AIR.

© 1992 USCEA

As seen in April 1992 issues of The Washington Post, FORTUNE, and National Journal; May 1992 issues of TIME, Newsweek, Washington Post National Weekly and Congressional Quarterly; June 1992 issues of National Geographic, Smithsonian, New Choices and Christian Science Monitor; July 1992 issue of Forbes; August 1992 issue of World Monitor; September 1992 issue of Ladies' Home Journal and Natural History; October 1992 issues of Good Housekeeping, Atlantic and American Heritage; and November 1992 issue of Reader's Digest.

Popular Appeals: Spending Our Money

How do all three of the following advertisements employ variations of the "bandwagon" or "transfer of virtue" appeal, discussed on pages 297–298?

In the American Century ad, what sort of company identity is created with the story of the boss's lunch? Why might an investment service want this image? To what kind of person does this ad appeal?

The TagHeuer watch ad may appeal to a different audience in its use of award-winning movie star Leonardo Dicaprio, known for his screen portrayals of both strong, intriguing characters (*Inception, Blood Diamond, The Departed*) and sensitive romantics (*Titanic, The Great Gatsby*); he is also well-known as a committed environmentalist. Given the actor's professional reputation, celebrity status, and personal attractiveness, what is the appeal of the ad's question, "What are you made of?" What connection between the consumer and Dicaprio does the watch company wish to establish? To whom is this ad primarily directed, and is this ad effective? Why or why not?

The advertisement on page 320, sponsored by People for the Ethical Treatment of Animals (PETA), is one of a series of anti-fur ads featuring media celebrities, such as Oscar-winning Charlize Theron (shown here), TV personalities Oprah Winfrey and Simon Cowell, singers Lady Gaga and Mariah Carey, and athletes Tony Gonzales and Willis McGaghee, among many others. In addition to its bandwagon appeal, this ad argues its cause by promoting what comparison or analogy (X is like Y) in the reader's mind? Do you find this ad's argument logical and persuasive? Why or why not? (◆ If it's helpful, review the discussions of analogies on pages 244–246 and 298.)

AMERICAN VALUES

Every day, our founder has the same lunch. It isn't lobster tail. ═══════

It's a true story. At noon, he sits down in the cafeteria and eats a peanut butter sandwich. When he's done, he folds up his paper sack so it can be used again tomorrow.

It's a tradition around here. One of the many we've created in our 44 years of managing investments. Over time we've grown, but two things have remained constant. His lunch. And our values. Your success is still our first priority. The proof is in the peanut butter.

AMERICAN CENTURY.

Investment Managers

Courtesy of American Values

Practicing What You've Learned

Continue practicing your critical thinking skills by analyzing the 1920s advertisement that appears here. Who was the likely target audience in terms of gender, age, socioeconomic group, and marital status? Why might this ad have appealed to its audience at that time in our country?

After analyzing this ad, compare it to an advertisement for one of today's cars, SUVs, or trucks. Has the audience changed? What kinds of arguments, appeals, and language are employed to sell the vehicle in the current ad? In what ways do you find the two ads similar and different in their persuasive techniques?

A Revision Worksheet

As you write your rough drafts, consult Chapter 5 for guidance through the revision process. In addition, here are a few questions to ask yourself as you revise your argumentative essay:

1. Does this essay present a clear thesis limited to fit the assigned length of this paper?

continued on next page

2. Does this essay contain a number of strong, persuasive points in support of its thesis?

3. Is the essay organized in an easy-to-follow pattern that avoids repetition or confusion?

4. Does the essay present enough supporting evidence to make each of its points convincing? Where could additional examples, factual information, testimony, or other kinds of supporting material be added to make the arguments even more effective?

5. Will all the supporting evidence be clear to the essay's particular audience? Do any terms or examples need additional explanation or special definition?

6. Has at least one major opposing argument been addressed?

7. Does the essay avoid any logical fallacies or problems in tone?

Collaborative Activity: After you've revised your essay extensively, exchange rough drafts with a classmate and answer these questions for each other, making specific suggestions for improvement wherever appropriate. (◆ For advice on productive participation in classroom workshops, see pages 116–120.)

Reviewing Your Progress

After you have completed your argument essay, take a moment to measure your progress as a writer by responding to the following questions. Such analysis will help you to recognize growth in your writing skills and may enable you to identify areas that are still problematic.

1. Which part of your essay do you like best? Why?

2. After analyzing your essay's reasoning and evidence, which particular argument or point do you consider the strongest? What makes it so convincing?

3. What part of your essay gave you the most trouble? How did you overcome the problem?

4. If you had more time to work on this essay, what would receive additional attention? Why?

5. What did you learn about your topic from writing this essay? About yourself as a writer?

Chapter 11

Description

···

The writer of description creates a word-picture of people, places, objects, and emotions, using a careful selection of details to make an impression on the reader. If you have already written expository or argumentative essays in your composition course, you almost certainly have written some descriptive prose. Nearly every essay, after all, calls for some kind of description; for example, in the student comparison/contrast essay (pages 232–233) the writer describes two kinds of stores; in the professional process essay (pages 216–220) the writer describes the embalming procedure in great detail. To help you write better description in your other essays, however, you may want to practice writing descriptive paragraphs or a short descriptive essay.

How to Write Effective Description

When descriptive prose is called for in your writing, consider these four basic suggestions:

Recognize your purpose. Description is not free-floating; it appears in your writing for a particular reason: to help you inform, clarify, persuade, or create a mood. In some essays you will want your description as *objective*—without personal impressions—as you can make it; for example, you might describe a scientific experiment or a business transaction in straight factual detail. Other times, however, you will want to convey a particular attitude toward your subject; this approach to description is called *subjective* or *impressionistic*. Note the differences between the following two descriptions of a tall, thin boy: the objective writer sticks to the facts by saying, "The eighteen-year-old boy was 6'1" and weighed 155 pounds," whereas the subjective writer gives an impressionistic description: "The young boy was as tall and scrawny as a birch tree in winter." Before you begin describing anything, you must first decide your purpose and whether it calls for objective or subjective reporting.

Describe clearly, using specific details. To make any description clear to your reader, you must include a sufficient number of details that are specific rather than fuzzy or vague. If, for example, your family dog were missing, you wouldn't call the animal shelter to ask if they'd seen a "big brown dog with a short tail"—naturally, you'd mention every distinguishing detail about your pet you could think of: size, color, breed, cut of ears, and special markings. Similarly, if your car had been stolen, you'd give the police as clear and as complete a description of your vehicle as possible. Look at the following sentence. Does it clearly identify a vaulting horse?

> A vaulting horse is a thing usually found in gyms that has four legs and a beam and is used by gymnasts making jumps.

If you didn't already know what a vaulting horse was, you might have trouble picking it out in a gymnasium crowded with equipment. A description with additional details would help you locate it:

> A vaulting horse is a piece of equipment used by gymnasts during competition to help propel them into the air when they perform any of a variety of leaps known as vaults. The gymnasts usually approach the vaulting horse from a running start and then place their hands on the horse for support or for a push off as they perform their vaults. The horse itself resembles a carpenter's sawhorse, but the main beam is made of padded leather rather than wood. The rectangular beam is approximately 5 feet, 3 inches long and 13$\frac{1}{2}$ inches wide. Supported by four legs usually made of steel, the padded leather beam is approximately 4 feet, $\frac{1}{2}$ inch above the floor in men's competitions and 3 feet, 7 inches in women's competitions. The padded leather beam has two white lines marking off three sections on top: the croup, the saddle, and the neck. The two end sections—the croup and the neck—are each 15$\frac{1}{2}$ inches long. Gymnasts place their hands on the neck or croup, depending on the type of vault they are attempting.

Moreover, the reader cannot imagine your subject clearly if your description is couched in vague generalities. The following sentence, for example, presents only a hazy picture:

> Larry is a sloppy dresser.

Revised, the picture is now sharply in focus:

> Larry wears dirty, baggy pants, shirts too small to stay tucked in, socks that fail to match his pants or each other, and a stained coat the Salvation Army rejected as a donation.

Specific details can turn cloudy prose into crisp, clear images that can be reproduced in the mind like photographs.

Select only appropriate details. In any description the choice of details depends largely on the writer's purpose and audience. However, many descriptions—especially the more subjective ones—will present a *dominant impression*; that is, the writer selects primarily those details that communicate a particular mood or feeling to the reader. The dominant impression is the controlling focus of a description; for example, if you wrote a description of your grandmother to show her thoughtfulness, you would select only those details that convey an impression of a sweet, kindly old lady. Here are two brief descriptions illustrating the concept of dominant impression. The first writer tries to create a mood of mystery:

> Down a black winding road stands the abandoned old mansion, silhouetted against the cloud-shrouded moon, creaking and moaning in the wet, chill wind.

The second writer tries to present a feeling of joy and innocence.

> A dozen kites filled the spring air, and around the bright picnic tables spread with hot dogs, hamburgers, and slices of watermelon, Tom and Annie played away the warm April day.

In the description of the deserted mansion, the writer would have violated the impression of mystery had the sentence read,

> Down the black winding road stands the abandoned old mansion, surrounded by bright, multicolored tulips in early bloom.

Including the cheerful flowers as a detail in the description destroys the dominant mood of bleakness and mystery. Similarly, the second example would be spoiled had the writer ended it this way:

> Tom and Annie played away the warm April day until Tom got so sunburned he became ill and had to go home.

Therefore, remember to select only those details that advance your descriptive purpose. Omit any details you consider unimportant or distracting.

See if you can determine the dominant impression of each of the following descriptions:

> The wind had curled up to sleep in the distant mountains. Leaves hung limp and motionless from the silent trees, while birds perched on the branches like little statues. As I sat on the edge of the clearing, holding my breath, I could hear a squirrel scampering through the underbrush. Somewhere far away a dog barked twice, and then the woods were hushed once more.

> This poor thing has seen better days, but one should expect the sofa in a fraternity house den to be well worn. The large, plump, brown corduroy pillows strewn lazily on the floor and propped comfortably against the threadbare arms bear the pencil-point scars of frustrated students and foam-bleeding cuts of multiple pillow wars. No fewer than four pairs of rotting Nikes stand twenty-four-hour guard at the corners of its carefully mended frame. Obviously the relaxed, inviting appearance masks the permanent odors of cheap cigars from Thursday night poker parties; at least two or three guests each weekend sift through the popcorn kernels and Doritos crumbs, sprawl face down, and pass out for a nap. However, frequent inhabitants have learned to avoid the brown stains courtesy of the house pup and the red fruit punch designs of the chapter klutz. Habitually, they strategically lunge over the back of the sofa to an unsoiled area easily identifiable in flight by the large depression left by previous regulars. The quiet *hmmph* of the cushions and harmonious squeal of the exhausted springs signal a perfect landing and utter a warm greeting from an old and faithful friend.

Make your descriptions vivid. By using clear, precise words, you can improve any kind of writing. ◆ Chapters 7 (on words) and 6 (on sentences) offer a variety of tips on clarifying your prose style. In addition to the advice given there, here are two other ways to enliven your descriptions, particularly those that call for a subjective approach:

Use sensory details. If it's appropriate, try using images that appeal to your readers' five senses. If, for example, you are describing your broken leg and the ensuing stay in a hospital, tell your readers how the place smelled, how it looked, what your cast felt like, how your pills tasted, and what noises you heard. Here are some specific examples using sensory details:

Sight	The clean white corridors of the hospital resembled the set of a sci-fi movie, with everyone scurrying around in identical starched uniforms.
Hearing	At night, the only sounds I heard were the quiet squeakings of sensible white shoes as the nurses made their rounds.
Smell	The green beans on the hospital cafeteria tray smelled stale and waxy, like crayons.
Touch	The hospital bed sheet felt as rough and heavy as a feed sack.
Taste	Every four hours they gave me an enormous gray pill whose aftertaste reminded me of the stale licorice my great-aunt kept in candy dishes around her house.

By appealing to the readers' senses, you better enable them to imagine the subject you are describing. Joseph Conrad, the famous nineteenth-century novelist, agreed, believing that all art "appeals primarily to the senses, and the artistic aim when expressing itself in written words must also make its appeal through the senses, if its highest desire is to reach the secret spring of responsive emotions." In other words, to make your readers feel, first make them "see."

Use figurative language when appropriate. As you may recall from Chapter 7, figurative language produces images or pictures in the readers' minds, helping them to understand unfamiliar or abstract subjects. Here are some devices you might use to clarify or spice up your prose:

1. Simile: a comparison between two things using the words "like" or "as" (◆ see also pages 171–172)

   Example   Seeing exactly the video game he wanted, he snatched it off the shelf as quickly as a starving teenager grabbing pie in a refrigerator full of leftover vegetables.

2. Metaphor: a direct comparison between two things that does not use "like" or "as" (◆ see also pages 171–172)

   Example   I was a puppet with my father controlling all the financial strings.

3. Personification: the attribution of human characteristics and emotions to inanimate objects, animals, or abstract ideas

   Example   The old teddy bear sat in a corner, dozing serenely before the fireplace.

4. Hyperbole: intentional exaggeration or overstatement for emphasis or humor

Example   The cockroaches in my kitchen had now grown to the size of carry-on luggage.

5. Understatement: intentional representation of a subject as less important than the facts would warrant (◆ see also irony, pages 157–158)

Example   "The reports of my death are greatly exaggerated."—Mark Twain

6. Synecdoche: a part of something used to represent the whole

Example   A hundred tired feet hit the dance floor for one last jitterbug. [Here "feet" stand for the dancing couples themselves.]

7. Allusion: a brief reference to real or fictitious people, places, events, or things to produce certain associations in the reader's mind

Example   She proofread her essay again and again, searching for errors with the tenacity of Captain Ahab. [Ahab, the ship captain in the novel Moby-Dick, was obsessively devoted to hunting the white whale.]

If you do choose to include figurative language in your descriptions, be sure you are creating the specific image and tone you want to convey. These similes, taken from actual student papers, may have a distracting (and/or humorous) effect:

- She grew on him like she was a colony of E. coli, and he was room-temperature Canadian beef.
- He had a deep, throaty, genuine laugh, like the sound a dog makes just before it throws up.
- He was deeply in love and when she spoke, he heard bells, as if she were a garbage truck backing up.
- Her face was a perfect oval, like a circle that had its two sides gently compressed by a ThighMaster.

And sometimes, as in the following case, a feeble comparison is worse than nothing at all!

The little boat gently drifted across the pond exactly the way a bowling ball wouldn't.

Used sparingly and with careful crafting, however, figures of speech can make your prose enjoyable (as expensive chocolate?) and memorable (as your best weekend ever?). (◆ For more discussion of figurative language, including mixed metaphors, see pages 171–173.)

Problems to Avoid

Keep in mind these three pieces of advice to solve problems that frequently arise in description:

Remember your audience. Sometimes the object of our description is so clear in our minds that we forget that our readers haven't seen it too. Consequently, the description we write turns out to be vague, bland, or skimpy ("The big tree was beautiful"). Ask yourself about your audience: what do they need to know to see this sight as clearly as I do? Then fill in your description with ample, precise details that reveal the best picture possible. Don't forget to define or explain any terms you use that may be puzzling to your audience. (◆ For more advice on clear, vivid language, see Chapter 7.)

Avoid an erratic organization of details.   Too often, descriptions are a hodgepodge of details, jotted down randomly. When you write a lengthy description, you should select a plan that will arrange your details in an orderly fashion. Depending on your subject matter and your purpose, you might adopt a plan calling for a description of something from top to bottom, left to right, front to back, and so on. For example, a description of a woman might begin at the head and move to the feet; furniture in a room might be described as your eyes move from one side of the room to another. A second plan for arranging details presents the subject's outstanding characteristics first and then fills in the lesser information; a child's red hair, for example, might be his most striking feature and therefore would be described first. A third plan presents details in the order you see them approaching: dust, then a car, then details about the car, its occupants, and so on. Or you might describe a subject as it unfolds chronologically, as in some kind of process or operation. Regardless of which plan of organization you choose, the reader should feel a sense of order in your description.

Avoid any sudden change in perspective.   If, for example, you are describing the White House from the outside, don't suddenly include details that could be seen only from the inside. Similarly, if you are describing a car from a distance, you might be able to tell the car's model, year, and color, but you could hardly describe the upholstery or reveal the mileage. It is, of course, possible for you—or your observer—to approach or move around the subject of your description, but the reader must be aware of this movement. Any shift in point of view must be presented clearly and logically, with no sudden, confusing leaps from a front to a back view, from outside to inside, and so on.

Practicing What You've Learned

A. Choose sensory details (sight, taste, smell, touch, and hearing) and/or figurative language (similes, metaphors, personification, etc.) to vividly describe each of the following in a few sentences. Avoid clichés and Insta-Prose by creating memorable new images (serious or humorous) for your reader.

1. A dessert

2. A pair of jeans

3. A pet

© Canstock Images, Inc./ Index Stock Imagery

continued on next page

   4. The floor of a theater following a kids' movie

   5. A sunset

   6. February

   7. A scene in nature or in the city

   8. Your favorite pillow

   9. A dentist's office

  10. Yourself in either a happy or grouchy mood

B. Describe a confined or small familiar place (your classroom, bedroom, work cubical, inside of your car, etc.) in a paragraph using language that presents a positive impression; then rewrite your paragraph creating a negative view of the same space. Which details are the most effective in each paragraph, and why?

C. *Collaborative Activity:* Bring a small (palm-sized), inexpensive, unbreakable object from home to class. This might be a household or personal item (such as a fork or a key) or perhaps something from nature (a rock or leaf) or even something left over from your lunch (a piece of fruit or candy). With your classmates, deposit each object in a large bag or cardboard box that your instructor has brought. Join two other students and direct a group representative to choose, without peeking, an object from the bag or box, one item that no one in your group contributed to the collection. Together, practice your objective descriptive skills by composing a detailed, factual picture of this object in a paragraph of at least five sentences. If time permits, write another paragraph describing the same object subjectively, using colorful language to offer a dominant impression. Which description was easier for your group? Be ready to read your paragraphs to the rest of the class.

Assignment

Use the painting reproduced here to practice your descriptive writing skills. Often influenced by his Russian-Jewish heritage, artist Marc Chagall (1887–1985) painted this picture titled *Birthday* in 1915. Describe what you feel is the dominant mood of this picture, pointing out some  of the details that communicate that tone to you. Consider the painting's people, setting, colors, and even shapes. In a short descriptive essay, re-create this painting as you see it for someone unfamiliar with the work. To get you started, ponder this: some viewers have questioned whether the male figure is "floating on air" with happiness or is instead an imaginary guest, perhaps even someone deceased. What do *you* think? (◆ For more help writing about art, see Chapter 17.)

continued on next page

Birthday (L'Anniversaire), 1915, by Marc Chagall

(◆ For additional advice and exercises designed to improve descriptive writing skills, see pages 141–142 and 162–165 in Part One of this text.)

Essay Topics

Here are some suggestions for a descriptive paragraph or essay; focus your topic to fit your assignment. Don't forget that every description, whether objective or subjective, has a purpose and that your details should support that purpose. ◆ For additional ideas, see "Suggestions for Writing" on page 338.

1. A favorite painting, photograph, poster, or sculpture (Or choose one of the many artworks in this textbook. A list of the visual art follows the Table of Contents.)

2. One dish or foodstuff that should be forever banned

3. A piece of equipment important to your major, a hobby, or a favorite sport

4. A childhood object you have kept (or wished that you had)

continued on next page

5. Your most precious material possession (Consider: after people and pets, what would you save first if you had fifteen minutes to evacuate your home as a fire approached?)

6. Yourself (how you looked at a certain age or on a memorable occasion or in a particular photograph)

7. A product or purchase whose ownership has disappointed you

8. The ugliest/most beautiful place or building on your campus or in town

9. A holiday, celebration, or ritual in your family

10. Your first or worst car or apartment

11. A piece of clothing that reveals the real "you" (or your favorite disguise)

12. A common object with uncommon beauty

13. A poster for a movie, concert, or campus event or an album cover by a favorite band

14. A good-luck object

15. One brief but unforgettable moment

16. An event, element, or creature in nature

17. A shopping mall, student cafeteria, or other crowded public place

18. The inside of your refrigerator, your closet, or some other equally loathsome place in your home

19. A treasure from a personal collection or a family heirloom

20. A Special Place (Perhaps your place offers you solitude, beauty, or renewed energy. The scene shown here was painted over a half-dozen different ways by nineteenth-century artist Claude Monet, who loved this tranquil lily pond near his farmhouse in France. Re-create your special place for your readers by choosing the right descriptive words, just as Monet did with each brushstroke of color.)

The Water-Lily Pond, 1899, by Claude Monet

SuperStock

A Topic Proposal for Your Essay

Selecting the right subject matter is important to every writer. To help you clarify your ideas and strengthen your commitment to your topic, here is a proposal sheet that asks you to describe some of your preliminary ideas about your subject before you begin drafting. Although your ideas may change as you write (they will almost certainly become more refined), thinking through your choice of topic now may help you avoid several false starts.

1. What subject will your essay describe? Will you describe this subject objectively or subjectively? Why?

2. Why are you interested in this topic? Do you have a personal or professional connection to the subject? State at least one reason for your choice of topic.

3. Is this a significant topic of interest to others? Why? Who specifically might find it interesting, informative, or entertaining?

4. What is the main purpose of your description? In one or two sentences describe the major effect you'd like your descriptive essay to have on your readers. What would you like for them to understand or "see" about your subject?

5. List at least three details that you think will help clarify your subject for your readers.

6. What difficulties, if any, might arise during drafting? For example, what organizational strategy might you think about now that would allow you to guide your readers through your description in a coherent way?

Sample Student Essay

In her descriptive essay, this student writer recalls her childhood days at the home of her grandparents to make a point about growing up. Notice that the writer uses both figurative language and contrasting images to help her readers understand her point of view.

TREECLIMBING

Introduction: The conversation that triggers her memory

1   It was Mike's eighteenth birthday and he was having a little bit of a breakdown. "When was the last time you made cloud pictures?" he asked me absently as he stared up at the ceiling before class started. Before I could answer, he continued, "Did you know that by the time you're an adult, you've lost 85 percent of your imagination?" He paused. "I don't want to grow up." Although I doubted the authenticity of his facts, I understood that Mike—the hopeless romantic with his long ponytail,

---

sullen black clothes, and glinting dark eyes—was caught in a Peter Pan complex. He drew those eyes from the ceiling and focused on me: "There are two types of children. Tree children and dirt children. Kids playing will either climb trees or play in the dirt. Tree children are the dreamers—the hopeful, creative dreamers. Dirt children, they just stay on the ground. Stick to the rules." He trailed off, and then picked up again: "I'm a tree child. I want to make cloud pictures and climb trees. And I don't ever want to come down." Mike's story reminded me of my own days as a tree child, and of the inevitable fall from the tree to the ground.

2   My childhood was a playground for imagination. Summers were spent surrounded by family at my grandparents' house in Milwaukee, Wisconsin. The rambling Lannonstone bungalow was located on North 46th Street at Burleigh, a short drive from center-city Milwaukee and the historic Schuster's department store. In the winter, all the houses looked alike, rigid and militant, like white-bearded old generals with icicles hanging from their moustaches. One European-styled house after the other lined the streets in strict parallel formation, block after block.

> The grandparents' neighborhood remembered in military images and sensory details

3   But in the summer it was different . . . softer. No subzero winds blew lonely down the back alley. Instead, kids played stickball in it. I had elegant, grass-stained tea parties with a neighborhood girl named Shelly, while my grandfather worked in his thriving vegetable garden among the honeybees, and watched sprouts grow. An ever-present warming smell of yeast filtered down every street as the nearby breweries pumped a constant flow of fresh beer. Above, the summer sky looked like an Easter egg God had dipped in blue dye.

4   Those summer trips to Milwaukee were greatly anticipated events back then. My brother and I itched with repressed energy throughout the long plane ride from the West Coast. We couldn't wait to see Grandma and Papa. We couldn't wait to see what presents Papa had for us. We couldn't wait to slide down the steep, blue-carpeted staircase on our

> Use of parallel sentences to emphasize anticipation

bottoms, and then on our stomachs. Most of all, we couldn't wait to go down to the basement.

5   The basement was better than a toy store. Yes, the old-fashioned milk cabinet in the kitchen wall was enchanting, and the laundry chute was fun because it was big enough to throw down Ernie, my stuffed dog companion, so my brother could catch him below in the laundry room, as our voices echoed up and down the chute. But the basement was better than all of these, better even than sliding down those stairs on rug-burned bottoms.

The basement in contrast to other parts of the house

6   It was always deliciously cool down in the basement. Since the house was built in the 1930s, there was no air conditioning. Upstairs, we slept in hot, heavy rooms. My nightgown stuck to the sheets, and I would lie awake, listening to crickets, inhaling the beer-sweet smell of the summer night, hoping for a cool breeze. Nights were forgotten, however, as my brother and I spent hours every day in the basement. There were seven rooms in the basement; some darker rooms I had waited years to explore. There was always a jumbled heap of toys in the middle room, most of which were leftovers from my father's own basement days. It was a child's safe haven; it was a sacred place.

7   The hours spent in the basement were times of a gloriously secure childhood. Empires were created in a day with faded colored building blocks. New territories were annexed when either my brother or I got the

Adventures in the basement

courage to venture into one of those Other Rooms—the dark, musty ones without windows—and then scamper back to report of any sightings of monsters or other horrific childhood creatures. In those basement days everything seemed safe and wholesome and secure, with my family surrounding me, protecting me. Like childhood itself, entering the basement was like entering another dimension.

8   Last summer I returned to Milwaukee to help my grandparents pack to move into an apartment. I went back at seventeen to find the house—

my kingdom—up for sale. I found another cycle coming to a close, and I found myself separated from what I had once known. I looked at the house. It was old; it was crumbling; it needed paint. I looked down the back alley and saw nothing but trash and weeds. I walked to the corner and saw smoke-choked, dirty streets and thick bars in shop windows, nothing more than another worn-out Midwestern factory city. I went back to the house and down to the basement, alone.

The house and neighborhood years later

9   It was gray and dark. Dust filtered through a single feeble sunbeam from a cracked window pane. It was empty, except for the overwhelming musty smell. The toys were gone, either packed or thrown away. As I walked in and out of rooms, the quietness filled my ears, but in the back of my head the sounds of childhood laughter and chatter played like an old recording.

The basement years later

10   The dark rooms were filled not with monsters but with remnants of my grandfather's business. A neon sign was propped against the wall in a corner: Ben Strauss Plumbing. Piles of heavy pipes and metal machine parts lay scattered about on shelves. A dusty purple ribbon was thumbtacked to a door. It said SHOOT THE WORKS in white letters. I gently took it down. The ribbon hangs on my door at home now, and out of context it somehow is not quite as awe-inspiring and mystifying as it once was. However, it does serve its purpose, permanently connecting me to my memories.

11   All children are tree children, I believe. The basement used to be my tree, the place I could dream in. That last summer I found myself, much to Mike's disappointment, quite mature, quite adult. Maybe Mike fell from his tree and was bruised. Climbing down from that tree doesn't have to be something to be afraid of. One needn't hide in the tree for fear of touching the ground and forgetting how to climb back up when necessary. I think there is a way to balance the two extremes. Climb down gracefully as you grow up, and if you fall, don't land in quicksand. I like to think I'm more of a shrubbery child: not so low as to get stuck in the mud and just high enough to look at the sky and make cloud pictures.

Conclusion: A return to the introduction's images and some advice

Professional Essay*

Still Learning from My Mother**

Cliff Schneider

Cliff Schneider is a graduate of Cornell and a retired freshwater fisheries biologist who worked for the Department of Environmental Conservation in New York. Much of his research and writing has focused on his work studying Lake Ontario. This essay, a personal tribute to his seventy-nine-year-old mother, was first published in the "My Turn" column of *Newsweek* magazine in March 2000.

> **Pre-reading Thoughts:** As you moved through your childhood, teenage, or young-adult years, what person had the most powerful positive effect on you? What important values or lessons did you learn from this person?

1   When I was a young boy growing up on New York's Long Island in the 1950s, it was common to see boys and their fathers gathering in the roads in front of their homes on warm summer evenings to "have a catch." That was the term we had for tossing a baseball while we talked about school, jobs and life in general. Although my dad and I had many catches together, my most memorable ones were with my mother. She would happily grab a glove, run out to the road and then fire fast-balls at me that cracked my glove and left my hand stinging. She never showed any motherly concern, though, just a broad grin with the tip of her tongue exposed in the corner of her mouth. This was her game face. I can still recall how delighted I was tossing the ball with Mom and hearing the comments from my friends and neighbors: "Where did your mother learn to throw a ball like that?"

2   My mother, you see, was a jock long before Title IX unleashed the explosion of modern women's athletics. She lettered in field hockey and basketball while attending Hofstra University in the late 1930s. This was a time when it wasn't very fashionable for women to go running after a ball and work up a sweat. Luckily for me, Mom never worried about what was fashionable. She loved sports, loved being active and, most of all, loved the competition. Mom was kind to her kids until we played ball. Then we'd notice this gleam in her eye, the broad grin and the famil-iar tongue that told us she was ready for action and ready to have some fun. No matter what game she played, Mom had class. She played hard, she laughed a lot and, win or lose, she was always gracious.

3   The years have diminished Mom's physical abilities, as they would have for any-one who is about to become an octogenarian. Her back is a little bent, and she complains occasionally about her hip. Her biggest concession to the aging process, however, is that she has had to lighten up on her bowling ball. As a young mother in suburban bowling leagues she toted a 15-pound ball, carried a 160 average and had a high game of 212. As she's grown older, her scores have declined. In recent years she's had to start using an eight-pound ball, which she protests is too light and "doesn't give enough pin action."

---

*◆ To help you read this essay analytically, review pages 179–181. For two other professional essays in Part Two that make extensive use of description, see "To Bid the World Farewell" (pages 216–220) and "Two Ways of Viewing the River" (pages 241–242).

**Cliff Schneider, "Still Learning from My Mother." Reprinted by permission.

4   For years I have had to listen to my mother's perennial battle cry as she begins each new bowling season—"This is the year I'm going to bowl a 200 game!" I've always smiled and nodded in agreement, which was my way of acknowledging her determination. During our regular Thursday-evening phone conversations (she bowls on Thursdays), she gives me a frame-by-frame description of her games, and gripes that she can't bowl the way she used to. She almost always slips in the comment "I'm going to make 200 if it kills me." I try to explain that she should be satisfied that she is at least able to play the game. "Try to make some concession to your age, Mom," I say. Of course, she will have none of this talk and this year bought a 10-pound ball in pursuit of her dream. Vince Lombardi would be proud.

5   A week after she started bowling with her new ball, I called to check on her progress. She no sooner said "Hi" than I could tell something big had happened in her life. I could feel the smile all the way from Hendersonville, N.C., to upstate New York. I shouted, "You bowled a 200 game!" knowing it could be the only reason for such a happy voice. She corrected me: "Not a 200 game; I got a 220." It was her highest score ever! She gave me a strike-by-strike description of her game, and we both celebrated over the phone. As she signed off and said her goodbyes, I could still sense the smile on her face. Her grin will probably fade in another month or two.

6   After some reflection, I am amazed by my mother's accomplishment. Whether it is baseball, tennis, golf or even bowling, I have never heard of anyone's peaking at 79. Yes, there is some degree of luck in every game, but in Mom's case she had the best game of her life because she persevered. Mom's achievement has lifted her spirits and made her feel young again. For someone who is too frequently reminded that she can't do what she used to, this experience could not have come at a better time in her life. I guess I'm not surprised that I can still learn from Mom—that you are never too old to dream and never too old to realize those dreams. I am not surprised, either, that in our most recent calls she talks about bowling a 250 game.

Questions on Content, Structure, and Style

1. Is Schneider's description of his mother primarily objective or subjective? Cite an example of his language to support your answer.

2. Why was his mother's behavior unusual in the 1950s? What does "before Title IX" (paragraph 2) mean?

3. What "dominant impression" of his mother does Schneider present in this essay? What are some of the details Schneider provides to help us understand this woman's character?

4. How does Schneider physically describe his mother so that readers can easily imagine those early games of catch? Why does she have "class"?

5. Examine some of Schneider's word choices. What, for example, is the effect of writing that his mother would "fire fastballs at me that cracked my glove and left my hand stinging" (paragraph 1) instead of "Mom could throw very hard"?

6. What does his mother's "perennial battle cry" at age seventy-nine reveal about her? Why does Schneider think football coach Vince Lombardi—for whom the Super Bowl trophy is named—would be proud of her?

7. What does Schneider's occasional use of dialogue add to this essay? Why, for example, does he quote his neighbors in paragraph 1 and his mother in paragraphs 3 and 4?

8. Why does Schneider organize his essay by starting with a description of his mother's younger days and concluding with a reference to "a 250 game"? How does this organization contribute to our understanding of his mother?

9. What has Schneider learned from his mother? In what way is this lesson an important part of this essay's purpose?

10. Did Schneider successfully create a picture of his mother? Could you suggest some ways he might improve his description? What language might have been more specific or vivid?

Vocabulary

Title IX (2)   octogenarian (3)   toted (3)
diminished (3)   concession (3)   perennial (4)

Suggestions for Writing

Try using Cliff Schneider's "Still Learning from My Mother" as a stepping-stone to your essay. Describe an unusual-but-wonderful relative or friend you admire for a particular trait. Consider including ample physical details, dialogue, and actions illustrating personality, as Schneider did, to make your description of this person vivid for your reader. Or write a description of an ancestor whose photograph has always intrigued you. What is the dominant impression of this picture? What does this person's face (or posture or choice of clothing) say to you about his or her character or style?

Perhaps you might choose to describe another mother figure, whose face is forever identified with the Great Depression. In 1936 photographer Dorothea Lange stopped on a dirt road in California to take a half-dozen pictures of a thirty-two-year-old woman and her children as they huddled in the rain under a lean-to tent. The woman told Lange they had been living off birds the children had killed and that she had just sold the tires off their car to buy food. Why do you think *Migrant Mother*, shown here, is considered one of the most affecting photographs of all time?

Library of Congress

Migrant Mother, 1936, by Dorothea Lange

A Revision Worksheet

As you write your rough drafts, consult Chapter 5 for guidance through the revision process. In addition, here are a few questions to ask yourself as you revise your description:

© Ryan McVay/
Photodisc/Getty Images

1. Is the descriptive essay's purpose clear to the reader?

2. Are there enough specific details in the description to make the subject matter distinct to readers who are unfamiliar with the scene, person, or object? Where might more detail be added?

3. Are the details arranged in an order that's easy to follow?

4. If the assignment called for an objective description, are the details as "neutral" as possible?

5. If the assignment called for a subjective description, does the writer's particular attitude come through clearly with a consistent use of well-chosen details or imagery?

6. Could any sensory details or figurative language be added to help the reader "see" the subject matter?

7. Does this essay end with an appropriate conclusion or does description merely stop?

Collaborative Activity: After you've revised your essay extensively, exchange rough drafts with a classmate and answer these questions for each other, making specific suggestions for improvement wherever appropriate. (◆ For advice on productive participation in classroom workshops, see pages 116–120.)

Reviewing Your Progress

After you have completed your descriptive essay, take a moment to measure your progress as a writer by responding to the following questions. Such analysis will help you recognize growth in your writing skills and may enable you to identify areas that are still problematic.

1. What is the best part of your essay? Why?

2. Which one descriptive detail or image do you think is the clearest or most vivid in your essay? Why does that one stand above the others?

3. What part of your essay gave you the most trouble? How did you overcome the problem?

4. If you had more time to work on this essay, what would receive additional attention? Why?

5. What did you learn about your topic from writing this essay? About yourself as a writer?

Chapter 12

Narration

• •

When many people hear the word "narrative," they think of a made-up story. But not all stories are fiction. In this chapter we are not concerned with writing literary short stories—that's a skill to develop in a creative writing class— but rather with nonfiction *expository narratives*, stories that are used to explain or prove a point. We most often use two kinds of these stories:

1. The *extended narrative*—a long episode that by itself illustrates or supports an essay's thesis

2. The *brief narrative*—a shorter incident that is often used in a body paragraph to support or illustrate a particular point in an essay.

Let's suppose, for example, you want to write an essay showing how confusing the registration system is at your school. To illustrate the problems vividly, you might devote your entire essay to the retelling of a friend's seven-hour experience signing up for classes last fall, thus making use of extended narration. Or take another example: in an argumentative essay advocating a new state law prohibiting drivers' use of cell phones in moving vehicles, you might include a brief narrative about a recent wreck to support a paragraph's point about the dangerous distraction of glancing at text messages. Regardless of which type of narrative best fits your purpose, the telling of a story or an incident can be an interesting, persuasive means of informing your readers.

Writing the Effective Narrative Essay

Know your purpose. What are you trying to accomplish by writing this narrative essay? Are you, for example, offering an *objective* retelling of a historical event (the dropping of the atomic bomb) to inform your readers who may not be acquainted with the facts? Or are you presenting a *subjective* narrative, which persuasively tells a story (Susan

B. Anthony's 1872 arrest for voting) from a clearly defined point of view? Perhaps your narrative is a personal story whose lesson you wish readers to share. Whatever your choice—an objective, factual retelling or a subjective interpretation—your narrative's purpose should be clear to your readers, who should never reach the end of the story wondering "What was that all about?" Knowing your purpose will help you select the information and language best suited to meet your audience's needs.

Present your main point clearly. To ensure that readers understand their purpose, many writers first state a thesis claim followed by a narrative that supports it. Sometimes writers begin with their narrative and use their concluding paragraph to state or sum up the point or "lesson" of their story. Still others choose to imply a main point or attitude through the unfolding action and choice of descriptive details. An implied thesis is always riskier than a stated one, so unless you are absolutely convinced that your readers could not possibly fail to see your point, work on finding a smooth way to incorporate a statement of your main idea into your essay.

Follow a logical time sequence. Many narrative essays—and virtually all brief stories used in other kinds of essays—follow a chronological order, presenting actions as they naturally occur in the story. Occasionally, however, a writer will use the flashback technique, which takes the readers back in time to reveal an event that occurred before the present scene of the essay. If you decide to use shifts in time, use transitional phrases or other signals to ensure that your readers don't become confused or lost.

Use sensory details to hold your readers' interest. For example, if the setting plays an important role in your story, describe it in vivid terms so that your readers can imagine the scene easily. Suppose you are pointing out the necessity of life preservers on sailboats by telling the story of how you spent a stormy night in the lake, clinging to a capsized boat. To convince your readers, let them "feel" the stinging rain and the icy current trying to drag you under; let them "see" the black waves and the dark menacing sky; let them "hear" the howling wind and the gradual splitting apart of the boat. Effective narration often depends on effective description, and effective description depends on vivid, specific detail. (◆ For more help on writing description, see Chapter 11; review Chapter 7 for advice on word choice.)

Create authentic characters. Again, the use of detail is crucial. Your readers should be able to visualize the people (or animals) in your narrative clearly; if your important characters are drawn too thinly, or if they seem phony or stereotyped, your readers will not fully grasp the meaning of your story. Show your readers the major characters as you see them by commenting unobtrusively on their appearances, speech, and actions. In addition, a successful narrative may depend on the reader's understanding of people's motives—why they act the way they do in certain situations. A narrative about your hometown's grouchiest miser who suddenly donated a large sum of money to a poor family isn't very believable unless we know the motive behind the action. In other words, let your readers know what is happening to whom by explaining or showing why.

Use dialogue realistically. Writers often use dialogue, their characters' spoken words, to reveal action or personality traits of the speakers. By presenting conversations, writers show rather than tell, often creating emphasis or a more dramatic effect. Dialogue may also help readers identify with or feel closer to the characters or action by creating a sense of "you are there." If your narrative would profit from dialogue, be certain the word choice and the manner of speaking are in keeping with each character's education, background, age, location, and so forth. Don't, for example, put a sophisticated philosophical treatise into the mouth of a ten-year-old boy or the latest campus slang into the speech of a fifty-year-old farmer from Two Egg, Florida. Also, make sure that your dialogue doesn't sound wooden or phony. The right dialogue can help make your story more realistic and interesting, provided that the conversations are essential to the narrative and are not merely padding the plot. (◆ For an example of dialogue in a narrative, read Langston Hughes' "Salvation" on pages 348–350. For help in punctuating dialogue, see pages 589–590 in the Handbook.)

Problems to Avoid

Weak, boring narratives are often the result of problems with subject matter or poor pacing; therefore, you should keep in mind the following advice:

Choose your subject carefully. Many of the best narrative essays come from personal experience or study, and the reason is fairly obvious: it's difficult to write convincingly about something you've never seen or done or read about. You probably couldn't, for instance, write a realistic account of a bullfight unless you'd seen one or at least had studied the subject in great detail. The simplest, easiest, most interesting nonfiction narrative you can write is likely to be about a subject with which you are personally familiar. This doesn't mean that you can't improvise many details, create a hypothetical story to illustrate a point, or recount an event you've learned about through research, as long as you identify the source of your borrowed material. Even so, you still may have more success basing your narrative—real or hypothetical—on something or someone you know well.

Limit your scope. When you wish to use an extended narrative to illustrate a thesis, don't select an event or series of actions whose retelling will be too long or complex for your assignment. In general, it's better to select one episode and flesh it out with many specific details so that your readers can clearly see your point. For instance, you may have had many rewarding experiences during the summer you worked as a lifeguard, but you can't tell them all. Instead, you might focus on one experience that captures the essence of your attitude toward your job—say, the time you saved a child from drowning—and present the story so vividly that the readers can easily understand your point of view.

Don't let your story lag or wander. At some time you've probably listened to a story-teller who became stuck on some insignificant detail ("Was it Friday or Saturday the letter came? Let's see now . . ."; "Then Joe said to me—no, it was Sally—no, wait, it was . . ."). And you've probably also heard bores who insist on making a short story long by including too many unimportant details or digressions. These mistakes ruin the *pacing* of their stories; in other words, the story's tempo or movement becomes bogged down until the readers are bored witless. To avoid creating a sleeping tonic in word form, dismiss all unessential information and focus your attention—and use of detail—on the important events, people, and places. Skip uneventful periods of time by using such phrases as "A week went by before Mr. Smith called . . ." or "Later that evening, around nine o'clock. . . ." In short, keep the story moving quickly enough to hold the readers' interest. Moreover, use a variety of transitional devices to move the readers from one action to another; don't rely continuously on the "and then . . . and then . . ." method.

Practicing What You've Learned

A. To practice collecting details that will strengthen your narrative, try this activity. Study the painting below, *Tornado Over Kansas*, and then list as many specific, descriptive details about the scene as you can see or imagine. For example, what do details about the setting and the family's appearance reveal about these people and where they live? What unusual noises, colors, and smells might be vividly described? What does each person's facial expression and body language tell you about his or her thoughts at this very moment? What words might be spoken by each person and in what tone of voice?

   Now think of a time in which you experienced a narrow escape or conquered a fearful moment—some event in your life that might be retold in an exciting

Tornado Over Kansas (oil on canvas), 1929, by John Steuart Curry

continued on next page

narrative essay. Using the impressions recorded from the painting as a guide to prompt your memory, compile a similar list of vivid, sensory details describing the people, setting, and action at the most dramatic point of your story. Which words or phrases on your list most effectively communicate your experience, and why?

B. *Collaborative Activity:* Think of an important event in your life that you would like known to future generations of your family. Or perhaps there is a story about your ancestors that you want to record so it is not forgotten. Draft some notes about your story, and then, in class, pair with another student. Take turns telling your stories; as each person talks, the partner should ask for more details. Simple questions such as "What did he look like at that moment?" or "Why was that decision so important?" or "What exactly did you say then?" can help a writer shape and invigorate a narrative. Incorporate any useful new details, descriptions, or dialogue into the final draft of your essay.

Essay Topics

© Inspirestock/CORBIS

Use one of the following topics to suggest an essay that is developed by narration. Remember that each essay must have a clear purpose. ◆ For additional ideas, see the "Suggestions for Writing" section following the professional essay (page 351); the quotations on pages 42–44 may also spark topics.

1. An experience revealing courage, loyalty, or generosity

2. An event of historical, medical, or scientific importance (◆ See Chapter 14 for help incorporating research material.)

3. An interaction that changed your thinking on a particular subject or informed an important decision

4. Your best/worst holiday, trip, or first day (school, job, camp, etc.)

5. A random act of kindness

6. Your worst accident or brush with danger

7. An unforgettable childhood experience

8. A memorable event governed by nature, a wild animal, or a pet

9. A time you gained self-confidence or improved your self-image

10. A meaningful event experienced in another culture or country

11. A triumph over prejudice, anger, or violence

12. A family story (perhaps one about you—for example, how did you get your name?)

continued on next page

13. The hardest or most satisfying work you've ever accomplished

14. A blessing in disguise

15. A gain or loss of something or someone important

16. A risk that paid off (or a triumph against the odds)

17. A nonacademic lesson learned at school, on a job, or on a team

18. An episode marking your passage from one stage of your life to another

19. A habit that got you into (or out of) trouble

20. Your participation in a civic event, social justice activity, or charity (an election campaign, voter registration work, Red Cross blood drive, Habitat for Humanity, etc.), showing how you were informed or changed

Jeff Greenberg/PhotoEdit

For many people, a first involvement in an exciting political campaign or in a helpful volunteer service organization can be a life-changing experience.

A Topic Proposal for Your Essay

Selecting the right subject matter is important to every writer. To help you clarify your ideas and strengthen your commitment to your topic, here is a proposal sheet that asks you to describe some of your preliminary ideas about your subject before you begin drafting. Although your ideas may change as you write (they will almost certainly become more refined), thinking through your choice of topic now may help you avoid several false starts.

1. In a sentence or two, briefly state the subject of your narrative. Did you or someone you know participate in this story?

2. Why did you select this narrative? Does it have importance for you personally, academically, or professionally? In some other way? Explain your reason, or purpose, for telling this story.

3. Will others be informed or entertained by this story? Who might be especially interested in hearing your narrative? Why?

4. What is the primary effect you would like your narrative to have on your readers? What would you like them to feel or think about after they read your story? Why?

5. What is the critical moment in your story? At what point, in other words, does the action reach its peak? Summarize this moment in a few descriptive words.

6. What difficulties, if any, might this narrative present as you are drafting? For example, if the story you want to tell is long or complex, how might you focus on the main action and pace it appropriately?

Sample Student Essay

In this narrative a student uses a story about a sick but fierce dog to show how she learned a valuable lesson in her job as a veterinarian's assistant. Notice the student's good use of vivid details that make this well-paced story both clear and interesting.

Never Underestimate the Little Things

Introduction: A misconception

1   When I went to work as a veterinarian's assistant for Dr. Sam Holt and Dr. Jack Gunn last summer, I was under the false impression that the hardest part of veterinary surgery would be the actual performance of an operation. The small chores demanded before this feat didn't occur

Thesis: Small preliminary details can be as important as the major action

to me as being of any importance. As it happened, I had been in the veterinary clinic only a total of four hours before I met a little animal who convinced me that the operation itself was probably the easiest part of treatment. This animal, to whom I owe thanks for so enlightening me, was a chocolate-colored chihuahua of tiny size and immense perversity named Smokey.

Description of the main character: His appearance

2   Smokey could have very easily passed for some creature from another planet. It wasn't so much his gaunt little frame and overly large head, or his bony paws with nearly saberlike claws, as it was his grossly infected eyes. Those once-shining eyes were now distorted and swollen into grotesque balls of septic, sightless flesh. The only vague similarity they had to what we'd normally think of as the organs of vision was a slightly upraised dot, all that was left of the pupil, in the center of a pink and

His personality

purply marble. As if that were not enough, Smokey had a temper to match his ugly sight. He also had surprisingly good aim, considering his largely diminished vision, toward any moving object that happened to place itself unwisely before his ever-inquisitive nose; with sudden and wholly vicious intent, he would snap and snarl at whatever blocked the little light that could filter through his swollen and ruptured blood vessels. Truly, in many respects, Smokey was a fearful dog to behold.

3   Such an appearance and personality did nothing to encourage my already flagging confidence in my capabilities as a vet's assistant. How was I supposed to get that little demon out of his cage? Jack had casually requested that I bring Smokey to the surgery room, but did he really expect me to put my hands into the cage of that devil dog? I suppose it must have been my anxious expression that saved me, for as I turned uncertainly toward the kennel, Jack chuckled nonchalantly and accompanied me to demonstrate how professionals in his line of work dealt with professionals in Smokey's. He took a small rope about four feet long with a no-choke noose at one end and unlatched Smokey's cage. Then cautiously he reached in and dangled the noose before the dog's snarling jaws. Since Smokey could only barely see what he was biting at, his attacks were directed haphazardly in a semicircle around his body. The tiny area of his cage led to his capture, for during one of Smokey's forward lunges, Jack dropped the noose over his head and moved the struggling creature out onto the floor. The fight had only just begun for Smokey, however, and he braced his feet against the slippery linoleum tiling and forced us to drag him, like a little pull toy on a string, to the surgery.

The difficulty of moving the dog to the surgery room

4   Once Smokey was in the surgery, however, the question that hung before our eyes like a veritable presence was how to get the dog from the floor to the table. Simply picking him up and plopping him down was out of the question. One glance at the quivering little figure emitting ominous and throaty warnings was enough to assure us of that. Realizing that the game was over, Jack grimly handed me the rope and reached for a muzzle. It was a doomed attempt from the start: the closer Jack dangled the tiny leather cup to the dog's nose, the more violent did Smokey's contortions and rage-filled cries become and the more frantic our efforts became to

The difficulty of moving the dog to the table

try to keep our feet and fingers clear of the angry jaws. Deciding that a firmer method had to be used, Jack instructed me to raise the rope up high enough so that Smokey would have to stand on his hind legs. This greatly reduced his maneuverability but served to increase his tenacity, for at this the little dog nearly went into paroxysms of frustration and rage. In his struggles, however, Smokey caught his forepaw on his swollen eye, and the blood that had been building up pressure behind the fragile cornea burst out and dripped to the floor. In the midst of our surprise and the twinge of panic startling the three of us, Jack saw his chance and swiftly muzzled the animal and lifted him to the operating table.

The difficulty of putting the dog to sleep before the surgery

5   Even at that point it wasn't easy to put the now terrified dog to sleep. He fought the local anesthesia and caused Jack to curse as he was forced to give Smokey more of the drug than should have been necessary for such a small beast. After what seemed an eternity, Smokey lay prone on the table, breathing deeply and emitting soft snores and gentle whines. We also breathed deeply in relief, and I relaxed to watch fascinated, while Jack performed a very delicate operation quite smoothly and without mishap.

Conclusion: The lesson she learned

6   Such was my harrowing induction into the life of a veterinary surgeon. But Smokey did teach me a valuable lesson that has proven its importance to me many times since: wherever animals are concerned, even the smallest detail is important and should never be taken for granted.

Professional Essay*

Salvation**

Langston Hughes

Langston Hughes was a poet and fiction writer who was an important part of the Harlem Renaissance of the 1920s. Creating innovative poetry that often incorporated the rhythms of jazz and vibrant dialect into his work, Hughes is admired for his insightful presentations of black life in America; his most famous poem is known as "Dream Deferred." This essay was first published as part of his autobiography, *The Big Sea* (1940).

Pre-reading Thoughts: Recall a family occasion from your childhood or adolescence in which you played—for better or worse—a major role. Why is this event still memorable for you? What details remain particularly vivid?

1   I was saved from sin when I was going on thirteen. But not really saved. It happened like this. There was a big revival at my Auntie Reed's church. Every night for weeks there had been much preaching, singing, praying, and shouting, and some very hardened sinners had been brought to Christ, and the membership of the church had grown by leaps and bounds. Then just before the revival ended, they held a special meeting for children, "to bring the young lambs to the fold." My aunt spoke of it for days ahead. That night I was escorted to the front row and placed on the mourners' bench** with all the other young sinners, who had not yet been brought to Jesus.

2   My aunt told me that when you were saved you saw a light, and something happened to you inside! And Jesus came into your life! And God was with you from then on! She said you could see and hear and feel Jesus in your soul. I believed her. I had heard a great many old people say the same thing and it seemed to me they ought to know. So I sat there calmly in the hot, crowded church, waiting for Jesus to come to me.

3   The preacher preached a wonderful rhythmical sermon, all moans and shouts and lonely cries and dire pictures of hell, and then he sang a song about the ninety and nine safe in the fold, but one little lamb was left out in the cold. Then he said: "Won't you come? Won't you come to Jesus? Young lambs, won't you come?" And he held out his arms to all us young sinners there on the mourners' bench. And the little girls cried. And some of them jumped up and went to Jesus right away. But most of us just sat there.

4   A great many old people came and knelt around us and prayed, old women with jet-black faces and braided hair, old men with work-gnarled hands. And the church sang a song about the lower lights are burning, some poor sinners to be saved. And the whole building rocked with prayer and song.

5   Still I kept waiting to *see* Jesus.

6   Finally all the young people had gone to the altar and were saved, but one boy and me. He was a rounder's [drunkard's] son named Westley. Westley and I were surrounded by sisters and deacons praying. It was very hot in the church, and getting late now. Finally Westley said to me in a whisper: ". . . I'm tired o' sitting here. Let's get up and be saved." So he got up and was saved.

7   Then I was left all alone on the mourners' bench. My aunt came and knelt at my knees and cried, while prayers and song swirled all around me in the little church. The whole congregation prayed for me alone, in a mighty wail of moans and voices. And I kept waiting serenely for Jesus, waiting, waiting—but he didn't come. I wanted to see him, but nothing happened to me. Nothing! I wanted something to happen to me, but nothing happened.

**At some revivals, a bench near the front of the church provided reserved seating for repentant sinners and others in sorrow.

8   I heard the songs and the minister saying: "Why don't you come? My dear child, why don't you come to Jesus? Jesus is waiting for you. He wants you. Why don't you come? Sister Reed, what is this child's name?"

9   "Langston" my aunt sobbed.

10   "Langston, why don't you come? Why don't you come and be saved? Oh, Lamb of God! Why don't you come?"

11   Now it was really getting late. I began to be ashamed of myself, holding everything up so long. I began to wonder what God thought about Westley, who certainly hadn't seen Jesus either, but who was now sitting proudly on the platform, swinging his knickerbockered legs and grinning down at me, surrounded by deacons and old women on their knees praying. God had not struck Westley dead for taking his name in vain or for lying in the temple. So I decided that maybe to save further trouble, I'd better lie, too, and say that Jesus had come, and get up and be saved.

12   So I got up.

13   Suddenly the whole room broke into a sea of shouting, as they saw me rise. Waves of rejoicing swept the place. Women leaped in the air. My aunt threw her arms around me. The minister took me by the hand and led me to the platform.

14   When things quieted down, in a hushed silence, punctuated by a few ecstatic "Amens," all the new young lambs were blessed in the name of God. Then joyous singing filled the room.

15   That night, for the last time in my life but one—for I was a big boy twelve years old—I cried. I cried, in bed alone, and couldn't stop. I buried my head under the quilts, but my aunt heard me. She woke up and told my uncle I was crying because the Holy Ghost had come into my life, and because I had seen Jesus. But I was really crying because I couldn't bear to tell her that I had lied, that I had deceived everybody in the church, that I hadn't seen Jesus, and that now I didn't believe there was a Jesus any more, since he didn't come to help me.

Questions on Content, Structure, and Style

1. What is Hughes' main purpose in this narrative? Why do you think this event was important in his life?

2. How does Hughes create the scene in the revival meeting? Which sensory details of sight and sound are particularly effective in helping the reader feel present at the church?

3. Which people in his life are pressuring the twelve-year-old Hughes to be "saved"?

4. Why does Hughes resist going to the altar with the rest of the children? What sense of conflict does he feel?

5. What does Hughes' use of dialogue add to his story? Which people speak directly and how do their words help the reader understand Hughes' emotional state?

6. Why does Hughes single out Westley's actions for description?

7. What are Hughes' reasons for finally joining the other children? Does he explain his thinking clearly enough for you to understand his decision?

8. How does Hughes use figurative language to capture a particular moment? (See, for example, "a sea of shouting . . . waves of rejoicing" in paragraph 13.)

9. Why is Hughes crying in bed after the service? How does his aunt perceive his tears?

10. Overall, how effective is Hughes' story about this childhood event? At the narrative's conclusion, did you empathize with him or have a different reaction?

Vocabulary

revival (1)
dire (3)
deacons (6)
serenely (7)

Suggestions for Writing

Try using Langston Hughes' essay as a stepping-stone to your writing. Remember a time you resisted or gave in to peer or family pressure. What insight did you gain from this experience? Given a second chance, would you make the same decision or a different one? Imagine that you are writing to an audience who might profit from hearing your story, such as high school or college students or members of a particular social group or organization facing a similar situation. Consider using sensory details, dialogue, or imagery, as Hughes did, to help your readers understand the people, places, and actions in your narrative.

A Revision Worksheet

© Ryan McVay/
Photodisc/Getty Images

As you write your rough drafts, consult Chapter 5 for guidance through the revision process. In addition, here are a few questions to ask yourself as you revise your narrative:

1. Is the narrative essay's purpose clear to the reader?

2. Is the thesis plainly stated or at least clearly implied?

3. Does the narrative convincingly support or illustrate its intended point? If not, how might the story be changed?

4. Does the story maintain a logical point of view and an understandable order of action? Are there enough transitional devices used to give the story a smooth flow?

5. Are the characters, actions, and settings presented in enough vivid detail to make them clear and believable? Where could more detail be effectively added? Would use of dialogue be appropriate?

continued on next page

6. Is the story coherent and well paced, or does it wander or bog down in places because of irrelevant or repetitious details? What might be condensed or cut? Could any bland or wordy description be replaced?

7. Does the essay end in a satisfying way, or does the action stop too abruptly?

Collaborative Activity: After you've revised your essay extensively, you might exchange rough drafts with a classmate and answer these questions for each other, making specific suggestions for improvement wherever appropriate. (◆ For advice on productive participation in classroom workshops, see pages 116–120.)

Reviewing Your Progress

After you have completed your narrative essay, take a moment to measure your progress as a writer by responding to the following questions. Such analysis will help you to recognize growth in your writing skills and may enable you to identify areas that are still problematic.

1. What do you like best about your narrative essay? Why?

2. After reading through your essay, select the description, detail, or piece of dialogue that you think best characterizes a major figure or most effectively advances the action in your story. Explain the reason for your choice in one or two sentences.

3. What part of your essay gave you the most trouble? How did you overcome the problem?

4. If you had more time to work on this essay, what would receive additional attention? Why?

5. What did you learn about your topic from writing this essay? About yourself as a writer?

Chapter 13

Writing Essays Using Multiple Strategies

I n Part Two of this text you have been studying essays developed primarily by a single mode or expository strategy. You may have, for example, written essays primarily developed by multiple examples, process analysis, or comparison/contrast. Concentrating on a single strategy in your essays has allowed you to practice, in a focused way, each of the patterns of development most often used in writing tasks. Although practicing each strategy in isolation this way is somewhat artificial, it is the easiest, simplest way to master the common organizational patterns. Consider the parallels to learning almost any skill: before you attempt a complex dive with spins and flips, you first practice each maneuver separately. Having understood and mastered the individual strategies of development, you should feel confident facing any writing situation, including those that would most profit from incorporating multiple strategies to accomplish their goal.

Most essays *do* call upon multiple strategies of development to achieve their purpose, a reality you have probably discovered for yourself as you studied various essays in this text. In fact, you may have found it difficult—or impossible—to avoid combining modes and strategies in your own essays. As noted in the introduction to Part Two, writers virtually always blend strategies, using examples in their comparisons, description in their definitions, causal analysis in their arguments, and so on. Therein is the heart of the matter: the single patterns of development you have been practicing are *thinking* strategies—ways of considering a subject and generating ideas—as well as organizing tools. Successful writers study their tasks and choose the strategies that will most effectively accomplish their purpose.

In addition, some writing tasks, often the longer ones, will clearly profit from combining multiple strategies in distinct ways to thoroughly address the essay's subject, purpose, and audience. Suppose, for example, you are given a problem-solving assignment in a business class: selling the City Council on a plan to build a student housing project in a particular neighborhood. You might call on your writing resources and use multiple strategies to

- Describe the project
- Explain the causes (the need for such a project)
- Argue its strengths; deflect opposing arguments
- Contrast it to other housing options
- Cite similar successful examples in other towns
- Explain its long-term beneficial effects on tenants, neighbors, businesses, etc.

Or perhaps you are investigating disciplinary action taken against a group of high school seniors for decorating their graduation caps and gowns. Your essay might combine strategies by first presenting examples of the controversy, explaining its causes and effects, and then contrasting the opinions of administrators, students, and parents. You might even conclude with a suggested process for avoiding future problems. In other words, many essay assignments—including the widely assigned summary-response paper*— might call for a multistrategy response.

As a writer who now knows how to use a variety of thinking and organizational methods, you can assess any writing situation and select the strategy—or strategies—that will work best for your topic, purpose, and audience.

Choosing the Best Strategies

To help you choose the best means of development for your essay, here is a brief review of the modes and strategies accompanied by some pertinent questions:

1. **Example**: Would real or hypothetical illustrations make my subject more easily understood?
2. **Process**: Would a step-by-step procedural analysis clarify my subject?
3. **Comparison/Contrast**: Would aligning or juxtaposing my subject to something else be helpful?
4. **Definition**: Would my subject profit from an extended explanation of its meaning?
5. **Division/Classification**: Would separating my subject into its component parts or grouping its parts into categories be useful?
6. **Causal Analysis**: Would explaining causes or effects add important information?
7. **Argument**: Would my position be advanced by offering logical reasons and/or addressing objections?
8. **Description**: Would vivid details, sensory images, or figurative language help readers visualize my subject?
9. **Narrative**: Would a story best illustrate some idea or aspect of my subject?

___

* ◆ For an in-depth look at this popular assignment, see pages 449–453.

Use these nine questions as prompts to help you generate ideas and select those strategies that best accomplish your purpose.

Problems to Avoid

Avoid overkill. Being prepared to use any of the writing strategies is akin to carrying many tools in your carpenter's bag. But just because you own many tools doesn't mean you must use all of them in one project; rather, you select only the ones you need for the specific job at hand. If you do decide to use multiple strategies in a particular essay, avoid a hodgepodge of information that runs in too many directions. Sometimes your essay's prescribed length means you cannot present all you know; again, let your main purpose guide you to selection of the best or most important ideas.

Organize logically. If you decide that multiple strategies will work best, you must find an appropriate order and coherent flow for your essay. In the hypothetical problem-solving essay on the housing project mentioned earlier, for instance, the writer must decide whether the long-term effects of the project should be discussed earlier or later in the paper. In the student essay that follows, the writer struggled with the question of discussing kinds of vegetarians before or after giving reasons for adopting vegetarianism. There are no easy answers to such questions—each writer must experiment with outlines and rough drafts to find the most successful arrangement, one that will offer the most effective response to the particular material, the essay's purpose, and the audience's needs. Be patient as you try various ways of combining strategies into a coherent rather than choppy paper.

Practicing What You've Learned

To help you recognize how writers often use multiple strategies in their writing, select one of the professional essays in Chapter 9 of this text. Identify at least two strategies at work, explaining their effectiveness and why you think the writer chose to make his or her point in this way.

© Canstock Images, Inc. / Index Stock Imagery

Sample Student Essay

In the essay that follows, the student writer responds to an assignment that asked her to write about an important belief or distinguishing aspect of her life. The purpose, audience, and development of her essay were left to her; the length was designated as 750 to 1,000 words. As a confirmed vegetarian for well over a decade, she often found herself questioned about her beliefs. After deciding to clarify (and encourage) vegetarianism for an audience of interested but often puzzled fellow students, she developed her essay by drawing on many strategies, including causal analysis, example, classification, contrast, argument, and process analysis. Because she found her early draft too long, the writer edited out an extended narrative telling the story of her own "conversion" to vegetarianism, viewing that section as less central to her essay's main purpose than the other parts.

PASS THE BROCCOLI—PLEASE!

Introduction: Famous examples

1   What do Benjamin Franklin, Charles Darwin, Leonardo da Vinci, Percy Bysshe Shelley, Mohandas Gandhi, Albert Einstein, and I have in common? In addition to being great thinkers, of course, we are all vegetarians, people who have rejected the practice of eating animals. Vegetarianism is growing rapidly in America today, but some people continue to see it as a strange choice. If you are thinking of making this decision yourself or are merely curious, taking time to learn about vegetarianism is worthwhile.

Thesis, purpose, audience

Contrast to other parts of the world

2   In a land where hamburgers, pepperoni pizza, and fried chicken are among our favorite foods, just why do Americans become vegetarians anyway? Worldwide, vegetarianism is often part of religious faith, especially to Buddhists, Hindus, and others whose spiritual beliefs emphasize nonviolence, karma, and reincarnation. But in this country the reasons for becoming vegetarian are more diverse. Some people cite ecological reasons, arguing that vegetarianism is best for our planet because it takes less land and food to raise vegetables and grain than livestock. Others choose vegetarianism because of health reasons. Repeated studies by groups such as the American Heart Association and the American Medical Association show that diets lower in animal fats and higher in fiber decrease the risk of heart disease, cancer, diabetes, hypertension, and osteoporosis.

Causal analysis: 3 reasons

3   Still other people's ethical beliefs bring them to vegetarianism. These people object to the ways that some animals, such as cows and chickens, are confined and are often fed various chemicals, such as growth hormones, antibiotics, and tranquilizers. They object to the procedures of slaughterhouses. They object to killing animals for consumption or for

their decorative body parts (hides, fur, skins, tusks, feathers, etc.) and to their use in science or cosmetic experiments. These vegetarians believe that animals feel fear and pain and that it is morally wrong for one species to inflict unnecessary suffering on another. I count myself among this group; consequently, my vegetarian choices extend to wearing no leather or fur, and I do not use household or cosmetic products tested on animals.

Personal example

4   Regardless of reasons for our choice, all vegetarians reject eating meat. However, there are actually several kinds of vegetarians, with the majority falling into three categories:

1. Ovo-lacto vegetarians eat milk, cheese, eggs, and honey;
2. Lacto vegetarians do not eat eggs but may keep other dairy products in their diet;
3. Vegans do not eat dairy products or any animal by-products whatsoever.

Classification: Three types

Many people, including myself, begin as ovo-lacto vegetarians but eventually become vegans, considered the most complete or pure type.

5   Perhaps the most common objection to any type of vegetarianism comes from a misconception about deficiencies in the diet, particularly protein. But it is a mistake to think only meat offers us protein. Vegetarians who eat dairy products, grains, vegetables, beans, and nuts receive more than enough nutrients, including protein. In fact, according to the cookbook *The Higher Taste*, cheese, peanuts, and lentils contain more protein per ounce than hamburger, pork, or a porterhouse steak. Many medical experts think that Americans actually eat too much protein, as seen in the revised food pyramid that now calls for an increase in vegetables, fruits, and grains over meat and dairy products. A vegetarian diet will not make someone a limp weakling. Kevin Eubanks, former *Tonight Show* band leader, is, for example, not only a busy musician but

Argument: Refutation, evidence, examples

also a weightlifter. A former "Mr. Universe," Bill Pearl, is a long-time vegetarian; many other successful athletes include Prince Fielder, Martina Navratilova, Hank Aaron, Billie Jean King, and Edwin Moses. Some current members of the Denver Broncos football team, according to their manager, no longer eat red meat at their training table.

6   For those who would like to give vegetarianism a try, here are a few suggestions for getting started:

Process: 4 steps to begin

1. Explore your motives. If you are only becoming a vegetarian to please a friend, for example, you won't stick with it. Be honest with yourself: the reasons behind your choice have a lot to do with your commitment.

2. Read more. The library can provide you with answers to your questions and concerns. There are hundreds of books full of ecological, medical, and ethical arguments for vegetarianism.

(More argument and examples)

3. Eat! Another popular misconception is that vegetarianism means a life of eating tasteless grass; nothing could be less true. Visit a vegetarian restaurant several times to see how many delicious dishes are available. Most grocery stores now carry a variety of vegetarian entrees. Or try one of the many vegetarian cookbooks on the market today. You may be surprised to discover that tofu enchiladas, soy burgers, and stuffed eggplant taste better than you could ever imagine.

4. Start slowly. You don't have to become a vegan overnight if it doesn't feel right. Some people begin by excluding just red meat from their diets. Feeling good as time goes by can direct your choices. Books, such as *The Beginning Vegetarian*, and magazines, such as *Vegetarian Times*, can offer encouragement.

7   It's never too late to change your lifestyle. Nobel Prize–winning author Isaac Bashevis Singer became a vegetarian at age fifty-eight. Making this choice now may allow you to live longer and feel better. In fifty years you

may be like playwright George Bernard Shaw, who at twenty-five was warned against a vegetarian diet. As a vigorous old man, Shaw wanted to tell all those people they were wrong, but noted he couldn't: "They all passed away years ago"!

Conclusion: Additional famous examples, witty quotation

Professional Essay*

Courage in Greensboro**

Owen Edwards

Owen Edwards is a freelance writer and author of *Elegant Solutions* (1989). For over a decade he has written the "Object at Hand" column for the *Smithsonian*, a magazine that supports the Smithsonian Institute.† This column highlights the stories behind historical and cultural objects in the Smithsonian's museum collections, ranging from George Washington's bed to Mr. Roger's cardigan sweater. This February 2010 column focuses on the lunch counter from a Woolworth's discount store, the scene of a 1960 protest considered a landmark event in the Civil Rights Movement.

Pre-reading Thoughts: Think about a possession that is important in your life or in your family's history—something personally meaningful rather than materially valuable. What is the "story" behind this object? Why do you treasure it?

1   On February 1, 1960, four young African-American men, freshmen at the Agricultural and Technical College of North Carolina, entered the Greensboro Woolworth's and sat down on stools that had, until that moment, been occupied exclusively by white customers. The four—Franklin McCain, Ezell Blair Jr., Joseph McNeil and David Richmond—asked to be served, and were refused. But they did not get up and leave. Indeed, they launched a protest that lasted six months and helped change America. A section of that historic counter is now held by the National Museum of American History, where the chairman of the division of politics and reform, Harry Rubenstein, calls it "a significant part of a larger collection about participation in our political system." The story behind it is central to the epic struggle of the civil rights movement.

---

* ◆ For help reading this essay analytically, review pages 179–181.

** Woolworth's Counter: Courage in Greensboro by Owen Edwards from SMITHSONIAN, February 28-29, 2010. Used by permission of the author.

† Located on the National Mall in Washington, D.C., the Smithsonian Institute is the world's largest museum complex, containing nineteen museums and galleries, including the American History Museum, the National History Museum, and the National Air and Space Museum. These museums are free and open every day except Dec. 25. The Smithsonian was originally funded by British scientist James Smithson (1765–1829), who left his estate to create an "institution for the increase and diffusion of knowledge." Mysteriously, Smithson had never visited America nor even corresponded with anyone in this country.

2   William Yeingst, chairman of the museum's division of home and community life, says the Greensboro protest "inspired similar actions in the state and elsewhere in the South. What the students were confronting was not the law, but rather a cultural system that defined racial relations."

3   Joseph McNeil, 67, now a retired Air Force major general living on Long Island, New York, says the idea of staging a sit-in to protest the ingrained injustice had been around awhile. "I grew up in Wilmington, North Carolina, and even in high school, we thought about doing something like that," he recalls. After graduating, McNeil moved with his family to New York, then returned to the South to study engineering physics at the technical college in Greensboro.

4   On the way back to school after Christmas vacation during his freshman year, he observed the shift in his status as he traveled south by bus. "In Philadelphia," he remembers, "I could eat anywhere in the bus station. By Maryland, that had changed." And in the Greyhound depot in Richmond, Virginia, McNeil couldn't buy a hot dog at a food counter reserved for whites. "I was still the same person, but I was treated differently." Once at school, he and three of his friends decided to confront segregation. "To face this kind of experience and not challenge it meant we were part of the problem," McNeil recalls.

5   The Woolworth's itself, with marble stairs and 25,000 square feet of retail space, was one of the company's flagship stores. The lunch counter, where diners faced rose-tinted mirrors, generated significant profits. "It really required incredible courage and sacrifice for those four students to sit down there," Yeingst says.

6   News of the sit-in spread quickly, thanks in part to a photograph taken the first day by Jack Moebes of the Greensboro Record [shown here] and stories in the paper by Marvin Sykes and Jo Spivey. Nonviolent demonstrations cropped up outside the store, while other protesters had a turn at the counter. Sit-ins erupted in other North Carolina cities and segregationist states.

7   By February 4, African-Americans, mainly students, occupied 63 of the 66 seats at the counter (waitresses sat in the remaining three). Protesters ready to assume their place crowded the aisles. After six months of diminished sales and unflattering publicity, Woolworth's desegregated the lunch counter—an astonishing victory for nonviolent protest. "The sit-in at the Greensboro Woolworth's was one of the early and pivotal events that inaugurated the student-led phase of the civil rights movement," Yeingst says.

8   More than three decades later, in October 1993, Yeingst learned Woolworth's was closing the Greensboro

Four students launch a six-month protest that helped change America.

store as part of a company-wide downsizing. "I called the manager right away," he recalls, "and my colleague Lonnie Bunch and I went down and met with African-American city council members and a group called Sit-In Movement Inc." (Bunch is now the director of the National Museum of African American History and Culture.)Woolworth's officials agreed that a piece of the counter belonged at the Smithsonian, and volunteers from the local carpenters' union removed an eight-foot section with four stools. "We placed the counter within sight of the flag that inspired the national anthem," Yeingst says of the museum exhibit.

9   When I asked McNeil if he had returned to Woolworth's to eat after the sit-in ended, he laughed, saying: "Well, I went back when I got to school the next September. But the food was bland, and the apple pie wasn't that good. So it's fair to say I didn't go back often."

Questions on Content, Structure, and Style

1. What is the main purpose of this article? What strategies are blended to achieve that purpose?
2. How does Edwards use the strategy of causal analysis to achieve this purpose?
3. Why is the narrative, or story, included here so important to the reader's understanding of the lunch counter's significance?
4. McNeil uses what strategy in paragraph 4 to explain his motivation for challenging segregation?
5. What descriptive details help the reader see the sit-in at Woolworth's?
6. How did the action of McNeil and his friends set in motion a causal chain of events in Greensboro and other locations?
7. According to William Yeingst, what important effect did the Greensboro protest have on the entire Civil Rights Movement?
8. Why include direct quotations from McNeil, Yeingst, and Rubenstein?
9. Why might the placement of the lunch counter exhibit in the museum by the flag that inspired our national anthem, "The Star-Spangled Banner," be considered highly appropriate?
10. Is "Courage in Greensboro" a fitting title for this article? In what way does this story offer a definition of courage?

Vocabulary

exclusively (1)	sit-ins (6)	pivotal (7)
ingrained (3)	diminished (7)	inaugurated (7)
segregation (4)	desegregated (7)	

Suggestions for Writing

Try using Owen Edwards' column "Courage in Greensboro" as a stepping-stone to an essay of your own. Joseph McNeil and his three friends were college freshmen when they bravely staged the Woolworth's sit-in, which in turn encouraged other students to become activists. How might students today make a difference for good in the world, or in a small corner of it? Perhaps you are currently involved in campus or local work (political, charitable, environmental, educational, etc.) dedicated to positive change. Or you might write about a time when you demonstrated a moment of personal courage in the face of someone's prejudice, stereotyping, or bullying. Perhaps you have overcome a prejudice of your own. Write an essay exploring discrimination, intolerance, or injustice that you have confronted. Use any of the organizational strategies you have studied in this text that would be helpful; you might, for instance, describe an incident or problem, discuss causes or effects, argue for change, or explain the steps you took that might help others in similar situations.

A Revision Worksheet

© Ryan McVay/
Photodisc/Getty Images

As you write your rough drafts, consult Chapter 5 for guidance through the revision process. In addition, here are a few questions to ask yourself before and during the early stages of your writing:

1. What is my main purpose in writing this particular essay? Who is my audience?

2. Does my assignment or the subject itself suggest a primary method of development or would combining several strategies be more effective?

3. Have I considered my subject from multiple directions, as suggested by the questions on page 354?

4. Have I selected the best strategies to meet the needs of my particular audience?

5. Would blending strategies help my readers understand my topic and my essay's purpose? Or am I trying to include too many approaches, move in too many directions, resulting in an essay that seems too scattered?

6. Have I considered an effective order for the strategies I've chosen? Do the parts of my essay flow together smoothly?

7. Have I avoided common weaknesses such as vague examples, fuzzy directions, circular definitions, overlapping categories, or logical falla-cies, as discussed in the "Problems to Avoid" sections of Chapters 9–12?

Collaborative Activity: After you've revised your essay extensively, exchange rough drafts with a classmate and answer these questions for each other, making spe-cific suggestions for improvement wherever appropriate. (◆ For advice on pro-ductive participation in classroom workshops, see pages 116–120.)

Reviewing Your Progress

After you have completed your essay, take a moment to measure your progress as a writer by responding to the following questions. Such analysis will help you recognize growth in your writing skills and may enable you to identify areas that are still problematic.

1. What do you like best about your essay? Why?

2. After considering the multiple strategies of development used in your essay, which one do you find most effective and why?

3. What part of your essay gave you the most trouble? How did you overcome the problem?

4. If you had more time to work on this essay, what would receive additional attention? Why?

5. What did you learn about your topic from writing this essay? About yourself as a writer?

Part 3

Special Assignments

The third section of this text addresses several kinds of assignments frequently included in composition classes and in many other college courses. Chapter 14 will first explain ways to conduct formal research on a topic and then show you how to best incorporate your research into your essay. Chapter 15, "Classroom Writing: Exams, Timed Essays, and Presentations," confronts the anxiety that writing under pressure may bring by helping you respond quickly but effectively to a variety of assignments, including the widely used summary-response (or reaction) essay. This chapter also contains a new section on presentations, with hints suggesting the best ways to write, adapt, and deliver your ideas in a classroom setting. Chapter 16, "Writing about Literature," illustrates several uses of poetry and short stories in the composition classroom and provides some guidelines for both close reading and analytical thinking. Chapter 17, "Writing about Visual Arts," offers suggestions for essays analyzing paintings, photographs, and sculptures. Chapter 18, "Writing about Film," is focused on thoughtful analysis of movies. The last chapter in Part Three, Chapter 19, "Writing in the World of Work," presents advice for effective business letters, memos, electronic-mail messages, and résumés.

If you have worked through Parts One and Two of this book, you have already practiced many of the skills demanded by these special assignments. Information in the next six chapters will build on what you already know about good writing.

Chapter 14

Writing a Paper
Using Research

••

Although the words "research paper" have been known to produce anxiety worse than that caused by the sound of a dentist's drill, you should try to relax. A research paper is similar to the kinds of expository and argumentative essays described in the earlier parts of this book, the difference being the use of documented source material to support, illustrate, or explain your ideas. Research papers still call for thesis statements, logical sequences of paragraphs, well-developed evidence, smooth conclusions—or in other words, all the skills you've been practicing throughout this book. By citing sources in your essays or reports, you show your readers that you have investigated your ideas and found support for them. By using your critical thinking skills to first analyze and then select the most thoughtful research from reliable sources, you demonstrate your own credibility—trustworthiness—as a writer, which in turn gives you the best chance of having others accept your ideas as valid. Last, using sources affords your readers the opportunity to look into your subject further if they so desire, consulting your references for additional information.

The process described in the next few pages should help you write a paper using research that is carefully and effectively documented. This chapter also contains sample citation forms for a variety of research sources, illustrated by sample student writing using both MLA and APA styles.

Focusing Your Topic

In some cases, you will be assigned your topic, and you will be able to begin your research right away. In other cases, however, you may be encouraged to select your own subject, or you may be given a general subject ("health-care reform," "recycling," "U.S. immigration policies") that you must narrow and then focus into a specific, manageable topic. If the topic is your choice, you need to do some preliminary thinking about what interests you; as in any assignment, you should make the essay a learning experience from which both you and your readers will profit. Therefore, you may want to brainstorm for a while on your general subject before you consult other sources, asking yourself questions about what you already know and don't know. Some of the most interesting papers are argumentative essays in which writers set out to find an answer to a controversy or to find support for a solution they suspected might work. Other papers, sometimes called "research reports," expose, explain, or summarize a situation or a problem for their audience.

Throughout this chapter, we will track the research and writing process of Kira Anzai, a composition student whose writing assignment called for an examination of major influences on the works of a noteworthy artist, musician, or writer. As an art major, Kira developed an interest in the twentieth-century artist Frida Kahlo (1907–1954) after discovering the painting *The Two Fridas*, found on page 490 in this textbook. From popular culture and her prior reading in an art history class, Kira was somewhat familiar with other arresting images and self-portraits by Frida Kahlo, but she knew very little about the artist's life. As she began her investigation of Kahlo's biography, Kira was able to think about her topic in terms of some specific *research questions*: What would research tell her about Frida Kahlo's personal life and career? How did the experiences and relationships in Kahlo's life influence her art? (◆ Kira's completed essay with MLA documentation appears on pages 423–430 and with APA documentation on pages 431–440.)

Beginning Your Library Research

Once you have a general topic (and perhaps have some research questions in mind), your next step is familiarizing yourself with the school or public library where you may do all or part of your research. Most college libraries today have both print and electronic resources to offer researchers, as well as access to the Internet. Your library most likely has an online central information system, which may include a catalog of its holdings, a number of selected databases, gateways to other libraries, and other kinds of resources. With appropriate computer connections, this system may be accessed from other places on or off campus, which is handy for those times when you cannot be in the library.

Most libraries also have information (printed or online) that will indicate the location of important areas, and almost all have reference librarians who can explain the various kinds of programs and resources available to you. The smartest step you may take is asking a librarian for help before you begin searching. Library staff members may be able to save you enormous amounts of research time by pointing you in just the right direction. Do not be shy about asking the library staff for help at any point during your research!

Once you are familiar with your library, you may find it useful to consult one or more of the following research tools.

General Reference Works

If you need a general overview of your subject, or perhaps some background or historical information, you might begin your library research by consulting an encyclopedia, a collection of biographical entries, or a world fact book, depending on your subject. You might use a comprehensive or specialized dictionary if your search turns up terms that are unfamiliar to you. These and many other library reference guides (in print and online) may also help you find a specific focus for your essay if you feel your topic is still too large or undefined at this point.

Online Catalogs

Today the online catalog has replaced the print catalog system as the primary guide to a library's holdings. You can access a library's catalog through on-site computer terminals or, in many cases, connect from off-site locations through the Internet to the library's Web page.

Most computer catalogs allow you to look for information by subject, author, and title as well as by keyword(s), by the ISBN (publisher's book number), by the call number, or by a series title (Time-Life books, for example). On-screen prompts will guide you through the process of searching. Because no two library catalog systems are exactly alike, never hesitate to ask a librarian for help if you need it.

Unless you are already familiar with authorities or their works on your topic, you might begin your search by typing in keywords or your general subject. For example, Kira Anzai began her search by typing in the subject words "Frida Kahlo," which produced a listing of sixty-five entries related to the artist. One book entitled *Frida Kahlo: The Brush of Anguish* looked particularly promising, so she pulled up the following screen to see more information.

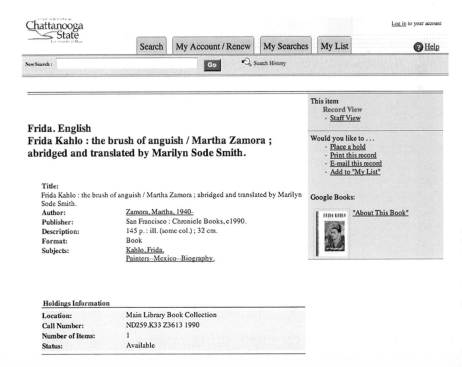

If you find a relevant book, as Kira did, look at the catalog record's *Subject* line to see additional headings ("Frida Kahlo" and "Painters–Mexico–Biography") that may lead you to other useful resources. Often these subject headings are linked to the online catalog, and, by clicking on one, you will be taken to resources related to the topic. For example, when Kira clicked on the "Frida Kahlo" subject heading, the library's online catalog provided a listing of more than a dozen alphabetically arranged categories, including "Kahlo, Frida Correspondence," "Kahlo, Frida Criticism and Interpretation," "Kahlo, Frida Diaries," and "Kahlo, Frida Exhibitions." Once you have a call number for a particular book, a library map will help you find its location on the shelves.

Databases

Most libraries across the country subscribe to a wide variety of information services that lead researchers to appropriate databases for their subjects. After you access your library's Web site, you might find an alphabetically arranged listing of the available databases. A list of this nature is often quite lengthy and not very easily navigated, so many libraries also provide headings (such as those shown in the following list) to organize the options into categories that are more easily searched:

Databases by Subject   Databases by Type
Full-Text Resources   Multidisciplinary Resources

If, indeed, you encounter these options and pursue the "Databases by Subject" link, you might find several headings (e.g., Business, Health, Literature, Music, Science, Social Sciences). Many of these categories may include other subheadings; for example, under "Science" you might find Biology, Chemistry, Environmental Science, and Physics. As you might expect, the organization of Web sites varies from library to library, so when you first visit your library's Web site, devote some time to becoming acquainted with the layout. And, of course, be willing to ask a librarian for assistance.

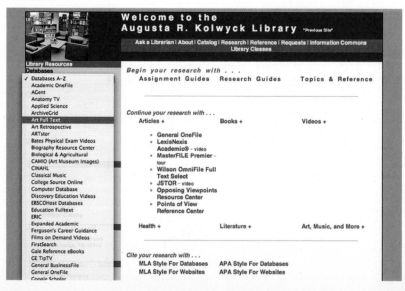

Chattanooga State Community College

At your library's Web site, you're likely to find one or more of the popular general databases, including *Academic Search Premier, Academic OneFile, General OneFile*, and *Info-Trac*. Any of these may serve as an excellent starting point for your research. Many college and university libraries subscribe to these databases because they provide access to millions of articles related to an exhaustive range of topics and derived from thousands of publications.

If your library's Web site also provides a listing of specialized categories, look for those that seem most appropriate to your topic. Because many college students write research papers about authors and their literary works, you might find that your library includes "Literature" among its specialized categories. Other categories might include "Science and Technology," "Career Search," "Health," or "Education."

Online databases are updated frequently—most on a daily basis—and almost certainly provide you with the most current sources for your research. Do note, however, that because libraries contract and pay a fee for database services, they must restrict most database access to on-site use or use by particular patrons (for example, enrolled students, faculty, and staff). Know, too, that each database may have its own search method. Always ask a librarian to help if you are struggling with a database search.

As you search your electronic sources, remember that you may have to try a variety of keywords (and their synonyms) to find what you need. Sometimes your keyword search may turn up too few leads—and sometimes you may be overwhelmed with too many matches! To save time and effort, you may be able to broaden or narrow your search by typing in words called *Boolean operators,** as illustrated here:

AND (Frida Kahlo AND Diego Rivera)—narrows your search to those references containing both Frida Kahlo and her husband, well-known artist Diego Rivera
OR (Frida Kahlo OR Diego Rivera)—broadens search to find items containing either term
NOT (Frida Kahlo NOT movie)—excludes items irrelevant to your search
NEAR (Frida Kahlo NEAR Surrealism)—finds references in which the terms occur within a set number of words (This option is not always available.)

Not all databases respond to Boolean operators, however, so it's always best to consult the searching advice offered by your particular information system.

While her school's library offered several database options, Kira selected *General One-File*. After accessing the *General OneFile* database, Kira clicked on the "Subject Guide Search" tab, typed "Frida Kahlo AND biography" in the "FIND" field, and limited the results "to documents with full text." This search yielded more than 400 potential sources—a bit overwhelming—but fortunately they were arranged in slightly over a dozen "subdivisions." Although Kira had begun her search with "biography" in mind, by clicking on the "subdivisions" link, she found several topics that she had not considered. The most promising, "Criticism and Interpretations," listed more than twenty potential sources spread among five categories (Academic Journals, Magazines, Books, News, and Multimedia).

---

*Named for the nineteenth-century British mathematician and logician George Boole

Kira also wanted to learn more about Kahlo's paintings, so she used *General OneFile*'s "Basic Search" option (rather than the "Subject Guide Search" that she used for "biography") and entered the keywords "Frida Kahlo AND paintings." Here is the *General OneFile* "keyword" search screen Kira used to look for more information on the important "Frida Kahlo AND paintings":

This search produced more than ninety potential sources, spread among the same five categories (Academic Journals, Magazines, Books, News, and Multimedia) that Kira had encountered in the "biography" search. With this list of ninety sources, Kira realized that she had some weeding out to do. Hoping to make the list more manageable, Kira sought advice from one of her school's librarians, who recommended that Kira sort the results by "relevance" as opposed to "publication date" (through a drop-down window located to the right and immediately below the category tabs). Selecting the "relevance" classification proved especially important in helping Kira quickly locate the most valuable articles for this particular topic. From the results, Kira came across the journal article shown in the screen that follows.

When Kira accessed the full-text version of this article (consisting of more than four thousand words), she found that it appeared on a single "page," making it difficult to include useful specific citations. She suspected that the article might also be available on the Smithsonian Institution's Web site, and a quick visit confirmed her suspicion. At the Web site, she found a version of the article spread over six numbered pages, so she was able to develop far more specific citations when she incorporated the article in her essay.

Once you have found useful information, remember that libraries have printers available to print out the on-screen data you wish to keep; you may have to pay a small fee for this printing, so it's a good idea to take some cash along, preferably in correct change. (Library users with personal computers or other kinds of technology can avoid this expense by e-mailing data to themselves.)

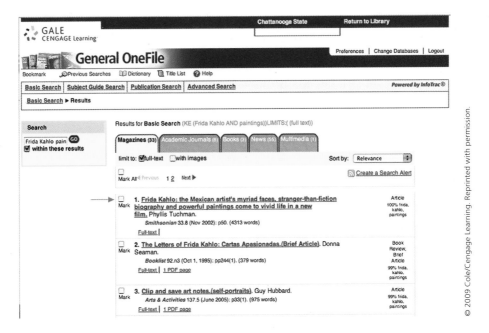

And once again, the very best advice bears repeating: never hesitate to ask your library staff for help.

The Internet

You may have access to the Internet through your library, through your school network, or through a personal account with a service provider of your choice. The Internet can offer great research opportunities, but in many cases, it may only supplement—not replace—the information you will need to collect through library sources.

The most effective approach to discovering useful material on the Internet may be through the use of search engines that produce a list of potential electronic documents or Web sites in response to your search. After you type in your keyword(s), the search engine explores its database for word or phrase matches; it then presents you with a list of potential sources, which include the Internet addresses (called URLs—"uniform resource locators"). You may access the sources that seem most promising (often those that appear first on the list), and you may also connect to other material by clicking on any highlighted words (hypertext links) appearing within the text of a particular document.

At this time, the most popular search engine is Google, but there are many more worldwide, including Bing, Yahoo!, and Ask; you might prefer meta-search engines (such as MetaCrawler or Dogpile), which simultaneously search the Internet's top search engines. Because each search engine pulls its results from a different (but often overlapping) pool of Web pages, and because each one offers distinct "extra features," it pays to try more than one. (If you aren't satisfied with your results, try another set of keywords before moving on.)

Most search engines have their own searching tips; to improve your chances for success, it's well worth the time to read the advice on conducting advanced searches. For example, Google's Advanced Search allows you to fill in such fields as "this wording or exact phrase," "all these words," "one or more of these words," or "none of these words." Other options narrow the search by designating certain reading levels, languages, specific dates, or particular kinds of materials. (Google Scholar, for example, will search among academic books, journals, theses, and abstracts.)

Some search engines allow use of Boolean operators (see page 371) to narrow or broaden your search. Some allow the use of plus and minus signs to show connected terms or unwanted matches:

> **Frida Kahlo + Diego Rivera** (find sources containing both Frida Kahlo and her artist husband)
> **Frida Kahlo – movie** (find sources about Frida Kahlo but exclude those that include the word "movie")

Some programs request quotation marks around a key term of multiple words ("Anne Frank"); some are case sensitive (capitalize proper nouns or not?); some use truncation to find various forms of a word ("myth*" will return "mythology" and "mythical"). Other search engines, such as Ask, allow users to ask questions in natural language ("Who was Frida Kahlo?"). As technology continues to improve, searching will no doubt become easier, so always take a moment to look at each search engine's current directions.

Here is one more hint for searching the Web: sometimes you can guess the URL you need. Simply fill in the name of a specific company, college, agency, or organization. Do not put spaces between words (usnews.com).

- **Businesses:** www.nameofcompany.com
- **Colleges:** www.nameofcollege.edu
- **Government agencies:** www.nameofagency.gov
- **Organizations:** www.nameoforganization.org

You may also consult specialized directories to discover the addresses you need.

Once you find a useful document, you may print it, add the reference to your "bookmarks" or "favorites" list, or copy it to a USB drive or to a home file if you are using your own computer. Whether at the library or at home, always keep a list of your important sites, their addresses, and the date you accessed them. You may need this information for an easy return to a particular document and also for your working bibliography.

To explore other ways to use the Internet for research, check your library's home page, which most likely will offer links to helpful search advice.

Words of Caution for Internet Users: Be Afraid, Be Very Afraid... The Internet offers researchers a wealth of information incredibly fast. However, the Internet poses problems, too. It may offer a great deal of information on your essay topic—but it may not always offer the *best* information, which might be found in a classic text on your library shelf. Background information or historical perspective may not be available; Web site information may be out of date. Moreover, simply finding the specific information you need can be frustrating and time-consuming, especially if your keywords and links don't lead in useful directions. The information superhighway is congested with scores of irrelevant distractions, so beware the wild Web chase.

There is, however, another much more serious problem: *not all material available on the Internet is accurate or reliable.* When an article is printed in a respected journal, for example, readers have assurances that editors have reviewed the information, writers have checked their facts, and authorities have been quoted correctly. However, Web sites may be created by anyone on any subject, from gene splicing to Elvis sightings, without any sort of editorial review. Opinions—wise or crackpot—may be presented as facts; rumors may be presented as reality.*

Because there is no "quality control" of Web sites, writers of research papers must evaluate their sources extremely carefully to avoid gathering unreliable information. For example, as Kira Anzai searched for information about Frida Kahlo, she consulted a number of Internet sites that were blogs written by a variety of Kahlo admirers. While these blogs frequently contained references to Kahlo's life, they often contained inaccurate details or rumored stories intermingled with personal interpretations, none of which was helpful to a serious investigation of Kahlo's art. Kira also checked several entries on *Wikipedia*, the popular general Web encyclopedia whose articles may be written or edited by anyone in the world, using a real identity or pseudonym. Although *Wikipedia* strives for information that may be verified and allows readers to demand better documentation (for example, a tag such as "citation needed" may appear after certain claims), Kira did in fact find information that contradicted details she was able to confirm in several other published sources. To be trusted as a reliable source of information by her own readers, Kira realized that she must always choose the most reliable, accurate sources herself; for that reason, she decided not to use *Wikipedia* as a resource for her essay. **

Apply your critical thinking skills to your selection of Internet sources by always asking the following questions about each Web site you consider:

- What is the purpose of this Web site? (To inform, persuade, market a product or service, share an interest, entertain?) To whom is this site primarily directed, and why?

- Who is the sponsor, author, or creator of the site? (A business, an educational institution, a nonprofit organization, a government agency, a news bureau, an individual?) Is the sponsor or author known and respected in the particular content area?

- Does the sponsor or author reveal a clear bias or strong opinion? Does such a slant undercut the usefulness of the information?

- When was this site produced? When was it last updated or revised? If links exist, are they still viable? Up to date?

- Is the information accurate? How might the material be cross-checked and verified?

---

* People sometimes circulate questionable information, stories, or pictures on the Internet as "proof" of their own political, social, or economic views. If you wish to check the validity of a particular message you have received, consider checking Snopes.com, a reference site devoted to killing rumors and exposing hoaxes, as well as identifying urban legends, folklore, and myths. Type in the name or some descriptive words associated with the story or picture you wish to check to see if it has already been identified as fake.

**On her own Web site, Pulitzer Prize-winning author Annie Dillard notes that "almost everything on Wikipedia about me is wrong" and identifies a number of false claims. She concludes with this advice: "Use Wikipedia only with caution."

If you have doubts about the accuracy of any material you discover on the Internet, find another authoritative source to validate the information or omit it from your essay. (◆ Following the guidelines on pages 386–388 will help you evaluate *all* your potential research sources; pages 102–105 may also be helpful.)

Special Collections

Your library may contain special collections that will help you research your subject. Some libraries, for example, have extensive collections of government documents or educational materials or newspapers from foreign cities. Other libraries may have invested in manuscripts from famous authors or in a series of works on a particular subject, such as your state's history. Remember, too, that some libraries contain collections of early films, rare recordings, or unique photographs. Consult your librarian or the information sources describing your library's special holdings.

Conducting Primary Research

To illustrate and support their points, most writers of research papers draw heavily on material found in articles, books, and other library sources. However, researchers sometimes find it useful to gather their own information. Collecting data firsthand is called *primary research* or *original research*, and it is valuable because it provides information not available from other sources.

Students often conduct primary research in a variety of college classes. For example, a chemistry major may gain new knowledge from a lab experiment; an English major may discover original insights reading a work of literature; a political science major may produce thoughtful analysis after studying local election results. In each case, the investigator collects information that was not already in existence.

Although there are many ways to conduct primary research, this section will present suggestions for conducting two strategies composition students may find most helpful: the *interview* and the *questionnaire*.

The Personal Interview

Depending on your choice of topic, you may find all the information you need for your essay by exploring sources through library and online research. However, sometimes you may discover that an authority on your subject lives in your town or works on your campus. In this case, you may wish to conduct a *personal interview* to gather valuable information for your essay.

Preparation is the key word governing a good interview. Here are some suggestions to help you collect useful data in the most effective way possible.

Before You Interview:

1. **Know your purpose.** If you have only a vague notion of why you are talking to the interviewee, you will waste everyone's time as the conversation roams like a lost hiker wandering from one clearing to the next. A close look at your essay's outline

or your early drafts should tell you why and how this person might contribute to your research. Be certain that the person you have selected for an interview is, in fact, the best source for the kind of information you are seeking. For example, if you are writing a paper on the campus program that assists students with learning disabilities, you might interview the program's director to obtain expert opinion; on the other hand, if you wish to know some specific ways in which the program has helped its participants, you might interview a student actively involved in the program for his or her personal response.

2. **Make an appointment.** Calling for an interview may make you a bit nervous, but remember that most people like to be asked for their opinions and are usually willing to help students with their research, if their schedules permit. Be sure the interviewee understands who you are, why you are asking for an interview, and approximately how much time you are requesting. Whenever possible, allow the interviewee to select the hour and place most convenient for him or her. Do adjust your schedule to give yourself time after the meeting in case the interview runs long and to allow yourself a few minutes to review and fill in your notes.

3. **Educate yourself.** Before the interview, read about your topic and your interviewee. You want to appear knowledgeable about your subject; you can also save time by skipping questions that have already been answered elsewhere. Busy experts appreciate not having to explain basic information that you could have— and should have—already looked up.

4. **Plan some questions.** Unless you have an excellent memory, it is best to prepare some specific questions to which you can refer during the interview. Some interviewers write each question at the top of an index card, and then use the rest of the card for their notes on the answer. Others use a notebook in which they write a question (or key words) at the top of each page. Try to create questions that are specific, clear, and logically ordered. Avoid "yes/no" questions that don't lead to discussion. If you have a complicated or convoluted issue you want to discuss, try breaking it into a series of simpler questions that can be tackled by the interviewee one at a time.

During the Interview:

5.   Make a good first impression. Always arrive on time, prepared with pens, paper, or any technology you may need. Some interviewers like to record comments, but you first must secure your interviewee's permission to do so. (Being recorded makes some people uncomfortably self-conscious and hesitant to speak freely, so consider whether the accuracy recording may provide is more important than the spontaneity it may kill.) Always begin by thanking your interviewee for his or her time and briefly say again why you think he or she can provide helpful information to you.

6.   Ask, listen, ask. Begin asking your prepared questions, but don't rush through them. Listen attentively to your interviewee's answers, and although it takes practice, try to maintain as much eye contact as possible as you take notes on the answers. Allow the interviewee to do almost all the talking; after all, you are there

to collect information, not participate in a debate. Do politely ask for clarification (unfamiliar terms, spelling of names, unclear references, and so on) when you need it.

7. Be flexible. Sometimes your interviewee will talk about something fascinating that never occurred to you when you prepared your original list of questions. Be ready to adapt your plan and ask new questions that follow up on unexpected commentary.

8. "Silence is golden," but . . . If an interviewee is quiet or hesitates to give the kind of detailed responses you are seeking, you may need to use phrases of this kind to draw out longer or more specific answers:

- Can you elaborate on that?
- Tell me more about X.
- Why did you think that?
- How did you react to that?
- When did you realize. . . ?
- Why do you believe that?
- What's your reading of that situation?
- Would you explain that for me?

As you ask for more details, try to use a friendly, conversational tone that will put your interviewee at ease.

On the other hand, sometimes interviewees talk too much! They become stuck on one aspect of a topic, going into unnecessary depth, or perhaps they begin to drift off the subject completely. Be courteous but firm in your resolve to redirect the flow of conversation. To get back to your topic, you may need to re-ask the original question, using slightly different words.

9. Conclude thoughtfully. At the end of the interview, ask for any additional comments the interviewee would like to offer and for any information (or other sources) he or she thinks you might find useful. Ask the interviewee if you may contact him or her again if you should have another brief question; if such permission is granted, ask for the best means of contact (a telephone number or e-mail address). Give the interviewee your most sincere thanks for his or her time and assistance.

After the Interview:

10. Review your notes immediately. Fill in gaps in your notes while your memory is fresh, and write out acronyms or abbreviations whose meanings you might forget in a few days. Make some notes to yourself about using the information in your essay.

Later, if the interview figures prominently in your essay, consider sending your interviewee a copy of your work. Within days of the interview, however, it is ALWAYS polite to send your interviewee a short thank-you note, acknowledging his or her help with your research project.

The Questionnaire

A questionnaire is a series of questions or statements designed to obtain people's opinions about certain ideas, products, issues, activities, or even other people. You have, no doubt, responded to a number of questionnaires yourself: in your school, you may have filled out course evaluation forms; in a store, you may have answered questions about a new product or service; at home, you may have replied to political pollsters or participated in a marketing survey.

Designing effective questionnaires is a complex business. There are, in fact, entire college courses devoted to the analysis and development of polls and surveys, courses often required for marketing majors and political science students. As daunting as composing a questionnaire may sound, student writers often find it useful to conduct small-scale surveys to gain wider opinions on a topic under research. For example, let's assume you've been assigned a paper calling for a specific recommendation to improve a campus service or agency. You have chosen the composition computer lab and, although you have a few ideas of your own, you think it would be valuable to know what other users of the lab would most like to see changed. You design a questionnaire asking lab users to identify their chief areas of concern, and, using that information, you write a persuasive essay calling for a specific change.

Here are some suggestions for designing, administering, and analyzing questionnaires, whose results might prove useful in your research.

Developing the Questionnaire

1. **Know your purpose and identify your target audience.** Writers of effective questionnaires have a specific goal in mind; articulating that goal clearly in writing will help you create the best survey questions. Ask yourself: what do I most want to know from this particular group of people? Which group of people will give me the information I want? Hint: Asking a particular population (computer lab users) to focus on a single issue (computer lab hours) will often produce the most precise responses.

2. **Encourage participation.** At the top of your questionnaire, briefly state your purpose and your request for response, giving pertinent (but not personal) information. People are more likely to participate if they know who is conducting the survey ("student in English 121"), what you want ("collecting composition students' opinions on . . ."), and how the results will be used ("data for essay whose purpose is . . ."). Some respondents will be naturally sympathetic to a hardworking student; others may need an answer to "what's in this for me?" If it's appropriate, you can appeal to your respondents' sense of the Common Good. In the case of the computer lab survey, for example, respondents might be encouraged to answer the questions if they thought the essay's recommendations would actually go to the lab supervisor, thus creating the possibility of improved service for all.

3. **Choose the most effective type of questionnaire for your purpose.** There are several kinds of questions or statements you may use to generate information; in a short survey, choose only one or two types to avoid confusing your participants.

Common methods include the following:

- *Yes/No* **Answers**
  Example: Do you use the computer lab at least once a week?
  ( ) Yes
  ( ) No

- **Multiple Choice**
  Example: Check one answer. How often do you use the computer lab?
  ( ) Once a week?
  ( ) Twice a week?
  ( ) More than twice a week?

- **Checklist**
  Example: Check all the statements with which you agree.
  ___ The current lab hours of operation are convenient for me.
  ___ The lab should be open on the weekends.
  ___ The lab needs extended evening hours.
  Etc.

- **Rank Order**
  Example: In the following list, identify the issues most important to you by marking the most important as "1" and the least important as "5."
  ___ Hours of operation
  ___ Updated equipment
  ___ Technical assistance available
  Etc.

- **Rating System**
  Example: Rate the following statements as SA (Strongly Agree), A (Agree), D (Disagree), SD (Strongly Disagree), or N (No Opinion).
  ___ The lab should be open on the weekends.
  ___ The lab should be open later at night.
  ___ The lab should have extended hours during final exams.
  Etc.

- **Open Questions**
  Example: If you could change the lab's hours of operation, what would an ideal schedule look like for you? Why would these hours be better than the current schedule?

Designers of questionnaires should note that although open questions may produce the most interesting answers to read, they are also the most difficult to tally objectively. Multiple-choice questionnaires may be the easiest to score, and their numbers may quickly be converted to percentages.

Once you have decided which method will best retrieve the kind of information you are seeking, clearly state the directions for following that method at the top of your questionnaire, after your statement of purpose. Consider using bold type to emphasize any important words in the instructions.

4. Watch your language. It's unfortunately easy to confuse your respondents or "contaminate" your survey with careless use of words or phrases. Avoid problems by remembering the following advice:

- Clarify vague references and avoid abbreviations your participants may not know.

Unclear	Are you in favor of or opposed to the proposed SB128?
Better	Are you in favor of or opposed to Colorado Senate Bill 128, which would raise the technology fees at this college by two percent?

- Rewrite any "loaded" questions or leading statements that attempt to shape the respondent's answer.

Biased	Should the university continue to waste your money on new, overpriced computer equipment?
Objective	Should the university purchase new computer equipment?

- Ask for one piece of information at a time.

Double question	Are the technical assistants at the lab helpful and friendly? Yes/No [Respondents might find the assistants friendly but not particularly helpful, or vice versa, so a single "yes" or a "no" answer would be misleading.]
Better questions	Do you find the technical assistants at the lab helpful? Yes/No Do you find the technical assistants in the lab friendly? Yes/No

5. Keep it short, simple, and smooth. People often cooperate with pollsters, but they don't want to be imposed on for too long. After you've drafted a number of potential questions for your survey, cut your list down to the most important ones. Unless you have an overwhelming reason to ignore this advice, limit your questionnaire to a single page. (Some pollsters also advise placing your most important questions first, in case respondents tire of answering and turn in incomplete forms.) Ask your questions in the clearest, most direct way possible to get the most straightforward answers.* Just as you know how to write coherent, smoothly linked paragraphs in your essays, group questions logically to move your respondents' thoughts easily from issue to issue.

Administering the Questionnaire

6. Secure a valid sampling. To get meaningful responses, you must survey the right people, ones with the knowledge or opinions that matter to your research. But at this point you must also ask yourself two other vitally important questions: are the people taking my survey truly representative of my target group as a whole? Does

---

*Some national pollsters believe that to obtain the most truthful responses, questionnaires should be answered anonymously; others suggest making signatures optional.

my sample—the number of people contacted—comprise a large enough part of the target group to merit the conclusions I might draw from their comments?

For valid results, first make sure that you are taking a *random sample*; that is, you must ensure that each member of the population has a fair and equal chance of being selected. In a survey on the computer center hours, for example, you would not get an accurate cross-section of opinions if you sampled only the work-study students staffing the lab or your best friends who feel as you do. Similarly, if you sample only a tiny fraction of the students who use the lab, your results will not provide strong support for any broad claims about student opinion. As you prepare to distribute your questionnaire, be sure you will address a significant number of randomly selected people who compose a cross-section of your target group.

7. **Perform a test run.** If time permits, ask several people in your target group to take the survey before you distribute it widely. If the questionnaire has problems or confusing spots, they will surface in time for you to fix them.

8. **Be prepared.** Plan ahead to discover how best to distribute your questionnaires. If you are handing out print copies on school or private property or making online surveys available on school computers, be sure you have permission to do so. If you are placing print questionnaires in a public place for respondents to pick up at their leisure, you'll need a secure drop-box for completed surveys that you can empty frequently. If your respondents are answering by hand, don't forget to provide an extra-large number of pencils or pens as they do "walk off" with great regularity. (For some types of inquiry, you might wish to check with one of several online survey services now available. Some professional services offer free design tools to help you create your own questionnaire, but others charge a fee for their templates, so do consult any Web-based business carefully.)

Totaling and Reporting Results

9. **Analyze your responses.** Depending on your method of surveying, you may simply add up the totals for each answer (in multiple-choice or checklist questionnaires, for example), or you may need to spend some time pondering the nuances of written comments. All returned, completed questionnaires must be included in your analysis. If you wish to convert questionnaire numbers into percentages, divide the number of responses to a particular answer by the total number of questionnaires returned and then multiply that figure by 100 (Example: five responses to one multiple-choice answer out of 25 questionnaires would be 0.20; multiplying $0.20 \times 100 = 20\%$). As you study your results, look for emerging patterns and repeated ideas. What conclusions can you draw based on these responses?

10. **Accurately report your findings.** If you base your essay's assertions, arguments, conclusions, or recommendations on your questionnaire's results, your readers will certainly need a clear understanding of how those results were obtained. To be persuaded that your research is valid, they may wish to know how the

questionnaire was designed and why, how many were distributed and completed, how the respondents were chosen, and other such information. Such explanations may appear within the body of your essay or in appropriately marked sections (such as "Purpose and Design," "Results," "Recommendations") or in an appendix; whichever method you choose, always attach a blank sample copy of the questionnaire to your essay.

Conducting research through the distribution of a questionnaire is a challenging but fascinating way to collect information about current unexplored topics. If you have collected data that would be valuable to people on your campus, at your workplace, or in your community, by all means communicate it to them. Your primary research, and your conclusions, could help someone make an important decision.

Preparing a Working Bibliography

As you search for information about your essay topic, keep a list of sources that you may want to use in your essay. This list, called a *working bibliography*, will grow as you discover potential sources, and it may shrink if you delete references that aren't useful. Ultimately, this working bibliography will become the list of references presented at the end of your essay.

There are several ways to record your sources. Some students prefer to make an index card for each title; others compile a list in a research notebook; still others use a word processing program or a computer database. (Potential time-saving hint: some of today's computer programs will format your information in the documentation style required for your essay, which may allow an easy transfer from your file to your paper's APA References or MLA Works Cited page.) However you choose to record your notes, you can avoid last-minute rechecking of your data by always including the following details, as appropriate for each source:

Book

1. Author's or editor's full name (and name of translator if given)
2. Complete title, including subtitle if one exists
3. Edition number
4. Volume number if the book is part of a series
5. City of publication and name of publisher
6. Date of publication
7. For a reading or article in an anthology, title and author
8. Page numbers of the information you need
9. Library call number or location of source

Article in a Journal, Magazine, or Newspaper

1. Author's full name (if given)
2. Title of the article

3. Title of the journal, magazine, or newspaper

4. Volume and issue number of the journal or magazine

5. Date of publication

6. Page numbers of the article (section and page numbers for newspaper)

Electronic Sources

1. Author's full name or name of sponsoring organization

2. Title of document

3. Information about print publication (book: place, publisher, date; periodical: title, volume and issue if given, date, pages)

4. Information about electronic publication (source, such as database or Web site; name of service; date of publication or most recent update)

5. Access information (URL, DOI, and date of access)

Interview

1. Interviewee's name and title

2. Interviewee's organization or company, job description, or other information regarding his or her expertise, including pertinent publications, studies, presentations, and so forth

3. Subject of interview

4. Date, place, and method of interview (e.g., in person, by telephone, by e-mail)

Here are four sample index cards that might appear in Kira Anzai's working bibliography:

Book

Zamora, Martha
Abridged and translated by Marilyn Sode Smith
Frida Kahlo: The Brush of Anguish
Chronicle Books, 1990
San Francisco, California
Call number: ND259.K33 Z3613 1990
TCU Library, Main Stacks

Article in a Scholarly Journal

Baddeley, Oriana
"'Her Dress Hangs Here': De-Frocking the Kahlo Cult"
Oxford Art Journal   Volume 14   Number 1   1991
pages 10-17
TCU Library, Periodicals

Electronic Source

Johnston, Jill
"Self-Portrait"
Rev. of *The Diary of Frida Kahlo: An Intimate Self-Portrait*
by Sarah M. Lowe
Art in America Volume 84   Number 3   March 1996
pages 31 and 33 (page 32 is skipped)
General OneFile   Gale
Accessed 24 March 2012

Interview

> Bryant, Jennifer (Dr.)
> Professor of Art History
> TCU Department of Art and Art History
> Teaches ART 20093, Art of Mexico from 1500 to the Present
> Interview subject: Frida Kahlo
> In-person interview: March 9, 2012
>
> Credentials:
> —specialist in Latin American art of the 20th Century
> —attended symposium on Mexican Modernism held in
>   Mexico City
> —saw exhibition of paintings by Frida Kahlo, Diego Rivera

Choosing and Evaluating Your Sources

After you have found a number of promising sources, take a closer look at them. The strength and credibility of your research paper will depend directly on the strength and credibility of your sources. In short, a research paper built on shaky, unreliable sources will not convince a thoughtful reader. Even one suspect piece of evidence may lead your reader to wonder about the validity—and integrity—of other parts of your essay.

As you review your potential sources, you must apply your *critical thinking skills.* Remember that critical thinking does not mean scattering negative criticism or hostility everywhere; it refers to the higher-order thinking that allows you to carefully examine and evaluate the validity of observations, experiences, and verbal or written communication. When you analyze the worth of someone's claims, evidence, or methodology presented in potentially useful sources, you may assess elements of accuracy, logic, breadth, depth, relevance, and fairness, among other considerations. (◆ For more discussion of critical thinking skills as applied to your own writing as well as that of others, see pages 102–105 in Chapter 5.)

To help you choose the best print and online sources, ask yourself the following questions as you decide which facts, figures, and testimonies will most effectively support or illustrate your ideas while lending credibility to you as a trustworthy, persuasive writer.

What do I know about the source's author? Does this person have any expertise or particular knowledge about the subject matter? If the author of an article about nuclear fusion is a physics professor at a respected university, her views may be more informed than those of a writer of popular science. Although books and scholarly journals generally cite their author's qualifications, the credentials of journalists and magazine writers may be harder to evaluate. Some kinds of Internet sources, as mentioned earlier, may be highly suspect. In cases in which the background of a writer is unknown, you might examine the writer's use of his or her own sources. Can sources for specific data or opinions be checked or verified? In addition, the objectivity of the author must be considered: some authors are clearly biased and may even stand to gain economically or politically from taking a particular point of view. The president of a tobacco company, for instance, might insist that secondary smoke from the cigarettes of others will not harm nonsmokers, but does he or she have an objective opinion? Try to present evidence only from those authors whose views will sway your intelligent readers.

What do I know about the publisher? Who published your sources? Major, well-known publishing houses can be one indication of a book's credibility. (If you are unfamiliar with a particular publisher, consult a librarian or professor in that field.) Be aware that there are many companies who publish books supporting only a specific viewpoint; similarly, many organizations support Web sites to further their causes. The bias in such sources may limit their usefulness to your research.

For periodicals, consider the nature of the journal, magazine, or newspaper. Who is its intended audience? A highly technical paper on sickle-cell anemia, for example, may be weakened by citing an introductory-level discussion of the disease from a general-readership health magazine; an article from the *Journal of the American Medical Association*, however, may be valuable. Is it a publication known to be fairly objective (the *New York Times*) or does it have a particular cause to support (the *National Sierra Club Bulletin*)? Looking at the masthead of a journal or other publication will often tell you whether articles are subjected to stringent review before acceptance for publication. In general, articles published in "open" or nonselective publications should be examined closely for credibility. For example, the newsletter for Mensa—a well-known international society for individuals who have documented IQs in the top 2 percent of the population—once created a furor when an article appeared recommending the euthanasia of the mentally and physically disabled, the homeless, and other so-called "nonproductive" members of society. The newsletter editor's explanation was that all articles submitted for publication were generally accepted.

Is my research reasonably balanced? Your treatment of your subject—especially if it is a controversial one—should show your readers that you investigated all sides of the issue before reaching a conclusion. If your sources are drawn only from authorities well known for voicing one position, your readers may be skeptical about the quality of your research. For instance, if in a paper arguing against a new gun-control measure, you cite only the opinions voiced by the officers of the National Rifle Association, you may antagonize the reader who wants a thorough analysis of all sides of the question. Do use sources that support your position, but don't limit your research to obviously biased sources.

Are my sources reporting valid research? Is your source the original researcher, or is he or she reporting someone else's study?* If the information is being reported

---

*Interviews, surveys, studies, and experiments conducted firsthand are referred to as *primary sources*; reports and studies written by someone other than the original researcher are called *secondary sources*.

secondhand, has your source been accurate and clear? Is the original source named or referenced in some way so that the information could be checked?

A thorough researcher might note the names of authorities frequently cited by other writers or researchers and try to obtain the original works by those authorities. This tip was useful for Kira Anzai as she found researcher Hayden Herrera, whose exhaustive book, *Frida: A Biography of Frida Kahlo*, was mentioned in a number of magazine articles. Once she obtained a copy of this often-quoted book, she had additional information to consider for her paper.

Look too at the way information in your source was obtained in the first place. Did the original researchers themselves draw logical conclusions from their evidence? Did they run their study or project in a fair, impartial way? For example, a survey of people whose names were obtained solely from the rolls of one political party will hardly constitute a representative sampling of voters' opinions on an upcoming election.

Moreover, be especially careful with statistics because they can be manipulated quite easily to give a distorted picture. A recent survey, for instance, asked a large sample of people to rate a number of American cities based on questions dealing with quality of life. Pittsburgh—a lovely city to be sure—came out the winner, but only if one agrees that all the questions should be weighted equally; that is, the figures gave Pittsburgh the highest score only if one rates "weather" as equally important as "educational opportunities," "number of crimes," "cultural opportunities," and other factors. In short, always evaluate the quality of your sources' research and the validity of their conclusions before you decide to incorporate their findings into your own paper. (And don't forget Mark Twain's reference to "lies, damned lies, and statistics.")

Are my sources still current? Although some famous experiments or studies have withstood the years, many topics demand research as current as possible. What was written two years or even two weeks ago may have been disproved or surpassed since, especially in our rapidly changing political world and ever-expanding fields of technology. A paper on the status of the U.S. space program, for example, demands recent sources, and research on tablet computer use in the United States might be severely weakened by the use of a text published as recently as last year for "current" statistics.

If they're appropriate, journals and other periodicals may contain more up-to-date reports than books printed several years ago; library database searches can often provide the most current information. On the other hand, you certainly shouldn't ignore a "classic" study on your subject, especially if it is the one against which all the other studies are measured. A student researching the life of Abraham Lincoln, for instance, might find Carl Sandburg's multivolume biography of over seventy years ago as valuable as more recent works. Be aware, too, that even though Web sites can be continually revised, they are sometimes neglected; always check to see if a "last updated" date has been posted or if the material contains current dates or references.

◆ REMEMBER: For more advice to help you think critically about your sources, see pages 102–105 in Chapter 5.

Preparing an Annotated Bibliography

While you are gathering and assessing your sources, you may be asked to compile an annotated bibliography—a description of each important source that includes the basic bibliographic facts as well as a brief summary of each entry's content. After reading multiple articles or books on your subject over a period of days or even weeks, you may discover that the information you've found has begun to blur in your head. Annotating each of your sources will help you remember the specific data in each one so that you can locate the material later in the planning and drafting stages of your writing process.

Here is a sample taken from Kira Anzai's annotated bibliography:

> Herrera, Hayden. *Frida: A Biography of Frida Kahlo*. 1983. New York: Perennial-Harper, 2002. Print.
>
> Art historian Hayden Herrera's detailed biography of Frida Kahlo explores her personal life, career, and vibrant personality within the context of Mexico's cultural and political atmosphere. The book frequently draws on Kahlo's own writing—her diary entries, letters, and poetry—as well as the views of her friends, relatives, and other contemporaries.

Compiling an annotated bibliography will also give you a clear sense of how complete and balanced your sources are in support of your ideas, perhaps revealing gaps in your evidence that need to be filled with additional research data. Later, when your essay is finished, your annotated bibliography might provide a useful reference for any of your readers who are interested in exploring your subject in more depth.

Taking Notes

As you evaluate and select those sources that are both reliable and useful, you will begin taking notes on their information. Most researchers use one or more of the following three methods of note-taking.

1. Some students prefer to make their notes on index cards rather than on notebook paper because a stack of cards may be added to, subtracted from, or shuffled around more easily when it's time to plan the essay. You may find it useful to label each card with a short topic heading that corresponds to a major idea in your essay. Then, as you read, put pertinent information on its appropriate card. Be sure to identify the source of all your notes. (Hint 1: If you have used bibliography cards, take your notes on cards of different sizes or colors to avoid any confusion; write on only one side of each card so that all your information will be in sight when you draft your essay.)

2. Students with personal computers may prefer to store their notes as computer files because of the easy transfer of quoted material from file to essay draft. (Hint 2: This is a great use for a USB drive.) Always make a hard copy of your notes and back up your files frequently. You may find yourself taking notes by hand on any occasions when you are without your computer (classroom, interview, public speech, etc.), so carry index cards with you and transcribe your notes into your files later.

3. Other students rely on photocopies or printouts of sources, highlighting or under-lining important details. (Hint 3: Copy a source's title page and other front matter so that you can clip complete bibliographic information to your pages.)

Whichever note-taking methods you choose, always remember to record biblio-graphic information and the specific page numbers (in printed sources) or paragraph numbers (in some electronic sources) from which your material is taken. Your notes may be one of the following kinds:

1. **Direct quotations.** When you use material word for word, you must always enclose it in quotation marks and note the precise page number of the quotation, if given.* If the quoted material runs from one printed page onto another, use some sort of signal to yourself, such as a slash bar (child/abuse) or arrow ($\rightarrow$ p. 162) at the break so if you use only part of the quoted material in your paper, you will know on which page it appeared. If the quoted material contains odd, archaic, or incorrect spelling, punctuation marks, or grammar, insert the word *sic* in brackets next to the item in question; [*sic*] means "this is the way I found it in the original text," and such a symbol will remind you later that you did not miscopy the quotation. In any case, always double-check to make sure you did copy the material accurately and completely to avoid having to come back to the source as you prepare your essay.

2. **Paraphrase.** You paraphrase when you put into your own words what someone else has written or said. Please note: *paraphrased ideas are borrowed ideas, not your original thoughts, and, consequently, they must be attributed to their owner just as direct quotations are.*

   To remind yourself that certain information in your notes is paraphrased, always introduce it with some sort of notation, such as a handwritten Ⓟ or a typed P//. Quotation marks will always tell you what you borrowed directly, but sometimes when writers take notes one week and write their first draft a week or two later, they cannot remember if a note was paraphrased or if it was an original thought. Writ-ers occasionally plagiarize unintentionally because they erroneously believe that only direct quotations and statistics must be attributed to their proper sources, so make your notes as clear as possible. (◆ For more information on avoiding plagia-rism, see pages 394–396.)

3. **Summary.** You may wish to condense a piece of writing so you can offer it as support for your own ideas. Using your own words, you should present in shorter form the writer's thesis and supporting ideas. You may find it helpful to include a few direct quotations in your summary to retain the flavor of the original work. Of course, you will tell your readers what you are summarizing and by whom it was written. Remem-ber to make a note (sum:) to yourself to indicate summarized, rather than original, material. (◆ For more information on writing a summary, see also pages 184–185.)

4. **Your own ideas.** Your notes may also contain your personal comments (judg-ments, flashes of brilliance, questions, notions of how to use something you've just read, notes to yourself about connections between sources, and so forth) that will aid you in the writing of your paper. In handwritten notes, you might jot these

---

*All tables, graphs, and charts that you copy must also be directly attributed to their sources, though you do not enclose graphics in quotation marks.

down in a different-colored pen or put them in brackets that you've initialed, so that you will recognize them later as your own responses.

Distinguishing Paraphrase from Summary

Because novice writers sometimes have a hard time understanding the difference between paraphrase and summary, here is an explanation and a sample of each. The original paragraph that appears here was taken from a magazine article describing an important 1984 study still frequently cited:

> Another successful approach to the prevention of criminality has been to target very young children in a school setting before problems arise. The Perry Preschool Program, started 22 years ago in a low socioeconomic area of Ypsilanti, Michigan, has offered some of the most solid evidence to date that early intervention through a high-quality preschool program can significantly alter a child's life. A study released this fall tells what happened to 123 disadvantaged children from preschool age to present. The detention and arrest rate for the 58 children who had attended the preschool program was 31 percent, compared to 51 percent for the 65 who did not. Similarly, those in the preschool program were more likely to have graduated from high school, have enrolled in postsecondary education programs and be employed, and less likely to have become pregnant as teenagers.
>
> —from "Arresting Delinquency," Dan Hurley,
> Psychology Today *March 1985, page 66*

Paraphrase

A *paraphrase* puts the information in the researcher's own words, but it does follow the order of the original text, and it does include the important details:

> Quality preschooling for high-risk children may help stop crime before it starts. A 1984 study from the Perry Preschool Program located in a poor area of Ypsilanti, Michigan, showed that of 123 socially and economically disadvantaged children, the 58 who attended preschool had an arrest rate of 31 percent compared to 51 percent for those 65 who did not attend. The adults with preschool experience had also graduated from high school in larger numbers; in addition, more of them had attended postsecondary education programs, were employed, and had avoided teenage pregnancy (Hurley 66).

Summary

A *summary* is generally much shorter than the original; the researcher picks out the key ideas but often omits many of the supporting details:

> A 1984 study from the Perry Preschool Program in Michigan suggests that disadvantaged children who attend preschool are less likely to be arrested as adults. They choose more education, have better employment records, and avoid teenage pregnancy more often than those without preschool (Hurley 66).

REMEMBER: Both paraphrased and summarized ideas must be attributed to their sources, even if you do not reproduce exact words or figures.

Incorporating Your Source Material

Be aware that a research paper is not a massive collection of direct quotations and paraphrased ideas glued together with a few transitional phrases. It is, instead, an essay in which you offer your thesis and ideas based on and supported by your research. Consequently, you will need to incorporate and blend in your reference material in a variety of smooth, persuasive ways. Here are some suggestions:

Use your sources in a clear, logical way. Make certain that you understand your source material well enough to use it in support of your own thoughts. Once you have selected the best references to use, be as convincing as possible. Ask yourself if you're using enough evidence and if the information you're offering really does clearly support your point. As in any essay, you need to avoid oversimplification, hasty generalizations, *non sequiturs*, and other problems in logic. (◆ For a review of common logical fallacies, see pages 295–299.) Resist the temptation to add quotations, facts, or statistics that are interesting but not really relevant to your paper.

Don't overuse direct quotations. It's best to use a direct quotation *only* when it expresses a point in a far more impressive, emphatic, or concise way than you could say it yourself. Suppose, for instance, you were analyzing the films of a particular director and wanted to include a sample of critical reviews:

> As one movie critic wrote, "This film is really terrible, and people should ignore it" (Dennison 14).

The direct quotation above isn't remarkable and could be easily paraphrased. However, you might be tempted to quote the following line to show your readers an emphatically negative review of this movie:

> As one movie critic wrote, "This film's plot is so idiotic it's clearly intended for people who move their lips not only when they read but also when they watch TV" (Dennison 14).

When you do decide to use direct quotations, don't merely drop them into your prose as if they had fallen from a tall building onto your page. Instead, lead into them smoothly so that they obviously support or clarify what you are saying.

Dropped in	Scientists have been studying the ill effects of nitrites on test animals since 1961. "Nitrites produced malignant tumors in sixty-two percent of the test animals within six months" (Smith 109).
Better	Scientists have been studying the ill effects of nitrites on test animals since 1961. According to Dr. William Smith, head of the Farrell Institute of Research, who conducted the largest experiment thus far, "Nitrites produced malignant tumors in sixty-two percent of the test animals within six months" (109).

Vary your sentence pattern when you present your quotations. Here are some sample phrases for introducing quotations:

> In her introduction to *The Great Gatsby*, Professor Wilma Smith points out that Fitzgerald "wrote about himself and produced a narcissistic masterpiece" (5).

Wilma Smith, author of *Impact*, summarized the situation this way: "Eighty-eight percent of the sales force threatens a walkout" (21).

"Only the President controls the black box," according to White House Press Secretary Wilma Smith.

As drama critic Wilma Smith observed last year in the *Saturday Review*, the play was "a rousing failure" (212).

Perhaps the well-known poet Wilma Smith expressed the idea best when she wrote, "Love is a spider waiting to entangle its victims" (14).

"Employment figures are down three percent from last year," claimed Senator Wilma Smith, who leads opposition to the tax cut (32).

In other words, don't simply repeat "Wilma Smith said," "John Jones said," "Mary Brown said."

Punctuate your quotations correctly. The proper punctuation will help your reader understand who said what. ◆ For information on the appropriate uses of quotation marks surrounding direct quotations, see pages 589–590 in Part Four. If you are incorporating a long quoted passage into your essay, one that appears as more than four lines in your text, you should present it in block form without quotation marks, as described on pages 399–400. To omit words in a quoted passage, use ellipsis points, explained on pages 597–598.

Make certain your support is in the paper, not still in your head or back in the original source. Sometimes after you've read a number of persuasive facts in an article or a book, it's easy to forget that your reader doesn't know them as you do now. For instance, the writer of the following paragraph isn't as persuasive as she might be because she hides the support for her controversial point in the reference to the article, forgetting that the reader needs to know what the article actually said:

An organ transplant from one human to another is becoming a common occurrence, an operation that is generally applauded by everyone as a lifesaving effort. But people are overlooking many of the serious problems that come with the increase in transplant surgery. A study shows that in Asia there may be a risk of traffic in organs on the black market. Figures recorded recently are very disturbing (Wood 35).

For the reader to be persuaded, he or she needs to know what the writer learned from the article: what study? What figures and what exactly do they show? Who has recorded these? Is the source reliable? Instead of offering the necessary support in the essay, the writer merely points to the article as proof. Few readers will take the time to look up the article to find the information they need to understand or believe your point. Therefore, when you use source material, always be sure that you have remembered to put your support on the page, *in the essay itself*, for the reader to see. Don't let the essence of your point remain hidden, especially when the claim is controversial.

Don't let reference material dominate your essay. Remember that your reader is interested in *your* thesis and *your* conclusions, not just in a string of references. Use your researched material wisely whenever your statements need clarification, support, or amplification. But don't use quotations, paraphrases, or summarized material at every turn, just to show that you've done your homework.

Avoiding Plagiarism

Unfortunately, most discussions of research must include a brief word about plagiarism. Novice writers often unintentionally plagiarize, as noted before, because they fail to recognize the necessity of attributing paraphrased, summarized, and borrowed ideas to their original owners. And indeed it is sometimes difficult after days of research to know exactly what one has read repeatedly and what one originally thought. Also, there's frequently a thin line between general or common knowledge ("Henry Ford was the father of the automobile industry in America") that does not have to be documented and those ideas and statements that do ("USX reported an operating loss of four million dollars in its last quarter"). As a rule of thumb, ask yourself whether the majority of your readers would recognize the fact or opinion you're expressing or if it's repeatedly found in commonly used sources; if so, you may not need to document it. For example, most people would acknowledge that the Wall Street crash of 1929 ushered in the Great Depression of the 1930s, but the exact number of bank foreclosures in 1933 is not common knowledge and, therefore, needs documenting. Similarly, a well-known quotation from the Bible or Mother Goose or even the Declaration of Independence might pass without documentation, but a line from the vice president's latest speech needs a reference to its source. Remember, too, that much of the material on the Internet is copyrighted. When in doubt, the best choice is to document anything that you feel may be in question.

To help you understand the difference between plagiarism and proper documentation, here is a passage taken from the book *Criminal Investigation*, followed by both incorrect and correct ways of using its information in a paper of your own:

Original   As bicycles have increased in popularity, so has bicycle theft. According to the Web site of the National Bike Registry (www.nationalbikeregistry .com), more than 1.5 million bicycles, worth an estimated $200 million, are stolen each year in the United States. Experienced thieves can steal a locked bike in less than 20 seconds. And while nearly 50 per cent of all stolen bicycles are recovered every year by law enforcement, only 5 per cent are returned to their owners, because most bikes are unregistered.

—from *Criminal Investigation* (8th edition)
Wayne W. Bennett and Karen M. Hess
Wadsworth, 2007, page 400

Plagiarized   As more people ride bicycles today, bike theft is on the rise. Over 1.5 million bikes are stolen every year in the United States, at a loss of approximately $200 million. A locked bike can be stolen by a good thief in as little as 20 seconds, and even though police recover almost half of them, only 5 percent of owners ever see their rides again because the bikes are unregistered.

The writer of the preceding paragraph paraphrased the original—changed some words and sentences. But because the writer borrowed the ideas and the statistics without crediting the original source, the passage is plagiarized.

Also plagiarized   Got a nice bicycle? Watch out, as it may become one of the 1.5 million bikes stolen this year alone, with bike theft on the rise (Bennett and Hess 400). Campus is a prime place for such theft, as I know from personal experience, despite use of a heavy lock and chain. But even if police or campus cops find your bike—and they do recover nearly half of them—you still may not get your transportation back if you are one of the 95 percent who have not registered your bike. You'll join the other U.S. bikers who all together will lose some $200 million this year.

The writer of the preceding paragraph did show the source of the number of stolen bikes, but the rest of the paragraph contains borrowed material that also must be clearly attributed.

Properly documented   This week campus police are holding their annual bicycle registration drive. Unfortunately, too many students ignore this simple procedure—and pay the price. I know I did last year when my new bike was stolen from the rack in front of the Chemistry Building, despite its heavy lock and chain. I'm not the only one to lose my transportation, of course. According to figures from the National Bike Registry, over 1.2 million bikes are stolen each year, but, more importantly, despite recovery of almost half of them, only 5 percent of owners could claim their recovered bikes through proper registration (Bennett and Hess 400). Learn from my mistake: it's worth the five-minute hassle of filling out a form. Walk—or ride the bike you want to keep—over to the Student Center any afternoon this week from 2 to 4.

The writer of the preceding paragraph used the properly documented information to support her own point about the value of campus bike registration. She has not tried to pass off any of the facts about national bike loss and recovery as her own, and her readers will know where to find the data should they wish more information.

Although plagiarism is often unintentional, it's your job to be as honest and careful as possible. If you're in doubt about your use of a particular idea, study, statistics or any other kind of borrowed material, consult your instructor for a second opinion.

Here's a suggestion that might help you avoid plagiarizing by accident. When you are drafting your essay and come to a spot in which you want to incorporate the ideas of someone else, think of the borrowed material as if it were in a window.* Always frame the window at the top with some sort of introduction that identifies the author (or source) and frame the window on the bottom with a reference to the location of the material, as illustrated on the following page.

---

*I am indebted to John Clark Pratt, Professor Emeritus of English, Colorado State University, for this useful suggestion. Professor Pratt is the author of *Writing from Scratch: The Essay* (1987), published by Hamilton Press, and the editor of the *Writing from Scratch* series.

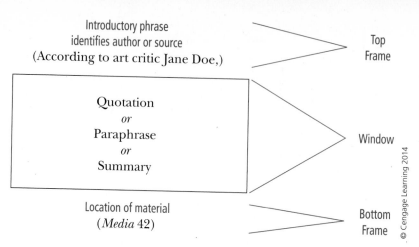

Introductory phrase
identifies author or source
(According to art critic Jane Doe,)

Top
Frame

Quotation
or
Paraphrase
or
Summary

Window

Location of material
(*Media* 42)

Bottom
Frame

© Cengage Learning 2014

A sample might look like this:

Introductory phrase identifies author

As humorist Mike McGrady once said about housekeeping, "Any job that requires six hours to do and can be undone in six minutes by one small child carrying a plate of crackers and a Monopoly set—this is not a job that will long capture my interest" (13).

Window

Location

In a later draft, you'll probably want to vary your style so that all your borrowed material doesn't appear in exactly the same "window" format (◆ see pages 392–393 for suggestions). But until you acquire the habit of always documenting your sources, you might try using the "window" technique in your early drafts.

Practicing What You've Learned

© Canstock Images, Inc./
Index Stock Imagery

A. As Kira Anzai researched the life of Frida Kahlo, she found the following commentary on one of the artist's paintings. To practice some of the skills you've learned, read the passage and perform the tasks that follow it.

Another Mexican artist, Frida Kahlo, moved in a different direction than the Mexican muralists. Although her work has been associated with the Surrealists, she was an independent like Klee and Miro. Using the visual vocabulary of Mexican folk art, she drew directly on the events of her life, particularly the accident that left her partly crippled and in pain. In *Self-Portrait with Thorn Necklace and Hummingbird* . . . the prickly thorns represent the ache of body and soul. The monkey and the cat refer to the jungle and the fact that she was part

continued on next page

Harry Ransom Humanities Research Center, The University of Texas at Austin. © 2012 Banco de Mexico Diego Rivera Frida Kahlo Museums Trust, Mexico, D.F. / Artists Rights Society (ARS), New York

Self-Portrait with Thorn Necklace and Hummingbird, 1940, by Frida Kahlo.

Indian. The hummingbird that hangs around her neck is a symbol of those who have lost love. In particular, it refers to her recent divorce from muralist Diego Rivera, whom she soon remarried.

1. The book from which the passage was taken contains the following information. Select the appropriate data and prepare a working bibliography card.

   Fleming's Arts & Ideas
   Tenth Edition
   Wadsworth/Cengage Learning, publishers
   Boston, MA
   Printed in the USA by Graphic World Inc.
   23 chapters plus glossary, 704 pages
   Library of Congress Control Number 2004107621
   Chapter 21
   Copyright 2005
   Authors: Mary Warner Marien, Professor, Syracuse University, and William Fleming, Professor Emeritus, Syracuse University
   Pages 585-586
   ISBN 0-534-61381-0

continued on next page

2. Paraphrase the first three sentences, showing how you would credit the source of your words in an essay of your own.

3. Practice summarizing the paragraph; do not quote directly from it.

4. Select an idea from the passage to quote directly. Using the "window" technique described on pages 395–396, lead into the quotation with a smooth acknowledgment of its source or authors in the top frame and conclude with the correct location of the material in the bottom frame.

5. Select an idea or take a direct quotation from the passage and use it as support for a point of your own, being careful not to plagiarize the borrowed material.

B. Using library or Internet resources, look up a newspaper* from any city and find the issue published on the day of your birth or on some other significant date. Prepare a bibliography card and then summarize an important article that interests you. (Don't forget to acknowledge the source of your summary.)

Assignment

© CORBIS

A. To practice searching for and choosing source material, find three recent works on your essay topic available in your library. If you don't have an essay topic yet, pick a subject that interests you, one that is likely to appear in both print and electronic sources (Baseball Hall of Fame, stamp collecting, the *Titanic* disaster, king cobras, etc.). If possible, try to find three different kinds of sources, such as a book, a journal or magazine article, and a Web site. After you have recorded bibliographic information for each source, locate and evaluate the works. Do all of these sources provide relevant, reliable information? In a few sentences explain why you believe each one would or would not be an appropriate source for your research essay.

B. *Collaborative Activity:* To help you focus your essay topic, engage in a "talk-write" session with another student. Before class, review your research thus far, selecting the most interesting, surprising, or puzzling piece of information you have found. In class, explain your findings to a classmate, and together brainstorm ways this information might be most effectively incorporated into your essay. Take notes on any useful suggestions or unexpected reactions that might help you see a new possibility for the direction of your essay. Also, if time permits, help each other problem-solve any difficulties with a particular research method or source.

---

*If the newspaper is not accessible, you might substitute a weekly news magazine, such as *Time* or *Newsweek*.

Choosing the Documentation Style for Your Essay

Once you begin to write your paper incorporating your source material, you need to know how to show your readers where your material came from. You may have already learned a documentation system in a previous writing class, but because today's researchers and scholars use a number of different documentation styles, it's important that you know which style is appropriate for your current essay. In some cases, your instructors (or the audience for whom you are writing) will designate a particular style; at other times, the choice will be yours.

In this chapter, we will look at two widely used systems—MLA style and APA style—and also briefly review use of the traditional footnote/bibliography format.

MLA Style

Most instructors in the humanities assign the documentation form prescribed by the Modern Language Association of America (MLA). Since 1984, the MLA has recommended a form of documentation that no longer uses traditional footnotes or endnotes to show references.* The current form calls for *parenthetical documentation*, most often consisting of the author's last name and the appropriate page number(s) in parentheses immediately following the source material in your paper. At the end of your discussion, readers may find complete bibliographic information for each source on a Works Cited page, a list of all the sources in your essay.

MLA Citations in Your Essay

Here are some guidelines for using the MLA parenthetical reference form within your paper.

1. If you use a source by one author, place the author's name and page number after the quoted, paraphrased, or summarized material. Note that the parentheses go *before* the end punctuation, and there is no punctuation between the author's name and the page number. (Use the author's name and omit the page reference when citing a complete work or a one-page work.)

   Example   Although pop art often resembles the comic strip, it owes a debt to such painters as Magritte, Matisse, and de Kooning (Rose 184).

2. If you use a source by one author and give credit to that author by name in your paper, you need only give the page number in the parentheses.

   Example   According to art critic Barbara Rose, pop art owes a large debt to such painters as Magritte, Matisse, and de Kooning (184).

3. If you are directly quoting material that extends to more than four print lines, indent the material one inch from the left margin, double-space, and do not

---

*If you wish a more detailed description of the current MLA form, ask your local bookstore or library for the *MLA Handbook for Writers of Research Papers*, 7th ed. (New York: MLA, 2009) and also the *MLA Style Manual and Guide to Scholarly Publishing*, 3rd ed. (New York: MLA, 2008). The most up-to-date documentation information may be found on the MLA Web site.

use quotation marks. Do not change the right margin. Note that in this case, the parentheses appear *after* the punctuation that ends the quoted material.

Example   In addition to causing tragedy for others, Crane's characters who are motivated by a desire to appear heroic to their peers may also cause themselves serious trouble. For example, Collins, another Civil War private, almost causes his own death because of his vain desire to act bravely in front of his fellow Union soldiers. (Hall 16)

4. If you are citing more than one work by the same author, include a short title in the parentheses.

Example   Within fifty years, the Inca and Aztec civilizations were defeated and overthrown by outside invaders (Thomas, *Lost Cultures* 198).

5. If you are citing a work by two or three authors, use all last names and the page number.

Examples   Prisons today are overcrowded to the point of emergency; conditions could not be worse, and the state budget for prison reforms is at an all-time low (Smith and Jones 72).

Human infants grow quickly, with most babies doubling their birth weight in the first six months of life and tripling their weight by their first birthday (Pantell, Fries, and Vickery 52).

6. For more than three authors, use all the last names or use the last name of the first author plus "et al." (Latin for "and others") and the page number. There is no comma after the author's name.

Example   Casualties of World War II during 1940-45 amounted to more than twenty-five million soldiers and civilians (Blum et al. 779).

7. If you cite a work that has no named author, use the work's title and the page number.

Example   Each year 350,000 Americans will die of a heart attack before reaching a hospital ("First Aid for Heart Attacks" 88).

8. If the work you are citing appears in a series, include the volume and page number with the author's name.

Example   On August 28, 1963, King delivered his "I Have a Dream" address to more than 200,000 civil rights supporters in Washington, DC, a speech that added momentum to the passage of the 1964 Civil Rights Act (Lopez 1: 270).

9. If your source is an electronic document, treat it as you would a print source. If you are citing an entire work from an electronic source that has no page, paragraph, or screen numbers, it is preferable to use the name of the author or editor in the text, rather than in a parenthetical reference. If the author's or editor's name is unavailable, use the work's title (shortened or in full).

Example   Cannon College Economics Professor John Thompson argues a different view of the Chinese role in Indonesia's economy.

Some electronic documents include paragraph or screen numbers. When citing these documents, include the appropriate number, preceded by "par." or "pars." for paragraph(s), or "screen." If the paragraphs are not numbered in the original source, however, do not impose your own numbering system.

Example   The Chinese in Indonesia account for only 4% of the population but control 70% of the economy (Thompson, par. 6).

10. If the material you are citing contains a passage quoted from another source, indicate your source for the quotation in the parentheses.

Example   According to George Orwell, "Good writing is like a window-pane" (qtd. in Murray 142).

11. If the work you are citing is a nonprint source with no reference markers, such as an interview, lecture, television show, film, or performance, include in the text the name of the person or the title (e.g., *60 Minutes*) that begins the corresponding entry in the Works Cited list.

Example   In a March 12, 2012, telephone interview, Kate Hall, Chair of the Chipeta Preservation Association, expressed her satisfaction with the progress being made in the negotiations for rebuilding the Red Feather Cafe.

Compiling a Works Cited List: MLA Style

If you are using the MLA format, at the end of your essay do include a Works Cited page—a formal listing of the sources you used in your essay. (If you wish to show all the sources you consulted, but did not cite, add a Works Consulted page.) Arrange the entries alphabetically by the authors' last names; if no name is given, alphabetize the source by the first important word of its title. Double-space each entry, and double-space between entries. If an entry takes more than one line, indent the subsequent lines one-half inch. MLA guidelines indicate one space following end punctuation marks.

Sample Entries: MLA Style*

Here are some sample entries to help you prepare a Works Cited page according to the MLA guidelines. Please note that MLA style recommends using shortened forms of publishers' names and omitting business descriptions, such as Inc., Co., Press, or House.

- For publishers' names that include the name of one person:

    Alfred A. Knopf becomes **Knopf**   **John Wiley** becomes **Wiley**

- For publishers' names that include the name of more than one person:

    Harper and Row becomes **Harper**   **Houghton Mifflin** becomes **Houghton**

- To cite a university press, use "U" and "P" appropriately:

    Oxford UP for **Oxford University Press**
    U of Illinois P for **University of Illinois Press**

---

*To conserve the number of pages in this chapter, sample entries are shown single-spaced. Double-space the entries in your essay.

- For publishers' names that include articles, business abbreviations, and descriptive words:

The Denali Press becomes **Denali**   **Stemmer House Publishers, Inc.** becomes **Stemmer**

Print titles of books and journals should be italicized; handwritten titles should be underlined. The titles of articles, essays, and chapters should be enclosed in quotation marks. Capitalize the first word, last word, and all important words in a title or subtitle. Do not capitalize the following parts of speech (unless they appear as the first or last word):

articles ("a," "an," "the," as in "Crossing the Bar")

prepositions (e.g., "across," "behind," "at," "of," "up," "down," as in "The Jilting of Granny Weatherall")

coordinating conjunctions ("and," "but," "for," "nor," "or," "so," "yet," as in *Romeo and Juliet*)

the "to" in infinitives ("A Good Man Is Hard to Find")

Books (Print)

- **A book with one author**

    Davis, Bertram H. *A Proof of Eminence: The Life of Sir John Hawkins*. Bloomington: Indiana UP, 1973. Print.

- **Two books by the same author**

    Davis, Bertram H. *A Proof of Eminence: The Life of Sir John Hawkins*. Bloomington: Indiana UP, 1973. Print.

    ---. *Thomas Percy: A Scholar-Cleric in the Age of Johnson*. Philadelphia: U of Pennsylvania P, 1989. Print.

    Include the author's name in only the first entry. In each subsequent entry, type three hyphens followed by a period. The three hyphens stand for exactly the same name as in the preceding entry. The hyphens do not represent any role other than author (for example, a comma and "ed." are added after the hyphens to indicate the role as editor). Such a label (e.g., "comp.," "ed.," or "trans.") does not affect the order in which the entries appear. For works listed under the same name, alphabetize them by title.

- **A book with two or three authors**

    McDonough, James Lee, and Thomas L. Connelly. *Five Tragic Hours: The Battle of Franklin*. Knoxville: U of Tennessee P, 1983. Print.

    Note that only the name of the first author is inverted.

- **A book with more than three authors**

    Guerin, Wilfred L., et al. *A Handbook of Critical Approaches to Literature*. 5th ed. New York: Oxford UP, 2004. Print.

Guerin, Wilfred L., Earle Labor, Lee Morgan, Jeanne C. Reesman, and John R. Willingham. *A Handbook of Critical Approaches to Literature*. 5th ed. New York: Oxford UP, 2004. Print.

You may use "et al." (meaning "and others") for the other names, or you may give all names in full in the order they appear on the book's title page.

- **A book with author and editor**

 Chaucer, Geoffrey. *The Tales of Canterbury*. Ed. Robert Pratt. Boston: Houghton, 1974. Print.

- **A book with corporate authorship**

 National Fire Safety Council. *Stopping Arson before It Starts*. Washington: Edmondson, 1992. Print.

 Omit any initial article ("A," "An," "The") in the name of a corporate author, and do not abbreviate its name.

- **A book with an editor**

 Knappman, Edward W., ed. *Great American Trials: From Salem Witchcraft to Rodney King*. Detroit: Visible Ink, 1994. Print.

- **A selection or chapter from an anthology or a collection with an editor**

 O'Connor, Flannery. "A Good Man Is Hard to Find." *Literature: Reading, Reacting, Writing*. Ed. Laurie G. Kirszner and Stephen R. Mandell. 8th ed. Boston: Wadsworth-Cengage, 2013. 405-15. Print.

 Following the date of publication and period, include the page numbers on which the work appears.

- **One volume of a multivolume work**

 Delaney, John J., ed. *Encyclopedia of Saints*. Vol. 4. New York: Doubleday, 1998. Print.

- **A work in more than one volume**

 Piepkorn, Arthur C. *Profiles in Belief: The Religious Bodies of the United States and Canada*. 2 vols. New York: Harper, 1976-78. Print.

 If the volumes were published over a period of years, give the inclusive dates after the publisher's name.

- **A work in a series**

 Vance, John A. *Joseph and Thomas Warton*. Ed. Sarah Smith. Boston: Twayne-Hall, 1983. Print. Twayne English Authors Ser. 380.

 After the medium of publication, include the series name and the series number (if any) followed by a period.

- **A translation**

 Zamora, Martha. *Frida Kahlo: The Brush of Anguish*. Trans. Marilyn Sode Smith. San Francisco: Chronicle, 1990. Print.

- **A reprint**

 Thaxter, Celia. *Among the Isles of Shoals*. 1873. Ed. Leslie Dunn. Hampton: Heritage, 1978. Print.

Note that the previous citation presents two dates: the date of original publication (1873) and the date of the reprinted work (1978).

- **An introduction, preface, foreword, or afterword**

    Soloman, Barbara H. Introduction. *Herland*. By Charlotte Perkins Gilman. New
        York: Penguin, 1992. xi-xxxi. Print.

    Begin the citation with the name of the writer of the section you are citing; then identify the section but do not italicize or use quotation marks around the word. Next, give the name of the book and the name of its author, preceded by the word "By" and followed by a period.

Periodicals (Magazines, Journals, Newspapers)

MLA guidelines stipulate that you should omit any introductory article in the title of an English-language magazine (*New Republic* rather than *The New Republic*) or scholarly journal (*Kenyon Review* rather than *The Kenyon Review*). In citing an English-language newspaper, give the name as it appears on the masthead, but omit any introductory article (*New York Times* rather than *The New York Times*; *Washington Post* rather than *The Washington Post*).

Scholarly and professional journals require volume and issue numbers; magazines and newspapers for general readers do not.

If an article is not printed on consecutive pages (for example, if the article begins on page 51, runs through page 55, resumes on page 112, and concludes on page 113), use the first page number and a plus sign with no space between them.

Except for May, June, and July, the months of the year are abbreviated. Use the first three letters for all other months (e.g., Jan., Feb., Mar.) except September (Sept.).

- **A signed article in a magazine published every week or every two weeks**

    Klein, Joe. "Ten Is Enough." *Time* 2 Apr. 2012: 20. Print.

    Note that the magazine title is not followed by a period.

- **An unsigned article in a magazine published every week or every two weeks**

    "Exit Ramp Poses Difficulty for Local Residents." *East Hamilton Weekly* 16 Mar.
        2009: 42-44. Print.

- **An article in a magazine published every month or every two months**

    Edwards, Owen. "Courage in Greensboro." *Smithsonian* Feb. 2010: 28-29. Print.

    To cite this article from an electronic source, refer to "An article in an online monthly magazine" and "An article in a periodical publication in an online database" later in this section.

- **A review in a magazine published every month or every two months**

    Rodwan, John. "The Great Migration." Rev. of *The Warmth of Other Suns*, by Isa-
        bel Wilkerson. *American Interest* Sept./Oct. 2011: 95-99. Print.

- **A signed article in a scholarly journal**

    Webb, Allen. "Digital Texts and the New Literacies." *English Journal* 97.1 (2007):
        83-88. Print.

Note that the journal title is not followed by a period. One space after the title of a scholarly journal, include the volume and issue numbers separated by a period. The year but not the month of publication is placed inside parentheses.

- **A signed article in a newspaper**

  Sohn, Pam. "City, County Burning Ban Begins Friday." *Chattanooga Times Free Press* 27 Apr. 2009: B1+. Print.

  Brooks, Jennifer. "Belmont to Stop Selling Bottled Water at School." *Tennessean* [Nashville] 22 Apr. 2009: 1B+. Print.

  Note that the newspaper title is not followed by a period. When it is not a part of the newspaper's title, add the city name in brackets after the title. Omit any introductory article (*Chattanooga Times Free Press* instead of *The Chattanooga Times Free Press*; *Miami Herald* instead of *The Miami Herald*). Note that section designation and page number are often combined (B1 or 1B); record the page numbers exactly as they appear.

- **An unsigned article in a newspaper**

  "Workforce Center Offers Youth Activities." *Denver Post* 28 Mar. 2012: B1. Print.

- **A signed editorial in a newspaper**

  Ball, George. "We Can't Spring Forward Fast Enough to Catch Nature." Editorial. *Atlanta Journal-Constitution* 15 Apr. 2009: A11. Print.

- **An unsigned editorial in a newspaper**

  "Environmental Rules at Risk." Editorial. *Chattanooga Times Free Press* 30 Apr. 2009: B6. Print.

- **A letter to the newspaper**

  Byrd, Charles. Letter. *Denver Gazette* 10 Jan. 2012: A10. Print.

Encyclopedias, Pamphlets, Dissertations

- **A signed article in an encyclopedia (full reference)**

  Collins, Dean R. "Light Amplifier." *McGraw-Hill Encyclopedia of Science and Technology*. Ed. Justin Thyme. 3 vols. Boston: McGraw, 1997. Print.

  Use full publication information for reference works, such as encyclopedias and dictionaries, unless they are familiar and often revised. Volume and page numbers are not needed if the information is in alphabetical order.

- **An unsigned article in a well-known encyclopedia**

  "Sailfish." *Encyclopedia Britannica*. 15th ed. 2010. Print.

- **A pamphlet**

  Young, Leslie. *Baby Care Essentials for the New Mother*. Austin: Hall, 2012. Print.

  Atlanta Builders Association. *Have Confidence in Your Builder*. Atlanta: Brown, 2009. Print.

- **A government document**

  United States. National Institute on Drug Abuse. *Drug Abuse Prevention*. Washington: GPO, 2008. Print.

  Many documents issued by the U.S. government are published by the Government Printing Office (GPO) in Washington, DC.

- **An unpublished dissertation or thesis**

  Harmon, Gail A. "Poor Writing Skills at the College Level: A Program for Correction." Diss. U of Colorado, 2012. Print.

Films, Television, Radio, Performances, Recordings, Digital Files

- **A film**

  Frida. Dir. Julie Taymor. Perf. Salma Hayek and Alfred Molina. Miramax, 2002. Film.

  Begin with the title (italicized) followed by the director, the distributor, the year of release, and the medium (Film). You may also include other data, such as the star performers, writer, or producer.

  Taymor, Julie, dir. *Frida*. Perf. Salma Hayek and Alfred Molina. 2002. Miramax, 2003. DVD.

  If you are referring to the contribution of a particular individual, such as the director, writer, actor, or composer, begin with that person's name. Cite a videocassette, DVD, or laser disc as a film but also include its distributor, its distribution date, and its medium.

- **A television or radio show**

  Antiques Roadshow. PBS. WGBH, Boston, 28 May 2012. Television.

  Conan, Neal, narr. "The 'Lost Magic' of the Irish Pub." *Talk of the Nation*. Natl. Public Radio. WSMC, Collegedale, 16 Mar. 2009. Radio.

  Dugan, David, dir. "Lord of the Ants." Narr. Harrison Ford. *NOVA*. PBS. WTCI, Chattanooga, 9 June 2009. Television.

  "The One with the Late Thanksgiving." By Shana Goldberg-Meehan. Dir. Gary Halvorson. Perf. Jennifer Aniston, Courteney Cox, Lisa Kudrow, Matt LeBlanc, Matthew Perry, and David Schwimmer. *Friends*. Fox. WASK, Boulder, 4 Apr. 2012. Television.

  If you are referring to a particular episode or person associated with the show, cite that name first, before the show's name.

- **Performances (plays, concerts, ballets, operas)**

  Messiah. By George Frideric Handel. Cond. Laurie Redmer Minner. Perf. Julie Penner, Martha Boutwell, Michael Kull, and Brett Hyberger. Collegedale Church of Seventh-day Adventists, Collegedale. 1 Apr. 2009. Performance.

  Cardillo, Ken, cond. "Rhapsody in Blue." By George Gershwin. Perf. Beth Douglass. Chattanooga Symphony Orch. Tivoli Theatre, Chattanooga. 18 May 2009. Performance.

If you are referring to the contribution of a particular person associated with the performance, put that person's name first.

- **A sound recording**

  Celtic Woman. *The Greatest Journey: Essential Collection*. Perf. Chloë Agnew, Órla Fallon, Lynn Hilary, Lisa Kelly, Méav Ni Mhaolchatha, Máiréad Nesbitt, and Alex Sharpe. Manhattan Records, 2008. CD.

  Zapen, Rebecca. "Shower #2." Rec. 2 Feb. 2004. *Japanese Bathhouse*. Bashert Records, 2005. CD.

  You may cite an entire sound recording (with its title italicized) or a specific song (with its title in quotation marks). Depending on what information you wish to emphasize, you may begin with the composer, conductor, or performers, followed by the title of the recording, artists other than the group or person listed first, the manufacturer, and the year of issue. Conclude with the medium (Audiocassette, CD [compact disc], or LP [long-playing record]), neither italicized nor in quotation marks.

- **Digital files**

  Gershwin, George. *Rhapsody in Blue*. ProMusic, 2001. MP3.

  Conclude the entry (e.g., article, sound recording, image) with the name of the digital format (e.g., MP3, PDF, JPEG). If the name of the medium is unknown, use "Digital file."

Letters, Lectures, and Speeches

- **An unpublished letter, archived**

  Steinbeck, John. Letter to Elizabeth R. Otis. 11 Nov. 1944. TS. Steinbeck Collection. Stanford U Lib., Stanford.

- **A letter received by the author**

  Hall, Sarah. Letter to the author. 10 May 2012. MS.

  For a letter, indicate the form by including "TS" for typescript (prepared by machine) or "MS" for manuscript (written by hand).

- **A lecture, speech, or other oral presentation**

  Dippity, Sarah N. "The Importance of Prewriting." CLASS Convention. President Hotel, Colorado Springs. 15 Feb. 2012. Keynote speech.

  Give the speaker's name and, if known, the title of the presentation (in quotation marks) followed by the meeting and the sponsoring organization (if appropriate), the location, the date, and the delivery format (e.g., Address, Lecture, Reading), neither italicized nor in quotation marks.

Interviews

- **A broadcast or published interview**

  Catanzaro, James L. Interview by Ray Bertani. *Around the Scenic City*. PBS. WTCI, Chattanooga. 28 Mar. 2009. Television.

Hewlett, F. D. "Expansion along the River." Interview by Tim Dills. *Chattanooga Times Free Press* 15 Feb. 2009: C12. Print.

Cite the person interviewed first and the title of the interview, if any. Use the word "Interview" (neither italicized nor in quotation marks) if the interview has no title. The interviewer's name may be added if relevant. Conclude with the publication or broadcast information and medium of publication.

- **A personal interview**

   Keen, Mary. Personal interview. 11 Jan. 2012.

   Payne, Linda. Telephone interview. 13 Apr. 2012.

   Give the name of the person interviewed, the kind of interview, and the date.

Visual Arts (Paintings, Sculptures, Photographs)

Green, Jon. *Alaskan Landscape*. 1972. Oil on canvas. Indianapolis Museum of Art, Indianapolis.

State the artist's name, the name of the work, and its date of completion (use N.d. if the year is unknown). Indicate the medium of composition (e.g., watercolor, photograph, marble) and identify both the institution (or private collection) that houses the work and the city in which it is located.

Advertisements

Nissan Maxima. Advertisement. *Sports Illustrated* 5 Sept. 2011: 41. Print.

Southwest Airlines. Advertisement. WRPQ. 13 Jan. 2012. Television.

Electronic Sources: MLA Style

The purpose of a citation for an electronic source is the same as that for printed matter: identification of the source and the best way to locate it. All citations basically name the author and the work and identify publication information. Citations for various types of electronic sources, however, must also include different kinds of additional information to help researchers locate the sources in the easiest way.

It's important to remember, too, that forms of electronic sources continue to change rapidly. As technology expands, new ways of documenting electronic sources must also be created. The problem is further complicated by the fact that some sources will not supply all the information you might like to include in your citation. In these cases, you simply have to do the best you can by citing what is available.

The guidelines and sample entries that follow are designed merely as an introduction to citing electronic sources according to MLA style. If you need additional help citing other kinds of electronic sources, consult the most up-to-the-minute documentation guide available, such as the current *MLA Handbook for Writers of Research Papers*. See the MLA Web site for more information.

Before looking at the sample citations given here, you should be familiar with the following information regarding dates, addresses, and reference markers in online sources.

Use of multiple dates. Because online sources may change or be revised, a citation may contain more than one date. For a document that appeared previously in print form, use the original date. For a Web-only document, use the date of its electronic publication. If no date is given, use "n.d." Your entry should also include a "date of access," indicating the day you found the particular source.

Use of network addresses. The *MLA Handbook* no longer requires the inclusion of a URL (uniform resource locator) in a Works Cited entry. But MLA guidelines continue to encourage that a URL be included when the reader probably cannot locate the source without it. If you choose to include the URL, place it immediately following the date of access, a period, and a space. Enclose the URL in angle brackets and conclude with a period. If you must divide a URL at the end of a line, break it only after a slash mark. Do not use a hyphen at the break as this will distort the address. URLs are often long and easy to misread, so take extra time to ensure that you are copying them correctly.

Important note: Many online databases and some online library catalogs now include a persistent link or URL to their records; do use this link in your citations for online works.

Use of reference markers. Unfortunately, many online sources do not use markers such as page or paragraph numbers. If such information is available to you, include it in your citations by all means; if it does not exist, readers must fend for themselves when accessing your sources. (Some readers might locate particular information in a document by using the "Find" tool in their computer program, but this option is not always available or useful.)

Nonperiodical Publications

Some works on the Web are classified as "nonperiodical publications" because they are not released on a regular schedule (i.e., weekly or monthly). An entry for a nonperiodical publication includes the following information, *if available*: name of the author, editor, or compiler; title of the work; title of the Web site (italicized) if distinct from the title of the work; version or edition number; publisher or sponsor of the Web site; date of publication; medium of publication; and date of access.

> Cohen, Elizabeth. "Five Ways to Avoid Germs While Traveling." *CNN.com*. Cable News Network, 27 Nov. 2008. Web. 14 Mar. 2012.
>
> "San Francisco, California." Map. *Google Maps*. Google, 5 Apr. 2012. Web. 5 Apr. 2012.
>
> Neary, Lynn. "Did Shakespeare Want to Suppress His Sonnets?" *Morning Edition*. Nat'l. Public Radio, 20 May 2009. Web. 22 May 2009.
>
> Parker, Deborah, gen. ed. *The World of Dante*. Inst. for Advanced Technology in the Humanities, U of Virginia, n.d. Web. 7 May 2012.

If a Web site indicates no date of publication, include "n.d." (neither italicized nor in quotation marks) where the date of publication would ordinarily appear.

Also within this group are Web sites sponsored by newspapers and magazines (discussed in the following section), which can post updated revisions after the original print version as well as reporters' blogs written only for the Web site.

Articles in Online Periodicals (Magazines and Newspapers)

Guidelines for citing online magazines and newspapers are based on the guidelines for citing their print counterparts. Begin with the author's name; if no author is given, begin with the title of the article (in quotation marks) and continue with the name of the periodical (italicized). At this point, the guidelines vary from those for the print version. After the name of the periodical, provide the sponsor of the publication, date of publication, medium of publication (Web), and date of access. Note that page numbers are not included in citations for online magazines and newspapers.

- **An article in an online monthly magazine**

  Edwards, Owen. "Courage in Greensboro." *Smithsonian*. Smithsonian Inst., Feb. 2010. Web. 30 Apr. 2012.

  After the publication (*Smithsonian*) include the publisher or sponsor of the site (Smithsonian Inst.) followed by a comma and the date of publication. Next is the medium of publication (Web) followed by the date of access. Note that periods follow each item—except after the publisher or sponsor of the site. Page numbers are not included.

- **A signed article in an online weekly magazine**

  Carter, Stephen. "My Lai Revisited." *Newsweek*. Newsweek, 19 Mar. 2012. Web. 7 May 2012.

  After the publication (*Newsweek*) include the publisher or sponsor of the site (Newsweek) followed by a comma and the date of publication. Next is the medium of publication (Web) followed by the date of access. Note that periods follow each item—except after the publisher or sponsor of the site. Page numbers are not included.

- **An unsigned article in an online weekly magazine**

  "10 Things You Didn't Know about Abraham Lincoln." *usnews.com*. U.S. News & World Report, 10 Feb. 2009. Web. 7 May 2012.

  Because this title begins with a numeral, the article should be alphabetized as if the numeral were spelled out ("Ten Things You Didn't Know about Abraham Lincoln").

- **An article in an online newspaper**

  Lubell, Sam. "Of the Sea and Air and Sky." *New York Times*. New York Times, 26 Nov. 2008. Web. 14 Mar. 2012.

  Spirrison, Brad. "Biotech 'Moon Shot' Starts in Classroom." *Chicago Sun-Times*. Sun-Times News Group, 27 Apr. 2009. Web. 13 Apr. 2012.

  After the publication (*New York Times* or *Chicago Sun-Times*) is the publisher or sponsor of the site (New York Times or Sun-Times News Group) followed by a comma and the date of publication. Next is the medium of publication (Web) followed by the date of access. Note that periods follow each item—except after the publisher or sponsor of the site. Page numbers are not included.

- **An editorial in an online newspaper**

  "As Fire Spread, So Did the Confusion." Editorial. *DenverPost.com*. Denver Post, 6 Apr. 2012. Web. 6 Apr. 2012.

- **A review in an online newspaper**

    Wisniewski, Mary. "Sundance's Girlfriend." Rev. of *Etta*, by Gerald Kolpan. *Chicago Sun-Times*. Sun-Times News Group, 5 Apr. 2009. Web. 23 Apr. 2012.

Articles in Online Scholarly Journals

As with online magazines and newspapers, the guidelines for citing online scholarly journals are based on the guidelines for citing their print counterparts. Begin with the author's name; if no author is given, begin with the title of the article (in quotation marks) and continue with the name of the periodical (italicized), the volume and issue numbers (if available), the year of publication (in parentheses) followed by a colon, and the page numbers followed by a period. At this point, the guidelines vary from those for the print version. Conclude the entry with the medium of publication (Web) and date of access.

    Fetters, Allison. "Intrigue in Shakespeare's Sonnets." *Midlothian Review* 28.3 (2009): 17-27. Web. 8 Apr. 2012.

    Shapiro, Stephen. "Intellectual Labor Power, Cultural Capital, and the Value of Prestige." *South Atlantic Quarterly* 108.2 (2009): 249-64. Web. 9 May 2012.

    Wright, Patrick. "Coleridge's Translucence: A Failed Transcendence." *RaVoN: Romanticism and Victorianism on the Net* 50 (2008): n. pag. Web. 7 May 2012.

If the page numbers are not indicated, you should include "n. pag." (neither italicized nor in quotation marks) to indicate "no pagination." Place "n. pag." where the page numbers would ordinarily appear.

Articles Accessed through an Online Database

To cite a source that you have found through one of your library's databases, begin by following the guidelines for citing their print counterparts. To this information, add the title of the database (italicized), medium of publication (Web), and date of access. For all periodical publications—magazines, newspapers, and scholarly journals—accessed through a database, provide the page numbers. If this information is not available, use "n. pag." (no pagination).

- **An article in a periodical publication in an online database**

    Edwards, Owen. "Courage in Greensboro." *Smithsonian* Feb. 2010: n. pag. *General OneFile*. Web. 30 Apr. 2012.

Compare this entry with other Edwards entries found at "An article in a magazine published every month or every two months" and at "An article in an online monthly magazine" earlier in this section. All three entries refer to the same *Smithsonian* article—one in print, one from the publication's Web site, and one accessed through an online database.

- **A review in a periodical publication in an online database**

    Johnston, Jill. "Self-Portrait." Rev. of *The Diary of Frida Kahlo: An Intimate Self-Portrait*, by Sarah M. Lowe. *Art in America* Mar. 1996: 31, 33. *General OneFile*. Web. 24 Mar. 2012.

Personal or Professional Web Sites

In citing Web sites, begin with the name of the person who created the site, if appropriate. If no name is given, begin with the title of the work (italicized if the work is independent; in quotation marks if the work is part of a larger work). For an untitled work, use a descriptive label such as "Advertisement," "Home page," "Online posting," or "Preface" (but do not italicize or enclose a description in quotation marks). Next, provide the title of the overall Web site (italicized), if it is different from the title of the work. Then, if appropriate, identify the version or edition. Continue with the Web site's publisher or sponsor; if this information is not available, use "N.p." (not italicized or enclosed in quotation marks). Then include the date of publication; if this information is not available, use "n.d." (not italicized nor enclosed in quotation marks). Conclude with the medium of publication (Web) and the date of access.

> "Humanities and Fine Arts." *Chattanooga State Technical Community College.* Chattanooga State Technical Community College, 25 Feb. 2009. Web. 9 May 2011.

> Williford, Sandra. Home page. *Teach Yourself to Paint Portraits*. N.p. 29 Sept. 2008. Web. 22 Apr. 2012.

Online Books

With the texts of countless books now available online, many students prefer to access copies in this format. To cite an online version of a book, begin the entry with the author's name, the book's name, and any publication information given in the source (city of publication, publisher, date). Then list the title of the Web site (italicized), the medium of publication, and the date of access.

> Dickens, Charles. *Oliver Twist*. London, 1897. *Electronic Text Center, U of Virginia.* Web. 22 May 2012.

> Goldsmith, Oliver. *The Vicar of Wakefield*. 1766. Google Book Search. Web. 22 May 2012.

Nonperiodical Publications on CD-ROM, Diskette, or Magnetic Tape

Nonperiodical electronic citations are similar to those for a print book, but also include the medium of publication (CD-ROM, Diskette, Magnetic tape). If you are citing a specific entry, article, essay, poem, or short story, enclose the title in quotation marks.

> "Acupuncture." *Oxford English Dictionary*. 2nd ed. Oxford: Oxford UP, 1992. CD-ROM.

> Ontag, Jennifer. "Aphra Behn's Spark." *Eighteenth-Century Drama*. Ed. Erica Lux. Knoxville: U of Tennessee P, 2009. CD-ROM.

E-Mail Communications

Begin with the writer's name, followed by the title from the subject line, "Message to" with recipient's name (or "Message to the author"), date of the message, and medium.

> Carroll, Jean. "Family Celebration." Message to Leti Carpenter. 12 Feb. 2012. E-mail.

Tweets

Begin with the sender's name, followed by the Twitter user name within parentheses, the message within quotation marks (without change in punctuation or capitalization), both the date and time (reflecting the reader's time zone), and the medium ("Tweet").

> Wheeler, Jane (JaneWriter). "Good luck with new book." 6 Apr. 2012, 3:01 p.m. Tweet.

APA Style

The American Psychological Association (APA) recommends a documentation style for research papers in the behavioral and social sciences.* Your instructors in psychology and sociology classes, for example, may prefer that you use the APA form when you write essays for them.

If you are using APA style in an academic paper, put your work's title, your name, the school's name, the instructor's name, the course name and section number, and the date on a title page, numbered as page 1. Writers following APA guidelines often include an *abstract* on page 2. An abstract is a short summary of your research; it may contain the following parts: a statement of the problem or your reason for undertaking this topic; your research methods; the results, findings, or product of this work; your conclusions; and, if appropriate, a statement of any larger implications. The essay itself begins on page 3. The APA style manual recommends inclusion of a shortened version (maximum 50 characters) of the essay's title as a running head in uppercase letters in the top left corner of all pages. Insert the words "Running head:" before the running head only on the title page. Some papers using APA style also include headings to identify major sections ("Methods," "Results") or key points in the discussion.

The APA style is similar to the MLA style in that it calls for parenthetical documentation within the essay itself, although the information cited in the parentheses differs slightly from that presented according to the MLA format. For example, you will note that in the APA style the date of publication follows the author's last name and precedes the page number in the parentheses. Instead of a Works Cited page, the APA style uses a References page at the end of the essay to list those sources cited in the text. In some instances, your instructor might prefer that you include a Bibliography page, which differs from the References page by listing all works that were consulted. Another important difference concerns capitalization of book and article titles in the reference list: in the MLA style, the first letter of each important word is capitalized, but in the APA style, only proper names, the first word of titles, and the first word appearing after a colon are capitalized.

---

*If you wish a more detailed description of the APA style, consult the *Publication Manual of the American Psychological Association*, 6th ed. (Washington, DC: American Psychological Association, 2010); your school's library probably has a copy. The most up-to-date documentation forms may be found on the APA Web site.

APA Citations in Your Essay

Here are some guidelines for using the APA parenthetical form within your paper:

1. APA style typically calls for an "author, publication year" method of citation, with the name and date inserted in the text at an appropriate place in the reference.

   Examples A recent study (Jones, 2012) found no discernible differences in the absentee rate of men and women students on the main campus.

   Jones (2012) contrasted the absentee rates of men and women students on the main campus but found no discernible differences.

2. When you are quoting directly, place the author's name, the publication year, and the page number in parentheses following the quoted material. Note that in APA style, you place commas between the items in the parentheses, and you do include the "p." and "pp." abbreviations for "page" and "pages" (these are omitted in MLA style).

   Example One crucial step in developing an anti-social personality may, in fact, be "the experience of being caught in some act and consequently being publicly labeled as a deviant" (Becker, 2008, p. 31).

3. If you use a print source by one author and give credit to that author by name within your paper, you need give only the date and the page number in parentheses. Note that the publication date follows directly after the name of the author.

   Example According to Green (2006), gang members from upper-class families are rarely convicted for their crimes and are "almost never labeled as delinquent" (p. 101).

4. If you are citing a work with more than two authors, but fewer than six, list all names in the first reference; in subsequent references, use only the first author's last name and "et al." (which means "and others"). For six or more authors, use only the last name of the first author followed by "et al." for all citations, including the first. Note the use of "&" instead of "and" within parentheses.

   Example *First reference:* After divorce, men's standard of living generally rises some 42%, whereas women's falls to approximately 27% of what it once was (Bird, Gordon, & Smith, 2012, p. 203).

   Subsequent references: Almost half of all the poor households in America today are headed by single women, most of whom are supporting a number of children (Bird et al., 1992, p. 285).

5. If you cite a work that has a corporate author, cite the group responsible for producing the work.

   Example In contrast, the State Highway Research Commission (2012) argues, "The return to the sixty-five-miles-an-hour speed limit on some of our state's highways has resulted in a decrease in traffic fatalities" (p. 3).

6. Private interviews, e-mail messages, and other personal communications should be referred to in your text but *not* in your reference list. Provide the initials and

last name of the communicator, the words "personal communication," and the date in your paper.

Example   Sierra Club leader C. L. Byrd confirmed that the fall trip to Cinque Terre would be September 15, 2012 (personal communication, January 18, 2012).

Compiling a Reference List: APA Style

If you are using the APA style, at the end of your essay you should include a page labeled References—a formal listing of the sources you cited in your essay. Arrange the entries alphabetically by the authors' last names; use initials for the authors' first and middle names. All authors' names are inverted (Forst, M. L, & Hall, S. L.). Note that with two to seven authors, an ampersand (&) appears before the last author. If a work has more than seven authors, APA lists the first six followed by an ellipsis and the last author's name, omitting the customary ampersand (&). If there are two or more works by one author, list them chronologically, beginning with the earliest publication date. If an author published two or more works in the same year, the first reference alphabetically is designated "a," the second "b," and so on (Feinstein 2012a; Feinstein 2012b). Double-space each entry and between each one. Lines subsequent to the first are indented one-half inch.

Remember in APA style, you italicize book and journal titles, volume numbers, and their associated punctuation, but you do not put the names of articles in quotation marks. Although you do capitalize the major words in the titles of magazines, newspapers, and journals, you do not capitalize any words in the titles of books or articles except the first word in each title, the first word after a colon or dash, and all proper names.

In a reference entry that includes the publisher, APA requires the publisher's location—city and state for those in the United States (using the official two-letter U.S. Postal Service abbreviation), and city and country for those outside the United States. If the publisher is a university press whose name includes the state, don't repeat the state in the publisher location. Use the full names of publishers, including the words "Books" and "Press," but omit terms such as "Publishers," "Co.," or "Inc."

Sample Entries: APA Style

Please note: Although the *Publication Manual of the American Psychological Association* (sixth edition) provides many examples illustrating APA format for references, it does not offer specific guidance for some sources commonly used today. APA advises writers to choose the example most like the source in question and to follow that format, offering as much useful information as possible. Checking the APA style Web site may also prove helpful.

Books (Print)

- **A book with one author**

    Isaacson, W. (2007). *Einstein: His life and universe*. New York, NY: Simon & Schuster.

- **A book with two authors**

  Forst, M. L., & Blomquist, M. (1991). *Missing children: Rhetoric and reality*. New York, NY: Lexington Books.

- **Books by one author published in the same year**

  Hall, S. L. (2012a). *Attention deficit disorder*. Denver, CO: Bald Mountain Press.

  Hall, S. L. (2012b). *Taming your adolescent*. Detroit, MI: Morrison Books.

- **A book with an editor**

  Banks, A. S. (Ed.). (1988). *Political handbook of the world*. Binghamton, NY: CSA.

- **A chapter from a book with an editor**

  Newcomb, T. M. (1958). Attitude development as a function of reference groups: The Bennington study. In E. Maccoby, T. M. Newcomb, & E. L. Hartley (Eds.), *Readings in social psychology* (pp. 10–12). New York, NY: Holt, Rinehart & Winston.

- **A book with a corporate author**

  Mentoring Group. (1997). *The new mentors and protégés: How to succeed with the new mentoring partnerships*. Grass Valley, CA: Author.

  This method indicates that the corporate author is also the publisher.

- **A reference book**

  Rothman, B. K. (Ed.). (1993). *Encyclopedia of childbearing: Critical perspectives*. Phoenix, AZ: Oryx Press.

  Remember that reference books are not cited in the body of the essay.

- **One volume in a multivolume work**

  Venegas, L. (Ed.). (2010). *The principles of animation: A beginner's guide* (Vol. 2). London, England: Neman & Hartham.

- **Several volumes in a multivolume work**

  Gregor, T. (Ed.). (2007). *Great thinkers throughout history* (Vols. 1–3). New York, NY: Seville.

- **A translation**

  Zamora, M. (1990). *Frida Kahlo: The brush of anguish* (M. S. Smith, Trans.). San Francisco, CA: Chronicle Books.

- **A reprint**

  Herrera, H. (2002). *Frida: A biography of Frida Kahlo*. New York, NY: Perennial-Harper. (Original work published 1983)

Articles (Print)

APA reference entries for articles in print periodicals (journals, magazines, newspapers, newsletters) follow a pattern similar to that used for books. The author is followed by the date of publication (in parentheses). Note that journals include only the year; magazines and newspapers include the complete date. Do not abbreviate names of months.

Next is the article's title, capitalizing the first word and any proper nouns. Then provide the periodical's name and volume number, italicized. If each issue of the journal begins on page one, place the issue number in parentheses immediately following the volume number. Use "p." or "pp." with page numbers in newspapers but not in magazines or journals. Unlike MLA style, numbers are not clipped in APA style (e.g., APA prefers 360–378, while MLA favors 360–78).

- **An article in a journal**

    Morrison, G. B., & Byers, B. D. (2007). Criminal justice career fairs: Addressing recruiting challenges through practitioner and academic collaboration. *Law Enforcement Journal, 7*(5), 107–124.

    Because this journal begins each issue on page one, the issue number in parentheses follows immediately after the volume number.

- **A signed article in a magazine**

    Halverson, N. (2009, May). Home gardening: Therapy for the heart and mind. *Today's Gardener, 25*(5), 22–31.

- **An unsigned article in a magazine**

    Reduce the risk of breast cancer. (2011, September 1). *Wellness Magazine, 37,* 14–17.

- **A signed article in a newspaper**

    Gascay, G. (2009, June 19). Strong winds, hail damage crops in three counties. *The Athens Eagle*, p. C1.

    Note the inclusion of the newspaper's entire title as it appears on the masthead. For newspaper articles, page numbers should be preceded by "p." or "pp."

- **An unsigned article in a newspaper**

    City unveils plans for tourist information center. (2009, May 21). *The Central Courier*, pp. D2, D10–D11.

    If an article is not printed on consecutive pages (for example, if the article begins on page D2, continues on page D10, and concludes on page D11), provide all page numbers separated by a comma and a space.

- **An unsigned editorial**

    Editorial: "Where there's smoke . . ." [Editorial]. (2011, June 2). *Montana Gazette*, pp. B2, B5.

Reference Books, Reports, Dissertations

- **An unsigned article in encyclopedia or reference book**

    Bullying. (2012). In A. Young (Ed.), *Encyclopedia of clinical psychology*. (2nd ed., Vol. 1, pp. 66–69). London, England: Society of Clinical Psychology.

- **A corporate or government authored report or document**

    National Weather Service. (2000). *Public fire danger statement* (NWS Publication No. 03-319). Washington, DC: U.S. Government Printing Office.

- **An unpublished dissertation or thesis**

  > Wilson, L. M. (2010). *Professional growth and job satisfaction in early career special education teachers* (Unpublished doctoral dissertation). Arizona State University, Phoenix.

Audio-Visual Media (Films, Television, Radio, Recordings, Artwork)

List the artist or contributor in the author position, using a descriptive word in parentheses to identify the particular role, such as writer or director. Use brackets to enclose the medium, such as motion picture, DVD, or CD.

- **A film**

  > Panem, P. S. (Producer), & Lupin, R. J. (Director). (2007). *The red wolf* [Motion picture]. United States: Spotlight Pictures.

- **An episode from a television or radio series**

  > Davies, R. (Writer), & Harper, G. (Director). (2006). Doomsday [Television series episode]. In P. Collinson (Producer), *Doctor Who*. Westminster, England: British Broadcasting.

  To cite a particular episode, list the writer and director in the author position, but put the producer in the editor position.

- **A music recording**

  > Heap, I. (2005). Hide and seek. On *Speak for yourself* [CD]. New York, NY: White Rabbit Recordings.

  Place the medium of recording, such as CD or cassette, in brackets following the title of the album.

- **An artwork**

  > Carpenter, L. (Artist). (1910). *Country brook* [Watercolor]. Texarkana, TX: Hazel Collection.

  Place the medium (oil, etching, photograph, etc.) in brackets, and identify the location of the artwork (city, state, country, as appropriate, and the name of the museum, private collection, gallery, etc.).

Letters, Lectures, Speeches, and Archived Interviews

- **Letter, private collection**

  > Merrill, Alison. (2012, February 2). [Letter to Jane Wheeler]. Copy in possession of Jane Wheeler.

- **An unpublished letter, archived**

  > Shulz, E. M. (1983–1994). Correspondence. Elizabeth M. Shulz Papers. Green University Archives, Silverton, VT.

- **A speech or presentation**

  > Harsin, P. J. (2012, May). *Red Feather Lakes living*. Paper presented at the meeting of Northern Colorado Realtors, Loveland, CO.

- **Unpublished papers, lectures**

  Ullman, D. (1999). *Taking action on homelessness and hunger lecture notes*. Daisy Ullman Memoirs (Box L 12). Archives of the Social Work Association, University of Oklahoma, Norman, OK.

- **An interview recorded, archived**

  Scott, J. M. (1972, November 1). Interview by K. J. Bolin [Tape recording]. Arts Oral History Project, Peabody Institution. Archives of European Art, Washington, DC.

Electronic Sources: APA Style

As with print versions of periodicals, APA guidelines for citing electronic versions of periodicals differ considerably from MLA methods. For all electronic sources, the APA prefers to include the DOI (digital object identifier) if it is available. Publishers who participate in the DOI system assign each publication a unique alphanumeric sequence intended to provide a persistent link to its location on the Internet. To help you recognize a DOI, understand that it begins with a "10" and is often placed on the first page of the electronic journal article, near the copyright notice.

If the DOI is available, include it in the citation at the location indicated in the following examples. Because the DOI is extremely long, try to copy and paste the DOI for accuracy. Note that a space does not follow the colon after "doi." If you use the DOI, no further retrieval information (such as the URL) is necessary to identify or locate the content.

If the DOI is not available, the APA prefers that you include the home page URL of the journal or of the book publisher. Before the URL, include "Retrieved from" and do not include angle brackets or conclude with a period (to avoid confusion that it is part of the URL). Break a URL only *before* a period or slash mark (but retain "http://" as a unit). Note that the location of this separation point differs from MLA guidelines, which call for a break after a slash mark.

For more about APA guidelines related to electronic citations, visit the APA Web site.

- **An electronic version of a print book**

  Isaacson, W. (2007). *Einstein: His life and universe* [XYZ Reader version]. Retrieved from http://ebookstore.sony.com

- **An electronic-only book**

  Stevens, K. (n.d.). *The dreamer and the beast*. Retrieved from http://www .onlineoriginals.com/

  Because no publication date is provided for this online book, "n.d." appears in parentheses where the year of publication would appear if it were available.

- **A signed entry in an online reference work**

  Brownlee, K. (2007). Civil disobedience. In E. N. Zalta (Ed.), *The Stanford encyclopedia of philosophy* (Fall 2008 ed.). Retrieved from http://plato.stanford .edu/entries/civil-disobedience/

- **An article in an online journal with DOI**

  Kubzansky, L. D., Martin, L. T., & Buka, S. L. (2009). Early manifestations of person-
     ality and adult health: A life course perspective. *Health Psychology, 28,*
     364–372. doi:10.1037/a0014428

- **An article in an online journal without DOI**

  Lane, A. M., Thelwell, R., & Devonport, T. J. (2009). Emotional intelligence and
     mood states associated with optimal performance. *E-Journal of Applied
     Psychology, 5*(1), 67–73. Retrieved from http://ojs.lib.swin.edu.au/index
     .php/ejap/index

  Because no DOI has been assigned, the URL for the journal's home page is
  included. Each issue of the journal begins on page one, so the issue number is
  included in parentheses. No retrieval date is necessary.

- **A signed article in an online magazine**

  Clover, F. (2011, February). Media and the message. *Digital Gateway, 4*(2).
     Retrieved from http://digitalgatewaymagazine.com/

- **An unsigned article in an online magazine**

  Investigative journalism: gaining access and protecting identities. (2010, May).
     Journalism Undercover, 11(5). Retrieved from http://journalismundercover
     .com/jkkm1354/articleone/

- **Non-periodical Web pages/Web documents**

  Sayers, B. (2011, January 20). Today's Sayers files. [Web log post]. Retrieved from
     http://sayersfiles.com/homepage/2011/20/todays_sayers_files

- **An article in an online newspaper**

  Murray, S. (2009, July 17). Health bill advances in the House. *The Washington Post.*
     Retrieved from http://www.washingtonpost.com/

  To avoid complex URLs that might move or be modified over time, APA recommends providing the URL of the home page when the online version of the article is available by search.

- **A review of a book, retrieved online**

  Johnston, J. (1996, March). Self-portrait. [Review of the book *The diary of Frida
     Kahlo: An intimate self-portrait,* by S. M. Lowe]. *Art in America, 84,* 31, 33.
     Retrieved from http://www.artinamericamagazine.com/

Footnote and Bibliography Form

Most research papers today use a parenthetical documentation style, as illustrated in
the MLA and APA sections of this chapter. However, in the event you face a writing situation that calls for use of traditional footnotes and bibliography page, here is a brief
description of one version of that format. This section will also help you understand
the citation system of older documents you may be reading, especially those using Latin
abbreviations.

   If you are writing a paper using this format, each idea you borrow and each quotation
you include must be attributed to its author(s) in a footnote that appears at the bottom

of the appropriate page.* Number your footnotes consecutively throughout the essay (do not start over with "1" on each new page), and place the number in the text to the right of and slightly above the end of the passage, whether it is a direct quotation, a paraphrase, or a summary. Place the corresponding superscript number, indented one-half inch, before the note at the bottom of the page. Single-space each entry, and double-space after each footnote if more than one appears on the same page. Once you have provided a first full reference, subsequent footnotes for that source may include only the author's last name and page number. (See the examples that follow. Please note that today many word-processing programs include a function for formatting footnotes.)

You may notice the use of Latin abbreviations in the notes of some documents, such as "ibid." ("in the same place") and "op. cit." ("in the work cited"). In such documents, "ibid." indicates the same author's name, title, and publication information as in the preceding footnote; there will be a new page number only if the reference differs from the one in the previous footnote. Writers use "op. cit." with the author's name to substitute for the title in second and subsequent references.

In the Bibliography at the end of the document, sources are listed by author in alphabetical order (or by title if no author is given). The first lines are flush left; subsequent lines are indented a half-inch.

First footnote reference

[5]Garrison Keillor, *Leaving Home* (New York: Viking, 1987), 23.

Next footnote

[6]Keillor, 79.   or   [6]*Ibid.,* 79.

Later reference

[12]Keillor, 135.

Bibliographic entry

Keillor, Garrison. *Leaving Home.* New York: Viking, 1987.

Practicing What You've Learned

Collaborative Activity: Increase your understanding of documentation styles and practice your editing skills by exchanging your MLA Works Cited page (or APA Reference list or Bibliography page) with a classmate. Using the sample entries on the appropriate pages of this chapter, check the accuracy of the forms on the page. Circle any errors you see, but do not correct the problems. Use both the feedback you give and receive as encouragement to proofread your own documentation carefully several more times.

---

*Some documents use endnotes that appear in a list on a page immediately following the end of the essay, before the bibliography page.

Using Supplementary Notes

Sometimes when writers of research papers wish to give their readers additional information about their topic or about a particular piece of source material, they include *supplementary notes*. If you are using the MLA or APA format, these notes should be indicated by using a superscript number in your text (The study seemed incomplete at the time of its publication.[2]); the explanations appear on a page called "Notes" that precedes the Works Cited page (MLA) or "Footnotes" that follows the References page (APA). If you are using traditional footnote form, simply include the supplementary notes in your list of footnotes at the bottom of the page or in the list of endnotes following your essay's conclusion.

Supplementary notes can offer a wide variety of additional information.

Examples (MLA Style)

1. For a different interpretation of this imagery, see Spiller 63-67.

2. Simon and Brown have also contributed to this area of investigation. For a description of their results, see *Report on the Star Wars Project* 98-102.

3. It is important to note here that Brown's study followed Smith's by at least six months.

4. Later in his report Carducci himself contradicts his earlier evaluation by saying, "Our experiment was contaminated from the beginning" (319).

Use supplementary notes only when you think the additional information would be truly valuable to your readers. Obviously, information critical to your essay's points should go in the appropriate body paragraphs. (◆ See pages 429 and 440 for additional examples.)

Sample Student Essay Using MLA Style

Here is the result of Kira Anzai's research on the biographical events influencing the art of painter Frida Kahlo. To see the portrait that inspired Kira's essay, *The Two Fridas*, turn to page 490 in Chapter 17; another portrait mentioned in this essay, *Self-Portrait with Thorn Necklace and Hummingbird*, appears on page 397.

As you read this essay, evaluate its effectiveness: does Kira successfully support her thesis? Point out major strengths and any weaknesses you see. If you wanted more information on Kahlo's life and work, how might Kira's sources help you begin your search? Be aware that the paragraphs in Kira's essay have been numbered for easy reference during class discussion. Do *not* number the paragraphs in your own essay.

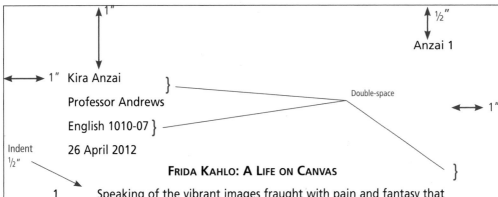

1"
Anzai 1 ½"

1" Kira Anzai

Professor Andrews

English 1010-07

Double-space

26 April 2012

Indent ½"

FRIDA KAHLO: A LIFE ON CANVAS

1   Speaking of the vibrant images fraught with pain and fantasy that filled her canvas, Frida Kahlo commented that "I paint my own reality" (qtd. in Herrera xi). Many viewers must wonder what sort of "reality" prompted the artist to paint pictures such as *The Two Fridas*, a double self-portrait in which her two selves—one in a snow-white dress, the other draped in colorful Mexican costume—sit connected by clasped hands, a blood-dripping artery, and mirrored expressions accentuated by distinctive dark eyebrows. An exploration of Frida Kahlo reveals that her art did indeed reflect her life, which was largely characterized by physical and emotional anguish. A tragic accident in her youth and a tumultuous marriage, mingled with deep personal and political ties to her native country, shaped the woman and work that continue to captivate viewers today.

Thesis: Kahlo's often-tragic life influenced her art

Essay Map: Accident, marriage, heritage

2   Born on July 6, 1907, Kahlo passed her childhood and adolescence on the outskirts of Mexico City. She would always identify herself as a daughter of the Mexican Revolution, which broke out in 1910 and exposed her to scenes of violent fighting in the streets near her home (Herrera 4). At age six, however, a severe bout with polio confined her indoors for nine months, leaving her socially isolated (14). The girlish Kahlo who appears in paintings created years later usually stands by herself, suggesting that the artist's "painted memories contain much truth about the past" (16). Loneliness would be a recurring theme throughout her life and art. Nevertheless, by the time Kahlo entered the

Early life in Mexico

1"

National Preparatory School in 1922, she was a mischievous extrovert aspiring to a future in medicine. Her study of anatomy lent accuracy to later paintings, including the detailed human heart in *The Two Fridas* (Tuchman 2). Beyond her intellectual pursuits, Kahlo delighted in practical joking and frequently targeted Diego Rivera, the famous muralist commissioned to paint the school auditorium. She teasingly nicknamed him Panzón ("fat belly") and entertained romantic notions in spite of their twenty-one-year age difference (Herrera 31-32).

Traumatic accident, lifelong pain

3   The desired liaison did not materialize, for Kahlo's life was altered by a tragic accident at age eighteen. On September 17, 1925, she and her boyfriend, Alejandro, hopped onto a wooden bus just before it was rammed by a trolley car. Alejandro recalled that the bus "burst into a thousand pieces," sending an iron handrail through Kahlo's abdomen; her "screaming was louder than the siren" of the arriving ambulance (qtd. in Herrera 48). The trauma broke her spine in three places, crushed her pelvis, and severely damaged her right leg and foot. Against all odds, Kahlo began a slow recovery, but the images of intense agony that characterized her art in ensuing years largely reflected her unending battle with physical pain. For the next three decades, she wore various plaster corsets to support her improperly healed spine and underwent taxing operations that provided temporary relief at best (Tuchman 2). Ironically, the accident that haunted Kahlo with thoughts of death was critical to rousing the artist inside her. During the months of her recuperation, she began painting portraits to pass the time, taking her first steps as an artist while still physically bedridden (Zamora 26-27).

Marriage to famous painter

4   After she regained mobility, financial difficulties prevented Kahlo's return to school, but an interest in leftist politics renewed her acquaintance with the highly political Diego Rivera in 1928 (Zamora 31). Kahlo sought the muralist's assessment of her paintings, and he

Anzai 3

instantly recognized her inborn talent. Rivera was equally drawn to the petite young woman—no longer a schoolgirl—whose "delicate face" was adorned by graceful black eyebrows he admirably compared to "the wings of a blackbird" (qtd. in Tuchman 3). In contrast, the heavyset Rivera was commonly described as having the features of a frog (Hardin 37). Despite these sharp contrasts, the mismatched couple struck up a courtship that led to their marriage on August 21, 1929. Rivera had a significant impact on his wife's artistic development. By observing his creation of historical murals, she "learned how to tell a story in paint," an ability that contributed to the frequently autobiographical nature of her later art (Tuchman 4).

5   After their wedding, Kahlo followed Rivera to the United States, where he accepted a series of commissions while she honed her portraiture and garnered public attention for her native Mexican attire. Bright blouses and skirts, stone bead necklaces, and upswept braids appeased Rivera's preference that she dress in the Tehuana Indian style and, more importantly, allowed Kahlo to openly celebrate her culture and nationalist sentiments (Baddeley 12-13). Most of the self-portraits she painted in subsequent decades, including her colorfully costumed self in *The Two Fridas*, capture this personal identification with Mexico. Despite the gratifying attention of the American press, the Riveras' time in the States was marred by tragedy when Kahlo suffered a miscarriage in 1932.[1] Her bloody and fantastical portrayal of the experience in the painting *Henry Ford Hospital* diverged from the portraits that typify her body of work up to that point. The loss of her child, accompanied by her mother's death the same year, marked a shift in Kahlo's subject matter. Elements of fantasy increasingly appeared in the paintings, which were "beginning to emphasize terror, suffering, wounds, and pain," both physical and psychological (Zamora 46).

> Identification with heritage

> Loss of child and mother

6 The return to Mexico in 1933 brought Kahlo some relief but did not restore her happiness, as her marriage felt the mounting pressure of her husband's infidelity. Although she had long tolerated Rivera's string of casual affairs, Kahlo's increasing anguish prompted her to move into her own apartment for several months (Zamora 46-47). Author Terri Hardin argues that Rivera's betrayal and the couple's ensuing separation freed her from convention and "removed the final impediments to her progress as an artist" whose vision was inimitable (49). Kahlo returned to Rivera in 1935, but their reconciliation left Kahlo far from comfortable. To cope with the duress of this situation, Kahlo channeled her feelings into her art (Zamora 50). The productive years that followed led to the inclusion of two paintings in a 1938 exhibit in Paris, where their shocking fantastical elements earned her praise as a Surrealist (56).[2] Fresh devastation replaced her confidence, however, when, shortly after her return from France, Rivera requested a divorce (62).

Tumultuous marriage, divorce, remarriage reflected in her art

7 The dissolution of their disintegrating marriage in 1939 coincided with the creation of emotionally charged paintings like *The Two Fridas*. Some critical interpretations of the double self-portrait conclude that it directly responded to the divorce, hence the depiction of the left-hand Kahlo wearing Rivera's favored Tehuana costume. She shares a severed artery with the opposing white-clad Kahlo, who displays a "broken" heart in her bisected chest; this second self stops the artery's blood flow with a clamp, suggesting that "the Frida independent of Rivera holds the means of self-rescue" (Hardin 68). *The Two Fridas*, in essence, conveys two sides of the artist's personality, a hallmark of additional self-portraits (captured on canvas and in her diary) that explore her distinct feminine and masculine identities. In *Self-Portrait with Cropped Hair*, completed the year after her divorce, Kahlo poses in a man's suit, as opposed to her

Anzai 5

typical Mexican dress and flower-bedecked braids. She is surrounded by long strands of sheared-off hair, a sign of despair and retaliation against Rivera (Johnston 33). *Self-Portrait with Thorn Necklace and Hummingbird*, painted in 1940, likewise expresses her woe through the symbolism of the dead bird hanging from her neck (Hardin 70-71). Without her husband, Kahlo felt an isolation reminiscent of her childhood and explained her profusion of self-portraits by stating simply, "I am all alone" (qtd. in Zamora 102). Regardless of their former troubles, Rivera was likewise plagued by separation from Kahlo, and they chose to remarry in 1940 (70). Kahlo expressed her renewed devotion to Rivera in the 1943 painting *Roots*, symbolically binding herself to the landscape where they built a home together (Herrera 312-14).

8   The last several years of Kahlo's life were disrupted by numerous operations as her health declined, but she continued to paint her signature self-portraits and fantastical scenes. In *The Dream* (1940), the skeleton over her canopied bed speaks to the psychological effects of her physical condition, while *The Wounded Deer* (1946) suggests her identification with a bleeding animal, as her head is fixed to a deer's arrow-pierced body (Hardin 70, 103). The pain that began in her youth now became unbearable, and Kahlo's reliance on stimulants and strong medication for relief revealed itself in her slightly frenetic brushwork (Tuchman 5). In 1953, her ailing lower right leg was amputated, but the restraints of an artificial limb and wheelchair did not prevent Kahlo from resolutely accompanying Rivera to leftist political demonstrations. Similarly, she had insisted upon attending her long-awaited one-person exhibition in Mexico City earlier that year despite serious illness. Kahlo was delivered to the gallery by ambulance and enjoyed the festive event from the comfort of a canopied bed (Hardin 108). She told attentive

Broken health and pain influence portraits

Anzai 6

reporters for *Time* magazine, "I am not sick. I am broken. But I am happy to be alive as long as I can paint" (qtd. in Zamora 126).

Conclusion: Shaped by pain and a beloved heritage, Kahlo's art continues to fascinate

9   Kahlo's artistic career was cut short by her death on July 13, 1954, when she was forty-seven years old, but over the course of three decades, she completed approximately two hundred paintings (Tuchman 1).[3] They have since fascinated a worldwide audience with their striking originality, which must be attributed to a life and artistic vision shaped by painful personal experiences and deep ties to Mexico. Kahlo consistently exhibited a concern with keeping her memory alive in people's minds, frequently beseeching her acquaintances, "Don't forget me!" (qtd. in Zamora 102). Her evocative images ensure that Frida Kahlo—the woman and the artist—will continue to be remembered by the legacy she left on canvas.

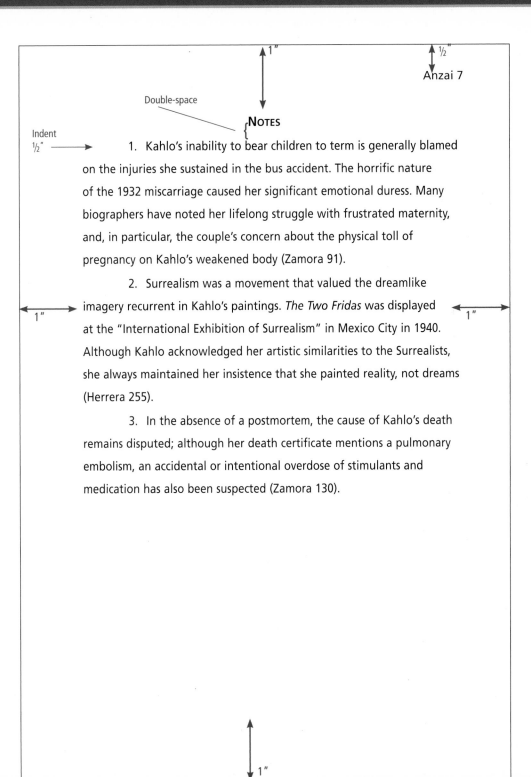

Anzai 7

Double-space

Indent
½"

NOTES

1. Kahlo's inability to bear children to term is generally blamed on the injuries she sustained in the bus accident. The horrific nature of the 1932 miscarriage caused her significant emotional duress. Many biographers have noted her lifelong struggle with frustrated maternity, and, in particular, the couple's concern about the physical toll of pregnancy on Kahlo's weakened body (Zamora 91).

2. Surrealism was a movement that valued the dreamlike imagery recurrent in Kahlo's paintings. *The Two Fridas* was displayed at the "International Exhibition of Surrealism" in Mexico City in 1940. Although Kahlo acknowledged her artistic similarities to the Surrealists, she always maintained her insistence that she painted reality, not dreams (Herrera 255).

3. In the absence of a postmortem, the cause of Kahlo's death remains disputed; although her death certificate mentions a pulmonary embolism, an accidental or intentional overdose of stimulants and medication has also been suspected (Zamora 130).

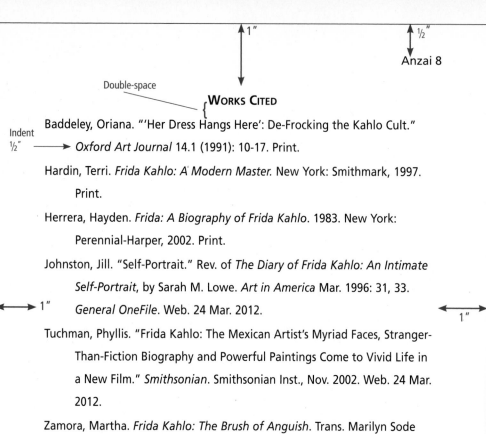

WORKS CITED

Baddeley, Oriana. "'Her Dress Hangs Here': De-Frocking the Kahlo Cult." *Oxford Art Journal* 14.1 (1991): 10-17. Print.

Hardin, Terri. *Frida Kahlo: A Modern Master.* New York: Smithmark, 1997. Print.

Herrera, Hayden. *Frida: A Biography of Frida Kahlo.* 1983. New York: Perennial-Harper, 2002. Print.

Johnston, Jill. "Self-Portrait." Rev. of *The Diary of Frida Kahlo: An Intimate Self-Portrait,* by Sarah M. Lowe. *Art in America* Mar. 1996: 31, 33. *General OneFile.* Web. 24 Mar. 2012.

Tuchman, Phyllis. "Frida Kahlo: The Mexican Artist's Myriad Faces, Stranger-Than-Fiction Biography and Powerful Paintings Come to Vivid Life in a New Film." *Smithsonian.* Smithsonian Inst., Nov. 2002. Web. 24 Mar. 2012.

Zamora, Martha. *Frida Kahlo: The Brush of Anguish.* Trans. Marilyn Sode Smith. San Francisco: Chronicle, 1990. Print.

Sample Student Essay Using APA Style

To illustrate the differences between MLA and APA documentation styles, here is the student essay from the previous pages rewritten to show the most current APA guidelines for in-text citations and a References page. This assignment also includes an abstract, which appears on page 2. To see the portrait that inspired Kira's essay, *The Two Fridas*, turn to page 490 in Chapter 17; another portrait mentioned in this essay, *Self-Portrait with Thorn Necklace and Hummingbird*, appears on page 397.

As you read this essay, evaluate its effectiveness: does Kira successfully support her thesis? Point out major strengths and any weaknesses you see. If you wanted more information on Kahlo's life and work, how might Kira's sources help you begin your search? Be aware that the paragraphs in Kira's essay have been numbered for easy reference during class discussion. Do *not* number the paragraphs in your own essay.

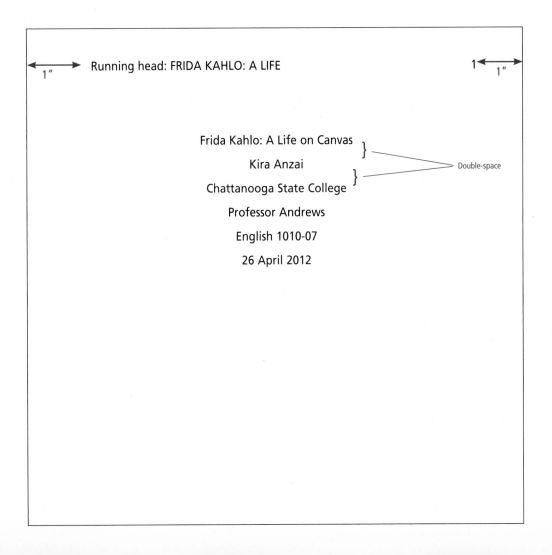

FRIDA KAHLO: A LIFE   1″   2

ABSTRACT   Double-space

No indent → The captivating, often surreal paintings of twentieth-century artist Frida Kahlo were directly influenced by significant events and relationships in her personal life. Examination of biographical sources and analyses of important paintings clarify the connection between her artistic style and a life dominated by physical and emotional pain. Major influences on her work include a tragic accident in her youth, a turbulent marriage to well-known muralist Diego Rivera, and a strong identification with Mexican culture. Knowledge of these influences adds to the understanding of Kahlo's art.

1″   1″

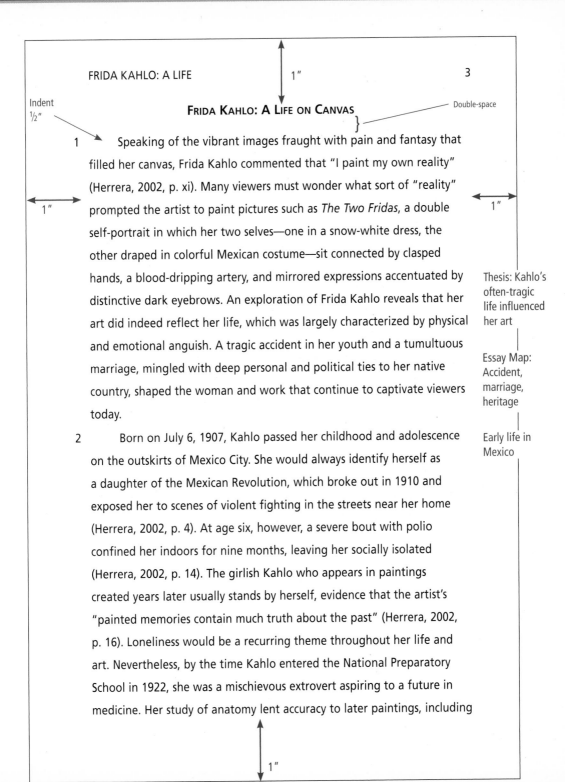

Indent
½"

FRIDA KAHLO: A LIFE ON CANVAS

Double-space

1   Speaking of the vibrant images fraught with pain and fantasy that filled her canvas, Frida Kahlo commented that "I paint my own reality" (Herrera, 2002, p. xi). Many viewers must wonder what sort of "reality" prompted the artist to paint pictures such as *The Two Fridas*, a double self-portrait in which her two selves—one in a snow-white dress, the other draped in colorful Mexican costume—sit connected by clasped hands, a blood-dripping artery, and mirrored expressions accentuated by distinctive dark eyebrows. An exploration of Frida Kahlo reveals that her art did indeed reflect her life, which was largely characterized by physical and emotional anguish. A tragic accident in her youth and a tumultuous marriage, mingled with deep personal and political ties to her native country, shaped the woman and work that continue to captivate viewers today.

Thesis: Kahlo's often-tragic life influenced her art

Essay Map: Accident, marriage, heritage

2   Born on July 6, 1907, Kahlo passed her childhood and adolescence on the outskirts of Mexico City. She would always identify herself as a daughter of the Mexican Revolution, which broke out in 1910 and exposed her to scenes of violent fighting in the streets near her home (Herrera, 2002, p. 4). At age six, however, a severe bout with polio confined her indoors for nine months, leaving her socially isolated (Herrera, 2002, p. 14). The girlish Kahlo who appears in paintings created years later usually stands by herself, evidence that the artist's "painted memories contain much truth about the past" (Herrera, 2002, p. 16). Loneliness would be a recurring theme throughout her life and art. Nevertheless, by the time Kahlo entered the National Preparatory School in 1922, she was a mischievous extrovert aspiring to a future in medicine. Her study of anatomy lent accuracy to later paintings, including

Early life in Mexico

1"

1"

1"

the detailed human heart in *The Two Fridas* (Tuchman, 2002, p. 2). Beyond her intellectual pursuits, Kahlo delighted in practical joking and frequently targeted Diego Rivera, the famous muralist commissioned to paint the school auditorium. She teasingly nicknamed him Panzón ("fat belly") and entertained romantic notions in spite of their twenty-one-year age difference (Herrera, 2002, pp. 31–32).

Traumatic accident, lifelong pain

3   The desired liaison did not materialize, for Kahlo's life was altered by a tragic accident at age eighteen. On September 17, 1925, she and her boyfriend, Alejandro, hopped onto a wooden bus just before it was rammed by a trolley car. Alejandro recalled that the bus "burst into a thousand pieces," sending an iron handrail through Kahlo's abdomen; her "screaming was louder than the siren" of the arriving ambulance (Herrera, 2002, p. 48). The trauma broke her spine in three places, crushed her pelvis, and severely damaged her right leg and foot. Against all odds, Kahlo began a slow recovery, but the images of intense agony that characterized her art in ensuing years largely reflected her unending battle with physical pain. For the next three decades, she wore various plaster corsets to support her improperly healed spine and underwent taxing operations that provided temporary relief at best (Tuchman, 2002, p. 2). Ironically, the accident that haunted Kahlo with thoughts of death was critical to rousing the artist inside her. During the months of her recuperation, she began painting portraits to pass the time, taking her first steps as an artist while still physically bedridden (Zamora, 1990, pp. 26–27).

Marriage to famous painter

4   After she regained mobility, financial difficulties prevented Kahlo's return to school, but an interest in leftist politics renewed her acquaintance with the highly political Diego Rivera in 1928 (Zamora,

FRIDA KAHLO: A LIFE 5

1990, p. 31). Kahlo sought the muralist's assessment of her paintings, and he instantly recognized her inborn talent. Rivera was equally drawn to the petite young woman—no longer a schoolgirl—whose "delicate face" was adorned by graceful black eyebrows he admirably compared to "the wings of a blackbird" (Tuchman, 2002, p. 3). In contrast, the heavyset Rivera was commonly described as having the features of a frog (Hardin, 1997, p. 37). Despite these sharp contrasts, the mismatched couple struck up a courtship that led to their marriage on August 21, 1929. Rivera had a significant impact on his wife's artistic development. By observing his creation of historical murals, she "learned how to tell a story in paint," an ability that contributed to the frequently autobiographical nature of her later art (Tuchman, 2002, p. 4).

5   After their wedding, Kahlo followed Rivera to the United States, where he accepted a series of commissions while she honed her portraiture and garnered public attention for her native Mexican attire. Bright blouses and skirts, stone bead necklaces, and upswept braids appeased Rivera's preference that she dress in the Tehuana Indian style and, more importantly, allowed Kahlo to openly celebrate her culture and nationalist sentiments (Baddeley, 1991, pp. 12–13). Most of the self-portraits she painted in subsequent decades, including her colorfully costumed self in *The Two Fridas*, capture this personal identification with Mexico. Despite the gratifying attention of the American press, the Riveras' time in the States was marred by tragedy when Kahlo suffered a miscarriage in 1932.[1] Her bloody and fantastical portrayal of the experience in the painting *Henry Ford Hospital* diverged from the portraits that typify her body of work up to that point. The loss of her child, accompanied by her mother's death the same year, marked a shift

Identification with heritage

Loss of child and mother

in Kahlo's subject matter. Elements of fantasy increasingly appeared in the paintings, which were "beginning to emphasize terror, suffering, wounds, and pain" (Zamora, 1990, p. 46), both physical and psychological.

6   The return to Mexico in 1933 brought Kahlo some relief but did not restore her happiness, as her marriage felt the mounting pressure of her husband's infidelity. Although she had long tolerated Rivera's string of casual affairs, Kahlo's increasing anguish prompted her to move into her own apartment for several months (Zamora, 1990, pp. 46–47). Author Terri Hardin (1997) argues that Rivera's betrayal and the couple's ensuing separation freed her from convention and "removed the final impediments to her progress as an artist" (p. 49) whose vision was inimitable. Kahlo returned to Rivera in 1935, but their reconciliation left Kahlo far from comfortable. To cope with the duress of this situation, Kahlo channeled her feelings into her art (Zamora, 1990, p. 50). The productive years that followed led to the inclusion of two paintings in a 1938 exhibit in Paris, where their shocking fantastical elements earned her praise as a Surrealist (Zamora, 1990, p. 56).[2] Fresh devastation replaced her confidence, however, when, shortly after her return from France, Rivera requested a divorce (Zamora, 1990, p. 62).

Tumultuous marriage, divorce, remarriage reflected in her art

7   The dissolution of their disintegrating marriage in 1939 coincided with the creation of emotionally charged paintings like *The Two Fridas*. Some critical interpretations of the double self-portrait conclude that it directly responded to the divorce, hence the depiction of the left-hand Kahlo wearing Rivera's favored Tehuana costume. She shares a severed artery with the opposing white-clad Kahlo, who displays a "broken" heart in her bisected chest; this second self stops the artery's blood flow with a clamp, suggesting that "the Frida independent of Rivera holds the

means of self-rescue" (Hardin, 1997, p. 68). *The Two Fridas*, in essence, conveys two sides of the artist's personality, a hallmark of additional self-portraits (captured on canvas and in her diary) that explore her distinct feminine and masculine identities. In *Self-Portrait with Cropped Hair*, completed the year after her divorce, Kahlo poses in a man's suit, as opposed to her typical Mexican dress and flower-bedecked braids. She is surrounded by long strands of sheared-off hair, a sign of despair and retaliation against Rivera (Johnston, 1996, p. 33). *Self-Portrait with Thorn Necklace and Hummingbird*, painted in 1940, likewise expresses her woe through the symbolism of the dead bird hanging from her neck (Hardin, 1997, pp. 70–71). Without her husband, Kahlo felt an isolation reminiscent of her childhood and explained her profusion of self-portraits by stating simply, "I am all alone" (Zamora, 1990, p. 102). Regardless of their former troubles, Rivera was likewise plagued by separation from Kahlo, and they chose to remarry in 1940 (Zamora, 1990, p. 70). Kahlo expressed her renewed devotion to Rivera in the 1943 painting *Roots*, symbolically binding herself to the landscape where they built a home together (Herrera, 2002, pp. 312–314).

8   The last several years of Kahlo's life were disrupted by numerous operations as her health declined, but she continued to paint her signature self-portraits and fantastical scenes. In *The Dream* (1940), the skeleton over her canopied bed speaks to the psychological effects of her physical condition, while *The Wounded Deer* (1946) suggests her identification with a bleeding animal, as her head is fixed to a deer's arrow-pierced body (Hardin, 1997, pp. 70, 103). The pain that began in her youth now became unbearable, and Kahlo's reliance on stimulants and strong medication for relief revealed itself in her slightly frenetic

Broken health and pain influence portraits

brushwork (Tuchman, 2002, p. 5). In 1953, her ailing lower right leg was amputated, but the restraints of an artificial limb and wheelchair did not prevent Kahlo from resolutely accompanying Rivera to leftist political demonstrations. Similarly, she had insisted upon attending her long-awaited one-person exhibition in Mexico City earlier that year despite serious illness. Kahlo was delivered to the gallery by ambulance and enjoyed the festive event from the comfort of a canopied bed (Hardin, 1997, p. 108). She told attentive reporters for *Time* magazine, "I am not sick. I am broken. But I am happy to be alive as long as I can paint" (Zamora, 1990, p. 126).

Conclusion: Shaped by pain and a beloved heritage, Kahlo's art continues to fascinate

9   Kahlo's artistic career was cut short by her death on July 13, 1954, when she was forty-seven years old, but over the course of three decades, she completed approximately two hundred paintings (Tuchman, 2002, p. 1).[3] They have since fascinated a worldwide audience with their striking originality, which must be attributed to a life and artistic vision shaped by painful personal experiences and deep ties to Mexico. Kahlo consistently exhibited a concern with keeping her memory alive in people's minds, frequently beseeching her acquaintances, "Don't forget me!" (Zamora, 1990, p. 102). Her evocative images ensure that Frida Kahlo—the woman and the artist—will continue to be remembered by the legacy she left on canvas.

FRIDA KAHLO: A LIFE   1″   9

REFERENCES

Baddeley, O. (1991). "Her dress hangs here": De-frocking the Kahlo cult.

Indent ½″ → *Oxford Art Journal, 14,* 10–17.

Hardin, T. (1997). *Frida Kahlo: A modern master.* New York, NY:

Smithmark.

Herrera, H. (2002). *Frida: A biography of Frida Kahlo.* New York, NY:

1″   Perennial-Harper. (Original work published 1983)

Johnston, J. (1996, March). Self-portrait. [Review of the book *The diary of*

Frida Kahlo: An intimate self-portrait, by S. M. Lowe]. *Art in America,*

84, 31, 33. Retrieved from http://www.artinamericamagazine.com/

Tuchman, P. (2002, November). Frida Kahlo: The Mexican artist's myriad

faces, stranger-than-fiction biography and powerful paintings come

to vivid life in a new film. *Smithsonian, 33*(11). Retrieved from http://

www.smithsonianmag.com/

Zamora, M. (1990). *Frida Kahlo: The brush of anguish* (M. S. Smith, Trans.).

San Francisco, CA: Chronicle Books.

1″

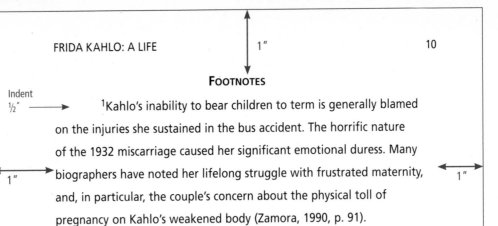

Footnotes

Indent ½″ →

[1]Kahlo's inability to bear children to term is generally blamed on the injuries she sustained in the bus accident. The horrific nature of the 1932 miscarriage caused her significant emotional duress. Many biographers have noted her lifelong struggle with frustrated maternity, and, in particular, the couple's concern about the physical toll of pregnancy on Kahlo's weakened body (Zamora, 1990, p. 91).

[2]Surrealism was a movement that valued the dreamlike imagery recurrent in Kahlo's paintings. *The Two Fridas* was displayed at the "International Exhibition of Surrealism" in Mexico City in 1940. Although Kahlo acknowledged her artistic similarities to the Surrealists, she always maintained her insistence that she painted reality, not dreams (Herrera, 2002, p. 255).

[3]In the absence of a postmortem, the cause of Kahlo's death remains disputed; although her death certificate mentions a pulmonary embolism, an accidental or intentional overdose of stimulants and medication has also been suspected (Zamora, 1990, p. 130).

1″

Part 4

A Concise Handbook

Part Four of this text begins with an overview of the parts of speech, followed by a brief discussion of sentence components and types. These pages present explanations, definitions, and illustrations to help you better understand the grammatical conventions and terms used in the handbook chapters that follow. Chapters 20, 21, and 22 will address major errors in grammar, punctuation, and mechanics, showing you how to recognize and correct these problems. Each chapter begins with a diagnostic test to help you identify the rules you may need to review. Then each rule will be explained as simply as possible, with a minimum of technical language. Beside each rule you will find the editing mark or abbreviation that most instructors use to identify that error; each rule is also numbered for easy reference. Exercises placed throughout each chapter offer opportunities to practice the advice; collaborative assignments may also promote improved editing and proofreading skills.

Parts of Speech

The following section offers an overview of the eight groups of words called *parts of speech*. Knowing how a word or phrase is properly used may help you produce sentences that are clear, correct, and pleasing to your readers. In addition, recognizing commonly used grammatical terms may make it easier for you to understand your instructor's advice as well as the explanations of major errors in usage and punctuation that appear in the following handbook chapters.

The eight parts of speech are *nouns, pronouns, verbs, adjectives, adverbs, prepositions, conjunctions,* and *interjections.** The group to which a word belongs is determined by its function in a particular sentence; consequently, a word may be one part of speech in one sentence and a different part of speech in another. (For example, note that "rock" is a noun—a thing—in "Put down that rock!" but also a verb—a word expressing action—in "Don't rock the boat!")

Here is a brief introduction to the parts of speech. You will also see some of these definitions repeated in the various sections on grammatical errors in Chapter 20. Moving back and forth between this overview and the advice in that chapter should help you improve your grammatical skills as you draft and revise your sentences.

1. **Nouns** name persons, places, things, and concepts. *Proper nouns* are the names of particular people, places, and things and should be capitalized; *common nouns,* referring to any person, place, or thing, are not capitalized. *Gerunds* are nouns formed from verbs ending in "-ing."

Examples of Common Nouns	The *girl* sold her *car* in *town*.
Examples of Proper Nouns	*Rachel* sold her *Honda* in *Denver*.
Example of a Gerund	*Dancing* is fun.

   (◆ For additional information on the uses of nouns, see pages 554–555.)

2. **Pronouns** take the place of nouns. By using pronouns, you can avoid repeating nouns in the same sentence or group of sentences.

   Example   We saw Hortense across the parking lot and waved to *her*. [Use of "her" avoids the awkward repetition of "We saw Hortense across the parking lot and waved to Hortense."]

   There are several classes of pronouns, including these six important kinds:

   - *Personal pronouns* refer to specific people; they include such words as "I," "you," "he," "her," "it," and "them." (*Compound personal pronouns*—sometimes called reflexive pronouns—add "-self" or "-selves" to some of the simple personal ones: "himself," "herself," "themselves.")

     Example   *You* and *I* will meet *him* at the movies.

---

*Some authorities claim nine parts of speech, adding the group of words called *articles*: "a," "an," and "the." In English "a" generally precedes nouns beginning with consonants (*a* cat); "an" generally precedes nouns beginning with vowels (*an* island).

- *Indefinite pronouns* refer to nonspecific people or things and include such words as "everyone," "everything," "someone," "anyone," and "anybody."

   Example   Everyone should use caution crossing that busy street.

- *Possessive pronouns* (such as "his," "hers," "its," "ours," "theirs") show ownership.

   Example   *His* passport was about to expire; *its* renewal deadline was March 15.

- *Demonstrative pronouns* refer the reader to previous references.

   Example   *That* is my house, *those* are my prize roses, and *this* is my cat.

- *Interrogative pronouns* introduce questions.

   Example   *Which* house? *What* roses? *Who* is asking all these questions?

- *Relative pronouns* join a dependent clause to the main clause of a sentence and describe a previous noun or pronoun. Commonly used relative pronouns are "who," "which," "that," and "whose."

   Examples   The singer *who* won the competition is holding a free concert.
   I found the purse *that* I thought I had lost at the restaurant.

(◆ For more information on the uses of pronouns, see pages 555–558.)

3. **Verbs** express action ("walk," "yell," "swim") and states of being ("am," "is," "are"). A verb phrase may be composed of several words: "should have written," "might have called."

   Three important kinds of verbs include the following:

- *Action verbs* express physical or mental activity.

   Examples   Birds *fly* through the yard.
   I *dream* of beaches in Hawaii.

- *Linking verbs* (such as "is, "are," "was," "were,") show states of being; they may also show connections between ideas or relationships of one thing to another.

   Examples   Shameka *is* twenty-eight years old.
   Austin *was* the youngest child.

- *Auxiliary verbs* are sometimes referred to as "helper verbs" because they assist the main verbs in communicating meaning or time of action. Common auxiliary verbs include forms of "do," "have," "may," "can," and "will."

   Examples (Auxiliary + Main Verbs)   Good students *do proofread* their essays.
   Revising *will help* your writing.

   Also note that verbs may be described as being in the *active voice* or the *passive voice*.

- Active voice denotes that the subject of the verb is performing the action:
   The house-sitter *watered* the lawn.

- Passive voice denotes that the subject of the verb is acted upon:
   The lawn was *watered* by the house-sitter.

Verbs come in many forms, but three to remember as you revise your prose include the *infinitive*, the *participle*, and the *gerund*.

- An infinitive is a verb introduced by the word "to": I like to *read*.

- A participle may share the properties of both a verb and a modifier; present participles end in "-ing": *Watching* the rain fall, we anticipated summer flowers.

- A gerund is a verb plus "-ing" used as a noun: *Swimming* is wonderful exercise.

(◆ For advice addressing some of the common errors with verbs, see pages 548–553.)

4. **Adjectives** modify or describe nouns and pronouns. *Proper adjectives* derived from proper nouns are usually capitalized. *Predicate adjectives* may follow the word they modify.

   Examples   I bought a *red* sweater, just the *perfect* weight for *Colorado* evenings.
   Her answer was *wrong*.

5. **Adverbs** most often modify or describe verbs, adjectives, and other adverbs. They frequently answer "how" or "how much" and end in "-ly."

   Examples   My father drove *slowly*. ["Slowly" modifies the verb, describing how he drove.]
   Her answer was *partially* wrong. ["Partially" modifies the adjective "wrong," describing how incorrect the answer was.]

   She appeared *mildly* amused. ["Mildly" modifies the adverb "amused," describing the extent of her delight.]

(◆ For additional information on the use of adjectives and adverbs, see pages 560–561.)

6. **Prepositions** are words that most often show locations and relationships in time, place, and direction. The following are some common prepositions:

to	under	in	during
on	with	at	upon
about	by	for	since
between	through	from	after
of	before	over	

   A preposition and its object make up a *prepositional phrase*, which may be used as an adjective or adverb.

   Example   *During Spring Break*, we took a vacation *to the city*. [The first prepositional phrase is used as an adverb to tell when and the other is used as an adjective to describe the place of the vacation.]

Writers should avoid ending sentences with prepositions when possible. Recast the sentence, or simply drop an unnecessary (and ungrammatical) preposition: "Where are you sitting at?" becomes "Where are you sitting?"

7. **Conjunctions** connect words ("dogs *and* cats") or groups of words ("please return the acceptance card *or* send a note of regret").

There are two kinds of conjunctions for you to recognize:

- *Coordinating conjunctions* connect two words, phrases, or clauses of equal kind or rank. The most commonly used coordinating conjunctions are "for," "and," "nor," "but," "or," "yet," and "so."

  Examples   He promises an evening of singing *and* dancing. [connecting two words]

  We can either hail a cab *or* catch the subway. [connecting two phrases]

  I have to be home early, *but* you can stay out late. [connecting two clauses]

- *Subordinating conjunctions* connect two clauses of unequal rank; as their name indicates, they connect one clause that is subordinate to—that is, dependent for meaning upon—its main clause. Common subordinating conjunctions include "because," "when," "if," "as," "since," "after," and "although."

  Example   *Because* his songs promote violence, I won't buy albums by that recording artist.

  In most cases when a subordinate clause begins the sentence, it is followed by a comma, as shown above.

  (◆ Understanding how to use coordinating and subordinating conjunctions is important as you learn to create sentence variety and also how to avoid fragment, run-on, or spliced sentences. For more information, see pages 563–564 and 565–567.)

8. **Interjections** are exclamatory words that frequently express strong, sudden, or contrary emotions. They may stand alone or they may be part of a sentence.

  Examples   *Ouch! Help!* Call an ambulance!
  Oh, never mind. The movie was, *alas,* already sold out.

Sentence Components and Classifications

In addition to recognizing the parts of speech, you may find it helpful to understand some of the grammatical terms used to describe sentence components and types. Here are a few common terms, their definitions, and examples.

1. A *sentence* is most often a group of words that expresses a complete thought.
   - The squirrel ate the bird seed.

2. A sentence contains a *subject* and a *predicate*, either expressed or understood. The subject is the performer or receiver of the action or state of being expressed in the predicate, which gives information about the subject.
   - The squirrel [subject] ate the bird seed [predicate].

   A subject may be implied rather than stated.
   - Stop talking! Run for your life! ["You" is implied.]

3. A *direct object* receives the action of the verb. It often answers the question "what?"
   - We caught a *skunk* [direct object] in a trap from the Humane Society.

4. An *indirect object* names the person or thing to whom or for whom the action is done.
   - We gave the *dog* [indirect object] some special treats [direct object].

5. A *modifier* is a word or group of words used to describe, characterize, or change the meaning of other words in the sentence. Adjectives and adverbs are common modifiers.
   - The *starving* teenager *happily* gobbled the *cold* pizza.

6. A *phrase* is a group of related words in a sentence that do not contain a subject or predicate. Phrases do not stand alone. Common forms include prepositional, infinitive, and verbal phrases.
   - He accidentally set up the tent *on an ant hill.* [prepositional phrase]
   - *Waving frantically,* he ran toward the river. [verbal phrase, using participle "ing" form of the verb "wave"]

7. A *clause* is a group of related words in a sentence that do have a subject and a predicate. Independent clauses stand alone and are complete thoughts; they are, in essence, what we call sentences. Dependent clauses, on the other hand, need to be attached for their meaning to a main clause; they are considered fragments if they stand alone.
   - Abraham Lincoln was the first president to sport a beard. [independent clause]
   - Although my history book fails to mention this fact [dependent clause], Abraham Lincoln was the first president to sport a beard [independent clause].

8. The word "compound" is often used to indicate parts of sentences that appear in multiple forms, such as compound subjects, predicates, clauses, and objects.

   - *Sarah* and *Kate* received their Master's Degrees on the same day. [compound subject]

   - The girls *found interesting jobs* and *moved to different states*. [compound predicate]

9. Sentences themselves may be classified according to their structures as four types: simple, compound, complex, and compound-complex.

   A *simple sentence* has one independent clause.

   - She practices yoga.

   A *compound sentence* has two or more independent clauses. (Expressed another way, a compound sentence is two simple sentences joined by a conjunction.)

   - Sarah moved to Berkeley, and Kate stayed in Washington.

   A *complex sentence* may consist of one independent clause and one or more dependent clauses.

   - If we are thoughtful enough [dependent clause], we usually can find an important lesson in every disappointment [independent clause].

   A *compound-complex* sentence includes two or more independent clauses and at least one dependent clause.

   - Thomas Jefferson is a much-admired president [independent clause], but he is especially honored in Virginia [independent clause], where he founded the state university [dependent clause].

10. Sentences may also be classified by purpose:

    Declarative: makes a statement (The day is sunny.)

    Imperative: gives a command (Do not pass that car.)

    Interrogative: asks a question (Why are you here?)

    Exclamatory: expresses strong emotion (How lovely you look tonight!)

Chapter 20

Major Errors in Grammar

· ·

Assessing Your Skills: Grammar

To help you focus your study of this chapter, take the self-graded test that follows. Each of the sentences below contains one or more errors discussed in this chapter. See how much you already know by correcting the sentences and then checking the answers on pages 572–573. By taking this test, you will be better able to evaluate your knowledge of grammar and direct your attention to those rules governing the errors you missed.*

1. Almost everyone today recognize the Statue of Liberty, but not everybody know its history.

2. Plans for the statue was first began in 1865 by Frenchman Edouard de Laboulaye. In honor of the United States' love of democracy and French-American friendship; according to the National Parks Service.

3. Commissioned to design the work, Bedloe's Island in the New York Harbor was chosen as the location by artist Frederic-Auguste Bartholdi. Because of how it could be seen by boats of immigrants thousands of who was entering the country via Ellis Island and was government owned.

4. The project was a joint effort between the two countries the French agreed to build the statue the U.S. building the pedestal.

5. Money was raised by France by entertainment, selling items with the statue's picture on it, and they charged some public fees. (Though between you and I, this seems difficult and in fact didn't work out so good in the U.S.)

---

*Historical information included in this assessment test provided by the National Parks Service; for more interesting details about the Statue of Liberty and other famous U.S. landmarks, see the National Parks Service's Website at <www.nps.gov/>.

6. The statue has a steel framework designed by Alexandre Gustave Eiffel, who previous had designed the famous Eiffel Tower, covered with a flexible copper skin the width of two pennies that don't crack in high winds.

7. The statue face was modeled on Bartholdi's mother, each of the seven rays of her crown represent one of the seven seas and continents of the world, the torch is a symbol of enlightenment, broken chains at its feet representing freedom from oppression, the tablet in her arm would stand for law.

8. Completed in France in the summer of 1884, the parts had to carefully be disassembled and shipped separate to New York.

9. Reassembled after four months, thousands of spectators watched the massive 305 feet high statue dedication on October 28, 1886.

10. Both you and me can't hardly disagree with the National Parks Service when they call the Statue of Liberty one of the more better recognized icons of democracy in the world, for more information; you may go online to <www.nps .gov/stli/historyculture>.

Errors with Verbs

Verbs express action ("run," "walk," "kick") or state of being ("is," "are," "was").

20a Faulty Agreement   S-V Agr

Make your verb agree in number with its subject; a singular subject takes a singular verb, and a plural subject takes a plural verb.

Incorrect	*Lester Peabody*, principal of the Kung Fu School of Grammar, *don't* agree that gum chewing should be banned in the classroom.
Correct	*Lester Peabody*, principal of the Kung Fu School of Grammar, *doesn't* agree that gum chewing should be banned in the classroom.
Incorrect	The *actions* of the new senator *hasn't* been consistent with her campaign promises.
Correct	The *actions* of the new senator *haven't* been consistent with her campaign promises.

Compound subjects joined by "and" take a plural verb, unless the subject refers to a single person or a single unit.

Examples	*Bean sprouts* and *tofu are* dishes Jim Bob won't consider eating. ["Bean sprouts" and "tofu" are a compound subject joined by "and"; therefore, use a plural verb.]
	The *winner* and *new champion refuses* to give up the microphone at the news conference. ["Winner" and "champion" refer to a single person; therefore, use a singular verb.]

Listed here are some of the most confusing subject-verb agreement problems:

1. With a collective noun: a singular noun referring to a collection of elements as a unit generally takes a singular verb.

Incorrect	During boring parts of the Transcendental Vegetation lecture, the *class* often *chant* to the music of Norman Bates and the Shower Heads.
Correct	During boring parts of the Transcendental Vegetation lecture, the *class* often *chants* to the music of Norman Bates and the Shower Heads.
Incorrect	The *army* of the new nation *want* shoes, bullets, and weekend passes.
Correct	The *army* of the new nation *wants* shoes, bullets, and weekend passes.

2. With a relative pronoun ("that," "which," and "who") used as a subject: the verb agrees with its antecedent, the word being described.

Incorrect	The boss rejected a shipment of *shirts, which was* torn.
Correct	The boss rejected a shipment of *shirts, which were* torn.

3. With "each," "everybody," "everyone," and "neither" as the subject: use a singular verb even when followed by a plural construction.

Incorrect	*Each* of the children *think* Mom and Dad are automatic teller machines.
Correct	*Each* of the children *thinks* Mom and Dad are automatic teller machines.
Incorrect	Although only a few of the students saw the teacher pull out his hair, *everybody know* why he did it.
Correct	Although only a few of the students saw the teacher pull out his hair, *everybody knows* why he did it.
Incorrect	*Neither have* a dime left by the second of the month.
Correct	*Neither has* a dime left by the second of the month.

4. With "either . . . or" and "neither . . . nor": the verb agrees with the nearer item.

Incorrect	Neither rain nor dogs nor *gloom of night keep* the mail carrier from delivering bills.
Correct	Neither rain nor dogs nor *gloom of night keeps* the mail carrier from delivering bills.
Incorrect	Either Betty or her *neighbors is* hosting a come-as-you-are breakfast.
Correct	Either Betty or her *neighbors are* hosting a come-as-you-are breakfast.

5. With "here is (are)" and "there is (are)": the verb agrees with the number indicated by the subject following the verb.

Incorrect	*There is* only two good *reasons* for missing this law class: death and jury duty.
Correct	*There are* only two good *reasons* for missing this law class: death and jury duty.
Incorrect	To help you do your shopping quickly, Mr. Scrooge, *here are* a *list* of gifts under a dollar.
Correct	To help you do your shopping quickly, Mr. Scrooge, *here is* a *list* of gifts under a dollar.

6. With plural nouns intervening between subject and verb: the verb still agrees with the subject.

   Incorrect   The *jungle*, with its poisonous plants, wild animals, and biting insects, *make* Herman long for the sidewalks of Topeka.
   Correct   The *jungle*, with its poisonous plants, wild animals, and biting insects, *makes* Herman long for the sidewalks of Topeka.

7. With nouns plural in form but singular in meaning: a singular verb is usually correct.

   Examples   *News travels* slowly if it comes through the post office.
   Charades is the exhibitionist's game of choice.
   Politics is often the rich person's hobby.

8. As you revise your prose, use a dictionary if you need help determining whether a word is singular or plural. For example, two common subject-verb agreement errors occur with the words "media" and "data," which, despite colloquial usage, should be treated as plurals in formal writing.

   Correct   The *data were* faulty.
   The media often *influence* public opinion polls.

Practicing What You've Learned

© Canstock Images, Inc./ Index Stock Imagery

Errors with Verbs: Subject-Verb Agreement
The following sentences contain subject-verb agreement errors. Correct the problems by changing the verbs. Some sentences contain more than one error.

1. A recent report on Cuban land crabs show that they can run faster than horses.

2. The team from Snooker Hollow High School are considering switching from basketball to basket weaving because passing athletics are now required for graduation.

3. Neither of the students know that both mystery writer Agatha Christie and inventor Thomas Edison was dyslexic.

4. Each of the twins have read about Joseph Priestley's contribution to the understanding of oxygen, but neither were aware that he also invented the pencil eraser.

5. Clarity in speech and writing are absolutely essential in the business world today.

continued on next page

6. Historical data suggests that the world's first money, in the form of coins, were made in Lydia, a country that is now part of Turkey.

7. Bananas, rich in vitamins and low in fat, is rated the most popular fruit in America.

8. There is many children in this country who appreciate a big plate of hot grits, but none of the Hall kids like this Southern dish.

9. Either the Labrador Retriever or the German Shepherd hold the honor of being the most popular breed of dogs in the United States, say the American Kennel Club.

10. Many people considers Johnny Appleseed a mythical figure, but now two local historians, authors of a well-known book on the subject, argues that he was a real person named John Chapman.

20b   Subjunctive   V Sub

When you make a wish or a statement that is contrary to fact, use the subjunctive verb form "were."

Incorrect	I wish I *was* queen so I could levy a tax on men who spit.
Correct	I wish I *were* queen so I could levy a tax on men who spit. [This expresses a wish.]
Incorrect	If "Fightin' Henry" *was* a foot taller and thirty pounds heavier, we would all be in trouble.
Correct	If "Fightin' Henry" *were* a foot taller and thirty pounds heavier, we would all be in trouble. [This proposes a statement contrary to fact.]

20c   Tense Shift   T

In most cases, the first verb in a sentence establishes the tense of any later verb. Keep your verbs within the same time frame to avoid confusing your readers.

Incorrect	Big Joe *saw* the police car coming up behind, so he *turns* into the next alley.
Correct	Big Joe *saw* the police car coming up behind, so he *turned* into the next alley.
Incorrect	Horace *uses* an artificial sweetener in his coffee all day, so he *felt* a pizza and a hot-fudge sundae *were* fine for dinner.
Correct	Horace *uses* an artificial sweetener in his coffee all day, so he *feels* a pizza and a hot-fudge sundae *are* fine for dinner.
Incorrect	Rex the Wonder Horse *was* obviously very smart because he *taps* out the phone numbers of the stars with his hoof.
Correct	Rex the Wonder Horse *was* obviously very smart because he *tapped* out the phone numbers of the stars with his hoof.

20d   Split Infinitive   **Sp I**

Many authorities insist that "to" never be separated from its verb; today, however, some grammarians allow the split infinitive except in the most formal kinds of writing.

Nevertheless, because the split offends some readers, it is probably best to avoid the construction unless clarity or emphasis is clearly served by its use.

Traditional	A swift kick is needed *to start* the machine properly.
Untraditional	A swift kick is needed *to* properly *start* the machine.
Traditional	The teacher wanted Lori *to communicate* her ideas clearly.
Untraditional	The teacher wanted Lori *to* clearly *communicate* her ideas.

20e   Double Negatives   **D Neg**

1. Rewrite sentences that use two negatives to communicate a single negative idea.

Incorrect	He *didn't* need *no* fancy car to impress her.
Correct	He *didn't* need a fancy car to impress her.
Incorrect	They *couldn't* find *no* record of my purchase.
Correct	They *could* find *no* record of my purchase.
Also Correct	They *couldn't* find *any* record of my purchase.

2. Don't use a negative verb and a negative qualifier ("hardly," "barely," "scarcely") together.

Incorrect	I *can't hardly* wait until Jim Bob gets his jaw out of traction, so I can challenge him to a bubblegum-blowing contest.
Correct	I *can hardly* wait until Jim Bob gets his jaw out of traction, so I can challenge him to a bubblegum-blowing contest.
Incorrect	Even when he flew his helicopter upside-down over her house, she *wouldn't barely* look at him.
Correct	Even when he flew his helicopter upside-down over her house, she *would barely* look at him.

20f   Passive Voice   **Pass**

"Active voice" refers to sentences in which the subject performs the action. "Passive voice" refers to sentences in which the subject is acted upon.

Active	The police *pulled over* the speeding van full of ski sweaters.
Passive	The speeding van full of ski sweaters *was pulled over* by the police.

The passive voice is a logical construction when the person or thing performing the action is unknown or of lesser importance than the event or action.

Examples	My car was stolen last night.
	The soldier was buried with full military honors.

Some disciplines, particularly those in science and engineering, may prefer the passive voice: "All results were triple verified." Nevertheless, your prose style will improve if you choose strong, active-voice verbs over wordy, awkward, or unclear passive constructions.

Awkward Passive Construction	The call for volunteers was responded to by many students.
Active Verb	Many students responded to the call for volunteers.
Unclear Passive Construction	Much protest is being voiced over the new electric fireworks. [Who is protesting?]
Active Verb	Members of the Fuse Lighters Association are protesting the new electric fireworks.

(◆ For more examples of active- and passive-voice verbs, see page 138.)

20g Irregular Verbs **Irreg V**

Most verbs form their past tense by adding "-ed" ("ask/asked," "walk/walked"). However, some verbs form their past tenses by changing a vowel ("begin/began," "write/wrote"); others indicate past tense with an entirely new spelling or word ("go/went," "strike/struck").

Consult your dictionary when you are uncertain of the correct verb form you need. Remember that some verbs simply do not behave themselves!

Incorrect	Irregular verbs have *creeped* into our language.
Correct	Irregular verbs have *crept* into our language.
Incorrect	She *shaked* the piggy bank as hard as she could.
Correct	She *shook* the piggy bank as hard as she could.
Incorrect	I don't know the current price of ant farms because I haven't *boughten* one since grade school.
Correct	I don't know the current price of ant farms because I haven't *bought* one since grade school.

Practicing What You've Learned

© Canstock Images, Inc./
Index Stock Imagery

Errors with Verbs: Form, Tense Shift, and Double Negatives

A. The following sentences contain incorrect verb forms, tense shifts, and double negatives. Correct any problems you see, and rewrite any sentences whose clarity or conciseness would be improved by using active rather than passive verbs.

1.   He couldn't hardly wait to hear country star Sue Flay sing her version of "I've Been Flushed from the Bathroom of Your Heart."

continued on next page

2. "If you was in Wyoming and couldn't hear no wind blowing, what would people call you?" asked Jethro. "Dead," replies his buddy Herman.

3. It was believed by Aztec ruler Montezuma that chocolate had magical powers and can act as an aphrodisiac.

4. Tammy's favorite band is Opie Gone Bad, so she always was buying their concert tickets, even though she can't hardly afford to.

5. Suspicions of arson are being raised by the fire department following the burning of the new Chip and Dale Furniture Factory.

B. Revise any incorrect verbs in the following sentences.

1. I seen what she was hiding behind her back.

2. He come around here yesterday asking questions, but we're use to that.

3. Having forget the combination to the safe, the burglar quietly snuck out the back door.

4. Austin don't like to be awokened until noon.

5. The kids done good work all day.

Errors with Nouns   N

Nouns name people, places, and things ("boy," "kitchen," "car"). Proper nouns name specific people, places, and things ("Zora Neale Hurston," "Texas," "Chevrolet") and are capitalized.

 Possessive with "-ing" Nouns

When the emphasis is on the action, use the possessive pronoun plus the "-ing" noun.

Example   He hated *my* singing around the house, so I made him live in the garage. [The emphasis is on *singing*.]

When the emphasis is not on the action, you may use a noun or pronoun plus the "-ing" noun.

Example   He hated *me* singing around the house, so I made him live in the garage. [The emphasis is on the person singing—me—not the action; he might have liked someone else singing.]

20i **Misuse of Nouns as Adjectives**

Some nouns may be used as adjectives modifying other nouns ("horse show," "movie star," "theater seats"). But some nouns used as adjectives sound awkward or like jargon.

To avoid such awkwardness, you may need to change the noun to an appropriate adjective or reword the sentence.

Awkward	The group decided to work on local *environment* problems.
Better	The group decided to work on local *environmental* problems.
Jargon	The executive began a *cost estimation comparison study* of the two products.
Better	The executive began a *comparison study* of the two products' costs.

(◆ For more information on ridding your prose of multiple nouns, see page 143.)

20j Plurals of Proper Nouns

Add an "s" to indicate plural proper nouns.

Examples	Both *Keishas* volunteered for the charity drive.
	The *Halls* were home for the holidays, enjoying their new *Frisbees* every afternoon.

(◆ For practice correcting errors with nouns, turn to pages 558–559.)

Errors with Pronouns

A pronoun ("he," "she," "it") takes the place of a noun. Possessive pronouns ("his," "hers," "its," "theirs") show ownership.

20k Faulty Agreement   Pro Agr

A pronoun should agree in number and gender with its antecedent (that is, the word the pronoun stands for).

Incorrect	To get a temperamental *actress* to sign a contract, the director would lock *them* in the dressing room.
Correct	To get a temperamental *actress* to sign a contract, the director would lock *her* in the dressing room.

Use the singular pronoun with "everyone," "anyone," and "each."

Incorrect	When the belly dancer asked for a volunteer partner, *everyone* in the men's gym class raised *their* hand.
Correct	When the belly dancer asked for a volunteer partner, *everyone* in the men's gym class raised *his* hand.
Incorrect	*Each* of the new wives decided to keep *their* own name.
Correct	*Each* of the new wives decided to keep *her* own name.

In the past, writers have traditionally used the masculine pronoun "he" when the gender of the antecedent is unknown, as in the following: "If a *spy* refuses to answer questions, *he* should be forced to watch James Bond movies until *he* cracks." Today, however, some authorities prefer the nonsexist "she or he," even though the construction can be awkward when maintained over a stretch of prose. Perhaps the best solution is to use the impersonal "one" when possible or simply rewrite the sentence in the plural: "If *spies* refuse to answer questions, *they* should be forced to watch James Bond movies until *they* crack." (◆ For more advice and examples, see pages 169–171.)

20l Vague Reference Ref

Your pronoun references should be clear.

Vague	If the trained seal won't eat its dinner, throw *it* into the lion's cage. [What goes into the lion's cage?]
Clear	If the trained seal won't eat its dinner, throw *the food* into the lion's cage.
Vague	After the dog bit Harry, *he* raised such a fuss at the police station that the sergeant finally had *him* impounded. [Who raised the fuss? Who was impounded?]
Clear	After being bitten, *Harry* raised such a fuss at the police station that the sergeant finally had the *dog* impounded.

Sometimes you must add a word or rewrite the sentence to make the pronoun reference clear:

Vague	I'm a lab instructor in the biology department and am also taking a statistics course. *This* has always been difficult for me. [What is difficult?]
Clear	I'm a lab instructor in the biology department and am also taking statistics, a *course* that has always been difficult for me.
Clear	I'm a lab instructor in the biology department and am also taking a statistics course. Being a teacher and a student at the same time has always been difficult for me.

In many cases, simply inserting a noun after a vague use of "this" or "that" will clarify meaning.

Vague	I visited with my grandmother while we watched the lunar eclipse. That was so special. [What was special? The visit? The eclipse?]
Clear	I visited with my grandmother while we watched the lunar eclipse. That *evening* was so special.

As you revise your prose, train yourself to catch any sentences that begin with "this" or "that" and see whether adding a noun or phrase will help communicate your meaning more effectively.

20m Shift in Pronouns P Sh

Be consistent in your use of pronouns; don't shift from one person to another.

Incorrect	*One* shouldn't eat pudding with *your* fingers.
Correct	*One* shouldn't eat pudding with *one's* fingers.

Correct   *You* shouldn't eat pudding with *your* fingers.
Incorrect   *We* left-handed people are at a disadvantage because most of the time *you* can't rent left-handed golf clubs or bowling balls.
Correct   *We* left-handed people are at a disadvantage because most of the time *we* can't rent left-handed golf clubs or bowling balls.

(◆ For additional examples, see pages 143–144.)

20n Incorrect Case   **Ca**

1. The case of a pronoun is determined by its function in the particular sentence. If the pronoun is a subject, use the nominative case: "I," "he," "she," "we," and "they"; if the pronoun is an object, use the objective case: "me," "him," "her," "us," and "them." To check your usage, all you need to do in many instances is isolate the pronoun in the manner shown here and determine whether it sounds correct alone.

Incorrect   Give the treasure map to Frankie and *I*.
Isolated   Give the treasure map to *I*. [awkward]
Correct   Give the treasure map to Frankie and *me*.
Incorrect   Bertram and *her* suspect that the moon is hollow.
Isolated   *Her* suspects that the moon is hollow. [awkward]
Correct   Bertram and *she* suspect that the moon is hollow.
Incorrect   The gift is from Annette and *I*.
Isolated   The gift is from *I*. [awkward]
Correct   The gift is from Annette and *me*.

Sometimes the "isolation test" doesn't work, so you just have to remember the rules. A common pronoun problem involves use of the preposition "between" and the choice of "me" or "I." Perhaps you can remember this rule by recalling there is no "I" in "between," only "e's" as in "me."

Incorrect   Just *between you and I*, the Russian housekeeper is a good cook, but she won't iron curtains.
Correct   Just *between you and me*, the Russian housekeeper is a good cook, but she won't iron curtains.

In other cases, to determine the correct pronoun, you will need to add implied but unstated sentence elements:

Examples   Mother always liked Dickie more than *me*. [Mother liked Dickie more than *she liked* me.]
                 She is younger than *I* by three days. [She is younger than I *am* by three days.]
                 Telephone exchange: May I speak to Kate? This is *she*. [This is she *speaking.*]

2. To solve the confusing *who/whom* pronoun problem, first determine the case of the pronoun in its own clause in each sentence.

    A. If the pronoun is the subject of a clause, use "who" or "whoever."

        Examples   I don't know *who* spread the peanut butter on my English paper. ["Who" is the subject of the verb "spread" in the clause "who spread the peanut butter on my English paper."]
Rachel is a librarian *who* only likes books with pictures. ["Who" is the subject of the verb "likes" in the clause "who only likes books with pictures."]
He will sell secrets to *whoever* offers the largest sum of money. ["Whoever" is the subject of the verb "offers" in the clause "whoever offers the largest sum of money."]

    B. If the pronoun occurs as the object of a preposition, use "whom," especially when the preposition immediately precedes the pronoun.

        Examples   *With whom* am I speaking?
To whom is the letter addressed?
Do not ask *for whom* the bell tolls.

    C. If the pronoun is the object of a verb, use "whom" or "whomever."

        Examples   Sid is a man *whom* I distrust. ["Whom" is the direct object of the verb "distrust."]
Who's calling *whom* a sore loser now? ["Whom" is the direct object of the verb "calling."]

20o Incorrect Compound Forms

Compound personal pronouns are formed by adding "-self" or "-selves" to some of the simple personal pronouns ("my," "you," "her," "him"). Use a dictionary if you are unsure of a correct form.

    Correct   myself, yourself, himself, themselves
    Incorrect   hisself, theirselves

Practicing What You've Learned

Errors with Nouns and Pronouns

A. In the following sentences, select the proper nouns and pronouns.

    1. Please buy a copy of the book *The Celery Stalks at Midnight* for my sister and (I, me).

continued on next page

2. Between you and (I, me), some people define a Freudian slip as saying one thing but meaning your mother.

3. (Who, Whom) is the singer of the country song "You Can't Make a Heel Toe the Mark"?

4. Aunt Beulah makes better cookies than (I, me).

5. (Her and me, She and I) are going to the movies to see *Attack of the Killer Crabgrass.*

6. I'm giving my accordion to (whoever, whomever) is carrying a grudge against our new neighbors, the (Smith's, Smiths).

7. The Botox surprise party was given by Paige Turner, Justin Case, and (I, me).

8. She is the kind of person for (who, whom) housework meant sweeping the room with a glance.

9. (Her and him, She and he) are twins (who, whom) are always finding (theirselves, themselves) in financial trouble.

10. The judge of the ugly feet contest announced (his self, him self, himself) the winner.

B. The following sentences contain a variety of errors with nouns and pronouns. Some sentences contain more than one error; skip any correct sentences you may find.

1. Clarence and me have an uncle who is so mean he writes the name of the murderer on the first page of mystery novels that are passed around the family.

2. Of whom did Oscar Wilde once say, "He hasn't a single redeeming vice"?

3. It was a surprise to both Mary and I to learn that Switzerland didn't give women the right to vote until 1971.

4. Each of the young women in the Family Life class decided not to marry after they read that couples today have 2.3 children.

5. Jim Bob explained to Frankie that the best way for him to avoid his recurring nosebleeds was to stay out of his cousin's marital arguments.

6. Those of us who'd had the flu agreed that one can always get a doctor to return your call quicker if you get in the shower, but let's keep this tip confidential between you and I.

7. The stranger gave the free movie tickets to Louise and I after he saw people standing in line to leave the theater.

continued on next page

8. The personnel director told each of the employees, most of who opposed him, to signify their "no" vote by saying, "I resign."

9. A person knows he's in trouble when their salary undergoes a modification reduction adjustment of 50 percent.

10. One of the first movies to gross over one million dollars was *Tarzan of the Apes* (1932), starring Johnny Weissmuller, a former Olympic star who became an actor. This didn't happen often in the movie industry at that time.

Errors with Adverbs and Adjectives

 Incorrect Usage **Adv Adj**

Incorrect use of adverbs and adjectives often occurs when you confuse the two modifiers. Adverbs qualify the meanings of verbs, adjectives, and other adverbs; they often answer the questions "how?" "when?" or "where?" and they frequently end in "-ly."

Incorrect   After Kay argued with the mechanic, she drove *slow* all the way home.
Correct   After Kay argued with the mechanic, she drove *slowly* all the way home.

Adjectives, on the other hand, commonly describe or qualify the meanings of nouns only.

Example   The *angry* mechanic neglected to put oil into Kay's *old* car.

One of the most confusing pairs of modifiers is "well" and "good." We often use "good" as an adjective modifying a noun and "well" as an adverb modifying a verb.

Examples   A *Sap's Fables* is a *good* book for children, although it is not *well* organized.
Bubba was such a *good* liar his wife had to call in the children at suppertime.
After eating Rocky Mountain oysters, Susie yodels exceptionally *well*.
Did you do *well* on your math test?

If you cannot determine whether a word is an adverb or an adjective, consult your dictionary.

 Faulty Comparison **Comp**

When you compare two elements to a higher or lower degree, you often add "-er" or "-r" to the adjective.

Incorrect   Of the two sisters, Selene is the *oldest*.
Correct   Of the two sisters, Selene is the *older*.

When you compare more than two elements, you often add "-est" to the adjective.

Example   Selene is the *oldest* of the four children in the family.

Other adjectives use the words "more," "most," "less," and "least" to indicate comparison.

Examples   Béla Lugosi is *more* handsome than Lon Chaney but *less* handsome than Vincent Price.
Of all the horror film stars, Boris Karloff is the *most* handsome, and Christopher Lee is the *least* handsome.

Beware using a double comparison when it is unnecessary:

Incorrect   It was the *most saddest* song I've ever heard.
Correct   It was the *saddest* song I've ever heard.

Note, too, that for most authorities, the word "unique" is a special adjective, one without a degree of comparison. Despite common usage to the contrary, an experience or thing may be unique—that is, one of a kind—but it may not be "very unique."

Practicing What You've Learned

Errors with Adverbs and Adjectives
Choose the correct adverbs and adjectives in the following sentences.

1. After the optometrist pulled her eye tooth, Hortense didn't behave very (good, well) in the waiting room.

2. Which is the (worser, worse, worst) food, liver or buttermilk?

3. I didn't do (good, well) on my nature project because my bonsai sequoia tree grew (bad, badly) in its tiny container.

4. Don't forget to dress (warm, warmly) for the Arctic freestyle race.

5. Of the twins, Teensie is (more tall, taller) than Egore.

6. Watching Joe Bob eat candied fruit flies made Jolene feel (real, really) ill, and his table manners did not make her feel (more better, better).

7. The Roman toothpick holder was (very unique, the uniquest, unique).

8. That was the (funniest, most funniest) flea circus I have ever seen.

9. Does the instructional guide *Bobbing for Doughnuts* still sell (good, well)?

10. The Fighting Mosquitoes were trained (well, good), but they just didn't take practices (serious, seriously).

Errors in Modifying Phrases

 20r Dangling Modifiers   **DM**

A modifying—or descriptive—phrase must have a logical relationship to some specific words in the sentence. When those words are omitted, the phrase "dangles" without anything to modify. Dangling modifiers frequently occur at the beginnings of sentences and often can be corrected by adding the proper subjects to the main clauses.

Dangling	Not knowing how to swim, buying scuba gear was foolish.
Correct	Not knowing how to swim, *we* decided that buying scuba gear was foolish.
Dangling	Feeling too sick to ski, her vacation to the mountains was postponed.
Correct	Feeling too sick to ski, *she* postponed her vacation to the mountains.

(◆ For additional examples, see pages 131–132.)

 20s Misplaced Modifiers   **MM**

When modifying words, phrases, or clauses are not placed near the word they describe, confusion or unintentional humor often results.

Misplaced	Teddy swatted the fly still dressed in his pajamas.
Correct	Still dressed in his pajamas, Teddy swatted the fly.
Misplaced	There are many things people won't eat, especially children.
Correct	There are many things people, especially children, won't eat.

(◆ For additional examples, see page 132.)

Practicing What You've Learned

Errors in Modifying Phrases
Correct the errors in dangling and misplaced modifiers by rearranging or rewriting the following sentences.

1. After boarding Hard Luck Airlines, the meals convinced us to return by ship.

2. Here is the new phone number for notifying the fire department of any fires that may be attached to your office telephone.

3. The prize-winning ice sculptor celebrated her new open-air studio in Aspen, where she lives with her infant daughter, purchased for $10,000.

4. The movie star showed off letters from admirers that were lying all over his desk.

continued on next page

5. Running too fast during a game of "Kick the Can," my face collided with the flagpole.

6. Eloise bought a computer from her neighbor with faulty memory.

7. Baggy, wrinkled, and hopelessly out of style, Jean tossed the skirt from her closet.

8. Forgetting to pack underwear, the suitcase had to be reopened.

9. Blanche plans to teach a course next spring incorporating her research into the mating habits of Big Foot on the campus of Slippery Rock College.

10. After spending all night in the library, Kate's friends knew she'd need a trip to Special Coffee.

11. Squeezing the can, the tomatoes didn't seem ripe to DeeDee.

12. From birth to twelve months, parents don't have to worry about solid food.

13. He didn't think the bicycles would make it over the mountains, being so old.

14. I've read that a number of modern sailors, like Thor Heyerdahl, have sailed primitive vessels across the ocean in books from the public library.

15. Proofreading carefully, dangling modifiers may be spotted and corrected easily.

Errors in Sentences

 20t **Fragments** **Frag**

A complete sentence must contain a subject and a verb. A fragment is an incomplete sentence; it is often a participial ("-ing") phrase or dependent clause that belongs to the preceding sentence. To check for fragments, try reading your prose one sentence at a time, starting at the *end* of your essay. If you find a "sentence" that makes no sense alone, it's probably a fragment that should be either rewritten or connected to another sentence.

Incorrect	Bubba's parents refuse to send him to a psychiatrist. Although they both know he eats shoelaces and lightbulbs.
Correct	Bubba's parents refuse to send him to a psychiatrist, although they both know he eats shoelaces and lightbulbs.
Incorrect	This recording of the symphony's latest concert is so clear you can hear every sound. Including the coughs and whispers of the audience.

Correct	This recording of the symphony's latest concert is so clear you can hear every sound, including the coughs and whispers of the audience.
Incorrect	Francis named her new mutt Super Dog. Because he could leap fences in a single bound.
Correct	Francis named her new mutt Super Dog because he could leap fences in a single bound.

You can also try this test to see whether a group of words is a fragment: say the phrase "It is true that" in front of the words in question. In most cases, a complete sentence will still make sense, but a fragment won't.

Examples	Francis named her new mutt Super Dog. Because he could leap fences in a single bound. [Which is a fragment?]
	It is true that *Francis named her new mutt Super Dog.* [This sentence makes sense so it is not a fragment.]
	It is true that *because he could leap fences in a single bound.* [Yes, this is the fragment.]

Sentence fragments are often used in conversations ("yes," "maybe," "just a minute") and in informal or personal writing (notes, letters, e-mail, etc.). In some professional and academic writing, *intentional fragments* or abbreviated sentences may be used occasionally for emphasis or to convey a particular tone, such as playfulness, anger, or scorn. However, intentional fragments should be just that: created on purpose to achieve a specific rhetorical goal.

Intentional Fragments	After cleaning out the attic, Eloise felt terrible. *Hot. Tired. Cranky with the world.*
	She agreed to hand over the jewels. *Just exactly what he had had in mind all along.*

As a general rule, fragments should be avoided in formal writing. Ask your instructor whether intentional fragments are permitted in your essays.

(◆ For more discussion of fragments, see pages 129–130.)

Practicing What You've Learned

Sentence Fragment Errors

A. Using the "It is true that" test, identify the fragments and the complete sentences in the following samples.

© Canstock Images, Inc./ Index Stock Imagery

1. The first drive-in theaters opened in New Jersey in 1933. Which was in the middle of the Great Depression when money was scarce.

2. By 1958 there were over 4,000 drive-ins in the United States. As recorded by the United Drive-in Theatre Owners Association.

continued on next page

3. The number of drive-ins has fallen drastically. Perhaps because escalating land prices make property too valuable for use in this way. Or the fact that they are open only during the summer months in some areas.

4. There are only 430 drive-ins left in the country. Including the American territories.

5. Other outdoor summer activities are also endangered. For instance, the miniature golf industry, down from 50,000 courses in the 1930s to fewer than 15,000 today.

B. Rewrite the following sentences so that there are no fragments.

1. The idea of a credit card first appeared in 1887. According to Lawrence M. Ausbel, author of "Credit Cards," in the *McGraw-Hill Encyclopedia of Economics.*

2. Originally an imaginary concept in a futurist novel by Edward Bellamy. The card allowed characters to charge against future earnings.

3. Around the turn of the twentieth century some American stores issued paper or metal "shoppers' plates." Although they were only used by retailers to identify their credit customers.

4. The first real credit card was issued in 1947 by a New York bank and was a success. Despite the fact that customers could charge purchases only in a two-block area in Brooklyn.

5. Travel and entertainment cards soon appeared that allowed customers to charge items and services across the country. For example, the American Express card in 1958 and Carte Blanche in 1959.

20u Run-on (or Fused) Sentence R-O

Don't run two sentences together without any punctuation. Use a period, a semicolon, or a comma plus a coordinating conjunction (if appropriate), or subordinate one clause.

Incorrect	The indicted police chief submitted his resignation the mayor accepted it gratefully.
Correct	The indicted police chief submitted his resignation. The mayor accepted it gratefully.
Correct	The indicted police chief submitted his resignation; the mayor accepted it gratefully.
Correct	The indicted police chief submitted his resignation, and the mayor accepted it gratefully.
Correct	When the indicted police chief submitted his resignation, the mayor accepted it gratefully.

Do not try to correct a run-on by inserting a comma between the two sentences; doing so without a coordinating conjunction will produce an error called a *comma splice*, discussed below and on page 577. Punctuate correctly or rewrite the run-on to best communicate your meaning.

Incorrect (run-on)	Victoria Woodhull was the first American woman to run for the presidency she was defeated in 1872 by Ulysses S. Grant.
Incorrect (comma splice)	Victoria Woodhull was the first American woman to run for the presidency, she was defeated in 1872 by Ulysses S. Grant.
Correct	Victoria Woodhull was the first American woman to run for the presidency. She was defeated in 1872 by Ulysses S. Grant.
Correct	Victoria Woodhull was the first American woman to run for the presidency; she was defeated in 1872 by Ulysses S. Grant.
Correct	Victoria Woodhull was the first American woman to run for the presidency, but she was defeated in 1872 by Ulysses S. Grant.
Correct	Victoria Woodhull, the first American woman to run for the presidency, was defeated in 1872 by Ulysses S. Grant.

Practicing What You've Learned

© Canstock Images, Inc./ Index Stock Imagery

Run-On Errors

Correct the following run-on sentences. Try to use several different methods of correcting the errors.

1. Workers in the United States take an average of thirteen days of vacation a year in Italy they take forty-two.

2. In 1901 a schoolteacher named Annie Edson Taylor became the first person to go over Niagara Falls in a wooden barrel she is the only woman known to have survived this risky adventure.

3. The minister preached his farewell sermon the choir sang "Break Forth into Joy."

4. The first microwave oven marketed in 1959 was a built-in unit it cost a whopping $2,595.

5. Coffee was considered a food in the Middle Ages travelers who found it growing in Ethiopia mixed it with animal fat.

(◆ For additional practice, turn to exercise "B" on pages 567–568.)

20v Comma Splice CS

A comma splice occurs when two sentences are linked with a comma. To correct this error, you can (1) separate the two sentences with a period, (2) separate the two sentences with a semicolon, (3) insert a coordinating conjunction ("for," "but," "and," "or," "nor," "so," "yet") after the comma, or (4) subordinate one clause.

Incorrect	Grover won a stuffed gila monster at the church raffle, his mother threw it away the next day while he was in school.
Correct	Grover won a stuffed gila monster at the church raffle. His mother threw it away the next day while he was in school.
Correct	Grover won a stuffed gila monster at the church raffle; his mother threw it away the next day while he was in school.
Correct	Grover won a stuffed gila monster at the church raffle, but his mother threw it away the next day while he was in school.
Correct	Although Grover won a stuffed gila monster at the church raffle, his mother threw it away the next day while he was in school.

(◆ For more help on correcting comma splices, see page 577 in the following chapter on punctuation; coordination and subordination are discussed in detail on pages 146–148.)

Practicing What You've Learned

© Canstock Images, Inc./
Index Stock Imagery

Comma Splice Errors

A. Correct the comma splices that appear in the following sentences. Use more than one method of correcting the errors.

1. Most people know that the likeness of Susan B. Anthony appeared on an American dollar coin in the 1990s, fewer people know exactly who she was or why she is so important.

2. For most of her life Anthony fought for women to obtain the right to vote, she was an organizer of the world's first women's rights convention in 1848.

3. Anthony often risked her safety and her freedom for her beliefs, she was arrested in 1872 for the crime of voting in an election.

4. She also worked to secure laws to protect working women, at that time all of a woman's wages automatically belonged to her husband.

5. Unfortunately, Anthony did not live to see the 1920 passage of the Nineteenth Amendment giving women the right to vote, she died in 1906.

B. Correct any run-on sentences or comma splice errors you see. Skip any correct sentences you find.

1. My mother is very politically conservative, she's written in King George III for president in the last two elections.

2. Mary Lou decided not to eat the alphabet soup the letters spelled out "botulism."

3. A dried gourd containing seeds probably functioned as the first baby rattle, ancient Egyptian wall paintings show babies with such gourds clutched in their fingers.

continued on next page

4. Opportunists who came to the South after the Civil War were often called "carpetbaggers," they carried their belongings in cheaply produced travel bags made of Belgian carpet.

5. A friend of mine offers a good definition of nasty theater critics on opening night, according to him, they're the people who can't wait to stone the first cast.

6. When English scientist James Smithson died in 1829, he willed his entire fortune to the United States to establish a foundation for knowledge, that's how the Smithsonian Institution was started.

7. The word "jack-o'-lantern" may have come from the legend of Irish Jack, a mean old man in life, he was condemned after death to wander the earth carrying a hollow turnip with a lump of burning coal inside.

8. People forget how large the blue whale is it has a heart as large as a Volkswagen Beetle and can hold an elephant on its tongue.

9. According to a study by the Fish and Wildlife Service, Americans' favorite animals are dogs, horses, swans, robins, and butterflies; their least favorite are cockroaches, mosquitos, rats, wasps, and rattlesnakes.

10. The famous Eiffel Tower, built for the 1889 Paris Exposition, has inspired many crazy stunts, for example, in 1891 Silvain Dornon climbed the 363 steps on stilts.

Assignment

Collaborative Activity: To continue practicing revision of major sentence errors, join two classmates, each with a current essay draft in hand. Each person should select and then study independently one of the following sections in this chapter: sentence fragments (pages 563–564), run-on sentences (pages 565–566), or comma splices (pages 566–567). After a study period of ten minutes, regroup and take turns explaining each error—and a way to eliminate it. Next, pass around and read all three essay drafts, marking the particular sentence error you studied if you find it in a classmate's paper. How might you help your classmate correct this error?

© CORBIS

20w Faulty Parallelism //

Parallel thoughts may be expressed in similar grammatical constructions. Repeated sentence elements, such as verbs, nouns, pronouns, and phrases, often appear in parallel form to emphasize meaning and to promote sentence flow.

Examples

Parallel verbs: In his vaudeville act he *sang*, *danced*, and *juggled*.

Parallel prepositional phrases: She ran *through the door*, *across the yard*, and *into the limo*.

You might find it helpful to isolate the repeated elements in a sentence to see whether they are parallel.

She ran

(1) through the door
(2 across the yard   } parallel
(3) into the limo

Faulty Parallelism	Boa constrictors like *to lie* in the sun, *to hang* from limbs, and *swallowing* small animals.
Isolated	(1) to lie
	(2) to hang
	(3) swallowing [not parallel to #1 and #2]
Revised	Boa constrictors like *to lie* in the sun, *to hang* from limbs, and *to swallow* small animals.
Faulty Parallelism	Whether *working* on his greasy car, *fistfighting* at the hamburger stand, or *in bed*, my brother always kept his hair combed.
Revised	Whether *working* on his greasy car, *fistfighting* at the hamburger stand, or *lounging* in bed, my brother always kept his hair combed.

Practicing What You've Learned

Errors in Parallelism

Revise the following sentences so that the parallel ideas are expressed in similar grammatical constructions.

1. Is it true that Superman could leap tall buildings, run faster than a locomotive, and that bullets would bounce off his skin?

2. To celebrate the canned pork product called Spam, for many years we attended the Texas Spamarama Festival to participate in the Spambalaya cook-off, the Spam slab toss, the Spam relay race, and were dancing to such favorites as "Twist and Snout."*

continued on next page

*Yes, readers, there really was a Spamarama Festival, a silly outdoor charity event in Austin, Texas, with music (SpamJam) and games (Spamolympics) for all ages. Held annually around April Fool's Day for thirty years, the Festival sadly reached its expiration date in 2008.

3. My Aunt Clara swears she has seen Elvis snacking at the deli, browsing at the supermarket, munching at the pizza parlor, and in the cookbook section of a local bookstore.

4. According to my husband, summer air in Louisiana is 2 percent oxygen, 8 percent water, and the rest is mosquitoes, about 90 percent.

5. Many teachers believe that the most important keys to success for students in college include attending class, keep up with reading assignments, and being brave enough to ask questions.

6. Yoga encourages its participants to work on their flexibility, strength, and how they can reduce their stress levels.

7. Drivers should hang up their cell phones, refrain from eating, and drinking too, leaving the radio buttons alone.

8. Smart people learn from their own mistakes; learning from the mistakes of others is what even smarter people do.

9. Theater class helped me overcome my shyness, make new friends, and my confidence to do other activities was improved.

10. The writer Oscar Wilde, the dancer Isadora Duncan, the painter Max Ernst, and Jim Morrison, who was a rock star, are all buried in the same Paris cemetery.

20x False Predication   Pred

This error occurs when the predicate (that part of the sentence that says something about the subject) doesn't fit properly with the subject. Illogical constructions result.

If it's helpful in some cases, remember that the verbs "is" and "was" often mean "equates to."

Incorrect	Energy is one of the world's biggest problems. ["Energy" itself is not a problem.]
Correct	The lack of fuel for energy is one of the world's biggest problems.
Incorrect	My roommate is why I'm moving to a new apartment. [A roommate is not a reason.]
Correct	My roommate's habit of talking nonstop is driving me to find a new apartment.
Also Correct	Because of my annoying roommate, I'm moving to a new apartment.
Incorrect	Her first comment after winning the lottery was exciting. [Her comment wasn't exciting; she was excited.]
Correct	Her first comment after winning the lottery expressed her excitement.

Incorrect	True failure is when you make an error and don't learn anything from it. [Avoid all "is when" and "is where" constructions. The subject does not denote a time, so the predicate is faulty.]
Correct	You have truly failed only when you make an error and don't learn anything from it.

(◆ For other examples of faulty predication, see pages 132–133.)

 20y **Mixed Structure** **Mix S**

"Mixed structure" is a catchall term that applies to a variety of sentence construction errors. Usually, the term refers to a sentence in which the writer begins with one kind of structure and then shifts to another in midsentence. Such a shift often occurs when writers are in a hurry and their minds have already jumped ahead to the next thought.

Confused	By the time one litter of cats is given away seems to bring a new one.
Clear	Giving away one litter of cats seems to tell the mother cat that it's time to produce a new batch.
Confused	The bank robber realized that in his crime spree how very little fun he was having.
Clear	The bank robber realized that he was having very little fun in his crime spree.
Confused	The novel is too difficult for what the author meant.
Clear	The novel is too difficult for me to understand what the author meant.
Confused	Children with messages from their parents will be stapled to the bulletin board.
Clear	To find messages from their parents, children should look at the bulletin board.

(◆ For other examples of mixed structure, see pages 132–133.)

Practicing What You've Learned

Errors of False Predication and Mixed Structure
Rewrite the following sentences so that each one is clear and coherent.

1. The team's quarterback A. M. Hall's broken finger, which sidelined him last week for the Raiders' game, is expected to play in tonight's game.

2. The groom is a graduate of Centerville High School where he lived all his life.

3. On my way to the doctor's office, my universal joint went out, causing even more body damage after hitting the tree.

continued on next page

4. An example of his intelligence is when he brought home a twenty-pound block of ice after ice fishing all day.

5. For those new residents who have children and don't know about it, the town offers low-cost daycare services.

6. According to the nineteenth-century cynic Ambrose Bierce, marriage is when there is "a master, a mistress, and two slaves, making in all, two."

7. Another situation when I get so mad is the plumber showing up three hours late.

8. My drama teacher is a big reason why I am a star today.

9. Some folks argue that sound travels slower than light such as when advice parents give their teenagers doesn't reach them until they're forty.

10. Hearing his cries for help is how he came to be found in a ditch by some stray cows.

Answers to the Grammar Assessment, Pages 547–548

Please note that some of the problems in grammar and sentence construction in this test could be corrected in more than one way. Here are some sample corrections.

1. Almost everyone today recognizes the Statue of Liberty, but not everybody knows its history.

2. According to the National Parks Service, plans for the statue were first begun in 1865 by Frenchman Edouard de Laboulaye in honor of the United States' love of democracy and French-American friendship.

3. Commissioned to design the work, artist Frederic-Auguste Bartholdi chose Bedloe's Island in the New York Harbor as the location because the island was government owned and the statue would be seen by thousands of immigrants entering the country through Ellis Island.

4. The project was a joint effort between the two countries: the French agreed to build the statue, and the U.S. agreed to build the pedestal.

5. The French raised money by sponsoring entertainment events, by selling souvenir items, and by charging some public fees. (Between you and me, these fund-raising methods seem difficult, and in fact didn't work very well in the U.S.)

6. Alexandre Gustave Eiffel, who had previously designed the famous Eiffel Tower, designed the statue's steel framework, which was covered with a flexible copper skin the width of two pennies so that the statue would not crack in high winds.

7. The statue's face is modeled on Bartholdi's mother. Each of the seven rays of her crown represents one of the seven seas and continents of the world; the torch symbolizes enlightenment; the broken chains at her feet signify freedom from oppression; the tablet in her arm stands for law.

8. Completed in France in the summer of 1884, the statue had to be carefully disassembled and the parts shipped separately to New York.

9. Following a reassembly process that took four months, thousands of spectators watched the massive 305-feet-high statue's dedication ceremony on October 28, 1886.

10. Both you and I can hardly disagree with the National Parks Service when it calls the Statue of Liberty one of the most recognized icons of democracy in the world. For more information, you may go online to <www.nps.gov/stli/historyculture>.

Chapter 21

A Concise Guide to Punctuation

Assessing Your Skills: Punctuation

To help you focus your study of this chapter, take the self-graded test that follows. Each of the sentences below contains one or more errors discussed in this chapter. See how much you already know by correcting the sentences and then checking the answers on page 600. By taking this test, you will be better able to evaluate your knowledge of punctuation and direct your attention to those rules governing the errors you missed.*

1. An interesting article appeared recently in the online version of The Writer's Almanac, it gave a brief history of sliced bread

2. Before 1928 bread was sold in solid loaves; or, baked at home.

3. Otto F. Rohwedder [a jeweler from Iowa] had invented a bread slicing machine, however, bakers' rejected it because they thought the bread would go dry stale or moldy too quickly.

4. Rohwedder tried many solutions to the dry—bread problem. Including sticking the slices together with hatpins.

5. He ultimately solved the problem by wrapping the sliced bread in wax paper but he still couldn't sell his machine.

6. Finally a baker in Chillicothe Missouri agreed to try Rohwedders plan.

7. The baker (Frank Bench installed the machine in his bakery. Despite it's bulky size. (three by five feet)

---

*Historical information included in this assessment test provided by *The Writer's Almanac with Garrison Keillor* on July 7, 2011, and may be accessed at <http://writersalmanac.publicradio.org/index.php?date=2011/07/07>.

8. Newspaper ad's announced the machines arrival; The Greatest Step Forward in the Baking Industry Since Bread Was Wrapped-Sliced Kleen Maid Bread".

9. Sales' were huge, a modern convenience was born.

10. Moreover the English-language gained an emphatic new phrase to express brilliance . . . Its the best thing since sliced bread

Punctuation Guidelines

Punctuation marks do not exist, as one student recently complained, to make your life complicated. They are used to clarify your written thoughts so that the reader understands your meaning. Just as traffic signs and signals tell a driver to slow down, stop, or go, so punctuation is intended to guide the reader through your prose. Look, for example, at the confusion in the following sentences when the necessary punctuation marks are omitted:

Confusing	Has the tiger been fed Bill? [Bill was the tiger's dinner?]
Clear	Has the tiger been fed, Bill?
Confusing	After we had finished raking the dog jumped into the pile of leaves. [Raking the dog?]
Clear	After we had finished raking, the dog jumped into the pile of leaves.
Confusing	The coach called the swimmers names. [Was the coach fired for verbally abusing the swimmers?]
Clear	The coach called the swimmers' names.

Because punctuation helps you communicate clearly with your reader, you should familiarize yourself with the following rules.

21a The Period (.) P

1. Use a period to end a sentence that makes a statement.

   Examples Employees at that company are not allowed to go on coffee breaks.
   It takes too long to retrain them.

2. Use a period at the end of a sentence that makes a direct command or request.

   Examples Don't walk on the grass.
   Please give me your new address.

3. Use a period after initials and many abbreviations.

   Examples W. B. Yeats, 12 A.M., Dr., etc., Ms.

4. Only one period is necessary if the sentence ends with an abbreviation.

   Examples The elephant was delivered C.O.D.
   To find a good job, you should obtain a B.S. or B.A.

21b The Question Mark (?) P

1. Use a question mark after every direct question.

> **Examples**   May I borrow your boots?
>
>   Is the sandstorm over now?

2. No question mark is necessary after an indirect question.

> **Examples**   Jean asked why no one makes a paper milk carton that opens without tearing.
>
>   Dave wondered how the television detective always found a parking place next to the scene of the crime.

21c The Exclamation Point (!) P

The exclamation point follows words, phrases, or sentences to show strong feelings.

> **Examples**   Fire! Call the rescue squad!
>
>   The Broncos finally won the Super Bowl!

Practicing What You've Learned

Errors Using Periods, Question Marks, and Exclamation Points

Correct the following sentences by adding, deleting, or changing periods, question marks, or exclamation points, where appropriate.

© Canstock Images, Inc./ Index Stock Imagery

1. The space program sent some cows into orbit last year I think they are now known as the herd shot around the world

2. Ms Anita Bath wants to know why erasers never outlast their pencils?

3. Her French class at St Claire's School on First Ave was taught by Madame Beau V Rhee, Ph.D. .

4. Where do all the birds go when it's raining

5. I have wonderful news I won the lottery

21d The Comma (,) P

1. Use a comma to separate two independent clauses* joined by a coordinating conjunction. To remember the coordinating conjunctions, think of the acronym

---

*An independent clause looks like a complete sentence; it contains a subject and a verb, and it makes sense by itself.

FANBOYS: "for," "and," "nor," "but," "or," "yet," and "so." Always use one of the FANBOYS and a comma when you join two independent clauses.

Examples   You can bury your savings in the backyard, *but* don't expect Mother Nature to pay interest.

I'm going home tomorrow, *and* I'm never coming back.

After six weeks Louie's diet was making him feel lonely and depressed, *so* he had a bumper sticker printed that said, "Honk if you love groceries."

Do *not* join two sentences with a comma only; such an error is called a *comma splice.* Use a comma plus one of the coordinating conjunctions listed previously, a period, a semicolon, or subordination.

Comma Splice	Beatrice washes and grooms the chickens, Samantha feeds the spiders.
Correct	Beatrice washes and grooms the chickens, and Samantha feeds the spiders.
Correct	Beatrice washes and grooms the chickens. Samantha feeds the spiders.
Correct	Beatrice washes and grooms the chickens; Samantha feeds the spiders.
Correct	When Beatrice washes and grooms the chickens, Samantha feeds the spiders.
Comma Splice	Juan doesn't like singing groups, he won't go with us to hear Fed Up with People.
Correct	Juan doesn't like singing groups, so he won't go with us to hear Fed Up with People.
Correct	Juan doesn't like singing groups. He won't go with us to hear Fed Up with People.
Correct	Juan doesn't like singing groups; he won't go with us to hear Fed Up with People.
Correct	Because Juan doesn't like singing groups, he won't go with us to hear Fed Up with People.

(◆ For additional help, see pages 566–567; for practice exercises, see pages 567 and 581.)

Beware the tricky word "however." "However" is *not* one of the FANBOYS (coordinating conjunctions) and consequently can never be used to join two independent clauses. Incorrect use of "however" most often results in a comma splice.

Comma Splice	The police arrested the thief, *however,* they had to release him because the plant wouldn't talk.
Correct	The police arrested the thief; *however,* they had to release him because the plant wouldn't talk.
Also Correct	The police arrested the thief. *However,* they had to release him because the plant wouldn't talk.

2. Set off with a comma an introductory phrase or clause.

Examples   After we had finished our laundry, we discovered that one sock was missing.

According to the owner of the Hall Laundry House, customers have conflicting theories about missing laundry.

For example, one man claims his socks make a break for freedom when no one is watching the dryers.

3. Set off nonessential phrases and clauses. If the information can be omitted without changing the meaning of the main clause, then the phrase or clause is nonessential. Do not set off clauses or phrases that are essential to the meaning of the main clause.

Essential   He looked worse than my friend *who gets his clothes from the "lost and found" at the bus station*. [The "who" clause is essential to explain which friend.]

The storm *that destroyed Mr. Peartree's outhouse* left him speechless with anger. [The "that" clause is essential to explain which storm angered Mr. Peartree.]

The movie *now showing at the Ritz* is very obscene and very popular. [The participial phrase is essential to identify the particular movie.]

Nonessential   Joe Medusa, *who won the jalapeno-eating contest last year*, is this year's champion cow-chip tosser. [The "who" clause is nonessential because it only supplies additional information to the main clause.]

Black widow spiders, *which eat their spouses after mating*, are easily identifiable by the orange hourglass design on their abdomens. [The "which" clause is nonessential because it only supplies additional information.]

The jukebox, *now reappearing in local honky-tonks*, first gained popularity during the 1920s. [The participial phrase is nonessential because it only supplies additional information.]

4. Conjunctive adverbs, such as "however," "moreover," "thus," "consequently," and "therefore," are used to show continuity and are frequently set off by commas when they appear in midsentence.

Examples   She soon discovered, *however*, that he had stolen her monogrammed towels in addition to her pet avocado plant.

She felt, *consequently*, that he was not trustworthy.

When a conjunctive adverb occurs at the beginning of a sentence, it may be followed by a comma, especially if a pause is intended. If no pause is intended, you may omit the comma, but inserting the comma is never wrong.

Examples   *Thus*, she resolved never to speak to him again.

Thus she resolved never to speak to him again.

Therefore, he resolved never to speak to her again.

Therefore he resolved never to speak to her again.

(◆ For practice of comma rules 1–4, turn to page 581.)

5. Use commas to separate items in a series of words, phrases, or clauses.

Examples   Julio collects coins, stamps, bottle caps, erasers, and pocket lint.

Mrs. Jones chased the burglar out the window, around the ledge, down the fire escape, and into the busy street.

Do note that there is no comma separating "such as" and the first word in the list of items that follow.

Incorrect   Sarah eats a variety of vegetarian foods, such as, tofu, nuts, and fruit.

Correct   Sarah eats a variety of vegetarian foods, such as tofu, nuts, and fruit.

Although journalists and some grammarians permit the omission of the last comma before the "and," many authorities believe the comma is necessary for clarity. For example, how many pints of ice cream are listed in the sentence below?

Please buy the following pints of ice cream: strawberry, peach, coffee, vanilla and chocolate swirl.

Four or five pints? Without a comma before the "and," the reader doesn't know whether vanilla and chocolate swirl are (is?) one item or two. By inserting the last comma, you clarify the sentence:

Please buy the following pints of ice cream: strawberry, peach, coffee, vanilla, and chocolate swirl.

6. Use commas to separate adjectives of equal emphasis that modify the same noun. To determine whether a comma should be used, see if you can insert the word "and" between the adjectives; if the phrase still makes proper sense with the substituted "and," use a comma.

Examples   She finally moved out of her cold, dark apartment.

She finally moved out of her cold and dark apartment.

I have a sweet, handsome husband.

I have a sweet and handsome husband.

He called from a convenient telephone booth.

But not: He called from a convenient and telephone booth. ["Convenient" modifies the unit "telephone booth," so there is no comma.]

Hand me some of that homemade pecan pie.

But not: Hand me some of that homemade and pecan pie. ["Homemade" modifies the unit "pecan pie," so there is no comma.]

7. Set off a direct address with commas.

Examples   Gentlemen, keep your seats.

Car fifty-four, where are you?

Not now, Eleanor, I'm busy.

8. Use commas to set off items in addresses and dates.

   Examples   The sheriff followed me from Austin, Texas, to question me about my uncle.

   He found me on February 2, 1978, when I stopped in Fairbanks, Alaska, to buy sunscreen.

9. Use commas to set off a degree or title following a name.

   Examples   John Dough, M.D., was audited when he reported only $5.68 in taxable income last year.

   The Neanderthal Award went to Samuel Lyle, Ph.D.

10. Use commas to set off dialogue from the speaker.

    Examples   Alexander announced, "I don't think I want a second helping of possum."

    "Eat hearty," said Marie, "because this is the last of the food."

    Note that you do not use a comma before an indirect quotation or before titles in quotation marks following the verbs "read," "sang," or "wrote."

    Incorrect   Bruce said, that cockroaches have portions of their brains scattered throughout their bodies.

    Correct   Bruce said that cockroaches have portions of their brains scattered throughout their bodies.

    Incorrect   One panel member read, "Aunt Jennifer's Tigers," and the other sang, "Song for My Father."

    Correct   One panel member read "Aunt Jennifer's Tigers," and the other sang "Song for My Father."

11. Use commas to set off "yes," "no," "well," and other weak exclamations.

    Examples   Yes, I am in the cat condo business.

    No, all the units with decks are sold.

    Well, perhaps one with a pool will do.

12. Set off interrupters or parenthetical elements appearing in the middle of a sentence. A parenthetical element is additional information placed as explanation or comment within an already complete sentence. This element may be a word (such as "certainly" or "fortunately"), a phrase ("for example" or "in fact"), or a clause ("I believe" or "you know"). The word, phrase, or clause is parenthetical if the sentence parts before and after it fit together and make sense.

    Examples   Jack is, *I think*, still a compulsive gambler.

    Harvey, *my brother*, sometimes has breakfast with him.

    Jack cannot, *for example*, resist shuffling the toast or dealing the pancakes.

13. Resist the temptation to pepper your prose with commas when you have no good reason to use them. Not all sentences containing "and" take a comma. In

the following sentence, for example, "and" separates a compound predicate; it is not used as one of the FANBOYS (a coordinating conjunction) separating two independent clauses.

Incorrect   She ate a biscuit, and drank a cup of tea. [The comma here incorrectly separates the verb "drank" from its subject "she."]

Correct   She ate a biscuit and drank a cup of tea.

On the other hand, writers may use commas when necessary to improve sentence clarity.

Confusing   Unlike Mary Jo never learned to cook.

Clear   Unlike Mary, Jo never learned to cook.

Confusing   Whatever will be will be.

Clear   Whatever will be, will be.

Practicing What You've Learned

Comma Errors

© Canstock Images, Inc./
Index Stock Imagery

A. Study the comma rules numbered 1–4 on pages 576–579. Correct any comma errors you see in the following sentences.

1. In 1886 temperance leader Harvey Wilcox left Kansas, he purchased 120 acres near Los Angeles to develop a new town.

2. Although there were no holly trees growing in that part of California Mrs. Wilcox named the area Hollywood.

3. Mrs. Wilcox may have named the place after a home, owned by a friend living in Illinois.

4. During the early years settlers who shared the Wilcoxes' values moved to the area and banned the recreational drinking of alcoholic beverages, however, some alcohol consumption was allowed for medicinal purposes.

5. Nevertheless by 1910 the first film studio opened its doors inside a tavern on Sunset Boulevard, within seven short years the quiet community started by the Wilcoxes had vanished.

B. Study the comma rules 5–13 on pages 579–581. Correct any comma errors you see in the following sentences.

1. Yes Hortense in the 1920s young women did indeed cut their hair raise their hemlines dab perfume behind their knees and dance the Charleston.

continued on next page

2. In 1873 Cornell University cancelled the school's first intercollegiate football game with Michigan when the president announced "I will not permit thirty men to travel four hundred miles merely to agitate a bag of wind."

3. Jane Marian Donna Ann and Cissy graduated from high school on June 5 1964 in Texarkana Texas in the old Walnut Street Auditorium.

4. "I may be a man of few opinions" said Henry "but I insist that I am neither for nor against apathy."

5. Did you know for instance that early American settlers once thought the tomato was so poisonous they used the plant only for decoration?

C. The following sentences contain many kinds of comma errors, including the comma splice. Correct any errors you see by adding, deleting, or changing the commas as needed.

1. The father decided to recapture his youth, he took his son's car keys away.

2. Although ice cream didn't appear in America until the 1700s our country now leads the world in ice cream consumption, Australia is second I think.

3. Last summer the large friendly family that lives next door flew Discount Airlines and visited three cities on their vacation, however, their suitcases visited five.

4. Researchers in Balboa, Panama have discovered that the poisonous, yellow-belly, sea snake which descended from the cobra, is the most deadly serpent in the world.

5. Lulu Belle, my cousin, spent the week of Sept. 1–7, 1986 in the woods near Dimebox, Texas looking for additions to her extinct, butterfly collection, however she wasn't at all successful in her search.

(◆ For additional practice correcting comma splice errors, see pages 567–568 in Chapter 20.)

21e   The Semicolon (;)   P

1. Use a semicolon to link two closely related independent clauses.

Examples   Anthropologists believe popcorn originated in Mexico; they have found popcorn poppers that are over 1,500 years old.

Kate's mother does not have to begin a jogging program; she gets all the exercise she needs by worrying in place.

Avoid a "semicolon fragment" error by making sure there is an independent clause—a complete sentence, not a fragment—on either side of the semicolon.*

Semicolon fragment	Cutting your lawn with a push mower burns 420 calories; according to *Vitality* magazine. ["According to *Vitality* magazine" is a fragment. In this case, a comma, not a semicolon, is needed.]
Correct	Cutting your lawn with a push mower burns 420 calories, according to *Vitality* magazine.

◆ If you are unsure about recognizing a fragment, try using the "It is true that" test as described on page 564.

2. Use a semicolon to avoid a comma splice when connecting two independent clauses with words like "however," "moreover," "thus," "therefore," and "consequently."

Examples	Vincent van Gogh sold only one painting in his entire life; however, in 1987 his *Sunflowers* sold for almost $40 million.
	All Esmeralda's plants die shortly after she gets them home from the store; consequently, she has the best compost heap in town.
	This town is not big enough for both of us; therefore, I suggest we expand the city limits.

3. Use a semicolon in a series between items that already contain internal punctuation.

Examples	Last year the Wildcats suffered enough injuries to keep them from winning the pennant, as Jake Pritchett, third baseman, broke his arm in a fight; Hugh Rosenbloom, starting pitcher, sprained his back on a trampoline; and Boris Baker, star outfielder, ate rotten clams and nearly died.
	Her children were born a year apart: Moe, 1936; Curley, 1937; and Larry, 1938.

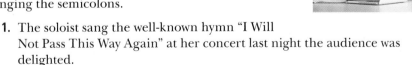

Practicing What You've Learned

© Canstock Images, Inc./ Index Stock Imagery

Semicolon Errors

Correct the sentences that follow by adding, deleting, or changing the semicolons.

1. The soloist sang the well-known hymn "I Will Not Pass This Way Again" at her concert last night the audience was delighted.

continued on next page

---

*Some folks have noted that the semicolon might be better named the "semi-period" in that it functions like a weak period, joining two complete sentences together but with a weaker stop between thoughts than a period demands.

2. Apples have long been associated with romance for example, one legend says if you throw an apple peel over your shoulder, it will fall into the shape of your true love's initial.

3. According to an 1863 book of etiquette, the perfect hostess will see to it that the works of male and female authors are properly separated on her bookshelves, however, if the authors happen to be married, their proximity may be tolerated.

4. Today, there are some 60,000 Americans older than 100 in 1960, there were only 3,222; according to *Health* magazine.

5. The sixth-grade drama club will present their interpretation of *Hamlet* tonight in the school cafeteria all parents are invited to see this tragedy.

6. Some inventors who named weapons after themselves include Samuel Colt, the Colt revolver, Henry Deringer, Jr., the derringer pistol, Dr. Richard J. Gatling, the crank machine gun, Col. John T. Thompson, the submachine or "tommy" gun, and Oliver F. Winchester, the repeating rifle.

7. My doctor failed in his career as a kidnapper, no one could read his ransom notes.

8. The highest point in the United States is Mt. McKinley at 20,320 feet, in contrast, the lowest point is Death Valley at 282 feet below sea level.

9. As we drove down the highway, we saw a sign that said "See the World's Largest Prairie Dog Turn Right at This Exit," therefore we immediately stopped to look.

10. The next billboard read "See Live Jackalopes"; making us want to stop again.

21f The Colon (:) P

1. Use a colon to introduce a long or formal list, but do not use one after "to be" verbs.

Example	Please pick up these items at the store: garlic, wolfbane, mirrors, a prayer book, a hammer, and a wooden stake.
Incorrect	Jean is such a bad cook that she thinks the four basic food groups are: canned, frozen, ready-to-mix, and take-out.
Correct	Jean is such a bad cook that she thinks the four basic food groups are canned, frozen, ready-to-mix, and take-out.

Avoid needless colons.

Incorrect	At the store I couldn't find: wolfbane or a wooden stake.
Correct	At the store I couldn't find wolfbane or a wooden stake.

2. A colon may be used to introduce a quotation or definition.

Examples Nineteenth-century writer Ambrose Bierce offers this definition of a bore: "A person who talks when you wish him to listen."

Critic Dorothy Parker was unambiguous in her review of the book: "This is not a novel to be tossed aside lightly; it should be thrown with great force."

In singer Jimmy Buffett's Margaritaville store in Key West, a sign warns: "Shoplifters will be forced to listen to Barry Manilow."

3. Use a colon to introduce a word, phrase, or sentence that emphatically or humorously explains, summarizes, or amplifies the preceding sentence.

Examples To her delight, we fed our pet lamb her favorite dish: shepherd's pie.

According to Kira, Colorado has four seasons: last winter, this winter, next winter, and July.

After marrying nine times, glamour queen Zsa Zsa Gabor had simple advice for becoming a marvelous housekeeper: every time you leave a relationship, keep the house.

4. Use a colon in the salutations of business or professional correspondence. Colons may also follow headings in memos.

Examples Dear Professor Stallones:

To:

Subject:

Date:

Practicing What You've Learned

Errors with Colons

Correct the following errors by adding, deleting, or substituting colons for faulty punctuation. Skip any correct sentences.

1. Experts have discovered over thirty different kinds of clouds but have separated them into three main types cirrus, cumulus, and stratus.

2. To those folks who may talk too much, Abraham Lincoln gives the following advice: "It is better to remain silent and be thought a fool than to speak out and remove all doubt."

3. A recent Gallup poll found that Americans consider only one activity more stressful than visiting the dentist hosting a dinner party.

4. Mr. and Mrs. Garden Slug hated their wedding gift a set of salt and pepper shakers.

5. Please remember to buy the following at the pet store, one pound of cat food, two flea collars, kitty fang floss, a bag of catnip, and thirty-six lint rollers.

continued on next page

6. A Director of Academic Services at Pennsylvania State University once nominated this sentence for Punctuation Error of the Year; "I had to leave my good friend's behind and find new ones."

7. Some of the cars manufactured between 1907 and 1912 that didn't achieve the popularity of the Model T were: the Black Crow, the Swallow, the Bugmobile, and the Carnation.

8. There's only one thing that can make our lawn look as good as our neighbor's; snow.

9. In a Thurmont, Maryland, cemetery can be found this epitaph "Here lies an Atheist, all dressed up, and no place to go."

10. George Bernard Shaw, the famous playwright, claimed he wanted the following epitaph on his tombstone: "I knew if I stayed around long enough, something like this would happen."

21g   The Apostrophe (')   AP

1. Use an apostrophe to indicate omitted letters in a contraction ("cannot" = "can't").

Examples   *It's* too bad your car burned.

Wouldn't the insurance company believe your story?

Many people today confuse "it's" (the contraction for "it is") and "its" (the possessive pronoun, which never takes an apostrophe).

   Its = shows possession, functioning like "his" or "her"
   It's = contraction for "it is"

Examples   The car is old, but *its* paint is new. ["Its" shows the car's possession of paint.]

The car is old, but *it's* reliable. ["It's" is a contraction for "it is."]

If you are ever in doubt about your choice, read the sentence aloud, saying the words "it is" in place of the *its/it's* in question. If the sentence becomes nonsensical (The car is old but it is coat of paint is new), then the possessive form "its" is probably what you need.

   Special note: There is no "its'." No such word exists in the English language! Forget you even thought about it!

2. Add an apostrophe plus "s" to a noun to show possession.

Examples   *Jack's* dog ate the *cat's* dinner.

The *veterinarian's* assistant later doctored the *puppy's* wounds.

3. Add only an apostrophe to a plural noun ending in "s" to show possession.

Examples   Goldilocks invaded the *bears'* house.

She ignored her *parents'* warning about breaking and entering.

4. To show joint possession between two people or things, you need to add an apostrophe and "s" only to the second noun. To show separate ownership, add an apostrophe plus "s" to both nouns.

> **Examples**   Isabel and *Sharona's* design project will be presented today. [one project]
>
>   *Isabel's* and *Sharona's* design projects will be presented today. [separate projects]

5. Be careful to avoid adding an apostrophe when the occasion simply calls for the plural use of a word.

> **Incorrect**   *Apple's* are on sale now.
>
> **Correct**   *Apples* are on sale now.
>
> **Incorrect**   We ordered *chip's* and dip.
>
> **Correct**   We ordered *chips* and dip.

6. In some cases you may add an apostrophe plus "s" to a singular word ending in "s," especially when the word is a proper name or for ease of pronunciation.

> **Examples**   *Doris's* name was popular in the 1950s.
>
>   The silent screen *actress's* favorite flowers were mums.

7. To avoid confusion, you may use an apostrophe plus "s" to form the plurals of letters and words discussed as words. An apostrophe is not used on plural numbers (1960s, 80s, nines) or abbreviations (MAs, DVDs, CDs).

> **Examples**   He made four *"C's"* last fall. [or "Cs"]
>
>   You use too many *"and's"* in your sentence. [or "ands"]

Practicing What You've Learned

Errors with Apostrophes

© Canstock Images, Inc./
Index Stock Imagery

A. Correct the apostrophe errors you see in the following phrases.

   1. A horses' pajamas

   2. The queens throne

   3. A families' vacation

   4. Ten students grades

   5. The Depression of the 1930s' was over.

   6. That dress of hers'

continued on next page

7. The childrens' toys

8. Worm's for sale

9. Bill Jones car

10. All essay's are due today.

11. Sign both the painters and the roofer's contracts.

12. Womens hats with feather's for decoration

B. Show that you understand the difference between "it's" and "its" by correcting any errors in the sentences that follow. Skip any correct use you see.

1. Its unfortunate that the game ended in a tie.

2. The tree lost its leaves.

3. Its beginning to feel like fall now.

4. The library was closing its' doors.

5. I realize its none of my business.

(◆ For more practice, turn to pages 590–591.)

Assignment

© CORBIS

Collaborative Activity: Continue working on your punctuation skills by editing the following paragraph for errors in commas, semicolons, colons, and apostrophes. Form a group with two other students and compare your corrections. Did you find and fix the same errors? If your group disagrees about a particular punctuation mark, consult the appropriate pages in this chapter. Once your group has agreed on a corrected paragraph, compare your work with that of other groups in the class. Later, when you are revising your own writing, proofread carefully for any of the errors you found in this exercise.

During winter parties theres often one ignored dessert on the buffet table; the fruitcake. If you're a fruitcake-hater on someones' annual holiday gift list don't just throw it out—dump it in style! Attend the Great Fruitcake Toss in Manitou Springs Colorado; a whacky series of contests held every first Saturday in January since 1996. Contestants' vie for the longest throw for the most accurate toss and for the most creative launching device. In years past hurlers have used catapults, cannons slingshots, bows and arrows, and giant rubber-band contraptions to fling their fruitcakes, only eating is strictly forbidden. Its all done for charity, the entrance fee of one nonperishable item for the towns local food bank fills the shelves for weeks.

21h Quotation Marks (" " and ' ') P

1. Use quotation marks to enclose someone's spoken or written words.

Examples   "Watch out for that left hook," said Tinkerbell to Peter Pan, just before his fight with the pirate captain.

Upon the opening of the world's first underground passenger train in 1863, the editor of the *London Times* wrote that it was "an insult to common sense to think that people would choose to travel in darkness across London."

Note that when a quotation is interrupted, an extra set of marks should be used.

Example   "Today, American coins of ten cents or more have grooved edges," explained the numismatist, "because decades ago our government wanted to stop thieves from shaving the edges of silver and gold coins."

Use quotation marks around the titles of essays,* articles, chapter headings, short stories, short poems, and songs.

Examples   "How to Paint Ceramic Ashtrays"

"The Fall of the House of Usher"

"Stopping by Woods on a Snowy Evening"

"Yankee Doodle"

2. Place quotation marks around a word, phrase, or letter used as the subject of discussion when italics are not available or preferred.

Examples   Never use "however" as a coordinating conjunction.

The word "bigwig," meaning an important person, is derived from the large wigs worn by seventeenth-century British judges.

Is your middle initial "X" or "Y"?

Her use of such adjectives as "drab," "bleak," and "musty" gives the poem a somber tone.

3. Place quotation marks around uncommon nicknames and words used ironically. Do not, however, try to apologize for slang or clichés by enclosing them in quotation marks; instead, substitute specific words.

Examples   "Scat-cat" Malone takes candy from babies.

Her "friend" was an old scarecrow in an abandoned barn.

Slang   After work Chuck liked to "simple out" in front of the television.

Specific   After work Chuck liked to relax by watching old movies on television.

4. The period and the comma go inside quotation marks; the semicolon and the colon go outside. If the quoted material is a question, the question mark goes

---

*Do *not*, however, put quotation marks around your own essay's title on either the title page or the first page of your paper.

inside; if the quoted material is a part of a whole sentence that is a question, the mark goes outside. The rules for exclamation points are the same as those for question marks.

Examples According to cartoonist Matt Groening, "Love is a snowmobile racing across the tundra; suddenly it flips over, pins you underneath, and at night the ice weasels come."

"Love is a snowmobile racing across the tundra; suddenly it flips over, pins you underneath, and at night the ice weasels come," says cartoonist Matt Groening.

According to cartoonist Matt Groening, "Love is a snowmobile . . . suddenly it flips over, pins you underneath, and at night the ice weasels come"; Groening also advises that bored friends are one of the first signs that you're in love.

Did he really say, "At night the ice weasels come"?

Lisa asked, "Do you think you're in love or just in a snowmobile?"

As usual, Homer replied, "D'oh!"

5. Use single quotation marks to enclose a quotation (or words requiring quotation marks) within a quotation.

Examples Professor Hall asked his class, "Do you agree with Samuel Johnson, who once said that a second marriage represents 'the triumph of hope over experience'?"

"One of my favorite songs is 'In My Life' by the Beatles," said Jane.

"I'm so proud of the 'A' on my grammar test," Sue told her parents.

6. If you are quoting fewer than four lines of poetry, enclose them within quotation marks, using a slash to indicate each line division.

Example In possibly the first love poem ever published in America, Anne Bradstreet wrote these opening lines in 1678: "If ever two were one, then surely we. / If ever man were loved by wife, then thee."

Practicing What You've Learned

Errors with Apostrophes and Quotation Marks

Correct the following errors by adding, changing, or deleting apostrophes and quotation marks.

1. Its true that when famous wit Dorothy Parker was told that President Coolidge, also known as Silent Cal, was dead, she exclaimed, How can they tell?

2. When a woman seated next to Coolidge at a dinner party once told him she had made a bet with a friend that she could get more than two words out of him, he replied You lose.

continued on next page

3. Twenty-one of Elvis Presleys albums have sold over a million copies; twenty of the Beatles albums have also done so.

4. Cinderellas stepmother wasn't pleased that her daughter received an F in her creative writing class on her poem Seven Guys and a Gal, which she had plagiarized from her two friend's Snow White and Dopey.

5. Wasn't it Mae West who said, When choosing between two evils, I always like to try the one I've never tried before? asked Olivia.

6. Horace said Believe me, its to everybodies' advantage to sing the popular song You Stole My Heart and Stomped That Sucker Flat, if thats what the holdup man wants.

7. A scholars research has revealed that the five most commonly used words in written English are the, of, and, a, and to.

8. The triplets mother said that while its' hard for her to choose, O. Henrys famous short story The Ransom of Red Chief is probably her favorite.

9. Despite both her lawyers advice, she used the words terrifying, hideous, and unforgettable to describe her latest flight on Golden Fleece Airways, piloted by Jack One-Eye Marcus.

10. Its clear that Bubba didnt know whether the Christmas' tree thrown in the neighbors yard was ours, theirs,' or your's.

21i Parentheses ( )   P

1. Use parentheses to set off words, dates, or statements that give additional information, explain, or qualify the main thought.

Examples   To encourage sales, some automobile manufacturers name their cars after fast or sleek animals (Impala, Mustang, and Thunderbird, for example).

Popular American author Mark Twain (Samuel Clemens) described many of his childhood experiences in *Tom Sawyer* (1876).

The Ford Motor Company once rejected the name Utopian Turtletop for one of its new cars, choosing instead to call it the Edsel (a name that obviously didn't help sales either).

2. The period comes inside the close parenthesis if a complete sentence is enclosed; it occurs after the close parenthesis when the enclosed matter comes at the end of the main sentence and is only a part of the main sentence.

Examples   The Colorado winters of 1978 and 1979 broke records for low temperatures. (See pages 72–73 for temperature charts.)

Jean hates Colorado winters and would prefer a warmer environment (such as Alaska, the North Pole, or a meat locker in Philadelphia).

3. If you are confused trying to decide whether information should be set off by commas, parentheses, or dashes, here are three guidelines:

   A. Use commas to set off information closely related to the rest of the sentence.

   Example   When Billy Clyde married Maybelle, his brother's young widow, the family was shocked. [The information identifies Maybelle and tells why the family was shocked.]

   B. Use parentheses to set off information loosely related to the rest of the sentence or material that would disturb the grammatical structure of the main sentence.

   Examples   Billy Clyde married Maybelle (his fourth marriage, her second) in Las Vegas on Friday. [The information is merely additional comment not closely related to the meaning of the sentence.]

   Billy Clyde married Maybelle (she was previously married to his brother) in Las Vegas on Friday. [The information is an additional comment that would also disturb the grammatical structure of the main sentence were it not enclosed in parentheses.]

   C. Use dashes to set off information dramatically or emphatically.

   Example   Billy Clyde eloped with Maybelle—only three days after her husband's funeral—without saying a word to anyone in the family.

4. For clarity, parentheses may be used to set off numbers in a list that appears within prose.

   Example   Urban legends are popular stories that almost always share these characteristics: (1) they are spread through person-to-person communication; (2) they are virtually untraceable to a single source, such as a book or newspaper; (3) they involve outlandish, humorous, or terrifying events; and (4) they carry an unstated warning or moral.

5. Parentheses may enclose the first-time use of acronyms (words formed from the initials of several words) or abbreviations.

   Examples   National Aeronautics and Space Administration (NASA)
   University of California at Los Angeles (UCLA)
   Museum of Modern Art (MoMA)

21j   Brackets [ ]   P

1. Use brackets to set off editorial explanations in the work of another writer.

   Examples   According to the old letter, the treasure map could be found "in the library taped to the back of the portrait [of Gertrude the Great] that faces north."

   The country singer ended the interview by saying, "My biggest hit so far is 'You're the Reason Our Kids Are Ugly' [original version by Sarah Bellham]."

2. Use brackets to set off editorial corrections in quoted material. By placing the bracketed word "sic" (meaning "thus") next to an error, you indicate that the mistake appeared in the original text and that *you* are not misquoting or misspelling.

Examples   The student wrote, "I think it's unfair for teachers to count off for speling [sic]." ["Sic" in brackets indicates that the student who is quoted misspelled the word "spelling."]

The highway advertisement read as follows: "For great stakes [sic], eat at Joe's, located right behind Daisy's Glue Factory." [Here, "sic" in brackets indicates an error in word choice; the restaurant owner incorrectly advertised "stakes" instead of "steaks."]

3. If additional information needs to appear in material already enclosed in parentheses, use brackets to avoid the confusion of double parenthesis marks.

Example   Nineteenth-century author Kate Chopin often found herself in the midst of controversy. (For example, *The Awakening* [1899] was considered so scandalous that it was banned by the St. Louis Library.)

21k   The Dash (—)*   P

1. Use a dash to indicate a strong or sudden shift in thought.

Examples   Now, let's be reasonable—wait, put down that ice pick!

"It's not athlete's foot—it's deadly coreopsis!" cried Dr. Mitty.

2. Use dashes to set off parenthetical matter that deserves more emphasis than parentheses denote.

Examples   Wanda's newest guru—the one who practiced catatonic hedonism— taught her to rest and play at the same time.

He was amazed to learn his test score—a pitiful 43.

(◆ To clear up any confusion over the uses of dashes, commas, and parentheses, see the guidelines on page 392.)

3. Use a dash before a statement that summarizes or amplifies the preceding thought. (Dashes can also be used to introduce a humorous or ironic twist on the first idea in the sentence.)

Examples   Aged wine, delicious food, someone else picking up the check—the dinner was perfect.

Not everyone agrees with football coach Vince Lombardi, who said, "Winning isn't everything—it's the only thing."

According to Hollywood star Cher, "The trouble with some women is that they get all excited about nothing—and then marry him."

---

*Do not confuse the dash with the hyphen. In typed work, a dash is indicated by *two* bar marks ("—"); one bar mark ("-") indicates a hyphen. Some word processing programs will automatically convert two bar marks to a dash.

Practicing What You've Learned

© Canstock Images, Inc./
Index Stock Imagery

Errors with Parentheses, Brackets, and Dashes

Show that you understand the different uses of parentheses, brackets, and dashes by selecting the best choice in the sentences that follow. Skip any correct sentences you see. (◆ For additional practice, see also the exercise that appears on pages 599–600.)

1. George Eliot (the pen name of Mary Ann Evans) wrote the novel *Middlemarch.*

2. The Apostrophe Protection Society, founded in London in 2001, fights against the gross misuse of this mark of punctuation. Editor's note: For help with apostrophes, see pages 586–587 in this text.

3. A Russian woman holds the record for the highest number of children born to one mother: sixty-nine babies in a total of twenty-seven pregnancies sixteen pairs of twins, seven sets of triplets, and four sets of quadruplets.

4. More men holding first-class tickets on the *Titanic* were saved than childrens (sic) in the third-class section of the ship.

5. Billy Clyde could stay married to Maybelle as long as he played his cards right [his Visa card, his Mastercard, his American Express card.]

21l   The Hyphen (-)*   P

1. Use a hyphen to join words into a single adjective before a noun.

   Examples   a wind-blown wig

   the mud-caked sneakers

   a made-for-television movie

   a well-written essay

   a five-year-old boy

Do not use a hyphen when the modifier ends in "-ly."

   Examples   a highly regarded worker

   a beautifully landscaped yard

2. Writers who create original compound adjectives often join the words with hyphens.

   Examples   Compulsive shoppers suffer from stuff-lust syndrome.

   She prefers novels with they-lived-wretchedly-ever-after endings.

---

*Do not confuse the hyphen with the dash. In typed work, a hyphen is indicated by *one* bar mark ("-"); a dash is indicated by *two* bar marks or one long mark ("—").

3. Some compound words are always spelled with a hyphen; check your dictionary when you're in doubt. Note that compound numbers from twenty-one to ninety-nine use a hyphen.

Examples   mother-in-law

president-elect

runner-up

good-for-nothing

twenty-nine

Compound words made from combining verb forms are frequently hyphenated: The psychiatrist insisted his birthday presents be *shrink-wrapped*.

4. Some words with prefixes use a hyphen; again, check your dictionary if necessary. (Hint: If the second word begins with a capital letter, a hyphen is almost always used.)

Examples   ex-wife

self-esteem

all-American

non-English

5. In a series of compound adjectives, place a space (or a comma and a space, when appropriate) following the hyphen in every item except the last one.

Examples   They surveyed students at both two- and four-year colleges.

She found herself on both the best- and the worst-dressed lists.

He suffered first-, second-, and third-degree burns on his arms.

6. Use a hyphen to mark the separation of syllables when you divide a word at the end of a line. Do not divide one-syllable words; do not leave one or two letters at the end of a line. (In most dictionaries, dots are used to indicate the division of syllables: va • ca • tion.)

Examples   In your essays you should avoid using fragment sentences.

Did your father try to help you with your homework?

Practicing What You've Learned

Errors with Hyphens

Correct the errors in the phrases that follow by adding, deleting, or changing hyphens. Skip any correct uses you see.

1. A first class event

2. The well done steak

3. A self employed person

continued on next page

4. His completely fabricated story

5. Her one word answer

6. Pre-Columbian art

7. A once in a lifetime experience

8. A fifteen year-old girl

9. The overly-excited dog

10. His fifty sixth birthday

11. fourth- and fifth-place trophies

12. The hard boiled detective o-
mitted an important detail in his report.

(◆ For additional practice, turn to the exercise on pages 599–600.)

 Italics (Ital) and Underlining ( )   P

Today, many style manuals recommend the use of italics in printed matter in place of underlining. Ask your instructor whether the use of italics or underlining is preferred. In handwritten material, you may use underlining in the cases described below.

1. Underline, italicize, or place quotation marks around a word, phrase, or letter used as the subject of discussion. Whether you underline, italicize, or use quotation marks, always be consistent. (◆ See also pages 589–590.)

   Examples   No matter how I spell <u>offered</u>, it always looks wrong.

   Is your middle initial "X" or "Y"?

   Her use of such words as *drab, bleak,* and *musty* give the poem a somber tone.

2. Underline or italicize the title of books, plays, magazines, newspapers, movies, works of art, television programs (but use quotation marks for individual episodes), airplanes, trains, and ships.

   Examples   <u>Moby-Dick</u>   or   *Moby-Dick*

   <u>Reader's Digest</u>   *Reader's Digest*

   <u>Texarkana Gazette</u>   *Texarkana Gazette*

   <u>Gone with the Wind</u>   *Gone with the Wind*

   <u>Mona Lisa</u>   *Mona Lisa*

   <u>60 Minutes</u>   *60 Minutes*

   <u>Spirit of St. Louis</u>   *Spirit of St. Louis*

   <u>Titanic</u>   *Titanic*

Exceptions: Do not italicize or underline the names of sacred texts (Bible, Torah, Koran), the titles of legal documents (United States Constitution, Magna Carta), or the name of your own essay when it appears on your title page. Do not italicize or underline the city in a newspaper title unless the city's name is actually part of the newspaper's title.

3. Underline or italicize foreign words that are not commonly regarded as part of the English language.

Examples   He shrugged and said, "*C'est la vie.*"

   Under the "For Sale" sign on the old rusty truck, the farmer had written *caveat emptor*, meaning "let the buyer beware."

4. Use underlining or italics sparingly to show emphasis.

Examples   Everyone was surprised to discover that the butler <u>didn't</u> do it.

   "Do you realize that *your* son just ate a piece of my priceless sculpture?" the artist screamed at the museum director.

Practicing What You've Learned

Errors with Italics and Underlining

Which of the following words should be italicized or underlined in your essay?

© Canstock Images, Inc./ Index Stock Imagery

1. page six of the New York Times

2. the popular novel The Great Gatsby

3. an article in Time magazine

4. watching the episode The Puffy Shirt on Seinfeld

5. movie stars in The Dark Knight

6. confusing the words to, too, and two

7. the first act of Death of a Salesman

8. remembering the words to The Star-Spangled Banner

9. the sinking of the Edmund Fitzgerald

10. missing my abuela in Texas

(◆ For additional practice, turn to pages 599–600.)

21n Ellipsis Points (. . . or . . . .) P

1. To show an omission in quoted material within a sentence, use three periods, with spaces before and after each one.

Original	Every time my father told the children about his having to trudge barefooted to school in the snow, the walk got longer and the snow got deeper.
Quoted with Omission	In her autobiography, she noted, "Every time my father told the children about his having to trudge barefooted to school . . . the snow got deeper."

Note: Never begin a sentence with ellipsis points.

2. Three points with spaces may be used to show an incomplete or interrupted thought.

   Example   My wife is an intelligent, beautiful woman who wants me to live a long time. On the other hand, Harry's wife . . . oh, never mind.

3. If you omit any words at the end of a quotation and you are also ending your sentence, use three points plus a fourth to indicate the period.

   Example   Lincoln wrote, "Four score and seven years ago our fathers brought forth, upon this continent, a new nation. . . ."

   Note: If a parenthetical reference follows ellipses at the end of your sentence, use three points with a space before each and put a period after the parenthesis:

   Example   Lincoln wrote, "Four score and seven years ago our fathers brought forth, upon this continent, a new nation . . ." (139-140).

4. If the omission of one or more sentences occurs at the end of a quoted sentence, use four points with no space before the first point.

   Example   "The Lord is my shepherd; I shall not want. . . . I will fear no evil."

5. Use a row of ellipsis points to indicate one or more missing lines of poetry.

   Example   Failing to fetch me at first keep encouraged.
   ·
   I stop somewhere waiting for you.
   —Walt Whitman, "Song of Myself"

6. Ellipsis points can occasionally be used to show hesitation or a pause in thought.
   Example   "Yes, I'm leaving . . . I need to find myself," said Waldo.

210 The Slash (/)   P

1. Use a slash between terms to indicate that either is acceptable. Do not put a space on either side of the slash.

   Examples   Bring a salad *and/or* a dessert to share at the picnic.

   Be careful to avoid the *either/or* fallacy in your argument paper.

2. Use a slash to mark line divisions in quoted poetry. Do use a space both before and after the slash.

   Example   In this poem Shakespeare describes love as "an ever-fixed mark / That looks on tempests and is never shaken."

Practicing What You've Learned

Errors with Parentheses, Brackets, Dashes, Hyphens, Italics, Ellipses, and Slashes

Correct the following errors by adding, changing, or deleting parentheses, brackets, dashes, hyphens, italics, ellipsis points, and slashes.

1. Many moviegoers know that the ape in King Kong the original 1933 version, not the re-make was only an eighteen inch tall animated figure, but not everyone realizes that the Red Sea Moses parted in the 1923 movie of The Ten Commandments was a quivering slab of Jell O sliced down-the-middle.

2. We recall the last words of General John B. Sedgwick at the Battle of Spotsylvania in 1864: "They couldn't hit an elephant at this dist ."

3. In a person to person telephone call the twenty five year old starlet promised the hard working gossip columnist that she would "tell the truth . . . and nothing but the truth" about her highly-publicized feud with her exhusband, editor in chief of Meat Eaters Digest.

4. While sailing across the Atlantic on board the celebrity filled yacht Titanic II, Dottie Mae Haskell she's the author of the popular new self help book Finding Wolves to Raise Your Children confided that until recently she thought chutzpah was an Italian side dish.

5. During their twenty four hour sit in at the melt down site, the anti-nuclear protestors began to sing, "Oh, say can you see . . ."

6. Few people know that James Arness later Matt Dillon in the long running television series Gunsmoke got his start by playing the vegetable creature in the postwar monster movie The Thing 1951.

7. If you do not pay your rent on time, your landlord has the right to charge a late fee and-or begin an eviction procedure.

8. A French chemist named Georges Claude invented the first neon sign in 1910. For additional information on his unsuccessful attempts to use seawater to generate electricity, see pages 200-205.

9. When Lucille Ball, star of I Love Lucy, became pregnant with her first child, the network executives decided that the word expecting could be used on the air to refer to her condition, but not the word pregnant.

10. In mystery stories the detective often advises the police to cherchez la femme. Editor's note: Cherchez la femme means "look for the woman."

Answers to the Punctuation Assessment, Pages 574–575

Please note that some of the punctuation errors in this test could be corrected in more than one way. Here are some sample corrections.

1. An interesting article appeared recently in the online version of *The Writer's Almanac*; it gave a brief history of sliced bread.

2. Before 1928, bread was sold in solid loaves or baked at home.

3. Otto F. Rohwedder, a jeweler from Iowa, had invented a bread slicing machine; however, bakers rejected it because they thought the bread would go dry, stale, or moldy too quickly.

4. Rohwedder tried many solutions to the dry-bread problem, including sticking the slices together with hatpins.

5. He ultimately solved the problem by wrapping the sliced bread in wax paper, but he still couldn't sell his machine.

6. Finally, a baker in Chillicothe, Missouri, agreed to try Rohwedder's plan.

7. The baker, Frank Bench, installed the machine in his bakery, despite its bulky size (three by five feet).

8. Newspaper ads announced the machine's arrival: "The Greatest Step Forward in the Baking Industry Since Bread Was Wrapped – Sliced Kleen Maid Bread."

9. Sales were huge; a modern convenience was born.

10. Moreover, the English language gained an emphatic new phrase to express brilliance: "It's the best thing since sliced bread!"

Chapter 22

A Concise Guide to Mechanics

••

Assessing Your Skills: Mechanics

To help you focus your study of this chapter, take the self-graded test that follows. Each of the sentences below contains one or more errors discussed in this chapter. See how much you already know by correcting the sentences and then checking the answers on pages 609–610. By taking this test, you will be better able to evaluate your knowledge of mechanics and direct your attention to those rules governing the errors you missed.*

1. According to "a monopoly anniversary," a december 1 2010 article in the *denver post* newspaper, the board game called monopoly is 75 years old.

2. charles darrow of Pa. was struggling through the great depression and looking for extra income to support his Family.

3. he sketched a game on a tablecloth, including street names, such as baltic avenue, found in atlantic city, a favorite vacation spot.

4. Darrow and his wife invited neighbors to play, & alot of them wanted there own set to keep at home.

5. The inventor made 2 sets a day and sold them to a store in philadelphia.

6. 5,000 people bought the game from Darrow before the parker bros. company agreed to manufacture and sell the game for him in 1935.

---

*Historical information in this assessment test originally found in "A Monopoly Anniversary," a December 1, 2010, article in "The Mini Page," a weekly section for young readers and adults in the *Denver Post* newspaper.

7. Some people believe that Darrow based his game on one called the landlord's game designed by a quaker woman named lizzie j. magie in 1903.

8. Today monopoly is not only produced in english and spanish but in more than 40 other languages, as well as in a braille version for people who are visually impaired.

9. Mister Green likes to play the game with his friends in the conservatory on new year's day.

10. Ms. Scarlett, who grew up in the south, asks, "would you rather play a board game or watch the nfl game?"

22a Capitalization   Cap

1. Capitalize the first word of every sentence.

   Example   The lazy horse leans against a tree all day.

2. Capitalize proper nouns—the specific names of people, places, and products— and also the adjectives formed from proper nouns.

   Examples   John Doe

   Austin, Texas

   First National Bank

   the Eiffel Tower

   Chevrolets

   Japanese cameras

   Spanish class

   an English major

3. Always capitalize the days of the week, the names of the months, and holidays.

   Examples   Saturday, December 14

   Tuesday's meeting

   Halloween parties

   Special events are often capitalized: Super Bowl, World Series, Festival of Lights.

4. Capitalize titles when they are accompanied by proper names.

   Examples   President Jones, Major Smith, Governor Brown, Judge Wheeler, Professor Plum, Queen Elizabeth

5. Capitalize all the principal words in titles of books, articles, stories, plays, movies, and poems. Prepositions, articles, and conjunctions are not capitalized unless they begin or end the title.

   Examples   "The Face on the Barroom Floor"

   A Short History of the Civil War

   For Whom the Bell Tolls

6. Capitalize the first word of a direct quotation.

   Examples   Shocked at actor John Barrymore's use of profanity, the woman said, "Sir, I'll have you know I'm a lady!"

   Barrymore replied, "Your secret is safe with me."

7. Capitalize "east," "west," "north," and "south" when they refer to particular sections of the country but not when they merely indicate direction.

   Examples   The South has produced many excellent writers, including William Faulkner and Flannery O'Connor. ["South" here refers to a section of the country.]

   If you travel south for ten miles, you'll see the papier-mâché replica of the world's largest hamburger. [In this case, "south" is a direction.]

   Capitalize a title when referring to a particular person;* do not capitalize a title if a pronoun precedes it.

   Examples   The President announced a new national holiday honoring Frank H. Fleer, inventor of bubble gum.

   The new car Dad bought is guaranteed for 10,000 miles or until something goes wrong.

   My mother told us about a Hollywood party during which Zelda and F. Scott Fitzgerald collected and boiled all the women's purses.

8. Capitalize important historic movements, documents, and events.

   Examples   the Civil Rights Movement

   World War I

   Impressionism

   Declaration of Independence

   D-Day

9. Capitalize the names of religions, their followers, revered books, and holidays.

   Examples   Islam

   Methodists

   Torah

   Bible

   Easter

10. Capitalize the letters that make up abbreviations for organizations, companies, agencies, and well-known people, places, and events.

    Examples   NFL

    CBS

    FEMA

    JFK

    USA

    WW II

*Some authorities disagree; others consider such capitalization optional.

© Canstock Images, Inc./
Index Stock Imagery

Practicing What You've Learned

Errors with Capitalization

A. Correct the errors in capitalization in the following phrases.

1. delicious chinese food

2. memorial day memories

3. fiery southwestern salsa

4. his latest novel, entitled *a prince at work*

5. bible study at the baptist church

6. count Dracula's castle in transylvania

7. african-american heritage

8. a dodge van driven across the golden gate bridge

9. sunday morning programs on abc

10. the british daughter-in-law of senator Snort

B. Write a sentence in which the following pairs of words are capitalized correctly. Example: He joined the U.S. Navy wearing his best white shirt and navy pants.

1. street, Street

2. lake, Lake

3. mustang, Mustang

4. south, South

5. president, President

22b Abbreviations Ab

1. Abbreviate the titles "Mr.," "Mrs.," "Ms.," "St.," and "Dr." when they precede names.

   Examples   Dr. Scott, Ms. Steinham, Mrs. White, St. Jude

2. Abbreviate titles and degrees when they follow names.

   Examples   Charles Byrd, Jr.; David Hall, Ph.D.; Dudley Carpenter, D.D.S.

3. You may abbreviate the following in even the most formal writing: "A.M." (*ante meridiem*, before noon), "P.M." (*post meridiem*, after noon), "A.D." (*anno Domini*,

in the year of our Lord), "B.C." (before Christ), "C.E." (common era), "B.C.E." (before the common era), "etc." (*et cetera*, and others), "i.e." (*id est*, that is), and "e.g." (*exempli gratia*, for example).

4. In formal writing, do *not* abbreviate the names of days, months, centuries, states, countries, or units of measure. Do *not* use an ampersand (&) unless it is an official part of a title.

Incorrect in formal writing	Tues., Sept., 18th century, Ark., Mex., lbs.
Correct	Tuesday, September, eighteenth century, Arkansas, Mexico, pounds
Incorrect	Tony & Gus went to the store to buy ginseng root.
Correct	Tony *and* Gus went to the A&P to buy ginseng root. [The "&" in "A&P" is correct because it is part of the store's official name.]

5. In formal writing, do *not* abbreviate the words "page," "chapter," "volume," and so forth, except in footnotes and bibliographies, which have prescribed rules of abbreviation.

6. Except in formal writing, it is often permissible to use abbreviations or acronyms for well-known organizations or people. However, you should spell out the abbreviation the first time, to avoid any confusion.

Examples	Franklin Delano Roosevelt (FDR)
	National Public Radio (NPR)
	North Atlantic Treaty Organization (NATO)

(For additional information on proper abbreviation, consult your dictionary.)

22c Numbers Num

1. Use figures for dates; street, room, and apartment numbers; page numbers; phone numbers; numbers by percentage signs; and decimals.

Examples	April 22, 1946
	710 West 14th Street
	page 242
	room 17
	476–1423
	40%
	3.78 GPA

2. Use figures for hours with "A.M." and "P.M." but write out the time when you use "o'clock."

Examples	8:00 A.M. or 8 A.M.
	eight o'clock in the morning

3. Some authorities say to spell out numbers that can be expressed in one or two words; others say to spell out numbers under one hundred.

Examples   ten thousand dollars   or $10,000

twenty-four hours

thirty-nine years

five partridges

1,294 essays

4. When several numbers are used in a short passage, use figures.

Examples   In the anchovy-eating contest, Jennifer ate 22, Juan ate 21, Pete ate 16, and I ate 6.

According to the U.S. Census Bureau, on an average day 11,000 babies are born, 6,000 people die, 7,000 couples marry, and 3,000 couples divorce.

5. Never begin a sentence with a figure.

Incorrect   50 spectators watched the surfing exhibition at Niagara Falls.

Correct   Fifty spectators watched the surfing exhibition at Niagara Falls.

6. When a date containing a month, a day, and a year appears in that order within a sentence, always set off the year by placing commas on each side. No comma is necessary between a month or season and a year.

Examples   She married her first husband on February 2, 1978, in Texas.

The first birth on a commercial airliner occurred on October 28, 1929, as the plane cruised over Miami.

I graduated spring 2011; the job began May 2012.

Practicing What You've Learned

© Canstock Images, Inc./ Index Stock Imagery

Errors in Capitalization, Abbreviations, and Numbers

Correct the following errors by adding, deleting, or changing capitals, abbreviations, and numbers. Skip any correct words, letters, or numbers you may find.

1.   Speaking to students at Gallaudet university, Marian Wright Edelman, Founder and president of the Children's Defense Fund, noted that an american child is born into poverty every thirty seconds, is born to a teen mother every 60 seconds, is abused or neglected every 26 seconds, is arrested for a violent crime every five minutes, and is killed by a gun every two hours.

continued on next page

2. My sister, who lives in the east, was amazed to read studies by Thomas Radecki, MD, showing that 12-year-olds commit 300 percent more murders than did the same age group 30 years ago.

3. In C.E. sixty-seven the roman emperor Nero entered the chariot race at the olympic games, and although he failed to finish the race, the judges unanimously declared him the Winner.

4. According to John Alcock, a Behavioral Ecologist at Arizona State University, in the U.S.A. the chance of being poisoned by a snake is 20 times less than that of being hit by lightning and 300 times less than the risk of being murdered by a fellow American.

5. The official chinese news agency, located in the city of xinhua, estimates that there are ten million guitar players in their country today, an amazing number considering that the instrument was banned during the cultural revolution, which lasted 10 years, from nineteen sixty-six to nineteen seventy-six.

6. 231 electoral votes were cast for James Monroe but only 1 for John Quincy Adams in the 1820 Presidential race.

7. The british soldier T. E. Lawrence, better known as "lawrence of arabia," stood less than 5 ft. 6 in. tall.

8. Before my 10 A.M. english class, held in wrigley field every other friday except on New Year's day, I eat 3 pieces of french pastry.

9. When a political opponent once called him "two-faced," president Lincoln retorted, "if I had another face, do you think I would wear this one?"

10. Alexander Graham Bell, inventor of the telephone, died on aug. 2, 1922 in nova scotia; 2 days later, on the day of his burial, for 1 minute no telephone in north america was allowed to ring.

Assignment

© CORBIS

Collaborative Activity: After studying the rules in this chapter, write a paragraph of at least five sentences containing the following data. Create the information for a mythical person (Captain Glass Half-Full born in Optimism, Indiana? Your Evil Twin raised in Elbonia?). Exchange paragraphs with a classmate, and circle any errors you see in capitalization, abbreviations, or numbers. Work together to correct any errors you find.

Include this data:

City, state/province, and country of birth

continued on next page

Day, month, year, and century of birth
Exact time of birth
Current professional title and salary
Favorite holiday, book, and movie
Membership in a sports league or organization, name abbreviated
Number and kinds of pets

22d Spelling Sp

For some folks, learning to spell correctly is harder than trying to herd cats. Entire books have been written to teach people to become better spellers, and some of these are available at your local bookstore (and, no, not shelved under witchcraft). Here, however, are a few suggestions that seem to work for many students:

1. Keep a list of the little beasties you misspell. After a few weeks, you may notice that you tend to misspell the same words again and again or that the words you misspell tend to fit a pattern—that is, you can't remember when the *i* goes before the *e* or when to change the *y* to *i* before *-ed*. Try to memorize the words you repeatedly misspell, or at least keep the list somewhere handy (your journal?) so you can refer to it when you're editing your last draft (listing the words in a computer file or on the inside cover of your desk dictionary also makes sense).

2. Become aware of a few rules that govern some of our spelling in English. For example, many people know the rule in the jingle "*I* before *E* except after *C* or when sounded like *A* as in *neighbor* and *weigh*." Not everyone, however, knows the follow-up line, which contains many of the exceptions to that jingle: "Neither the weird financier nor the foreigner seizes leisure at its height."

3. Here are some other rules, without jingles, for adding suffixes (new endings to words), a common plague for poor spellers:

   • Change final *y* to *i* if the *y* follows a consonant.*

     bury → buried
     marry → marries

   • But if the suffix is *-ing*, keep the *y*.

     marry + ing = marrying
     worry + ing = worrying

   • If the word ends in a single consonant after a single vowel and the accent is on the last syllable, double the consonant before adding the suffix.

     occur → occurred
     cut → cutting
     swim → swimmer

---

*Reminder: Consonants are all the letters that are not vowels (*a, e, i, o, u*, and sometimes *y*).

- If a word ends in a silent *e*, drop the *e* before adding -*able* or -*ing*.

  love + able = lovable
  believe + able = believable

4. And here's an easy rule governing the doubling of letters with the addition of prefixes (new beginning syllables): Most of the time, you simply add all the letters you've got when you mix the word and the prefix.

   mis + spell = misspell
   un + natural = unnatural
   re + entry = reentry

5. Teach yourself to spell the words that you miss often by making up your own silly rules or jingles. For instance:

   - dessert (one *s* or two?): I always want two helpings so I double the *s*.

   - apparently (apparantly?): Ap*parent*ly, my *parent* knows the whole story.

   - separate (seperate?): I'd be *a rat* to sep*arat*e from you.

   - a lot (or alot?): A cot (not *acot*) provides *a lot* of comfort in a tent.

   - all right (or alright?): Think of the rhyme "all right, good night" and remember that both these phrases have two words. (No matter what Roger Daltrey and The Who said, the line should be "The kids are all right"!)

   - questionnaire (one *n* or two?): Questio*nn*aires have *n*umerous *n*umbered questions (two *n*'s).

   And so on.

6. Proofread your papers carefully. Anything that looks misspelled probably is and deserves to be looked up in your dictionary. Reading your paper one sentence at a time from the end helps, too, because you tend to start thinking about your ideas when you read from the beginning of your paper. If you are writing on a word processor that has a spell-checking program, don't forget to run it; however, do remember that such programs will skip over confused words (*to* for *too*, *there* for *their*) that are spelled correctly.

Although these few suggestions won't completely cure your spelling problems, they can make a dramatic improvement in the quality of your papers and give you the confidence to continue learning and practicing other rules that govern the spelling of our language. Good luck!

Answers to the Mechanics Assessment, Page 601

1. According to "A Monopoly Anniversary," a December 1, 2010, article in the *Denver Post* newspaper, the board game called Monopoly is seventy-five years old.

2. Charles Darrow of Pennsylvania was struggling through the Great Depression and looking for extra income to support his family.

3. He sketched a game on a tablecloth, including street names such as Baltic Avenue, found in Atlantic City, a favorite vacation spot.

4. Darrow and his wife invited neighbors to play, and a lot of them wanted their own set to keep at home.

5. The inventor made two sets a day and sold them to a store in Philadelphia.

6. Five thousand people bought the game from Darrow before the Parker Brothers Company agreed to manufacture and sell the game for him in 1935.

7. Some people believe that Darrow based his game on one called The Landlord's Game designed by a Quaker woman named Lizzie J. Magie in 1903.

8. Today Monopoly is not only produced in English and Spanish but in more than forty other languages, as well as in a Braille version for people who are visually impaired.

9. Mr. Green likes to play the game with his friends in the conservatory on New Year's Day.

10. Ms. Scarlett, who grew up in the South, asks, "Would you rather play a board game or watch the NFL game?"

Part 5

Additional Readings

Part Five offers thirty-three additional readings to help you improve your writing skills. In nine chapters, three selections illustrate each of the modes and strategies previously explained in Part Two. In addition, Chapter 32 includes a speech and two essays illustrating multiple strategies and styles for further analysis; Chapter 33 offers two poems and a story to supplement literary assignments. Overall, the readings in Part Five were selected not only to model methods of development but also to illustrate a variety of purposes, styles, and tones, including humor and irony.

A close reading of these selections can help you become a better writer in several ways. Identifying the various methods by which these writers focused, organized, and developed their material may spark new ideas as you plan and shape your own essay. Familiarizing yourself with different styles and voices may encourage new uses of language. Analyzing the rhetorical choices of other writers will also help you revise your prose because it promotes the habit of asking questions from the reader's point of view. Moreover, reading the opinions or sharing the experiences of these authors may suggest interesting topics for your own essays. In other words, to help yourself become a more effective writer, read as much and as often as you can.

Chapter 23

Exposition: Development by Example

···

Black Men and Public Space*

Brent Staples

Brent Staples is an editorial writer for the *New York Times* and has published essays and reviews in a number of other newspapers and magazines, including the *Chicago Sun-Times*, the *New York Review of Books*, and *Slate* magazine. He holds a Ph.D. in psychology from the University of Chicago, and his memoir *Parallel Time: Growing Up in Black and White* (1994) won the Anisfield Wolff Book Award. This essay first appeared in *Ms.* magazine in 1986.

1   My first victim was a woman—white, well dressed, probably in her late twenties. I came upon her late one evening on a deserted street in Hyde Park, a relatively affluent neighborhood in an otherwise mean, impoverished section of Chicago. As I swung onto the avenue behind her, there seemed to be a discreet, uninflammatory distance between us. Not so. She cast back a worried glance. To her, the youngish black man—a broad six feet two inches with a beard and billowing hair, both hands shoved into the pockets of a bulky military jacket—seemed menacingly close. After a few more quick glimpses, she picked up her pace and was soon running in earnest. Within seconds she disappeared into a cross street.

2   That was more than a decade ago. I was twenty-two years old, a graduate student newly arrived at the University of Chicago. It was in the echo of that terrified woman's footfalls that I first began to know the unwieldy inheritance I'd come into—the ability to alter public space in ugly ways. It was clear that she thought herself the quarry of a mugger, a rapist, or worse. Suffering a bout of insomnia, however, I was stalking sleep, not defenseless wayfarers. As a softy who is scarcely

---

* "Black Men and Public Space" first appeared in MS Magazine, 1986. Brent Staples writes editorials on politics and culture for The New York Times and is the author of the memoir PARALLEL TIME: GROWING UP IN BLACK AND WHITE. Reprinted by permission of the author.

able to take a knife to a raw chicken—let alone hold one to a person's throat—I was surprised, embarrassed, and dismayed all at once. Her flight made me feel like an accomplice in tyranny. It also made it clear that I was indistinguishable from the muggers who occasionally seeped into the area from the surrounding ghetto. That first encounter, and those that followed, signified that a vast, unnerving gulf lay between nighttime pedestrians—particularly women—and me. And I soon gathered that being perceived as dangerous is a hazard in itself. I only needed to turn a corner into a dicey situation, or crowd some frightened, armed person in a foyer somewhere, or make an errant move after being pulled over by a policeman. Where fear and weapons meet—and they often do in urban America—there is always the possibility of death.

3   In that first year, my first away from my hometown, I was to become thoroughly familiar with the language of fear. At dark, shadowy intersections, I could cross in front of a car stopped at a traffic light and elicit the *thunk, thunk, thunk, thunk* of the driver—black, white, male, or female—hammering down the door locks. On less traveled streets after dark, I grew accustomed to but never comfortable with people crossing to the other side of the street rather than pass me. Then there were the standard unpleasantries with policemen, doormen, bouncers, cabdrivers, and others whose business it is to screen out troublesome individuals *before* there is any nastiness.

4   I moved to New York nearly two years ago and I have remained an avid night walker. In central Manhattan, the near-constant crowd cover minimizes tense one-on-one street encounters. Elsewhere—in SoHo, for example, where sidewalks are narrow and tightly spaced buildings shut out the sky—things can get very taut indeed.

5   After dark, on the warrenlike streets of Brooklyn where I live, I often see women who fear the worst from me. They seem to have set their faces on neutral, and with their purse straps strung across their chests bandolier-style, they forge ahead as though bracing themselves against being tackled. I understand, of course, that the danger they perceive is not a hallucination. Women are particularly vulnerable to street violence, and young black males are drastically overrepresented among the perpetrators of that violence. Yet these truths are no solace against the kind of alienation that comes of being ever the suspect, a fearsome entity with whom pedestrians avoid making eye contact.

6   It is not altogether clear to me how I reached the ripe old age of twenty-two without being conscious of the lethality nighttime pedestrians attributed to me. Perhaps it was because in Chester, Pennsylvania, the small, angry industrial town where I came of age in the 1960s, I was scarcely noticeable against a backdrop of gang warfare, street knifings, and murders. I grew up one of the good boys, had perhaps a half-dozen fistfights. In retrospect, my shyness of combat has clear sources.

7   As a boy, I saw countless tough guys locked away; I have since buried several, too. They were babies, really—a teenage cousin, a brother of twenty-two, a childhood friend in his mid-twenties—all gone down in episodes of bravado played out in the streets. I came to doubt the virtues of intimidation early on. I chose, perhaps unconsciously, to remain a shadow—timid, but a survivor.

8   The fearsomeness mistakenly attributed to me in public places often has a perilous flavor. The most frightening of these confusions occurred in the late 1970s and early 1980s, when I worked as a journalist in Chicago. One day, rushing into the office of a magazine I was writing for with a deadline story in hand, I was mistaken for a burglar. The office manager called security and, with an ad hoc posse, pursued me through the labyrinthine halls, nearly to my editor's door. I had no way of proving who I was. I could only move briskly toward the company of someone who knew me.

9   Another time I was on assignment for a local paper and killing time before an interview. I entered a jewelry store on the city's affluent Near North Side. The proprietor excused herself and returned with an enormous red Doberman pinscher straining at the end of a leash. She stood, the dog extended toward me, silent to my questions, her eyes bulging nearly out of her head. I took a cursory look around, nodded, and bade her good night.

10   Relatively speaking, however, I never fared as badly as another black male journalist. He went to nearby Waukegan, Illinois, a couple of summers ago to work on a story about a murderer who was born there. Mistaking the reporter for the killer, police officers hauled him from his car at gunpoint and but for his press credentials would probably have tried to book him. Such episodes are not uncommon. Black men trade tales like this all the time.

11   Over the years, I learned to smother the rage I felt at so often being taken for a criminal. Not to do so would surely have led to madness. I now take precautions to make myself less threatening. I move about with care, particularly late in the evening. I give a wide berth to nervous people on subway platforms during the wee hours, particularly when I have exchanged business clothes for jeans. If I happen to be entering a building behind some people who appear skittish, I may walk by, letting them clear the lobby before I return, so as not to seem to be following them. I have been calm and extremely congenial on those rare occasions when I've been pulled over by the police.

12   And on late-evening constitutionals I employ what has proved to be an excellent tension-reducing measure: I whistle melodies from Beethoven and Vivaldi and the more popular classical composers. Even steely New Yorkers hunching toward nighttime destinations seem to relax, and occasionally they even join in the tune. Virtually everybody seems to sense that a mugger wouldn't be warbling bright, sunny selections from Vivaldi's *Four Seasons*. It is my equivalent of the cowbell that hikers wear when they know they are in bear country.

Metaphors for Life*

David Brooks

David Brooks is a journalist and Opinion-Editorial columnist for the *New York Times*, a political commentator on television's PBS *NewsHour*, and a frequent contributor to National Public Radio's *All Things Considered*. He has been an editor at the *Wall Street Journal*, *The Weekly Standard*, the *Atlantic Monthly* magazine, and *Newsweek*. His most recent book is *The Social Animal* (2011). This essay appeared April 12, 2011, in the *New York Times*.

1   Here's a clunky but unremarkable sentence that appeared in the British press before the last national election: "Britain's recovery from the worst recession in decades is gaining traction, but confused economic data and the high risk of hung Parliament could yet snuff out its momentum."

2   The sentence is only worth quoting because in 28 words it contains four metaphors. Economies don't really gain traction, like a tractor. Momentum doesn't literally get snuffed out, like a cigarette. We just use those metaphors, without even thinking about it, as a way to capture what is going on. In his fine new book, *I Is an Other*, James Geary reports on linguistic research suggesting that people use a metaphor every 10 to 25 words. Metaphors are not rhetorical frills at the edge of how we think, Geary writes. They are at the very heart of it.

3   George Lakoff and Mark Johnson, two of the leading researchers in this field, have pointed out that we often use food metaphors to describe the world of ideas. We devour a book, try to digest raw facts and attempt to regurgitate other people's ideas, even though they might be half-baked. When talking about relationships, we often use health metaphors. A friend might be involved in a sick relationship. Another might have a healthy marriage. When talking about argument, we use war metaphors. When talking about time, we often use money metaphors. But when talking about money, we rely on liquid metaphors. We dip into savings, sponge off friends or skim funds off the top. Even the job title stockbroker derives from the French word *brocheur*, the tavern worker who tapped the kegs of beer to get the liquidity flowing.

4   The psychologist Michael Morris points out that when the stock market is going up, we tend to use agent metaphors, implying the market is a living thing with clear intentions. We say the market climbs or soars or fights its way upward. When the market goes down, on the other hand, we use object metaphors, implying it is inanimate. The market falls, plummets or slides.

5   Most of us, when asked to stop and think about it, are by now aware of the pervasiveness of metaphorical thinking. But in the normal rush of events, we often see straight through metaphors, unaware of how they refract perceptions. So it's probably important to pause once a month or so to pierce the illusion that we see the world directly. It's good to pause to appreciate how flexible and tenuous our grip on reality actually is.

6   Metaphors help compensate for our natural weaknesses. Most of us are not very good at thinking about abstractions or spiritual states, so we rely on concrete or spatial metaphors to (imperfectly) do the job. A lifetime is pictured as a journey across a landscape. A person who is sad is down in the dumps, while a happy fellow is riding high. Most of us are not good at understanding new things, so we grasp them imperfectly by relating them metaphorically to things that already exist. That's a "desktop" on your computer screen.

7   To be aware of the central role metaphors play is to be aware of how imprecise our most important thinking is. It's to be aware of the constant need to question metaphors with data—to separate the living from the dead ones, and the authentic metaphors that seek to illuminate the world from the tinny advertising and political metaphors that seek to manipulate it. Most important, being aware of metaphors reminds you of the central role that poetic skills play in our thought. If

much of our thinking is shaped and driven by metaphor, then the skilled thinker will be able to recognize patterns, blend patterns, apprehend the relationships and pursue unexpected likenesses.

8   Even the hardest of the sciences depend on a foundation of metaphors. To be aware of metaphors is to be humbled by the complexity of the world, to realize that deep in the undercurrents of thought there are thousands of lenses popping up between us and the world, and that we're surrounded at all times by what Steven Pinker of Harvard once called "pedestrian poetry."

Word to Youth: Texting, Driving Don't Mix*

Larry Copeland

Larry Copeland is a national correspondent for the *USA Today* newspaper, which has published nearly a thousand of his stories, many of which focus on topics related to road and driving safety. His previous newspaper experience includes work as a reporter for the *Philadelphia Inquirer* and the *Atlantic Journal-Constitution*. This article, using tragic examples to emphasize its point, appeared in *USA Today* in March 2010.

1   Mariah West was a devoted texter.

2   At 18, she could hold dinner conversations with her family while surreptitiously texting with friends, hiding her cellphone under the table. Everyone in the Rogers, Ark., high school senior's circle had warned her about texting while driving; they'd see her car swerve and know what she was doing. It cost her her life.

3   Last May, on the day before graduation, Mariah was driving to a Minor League Baseball game in Springfield, Mo., texting with the player who'd invited her. As she was sending him a text, she lost control of the car, which clipped a bridge, skidded on its roof along the edge of the bridge and flipped back into oncoming traffic. Mariah, who had been getting directions to the Springfield Cardinals' stadium, was partially ejected, her skull crushed, says her mother, Merry Dye, 45. The last message Mariah got: "Where U At."

4   Now, Dye is working to spare other teens and their parents from a similar loss. She is part of a campaign against texting and driving that AT&T is launching today. The effort uses television, radio, print, the Internet, shopping malls, even the protective "clings" over the front of new cellphones, to target young drivers. "I know there are a lot of laws being passed, but that isn't what's going to stop it," says Dye, assistant program coordinator for a television station in Springdale, Ark. "The hope is to reach the hearts of these kids and their parents, to help them understand that nobody is immune."

5   In focus groups and exchanges on its popular Facebook site, the company has heard from many teens, says Daryl Evans, AT&T's vice president of consumer advertising. "In our focus groups, everybody acknowledged the dangers of texting while driving," he says. "But it was amazing how many people said, 'I know it's dangerous, but I've figured out how to do it safely' or 'I can put the phone on top of the steering wheel and do it.'" AT&T's "Txtng & Drivng . . . It Can Wait" campaign

features parents of young texting-and-driving victims and the final text messages the young drivers received just before they died. The campaign's theme: "No text is worth dying over."

6   It's difficult to know how successful such a campaign can be, says Peter Kissinger, president and CEO of the AAA Foundation for Traffic Safety. "The great majority of traditional public awareness campaigns on traffic safety have, unfortunately, not been terribly successful," he says. The successful model, he says, is the national Click It or Ticket seat belt campaign, which works because it has a law generally accepted by the public, a visible enforcement component and a big public awareness effort.

7   In 2008, 5,870 people died and more than a half-million were hurt in crashes involving a distracted or inattentive driver, according to the National Highway Traffic Safety Administration. Young, inexperienced drivers are disproportionately represented among these drivers.

Not worth dying for

8   The theme for AT&T's campaign grew out of one of its focus groups, Evans says. "The group leader said, 'Everybody pull out your phone. Pull up the very last text you had before you came in here.' He said, 'Are any of those texts worth dying for?' The air came out of the room. It went absolutely silent. And every time we did it after that, the same thing happened. We knew we had our aha! moment," he says. The campaign, which will include advertising in 72 shopping malls, also features an online resource center, att.com/txtngcanwait, where educators, parents and teens can download information about texting while driving and sign a pledge not to do it. AT&T also has launched a Facebook application, at facebook.com /att. Dallas-based AT&T, which serves about 85 million wireless customers, is the second communications company to enter the fray against texting while driving. Verizon Wireless launched its national "Don't Text and Drive" campaign last year.

9   The campaign comes as the movement against texting while driving nears critical mass. At least 23 states this year have considered bans on texting while driving; 10 of them restrict texting by novice drivers. Nineteen states and the District of Columbia prohibit texting while driving for all drivers, the Governors Highway Safety Association says. In January, the federal government banned texting on handheld devices while driving for bus drivers and commercial truckers. Allstate Insurance launched an anti-texting effort last year. Talk show host Oprah Winfrey devoted shows to the topic.

'He knew better'

10   A year ago, John Bradley Breen, known as "JB" to his friends in St. Francisville, Ill., was a young Marine, 23, who had a young daughter. He was home on leave preparing to deploy to Afghanistan. He was an avowed texter: The day before he died, Breen was helping to bury the family dog—and busily texting while digging, says his mother, Teresa Breen, 47. "My husband said, 'JB, put that phone down. You're obsessed with that thing. It's taking over your life.'" The next day, while driving and texting with a young woman, Breen lost control of his pickup. The

truck veered off the road. He was ejected and thrown 150-200 feet, his mother says. "He knew better," says Breen, a customer service representative at a seed company. "He couldn't do it on the base. He just came home and got lax."

11   Her son had been discussing a date with the young woman, Breen says. They had planned to get together soon. His last text message, which he never got to send: "Yeah T-." "The girl wondered why she never received a text message back," Breen says. "She never knew anything had happened until she got to work the next day."

Chapter 24

Exposition: Process Analysis

· ·

Family Feud: Resolving Holiday Conflict*

Stephen R. Covey

Stephen R. Covey was the author of eleven books and numerous articles on human relationships. His best-known work is *The Seven Habits of Highly Effective People*, which has sold more than twenty-five million copies since 1989. Based on advice in his last book, *The 3rd Alternative: Solving Life's Most Difficult Problems* (2011), this brief, three-step process for encouraging family tranquility appeared in the *USA Weekend* magazine just prior to the 2011 Thanksgiving holiday.

1   Family holiday togetherness. The thought may fill you with warmth—and quite another emotion: dread.

2   We all have dealt with family conflict. But over the holidays, it can be especially dicey to navigate. Whether an old or fresh, raw quarrel, you want to get past it. But how? And what about the other person? Isn't it his or her place to apologize to *you*?

3   Here are steps you can take:

1. Listen Without Losing It.

4   Take the chance over the holidays to connect with your relative. Find time for a one-on-one. This is not "We need to talk"; it's "I need to listen." Shut down that voice in your head that argues with everything the other person is saying. Try to see things through their eyes.

5   No question, this is hard to do. You might hear things that make your blood boil. But if you simply listen quietly, you'll accomplish two things. You'll understand

---

better where the other person is coming from (after all, you don't have a monopoly on the truth, either). Second, the other person airs it all out and *feels* understood, maybe for the first time.

2. Let Go.

6   Calmly say back to the other person what you understand about their point of view. Make sure they're satisfied that you really *do* understand. Then ask, "Now, would you be willing to understand my point of view?" If you have honestly understood theirs without lashing out, they will usually agree to hear yours, too.

7   When you're both satisfied that you understand each other's feelings and viewpoints, you naturally let go of your resentment.

3. Look for Third Alternatives.

8   You're no longer stuck with "my way" or "your way." You can go on to look for a third alternative, a better way than either of you has thought of before.

9   Here's an example. One woman was mad at her sister, who in her opinion "stole" Grandma's precious china collection. The sister insisted that Grandma had given it to her. After following the first two steps, they agreed on a third alternative—to have an expert value the collection, put it in a family trust for future generations, and share the use of it. Both sisters were happy, along with all the other family members.

10   Unless you're dealing with abusive or illegal behavior, this kind of family conflict can turn into a family miracle if even one person is willing to listen, let go, and look for third alternatives.

College Students: Protect Yourself from Identity Theft*

Luanne Kadlub

Luanne Kadlub is the Media Relations Manager at the Better Business Bureau (BBB) serving Northern Colorado and Wyoming, representing a national organization whose mission is "advancing marketplace trust." Kadlub wrote this *Coloradoan* newspaper article in 2011, in early August, just prior to the start of most college students' academic year, as part of the BBB's commitment to consumer education and protection.

1   In a few short weeks, college students will say goodbye to their families and head off to colleges near and far. But their academic adventures are not without risks, which makes now a good time for a refresher course on the importance of protecting their identities from potential identity thieves.

2   In 2010, 8.1 million Americans—or 3.5 percent of the population—became victims of identity theft, according to the 2011 Identity Fraud Survey conducted by Javelin Strategy & Research and sponsored by the Better Business Bureau. The average mean cost of identity theft is $631, and the average time to resolve identity fraud is 33 hours—valuable study time.

---

3   "Friendly fraud" accounts for 14 percent of all ID theft crimes. This means that new roommates and friends have just as much potential of being as dastardly as a foreign-based scam artist phishing on the Internet. And identity thieves—friend or foe—think nothing of Dumpster diving (or rifling through unattended trash cans) for unshredded paperwork or even taking mail from unlocked mailboxes (or off a desk). They even cruise social networking sites looking for some personal tidbit that can unlock a wealth of information elsewhere.

4   What to do?

5   • Keep sensitive information from prying eyes. Store personal and financial records in a locked storage device or in a password-protected file. Shred sensitive documents you don't intend to keep. (Note to parents: A paper shredder makes a great last-minute going-away gift for college students.)

6   • Be mindful of people in close proximity who could overhear or watch as sensitive financial or personal information is provided on the phone, websites or while shopping.

7   • Avoid providing your full nine-digit Social Security number whenever possible. Ask if you can provide alternate information instead.

8   • Don't carry Social Security cards or unnecessary credit cards or checks.

9   • Request electronic financial statements and use online bill pay whenever possible. Enroll in direct deposit, shred sensitive paper documents, and don't put checks in an unlocked mailbox.

10   • Install and update anti-virus and anti-malware software on your computer. Keep firewalls, browsers, applications and software updated as well.

11   • Don't publish birth date, email address, mother's maiden name, pet's name or other identifying personal information on social networking sites. Use privacy settings to control who has access to your profile.

12   • Use strong passwords that combine letters, numbers and symbols, and change them regularly. Don't access unsecure websites or type in personally identifiable information while using public Wi-Fi on mobile devices, laptops or computers. Turn off Bluetooth and Wi-Fi when they're not being used.

13   • If conducting business online, provide personal or financial information only on secure sites. To recognize these sites, look for a padlock symbol and an "s" after the "http" in the address bar.

14   • Be vigilant in monitoring bank and credit card statements to spot unauthorized activity. The most common method for fraudsters to take over a victim's account is by changing the physical address, so sign up for security alerts that are sent to your mobile phone or email account whenever changes are made to your account or personal information.

15   College students—and others—who believe they are victims of identity theft should immediately contact their bank and credit card companies, contact the Federal Trade Commission to fill out a complaint form, place a fraud alert on their credit report, and file a police report.

Bite-Sized History*

Carlton Stowers

Carlton Stowers is the author of more than two dozen works of nonfiction, including two Edgar Award-winning books, *Careless Whispers* (1986) and *To the Last Breath* (1998). As a journalist and feature writer, he has published stories in the *Dallas Morning News*, the *Dallas Observer*, *Time*, *Sports Illustrated*, and many other magazines. This article first appeared in *American Way* magazine in 2010.

1   For the most part, our historians have done a commendable job of reminding us of the milestone achievements that have greatly affected American lives. We know that Thomas Edison brought us out of the darkness with the invention of the lightbulb. Were it not for Alexander Graham Bell, our kids couldn't talk endlessly on the phone. We've duly credited Henry Ford for freeway traffic jams and the Wright brothers for [air travel].

2   But in no history book can I find mention of Charles Elmer Doolin and his Great Depression brainstorm that forever changed our nation's eating habits. If you ask me, the guy deserves a statue and a parade.

3   True, he may not have done my waistline much good, but over the years, he's added greatly to my enjoyment of county fairs, ballgames, late-night TV watching, backyard cookouts and long cross-country drives. His food-on-the-run invention has been my constant companion since boyhood days.

4   Think about it for a minute: Where would we be today without his crispy, salted corn chips, Fritos? If there were a Snack Food Hall of Fame, Doolin would get my vote for immediate induction.

5   His proud daughter, Kaleta, an accomplished Dallas artist and careful keeper of the family history, agrees. Her dad and his story are, she rightfully boasts, a need-to-know part of Americana. And she's the go-to source for how it all came about; she's even written a book, *Fritos Pie: Stories, Recipes and More*, that Texas A&M University Press will publish next fall.

6   You want an honest-to-goodness success tale, she's got a dandy.

7   In the early 1930s, C.E. Doolin was the proprietor of San Antonio's Highland Park Confectionary, constantly in search of new ways to lure customers into his establishment. In addition to the pastries, ice creams, soft drinks and candies he had to offer, he wanted some kind of bite-size treat he could place on his counter for arriving patrons.

8   Down the street, at a neighborhood service station, Gustavo Olguin had just the thing. Originally from Mexico, Olguin had brought the ideas of a popular Mexican beach food that he cooked, packaged and sold. It wasn't exactly the culinary version of rocket science. He shaped masa (a corn and water mixture) into small strips using a converted potato ricer, deep-fried and salted them, and then put the crispy chips into small bags. Records show that he started with a grand total of only nineteen customers. Aware that Olguin wanted badly to return to his homeland and to his love of coaching soccer, Doolin offered to buy him out. After considerable negotiation, the owner agreed to sell his recipe, customer list and cooking utensils for $100 cash.

---

* "Bite-Sized History," by Carlton Stowers, in American Way magazine, Nov. 1, 2010, page 104. Reprinted by permission.

9   Doolin's only problem was in getting his hands on that kind of money. Which is where his mother, Daisy Dean Doolin, enters our story. Demonstrating remarkable faith in her son's plan, she offered to pawn her wedding ring, an above-and-beyond gesture that raised $80. Gustavo Olguin loaned C.E. the additional $20, and thus was born The Frito Co. Its first headquarters was Daisy Doolin's kitchen when ten pounds of *fritos* (Spanish translation: "fried things") could be produced daily. Priced to sell for a nickel per package, on a good day the chips brought in a profit of two bucks.

10   That, as historians like to say, was how it all began.

11   In the years to come, Doolin became consumed with the notion that he had struck a food product gold mine. Eventually, production moved into a rented building that would house Doolin-designed cooking facilities, assembly-line conveyor belts, a packaging process and its own test kitchen for continued experimenting with the recipe. He even began growing and testing various types of corn in his search for the perfect masa. "We kids were his taste testers," recalls Kaleta. "He'd bring samples home, straight off the conveyor belt."

12   Fritos were a hit in the Doolin home as well as in food outlets nationwide. And not just as a snack but as an ingredient in recipes Daisy Doolin was coming up with to be printed on the back of each package. There were her Fritos Meatloaf, Fritos Squash and, most important, her famed Fritos Pie, that simple and tasty treat that remains the favorite of every high school football-stadium concession stand in the nation. You don't even need to write it down to remember it: Open a pack of Fritos, pour in a little chili, stir and enjoy. I can do it with my eyes closed.

13   But, back to our history lesson.

14   In 1934, the farsighted Doolin moved his operation to Dallas and ultimately had a fleet of delivery trucks on the road. By 1950, Fritos were being sold in every state in the U.S. A decade later, distribution had expanded to forty-eight countries.

15   Such was the ever-growing demand that he eventually sold a dozen manufacturing franchises. Among those who bought in was Herman Lay, a Nashville businessman who was also pioneering in the snack-food business. If you bought a bag of potato chips in the southeastern U.S. back in those days, it was most likely distributed by Lay's company. Ultimately, it was at Lay's suggestion that the companies merged into what would become the famous and mega-successful Frito-Lay Co.

16   Not a bad return on a $100 investment.

Chapter 25

Exposition: Comparison/Contrast

. . . .

My Real Car*

Bailey White

Georgia-born Bailey White has published stories and essays in many magazines, but she is perhaps best known as a commentator on National Public Radio's award-winning news program *All Things Considered*. Her essays and stories have been collected in *Mama Makes Up Her Mind and Other Dangers of Southern Living* (1993), *Sleeping at the Starlight Motel* (1995), and *Nothing with Strings* (2008); her novel is *Quite a Year for Plums* (1998). This selection was originally published in *Smithsonian* magazine in 1991.

1   It really makes you feel your age when you get a letter from your insurance agent telling you that the car you bought, only slightly used, the year you got out of college is now an antique. "Beginning with your next payment, your premiums will reflect this change in classification," the letter said.

2   I went out and looked at the car. I thought back over the years. I could almost hear my uncle's disapproving voice. "You should never buy a used car," he had told me the day I brought it home. Ten years later I drove that used car to his funeral. I drove my sister to the hospital in that car to have her first baby, and I drove to Atlanta in that car when the baby graduated from Georgia Tech with a degree in physics.

3   "When are you going to get a new car?" my friends asked me.

4   "I don't need a new car," I said. "This car runs fine."

5   I changed the oil often, and I kept good tires on it. It always got me where I wanted to go. But the stuffing came out of the backseat and the springs poked through, and the dashboard disintegrated. At 300,000 miles the odometer quit

---

* "My Real Car" from MAMA MAKES UP HER MIND AND OTHER DANGERS OF SOUTHERN LIVING by Bailey White, pp. 192–196. Copyright © 1993 by Bailey White. Reprinted by permission of Perseus Books Publishers, a member of Perseus Books, L.L.C.

turning, but I didn't really care to know how far I had driven. A hole wore in the floor where my heel rested in front of the accelerator, and the insulation all peeled off the fire wall. "Old piece of junk," my friends whispered. The seat-belt catch finally wore out, and I tied on a huge bronze hook with a fireman's knot.

6   Then one day on my way to work, the car coughed, sputtered and stopped. "This is it," I thought, and I gave it a pat. "It's been a good car."

7   The mechanic laughed at me. "You know what's wrong with that car?" he asked. "That car is out of gas." So I slopped some gas in the tank and drove ten more years.

8   The fuel gauge never worked again after that, but I got to where I could tell when the gas was low by the smell. I think it was the smell of the bottom of the tank. There was also a little smell of brake fluid, a little smell of exhaust, a little smell of oil and, after all the years, a little smell of me. Car smells.

9   And sounds. The wonderful sound when the engine finally catches on a cold day, and an ominous *tick tick* in July when the radiator is working too hard. The windshield wipers said, "Gracie Allen Gracie Allen Gracie Allen." I didn't like a lot of conversation in the car, because I had to keep listening for a little skip that meant I needed to jump out and adjust the carburetor. I kept a screwdriver close at hand, and a pint of brake fluid and a new rotor, just in case. "She's strange," my friends whispered. "And she drives so slow."

10   I don't know how fast I drove. The speedometer had quit working years ago. But when I would look down through the hole in the floor and see the pavement, a gray blur, whizzing by just inches away from my feet, and feel the tremendous heat from the internal-combustion engine pouring back through the fire wall into my lap, and hear each barely contained explosion, just as a heart attack victim is able to hear her own heartbeat, it didn't feel like slow to me. A whiff of brake fluid would remind me just what a tiny thing I was relying on to stop myself from hurtling along the surface of the Earth at an unnatural speed. When I arrived at my destination, I would slump back, unfasten the seat-belt hook with trembling hands and stagger out. I would gather up my things and give the car a last look. "Thank you, sir," I would say. "We got here one more time."

11   But after I received that letter I began thinking about buying a new car. I read the newspaper every night. Finally I found one that sounded good. It was the same make as my car, but almost new. "Call Steve," the ad said. I went to see the car. It was parked in Steve's driveway. It was a fashionable wheat color. There was carpet on the floor and the seats were covered with soft, velvety-feeling stuff. It smelled like acrylic, and vinyl, and Steve. I turned a knob. Mozart's Concerto for Flute and Harp poured out of four speakers. "But how can you listen to the engine with music playing?" I asked Steve.

12   I turned the key. The car started instantly. I fastened my seat belt. Nothing but a click. Steve got in the passenger seat, and we went for a test drive. We floated down the road. I couldn't hear a sound, but I decided it must be time to shift gears. I stomped around on the floor and grabbed Steve's knee before I remembered the car had automatic transmission.

13   "You mean you just put it in 'Drive' and drive?" I asked. Steve scrunched himself against his door and clamped his knees together. He tested his seat belt. "Have you ever driven before?" he asked.

14   I bought it. I rolled all the windows up by mashing a button beside my elbow, set the air-conditioning on "Recirc" and listened to Vivaldi all the way home.

15   So now I have two cars. I call them my new car and my real car. Most of the time I drive my new car. But on some days I go out to the barn and get in my real car. I shoo the rats out of the backseat and crank up the engine. Even without daily practice my hands and feet know just what to do. My ears perk up, and I sniff the air. I add a little brake fluid, a little water. I sniff again. It'll need gas next week, and an oil change. I back it out and we roll down the road. People stop and look. They smile. "Neat car!" they say.

The Myth of the Latin Woman: I Just Met a Girl Named Maria*

Judith Ortiz Cofer

Judith Ortiz Cofer is an award-winning poet, essayist, fiction writer, and professor of English and creative writing at the University of Georgia. Cofer often draws upon her Puerto Rican heritage as she explores cultural diversity issues in America. Her works include *If I Could Fly* (2011), *A Love Story Beginning in Spanish* (2005), *The Meaning of Consuelo* (2003), and *The Latin Deli* (1993), from which this essay is taken.

1   On a bus trip to London from Oxford University, where I was earning some graduate credits one summer, a young man, obviously fresh from a pub, spotted me and as if struck by inspiration went down on his knees in the aisle. With both hands over his heart he broke into an Irish tenor's rendition of "Maria" from *West Side Story.*** My politely amused fellow passengers gave his lovely voice the round of gentle applause it deserved. Though I was not quite as amused, I managed my version of an English smile: no show of teeth, no extreme contortions of the facial muscles—I was at this time of my life practicing reserve and cool. Oh, that British control, how I coveted it. But Maria had followed me to London, reminding me of a prime fact of my life: you can leave the Island [Puerto Rico], master the English language, and travel as far as you can, but if you are Latina, especially one like me who so obviously belongs to Rita Moreno's gene pool, the Island travels with you.

2   This is sometimes a very good thing—it may win you that extra minute of someone's attention. But with some people, the same things can *make you* an island—not so much a tropical paradise as an Alcatraz, a place nobody wants to visit. As a Puerto Rican girl growing up in the United States and wanting like most children to "belong," I resented the stereotype that my Hispanic appearance called forth from many people I met.

3   Our family lived in a large urban center in New Jersey during the sixties, where life was designed as a microcosm of my parents' *casas* [households] on the island. We spoke in Spanish, we ate Puerto Rican food bought at the *bodega* [grocery], and we practiced strict Catholicism complete with Saturday confession and Sunday

---

* "The Myth of the Latin Woman: I Just Met a Girl Named Maria" by Judith Ortiz Cofer from THE LATIN DELI: Prose and Poetry. Reprinted by permission of The University of Georgia Press.
**West Side Story* is a well-known musical (and movie) that sets the Romeo and Juliet story on the streets of New York amid gang rivalry. Puerto Rico-born actress Rita Moreno won an Oscar for her supporting role in the film version.

mass at a church where our parents were accommodated into a one-hour Spanish mass slot, performed by a Chinese priest trained as a missionary for Latin America.

4   As a girl I was kept under strict surveillance, since virtue and modesty were, by cultural equation, the same as family honor. As a teenager I was instructed on how to behave as a proper señorita. But it was a conflicting message girls got, since the Puerto Rican mothers also encouraged their daughters to look and act like women and to dress in clothes our Anglo friends and their mothers found too "mature" for our age. It was, and is, cultural, yet I often felt humiliated when I appeared at an American friend's party wearing a dress more suitable to a semiformal than a playroom birthday celebration. At Puerto Rican festivities, neither the music nor the colors we wore could be too loud. I still experience a vague sense of letdown when I'm invited to a "party" and it turns out to be a marathon conversation in hushed tones rather than a fiesta with salsa, laughter, and dancing—the kind of celebration I remember from my childhood.

5   I remember Career Day in our high school, when teachers told us to come dressed as if for a job interview. It quickly became obvious that to the barrio girls, "dressing up" sometimes meant wearing ornate jewelry and clothing that would be more appropriate (by mainstream standards) for the company Christmas party than as daily office attire. That morning I had agonized in front of my closet, trying to figure out what a "career girl" would wear because, essentially, except for Marlo Thomas* on TV, I had no models on which to base my decision. I knew how to dress for school: at the Catholic school I attended we all wore uniforms; I knew how to dress for Sunday mass, and I knew what dresses to wear for parties at my relatives' homes. Though I do not recall the precise details of my Career Day outfit, it must have been a composite of the above choices. But I remember a comment my friend (an Italian American) made in later years that coalesced my impressions of that day. She said that at the business school she was attending the Puerto Rican girls always stood out for wearing "everything at once." She meant, of course, too much jewelry, too many accessories. On that day at school, we were simply made the negative models by the nuns who were themselves not credible fashion experts to any of us. But it was painfully obvious to me that to the others, in their tailored skirts and silk blouses, we must have seemed "hopeless" and "vulgar." Though I now know that most adolescents feel out of step much of the time, I also know that for the Puerto Rican girls of my generation that sense was intensified. The way our teachers and classmates looked at us that day in school was just a taste of the culture clash that awaited us in the real world, where prospective employers and men on the street would often misinterpret our tight skirts and jingling bracelets as a come-on.

6   Mixed cultural signals have perpetuated certain stereotypes—for example, that of the Hispanic woman as the "Hot Tamale" or sexual firebrand. It is a one-dimensional view that the media have found easy to promote. In their special vocabulary, advertisers have designated "sizzling" and "smoldering" as the adjectives of choice for describing not only the foods but also the women of Latin America.

---

*Marlo Thomas starred in the 1965–1971 series *That Girl* as a young single woman seeking an acting career in New York City.

From conversations in my house I recall hearing about the harassment that Puerto Rican women endured in factories where the "boss men" talked to them as if sexual innuendo was all they understood and, worse, often gave them the choice of submitting to advances or being fired.

7   It is custom, however, not chromosomes, that leads us to choose scarlet over pale pink. As young girls, we were influenced in our decisions about clothes and colors by the women—older sisters and mothers who had grown up on a tropical island where the natural environment was a riot of primary colors, where showing your skin was one way to keep cool as well as to look sexy. Most important of all, on the island, women perhaps felt freer to dress and move more provocatively, since, in most cases, they were protected by the traditions, mores, and laws of a Spanish/Catholic system of morality and machismo whose main rule was: *You may look at my sister, but if you touch her I will kill you.* The extended family and church structure could provide a young woman with a circle of safety in her small pueblo on the island; if a man "wronged" a girl, everyone would close in to save her family honor.

8   This is what I have gleaned from my discussions as an adult with older Puerto Rican women. They have told me about dressing in their best party clothes on Saturday nights and going to the town's plaza to promenade with their girlfriends in front of the boys they liked. The males were thus given an opportunity to admire the women and to express their admiration in the form of *piropos*: erotically charged street poems they composed on the spot. I have been subjected to a few *piropos* while visiting the Island and they can be outrageous, although custom dictates that they must never cross into obscenity. This ritual, as I understand it, also entails a show of studied indifference on the woman's part; if she is "decent," she must not acknowledge the man's impassioned words. So I do understand how things can be lost in translation. When a Puerto Rican girl dressed in her idea of what is attractive meets a man from the mainstream culture who has been trained to react to certain types of clothing as a sexual signal, a clash is likely to take place. The line I first heard based on this aspect of the myth happened when the boy who took me to my first formal dance leaned over to plant a sloppy overeager kiss painfully on my mouth, and when I didn't respond with sufficient passion said in a resentful tone: "I thought you Latin girls were supposed to mature early"—my first instance of being thought of as a fruit or vegetable—I was supposed to *ripen*, not just grow into womanhood like other girls.

9   It is surprising to some of my professional friends that some people, including those who should know better, still put others "in their place." Though rarer, these incidents are still commonplace in my life. It happened to me most recently during a stay at a very classy metropolitan hotel favored by young professional couples for their weddings. Late one evening after the theater, as I walked toward my room with my new colleague (a woman with whom I was coordinating an arts program), a middle-aged man in a tuxedo, a young girl in satin and lace on his arm, stepped directly into our path. With his champagne glass extended toward me, he exclaimed, "Evita!"*

---

*"Evita" refers to Eva Perón, popular wife of former Argentinean president Juan Perón, whose rags-to-riches life story was made into a hit musical and movie.

10   Our way blocked, my companion and I listened as the man half-recited, half-bellowed "Don't Cry for Me, Argentina." When he finished, the young girl said: "How about a round of applause for my daddy?" We complied, hoping this would bring the silly spectacle to a close. I was becoming aware that our little group was attracting the attention of the other guests. "Daddy" must have perceived this too, and he once more barred the way as we tried to walk past him. He began to shout-sing a ditty to the tune of "La Bamba"—except the lyrics were about a girl named Maria whose exploits all rhymed with her name and gonorrhea. The girl kept saying "Oh, Daddy" and looking at me with pleading eyes. She wanted me to laugh along with the others. My companion and I stood silently waiting for the man to end his offensive song. When he finished, I looked not at him but at his daughter. I advised her calmly never to ask her father what he had done in the army. Then I walked between them and to my room. My friend complimented me on my cool handling of the situation. I confessed to her that I really had wanted to push the jerk into the swimming pool. I knew that this same man—probably a corporate executive, well educated, even worldly by most standards—would not have been likely to regale a white woman with a dirty song in public. He would perhaps have checked his impulse by assuming that she could be somebody's wife or mother, or at least *somebody* who might take offense. But to him, I was just an Evita or a Maria; merely a character in his cartoon-populated universe.

11   Because of my education and my proficiency with the English language, I have acquired many mechanisms for dealing with the anger I experience. This was not true for my parents, nor is it true for the many Latin women working at menial jobs who must put up with stereotypes about our ethnic group, such as "They make good domestics." This is another facet of the myth of the Latin woman in the United States. Its origin is simple to deduce. Work as domestics, waitressing, and factory jobs are all that's available to women with little English and few skills. The myth of the Hispanic menial has been sustained by the same media phenomenon that made Mammy from *Gone with the Wind* America's idea of the black woman for generations: Maria, the housemaid or counter girl, is now indelibly etched into the national psyche. The big and the little screens have presented us with the picture of the funny Hispanic maid, mispronouncing words and cooking up a spicy storm in a shiny California kitchen.

12   This media-engendered image of the Latina in the United States has been documented by feminist Hispanic scholars, who claim that such portrayals are partially responsible for the denial of opportunities for upward mobility among Latinas in the professions. I have a Chicana friend working on a Ph.D. in philosophy at a major university. She says her doctor still shakes his head in puzzled amazement at all the "big words" she uses. Since I do not wear my diplomas around my neck for all to see, I too have on occasion been sent to that "kitchen," where some think I obviously belong.

13   One such incident that has stayed with me, though I recognize it as a minor offense, happened on the day of my first public poetry reading. It took place in Miami in a boat-restaurant where we were having lunch before an event. I was nervous and excited as I walked in with my notebook in my hand. An older woman motioned me to her table. Thinking (foolish me) that she wanted me to autograph

a copy of my brand-new slender volume of verse, I went over. She ordered a cup of coffee from me, assuming that I was the waitress. Easy enough to mistake my poems for menus, I suppose. I know that it wasn't an intentional act of cruelty, yet of all the good things that happened that day, I remember that scene most clearly, because it reminded me of what I had to overcome before anyone would take me seriously. In retrospect I understand that my anger gave my reading fire, that I have almost always taken doubts in my abilities as a challenge—and that the result is, most times, a feeling of satisfaction at having won a convert when I see the cold, appraising eyes warm to my words, the body language change, the smile that indicates that I have opened some avenue for communication. That day I read to that woman and her lowered eyes told me that she was embarrassed at her little faux pas, and when I willed her to look up at me, it was my victory, and she graciously allowed me to punish her with my full attention. We shook hands at the end of the reading, and I never saw her again. She has probably forgotten the whole thing, but maybe not.

14   Yet I am one of the lucky ones. My parents made it possible for me to acquire a stronger footing in the mainstream culture by giving me the chance at an education. And books and art have saved me from the harsher forms of ethnic and racial prejudice that many of my Hispanic *compañeras* [friends] have had to endure. I travel a lot around the United States, reading from my books of poetry and my novel, and the reception I most often receive is one of positive interest by people who want to know more about my culture. There are, however, thousands of Latinas without the privilege of an education or the entrée into society that I have. For them life is a struggle against the misconceptions perpetuated by the myth of the Latina as whore, domestic, or criminal. We cannot change this by legislating the way people look at us. The transformation, as I see it, has to occur at a much more individual level. My personal goal in my public life is to try to replace the old pervasive stereotypes and myths about Latinas with a much more interesting set of realities. Every time I give a reading, I hope the stories I tell, the dreams and fears I examine in my work, can achieve some universal truth which will get my audience past the particulars of my skin color, my accent, or my clothes.

15   I once wrote a poem in which I called us Latinas "God's brown daughters." This poem is really a prayer of sorts, offered upward but also, through the human-to-human channel of art, outward. It is a prayer for communication, and for respect. In it, Latin women pray "in Spanish to an Anglo God / with a Jewish heritage," and they are "fervently hoping / that if not omnipotent, / at least He be bilingual."

Once More to the Lake*

E. B. White

Elwyn Brooks White was an editor and writer for *The New Yorker* and a columnist for *Harper's* magazine. He is well known for his essays, collected in volumes including *One Man's Meat* (1943), *The Second Tree from the Corner* (1954), and *The Points of My Compass* (1962), and for his children's books, *Stuart Little* (1945) and *Charlotte's Web* (1952). This essay, written in 1941, originally appeared in *Harper's*.

---

1   One summer, along about 1904, my father rented a camp on a lake in Maine and took us all there for the month of August. We all got ringworm from some kittens and had to rub Pond's Extract on our arms and legs night and morning, and my father rolled over in a canoe with all his clothes on; but outside of that the vacation was a success and from then on none of us ever thought there was any place in the world like that lake in Maine. We returned summer after summer—always on August 1st for one month. I have since become a salt-water man, but sometimes in summer there are days when the restlessness of the tides and the fearful cold of the sea water and the incessant wind which blows across the afternoon and into the evening make me wish for the placidity of a lake in the woods. A few weeks ago this feeling got so strong I bought myself a couple of bass hooks and a spinner and returned to the lake where we used to go, for a week's fishing and to revisit old haunts.

2   I took along my son, who had never had any fresh water up his nose and who had seen lily pads only from train windows. On the journey over to the lake I began to wonder what it would be like. I wondered how time would have marred this unique, this holy spot—the coves and streams, the hills that the sun set behind, the camps and the paths behind the camps. I was sure the tarred road would have found it out and I wondered in what other ways it would be desolated. It is strange how much you can remember about places like that once you allow your mind to return into the grooves which lead back. You remember one thing, and that suddenly reminds you of another thing. I guess I remembered clearest of all the early mornings, when the lake was cool and motionless, remembered how the bedroom smelled of the lumber it was made of and of the wet woods whose scent entered through the screen. The partitions in the camp were thin and did not extend clear to the top of the rooms, and as I was always the first up I would dress softly so as not to wake the others, and sneak out into the sweet outdoors and start out in the canoe, keeping close along the shore in the long shadows of the pines. I remembered being very careful never to rub my paddle against the gunwale for fear of disturbing the stillness of the cathedral.

3   The lake had never been what you would call a wild lake. There were cottages sprinkled around the shores, and it was in farming country although the shores of the lake were quite heavily wooded. Some of the cottages were owned by nearby farmers, and you would live at the shore and eat your meals at the farmhouse. That's what our family did. But although it wasn't wild, it was a fairly large and undisturbed lake and there were places in it which, to a child at least, seemed infinitely remote and primeval.

4   I was right about the tar; it led to within half a mile of the shore. But when I got back there, with my boy, and we settled into a camp near a farmhouse and into the kind of summertime I had known, I could tell that it was going to be pretty much the same as it had been before—I knew it, lying in bed the first morning, smelling the bedroom, and hearing the boy sneak quietly out and go off along the shore in a boat. I began to sustain the illusion that he was I, and therefore by simple transposition, that I was my father. This sensation persisted, kept cropping up all the time we were there. It was not an entirely new feeling, but in this setting it grew much stronger. I seemed to be living a dual existence. I would be in the middle of

some simple act, I would be picking up a bait box or laying down a table fork, or I would be saying something, and suddenly it would be not I but my father who was saying the words or making the gesture. It gave me a creepy sensation.

5   We went fishing the first morning. I felt the same damp moss covering the worms in the bait can, and saw the dragonfly alight on the tip of my rod as it hovered a few inches from the surface of the water. It was the arrival of this fly that convinced me beyond any doubt that everything was as it always had been, that the years were a mirage and there had been no years. The small waves were the same, chucking the rowboat under the chin as we fished at anchor, and the boat was the same boat, the same color green and the ribs broken in the same places, and under the floor-boards the same fresh-water leavings and debris—the dead helgramite,* the wisps of moss, the rusty discarded fishhook, the dried blood from yesterday's catch. We stared silently at the tips of our rods, at the dragonflies that came and went. I low-ered the tip of mine into the water, tentatively, pensively dislodging the fly, which darted two feet away, poised, darted two feet back, and came to rest again a little farther up the rod. There had been no years between the ducking of this dragon-fly and the other one—the one that was part of memory. I looked at the boy, who was silently watching his fly, and it was my hands that held his rod, my eyes watch-ing. I felt dizzy and didn't know which rod I was at the end of.

6   We caught two bass, hauling them in briskly as though they were mackerel, pull-ing them over the side of the boat in a businesslike manner without any landing net, and stunning them with a blow on the back of the head. When we got back for a swim before lunch, the lake was exactly where we had left it, the same number of inches from the dock, and there was only the merest suggestion of a breeze. This seemed an utterly enchanted sea, this lake you could leave to its own devices for a few hours and come back to, and find that it had not stirred, this constant and trustworthy body of water. In the shallows, the dark, water-soaked sticks and twigs, smooth and old, were undulating in clusters on the bottom against the clean ribbed sand, and the track of the mussel was plain. A school of minnows swam by, each minnow with its small individual shadow, doubling the attendance, so clear and sharp in the sunlight. Some of the other campers were in swimming, along the shore, one of them with a cake of soap, and the water felt thin and clear and unsubstantial. Over the years there had been this person with the cake of soap, this cultist, and here he was. There had been no years.

7   Up to the farmhouse to dinner through the teeming, dusty field, the road under our sneakers was only a two-track road. The middle track was missing, the one with the marks of the hooves and the splotches of dried, flaky manure. There had always been three tracks to choose from in choosing which track to walk in; now the choice was narrowed down to two. For a moment I missed terribly the middle alternative. But the way led past the tennis court, and something about the way it lay there in the sun reassured me; the tape had loosened along the backline, the alleys were green with plantains and other weeds, and the net (installed in June and removed in September) sagged in the dry noon, and the whole place steamed

---

*A helgramite is an insect sometimes used for bait.

with mid-day heat and hunger and emptiness. There was a choice of pie for dessert, and one was blueberry and one was apple, and the waitresses were the same country girls, there having been no passage of time, only the illusion of it as in a dropped curtain—the waitresses were still fifteen; their hair had been washed, that was the only difference—they had been to the movies and seen the pretty girls with the clean hair.

8   Summertime, oh summertime, pattern of life indelible, the fade-proof lake, the woods unshatterable, the pasture with the sweet-fern and the juniper forever and ever, summer without end; this was the background, and the life along the shore was the design, the cottages with their innocent and tranquil design, their tiny docks with the flagpole and the American flag floating against the white clouds in the blue sky, the little paths over the roots of the trees leading from camp to camp and the paths leading back to the outhouses and the can of lime for sprinkling, and at the souvenir counters at the store the miniature birch-bark canoes and the post cards that showed things looking a little better than they looked. This was the American family at play, escaping the city heat, wondering whether the newcomers in the camp at the head of the cove were "common" or "nice," wondering whether it was true that the people who drove up for Sunday dinner at the farmhouse were turned away because there wasn't enough chicken.

9   It seemed to me, as I kept remembering all this, that those times and those summers had been infinitely precious and worth saving. There had been jollity and peace and goodness. The arriving (at the beginning of August) had been so big a business in itself, at the railway station the farm wagon drawn up, the first smell of the pine-laden air, the first glimpse of the smiling farmer, and the great importance of the trunks and your father's enormous authority in such matters, and the feel of the wagon under you for a long ten-mile haul, and at the top of the last long hill catching the first view of the lake after eleven months of not seeing this cherished body of water. The shouts and cries of the other campers when they saw you, and the trunks to be unpacked, to give up their rich burden. (Arriving was less exciting nowadays, when you sneaked up in your car and parked it under a tree near the camp and took out the bags and in five minutes it was all over, no fuss, no loud wonderful fuss about trunks.)

10   Peace and goodness and jollity. The only thing that was wrong now, really, was the sound of the place, an unfamiliar nervous sound of the outboard motors. This was the note that jarred, the one thing that would sometimes break the illusion and set the years moving. In those other summertimes all motors were inboard; and when they were at a little distance, the noise they made was a sedative, an ingredient of summer sleep. They were one-cylinder and two-cylinder engines, and some were make-and-break and some were jump-spark, but they all made a sleepy sound across the lake. The one-lungers throbbed and fluttered, and the twin-cylinder ones purred and purred, and that was a quiet sound too. But now the campers all had outboards. In the daytime, in the hot mornings, these motors made a petulant, irritable sound; at night, in the still evening when the afterglow lit the water, they whined about one's ears like mosquitoes. My boy loved our rented outboard, and his great desire was to achieve singlehanded mastery over it, and authority, and he soon learned the trick of choking it a little (but not too much), and the

adjustment of the needle valve. Watching him I would remember the things you could do with the old one-cylinder engine with the heavy flywheel, how you could have it eating out of your hand if you got really close to it spiritually. Motor boats in those days didn't have clutches, and you would make a landing by shutting off the motor at the proper time and coasting in with a dead rudder. But there was a way of reversing them, if you learned the trick, by cutting the switch and putting it on again exactly on the final dying revolution of the flywheel, so that it would kick back against compression and begin reversing. Approaching a dock in a strong following breeze, it was difficult to slow up sufficiently by the ordinary coasting method, and if a boy felt he had complete mastery over his motor, he was tempted to keep it running beyond its time and then reverse it a few feet from the dock. It took a cool nerve, because if you threw the switch a twentieth of a second too soon you would catch the flywheel when it still had speed enough to go up past center, and the boat would leap ahead, charging bull-fashion at the dock.

11   We had a good week at the camp. The bass were biting well and the sun shone endlessly, day after day. We would be tired at night and lie down in the accumulated heat of the little bedrooms after the long hot day and the breeze would stir almost imperceptibly outside and the smell of the swamp drift in through the rusty screens. Sleep would come easily and in the morning the red squirrel would be on the roof, tapping out his gay routine. I kept remembering everything, lying in bed in the mornings—the small steamboat that had a long rounded stern like the lip of a Ubangi, and how quietly she ran on the moonlight sails, when the older boys played their mandolins and the girls sang and we ate doughnuts dipped in sugar, and how sweet the music was on the water in the shining night, and what it had felt like to think about girls then. After breakfast we would go up to the store and the things were in the same place—the minnows in a bottle, the plugs and spinners disarranged and pawed over by the youngsters from the boys' camp, the fig newtons and the Beeman's gum. Outside, the road was tarred and cars stood in front of the store. Inside, all was just as it had always been, except there was more Coca-Cola and not so much Moxie and root beer and birch beer and sarsaparilla. We would walk out with a bottle of pop apiece and sometimes the pop would backfire up our noses and hurt. We explored the streams, quietly, where the turtles slid off the sunny logs and dug their way into the soft bottom; and we lay on the town wharf and fed worms to the tame bass. Everywhere we went I had trouble making out which was I, the one walking at my side, the one walking in my pants.

12   One afternoon while we were there at that lake a thunderstorm came up. It was like the revival of an old melodrama that I had seen long ago with childish awe. The second-act climax of the drama of the electrical disturbance over a lake in America had not changed in any important respect. This was the big scene, still the big scene. The whole thing was so familiar, the first feeling of oppression and heat and a general air around camp of not wanting to go very far away. In midafternoon (it was all the same) a curious darkening of the sky, and a lull in everything that had made life tick; and then the way the boats suddenly swung the other way at their moorings with the coming of a breeze out of the new quarter, and the premonitory rumble. Then the kettle drum, then the snare, then the bass drum and cymbals, then crackling light against the dark, and the gods grinning and

licking their chops in the hills. Afterward the calm, the rain steadily rustling in the calm lake, the return of light and hope and spirits, and the campers running out in the joy and relief to go swimming in the rain, their bright cries perpetuating the deathless joke about how they were getting simply drenched, and the children screaming with delight at the new sensation of bathing in the rain, and the joke about getting drenched linking the generations in a strong indestructible chain. And the comedian who waded in carrying an umbrella.

13   When the others went swimming my son said he was going in too. He pulled his dripping trunks from the line where they had hung all through the shower, and wrung them out. Languidly, and with no thought of going in, I watched him, his hard little body, skinny and bare, saw him wince slightly as he pulled up around his vitals the small, soggy, icy garment. As he buckled the swollen belt suddenly my groin felt the chill of death.

Chapter 26

Exposition: Definition

・・・

Celebrating Nerdiness*

Tom Rogers

A former chemical engineer, Tom Rogers now teaches advanced courses in physics, computer science, and statistics at a South Carolina high school and maintains a popular Web site, *Insultingly Stupid Movie Physics*, that has been featured on National Public Radio and in the *New York Times*. A companion book to the site was published in 2007. This essay appeared in *Newsweek* in 2000.

1   I'm a nerd. While the Internet boom has lent some respectability to the term, narrow-minded and thoughtless stereotypes still linger. Nerds are supposedly friendless, book-smart sissies who suck up to authority figures. Some of our image problems stem from our obsession with mastering every inane detail of our interests. But to call us suck-ups is nonsense. We often horrify those in authority with our inability to understand, let alone follow, societal norms.

2   Like most nerds, I didn't know I was one until I started school. There I quickly found out that my enthusiasm for answering the teacher's questions made others feel I was deliberately trying to make them look bad. My classmates were not shy about expressing their feelings on the playground. Fortunately, I was tall and stood my ground, a bluff that helped repel bullies. But mostly I survived by learning to keep quiet in the classroom.

3   I became a high-school teacher because I realized there were lots of young nerds growing up who needed to know that being a nerd was not just OK but something wonderful. Unfortunately, they weren't likely to hear this even from teachers, although virtually every modern blessing from democracy to electric motors originated with a nerd. Some, like Thomas Paine, were idealistic; others, like Tesla,

eccentric. Newton was arrogant and Einstein absent-minded. All of them are now considered geniuses. But make no mistake: 17-year-old versions of these men, placed in modern American high schools, would instantly be labeled as nerds.

4   I raised two nerd sons and a daughter, who describes herself as a nerd sympathizer, partly because I didn't have the cleverness to raise "cool" kids, but also because, selfishly, I wanted nerds to talk to. Every year I invite my Advanced Placement physics students to my house for study sessions before the AP test. Last year one student nerd's mother told me that her son had returned home and talked for hours about how awesome it was to have found a nerd family. Unfortunately, the world's response to our family has not always been so enthusiastic.

5   When my sons were still in school, they were often picked on by classmates. My older boy, a pale and unathletic kid, was an easy target. When his middle-school science teacher asked if anyone could name some elements, my son recited the periodic table from memory. Thanks to events like that, he endured nerd hell at the hands of bullies when waiting for the school bus every afternoon. We tried karate classes and pep talks to bolster his defenses, but he was never able to win his tormentors' respect. He was just too small.

6   My boys were often misunderstood by their teachers, too. My younger son's middle-school social-studies teacher rigidly insisted that he take notes. When he refused, she publicly told him he would never graduate from high school. My son was perfectly capable of taking notes, but in typical nerd fashion, he couldn't bring himself to comply because it was illogical. He could easily remember what the teacher had said. Writing it down cut into his thinking time.

7   Clearly, my son would have to give his teacher what she wanted, but it had to be done with style. We discussed options. These included taking notes in one of the foreign languages he studied as a hobby. I discouraged it because he had learned some colorful foreign terms and was capable of describing his teacher in ways that could make a sailor blush. Finally, we agreed he would write his notes backward.

8   For six months he transcribed his teacher's lectures backward. When I held my son's notes up to a mirror, they were perfectly readable. I shouldn't have been surprised. As a small child he'd entertained us by turning books upside down and reading them backward. I waited for a complaint from his teacher, but she never noticed.

9   Despite childhood trials, both of my sons remain devoted nerds. My older son became conversational in four foreign languages and has hitchhiked around Europe three times. And these days no one would mistake him for a sissy. On one occasion a group of Russian policemen threw him a party after he accepted their invitation to take a mid-December dip in a spring filled with near-freezing water.

10   My younger son proved his teacher wrong and graduated from high school. He scored 1600 on the SAT and was asked to give a speech before 500 educators and politicians who had gathered to honor education. It was his one moment of visibility. As I waited for him to talk, my stomach flip-flopped. I had no idea what he was going to say. He rose from his seat and delivered 10 minutes of stand-up comedy on being a nerd. The audience laughed until they cried. I cried. Afterward a young nerd paid him his highest compliment: "Thank you for what you've done for our people." No, our kind doesn't fit the stereotypes, but yes, there is something wonderful about being a nerd.

The Exam Dream*

Eric Hoover

Eric Hoover is a senior reporter for *The Chronicle of Higher Education*, a weekly news source for college faculty, administrators, staff, and students. Hoover often writes about college admissions, enrollment management, standardized testing, and issues facing non-traditional age students. Previously, he worked for the *C-Ville Weekly* (Charlottesville, Va.) and for the *Washington* [D.C.] *City Paper*. This article appeared in the *Chronicle* in March 2011.

1   *Once more I find myself on this strange but familiar campus. As always, I'm running, a madman with a bookbag, late for an appointment. . . . Down a hallway lies a classroom, and inside waits a desk—the desk of my doom. I sit down; then someone passes me the final exam. All semester I have not cracked a single book. Before me lie pages of questions for which I have no answers. I grip my pen. The pale eye of the clock glares. My palms turn to sponges, and*—and then . . . sweet relief . . . I wake up.

2   So goes my "exam dream," which I've had about once a month since the late 1990s. Odds are you've had some version of it, too. In this nation of tests, few dreams are so familiar, recurring long after we put away our No. 2 pencils and textbooks. For many of us, the exam dream is an albatross gliding evermore over the dark seas of sleep, calling us back to the long ago.

3   In sleep we return to the classrooms where we once fretted over questions and fumbled for the answers. And these settings are no coincidence. "Children start with test-taking very early—it's often their first school experience," says Eleanor Rosch, a professor of psychology at the University of California at Berkeley. Ms. Rosch recalls taking a spelling test in second or third grade. She wrote down the first few words, but then she froze. "There was this mounting terror of figuring out the next word," she says. Such moments, she explains, can imprint themselves in our memories, becoming symbols of emotions and fears we experience years, or even decades, later.

4   The dream can be especially powerful among those who never leave the land of learning. After all, even the highest positions come with scrutiny; the tenured merely trade tests for other trials. "You're being evaluated on your evaluation of someone else's journal article," Ms. Rosch says.

5   Like real exams, the exam dream may take many forms. William G. Durden, president of Dickinson College, sometimes dreams that he's an anxious student who's forgotten to write a paper. He must finish the assignment to graduate, but he cannot. That dream merges with another in which he's a college president with no degrees—a phony in plain sight. These nightmares, Mr. Durden believes, speak to his past: He was the first in his family to attend college, so he had grown up with no narrative for his eventual success. "At a very primordially emotional level," he says, "I appear to find it very hard to believe that I actually have a degree."

6   Over time, some dreamers of exam dreams experience a shift in perspective. As a history professor at Grinnell College, Marci Sortor long dreamed that she had exams in geometry and Spanish but had not been attending either class. In the dream, she couldn't remember where the classrooms were, or how to find her locker, which contained her textbooks. Eventually, Ms. Sortor's dream-self resolved to drop one course and study hard for the other. "Somehow my subconscious was

satisfied," she says. The dream vanished, only to return as the professor's version, in which she was late for class, frantically wondering how she would explain herself to her students and her department chair. "Meanwhile, I'm climbing mountains, jumping over crevasses, and swimming across moats," she says. That dream faded after Ms. Sortor became vice president for institutional planning. Now she dreams that she's late for an administrative meeting, a horror within a horror, if you will.

7   The venues of dreams may vary according to one's interests. Benjamin B. Dunlap, president of Wofford College, suspects that he's never had the exam dream because he's rarely doubted his intellectual abilities or verbal skills (Rhodes Scholars are like that, you know). Yet Mr. Dunlap—who's published poems, written television scripts, and danced for a ballet company—has long valued artistic excellence above other kinds. So perhaps it's not surprising that in his own recurring dream he's a pianist faking his way through a concerto before a large audience. "I'm improvising along with the orchestra, then I realize I've run out of gas, I'm not able to keep up, and I'm just seconds away from people discovering that I'm a total fraud," he says. "It's dreadful."

8   In other words, Mr. Dunlap, who likes to noodle about on the Steinway in the president's house, believes anxiety follows one's most profound aspirations into slumber. But that doesn't mean his dream lacks metaphysical ties to the present. After all, his job demands constant improvisation and buckets of confidence; he describes being a college president as "performance art." "These dreams represent a kind of psychic modesty or intellectual integrity," he says, "the uneasy feeling that you're getting away with something and might get called out."

9   That uneasy feeling can creep over anyone, be it a president or a plumber. By no means are dreams set in school or college the exclusive bane of those who work in education. Merely attending college is enough to get you into the club. My brother-in-law Greg Stuckey, a computer-systems analyst in Illinois, still dreams that he failed a college course, usually English, that kept him from graduation. Every couple of months, Elizabeth Brotherton, a writer I know in Washington, dreams that she must take an exam for a class she's skipped all semester; often the dream comes when she's feeling overwhelmed.

10   Ann McClure, a real-estate agent I know in Virginia, sometimes dreams that she's standing in her cap and gown when she realizes that she hasn't passed a class she needed to graduate. Martha Floyd, who works in the same office, still dreams about taking a big test for which she's not prepared, 32 years after graduating from college. And my dear friend Bryn Chalkley has a jarring version of the exam dream about twice a month, "Going into a situation blind definitely makes me nervous," she says, "and I guess this scenario is an easy or tangible experience for me to apply that kind of anxiety."

11   In some form, the exam dream may be more common among Americans than all but one other type—the nightmare in which we are running from someone or something. This is according to Dierdre Barrett, an assistant clinical professor of psychology at Harvard Medical School, who has reviewed more dream-frequency studies and surveys of dreamers than you ever knew existed. She suspects that people go on dreaming of academic tasks because much of our "symbolic imagery" is set during adolescence, when tests are literally an everyday burden. "This is when

our emotional wiring is getting laid down, and a lot of our emotions are associated with certain visual imagery," Ms. Barrett says. "People have basic anxieties about other people evaluating them. And our society puts a pretty strong value on test-taking."

12   A defining feature of many exam dreams is the dreamer's role in his or her own demise. The psychic gist isn't so much that the big test is a monster, but that one has somehow ushered the monster in, by skipping class or failing to prepare for a task. In the end, we seem to judge ourselves more harshly than the grader of any exam might.

13   So those who've never had such a dream should be very glad. To everyone else, there's just one more thing to say: See you in class.

What Is Poverty?*

Jo Goodwin Parker

When George Henderson, a professor at the University of Oklahoma, was writing his 1971 book, *America's Other Children: Public Schools outside Suburbia*, he received the following essay in the mail. It was signed "Jo Goodwin Parker" and had been mailed from West Virginia. No further information was ever discovered about the essay or its source. Whether the author of this essay was in reality a woman describing her own painful experiences or a sympathetic writer who had adopted her persona, Jo Goodwin Parker remains a mystery.

1   You ask me what is poverty? Listen to me. Here I am, dirty, smelly, and with no "proper" underwear on and with the stench of my rotting teeth near you. I will tell you. Listen to me. Listen without pity. I cannot use your pity. Listen with understanding. Put yourself in my dirty, worn out, ill-fitting shoes, and hear me.

2   Poverty is getting up every morning from a dirt- and illness-stained mattress. The sheets have long since been used for diapers. Poverty is living with a smell that never leaves. This is the smell of urine, sour milk, and spoiling food sometimes joined with the strong smell of long-cooked onions. Onions are cheap. If you have smelled this smell, you did not know how it came. It is the smell of the outdoor privy. It is the smell of young children who cannot walk the long dark way in the night. It is the smell of the mattresses where years of "accidents" have happened. It is the smell of the milk which has gone sour because the refrigerator long has not worked, and it costs money to get it fixed. It is the smell of rotting garbage. I could bury it, but where is the shovel? Shovels cost money.

3   Poverty is being tired. I have always been tired. They told me at the hospital when the last baby came that I had chronic anemia caused from poor diet, a bad case of worms, and that I needed a corrective operation. I listened politely—the poor are always polite. The poor always listen. They don't say that there is no money for iron pills, or better food, or worm medicine. The idea of an operation is frightening and costs so much that, if I had dared, I would have laughed. Who takes care of my children? Recovery from an operation takes a long time. I have

* "What Is Poverty?" by Jo Goodwin Parker in AMERICA'S OTHER CHILDREN: PUBLIC SCHOOLS OUTSIDE SUBURBIA by George Henderson. Reprinted by permission of University of Oklahoma Press.

three children. When I left them with "Granny" the last time I had a job, I came home to find the baby covered with fly specks, and a diaper that had not been changed since I left. When the dried diaper came off, bits of my baby's flesh came with it. My other child was playing with a sharp bit of broken glass, and my oldest was playing alone at the edge of a lake. I made twenty-two dollars a week, and a good nursery school costs twenty dollars a week for three children. I quit my job.

4   Poverty is dirt. You say in your clean clothes coming from your clean house, "Anybody can be clean." Let me explain about housekeeping with no money. For breakfast I give my children grits with no oleo or cornbread without eggs and oleo. This does not use up many dishes. What dishes there are, I wash in cold water and with no soap. Even the cheapest soap has to be saved for the baby's diapers. Look at my hands, so cracked and red. Once I saved for two months to buy a jar of Vaseline for my hands and the baby's diaper rash. When I had saved enough, I went to buy it and the price had gone up two cents. The baby and I suffered on. I have to decide every day if I can bear to put my cracked, sore hands into the cold water and strong soap. But you ask, why not hot water? Fuel costs money. Hot water is a luxury. I do not have luxuries. I know you will be surprised when I tell you how young I am. I look so much older. My back has been bent over the wash tubs for so long, I cannot remember when I ever did anything else. Every night I wash every stitch my school age child has on and just hope her clothes will be dry by morning.

5   Poverty is staying up all night on cold nights to watch the fire, knowing one spark on the newspaper covering the walls means your sleeping children die in flames. In summer poverty is watching gnats and flies devour your baby's tears when he cries. The screens are torn and you pay so little rent you know they will never be fixed. Poverty means insects in your food, in your nose, in your eyes, and crawling over you when you sleep. Poverty is hoping it never rains because diapers won't dry when it rains and soon you are using newspapers. Poverty is seeing your children forever with runny noses. Paper handkerchiefs cost money and all your rags you need for other things. Even more costly are antihistamines. Poverty is cooking without food and cleaning without soap.

6   Poverty is asking for help. Have you ever had to ask for help, knowing your children will suffer unless you get it? Think about asking for a loan from a relative, if this is the only way you can imagine asking for help. I will tell you how it feels. You find out where the office is that you are supposed to visit. You circle that block four or five times. Thinking of your children, you go in. Everyone is very busy. Finally, someone comes out and you tell her that you need help. That never is the person you need to see. You go see another person, and after spilling the whole shame of your poverty all over the desk between you, you find that this isn't the right office after all—you must repeat the whole process, and it never is any easier at the next place.

7   You have asked for help, and after all it has a cost. You are again told to wait. You are told why, but you don't really hear because of the red cloud of shame and the rising black cloud of despair.

8   Poverty is remembering. It is remembering quitting school in junior high because "nice" children had been so cruel about my clothes and my smell. The attendance officer came. My mother told him I was pregnant. I wasn't but she thought that I could get a job and help out. I had jobs off and on, but never long

enough to learn anything. Mostly I remember being married. I was so young then. I am still young. For a time, we had all the things you have. There was a little house in another town, with hot water and everything. Then my husband lost his job. There was unemployment insurance for a while and what few jobs I could get. Soon, all our nice things were repossessed and we moved back here. I was pregnant then. This house didn't look so bad when we first moved in. Every week it gets worse. Nothing is ever fixed. We now had no money. There were a few odd jobs for my husband, but everything went for food then, as it does now. I don't know how we lived through three years and three babies, but we did. I'll tell you something, after the last baby I destroyed my marriage. It had been a good one, but could you keep on bringing children in this dirt? Did you ever think how much it costs for any kind of birth control? I knew my husband was leaving the day he left, but there were no good-byes between us. I hope he has been able to climb out of this mess somewhere. He never could hope with us to drag him down.

9   That's when I asked for help. When I got it, you know how much it was? It was, and is, seventy-eight dollars a month for the four of us; that is all I ever can get. Now you know why there is no soap, no needles and thread, no hot water, no aspirin, no worm medicine, no hand cream, no shampoo. None of these things forever and ever and ever. So that you can see clearly, I pay twenty dollars a month rent, and most of the rest goes for food. For grits and cornmeal, and rice and milk and beans. I try my best to use only the minimum electricity. If I use more, there is that much less for food.

10   Poverty is looking into a black future. Your children won't play with my boys. They will turn to other boys who steal to get what they want. I can already see them behind the bars of their prison instead of behind the bars of my poverty. Or they will turn to the freedom of alcohol or drugs, and find themselves enslaved. And my daughter? At best, there is for her a life like mine.

11   But you say to me, there are schools. Yes, there are schools. My children have no extra books, no magazines, no extra pencils, or crayons, or paper and the most important of all, they do not have health. They have worms, they have infections, they have pinkeye all summer. They do not sleep well on the floor, or with me in my one bed. They do not suffer from hunger, my seventy-eight dollars keeps us alive, but they do suffer from malnutrition. Oh yes, I do remember what I was taught about health in school. It doesn't do much good. In some places there is a surplus commodities program. Not here. The county said it cost too much. There is a school lunch program. But I have two children who will already be damaged by the time they get to school.

12   But, you say to me, there are health clinics. Yes, there are health clinics and they are in the towns. I live out here eight miles from town. I can walk that far (even if it is sixteen miles both ways), but can my little children? My neighbor will take me when he goes; but he expects to get paid, *one way or another*. I bet you know my neighbor. He is that large man who spends his time at the gas station, the barbershop, and the corner store complaining about the government spending money on the immoral mothers of illegitimate children.

13   Poverty is an acid that drips on pride until all pride is worn away. Poverty is a chisel that chips on honor until honor is worn away. Some of you say that you

would do *something* in my situation, and maybe you would, for the first week or the first month, but for year after year after year?

14   Even the poor can dream. A dream of a time when there is money. Money for the right kinds of food, for worm medicine, for iron pills, for toothbrushes, for hand cream, for a hammer and nails and a bit of screening, for a shovel, for a bit of paint, for some sheeting, for needles and thread. Money to pay *in money* for a trip to town. And, oh, money for hot water and money for soap. A dream of when asking for help does not eat away the last bit of pride. When the office you visit is as nice as the offices of other governmental agencies, when there are enough workers to help you quickly, when workers do not quit in defeat and despair. When you have to tell your story to only one person, and that person can send you for other help and you don't have to prove your poverty over and over and over again.

15   I have come out of my despair to tell you this. Remember I did not come from another place or another time. Others like me are all around you. Look at us with an angry heart, anger that will help you help me. Anger that will let you tell of me. The poor are always silent. Can you be silent too?

Chapter 27

Exposition: Division/ Classification

• •

Party Manners*

Richard L. Grossman

Richard L. Grossman is a psychotherapist, medical educator, and author. He has written a number of books, many on health-related issues, including *Choosing & Changing: A Guide to Self-Reliance* (1978) and *The Other Medicines* (1986). His most recent work is *A Year with Emerson* (2003), a daybook that introduces readers to the writings of philosopher-poet Ralph Waldo Emerson. This 1983 article first appeared in *Health* magazine as part of Grossman's column called "Richard's Almanac."

1   The Romans had their Colosseum, the Elizabethans their village promenades and their Globe Theater. For centuries the French and Germans had their spectacular court balls. Queens and Presidents have their state dinners, complete with chamber music. And we ordinary moderns? We have *parties*.

2   From college "mixers" to suburban cocktail "standarounds," from children's ice-cream splattered birthday celebrations to retirement dinners, from political fundraisers to bridal showers, the party has become as ubiquitous an institution as the Internal Revenue Service. And familiar though it is, the party has a psychologically transforming effect on many of us. Somehow our attendance at a gathering called a "party" causes us to behave in ways we never do elsewhere, as though we were players in a drama meant to reveal some of the hidden parts of our personalities. The party setting seems to provide a license to unveil attitudes that we would never display at the office or the family dinner table. And though party behavior may not be a reliable guide to all our psychological tics, it is nevertheless a place to see how

we "go public" with some of our unresolved problems. Consider this cast of characters, for example:

The Cartoonist

3   Here's the person who has no other arena in his life in which to be a vocal social critic, who sees every party as an opportunity to be the local Andy Rooney.* No dancing or merrymaking for this one, but rather a steady stream of mini-lectures on the foibles and deficiencies of all the other guests. The Cartoonist is someone who does not want to be part of the crowd, but needs to keep his distance and act the reporting observer, drawing verbal caricatures of "them" as though he were sending communiqués back to Mars on the tribal rituals of the "Earthlings." What's really going on, of course, is that the fear of spontaneity and the relaxation of conventions are just too threatening, so the only safe stance is to play the part of the uninvolved expert.

The Spotter

4   This character is the familiar shopper for greener pastures. She is talking to you, but is looking over your shoulder the whole time, ever alert to someone just a little more interesting or a little more important who may be on the other side of the room. This person is usually the inside-dopester, the one who craves the latest information, who drops the trendiest names, who goes to the hottest events. The Spotter has the attention span of an alcoholic mayfly and cannot wait to move on, fearful that she is missing out on something better. The usual result, of course, is that she has a terrible time at parties and can't understand why all those other folks are laughing.

The Performer

5   He's often known as "the life of the party" and is the one for whom every party is the high school play in which he didn't get a part. Parties for this type are only an opportunity to grab the spotlight that he wants desperately but is being denied elsewhere. There are variations, of course: The Practical Joker, The Bathroom Comedian, The Barroom Baritone, The Poor Man's Rich Little**—but all are revealing only one sad fact: They are yearning for notoriety and attention.

The Wallflower

6   Here you have the reverse image of The Performer: The person who gains attention by a silent, martyred withdrawal from the center of the party. Sooner or later, someone will spot her standing in a corner with a rueful smile on her face, just waiting to be asked if something is wrong. If you should inquire, you'll hear that she "just isn't good in crowds," or "hates all that noise," or "never could learn to

---

*Andy Rooney, a television commentator on *60 Minutes* for over thirty years, was known for his cranky observations on the annoyances of everyday life.
**Rich Little is a comedian known for his impersonations of famous celebrities.

disco." Do not be deceived into thinking that you've discovered an authentically shy or lonely person. This routine is simply a device to get attention with a passive strategy. (The *really* shy one didn't come to the party.)

The Swashbuckler

7   Also known as "The Last of the Big Benders," this is a person who may be in real trouble. Something has gone drastically wrong somewhere in his life, and he is frightened or even desperate about the outcome. If he is not working on the problem in another corner of life or getting the help he really needs, then the only place for that terrified energy to go is into uncharacteristically heavy drinking and raucous, high-pitched haranguing. There are usually very real and troubling issues underlying this kind of behavior, and the party can, unfortunately, provide a convenient setting for acting out.

The Scarlet Pimpernel*

8   She's the person who sees every party invitation as an opportunity to project her romantic fantasy. Feeling frustrated by a humdrum, uneventful existence, such a person mentally writes out a script for Meryl Streep or Julie Christie** and goes off to the party prepared to try out the new role, altering the voice to sound sultry or provocative, speaking in cryptic or poetic language, gliding around the room like a visitor from the Court of St. James. Sometimes this is just playfulness or harmless flirtatiousness, but usually the pseudo-romantic is simply saying through her behavior that the rest of her life is dull and gray, and needs spicing up.

9   Now, a certain amount of nervousness and unease about going to a party is clearly normal, and it would be simple-minded to claim that even the types described above are necessarily displaying secret pathology. But if parties regularly call up odd or extraordinary behavior in you, or become a theater for exposing subterranean needs, it might be a good idea to look at the usual, non-partying areas of your life and see what's troubling you. Some parties are boring, to be sure, and a dose of silly, unplanned frolicking may liven them up. But we should remember that parties are usually designed as a means to gather in a friendly, open, genuine way; as a chance to enjoy the warmth and closeness of other human beings. If those are not reasons enough for going, if we need parties to ventilate other feelings, perhaps we should consider group therapy instead.

---

*This name is drawn from a 1905 novel by Baroness Emmuska Orczy, in which a British nobleman leads a double life as "the Scarlet Pimpernel," a sword-fighting rescuer of innocent people condemned to the guillotine during the French Revolution's Reign of Terror. Often credited as the first popular novel to establish the "dual identity" hero, the story paved the way for Superman, Batman, Zorro, and other modern superheroes in disguise.

**Meryl Streep is one of America's most highly regarded actresses, having won three Academy Awards; Julie Christie is a British actress, also an Academy Award winner, but possibly best known in this country for her role as Lara in the classic 1965 film *Dr. Zhivago*.

The Colorful Plate*

Dianne Moeller

Dianne Moeller spent many years as a registered dietitian at the Health District of Northern Larimer County, serving communities in northern Colorado. In addition to offering nutritional counseling to Health District clients, Moeller wrote a newspaper column called "Health and Fitness," in which she presented a variety of suggestions for improving and maintaining her readers' physical wellbeing. This column appeared in the Fort Collins, Colorado, *Coloradoan* in March 2011.

1   Spring is here, and with it comes the promise of more color in our yards and gardens. There's one place we should try to keep colorful throughout the year: the meal plate.

2   The vibrant hues of fruits and vegetables aren't just a feast for the eyes—they're a source of powerful compounds packed with health benefits. These compounds, called phytonutrients (or phytochemicals), help protect plants while they are growing. As part of our diet, they can help protect us from disease, and they are most heavily concentrated in colorful fruits and vegetables.

3   Phytonutrients can be grouped into families represented by different colors and health benefits. Generally the brighter the color, the bigger the benefit (as long as the color doesn't come from a dye). As with all foods we eat, variety is key. You get the most benefit by eating fruits and vegetables from several families. That's why experts now recommend that we "eat a rainbow" everyday.

4   Let's take a look at the color families.

5   **Red**—Tomatoes, watermelon and red grapefruit are rich in the antioxidant lycopene. Diets high in lycopene have been associated with reduced incidence of prostate and other cancers, cardiovascular disease and macular degeneration. Using salsa or other tomato products generously helps you get more lycopene. Also, cooking concentrates lycopene, so foods such as pasta sauce offer a bigger dose of this phytonutrient.

6   **Blue/Purple**—This family includes all berries (not just blue ones) because they contain similar compounds, which might help slow the aging process, protect against heart disease and cancer, prevent blood clots and fight inflammation and allergies. Use berries as toppings, snacks, or ingredients in smoothies. Juices, including grape and cranberry, are another way to get benefits from the blue/purple family. This family also extends to vegetables, including eggplant and purple cabbage.

7   **Orange**—Carrots, cantaloupe, apricots, sweet potatoes and squashes contain carotenoids and other compounds that are important for eye health and might protect against sun damage to the eyes and skin. Your best and safest source for carotenoids is food, as evidence suggests that beta-carotene supplements might have harmful effects, at least in smokers. Carrots, cooked or raw, shredded on salads or eaten as snacks, deliver plenty of carotenoids.

8   **Yellow**—Yellow fruits and vegetables, including citrus, pineapple, and white grapefruit, contain substances that inhibit cancer, macular degeneration and cataracts.

9   **Green**—Here darker is better. Green vegetables, whether cruciferous—such as broccoli—or leafy (spinach, kale, chard), offer up a host of powerful health-promoting compounds. The green family contains nutrients that protect against many cancers, help strengthen bones and teeth, sharpen eyesight and fight birth defects.

10   **White**—Yes, white is a color. Foods such as onions, garlic and mushrooms contain allicin, flavonoids and quercitin, which provide protection against heart disease and cancer. Other white foods, including bananas, cauliflower, and white peaches, have important phytonutrients.

11   So go ahead and turn your plate into a palette. The colorful scenes you create will help keep you healthy in addition to making your meals more attractive.

Four Kinds of Chance*

James H. Austin

James H. Austin is a Clinical Professor of Neurology at the University of Missouri Science Center and Emeritus Professor of Neurology at the University of Colorado Science Center, whose medical career has focused on brain research. He has received the American Association of Neuropathologists Prize and has published a number of books, including *Zen and the Brain* (1998) and *Meditating Selflessly* (2011). This essay, written for *Saturday Review*, also appears In *Chase, Chance, and Creativity: The Lucky Art of Novelty* (1978).

1   What is chance? Dictionaries define it as something fortuitous that happens unpredictably without discernable human intention. Chance is unintentional and capricious, but we needn't conclude that chance is immune from human intervention. Indeed, chance plays several distinct roles when humans react creatively with one another and with their environment.

2   We can readily distinguish four varieties of chance if we consider that they each involve a different kind of motor activity and a special kind of sensory receptivity. The varieties of chance also involve distinctive personality traits and differ in the way one particular individual influences them.

3   Chance I is the pure blind luck that comes with no effort on our part. If, for example, you are sitting at a bridge table of four, it's "in the cards" for you to receive a hand of all 13 spades, but it will come up only once in every 6.3 trillion deals. You will ultimately draw this lucky hand—with no intervention on your part—but it does involve a longer wait than most of us have time for.

4   Chance II evokes the kind of luck [American inventor] Charles Kettering had in mind when he said: "Keep on going and the chances are you will stumble on something, perhaps when you are least expecting it. I have never heard of anyone stumbling on something sitting down."

5   In the sense referred to here, Chance II is not passive, but springs from an energetic, generalized motor activity. A certain basal level of action "stirs up the pot," brings in random ideas that will collide and stick together in fresh combinations, lets chance operate. When someone, *anyone*, does swing into motion and keeps on

* Austin, James H., CHASE, CHANCE, AND CREATIVITY: The Lucky Art of Novelty, pp. excerpt from pages 70–77: "Four Kinds of Chance." © 2003 Massachusetts Institute of Technology, by permission of The MIT Press.

going, he will increase the number of collisions between events. When a few events are linked together, they can then be exploited to have a fortuitous outcome, but any others, of course, cannot. Kettering was right. Press on. Something will turn up. We may term this the Kettering Principle.

6   In the two previous examples, a unique role of the individual person was either lacking or minimal. Accordingly, as we move on to Chance III, we see blind luck, but in camouflage. Chance presents the clue, the opportunity exists, but it would be missed except by that one person uniquely equipped to observe it, visualize it conceptually, and fully grasp its significance. Chance III involves a special receptivity and discernment unique to the recipient. [Microbiologist] Louis Pasteur characterized it for all time when he said: "Chance favors only the prepared mind."

7   Pasteur himself had it in full measure. But the classic example of his principle occurred in 1928, when Alexander Fleming's mind instantly fused at least five elements into a conceptually unified nexus. His mental sequences went something like this: (1) I see that a mold has fallen by accident into my culture dish; (2) the staphylococcal colonies residing near it failed to grow; (3) the mold must have secreted something that killed the bacteria; (4) I recall a similar experience once before; (5) if I could separate this new "something" from the mold, it could be used to kill staphylococci that cause human infections.

8   Actually, Fleming's mind was exceptionally well prepared for the penicillin mold. Six years earlier, while he was suffering from a cold, his own nasal drippings had found their way into a culture dish, for reasons not made entirely clear. He noted that nearby bacteria were killed, and astutely followed up the lead. His observations led him to discover a bactericidal enzyme present in nasal mucus and tears, called lysozyme. Lysozyme proved too weak to be of medical use, but imagine how receptive Fleming's mind was to the penicillin mold when it later happened on the scene!

9   One word evokes the quality of the operations involved in the first three kinds of chance. It is *serendipity*. The term describes the facility for encountering unexpected good luck, as the result of: accident (Chance I), general exploratory behavior (Chance II), or sagacity (Chance III). The word itself was coined by the Englishman-of-letters Horace Walpole, in 1754. He used it with reference to the legendary tales of the Three Princes of Serendip (Ceylon), who quite unexpectedly encountered many instances of good fortune on their travels. In today's parlance, we have usually watered down *serendipity* to mean the good luck that comes solely by accident. We think of it as a result, not an ability. We have tended to lose sight of the element of sagacity, by which term Walpole wished to emphasize that some distinctive personal receptivity is involved.

10   There remains a fourth element in good luck, an unintentional but subtle personal prompting of it. The English Prime Minister Benjamin Disraeli summed up the principle underlying Chance IV when he noted that "we make our fortunes and we call them fate." Disraeli, a politician of considerable practical experience, appreciated that we each shape our own destiny, at least to some degree. One might restate the principle as follows: *Chance favors the individualized action.*

11   In Chance IV the kind of luck is peculiar to one person, and like a personal hobby, it takes on a distinctive individual flavor. This form of chance is

one-man-made, and it is as personal as a signature. . . . Chance IV has an elusive, almost mirage-like, quality. Like a mirage, it is difficult to get a firm grip on, for it tends to recede as we pursue it and advance as we step back. But we still accept a mirage when we see it, because we vaguely understand the basis for the phenomenon. A strongly heated layer of air, less dense than usual, lies next to the earth, and it bends the light rays as they pass through. The resulting image may be magnified as if by a telescopic lens in the atmosphere, and real objects, ordinarily hidden far out of sight over the horizon, are brought forward and revealed to the eye. What happens in a mirage then, and in this form of chance, not only appears farfetched but indeed is farfetched.

12   About a century ago, a striking example of Chance IV took place in the Spanish cave of Altamira.* There, one day in 1879, Don Marcelino de Sautuola was engaged in his hobby of archaeology, searching Altamira for bones and stones. With him was his daughter, Maria, who had asked him if she could come along to the cave that day. The indulgent father had said she could. Naturally enough, he first looked where he had always found heavy objects before, on the *floor* of the cave. But Maria, unhampered by any such preconceptions, looked not only at the floor but also all around the cave with the open-eyed wonder of a child! She looked up, exclaimed, and then he looked up, to see incredible works of art on the cave ceiling! The magnificent colored bison and other animals they saw at Altamira, painted more than 15,000 years ago, might lead one to call it "the Sistine Chapel of Prehistory." Passionately pursuing his interest in archaeology, de Sautuola, to his surprise, discovered man's first paintings. In quest of science, he happened upon Art.

13   Yes, a dog did "discover" the cave, and the initial receptivity was his daughter's, but the pivotal reason for the cave paintings' discovery hinged on a long sequence of prior events originating in de Sautuola himself. For when we dig into the background of this amateur excavator, we find he was an exceptional person. Few Spaniards were out probing into caves 100 years ago. The fact that he—not someone else—decided to dig that day in the cave of Altamira was the culmination of his passionate interest in his hobby. Here was a rare man whose avocation had been to educate himself from scratch, as it were, in the science of archaeology and cave exploration. This was no simple passive recognizer of blind luck when it came his way, but a man whose unique interests served as an active creative thrust—someone whose own actions and personality would focus the events that led circuitously but inexorably to the discovery of man's first paintings.

14   Then, too, there is a more subtle manner. How do you give full weight to the personal interests that imbue your child with your own curiosity, that inspire her to ask to join you in your own musty hobby, and that then lead you to agree to her request at the critical moment? For many reasons, at Altamira, more than the special receptivity of Chance III was required—this was a different domain, that of the personality and its actions.

---

*The cave had first been discovered some years before by an enterprising hunting dog in search of game. Curiously, in 1932 the French cave of Laseaux was discovered by still another dog.

15   A century ago no one had the remotest idea our caveman ancestors were highly creative artists. Weren't their talents rather minor and limited to crude flint chippings? But the paintings at Altamira, like a mirage, would quickly magnify this diminutive view, bring up into full focus a distant, hidden era of man's prehistory, reveal sentient minds and well-developed aesthetic sensibilities to which men of any age might aspire. And like a mirage, the events at Altamira grew out of de Sautuola's heated personal quest and out of the invisible forces of chance we know exist yet cannot touch. Accordingly, one may introduce the term *altamirage* to identify the quality underlying Chance IV. Let us define it as the facility for encountering unexpected good luck as the result of highly individualized action. Altamirage goes well beyond the boundaries of serendipity in its emphasis on the role of personal action in chance.

16   Chance IV is favored by distinctive, if not eccentric, hobbies, personal lifestyles, and modes of behavior peculiar to one individual, usually invested with some passion. The farther apart these personal activities are from the area under investigation, the more novel and unexpected will be the creative product of the encounter.

Chapter 28

Exposition: Causal Analysis

· ·

Mystery!*

Nicholas Meyer

Nicholas Meyer is a novelist, screenwriter, and film director-producer. Two of his three mystery novels, *The Seven-Per-Cent Solution* (1974) and *The West End Horror* (1976), have been made into successful movies. Meyer, also known for his contributions as a director and co-writer of the sci-fi movies *Star Trek II, IV*, and *VI*, has published *The View from the Bridge: Memories of Star Trek and a Life in Hollywood* (2009). This essay, originally published in *TV Guide* magazine in 1980, appeared in an earlier edition of this textbook and has returned in response to readers' requests.

1   Reading mysteries is a bedtime recreation for all segments of society—high, low and middle brow. It is the *divertissement*** of prime ministers and plumbers. Mysteries, whether they are on television, paper or movie screens, delight almost all of us. Everyone likes to "curl up" with a good mystery, and that makes this particular kind of literature unique in its ubiquitous appeal. No other genre so transcends what might otherwise appear to be significant differences in the social, educational and economic backgrounds of its audience.

2   Why, for heaven's sake? What is there about mystery and detective stories that fascinate so many of us, regardless of age, sex, color and national origin?

3   On the surface, it seems highly improbable that detective novels should provide such broad-based satisfaction. Their jacket blurbs and ad copy contain plenty of violent, even gory, references: "The body lay inert, the limbs dangling at unnatural angles, the head bashed in, clearly the result of a blunt instrument . . ." Who wants to read this stuff? Even assuming that there is a certain segment of society that

---

*Mystery! by Nicholas Meyer as appeared in TV Guide, 1980. Reprinted by permission of the author.
**A French word for diversion or entertainment.

delights in sadistic imagery and rejoices in thrills and chills and things that go bump in the night, it is hard to imagine that these sensibilities are in the majority.

4   As the Great Detective* himself might have observed, "It is a singular business, Watson, and on the surface, most unlikely." Yet as Holmes was wont to remark, evidence that appears to point in one unerring direction may, if viewed from a slightly altered perspective, admit of precisely the opposite interpretation. People do, in fact, like to "curl up" with a good mystery. They take the corpses and the murderers to bed with them as favorite nighttime reading. One could hardly imagine a more intimate conjunction!

5   But the phrase "curling up" does not connote danger; say rather the reverse. It conjures up snug, warm, secure feelings. Curling up with a good mystery is not exciting or thrilling; it is in fact oddly restful. It is reassuring.

6   Now why should this be? How is it possible that detective stories, with all the murder and blackmail and mayhem and mystery that pervades them, should provide us with feelings of security, coziness and comfort?

7   Well, detective stories have other things in them besides violence and blood. They have solutions, for one thing. Almost invariably, the murderer is caught, or at the very least identified. *As sure as God made little green apples, it all adds up to something.* If it doesn't, we aren't happy with the piece. A good detective story ties up all the loose ends; we resent motives and clues left unconnected.

8   Yes, detective stories have solutions. But life does not. On the contrary, life is an anarchic proposition in which meaningless events conspire daily to alter our destiny without rhyme or reason. Your plane crashes, or the one you were booked on crashes but you missed it; a flat tire, a missed phone call, an open manhole, a misunderstanding—these are the chaotic commonplaces of everyday existence. But they have no place in the mystery novel. In detective novels, nothing happens without a reason. Detective literature, though it may superficially resemble life, in fact has effected at least one profound alteration: mystery stories *organize* life and provide it with meaning and answers. The kind of confusion in which real people are forced to exist doesn't occur in detective stories. Whatever the various people's problems, the only serious difficulty confronting them in detective stories is the fact that they are suspected of committing the crime involved. Once cleared of that lowering cloud, they are free to pursue their lives with, presumably, successful results.

9   So we see that the coziness of detective and mystery stories is not entirely incomprehensible or inappropriate, after all. If we like to take such literature to bed with us and cuddle up with it, what we are really cuddling up to is a highly stylized literary formula, which is remarkably consistent in delivering to us that reassuring picture we all crave of an ordered world.

10   Sherlock Holmes, Philip Marlow, Miss Marple or Columbo**—the stories in which these characters appear all manage to delight us by reassuring us. The

---

*Sherlock Holmes

**These four characters are famous fictional detectives: Sherlock Holmes created by Arthur Conan Doyle; Philip Marlowe, by Raymond Chandler; Miss Marple, by Agatha Christie. Columbo solved crimes in a popular television series of the same name.

victim is usually only slightly known or not very well liked. The world seems better off without him, or else he is so sorely missed that tracking his (or her) murderer will be, in Oscar Wilde's* words, more than a duty, it will be a pleasure.

11   And pleasurable indeed is the process of watching the tracking. There are some highfalutin apologists of the detective genre who would have us believe it is the intellectual exercise of following the clues along with the detective—the reader's or viewer's participation in a kind of mental puzzle—that provides the satisfaction associated with detective stories. I believe such participation is largely illusory. We don't really ever have all the pieces at our disposal and most of us are not inclined to work with them very thoroughly, even in those rare cases when the author has been scrupulously "fair" in giving them to us. We enjoy the *illusion* of participation without really doing any of the mental legwork beyond the normal wondering "Whodunit?"

12   In any event, such a theory to justify the fascination exerted by detective and mystery stories is elitist and falsely elitist into the bargain. It distracts our attention with a pretentious and tenuous explanation in place of a much more interesting and persuasive one; namely, that detective stories are appealing because they depict life not as it is but in some sense as it ought to be.

The Mind Game**

Joshua Bell

Award-winning contemporary musician Joshua Bell has been called "the poet of the violin." Since the age of fourteen, he has appeared as a star performer with the premier orchestras of the world and is a frequent guest on popular television shows. He has recorded over thirty-five albums, winning both a Grammy and an Oscar for his music. This essay, on the mind game of performing, was published in *Newsweek* magazine's column called "My Favorite Mistake," in January 2012.

1   When I was twelve years old I entered my first violin competition, the Stulberg International String Competition. Almost everyone else was college-age, so I wasn't expecting to do very well. I was playing a violin concerto called *Symphonie Espagnole* by Lalo. It starts with a very difficult opening right off the bat, sort of like if a skating routine started with a triple axel. I began playing, and I messed it up worse than I ever could have imagined. I had never made such a terrible mistake at the beginning of a piece. My parents came all the way to Michigan for me to be in my first big competition, and it was a completely embarrassing way to start.

2   No one tells you what to do if you completely flop at the beginning of a performance. My teachers had never taught me, and I didn't know the etiquette, but I think I did the right thing in the moment. Instead of just playing on, finishing the piece, and feeling lousy, I completely stopped. I turned to the audience and said, "I'd really like to start over." I already felt like I'd lost the competition and the chance to do well, but I really wanted to try again.

---

*Oscar Wilde was a nineteenth-century English author and wit.
**Joshua Bell from Jan. 9 & 16, 2012, Newsweek column called "My Favorite Mistake" ("Violinist Joshua Bell on the mind game of performing," page 64).

3   It was a quick decision and could have been the worst performance after that because my confidence was down. I screwed up, and when you do something like that it can psychologically totally ruin your performance. But somehow it turned in the other direction. I got into this zone of feeling completely liberated and relaxed because I knew I had lost. I played the best I had ever played in my life. I felt like I couldn't make a mistake. I was elated, and it could have been the worst day of my twelve-year-old life.

4   I actually ended up getting third prize in the competition and went back the next year and won first prize, but that's not really the point. For me it was a major revelation, and it taught me that when you take your mind off worrying about being perfect all the time, sometimes amazing things can happen. So much of performing is a mind game. You're memorizing thousands of notes, and if you start thinking about it in the wrong way, everything can blow up in your face.

5   When I'm onstage and make a mistake, I remember back to that moment. I learned from that experience how to get into that zone. The competition ended up launching my career and my confidence in a lot of ways. It was a turning point and a lesson I use to this day.

Cell Phones and Social Graces*

Charles Fisher

Charles Fisher has been a professor of English at Aims Community College in northeastern Colorado for over twenty years and is the author of the composition textbook *Researching and Writing about Controversies*. He has taught a variety of college writing, research, and literature courses. Fisher uses this personal essay to spark discussion among his own composition students; it has been slightly adapted for this text.

1   I want to say first that I'm not a Luddite** like those who destroyed machinery in English factories during the Industrial Revolution. I have a computer, I manage my email, I can de-fragment my hard drive. But I draw the line at cell phones.

2   Cell phones are amazing creations. These brushed-silver and fluorescent-blue-lit devices do what home computers—not to mention *telephones*—could not do five years ago. They add and subtract. They enable Internet stock transactions. They download and play music. They allow real-time conversations through text messaging. They record videos. They identify who is calling by playing a particular tune. Last night my sister in Idaho knew I called because her phone tootled "Stars and Stripes Forever."

3   There are good reasons to own a cell phone. They provide a means to contact someone in an emergency: to call the insurance company after an accident on the interstate, to call the owner of a wandering dog with a phone number on its collar, to monitor children entrusted with the house for a day, and to coordinate

---

*Cell Phones and Social Graces by Charles Fisher. Used by permission of the author.
**Luddites were English workers who, having previously earned their living through handcrafts, participated in 1811–1812 raids that destroyed mechanized knitting and weaving machines. Today the term often refers to anyone who resists technology.

pick-ups and deliveries in multi-car soccer families. Still, until cell phones came along, business was conducted without catastrophe; folks wanting to contact me urgently enough left a voice-mail message on my home phone. Even if they could never make contact, *life went on anyway*. Domestic problems were addressed *at home*, not in public (I didn't appreciate the woman in Borders [bookstore] yesterday who argued over domestic relationships, complete with profanity, in full hearing of customers desiring quiet while they browsed). Grocery lists were compiled *before* one left for the store, and if one forgot something, then one could always go back (does it save *that* much time and gas?)—all without cell phones.

4   Cell phones enable a person simply to stay in constant contact. But what demon has convinced the cell-phone generation that it is a *good* thing to be constantly available? Whatever happened to *not* being available to everyone at all times?

5   I am not in the market for a cell phone for the simplest and most logical reason: I don't need one; our conventional phone serves us well enough. There are economic and technological reasons as well. For example, it costs more per month than my land-line, there are additional "roaming charges" and other fees for "exceeding one's minutes," and awful penalties are exacted for breaking a mandatory two-year contract. A final indignity is that if I own a cell phone, *I* am charged if someone calls *me*. Thus my younger sons remind me to call only on "free days."

6   From a technological standpoint, I have yet to communicate with anyone on a cell phone when the connection wasn't muffled, garbled, wavery, barrel-like, or disconnected without warning because a cell phone battery lost energy. And of course, we're all aware of the controversial safety record of drivers using cell phones. I myself have been nearly a victim twice of drivers on cell phones who nearly ran over me while I was biking to work.

7   But I refuse to buy a cell phone primarily because I'm afraid that if I yield to the siren-call of gadgetry and instant-constant access, I too will evolve into one of the many social troglodytes whom cell phones have created. I mourn the demise of courtesy and civility and refuse to become a life-long slave to the cell phone.

8   This slavish dependency is seen in countless ways. See me walking briskly around the local park lake on a delightful spring morning, enjoying the new duck family and the song of meadowlarks. See the woman approaching me, speed-walking with a cell-phone glued to her ear. Apparently, she cannot wait until she gets home to conduct this conversation. I don't even bother to say "Good morning"; she's not listening, anyway. So much for social interaction and pleasantries that enhance human contact.

9   Observe the Safeway shopper with a cell phone impaled in her ear, halted in the middle of the deli aisle, a far-off glaze in her eyes: "Well, as long as it has a ground-level bathroom." And why is it that people talking on cell phones in grocery stores feel the need to talk louder than normal? I'm sure *I* want to hear all about her husband's house-hunting. I simply don't want to hear about the problems a shopper is having with her husband while in the "foot remedies" aisle of Walgreens or while I'm trying to enjoy Rattlesnake Bites at the Texas Roadhouse. I would like to shop in peace and eat in peace.

10   I can no longer attend a movie without cell phones intruding like unwanted aliens into my enjoyment. If a cell phone doesn't go off, it's the sudden green glow

of one in the lap in front of me because the movie patron *is forced* to respond to urgent bee-vibration at his hip. He *must* answer the call of the text message or call-back number *right now.* "Oh, sorry, I've *got* to get this," we hear often. Well, no, one *doesn't have* to get that.

11   More slavishness: When my wife and I celebrated our anniversary at Disney World two years ago, I had the urge to say to the lady bobbing on a carousel stallion with her hand glued to her ear: "Do you *really* have to talk to someone? Couldn't you have waited the two minutes before the ride's end? Couldn't you just simply *enjoy* the ride and enter into the enjoyment of your daughter next to you for *two doggone minutes*?"

12   Such slavish dependency on cell phones is accompanied by the demise of common social courtesies. Perfectly decent people will flip open their cell phone at a call, identify the caller, and simply press a button to ignore the call. A friend or family member who will open their front door to cute little girls selling cookies will ignore me—their beloved father or valued friend—on their cell phone. What heady power to make someone disappear! I can understand not answering the doorbell to a man selling SuperScrub Concrete Cleaner. But I'm not that guy. I'm a family member. I'm a friend.

13   I know it's not the cell phone—it's how people use all those candy-store options. But the choices *encourage* rudeness in far too many cases. Scene: Commencement and graduation ceremonies at a northern California college. Two deans in full regalia are honored by being selected to pass out diplomas to students, many of whom they had in their classes. A name is called. Across the stage strides a cocky graduate, *talking to someone on his cell phone*, his hand pasted to his ear, a stupid grin on his face. He takes his diploma without making eye contact with the dean or saying so much as a "thank you" or indication of respect—he's too busy yakking as he bounds down the steps, oblivious to decorum.

14   Sadly, people I would least expect to be slavish and rude with cell phones—my church family—have committed some of the most odious offenses. A cell phone suddenly begins bleeping the brassy notes of "Für Elise" during the eulogy at a funeral several weeks ago. A few days later, while we shared prayer requests in our home Bible study, we all jumped as a rousing "Dixie" began emanating from one lady's purse—followed by the frantic fumbling to find the offending device, the embarrassed glance, and a quick apology and disabling of the phone—wait, *no!*— there was no embarrassed glance, no apology—instead, she said, "I've *got* to get this" and rushed, phone still ringing, into the hallway.

15   Yes, all of the above scenarios are the result of *choices* users make regarding their cell phones. They are sociological and cultural actions, and I don't have to do what they do if I ever do buy a cell phone. I could turn it off when I'm driving or shopping or eating, or attending a funeral or Bible study. No, I don't have to talk while at the carnival or while taking walks around the park. I don't have to know who's trying to call me, and I don't have to use instant messaging. In this cornucopia of choices, I don't have to choose *any* of those options. And I most likely wouldn't. And *that* is probably the main reason I don't have a cell phone.

Chapter 29

Argumentation

· ·

Guns on Campus: More Harm than Help*

The USA Today *Editorial Board*

USA Today is an American newspaper, begun in 1982 with special appeal to travelers. Today the newspaper claims the widest print circulation in the country. One of the paper's popular features is "Today's Debate," which expresses the opinion of the editors on a current topic and then offers an opposing view. This essay by the editorial board appeared in the "Debate" column in February 2011.

1 Could the answer to the problem of campus shootings be . . . more guns? That's what legislators in Texas and several other states are arguing as they push ill-conceived laws to allow concealed handguns on public college campuses, even if college officials are adamantly opposed.

2 A proposal with a good chance of passage in gun-friendly Texas would allow professors and students 21 and older to carry handguns on campus as long as they have a state permit to carry a concealed weapon. The idea is to deter attackers such as the one who killed 32 people at Virginia Tech in 2007, and send a message to criminals that they can't expect students to be unarmed.

3 Of the dozen states considering campus-carry laws, Texas is considered the likeliest to enact one this year. Interestingly, states that are otherwise supportive of guns-everywhere policies have consistently said "no" to this awful idea, on the sensible grounds that students and guns are a risky combination. More than 40 such proposals have died in state legislatures, and even Texas rejected a similar bill in 2009.**

** The Texas Senate did not pass the bill in 2011, though it continues to be re-introduced into legislation. Other states have moved in different directions; in 2012, for instance, a Colorado Supreme Court ruling forced the University of Colorado to allow concealed weapons on campus, including in dorms.

4   Memo to Gov. Rick Perry, a guns-on-campus supporter: Your state had it right the first time.

5   To believe that armed students and professors might stop campus crime is an alluring idea. But the tiny chance that someone with a gun might be in the right place—and have the necessary skill and nerve—to deter a criminal or an insane shooter isn't worth risking the way everyday gun carrying could change the atmosphere in classes and dorms, or the unintended dangers it would bring.

6   Mass attacks such as the one at Virginia Tech, as horrible as they are, are rare. And of the incidents that do occur, many either last long enough for armed campus security to respond, or are over before anyone can react. For example, the mentally disturbed community college student who shot an Arizona congresswoman [Gabrielle Giffords] and killed six people in January [2011] fired 32 bullets in 15 seconds. After unarmed bystanders wrestled him down and took his gun, a man with a concealed weapon burst on the scene and almost shot one of the Good Samaritans by mistake.

7   Statistics show that students are safer on campus than off, and college students are far more likely to be crime victims when they're away from campus. One reason legislators in most states have rejected guns-on-campus laws is probably because most were once college students themselves and can remember the binge drinking, drug taking and the bad judgment common at an age when science says brains haven't yet fully developed and the propensity for risky behavior is at its highest. The one state where college students are allowed to pack heat on public campuses statewide is Utah, where the influence of the Mormon church is strong and college drinking is lower than in other states.

8   The key to deterring campus massacres is to make it easier to identify individuals who pose a threat and harder for them to acquire rapid-fire weapons. The gunmen at Virginia Tech and in Arizona were both clearly disturbed, but both were able to get firearms and neither was in treatment. That has to change.

9   There are far smarter ways to keep students safe than arming them and asking them to shoot it out.

Putting Up with Hate*

The Denver Post *Editorial Board*

The *Denver Post* Editorial Board consists of William Dean Singleton, chair and publisher, Gerald Grilly, president and CEO, and eight of the newspaper's editors and columnists. This editorial, which appeared in March 2011, was the Board's response to the Supreme Court ruling that even the most vile protests near a soldier's funeral should be protected by the First Amendment to the Constitution, which guarantees the right of free speech.

1   The despicable Rev. Fred W. Phelps Sr. and his followers are a difficult price to pay for the First Amendment.

2   Their ugly protests at the funerals of dead soldiers are designed to shock and get attention for their anti-gay agenda. And even though their hateful words and actions have hurt and angered grieving families, they ought to be constitutionally protected.

---

* Putting Up with Hate, Editorial from THE DENVER POST, March 6, 2011. Used by permission.

3   The U.S. Supreme Court last week agreed, ruling that the First Amendment protects the church members who protest outside funerals. The 8-1 decision, with Justice Samuel Alito dissenting, upheld an appeals court ruling that tossed out a $5 million judgment to the father of a dead Marine who sued church members after they picketed his son's funeral.

4   In the court of public opinion, Phelps and his followers, most of whom are his extended family, lose. These characters flew 1,000 miles from the Westboro Baptist Church in Kansas to picket the 2006 funeral of Lance Cpl. Matthew Snyder, carrying signs with messages such as "Thank God for Dead Soldiers" and "You're going to hell." Somehow, according to the twisted beliefs of Phelps, Snyder's death was punishment from God for this country's tolerance of gays and lesbians, especially in the military. It doesn't matter that Snyder was not gay.

5   But in writing the court's opinion Chief Justice John Roberts said that free-speech rights shield the funeral protests, noting that they obeyed police directions and were 1,000 feet from the church. "Speech is powerful. It can stir people to action, move them to tears of both joy and sorrow, and—as it did here—inflict great pain. On the facts before us, we cannot react to that pain by punishing the speaker," Roberts said. "As a nation we have chosen a different course—to protect even hurtful speech on public issues to ensure that we do not stifle public debate."

6   The central question before the high court was whether Phelps' speech should lose its constitutional protections if it was deemed to be outrageous or cause severe emotional distress. Had a majority of the court sided with Alito, it would have set a dangerous precedent. If speech can be squelched because it is deemed to be "outrageous," how long would it be before other "outrageous" speech was curbed?

7   Rather than curbing speech, we prefer the way communities have neutralized the Phelps gang—with citizens lining the streets surrounding the funeral. They form a barrier between the ugly shouts of protesters and the grieving family members.

Judging by the Cover*

Bonny Gainley

Bonny Gainley is a marketing and management consultant, speaker, and author who writes on topics relating to the family and the workplace. In addition to articles based on her experiences in the high-tech industry, she has published *Look Before You Step: Advice for Potential Stepparents and Their Partners* (2002). This essay originally appeared in 2003 as an opinion column in the Fort Collins, Colorado, newspaper, the *Coloradoan*.

1   Spring is in the air, and those about to graduate are looking for jobs just like many of the rest of us. Competition is tough, so jobs seekers must carefully consider their personal choices.

2   Every person has a need to be accepted, ideally just as he or she is. Our family and friends may do that, but the workplace does not. An editorial a while back in one of our high school newspapers claimed it is unfair for professions such as business, public relations, teaching and others to discourage visible tattoos. While not

---

* "Judging by the Cover" by Bonny Gainley. Reprinted by permission.

specifically mentioned, piercings and perhaps even certain hairstyles or garments would fall into the same category.

3   They say you can't judge a book by its cover, yet some people "cover" themselves in ways intended to convey certain messages. The message may be "my uniform says I am a police officer" or "I like the latest fashions" or "I am a gang member."

4   We make assumptions about people based on their appearance every day, and often we assume exactly what they want us to assume. Just as people project messages about themselves with their appearance, so do businesses. Dress codes and standards exist in the professional world for a number of reasons. Sometimes the issue is safety; sometimes it is a matter of what clients will accept. As long as parents don't want pre-school teachers waving visible skull or profanity tattoos in front of their small children, those tattoos will be deemed inappropriate for that profession.

5   Some say this is an issue of human rights and freedom, but it is really about free enterprise. The bottom line is that businesses exist to make money. Whether it seems fair or not, most employers do care about the personal appearances of the people they hire because those people represent the business to its customers.

6   Discrimination on the basis of factors an applicant can't control is wrong and illegal. Choosing the candidate who displays the attributes and skills that best match a job description is not. Just as runners would put themselves at a disadvantage by choosing to run the 100 meters in combat boots, people who choose to wear rings through their noses are putting themselves at a disadvantage in the professional job market. Each of us can choose whether to conform to the rules of any organization, but that organization is also free to choose whether they want us associated with it.

7   I don't personally have issues with visible tattoos or piercings, but as a hiring manager I was paid to choose the people who would make the best impression on our customers. It comes down to this—there are plenty of well-qualified applicants and most present themselves in a way my industry considers professional, so there was no compelling reason to choose someone who might offend my customers or poorly represent my company. Even though I may be open minded, I can't count on my customers to be.

8   If people continue to tattoo and pierce, attitudes about the appropriateness of those adornments in the professional workplace will change over time, in the same way that pants have become appropriate for women, for example. When tattoos and piercings are generally accepted in the business world, there will be new things that aren't—maybe nudity or some other trend we can't even imagine. Whether our personal choices will be accepted or not, we each have the right to make them, but must also be willing to accept the related consequences.

9   How we dress, tattoo or pierce is an expression of who we are and a message to the people we encounter. Freedom of choice is a dual-edged sword—individuals are free to present their desired image, and others are free to react to it.

10   There is nobody to blame but yourself if your set of choices does not match those desired by your preferred employers. No organization should have to change to accommodate a candidate simply because that person is unwilling to respect its standards, as long as its standards are legal.

Chapter 30

Description

··

A Day at the Theme Park*

W. Bruce Cameron

W. Bruce Cameron began writing humorous features for the Denver newspaper the *Rocky Mountain News* in 1999; his column is now in national syndication. His book *8 Simple Rules for Dating My Teenage Daughter* (2001) was adapted into a television show of the same name; other books include *How to Remodel a Man* (2004), *A Dog's Purpose* (2010), and *Emory's Gift* (2011). As a father of three, Cameron often writes about the challenges facing parents, as illustrated in this 1999 column.

1   One of the most endearing traits of children is their utter trust that their parents will provide them with all of life's necessities, meaning food, shelter, and a weekend at a theme park.

2   A theme park is a sort of artificial vacation, a place where you can enjoy all your favorite pastimes at once, such as motion sickness and heat exhaustion. Adult tolerance for theme parks peaks at about an hour, which is how long it takes to walk from the parking lot to the front gate. You fork over an obscene amount of money to gain entrance to a theme park, though it costs nothing to leave (which is odd, because you'd pay anything to escape). The two main activities in a theme park are (a) standing in line, and (b) sweating. The sun reflects off the concrete with a fiendish lack of mercy. You're about to learn the boiling point of tennis shoes. Your hair is sunburned, and when a small child in front of you gestures with her hand she smacks you in the face with her cotton candy; now it feels like your cheeks are covered with carnivorous sand.

3   The ride your children have selected for you is a corkscrewing, stomach-compressing roller coaster built by the same folks who manufactured the baggage

---

delivery system at DIA.* Apparently the theme of this particular park is "Nausea." You sit down and are strapped in so tightly you can feel your shoulders grinding against your pelvis. Once the ride begins you are thrown about with such violence it reminds you of your teenager's driving. When the ride is over your children want to get something to eat, but first the ride attendants have to pry your fingers off the safety bar. "Open your eyes, please, sir," they keep shouting. They finally persuade you to let go, though it seems a bit discourteous of them to have used pepper spray. Staggering, you follow your children to the Hot Dog Palace for some breakfast.

4   Food at a theme park is so expensive it would be cheaper to just eat your own money. Your son's meal costs a day's pay and consists of items manufactured of corn syrup, which is sugar; sucrose, which is sugar; fructose, which is sugar; and sugar, which is sugar. He also consumes large quantities of what in dog food would be called "meat byproducts." When, after a couple of rides, he announces that he feels like he is going to throw up, you're very alarmed. Having seen his meal once, you're in no mood to see it again.

5   With the exception of that first pummeling, you manage to stay off the rides all day, explaining to your children that it isn't good for you when your internal organs are forcibly rearranged. Now, though, they coax you back in line, promising a ride that doesn't twist, doesn't hang you upside down like a bat, doesn't cause your brain to flop around inside your skull; it just goes up and then comes back down. That's it, Dad, no big deal. What they don't tell you is HOW it comes back down. You're strapped into a seat and pulled gently up into acrophobia, the city falling away from you. Okay, not so bad, and in the conversation you're having with God you explain that you're thankful for the wonderful view but you really would like to get down now.

6   And that's just how you descend: NOW. Without warning, you plummet to the ground in an uncontrolled free fall. You must be moving faster than the speed of sound because when you open your mouth, nothing comes out. Your life passes before your eyes, and your one regret is that you will not have an opportunity to punish your children for bringing you to this hellish place. Brakes cut in and you slam to a stop. You gingerly touch your face to confirm it has fallen off. "Wasn't that fun, Dad?" your kids ask. "Why are you kissing the ground?"

7   At the end of the day, you let your teenager drive home. (After the theme park, you are impervious to fear.)

Walking on the Moon**

David R. Scott

Following two prior flights into space, USAF Colonel David R. Scott commanded the 1971 Apollo 15 mission, the first extended scientific expedition to the moon. This description of his lunar experience is excerpted from a longer article written two years later for *National Geographic* magazine. After serving in various NASA administrative positions, the former astronaut is now president of Scott Science and Technology, Inc.

---

*Denver International Airport

** "Walking on the Moon" by David R. Scott from NATIONAL GEOGRAPHIC, September 1973, Volume 144, No. 3.

1   Sixty feet above the moon, the blast of our single rocket churns up a gray tumult of lunar dust that seems to engulf us. Blinded, I feel the rest of the way down "on the gauges." With an abrupt jar, our lunar module, or LM, strikes the surface and shudders to rest. We have hit our target squarely—a large amphitheater girded by mountains and deep canyon, at the eastern edge of a vast plain.

2   As Jim Irvin and I wait for the dust to settle, I recall the twelve revolutions we have just spent in lunar orbit aboard our Apollo 15 spaceship *Endeavour*. Each two hours found us completing a full circuit of earth's ancient satellite—one hour knifing through lunar night, then sunrise and an hour of daylight. As we orbited, I found a particular fascination in that sector of the darkened moon bathed in earthshine. The light reflected by our planet illuminates the sleeping moon much more brightly than moonlight silvers our own night. The mountains and crater rims are clearly seen.

3   I will always remember *Endeavor* hurtling through that strange night of space. Before us and above us stars spangled the sky with their distant icy fire; below lay the moon's far side, an arc of impenetrable blackness that blotted the firmament. Then, as our moment of sunrise approached, barely discernible streamers of light—actually the glowing gases of the solar corona millions of miles away—played above the moon's horizon. Finally the sun exploded into our view like a visual thunderclap. Abruptly, completely, in less than a second, its harsh light flooded into the spaceship and dazzled our eyes.

4   As we looked into the early lunar morning from *Endeavor*, the moonscape stretched into the distance, everything the color of milk chocolate. Long angular shadows accentuated every hill, every crater. As the sun arched higher, the plains and canyons and mountains brightened to a gunmetal gray, while the shadows shrank. At full lunar noontide, the sun glared down upon a bleached and almost featureless world.

5   Now we have come to rest on the moon, and the last of the dust settles outside the LM. We throw the switches that convert this hybrid vehicle from spacecraft to dwelling. Thus begin our 67 hours of lunar residence. We are on a still and arid world where each blazing day and each subfreezing night stretch through 355 earth hours. We have landed in the bright morning of a moon day. When we depart, the sun will not have reached zenith. . . .

6   Opening the top hatch for a preliminary reconnaissance, I peer out at a world seemingly embalmed in the epoch of its creation. Each line, each form blends into the harmonious whole of a single fluid sculpture. Craters left by "recent" meteorites—merely millions of years ago—stand out, startlingly white, like fresh scar tissue against the soft beige of the undulating terrain.

7   I steal a moment and glance straight up into the black sky where the crystalline sphere of earth—all blue and white, sea and clouds—gleams in the abyss of space. In that cold and boundless emptiness, our planet provides the only glow of color. For 30 minutes my helmeted head pivots above the open hatch as I survey and photograph the wonderland of the lunar surface. The incredible variety of landforms in this restricted area (on the moon, the horizon lies a scant mile and a half from a viewer) fills me with pleasant surprise. To the south an 11,000-foot ridge rises above the bleak plain. To the east stretch the hulking heights of an even higher

summit. On the west a winding gorge plunges to depths of more than 1,000 feet. Dominating the northeastern horizon, a great mountain stands in noble splendor almost three miles above us. Ours is the first expedition to land amid lunar mountains. Never quickened by life, never assailed by wind and rain, they loom still and serene, a tableau of forever. Their majesty overwhelms me.

8   Eight years' training in lunar geology makes me instantly aware of intriguing details. A dark line like a bathtub ring smudges the bases of the mountains. Was it left by the subsiding lake of lava that filled the immense cavity of Palus Putredinis, on the fringes of Mare Imbrium, billions of years ago? Mare Imbrium, on whose edge we have landed, stretches across the face of the moon for some 650 miles. The celestial projectile that excavated it must have been huge—perhaps as much as 50 miles across—and it slammed into the moon with a velocity many times greater than that of a rifle bullet.

9   When we descend the ladder of the LM and step onto the moon's surface, Jim and I feel a gratifying sense of freedom. For five days we have been crammed into the tight confines of the spacecraft that brought us here. Now, all at once, we regain the luxury of movement. But, we quickly discover, locomotion on the moon has its own peculiar restrictions. At one-sixth of earth's gravity, we weigh only a sixth our normal poundage. Our gait quickly evolves into a rhythmic, bounding motion that possesses all the lightness and ease of strolling on a trampoline.

10   At the same time, since the mass of our bodies and personal gear—and hence, our inertia—remains unchanged, starting and stopping require unusual exertion. I learn to get under way by thrusting my body forward, as though I were stepping into a wind. To stop, I dig in my heels and lean backward.

11   To fall on the moon—and I did several times—is to rediscover childhood. You go down in slow motion, the impact is slight, the risk of injury virtually nil. Forsaking the adult attitude that regards a fall not only as a loss of dignity but also a source of broken bones, the moon walker—like a child—accepts it as yet another diversion. Only the clinging moon dust, the untoward demand on the oxygen supply occasioned by the exertion of getting up, pall the pleasure of a tumble. Personally I find the one-sixth gravity of the moon more enjoyable than the soothing weightlessness of space. I have the same sense of buoyancy, but the moon provides a reassuringly fixed sense of up and down. . . .

12   The flowing moonscape, unmarred by a single jagged peak, reminds me of earth's uplands covered by a heavy blanket of fresh snow. Indeed, the dark-gray moon dust—its consistency seems to be somewhat between coal dust and talcum powder—mantles virtually every physical feature of the lunar surface. Our boots sink gently into it as we walk; we leave sharply chiseled footprints.

13   Color undergoes an odd transformation here. Everything underfoot or nearby is gray, yet this hue blends gradually into the uniform golden tan that characterizes distant objects. And this small spectrum moves with the walker. Most of the scattered rocks share the same gray tint as the dust, but we find two that are jet black, two of pastel green, several with sparkling crystals, some coated with glass, and one that is white. As we advance, we are surrounded by stillness. No wind blows. No sound echoes. Only shadows move. Within the space suit, I hear the reassuring purr of the miniaturized machines that supply vital oxygen and shield me from the blistering 150°F surface heat of the lunar morning. . . .

14   At first we experience a troubling deception with perspective. Without the familiar measuring sticks of our native planet—trees, telephone poles, clouds, and haze—we cannot determine whether an object stands close at hand or at a considerable distance, or whether it is large or small. Gradually our eyes learn to cope with the craters—mammoth, medium, and minuscule—that dot virtually every inch of the surface. And gradually the moon becomes a friendlier place. . . .

15   After each of our expeditions, we climb—sapped of energy—back into the LM. With its oxygen and food and water, it is a tiny artificial earth that comforts us in the void. Removing our space suits and attending to our housekeeping chores consumes two hours. For the first twenty minutes we are conscious of a pervasive odor, similar to that of gunpowder, from the moon dust we have tracked in. Our air-purifying system soon dispels the acrid scent, but the fine, adhesive dust clings to everything. Back on earth, no amount of cleaning will convert our space suits from the gray hue acquired on the moon to their once pristine and sparkling white. . . .

16   The thought haunts us that the end of the Apollo flights may mark man's last visit to the moon for a long time. American manned exploration of deep space is scheduled for an indefinite hiatus. Most scientists have already suggested that, when it resumes, all effort should concentrate upon reaching Mars and beyond. So our lunar artifacts—bypassed in the race to the planets—could remain undisturbed for eternity.

17   Clutching the ladder, I raise my eyes from the now-familiar moonscape to earth, glowing in the black heavens—that incredibly vivid sphere, so blue, so beautiful, so beloved. And so bedeviled: by ecological balances gone awry, by scattered starvation, by a shortage of energy that may motivate us to seek sources beyond our earth. Our Apollo crew believes that a technology capable of exploring space can and will help resolve such problems. We feel a sense of pride in the accomplishments of our program, yet we cannot escape a sense of deep concern for the fate of our planet and our species. This concern has led us to add certain items to the equipment we are leaving on the moon. The sum of these articles, we hope, will form a résumé of our era in the continuing story of the human race.

18   In eons to come, should astronauts from the deeps of space—from other solar systems in other galaxies—pass this way, they may find our spoor, our abandoned gear. A plaque of aluminum affixed to the deserted LM descent stage portrays the two hemispheres of our planet; upon it are engraved the name of our spacecraft, the date of our mission and a roster of the crew. From these data, the equipment, and even the dimensions of our footprints, intelligent beings will readily deduce what kind of creatures we were and whence we came. We leave a piece of fauna—a falcon feather—and of flora—a four-leaf clover.

19   In a little hollow in the moon dust we placed a stylized figurine of a man in a space suit and beside it another metal plaque bearing the names of the 14 spacemen—Russians and Americans—who have given their lives so that man may range the cosmos. Finally we deposit a single book: the Bible.

20   Our mission ends in fatigue and elation. Amazing success has rewarded the first extended scientific expedition to the moon. After debriefing and helping in the analyses of our findings, our crew disbands. . . .

21   Occasionally, while strolling on a crisp autumn night or driving a straight Texas road, I look up at the moon riding bright and proud over the clouds. My eye picks

out the largest circular splotch on the silvery surface: Mare Imbrium. There, at the eastern edge of that splotch, I once descended in a spaceship. Again I feel that I will probably never return, and the thought stirs a pang of nostalgia. For when I look at the moon I do not see a hostile, empty world. I see the radiant body where man has taken his first steps into a frontier that will never end.

The Battle of the Ants*

Henry David Thoreau

Henry David Thoreau was a nineteenth-century American author, naturalist, and proponent of Transcendentalism, a philosophical movement of the 1830s-1840s that emphasized the inherent goodness of humankind. Thoreau is perhaps best known today for his essay "Civil Disobedience" (1849) and for *Walden, or Life in the Woods* (1854), a memoir of living simply in nature, based on his two years in a cabin at Walden Pond, near Concord, Massachusetts. This excerpt is from Chapter 12 of that work.

1   You only need sit still long enough in some attractive spot in the woods that all its inhabitants may exhibit themselves to you by turns.

2   I was witness to events of a less peaceful character. One day when I went out to my wood-pile, or rather my pile of stumps, I observed two large ants, the one red, the other much larger, nearly half an inch long, and black, fiercely contending with one another. Having once got hold they never let go, but struggled and wrestled and rolled on the chips incessantly. Looking farther, I was surprised to find that the chips were covered with such combatants, that it was not a *duellum*,** but a *bellum*, a war between two races of ants, the red always pitted against the black, and frequently two red ones to one black. The legions of these Myrmidons† covered all the hills and vales in my wood-yard, and the ground was already strewn with the dead and dying, both red and black. It was the only battle which I have ever witnessed, the only battle-field I ever trod while the battle was raging; internecine war; the red republicans on the one hand, and the black imperialists on the other. On every side they were engaged in deadly combat, yet without any noise that I could hear, and human soldiers never fought so resolutely. I watched a couple that were fast locked in each other's embraces, in a little sunny valley amid the chips, now at noonday prepared to fight till the sun went down, or life went out. The smaller red champion had fastened himself like a vice to his adversary's front, and through all the tumblings on that field never for an instant ceased to gnaw at one of his feelers near the root, having already caused the other to go by the board; while the stronger black one dashed him from side to side, and, as I saw on looking nearer, had already divested him of several of his members. They fought with more pertinacity than bulldogs. Neither manifested the least disposition to retreat. It was evident that their battle-cry was "Conquer or die."

*Thoreau's WALDEN (the Battle of the Ants)
**Latin word for "duel."
†The Myrmidons were the troops led by the Greek hero, Achilles, during the Trojan War. Achilles is the central character in Homer's *Iliad*.

3   In the meanwhile there came along a single red ant on the hillside of this valley, evidently full of excitement, who either had dispatched his foe, or had not yet taken part in the battle; probably the latter, for he had lost none of his limbs; whose mother had charged him to return with his shield or upon it.* Or perchance he was some Achilles, who had nourished his wrath apart, and had now come to avenge or rescue his Patroclus.** He saw this unequal combat from afar—for the blacks were nearly twice the size of the red—he drew near with rapid pace till be stood on his guard within half an inch of the combatants; then, watching his opportunity, he sprang upon the black warrior, and commenced his operations near the root of his right foreleg, leaving the foe to select among his own members; and so there were three united for life, as if a new kind of attraction had been invented which put all other locks and cements to shame.

4   I should not have wondered by this time to find that they had their respective musical bands stationed on some eminent chip, and playing their national airs the while, to excite the slow and cheer the dying combatants. I was myself excited somewhat even as if they had been men. The more you think of it, the less the difference. And certainly there is not the fight recorded in Concord† history, at least, if in the history of America, that will bear a moment's comparison with this, whether for the numbers engaged in it, or for the patriotism and heroism displayed. For numbers and for carnage it was an Austerlitz or Dresden.†† Concord Fight! Two killed on the patriots' side, and Luther Blanchard wounded! Why here every ant was a Buttrick—"Fire! for God's sake fire!"—and thousands shared the fate of Davis and Hosmer.‡ There was not one hireling there. I have no doubt that it was a principle they fought for, as much as our ancestors, and not to avoid a three-penny tax on their tea; and the results of this battle will be as important and memorable to those whom it concerns as those of the battle of Bunker Hill, at least.

5   I took up the chip on which the three I have particularly described were struggling, carried it into my house, and placed it under a tumbler [a drinking glass] on my window-sill, in order to see the issue. Holding a microscope [a magnifying glass] to the first-mentioned red ant, I saw that, though he was assiduously gnawing at the near foreleg of his enemy, having severed his remaining feeler, his own breast was all torn away, exposing what vitals he had there to the jaws of the black warrior, whose breastplate was apparently too thick for him to pierce; and the dark

---

*Mothers of Spartan warriors supposedly told their sons to return from battle as either victors or dead soldiers (i.e., carried home upon their shields).

**In Homer's epic, Achilles had remained in camp until the death of his friend Patroclus, who had worn Achilles' armor into battle. Enraged over his friend's death, Achilles sought revenge.

†Concord, Massachusetts, was the site of the first shots fired in the American Revolution, in 1775.

††Austerlitz and Dresden were the sites of famous battles during the Napoleonic wars.

‡Thoreau includes various references to the American Revolution, including names of people, places, and issues his readers might recognize. During the Battle of Concord, British troops first wounded Luther Blanchard, though perhaps aiming for Major John Buttrick, militia commander, who then gave the order to return fire. Davis and Hosmer were the only colonists killed that day. Bunker Hill was another battle site in the American Revolution.

carbuncles of the sufferer's eyes shone with ferocity such as war only could excite. They struggled half an hour longer under the tumbler, and when I looked again the black soldier had severed the heads of his foes from their bodies, and the still living heads were hanging on either side of him like ghastly trophies at his saddle-bow, still apparently as firmly fastened as ever, and he was endeavoring with feeble struggles, being without feelers and with only the remnant of a leg, and I know not how many other wounds, to divest himself of them, which at length, after half an hour more, he accomplished. I raised the glass, and he went off over the window-sill in that crippled state. Whether he finally survived that combat, and spent the remainder of his days in some Hôtel des Invalides*, I do not know; but I thought that his industry would not be worth much thereafter.

6   I never learned which party was victorious, nor the cause of the war; but I felt for the rest of that day as if I had had my feelings excited and harrowed by witnessing the struggle, the ferocity and carnage, of a human battle before my door.

---

*Originally, the Paris hospital for veterans; now most famous as the site of Napoleon's elaborate 1840 tomb.

Chapter 31

Narration

· ·

---

38 Who Saw Murder Didn't Call the Police*

Martin Gansberg

Martin Gansberg was a reporter and editor for the *New York Times* for over 40 years, until his retirement in 1985. He also wrote for such magazines as *Diplomat*, *Catholic Digest*, and *Facts*. This often-reprinted article was first published in the *New York Times* in 1964, shortly after the murder of Kitty Genovese, a crime that has become synonymous with moral apathy.

1   For more than half an hour 38 respectable, law-abiding citizens in Queens watched a killer stalk and stab a woman in three separate attacks in Kew Gardens.

2   Twice the sound of their voices and the sudden glow of their bedroom lights interrupted him and frightened him off. Each time he returned, sought her out and stabbed her again. Not one person telephoned the police during the assault; one witness called after the woman was dead.

3   That was two weeks ago today. But Assistant Chief Inspector Frederick M. Lussen, in charge of the borough's detectives and a veteran of 25 years of homicide investigations, is still shocked.

4   He can give a matter-of-fact recitation of many murders. But the Kew Gardens slaying baffles him—not because it is a murder, but because the "good people" failed to call the police.

5   "As we have reconstructed the crime," he said, "the assailant had three chances to kill this woman during a 35-minute period. He returned twice to complete the job. If we had been called when he first attacked, the woman might not be dead now."

6   This is what the police say happened beginning at 3:20 A.M. in the staid, middle-class, tree-lined Austin Street area:

7   Twenty-eight-year-old Catherine Genovese, who was called Kitty by almost everyone in the neighborhood, was returning home from her job as manager of a bar in
Hollis. She parked her red Fiat in a lot adjacent to the Kew Gardens Long Island
Rail Road Station, facing Mowbray Place. Like many residents of the neighborhood, she had parked there day after day since her arrival from Connecticut a year
ago, although the railroad frowns on the practice.

8   She turned off the lights of her car, locked the door and started to walk the 100
feet to the entrance of her apartment at 82–70 Austin Street, which is in a Tudor
building, with stores on the first floor and apartments on the second.

9   The entrance to the apartment is in the rear of the building because the front
is rented to retail stores. At night the quiet neighborhood is shrouded in the slum-
bering darkness that marks most residential areas.

10   Miss Genovese noticed a man at the far end of the lot, near a seven-story apart-
ment house at 82–40 Austin Street. She halted. Then, nervously, she headed up
Austin Street toward Lefferts Boulevard, where there is a call box to the 102nd
Police Precinct in nearby Richmond Hill.

"He Stabbed Me"

11   She got as far as a street light in front of a bookstore before the man grabbed
her. She screamed. Lights went on in the 10-story apartment house at 82–67 Austin
Street, which faces the bookstore. Windows slid open and voices punctuated the
early-morning stillness.

12   Miss Genovese screamed: "Oh, my God, he stabbed me! Please help me! Please
help me!"

13   From one of the upper windows in the apartment house, a man called down:
"Let that girl alone!"

14   The assailant looked up at him, shrugged and walked down Austin Street
toward a white sedan parked a short distance away. Miss Genovese struggled to her
feet.

15   Lights went out. The killer returned to Miss Genovese, now trying to make her
way around the side of the building by the parking lot to get to her apartment. The
assailant stabbed her again.

16   "I'm dying!" she shrieked. "I'm dying!"

A City Bus Passed

17   Windows were opened again, and lights went on in many apartments. The assailant got into his car and drove away. Miss Genovese staggered to her feet. A city bus,
Q-10, the Lefferts Boulevard line to Kennedy International Airport, passed. It was
3:35 A.M.

18   The assailant returned. By then, Miss Genovese had crawled to the back of the
building, where the freshly painted brown doors to the apartment house held out
hope of safety. The killer tried the first door; she wasn't there. At the second door,
82–62 Austin Street, he saw her slumped on the floor at the foot of the stairs. He
stabbed her a third time—fatally.

19   It was 3:50 by the time the police received their first call, from a man who was a neighbor of Miss Genovese. In two minutes they were at the scene. The neighbor, a 70-year-old woman and another woman were the only persons on the street. Nobody else came forward.

20   The man explained that he had called the police after much deliberation. He had phoned a friend in Nassau County for advice and then he had crossed the roof of the building to the apartment of the elderly woman to get her to make the call.

21   "I didn't want to get involved," he sheepishly told the police.

Suspect Is Arrested

22   Six days later, the police arrested Winston Moseley, a 29-year-old business-machine operator, and charged him with homicide. Moseley had no previous record. He is married, has two children and owns a home at 133–19 Sutter Avenue, South Ozone Park, Queens. On Wednesday, a court committed him to Kings County Hospital for psychiatric observation.

23   When questioned by the police, Moseley also said that he had slain Mrs. Annie May Johnson, 24, of 146–12 133d Avenue, Jamaica, on Feb. 29 and Barbara Kralik, 15, of 174–17 140th Avenue, Springfield Gardens, last July. In the Kralik case, the police are holding Alvin L. Mitchell, who is said to have confessed [to] that slaying.

24   The police stressed how simple it would have been to have gotten in touch with them. "A phone call," said one of the detectives, "would have done it." The police may be reached by dialing "O" for operator or SPring 7-3100.

25   Today witnesses from the neighborhood, which is made up of one-family homes in the $35,000 to $60,000 range with the exception of the two apartment houses near the railroad station, find it difficult to explain why they didn't call the police.

26   A housewife, knowingly if quite casually, said, "We thought it was a lover's quarrel." A husband and wife both said, "Frankly, we were afraid." They seemed aware of the fact that events might have been different. A distraught woman, wiping her hands in her apron, said, "I didn't want my husband to get involved."

27   One couple, now willing to talk about that night, said they heard the first screams. The husband looked thoughtfully at the bookstore where the killer first grabbed Miss Genovese.

28   "We went to the window to see what was happening," he said, "but the light from our bedroom made it difficult to see the street." The wife, still apprehensive, added: "I put out the light and we were able to see better."

29   Asked why they hadn't called the police, she shrugged and replied: "I don't know."

30   A man peeked out from a slight opening in the doorway to his apartment and rattled off an account of the killer's second attack. Why hadn't he called the police at the time? "I was tired," he said without emotion. "I went back to bed."

31   It was 4:25 A.M. when the ambulance arrived to take the body of Miss Genovese. It drove off. "Then," a solemn police detective said, "the people came out."

Crossing the Great Divide*

Peter Fish

Peter Fish is an editor-at-large and award-winning writer for *Sunset*, a magazine of Western living that began publication in 1898. During the last decade Fish has written over two hundred articles for the magazine on a wide range of subjects including travel, history, science, food, and nature, in addition to a number of interviews and book reviews. This essay appeared in Fish's column, called "Western Wanderings," in 1998.

1   I went to South Pass, Wyoming, to mark my son's four-month birthday and my forty-third. People might think the middle of Wyoming a strange place to commemorate passing time, but I had my reasons. At forty-three, you look forward and backward, like a driver shifting his gaze from windshield to rearview mirror. At four months, you look straight ahead. From both my son's vantage point and mine, I thought South Pass would be enlightening.

2   We followed the Oregon Trail in from the east, past Independence Rock, where the wagon trains stopped to let emigrants carve their names in splintered granite. We crossed and recrossed the Sweetwater River. We rose with Wyoming toward the sky. At the end of a dirt road was a stone slab inscribed "Old Oregon Trail 1843–57." This was South Pass. Six generations ago my son's ancestors came here on their way to new lives in the West.

3   "South Pass is almost a religious experience," Terry Del Bene had told me a few days earlier. Before I dragged my wife and son into the sagebrush, I wanted to know where I was going. So I tagged along with Del Bene. He is an archaeologist for the Bureau of Land Management, the agency that manages South Pass National Historic Landmark, and he knows the place cold.

4   If South Pass did not exist, the history of the United States would be so different as to be unimaginable. The pass rests at 7,400 feet elevation and forms a broad gap in the otherwise unbroken mountain ranges we label the Rockies. It straddles the Continental Divide—"Splash your canteen and half the water would go to the Atlantic and half to the Pacific," says Del Bene—but does so gently enough to allow wagon travel. Without South Pass, there would have been no Oregon or Mormon or California Trail. The first emigrant wagon train came through in 1843. By the time the last recorded wagons rolled west (amazingly late, in 1912), 400,000 settlers had crossed South Pass.

5   Del Bene told me all this while steering his government truck down State Highway 28. He was dressed as a nineteenth-century sharpie in wool pants and a vest that resembled mattress ticking. Del Bene is not above spiking his history with theater, and perhaps South Pass needs that—though a national historic landmark, it is noticeably lacking in the visitor centers, interpretive trails, and gift shops with which Americans embalm their history.

6   But when Del Bene announced we had arrived at South Pass, I thought he was joking. This is not an uncommon response. "It ill comports with the ideas we have formed of a pass through the Rocky Mountains," wrote emigrant Cecelia Adams in 1852, "being merely a vast, level and sandy plain sloping a little on each side of the summit."

* "Crossing the Great Divide" by Peter Fish from SUNSET Magazine, May 1998, pp. 24, 28. Reprinted by permission of Sunset Publishing Corp.

7   Del Bene must have noticed my expression. Enthusiasm is one of his skills, and he went to work. "Look there," he said. "That's the trail. At the peak of the west-ward movement, wagons rolled through four or five abreast. The wagons tend to push dirt to the side, so you get those marks. The reason you still see them is that we have such a short growing season up here. We have the best wagon ruts in the country."

8   I squinted at where Del Bene was pointing, but, as usual when somebody tries to show me something important, I couldn't see what he was talking about. Still, South Pass began to make itself felt. The very absence of modern man's tampering helped. At South Pass it's just you and the weight of hopes so numerous they dent the earth a century and a half later.

9   For every traveler who disparaged South Pass, there was one who knew the most important landmarks are those you don't recognize at first, who understood that he or she had reached the point of no return in a great journey. Some travelers fired rifles in the air and shouted, "Huzzah!" Others turned introspective. "We have forever taken leave of the waters running toward the home of our childhood and youth," one woman recorded in her diary. Another wrote, "Now we are on the other side of the world."

10   We got back in Del Bene's truck so he could show me a sadder sight. When Charlotte Dansie traveled the trail in 1862, she was thirty-two and pregnant with her eighth child. She went into labor about a mile east of the pass. The child lived only long enough to be christened. Charlotte died minutes later. Wyoming was hard on the immigrants, Del Bene said. "One out of ten died. On average there should be a grave every tenth of a mile, but most of them are unmarked. Char-lotte's is marked."

11   We were looking at the gravestone when we heard the crunch of tires on gravel. Three people got out of the car: a man in his twenties, his mother, her mother. Descendants of Charlotte Dansie, they had driven up from Salt Lake City to put flowers on the grave. They knew her story, of course, but Del Bene told them things they hadn't heard. One account had her pleading with her husband: "She could stand her suffering no longer and asked him to pray to God that she might be released and return to her maker." The grandmother said it was merciful that Charlotte had died so quickly.

12   That night I went back to a motel in Rock Springs. I knew I had a long drive the next morning to pick up my wife and son, and I wanted to fall asleep. Instead I lay on the ugly brocade bedspread pondering why Charlotte Dansie's descendants had driven three hundred miles to honor sorrow so old, and why I felt it imperative that my son see South Pass before, say, Toys "R" Us. Venturing into the past is never about the past but about the present—we look for the courage and purity of intent that we cannot locate in the modern world.

13   It is bright and windy when I drive back to South Pass with my wife and son. Busty cumulus clouds tumble across a blue sky, and their shadows roll across the plain. Joseph is a good traveler: cheerful, unflappable. He squirms while his mother tells him ancestral stories—her ancestors, not mine, as she takes pains to point out. They were from Illinois, advised to go west by a family friend named Abraham Lincoln. It is good story, and possibly true.

14   We follow the dirt road and stop at the pass. I unbuckle Joseph from his car seat and lift him into the windy day. The world smells of sage and clean baby. His arrival was its own continental divide, and all the rivers of my life now run in a new direction. If there was water here, I would baptize us both, sprinkling droplets from the Atlantic slope and then from the Pacific. But all we have are sky and ground. I watch him take those in. "This is South Pass," I tell him. I want him to remember this place. I want it to be something he can carry with him on the rest of his trail.

Arrival at Manzanar*

Jeanne Wakatsuki Houston and James D. Houston

Born in California, Jeanne Wakatsuki Houston was seven years old when, during World War II, her family was moved to a Japanese-American internment camp, where they were held for four years. In collaboration with her husband, novelist James D. Houston, she recounts these experiences in *Farewell to Manzanar* (1973), from which this excerpt is taken. Individually and together, the couple has written a variety of books, films, and magazine articles. Wakatsuki Houston's most recent work is *The Legend of Fire Horse Woman* (2004); Houston's is *A Queen's Journey* (2011).

1   In December of 1941 Papa's disappearance didn't bother me nearly so much as the world I soon found myself in.

2   He had been a jack-of-all-trades. When I was born he was farming near Ingelwood. Later, when he started fishing, we moved to Ocean Park, near Santa Monica, and until they [the FBI] picked him up, that's where we lived, in a big frame house with a brick fireplace, a block back from the beach. We were the only Japanese family in the neighborhood. Papa liked it that way. He didn't want to be labeled or grouped by anyone. But with him gone and no way of knowing what to expect, my mother moved all of us down to Terminal Island. Woody** already lived there, and one of my older sisters had married a Terminal Island boy. Mama's first concern now was to keep the family together; and once the war began, she felt safer there than isolated racially in Ocean Park. But for me, at age seven, the island was a country as foreign as India or Arabia would have been. It was the first time I had lived among other Japanese, or gone to school with them, and I was terrified all the time. . . .

3   At the time it seemed we had been living under this reign of fear for years. In fact, we lived there about two months. Late in February the navy decided to clear Terminal Island completely. Even though most of us were American-born, it was dangerous having that many Orientals so close to the Long Beach Naval Station, on the opposite end of the island. We had known something like this was coming. But, like Papa's arrest, not much could be done ahead of time. There were four of us kids still young enough to be living with Mama, plus Granny, her mother, sixty-five then, speaking no English, and nearly blind. Mama didn't know where else she

---

* "Arrival at Manzanar" (originally titled "Shikata Ga Nai") from FAREWELL TO MANZANAR by James D. and Jeanne Wakatsuki Houston. Copyright © 1973 by James D. Houston. Reprinted by permission of Houghton Mifflin Harcourt Publishing Company. All rights reserved.
**An older brother.

could get work, and we had nowhere else to move *to*. On February 25 the choice was made for us. We were given forty-eight hours to clear out.

4   The secondhand dealers had been prowling around for weeks, like wolves, offering humiliating prices for goods and furniture they knew many of us would have to sell sooner or later. Mama had left all but her most valuable possessions in Ocean Park, simply because she had nowhere to put them. She had brought along her pottery, her silver, heirlooms like the kimonos Granny had brought from Japan, tea sets, lacquered tables, and one fine old set of china, blue and white porcelain, almost translucent. On the day we were leaving, Woody's car was so crammed with boxes and luggage and kids we had just run out of room. Mama had to sell this china.

5   One of the dealers offered her fifteen dollars for it. She said it was a full setting for twelve and worth at least two hundred. He said fifteen was his top price. Mama started to quiver. Her eyes blazed up at him. She had been packing all night and trying to calm down Granny, who didn't understand why we were moving again and what all the rush was about. Mama's nerves were shot, and now Navy jeeps were patrolling the streets. She didn't say another word. She just glared at this man, all the rage and frustration channeled at him through her eyes.

6   He watched her for a moment and said he was sure he couldn't pay more than seventeen fifty for that china. She reached into the red velvet case, took out a dinner plate and hurled it at the floor right in front of his feet.

7   The man leaped back shouting, "Hey! Hey, don't do that! Those are valuable dishes!"

8   Mama took out another dinner plate and hurled it at the floor; then another and another, never moving, never opening her mouth, just quivering and glaring at the retreating dealer, with tears streaming down her cheeks. He finally turned and scuttled out the door, heading for the next house. When he was gone she stood there smashing cups and bowls and platters until the whole set lay in scattered blue and white fragments across the wooden floor.

9   The American Friends Service helped us find a small house in Boyle Heights, another minority ghetto, in downtown Los Angeles, now inhabited briefly by a few hundred Terminal Island refugees. Executive Order 9066 had been signed by President Roosevelt, giving the War Department authority to define military areas in the western states and to exclude from them anyone who might threaten the war effort. There was a lot of talk about internment, or moving inland, or something like that in store for all Japanese Americans. I remember my brothers sitting around the table talking very intently about what we were going to do, how we would keep the family together. They had seen how quickly Papa was removed, and they knew now that he would not be back for quite a while. Just before leaving Terminal Island Mama had received her first letter, from Bismarck, North Dakota. He had been imprisoned at Fort Lincoln, in an all-male camp for enemy aliens.

10   Papa had been the patriarch. He had always decided everything in the family. With him gone, my brothers, like councilors in the absence of a chief, worried about what should be done. The ironic thing is, there wasn't much left to decide. These were mainly days of quiet, desperate waiting for what seemed at the time to be inevitable. There is a phrase the Japanese use in such situations, when

something difficult must be endured. You would hear the older heads, the Issei, telling others very quietly, "*Shikato ga nai*" (It cannot be helped). "*Shikata ga nai*" (It must be done).

11　Mama and Woody went to work packing celery for a Japanese produce dealer. Kiyo and my sister May and I enrolled in the local school, and what sticks in my memory from those few weeks is the teacher—not her looks, her remoteness. In Ocean Park my teacher had been a kind, grandmotherly woman who used to sail with us in Papa's boat from time to time and who wept the day we had to leave. In Boyle Heights the teacher felt cold and distant. I was confused by all the moving and was having trouble with the classwork, but she would never help me out. She would have nothing to do with me.

12　This was the first time I had felt outright hostility from a Caucasian. Looking back, it is easy enough to explain. Public attitudes toward the Japanese in California were shifting rapidly. In the first few months of the Pacific war, America was on the run. Tolerance had turned to distrust and irrational fear. The hundred-year-old tradition of anti-Orientalism on the west coast soon resurfaced, more vicious than ever. Its result became clear about a month later, when we were told to make our third and final move.

13　The name Manzanar meant nothing to us when we left Boyle Heights. We didn't know where it was or what it was. We went because the government ordered us to. And, in the case of my older brothers and sisters, we went with a certain amount of relief. They had all heard stories of Japanese homes being attacked, of beatings in the streets of California towns. They were as frightened of the Caucasians as Caucasians were of us. Moving, under what appeared to be government protection, to an area less directly threatened by the war seemed not such a bad idea at all. For some it actually sounded like a fine adventure.

14　Our pickup point was a Buddhist church in Los Angeles. It was very early, and misty, when we got there with our luggage. Mama had bought heavy coats for all of us. She grew up in eastern Washington and knew that anywhere inland in early April would be cold. I was proud of my new coat, and I remember sitting on a duffel bag trying to be friendly with the Greyhound driver. I smiled at him. He didn't smile back. He was befriending no one. Someone tied a numbered tag to my collar and to the duffel bag (each family was given a number, and that became our official designation until the camps were closed), someone else passed out box lunches for the trip, and we climbed aboard.

15　I had never been outside Los Angeles County, never traveled more than ten miles from the coast, had never even ridden on a bus. I was full of excitement, the way any kid would be, and wanted to look out the window. But for the first few hours the shades were drawn. Around me other people played cards, read magazines, dozed, waiting. I settled back, waiting too, and finally fell asleep. The bus felt very secure to me. Almost half its passengers were immediate relatives. Mama and my older brothers had succeeded in keeping most of us together, on the same bus, headed for the same camp. I didn't realize until much later what a job that was. The strategy had been, first, to have everyone living in the same district when the evacuation began, and then to get all of us included under the same family number, even though names had been changed by marriage. Many families weren't as lucky as ours and suffered months of anguish while trying to arrange transfers from one camp to another.

16   We rode all day. By the time we reached our destination, the shades were up. It was late afternoon. The first thing I saw was a yellow swirl across a blurred, reddish setting sun. The bus was being pelted by what sounded like splattering rain. It wasn't rain. This was my first look at something I would soon know very well, a billowing flurry of dust and sand churned up by the wind through Owens Valley.

17   We drove past a barbed-wire fence, through a gate, and into an open space where trunks and sacks and packages had been dumped from the baggage trucks that drove out ahead of us. I could see a few tents set up, the first rows of black barracks, and beyond them, blurred by sand, rows of barracks that seemed to spread for miles across this plain. People were sitting on cartons or milling around, with their backs to the wind waiting to see which friends or relatives might be on this bus. As we approached, they turned or stood up, and some moved toward us expectantly. But inside the bus no one stirred. No one waved or spoke. They just stared out the windows, ominously silent. I didn't understand this. Hadn't we finally arrived, our whole family intact? I opened a window, leaned out, and yelled happily. "Hey! This whole bus is full of Wakatsukis!"

18   Outside, the greeters smiled. Inside there was an explosion of laughter, hysterical, tension-breaking laughter that left my brothers choking and whacking each other across the shoulders.

19   We had pulled up just in time for dinner. The mess halls weren't completed yet. An outdoor chow line snaked around a half-finished building that broke a good part of the wind. They issued us army mess kits, the round metal kind that fold over, and plopped in scoops of canned Vienna sausage, canned string beans, steamed rice that had been cooked too long, and on top of the rice a serving of canned apricots. The Caucasian servers were thinking that the fruit poured over rice would make a good dessert. Among the Japanese, of course, rice is never eaten with sweet foods, only with salty or savory foods. Few of us could eat such a mixture. But at this point no one dared protest. It would have been impolite. I was horrified when I saw the apricot syrup seeping through my little mound of rice. I opened my mouth to complain. My mother jabbed me in the back to keep quiet. We moved on through the line and joined the others squatting in the lee of half-raised walls, dabbing courteously at what was, for almost everyone there, an inedible concoction.

20   After dinner we were taken to Block 16, a cluster of fifteen barracks that had just been finished a day or so earlier—although finished was hardly the word for it. The shacks were built of one thickness of pine planking covered with tarpaper. They sat on concrete footings, with about two feet of open space between the floorboards and the ground. Gaps showed between the planks, and as the weeks passed and the green wood dried out, the gaps widened. Knotholes gaped in the uncovered floor.

21   Each barracks was divided into six units, sixteen by twenty feet, about the size of a living room, with one bare bulb hanging from the ceiling and an oil stove for heat. We were assigned two of these for the twelve people in our family group; and our official family "number" was enlarged by three digits—6 plus the number of

this barracks. We were issued steel army cots, two brown army blankets each, and some mattress covers, which my brothers stuffed with straw.

22   The first task was to divide up what space we had for sleeping. Bill and Woody contributed a blanket each and partitioned off the first room: one side for Bill and Tomi, one side for Woody and Chizu and their baby girl. Woody also got the stove, for heating formulas.

23   The people who had it hardest during the first few months were young couples like these, many of whom had married just before the evacuation began, in order not to be separated and sent to different camps. Our two rooms were crowded, but at least it was all in the family. My oldest sister and her husband were shoved into one of those sixteen-by-twenty-foot compartments with six people they had never seen before—two other couples, one recently married like themselves, the other with two teenage boys. Partitioning off a room like that wasn't easy. It was bitter cold when we arrived, and the wind did not abate. All they had to use for room dividers were those army blankets, two of which were barely enough to keep one person warm. They argued over whose blanket should be sacrificed and later argued about noise at night—the parents wanted their boys asleep by 9:00 P.M.— and they continued arguing over matters like that for six months, until my sister and her husband left to harvest sugar beets in Idaho. It was grueling work up there, and wages were pitiful, but when the call came through camp for workers to alleviate the wartime labor shortage, it sounded better than their life at Manzanar. They knew they'd have, if nothing else, a room, perhaps a cabin of their own.

24   That first night in Block 16, the rest of us squeezed into the second room— Granny, Lillian, age fourteen, Ray, thirteen, May, eleven, Kiyo, ten, Mama, and me. I didn't mind this at all at the time. Being youngest meant I got to sleep with Mama. And before we went to bed I had a great time jumping up and down on the mattress. The boys had stuffed so much straw into hers, we had to flatten it some so we wouldn't slide off. I slept with her every night after that until Papa came back.

Chapter 32

Essays for Further Analysis: Multiple Strategies and Styles

· ·

I Have a Dream*

Martin Luther King, Jr.

The Rev. Martin Luther King, Jr., president of the Southern Christian Leadership Conference, was the best-known leader of the Civil Rights Movement of the 1960s and the recipient of the 1964 Nobel Peace Prize. King delivered this speech in 1963 at a celebration of the Emancipation Proclamation, before a crowd of 250,000 who had marched to the Lincoln Memorial on the National Mall in Washington, D.C. A memorial to King, the newest addition to monuments on the National Mall, was dedicated in October 2011.

1   Five score years ago, a great American, in whose symbolic shadow we stand, signed the Emancipation Proclamation. This momentous decree came as a great beacon light of hope to millions of Negro slaves who had been seared in the flames of withering injustice. It came as a joyous daybreak to end the long night of captivity.

2   But one hundred years later, we must face the tragic fact that the Negro is still not free. One hundred years later, the life of the Negro is still sadly crippled by the manacles of segregation and the chains of discrimination. One hundred years later, the Negro lives on a lonely island of poverty in the midst of a vast ocean of material prosperity. One hundred years later, the Negro is still languishing in the corners of American society and finds himself an exile in his own land. So we have come here today to dramatize an appalling condition.

---

3   In a sense we have come to our nation's capital to cash a check. When the architects of our republic wrote the magnificent words of the Constitution and the Declaration of Independence, they were signing a promissory note to which every American was to fall heir. This note was a promise that all men would be guaranteed the unalienable rights of life, liberty, and the pursuit of happiness.

4   It is obvious today that America has defaulted on this promissory note insofar as her citizens of color are concerned. Instead of honoring this sacred obligation, America has given the Negro people a bad check, a check which has come back marked "insufficient funds." But we refuse to believe that the bank of justice is bankrupt. We refuse to believe that there are insufficient funds in the great vaults of opportunity of this nation. So we have come to cash this check—a check that will give us upon demand the riches of freedom and the security of justice. We have also come to this hallowed spot to remind America of the fierce urgency of *now*. This is no time to engage in the luxury of cooling off or to take the tranquilizing drugs of gradualism. *Now* is the time to make real the promises of Democracy. *Now* is the time to rise from the dark and desolate valley of segregation to the sunlit path of racial justice. *Now* is the time to open the doors of opportunity to all of God's children. *Now* is the time to lift our nation from the quicksands of racial injustice to the solid rock of brotherhood.

5   It would be fatal for the nation to overlook the urgency of the moment and to underestimate the determination of the Negro. This sweltering summer of the Negro's legitimate discontent will not pass until there is an invigorating autumn of freedom and equality. Nineteen sixty-three is not an end, but a beginning. Those who hope that the Negro needed to blow off steam and will now be content will have a rude awakening if the nation returns to business as usual. There will be neither rest nor tranquility in America until the Negro is granted his citizenship rights. The whirl-winds of revolt will continue to shake the foundations of our nation until the bright day of justice emerges.

6   But there is something that I must say to my people who stand on the warm threshold which leads into the palace of justice. In the process of gaining our rightful place we must not be guilty of wrongful deeds. Let us not seek to satisfy our thirst for freedom by drinking from the cup of bitterness and hatred. We must forever conduct our struggle on the high plane of dignity and discipline. We must not allow our creative protest to degenerate into physical violence. Again and again we must rise to the majestic heights of meeting physical force with soul force. The marvelous new militancy which has engulfed the Negro community must not lead us to distrust of all white people, for many of our white brothers, as evidenced by their presence here today, have come to realize that their destiny is tied up with our destiny and their freedom is inextricably bound to our freedom. We cannot walk alone.

7   And as we walk, we must make the pledge that we shall march ahead. We cannot turn back. There are those who are asking the devotees of civil rights, "When will you be satisfied?" We can never be satisfied as long as the Negro is the victim of the unspeakable horrors of police brutality. We can never be satisfied as long as our bodies, heavy with the fatigue of travel, cannot gain lodging in the motels of the highways and the hotels of the cities. We cannot be satisfied as long as the Negro's

basic mobility is from a smaller ghetto to a larger one. We can never be satisfied as long as a Negro in Mississippi cannot vote and a Negro in New York believes he has nothing for which to vote. No, no, we are not satisfied, and we will not be satisfied until justice rolls down like waters and righteousness like a mighty stream.

8   I am not unmindful that some of you have come here out of great trials and tribulations. Some of you have come fresh from narrow jail cells. Some of you have come from areas where your quest for freedom left you battered by the storms of persecution and staggered by the winds of police brutality. You have been the veterans of creative suffering. Continue to work with the faith that unearned suffering is redemptive.

9   Go back to Mississippi, go back to Alabama, go back to South Carolina, go back to Georgia, go back to Louisiana, go back to the slums and ghettos of our northern cities, knowing that somehow this situation can and will be changed. Let us not wallow in the valley of despair.

10   I say to you today, my friends, that in spite of the difficulties and frustrations of the moment I still have a dream. It is a dream deeply rooted in the American dream.

11   I have a dream that one day this nation will rise up and live out the true meaning of its creed: "We hold these truths to be self-evident, that all men are created equal."

12   I have a dream that one day on the red hills of Georgia the sons of former slaves and the sons of former slaveowners will be able to sit down together at the table of brotherhood.

13   I have a dream that one day even the state of Mississippi, a desert state sweltering with the heat of injustice and oppression, will be transformed into an oasis of freedom and justice.

14   I have a dream that my four little children will one day live in a nation where they will not be judged by the color of their skin but by the content of their character.

15   I have a dream today.

16   I have a dream that one day the state of Alabama, whose governor's lips are presently dripping with the words of interposition and nullification, will be transformed into a situation where little black boys and black girls will be able to join hands with little white boys and white girls and walk together as sisters and brothers.

17   I have a dream today.

18   I have a dream that one day every valley shall be exalted, every hill and mountain shall be made low, the rough places will be made plain, and the crooked places will be made straight, and the glory of the Lord shall be revealed, and all flesh shall see it together.

19   This is our hope. This is the faith with which I return to the South. With this faith we will be able to hew out of the mountain of despair a stone of hope. With this faith we will be able to transform the jangling discords of our nation into a beautiful symphony of brotherhood. With this faith we will be able to work together, to pray together, to struggle together, to go to jail together, to stand up for freedom together, knowing that we will be free one day.

20   This will be the day when all of God's children will be able to sing with new meaning

> My country, 'tis of thee,
> Sweet land of liberty,
>   Of thee I sing:
> Land where my fathers died,
> Land of the pilgrims' pride,
> From every mountain-side
>   Let freedom ring.

21   And if America is to be a great nation this must become true. So let freedom ring from the prodigious hilltops of New Hampshire. Let freedom ring from the mighty mountains of New York. Let freedom ring from the heightening Alleghenies of Pennsylvania!

22   Let freedom ring from the snowcapped Rockies of Colorado!

23   Let freedom ring from the curvaceous peaks of California!

24   But not only that; let freedom ring from Stone Mountain of Georgia!

25   Let freedom ring from Lookout Mountain of Tennessee!

26   Let freedom ring from every hill and molehill of Mississippi. From every mountainside, let freedom ring.

27   When we let freedom ring, when we let it ring from every village and every hamlet, from every state and every city, we will be able to speed up that day when all of God's children, black men and white men, Jews and Gentiles, Protestants and Catholics, will be able to join hands and sing in the words of the old Negro spiritual, "Free at last! Free at last! thank God almighty, we are free at last!"

Take This Fish and Look at It*

Samuel H. Scudder

Samuel H. Scudder was a nineteenth-century entomologist—a zoologist who focuses on insects—whose scholarship in the natural and physical sciences was widely respected. His works include *A Century of Orthoptera* (1879) and *Fossil Insects of North America* (1890). This well-known 1874 essay describes the early lessons in observation and analysis Scudder received from the acclaimed naturalist Louis Agassiz, his professor at Harvard's Lawrence Scientific School.

1   It was more than fifteen years ago that I entered the laboratory of Professor Agassiz, and told him I had enrolled my name in the scientific school as a student of natural history. He asked me a few questions about my object in coming, my antecedents generally, the mode in which I afterwards proposed to use the knowledge I might acquire, and finally, whether I wished to study any special branch. To the latter I replied that while I wished to be well grounded in all departments of zoology, I purposed to devote myself specially to insects.

2   "When do you wish to begin?" he asked.

3   "Now," I replied.

4   This seemed to please him, and with an energetic "Very well," he reached from a shelf a huge jar of specimens in yellow alcohol.

---

* Scudder, Samuel H. "Take This Fish and Look at It"

5   "Take this fish," said he, "and look at it; we call it a haemulon; by and by I will ask what you have seen."

6   With that he left me, but in a moment returned with explicit instructions as to the care of the object entrusted to me.

7   "No man is fit to be a naturalist," said he, "who does not know how to take care of specimens."

8   I was to keep the fish before me in a tin tray, and occasionally moisten the surface with alcohol from the jar, always taking care to replace the stopper tightly. Those were not the days of ground glass stoppers and elegantly shaped exhibition jars; all the old students will recall the huge, neckless glass bottles with their leaky, wax-besmeared corks, half eaten by insects and begrimed with cellar dust. Entomology was a cleaner science than ichthyology, but the example of the professor, who had unhesitatingly plunged to the bottom of the jar to produce the fish, was infectious; and though this alcohol had "a very ancient and fish-like smell," I really dared not show any aversion within these sacred precincts, and treated the alcohol as though it were pure water. Still I was conscious of a passing feeling of disappointment, for gazing at a fish did not commend itself to an ardent entomologist. My friends at home, too, were annoyed, when they discovered that no eau de cologne would drown the perfume which haunted me like a shadow.

9   In ten minutes I had seen all that could be seen in that fish, and started in search of the professor, who had, however, left the Museum; and when I returned, after lingering over some of the odd animals stored in the upper apartment, my specimen was dry all over. I dashed the fluid over the fish as if to resuscitate the beast from a fainting fit, and looked with anxiety for a return of the normal, sloppy appearance. This little excitement over, nothing was to be done but return to a steadfast gaze at my mute companion. Half an hour passed—an hour—another hour; the fish began to look loathsome. I turned it over and around; looked it in the face—ghastly; from behind, beneath, above, sideways, at a three-quarters view—just as ghastly. I was in despair; at an early hour I concluded that lunch was necessary; so, with infinite relief, the fish was carefully replaced in the jar, and for an hour I was free.

10   On my return, I learned that Professor Agassiz had been at the Museum, but had gone and would not return for several hours. My fellow-students were too busy to be disturbed by continued conversation. Slowly I drew forth that hideous fish, and with a feeling of desperation again looked at it. I might not use a magnifying glass; instruments of all kinds were interdicted. My two hands, my two eyes, and the fish: it seemed a most limited field. I pushed my finger down its throat to feel how sharp the teeth were. I began to count the scales in the different rows until I was convinced that that was nonsense. At last a happy thought struck me—I would draw the fish; and now with surprise I began to discover new features in the creature. Just then the professor returned.

11   "That is right," said he; "a pencil is one of the best of eyes. I am glad to notice, too, that you keep your specimen wet, and your bottle corked."

12   With these encouraging words, he added, "Well, what is it like?"

13   He listened attentively to my brief rehearsal of the structure of parts whose names were still unknown to me: the fringed gill-arches and movable operculum; the pores of the head, fleshy lips and lidless eyes; the lateral line, the spinous fins, and forked tail; the compressed and arched body. When I had finished, he waited

as if expecting more, and then, with an air of disappointment: "You have not looked very carefully; why," he continued, more earnestly, "you haven't even seen one of the most conspicuous features of the animal, which is as plainly before your eyes as the fish itself; look again, look again!" and he left me to my misery.

14   I was piqued; I was mortified. Still more of that wretched fish! But now I set myself to my task with a will, and discovered one new thing after another, until I saw how just the professor's criticism had been. The afternoon passed quickly, and when, towards its close, the professor inquired:

15   "Do you see it yet?"

16   "No," I replied, "I am certain I do not, but I see how little I saw before."

17   "That is the next best," said he earnestly, "but I won't hear you now; put away your fish and go home; perhaps you will be ready with a better answer in the morning. I will examine you before you look at the fish."

18   This was disconcerting; not only must I think of my fish all night, studying without the object before me, what this unknown but most visible feature might be; but also, without reviewing my new discoveries, I must give an exact account of them the next day. I had a bad memory; so I walked home by the Charles River in a distracted state, with my two perplexities.

19   The cordial greeting from the professor the next morning was reassuring; here was a man who seemed to be quite as anxious as I that I should see for myself what he saw.

20   "Do you perhaps mean," I asked, "that the fish has symmetrical sides with paired organs?"

21   His thoroughly pleased "Of course! of course!" repaid the wakeful hours of the previous night. After he had discoursed most happily and enthusiastically—as he always did—upon the importance of this point, I ventured to ask what I should do next.

22   "Oh, look at your fish!" he said, and left me again to my own devices. In a little more than an hour he returned and heard my new catalogue.

23   "That is good, that is good!" he repeated; "but that is not all, go on"; and so for three long days he placed that fish before my eyes; forbidding me to look at anything else, or to use any artificial aid. "Look, look, look," was his repeated injunction.

24   This was the best entomological lesson I ever had—a lesson whose influence has extended to the details of every subsequent study; a legacy the professor has left to me, as he has left it to many others, of inestimable value, which we could not buy, with which we cannot part.

25   A year afterward, some of us were amusing ourselves with chalking outlandish beasts upon the Museum blackboard. We drew prancing star-fishes; frogs in mortal combat; hydra-headed worms; stately crawfishes, standing on their tails, bearing aloft umbrellas; and grotesque fishes with gaping mouths and staring eyes. The professor came in shortly after and was as amused as any at our experiments. He looked at the fishes.

26   "Haemulons, every one of them," he said; "Mr.——-drew them."

27   True; and to this day, if I attempt a fish, I can draw nothing but haemulons.

28   The fourth day, a second fish of the same group was placed beside the first, and I was bidden to point out the resemblances and differences between the two;

another and another followed, until the entire family lay before me, and a whole legion of jars covered the table and surrounding shelves; the odor had become a pleasant perfume; and even now, the sight of an old, six-inch worm-eaten cork brings fragrant memories!

29 The whole group of haemulons was thus brought in review; and, whether engaged upon the dissection of the internal organs, the preparation and examination of the bony framework, or the description of the various parts, Agassiz's training in the method of observing facts and their orderly arrangement, was ever accompanied by the urgent exhortation not to be content with them.

30 "Facts are stupid things," he would say, "until brought into connection with some general law."

31 At the end of eight months, it was almost with reluctance that I left these friends and turned to insects; but what I had gained by this outside experience has been of greater value than years of later investigation in my favorite groups.

A Modest Proposal*

Jonathan Swift

Born in 1667 in Ireland, Jonathan Swift was an Anglican priest who eventually became dean of St. Patrick's Cathedral in Dublin. He is best known for his satires, often addressing the English exploitation of the Irish, including his masterpiece *Gulliver's Travels* (1726). This essay, originally a pamphlet written in 1729 during a terrible famine and at a time when the English were proposing a severe tax on the Irish, uses irony and satiric exaggeration to emphasize Ireland's desperation and England's greed.

For Preventing the Children of
Poor People in Ireland
from Being a Burden to Their Parents
or Country,
and for Making Them Beneficial to the Public

1 It is a melancholy object to those who walk through this great town or travel in the country, when they see the streets, the roads, and cabin doors, crowded with beggars of the female sex, followed by three, four, or six children, all in rags and importuning every passenger for an alms. These mothers, instead of being able to work for their honest livelihood, are forced to employ all their time in strolling to beg sustenance for their helpless infants, who, as they grow up, either turn thieves for want of work, or leave their dear native country to fight for the Pretender in Spain, or sell themselves to the Barbadoes.

2 I think it is agreed by all parties that this prodigious number of children in the arms, or on the backs, or at the heels of their mothers, and frequently of their fathers, is in the present deplorable state of the kingdom a very great additional grievance; and therefore whoever could find out a fair, cheap, and easy method of making these children sound, useful members of the commonwealth would deserve so well of the public as to have his statue set up for a preserver of the nation.

---

* Jonathan Swift, a Modest Proposal

3   But my intention is very far from being confined to provide only for the children of professed beggars; it is of a much greater extent, and shall take in the whole number of infants at a certain age who are born of parents in effect as little able to support them as those who demand our charity in the streets.

4   As to my own part, having turned my thoughts for many years upon this important subject, and maturely weighed the several schemes of other projectors, I have always found them grossly mistaken in the computation. It is true, a child just dropped from its dam may be supported by her milk for a solar year, with little other nourishment; at most not above the value of two shillings, which the mother may certainly get, or the value in scraps, by her lawful occupation of begging; and it is exactly at one year old that I propose to provide for them in such a manner as instead of being a charge upon their parents or the parish, or wanting food and raiment for the rest of their lives, they shall on the contrary contribute to the feeding, and partly to the clothing, of many thousands.

5   There is likewise another great advantage in my scheme, that it will prevent those voluntary abortions, and that horrid practice of women murdering their bastard children, alas, too frequent among us, sacrificing the poor innocent babes I doubt, more to avoid the expense than the shame, which would move tears and pity in the most savage and inhuman breast.

6   The number of souls in this kingdom being usually reckoned one million and a half, of these I calculate there may be about two hundred thousand couples whose wives are breeders; from which number I subtract thirty thousand couples who are able to maintain their own children, although I apprehend there cannot be so many under the present distress of the kingdom; but this being granted, there will remain an hundred and seventy thousand breeders. I again subtract fifty thousand for those women who miscarry, or whose children die by accident or disease within the year. There only remain an hundred and twenty thousand children of poor parents annually born. The question therefore is, how this number shall be reared and provided for, which, as I have already said, under the present situation of affairs, is utterly impossible by all the methods hitherto proposed. For we can neither employ them in handicraft nor agriculture; we neither build houses (I mean in the country) nor cultivate land. They can very seldom pick up a livelihood by stealing till they arrive at six years old, except where they are of towardly parts; although I confess they learn the rudiments much earlier, during which time they can however be looked upon only as probationers, as I have been informed by a principal gentleman in the county of Cavan, who protested to me that he never knew above one or two instances under the age of six, even in a part of the kingdom so renowned for the quickest proficiency in that art.

7   I am assured by our merchants that a boy or a girl before twelve years old is no salable commodity; and even when they come to this age, they will not yield above three pounds, or three pounds and half a crown at most on the Exchange; which cannot turn to account either to the parents or kingdom, the charge of nutriment and rags having been at least four times that value.

8   I shall now therefore humbly propose my own thoughts, which I hope will not be liable to the least objection.

9   I have been assured by a very knowing American of my acquaintance in London, that a young healthy child well nursed is at a year old a most delicious, nourishing, and wholesome food, whether stewed, roasted, baked, or boiled; and I make no doubt that it will equally serve in a fricassee or a ragout.

10   I do therefore humbly offer it to public consideration that of the hundred and twenty thousand children, already computed, twenty thousand may be reserved for breed, whereof only one fourth part to be males, which is more than we allow to sheep, black cattle, or swine; and my reason is that these children are seldom the fruits of marriage, a circumstance not much regarded by our savages, therefore one male will be sufficient to serve four females. That the remaining hundred thousand may at a year old be offered in sale to the persons of quality and fortune through the kingdom, always advising the mother to let them suck plentifully in the last month, so as to render them plump and fat for a good table. A child will make two dishes at an entertainment for friends; and when the family dines alone, the fore or hind quarter will make a reasonable dish, and seasoned with a little pepper or salt will be very good boiled on the fourth day, especially in winter.

11   I have reckoned upon a medium that a child just born will weigh twelve pounds, and in a solar year if tolerably nursed increaseth to twenty-eight pounds.

12   I grant this food will be somewhat dear, and therefore very proper for landlords, who, as they have already devoured most of the parents, seem to have the best title to the children.

13   Infant's flesh will be in season throughout the year, but more plentiful in March, and a little before and after. For we are told by a grave author, an eminent French physician, that fish being a prolific diet, there are more children born in Roman Catholic countries about nine months after Lent, than at any other season; therefore, reckoning a year after Lent, the markets will be more glutted than usual, because the number of popish infants is at least three to one in this kingdom; and therefore it will have one other collateral advantage, by lessening the number of Papists among us.

14   I have already computed the charge of nursing a beggar's child (in which list I reckon all cottagers, laborers, and four-fifths of the farmers) to be about two shillings per annum, rags included; and I believe no gentleman would repine to give ten shillings for the carcass of a good fat child, which, as I have said, will make four dishes of excellent nutritive meat, when he hath only some particular friend or his own family to dine with him. Thus the squire will learn to be a good landlord, and grow popular among his tenants; the mother will have eight shillings net profit, and be fit for work till she produces another child.

15   Those who are more thrifty (as I must confess the times require) may flay the carcass; the skin of which artificially dressed will make admirable gloves for ladies, and summer boots for fine gentlemen.

16   As to our city of Dublin, shambles may be appointed for this purpose in the most convenient parts of it, and butchers we may be assured will not be wanting; although I rather recommend buying the children alive, and dressing them hot from the knife as we do roasting pigs.

17   A very worthy person, a true lover of his country, and whose virtues I highly esteem, was lately pleased in discoursing on this matter to offer a refinement upon

my scheme. He said that many gentlemen of this kingdom, having of late destroyed their deer, he conceived that the want of venison might be well supplied by the bodies of young lads and maidens, not exceeding fourteen years of age nor under twelve, so great a number of both sexes in every country being now ready to starve for want of work and service; and these to be disposed of by their parents, if alive, or otherwise by their nearest relations. But with due deference to so excellent a friend and so deserving a patriot, I cannot be altogether in his sentiments; for as to the males, my American acquaintance assured me from frequent experience that their flesh was generally tough and lean, like that of our schoolboys, by continual exercise, and their taste disagreeable; and to fatten them would not answer the charge. Then as to the females, it would, I think with humble submission, be a loss to the public, because they soon would become breeders themselves; and besides, it is not improbable that some scrupulous people might be apt to censure such a practice (although indeed very unjustly) as a little bordering upon cruelty; which, I confess, hath always been with me the strongest objection against any project, how well soever intended.

18   But in order to justify my friend, he confessed that this expedient was put into his head by the famous Psalmanazar, a native of the island Formosa, who came from thence to London above twenty years ago, and in conversation told my friend that in his country when any young person happened to be put to death, the executioner sold the carcass to persons of quality as a prime dainty; and that in his time the body of a plump girl of fifteen, who was crucified for an attempt to poison the emperor, was sold to his Imperial Majesty's prime minister of state, and other great mandarins of the court, in joints from the gibbet, at four hundred crowns. Neither indeed can I deny that if the same use were made of several plump young girls in this town, who without one single groat to their fortunes cannot stir abroad without a chair, and appear at the playhouse and assemblies in foreign fineries which they never will pay for, the kingdom would not be the worse.

19   Some persons of a desponding spirit are in great concern about that vast number of poor people who are aged, diseased, or maimed, and I have been desired to employ my thoughts what course may be taken to ease the nation of so grievous an encumbrance. But I am not in the least pain upon that matter, because it is very well known that they are every day dying and rotting by cold and famine, and filth and vermin, as fast as can be reasonably expected. And as to the young laborers, they are now in almost as hopeful a condition. They cannot get work, and consequently pine away for want of nourishment to a degree that if at any time they are accidentally hired to common labor, they have not strength to perform it; and thus the country and themselves are happily delivered from the evils to come.

20   I have too long digressed, and therefore shall return to my subject. I think the advantages by the proposal which I have made are obvious and many, as well as of the highest importance.

21   For first, as I have already observed, it would greatly lessen the number of Papists, with whom we are yearly overrun, being the principal breeders of the nation as well as our most dangerous enemies; and who stay at home on purpose to deliver the kingdom to the Pretender, hoping to take their advantage by the absence of so

many good Protestants, who have chosen rather to leave their country than to stay at home and pay tithes against their conscience to an Episcopal curate.

22   Secondly, the poorer tenants will have something valuable of their own, which by law may be made liable to distress, and help to pay their landlord's rent, their corn and cattle being already seized and money a thing unknown.

23   Thirdly, whereas the maintenance of an hundred thousand children, from two years old and upwards, cannot be computed at less than ten shillings a piece per annum, the nation's stock will be thereby increased fifty thousand pounds per annum, besides the profit of a new dish introduced to the tables of all gentlemen of fortune in the kingdom who have any refinement in taste. And the money will circulate among ourselves, the goods being entirely of our own growth and manufacture.

24   Fourthly, the constant breeders, besides the gain of eight shillings sterling per annum by the sale of their children, will be rid of the charge for maintaining them after the first year.

25   Fifthly, this food would likewise bring great custom to taverns; where the vintners will certainly be so prudent as to procure the best receipts for dressing it to perfection, and consequently have their houses frequented by all the fine gentlemen, who justly value themselves upon their knowledge in good eating; and a skillful cook, who understands how to oblige his guests, will contrive to make it as expensive as they please.

26   Sixthly, this would be a great inducement to marriage, which all wise nations have either encouraged by rewards or enforced by laws and penalties. It would increase the care and tenderness of mothers toward their children, when they were sure of a settlement for life to the poor babes, provided in some sort by the public, to their annual profit instead of expense. We should see an honest emulation among the married women, which of them could bring the fattest child to the market. Men would become as fond of their wives during the time of their pregnancy as they are now of their mares in foal, their cows in calf, or sows when they are ready to farrow; nor offer to beat or kick them (as is too frequent a practice) for fear of a miscarriage.

27   Many other advantages might be enumerated. For instance, the addition of some thousand carcasses in our exportation of barreled beef, the propagation of swine's flesh, and improvements in the art of making good bacon, so much wanted among us by the great destruction of pigs, too frequent at our tables, which are no way comparable in taste or magnificence to a well-grown, fat, yearling child, which roasted whole will make a considerable figure at a lord mayor's feast or any other public entertainment. But this and many others I omit, being studious of brevity.

28   Supposing that one thousand families in this city would be constant customers for infants' flesh, besides others who might have it at merry meetings, particularly weddings and christenings, I compute that Dublin would take off annually about twenty thousand carcasses, and the rest of the kingdom (where probably they will be sold somewhat cheaper) the remaining eighty thousand.

29   I can think of no one objection that will possibly be raised against this proposal, unless it should be urged that the number of people will be thereby much lessened

in the kingdom. This I freely own, and it was indeed one principal design in offering it to the world. I desire the reader will observe, that I calculate my remedy for this one individual kingdom of Ireland and for no other that ever was, is, or I think ever can be upon earth. Therefore, let no man talk to me of other expedients: of taxing our absentees at five shillings a pound: of using neither clothes nor household furniture except what is of our own growth and manufacture: of utterly rejecting the materials and instruments that promote foreign luxury: of curing the expensiveness of pride, vanity, idleness, and gaming in our women: of introducing a vein of parsimony, prudence, and temperance: of learning to love our country, in the want of which we differ even from Laplanders and the inhabitants of Topinamboo: of quitting our animosities and factions, nor acting any longer like the Jews, who were murdering one another at the very moment their city was taken: of being a little cautious not to sell our country and conscience for nothing: of teaching our landlords to have at least one degree of mercy towards their tenants: lastly, of putting a spirit of honesty, industry, and skill into our shopkeepers; who, if a resolution could now be taken to buy only our native goods, would immediately unite to cheat and exact upon us in the price, the measure, and the goodness, nor could ever yet be brought to make one fair proposal of just dealing, though often and earnestly invited to it.

30   Therefore, I repeat, let no man talk to me of these and the like expedients, till he hath at least some glimpse of hope that there will ever be some hearty and sincere attempt to put them into practice.

31   But as to myself, having been wearied out for many years with offering vain, idle, visionary thoughts, and at length utterly despairing of success, I fortunately fell upon this proposal, which, as it is wholly new, so it hath something solid and real, of no expense and little trouble, full in our own power, and whereby we can incur no danger in disobliging England. For this kind of commodity will not bear exportation, the flesh being of too tender a consistence to admit a long continuance in salt, although perhaps I could name a country which would be glad to eat up our whole nation without it.

32   After all, I am not so violently bent upon my own opinion as to reject any offer proposed by wise men, which shall be found equally innocent, cheap, easy, and effectual. But before something of that kind shall be advanced in contradiction to my scheme, and offering a better, I desire the author or authors will be pleased maturely to consider two points. First, as things now stand, how they will be able to find food and raiment for an hundred thousand useless mouths and backs. And secondly, there being a round million of creatures in human figure throughout this kingdom, whose sole subsistence put into a common stock would leave them in debt two millions of pounds sterling, adding those who are beggars by profession to the bulk of farmers, cottagers, and laborers, with their wives and children who are beggars in effect; I desire those politicians who dislike my overture, and may perhaps be so bold as to attempt an answer, that they will first ask the parents of these mortals whether they would not at this day think it a great happiness to have been sold for food at a year old in this manner I prescribe, and thereby have avoided such a perpetual scene of misfortunes as they have since gone through by the oppression of landlords, the impossibility of paying rent without money or

trade; the want of common sustenance, with neither house nor clothes to cover them from the inclemencies of the weather, and the most inevitable prospect of entailing the like or greater miseries upon their breed forever.

33   I profess, in the sincerity of my heart, that I have not the least personal interest in endeavoring to promote this necessary work, having no other motive than the public good of my country, by advancing our trade, providing for infants, relieving the poor, and giving some pleasure to the rich. I have no children by which I can propose to get a single penny; the youngest being nine years old, and my wife past childbearing.

INDEX